The Impact of EU Accession on the Legal Orders of New EU Member States and (Pre-)Candidate Countries

Hopes and Fears

T.M.C. ASSER INSTITUUT
The Hague

The Impact of EU Accession on the Legal Orders of New EU Member States and (Pre-)Candidate Countries

Hopes and Fears

Edited by

Alfred E. Kellermann
Jenő Czuczai
Steven Blockmans
Anneli Albi
Wybe Th. Douma

T·M·C·ASSER PRESS

Published by T·M·C·ASSER PRESS
P.O.Box 16163, 2500 BD The Hague, The Netherlands
<www.asserpress.nl>

T·M·C·ASSER PRESS English language books are distributed exclusively by:

Cambridge University Press, The Edinburgh Building, Shaftesbury Road,
Cambridge CB2 2RU, UK,
or
for customers in the USA, Canada and Mexico:
Cambridge University Press, 100 Brook Hill Drive, West Nyack, NY 10994-2133, USA

<www.cambridge.org>

ISBN 90-6704-217-X
ISBN 978-90-6704-217-8

T.M.C. Asser Instituut - Institute for Private and Public International Law, International Commercial Arbitration and European Law
Institute Address: R.J. Schimmelpennincklaan 20-22, 2517 JN The Hague, The Netherlands; P.O. Box 30461, 2500 GL The Hague, The Netherlands; Tel.: (31-70)3420300; Fax: (31-70)3420359; URL: <www.asser.nl>.
Over forty years, the T.M.C. Asser Institute has developed into a leading scientific research institute in the field of international law. It covers private international law, public international law, including international humanitarian law, the law of the European Union, the law of international commercial arbitration and increasingly, also, international economic law, the law of international commerce and international sports law. Conducting scientific research either fundamental or applied, in the aforementioned domains, is the main activity of the Institute. In addition, the Institute organizes congresses and postgraduate courses, undertakes contract-research and operates its own publishing house, T.M.C.ASSER PRESS. Because of its inter-university background, the Institute often cooperates with Dutch law faculties as well as with various national and foreign institutions. The Institute organizes Asser College Europe, a project in cooperation with East and Central European countries whereby research and educational projects are organized and implemented.

FOREWORD

This book deals with important issues related to the process of enlargement of the European Union. The publication is the result of a Matra Multi Country Project, which was implemented under the guidance of Alfred E. Kellermann and Steven Blockmans since 2002 and was concluded with a Final Conference held on 13 October 2004 in The Hague (Scheveningen).

The book focuses on the necessary adaptations of the law and policies of the new and (pre-)candidate Member States in view of their (future) membership of the EU. More particularly the compatibility of national constitutional texts and the preparedness of public authorities (the executive, the judiciary and national parliaments) for full membership will be discussed.

A group of distinguished experts has analyzed the legal situation in their respective states with regard to issues like:

- The compatibility of national constitutional texts with fundamental principles of EU law, such as the principle of supremacy and direct effect;
- The preparedness of the judiciary to guarantee the effectiveness of EU law;
- The existence of coordination mechanisms for the preparation of the national position in EU negotiations as well as for the implementation of EU law in the national legal order;
- The existence of controlling mechanisms enabling national parliaments to control the functioning of national politicians in the EU negotiating framework.

The question has also been raised whether the new European constitutional treaty, which was signed in Rome on 29 October 2004, may give rise to amendments of the national Constitutions. Of course, in view of the recent developments, most notably in France and The Netherlands, it remains to be seen whether this new European treaty will actually enter into force.

The interaction between national and European law and policies is thus the central theme of this book. A smooth organization of this interaction is of the utmost importance, not only for the Member States in view of their obligations following from Article 10 of the EC Treaty – the obligation to cooperate – but also in order to ensure the effectiveness of the EU legal system in the interest of the ordinary citizen.

The contributions by the different authors and the discussions during the Final Conference on 13 October 2004 offered a multitude of interesting insights, views and experiences. These views and experiences have now been laid down in this book, and so become accessible to a wider public.

The important results of the Matra Multi Country Project lend themselves for a repetition of a similar comparative analysis in a couple of years from now. By that time the European Union most probably will have welcomed Bulgaria and Romania as new Member States; negotiations will be underway with a number of candidate countries; and possibly new applications for membership will have been tabled.

All in all this book can be regarded as an important contribution to the ongoing process of European integration guaranteeing fundamental values such as peace, stability and prosperity to its Member States and citizens.

JAAP W. DE ZWAAN*

* Professor of the Law of the European Union at Erasmus University Rotterdam and Vice-President of the Executive Board of the T.M.C. Asser Institute. Since 1 September 2005, Director of the Netherlands Institute of International Relations 'Clingendael', The Hague.

ACKNOWLEDGEMENTS

In the first place, the initiator of the project from which this book has resulted is to be congratulated for having had yet another excellent idea: Alfred E. Kellermann. Secondly, the numerous authors who shared their views on the legal situation in their countries made for a rich source of information, and we are especially glad that many of them were able and willing to revise and update their texts for this publication after the conference at which their reports were originally presented. Then, the editors who helped in shaping the contributions into their present form and who presented such an elaborate introduction (Alfred E. Kellermann) and such thorough cross-cutting reports (Jenő Czuczai, Steven Blockmans and Anneli Albi) are to be thanked wholeheartedly.

We gratefully acknowledge the financial support received from the Ministry of Foreign Affairs of the Netherlands which has made this publication, and the project from which it originates, possible.

`For her excellent language revision work, we would like to thank Corinne van den Berg. A couple of chapters were language revised by Richard Strager and Carol Post, to whom we would also like to express our gratitude. We would like to thank Daniel Stephens for the typesetting and Mieke Eijdenberg for her help with the sub-editing. Last, but definitely not least, we especially would like to thank the central person at the T.M.C. Asser Institute that helped to produce this book, Inge van Dun-van den Bosch.

WYBE TH. DOUMA
The Hague, 30 November 2005

SUMMARY TABLE OF CONTENTS

Part III: New Member States

DETAILED TABLE OF CONTENTS

Part II: Comparative Analyses

Part III: New Member States

ABBREVIATIONS

AKP	Justice and Development Party
Berkeley J. Int'l L.	Berkeley Journal of International Law
Bull. EU	Bulletin of the European Union
BVerfGE	Entscheidungen des Bundesverfassungsgerichts
Cardozo L. Rev.	Cardozo Law Review
CARDS	Community Assistance for Reconstruction, Development and Stabilisation
CC	Constitutional Court
CCBE	Council of the Bars and Law Societies of the EU
CEEC	Central and Eastern European Countries
CFI	Court of First Instance
CFSP	Common Foreign and Security Policy
Chi. J. Int'l L.	Chicago Journal of International Law
CIG	Conférence intergouvernementale
CLR	Cyprus Law Reports
CMLR	Common Market Law Reports
CNB	Česká národní banka [Czech National Bank]
Coll.	Collection of laws
COM	European Commission document
Const.	Constitution
CONV	Convention
Coreper	Comité des Représentants Permanents (EU)
COSAC	Conference of Community and European Affairs Committees
DEI	Department for European Integration
DEP	Democracy Party
DG	Directorate General
DGM	State Security Court
EA	Europe Agreement
EAEC	European Atomic Energy Community
EC	European Community
ECA	European Communities Act
ECB	European Central Bank
ECHR	European Convention for the Protection of Human Rights and Fundamental Freedoms
ECJ	European Court of Justice
ECR	European Court Reports
ECSC	European Coal and Steel Community
ECtHR	European Court of Human Rights
EEC	European Economic Community
EFA Rev.	European Foreign Affairs Review
EFTA	European Free Trade Association

EJN	European Judicial Network in civil and commercial matters
ELR	European Law Review
EMU	Economic and Monetary Union
ENIC	European Network of Information Centres
EP	European Parliament
EPD	Enhanced Permanent Dialogue
ESDP	European Security and Defence Policy
EU	European Union
EUI	European University Institute, Florence
Euratom	European Atomic Energy Community
Eurojust	European Judicial Cooperation Unit
Fidesz	Fiatal Demokraták Szövetsége [Alliance of Young Democrats]
FRY	Federal Republic of Yugoslavia
GD	Government Decisions
GEO	Government Emergency Ordinance
GNA	Grand National Assembly
GoS	Government of Serbia
GRECO	Group of States against Corruption
HR	Republike Hrvatske
HSS	Hrvatska Seljacka Stranka [Croatian Farmers' Party]
ICC	International Criminal Court
ICTY	International Criminal Tribunal for the former Yugoslavia
IGC	Intergovernmental Conference
ILM	International Legal Materials
ILO	International Labor Organization
INTERREG	Interregional Cooperation
Int'l J. Legal Info	International Journal of Legal Information
IPR	intellectual property rights
ISPA	Instrument for Structural Policies for Pre-Accession
IT	Information Technology
JHA	Justice and Home Affairs (EU)
LL.B.	Bachelor of Laws
LL.M.	Legum Magister, Master of Laws
Matra	Maatschappelijke Transformatie
MEI	Ministry of European Integration
MEP	Member of the European Parliament
MEUSAC	Malta-EU Steering and Action Committee
MFA	Ministry of Foreign Affairs
MGIMO	Moscow State Institute of International Relations
MHP	Nationalist Movement Party
MIEREI	Ministry for International Economic Relations and European Integration
MP	Member of Parliament

MZZ	Ministrstvo za zunanje zadeve [Ministry of Foreign Affairs]
NA	National Assembly
NAPO	National Anti-corruption Prosecution Office
NARIC	National Academic Recognition Information Centres
NATO	North Atlantic Treaty Organization
NGO	Non-Governmental Organization
NPAA	National Programme for the Adoption of the Acquis
NPAR	National Programme for the Accession of Romania to the EU
NPIEU	National Programme for the Integration of the Republic of Croatia into the European Union
N.Y. Int'l L. Rev.	New York International Law Review
OECD	Organisation for Economic Co-operation and Development
OHIM	Office for Harmonisation in the Internal Market
OJ	Official Journal of the European Communities/Union
OLAF	European Anti-Fraud Office
OSCE	Organization for Security and Co-operation in Europe
PHARE	originally: Poland Hungary Assistance for the Reconstruction of the Economy
PM	Prime Minister
PSC	Political and Security Committee
RS	Republic of Slovenia
SAA	Stabilisation and Association Agreement
SAP	Stabilisation and Association Process
SAPARD	Special Accession Programme for Agriculture and Rural Development
SCM	Supreme Council of Magistrates
SC Res.	Security Council Resolution
SEIO	Serbian European Integration Office
SIGMA	Support for Improvement in Governance and Management in Central and Eastern European Countries
SME	small and medium-sized enterprises
SS	(Nazi) Schutzstaffel
SVEZ	Služba Vlade RS za evropske zadeve [Government Office for European Affairs]
TCE	Treaty establishing a Constitution for Europe
TEC	Treaty establishing the European Community
TEU	Treaty on European Union
TGNA	Turkish Grand National Assembly
TRIPS	WTO's Agreement on Trade-Related Aspects of Intellectual Property Rights
UCLAF	Anti-Fraud Coordination Unit
UK	United Kingdom
UN	United Nations

UNMIK	United Nations Interim Administration Mission in Kosovo
UNTS	United Nations Treaty Series
USSR	Union of Soviet Socialist Republics
UYAP	Ulusal Yargı Ağı Projesi
VAT	value-added tax
VSRH	Vrhovni sud Republike Hrvatske [Supreme Court of the Republic of Croatia]
WTO	World Trade Organization
YOK	Yuksek Ogretim Kurulu Baskanligi [The Council of Higher Education]
ZaöRV	Zeitschrift für ausländisches öffentliches Recht und Völkerrecht
ZSE	Zeitschrift für Staats- und Europawissenschaften

HOPES AND FEARS

Alfred E. Kellermann*

1. INTRODUCTION

This book entitled 'Hopes and Fears' of new Member States and (pre-)candidate countries is the result of a Matra Multi-Country Project entitled "Impact of EU Accession on the Legal Orders of New Member States and (Pre-)Candidate Countries". The project countries were Bulgaria, Romania, Turkey, Slovenia, Croatia and Serbia and Montenegro.

After the final Matra Conference which was held 13-16 October 2004 in The Hague (see the Annex to this introduction) and to which, besides experts from Slovenia, also experts from the other new EU Member States were invited, it was suggested to add the reports of these 9 new EU Member States to the 6 reports of the project countries for the sake of comparison. The 9 conference country reports had been drafted more or less according to the same reporter's guidelines but are generally shorter in length, since they were drafted only for the conference and not as part of the study in the framework of the Matra Multi-Country Project. Still, as a consequence, a total of 15 country reports are now included in this book. The editors of the book were Alfred E. Kellermann, Jenö Czuczai, Steven Blockmans and Anneli Albi. They all contributed to the realization of the project objectives by lecturing at the briefing seminars and by drafting the General Summary of the book. Wybe Douma was later added to the team of editors as managing editor.

As the final Matra Multi-County Conference had as its sub-title "Hopes and Fears" and many experts and participants expressed their Hopes and Fears during the debates, we considered it appropriate to use these words for the title of the present book. However, after the recent rejection by France and the Netherlands of the European Constitutional Treaty we may conclude that "Hopes and Fears" in respect of European integration are equally present in the old Member States!

In this introduction we will focus mainly on the realization of the project objectives, the impact of the project and the impact of EU accession on the national

* Dr A.E. Kellermann, Senior Legal and Policy Advisor T.M.C. Asser Institute; Visiting Professor in the Law of the EU; Project Director Matra Multi Country Project "the Impact of EU Accession on the national legal orders".

constitutional practice of the old Member States: what may be learnt from the constitutional experiences in the old Member States? The other editors in their contributions will focus on the impact of EU accession on the national constitution, national judiciary, the national executive and the national parliaments of the new EU Member States and the (pre-)candidate countries.

2. THE REALIZATION OF THE OBJECTIVES OF THE MATRA MULTI-COUNTRY PROJECT

Since the idea of this multi-country project proposal was launched during the Asser Colloquium "The Constitutional Impact of Enlargement at EU and National level" held from 20 to 23 September 2000 in The Hague many new developments have occurred at EU level. On 15 December 2001 the Laeken Declaration was adopted at the European Council Meeting. The European Council of Laeken stated that the Union "has to become more democratic, more transparent and more efficient". One of the ways of contributing to this general objective was through simplification and restructuring of the Treaties. On 13 June 2003 the Brussels Convention on the future of the EU presented a final draft of the restructured Treaty which they called "Constitution". In the meantime, many candidate countries signed and ratified the accession treaty and gained the status of acceding new Member State.

This had the following consequences for the qualification and labelling of the countries involved in the project: Slovenia was an acceding new Member State and is presently a new EU Member State; Bulgaria, Romania and Turkey are candidate countries; Croatia was an applicant country and is presently a candidate country and, finally, Serbia and Montenegro is a (pre-)candidate country.

For a proper understanding of this introduction, it is necessary to refer to the overall objective and the project goals as they were established on 3 December 2002 when the Multi-Country Project Proposal was finally accepted by the Dutch Ministry of Foreign Affairs.

The overall objective of this multi-country project was to improve the capacity to implement, enforce and apply Community and European Union law in the applicant countries through the sharing of experiences with the project activities in other candidate countries and EU Member States in a multi-country context.

The project goals were:

1. to improve the quality of the adoption of the *acquis communautaire* in the national legal orders of EU candidate countries by increasing the theoretical and practical knowledge of Community law of persons who are or will be involved in the preparation, implementation, interpretation and application of Community legislation;

2. to improve the capacity of the national judiciary to apply Community law, especially those principles which are relevant for the relationship between Community law and national law and to increase the awareness of the national judiciary of their role as Community courts through workshops, briefings and training sessions in the respective EU candidate countries;
3. to increase awareness of civil society, national parliaments and governments of EU candidate countries for the legal impact of EU accession through organizing debates, conferences and the dissemination of the project results (Country Reports, General Comparative Report and Final Report) in the national language of the respective candidate country and in English for reasons of comparison.

The following national rapporteurs and experts were invited in 2003, 2004 and 2005 to contribute to one or more of the following activities in their respective countries:

1. Completing a questionnaire, establishing national study or working parties and assisting in the drafting of country reports (in two languages: the national language of the country in question and English);
2. Lending support to the organization and implementation of training programmes and briefings (among other things, translation and interpretation services and providing complimentary rooms and premises at government offices or university buildings for the one-week training sessions);
3. Assisting in the dissemination of the project results (national reports) to national authorities (government, parliament, judiciary) and universities by organizing meetings, academic debates, press conferences, etc.
4. Participating in the international seminar and rapporteurs' meeting in Bucharest on 24 and 25 October 2003 and in the Final Multi-Country Matra Conference in The Hague from 13 to 16 October 2004.

Bulgaria: Evgeni Tanchev, Member of the Constitutional Court in Sofia and Professor at the Sofia and New Bulgarian University; Jenia Peteva, Assistant Professor at Sofia University.
Croatia: Siniša Rodin, University of Zagreb, Zagreb; Tamara Capeta, University of Zagreb, Zagreb; Daria Mihelin, Ministry of European Integration, Zagreb.
Romania: Vasile Puscas, Chief Negotiator with the EU, Ministry of European Integration, Government of Romania, Bucharest; Victor Duculescu, Professor of Constitutional Law and parliamentary counsellor; R. Adam, legal analyst with the Ministry of European Integration; Andrei Popescu, Secretary of State, Ministry of European Integration, Bucharest.

Slovenia: Miha Pogacnik, Head of the Institute of International Law and International Relations in Ljubljana; Primoz Vehar, National Assembly, Ljubljana; Marko Starman, State Secretary of Justice, Ljubljana.
Serbia and Montenegro: Dusko Lopandic, Assistant Minister at the Ministry of International Economic Relations in Belgrade; Slobodan Samardzic, Professor at Belgrade University.
Turkey: Kemal Baslar, Professor and Member of the Constitutional Court in Ankara; Erdogan Ishakoglu, Ministry of Justice, Ankara.

The country reports were drafted according to the following *rapporteurs' guidelines*:

General

National rapporteurs should base their papers (as far as applicable and necessary) on the non-exhaustive list of questions below. They are encouraged to include matters which are of utmost importance to the overall topic but which are not addressed in the questions. In our opinion, papers should not be longer than 20 to 25 pages.

I. National constitution

1. How does the constitution deal with the incorporation and implementation of international law in the national legal order? Does it provide for transfer of competences to international organizations or related legal concepts and to what extent?
2. Are there constitutional provisions regarding the supremacy of international law over national law? If so, do these provisions guarantee supremacy and direct effect of European law?
3. Would your constitution require amendment for the ratification of the EU Treaty, EC Treaty, Euratom Treaty? If so, what are currently the key practical problems in that respect and which procedures would have to be followed in order to overcome these problems?
4. Which constitutional provisions do you consider to be contrary to the *acquis communautaire*?
5. Which procedures will be followed to adapt the national constitutions to the *acquis communautaire* (parliamentary voting, referenda, etc.)?

II. Role of the judiciary (national courts, including special bodies with judiciary functions)

1. Do the national courts refer to and apply the Europe Agreement or Stabilization and Association Agreement (SAA)?
2. Has the judiciary already embraced the principles of supremacy and direct effect?
3. Does the judiciary recognize a rule of interpretation whereby prior and/or posterior national law must be interpreted in conformity with obligations resulting from primary and secondary EC legislation, before and/or after its entry into force (principle of indirect effect)?
4. Could you mention and comment on some interesting cases of your Supreme Court and/or Constitutional Court dealing with the problems raised above?
5. What impact do you expect EU accession to have on the structure, (rules of) procedure and practice (incl. workload) of the national courts?

III. Role of the executive (Government and administration)

1. To what extent do the central Government and the administration implement and/or apply the Europe Agreement or SAA?
2. Which administrative and/or legal measures have already been initiated by your Government to comply with the political criteria of Copenhagen?
3. What coordination mechanisms (between and/or within Ministries) have been envisaged for the preparation and implementation of EC/EU law?
4. What impact do you expect EU accession to have on the organization and practice of (a) central Government and Administration and (b) the decentralized authorities?

IV. Role of the national parliament

1. Is the national parliament prepared for the legal approximation of national legislation with EC/EU law? Are there any special instructions or committees for implementation of EC/EU law? Please elaborate.
2. To which extent will national parliament keep control over decisions taken by ministers in the Council of the European Union? Which views exist on this matter in your country?

Finally the following four experts were invited to contribute to the drafting of the General Report, based on the experiences emerging from the briefings and country reports: Alfred E. Kellermann and Steven Blockmans (The Netherlands – old Member State); Jenö Czuczai and Anneli Albi (Hungary and Estonia – new Member States).

The report is based on the following problem analysis. Practice has shown that there is a growing and continuous need – before as well as after accession – to adapt national legal, judicial and administrative practices, because:

- Firstly, in some applicant countries the adaptation of national legislation is necessary in order to be able to ratify the Treaty of the European Union. The wording of the national legal texts of the candidate countries must not act as an obstacle to the accession of candidate countries to international organizations like the EU. However, in a number of smaller candidate countries that only regained their independence since 1991 there are some political and psychological objections against, for example, the transfer of sovereignty or state powers.
- Secondly, the way in which the European integration process is dealt with in the national legislation of some candidates is politically and psychologically less fortunate. For example, where there is a lack of transparency concerning integration ("European deficit"). By its comparative approach, the project supports the efforts of the applicant countries to adopt a more or less uniform legal language and terminology concerning EU topics and stimulates the applicant countries to improve the wording of their legislative proposals in this respect. For political reasons it is important that the "European deficit" should be eliminated from the national constitutions.
- Thirdly, many national constitutional provisions are contrary to or do not comply with the *acquis communautaire*.
- Fourthly, the Copenhagen criteria for accession as listed in Agenda 2000 – the stability of institutions guaranteeing respect for the rule of law, democracy, protection of minorities and human rights – are topics which are generally laid down in national constitutional laws and judicial practice. For an assessment of how these principles work in practice and to evaluate whether the respective rights are also actually applied, an analysis of the national constitutional provisions and practice is necessary. This is done in the Progress Reports from the European Commission.

3. WHAT WAS THE IMPACT OF THE MULTI-COUNTRY PROJECT?

This joint effort has stimulated the applicant countries to draft better proposals for the amendment of constitutional texts. Political support for accession sometimes wavers in the candidate countries which could form an obstacle to the amendment of the constitutions, especially when the amendment procedure takes too much time. For this reason, proposals for improving these procedures are needed, as they are crucial to the efficient adaptation of legislation. The candidate countries have learned from each other's experiences in this respect during the discussions and debates organized in the framework of the multi-country project. In so doing, they avoided having to re-invent the wheel!

The stakeholders and target groups of the multi-country project consisted of scholars, civil servants, judges, prosecutors, (staff) members of national parliaments and government representatives from the participating countries.

3.1 New developments at EU level

Since the Declaration of Laeken of 15 December 2001, the Brussels Convention and the Draft EU Constitution of 18 June 2004, the objectives of this multi-country project and its project setting have been adapted accordingly and a new Constitutional dimension was added. Once it has been adopted by all the Member States, the European Constitution will change the *acquis communautaire* and thus impact the conditions for accession: the adoption of the European Constitution will become a new condition for accession. This meant that some new questions had to be included in the initial questionnaire. The following two new questions were suggested and added during the Rapporteurs' meeting in Bucharest on 24 and 25 October 2003:

A. Are there specific legal and constitutional problems and/or obstacles in your national legal order to the adoption of the European Constitution? Could you give an overview of the possible legal problems in your country with regard to impact on the constitution, the national judiciary, the executive and the parliament?
B. In your opinion, does the European Constitution improve the democracy, transparency and efficiency of EU decision making? Could you give some examples?

3.2 Why were the training sessions and briefings necessary?

Participation in the training sessions organized in the framework of the project has raised the awareness of the candidate countries' participating judges, prosecutors, and experts of the constitutional problems involved in accession and the impact of accession on the national legal order and on legal protection and the rule of law. This was necessary as the Copenhagen accession criteria explicitly refer to democracy, the rule of law, human rights and protection of minorities, topics that are generally regulated by the national constitutions. In complying with these criteria not only the national constitutions and legislation are relevant, but also and especially their application and interpretation ("living constitutions") by the national judiciary and prosecutors.

The project increased the national judiciary's awareness of their role as Community courts by training judges, prosecutors and lawyers in the candidate countries on European law. Training was required as European law requires that the candidate countries, as soon as they become Member States, should apply and give priority to Community law in their national legal order. To give a "briefing" to the judges, workshops were held on the comparative analysis of national court decisions (of Constitutional Courts, Supreme Courts, etc.) concerning the relationship between the national legal order and the Community legal order. On request, workshops concerning the relationship between substantive EU law and substantive national law were also organized. To complement these activities, meetings, academic debates and press conferences were held at the universities of the participating countries.

The case law of the European Court of Justice requires that candidate countries, once they become Member States, should apply and give priority to Community law in their national legal order. This made it necessary to train the national judiciary and prosecutors on the principles of primacy, direct effect and direct applicability of Community law and to prepare them for the impact of accession on their national legal order.

The project aimed to contribute to and improve the capacity to implement and apply Community law, not only during the current *pre-accession phase, but also after accession.*

Another result of the project was, however, that the participation of university teachers in the training sessions considerably increased their skills and knowledge of European and comparative national public and private law increased. In addition, the academic teaching of European law to law students in the candidate countries received new impetus and the multi-country project established an interregional network of co-operation between law professors in the participating countries. This network has since been strengthened especially after the participation in the Final Conference in The Hague in the framework of the Dutch EU Presidency.

Finally, the multi-country project contributed to the debate on the European Constitution as the views of the new Member States and (pre-)candidate countries were added to it during the briefing seminars and the Final Conference.

4. OLD AND NEW REASONS FOR APPROXIMATION AND ADAPTATION OF NATIONAL CONSTITUTIONS AND LAWS

The European Council of Laeken stated that the Union "has to become more democratic, more transparent and more efficient". The Convention was also intended to pave the way for enlargement of the Union to twenty-five and to cope with the ten new members. It is in the interest of an enlarged EU to increase the effectiveness of the EU legal order. The European Constitution may contribute to this effectiveness. The EC and EU proved to be a success story since after its existence many new countries have applied for membership and acceded to the European Community which is based on the rule of law. It was the rule of law as interpreted by the European Court of Justice which promoted further integration and not the rule of politics! To achieve security, democracy and effectiveness of the rule of law, it is necessary to have an effective and transparent administration, an independent judiciary and an adequate system of legal protection at EU and national level. The European Constitution will contribute to these objectives.

National constitutions and the national courts interpreting these constitutions play an important role in the legal protection of citizens in the European Union and the candidate countries. The national constitutional aspects are especially important in *the pre-accession period* as the national constitutions of the candidate countries determine the legal consequences of the rule of law in the national legal order: legal protection, direct applicability, direct effect and supremacy, primacy or priority of Community law. They determine the possibility to enforce Community law (e.g., the Europe Agreements) in the national legal order during the pre-accession period. For a satisfactory system of legal protection not only the national constitutions and constitution-based legislation are relevant, but also and especially their interpretation ("living constitutions") by the national judiciary. These constitutional aspects have to be addressed and regulated and adequate legal protection has to be established as far as possible before accession. However, adaptation of national constitutions also remains necessary after accession, as practice in respect of the constitutions of the "old" EU Member States has shown.

At the national level, enlargement will likely contribute to the constitutional modernization of the candidate countries. From the above it has already emerged that there is a growing and continuous need – before as well as after accession – to adapt national constitutions and constitutional laws and practice:

1. In some applicant countries the adaptation of the constitution is necessary in order to be able to ratify the EU Treaty. These constitutions must, for example, come to include provisions concerning the transfer to international organizations of state powers which are to be exercised jointly with the EC and EU. Any obstacles to accession to international organizations (like the EU) in the national constitutions must be eliminated. However, in a number of smaller candidate countries that only regained their independence since 1991 there are some political and psychological objections against, for example, the transfer of sovereign powers. Still, inclusion of relevant provisions is necessary to ward of possible future constitutional complaints.

2. In order to guarantee the required degree of uniformity of terminology concerning EU topics, applicant countries have to improve their drafting skills so as to produce better legislative proposals for the amendment of the Constitution. One example of the problems relating to terminology which may occur is the wording of the transfer of sovereignty in the official English translation of Article 90 of the Polish Constitution which speaks of *delegation* of the competence of state organs to an international organization, whereas the correct term is *transfer*. The meaning of *delegation* in constitutional law is limited to transfer of powers to a *lower* institution or organization. According to Community law, the transfer of sovereign or state powers to the European institutions is permanent, i.e., these powers cannot be reclaimed, which is, however, what the term delegation suggests.
3. The relationship between European law and national law should be more or less identically formulated in all candidate countries in order to have the same effect on the national legal orders in the pre-accession period. One question is whether in the future the national Constitutions may simply refer for this to the respective articles of a future European Constitution.
4. The way in which the European integration process is dealt with in some Constitutions is politically and psychologically less fortunate. For example, where there is a lack of transparency concerning integration ("European deficit"), as in the Dutch Constitution where no reference at all is made to the EC or EU.
5. At present, many provisions in national Constitutions are contrary to or do not comply with the *acquis communautaire* (for example, concerning extradition of own nationals). These provisions will have to be adapted.
6. The Copenhagen criteria for accession as included in Agenda 2000 – the stability of institutions guaranteeing respect for the rule of law, democracy, protection of minorities and human rights – are topics which are generally laid down in national constitutional laws and judicial practice. For an assessment of whether the national Constitutions comply with these criteria and how these principles work in practice and to evaluate whether the respective rights are also actually applied, an analysis of the national constitutional provisions and practice is necessary, possibly followed by relevant amendments to the Constitution. The attitude of the European Commission may in my view be characterized as slightly schizophrenic, as on the hand it considers the drafting of national Constitutions the exclusive domain of each accession country,[1]

[1] Alfred E. Kellermann, 'Preliminary Conference Findings, Results and Conclusions', in Alfred E. Kellermann, Jaap W. de Zwaan, Jenö Czuczai, eds., *EU Enlargement: The Constitutional Impact at EU and National Level* (The Hague, T.M.C. Asser Press 2001) pp. LVIII-LXI, especially Conclusion No. 8.

while on the other hand its Progress Reports focus on the operation in practice of the constitutional principles in these countries. The leading principle during the negotiations on accession to the European Union is the acceptance of the *acquis de l'Union* by the candidate country. An altogether different question is whether the candidate country can also be required to accept some kind of *acquis constitutionnel*: does membership of the European Union involve the adoption of particular rules and principles in *national constitutional law* which are modelled on the Constitutions of the present Member States?

7. Because the *acquis communautaire* is dynamic, the adaptation of national Constitutions is a continuous process, both before and after accession. With the adaptation of national Constitutions it is aimed to improve the capacity to implement and apply Community law both in the current pre-accession phase, but also after accession. The present EU members have also on occasion had to adapt their Constitutions after accession. This makes the Constitutions themselves dynamic too.

5. HOW TO PREPARE AN EFFICIENT AND EFFECTIVE STUDY AND COMPARATIVE ANALYSIS OF NATIONAL CONSTITUTIONS FROM THE VIEWPOINT OF ACCESSION?

1. For improving the capacity to prepare and adapt national Constitutions and constitutional practice in accordance with the requirements of Community law, the sharing of experiences with drafting in other current and candidate EU Member States can be extremely useful. Multi-country cooperation in adapting national Constitutions is improving the quality of European constitutional law. By its comparative approach, multi-country cooperation supports the efforts of the applicant countries to attain a more or less uniform legal language concerning EU topics and stimulates them to draft better constitutional texts. Multi-country discussion raises the awareness of politicians, judges and experts in the participating countries and improves the practical and theoretical knowledge of the national judiciary concerning concepts such as primacy, direct effect and direct applicability of Community law.

   To this, the following advantages may be added:

   - The project yields a useful overview of possible adaptations of the national Constitutions and constitutional practice in the applicant countries.
   - The process could continue to contribute after accession to proposals for adaptation or revision of national Constitutions which fully reflect the true importance of the European integration process.
   - The development and use of uniform European legal terminology in the national Constitutions where the relationship between Community law and

national law is concerned could also contribute to the development of the European Constitution.
- Participating countries are able to learn from each other's experiences during the discussions and debates in a multi-country context preventing them from having to reinvent the wheel.

2. The adaptation or amendment of national Constitutions is often achieved through complicated procedures which take a long period of time. In this respect, too, the sharing of experiences with lawyers in other candidate and Member States as well as with lawyers from the European institutions is very useful. It urges applicant countries to simplify their constitutional amendment procedures so as to be better equipped to deal with subsequent changes at EU level. Political support for accession wavers at times in the candidate countries, which could form an obstacle for necessary amendments of the Constitution, especially when amendment procedures take too much time. Improving these procedures is therefore necessary to enable efficient adaptation.

3. To ensure the effective implementation of the process of adaptation, the following groups of persons should be involved:

   - scholars, civil servants, judges, prosecutors, (staff) members of national parliaments and government representatives from (pre-)candidate countries;
   - EU experts from (pre-)candidate countries and EU Member States.

The theoretical and practical knowledge of Community law of persons who are or will be involved in the preparation, implementation, interpretation and application of national constitutional law and Constitutions must be improved. The awareness of citizens, national parliaments and governments of EU candidate countries of the constitutional impact of EU accession may be increased by organising debates and conferences and by the dissemination of reports in two languages, namely the national language of the respective candidate country and English, the latter for reasons of comparison.

4. The national judiciary's capacity to apply Community law, especially the principles concerning the relationship between Community law and national law, has to be enhanced and national judges must be made aware of their role as Community judges. This can be achieved through workshops, briefings and training sessions. European law explicitly requires that candidate countries once they become Member States should apply and give priority to Community law in their national legal orders. It is therefore necessary to train national judges and prosecutors in the principles of primacy, direct effect and direct

applicability of Community law and to make them aware of the constitutional impact of accession. Not only the wording of the national Constitutions is important, but especially their interpretation by the national judiciary and prosecutors to make them living Constitutions.

5. The project is expected to engender some common guidelines and instructions for the drafting and wording of national Constitutions to make them "EU-proof".

6. WHAT CAN BE LEARNT FROM THE EXPERIENCES IN THE EXISTING MEMBER STATES?

In order to be able to answer this we may focus on two specific constitutional provisions, namely provisions regulating the transfer of state powers and provisions regulating the relationship between the international/European legal order and the national legal order. In the following, an overview will be given of the relevant provisions in the Constitutions of the present EU Member States and how these provisions have been interpreted by the highest national courts after accession.[2]

6.1 The original six Member States

According to Bruno de Witte[3] there is simply no "common constitutional model" to be found in the six original Member States in respect of European integration; they can therefore not, as a group, act as a role model for the drafters of the Constitution in Central and Eastern Europe, Cyprus and Malta. However, the constitutional approach adopted by the individual countries making up the original membership may provide such constitutional inspiration, although no more so than could the experience of any of the other present Member States.

Constitutional impact of Schuman Plan / The European Coal and Steel Community

A major, and at the time startling, innovation of the "Schuman Plan", in contrast with earlier pre-war and post-war cooperation projects, was that sovereign states should agree to surrender their power over their coal and steel industries to a

---

[2] For an overview of the relevant texts of national constitutions of the EU Member States, see L.F.M. Besselink, et al., *De Nederlandse Grondwet en de Europese Unie* (Groningen, Europa Law Publishing 2002) Bijlage [Annex] 4, pp. 252-271.

[3] Bruno de Witte, 'Constitutional Aspects of European Union Membership in the Original Six Member States: Model Solutions for the Applicant Countries?', in Kellermann, et al., op. cit. n. 1, at pp. 65-79.

supranational body, the High Authority. By signing the European Coal and Steel Treaty, as it emerged from the "Schuman Plan" through negotiations in 1950, the governments of the Six agreed to relinquish national control over these two sectors of the economy and to allow the supranational High Authority to exercise autonomous "state" powers in their stead.

The way for this international innovation had been paved by the unprecedented openness to international cooperation displayed by the new post-war Constitutions of the three largest participants in the ECSC project. In *France*, *Italy* and *Germany*, the post-war restoration of democracy had been accompanied by the express constitutional recognition of the fact that effective international cooperation was necessary in order to prevent new wars and to avoid the excesses caused by unbridled state sovereignty. Each of these three new Constitutions contained a provision permitting limitations of sovereignty or transfer of sovereign powers to international institutions. All three provisions are still a part of the constitutional law of these countries today.

In *France*, paragraph 15 of the preamble of the Constitution of the Fourth Republic adopted in 1946 stated that "subject to reciprocity, France consents to limitations of sovereignty necessary for the realization and the defence of peace." Article 11 of the Italian Constitution of 1948 declares in strikingly similar terms that "Italy may consent, on equal terms with other States, to limitations of sovereignty necessary to establish an order ensuring peace and justice among nations, and it will favour international organizations which have that aim." Article 24(1) of the German Basic Law of 1949 expresses the same intention in active, rather than passive, wording: "The Federation may by legislation transfer sovereign powers to international institutions".

The function of each of these provisions was to facilitate the approval and entry into force of treaties for which otherwise a prior constitutional revision would have been needed. In the end all three countries approved both the ECSC Treaty and the Treaties of Rome (EEC and EAEC) on the basis of the "limitation of sovereignty" clause, and without making amendments to the text of their constitution.

The model set in the post-war years by the three leading Member States was imitated by *the Netherlands* and *Luxembourg* some years later, at a time when these countries had already joined the ECSC. *The Netherlands* adopted a constitutional amendment in 1953 (Art. 67 of the Constitution, now renumbered as Art. 92) allowing for the attribution of legislative, executive and judicial powers to international organizations. If such a transfer would deviate from the Constitution, it requires no more than an authorization by Act of Parliament approved by a two-thirds majority in both Houses of Parliament. There have been only three such deviations since 1953. Treaties such as the EEC Treaty and its later amendments have never required the qualified majority of two thirds of the votes cast.

Concerning the relationship between international law and domestic law, the Netherlands adheres to a monistic system: international law is "automatically" part of the national legal system.

In 1956, *Luxembourg* included Article 49bis in its Constitution, which reads as follows: "L'exercice d'attributions réservés par la Constitution aux pouvoirs législatif, exécutif, et judiciaire peut être temporairement dévolu par traité à des institutions de droit international."

The sixth member, *Belgium*, acted only much later. In this country, constitutional lawyers had expressed misgivings about the legality of joining the ECSC first, and the EEC and Euratom later, in the absence of any constitutional clause authorising the transfer of powers to international organizations, but it took until 1970, in the context of a much broader revision of the Belgian Constitution, before such an enabling provision was finally inscribed in the Constitution. In *Belgium*, Article 34 of the Constitution reads as follows: "The exercise of specific powers may be instructed by a treaty or by an act of organizations of international law".

The Contracting States were limiting their sovereign rights, transferring some of them to institutions over which they had no direct control. Two important cases concerning this transfer of rights were decided by the European Court of Justice, *Van Gend en Loos*[4] and *Costa* v. *ENEL*,[5] which both confirmed the precedence of Community law over national law. The strong submissions made on behalf of the governments in these cases indicate that at that time the concept of direct effect of Treaty provisions probably did not accord with the intention or understanding of those states when they became parties to the EEC.

One of the main challenges for all Member States' constitutional systems has been how to accommodate the primacy doctrine of the European Court of Justice and the exacting demands it makes on the national courts. There is a clear distinction to be made, in this respect, between the Six, for whom the *Costa* v. *ENEL* judgment of 1964 may have come as an unexpected surprise, and the states joining the EC at a time when primacy was a firmly established and widely publicized characteristic of the Community legal order for which they could (if necessary) make constitutional preparations.

Among the Six, the *Costa* v. *ENEL* judgment required no special efforts from the courts in *the Netherlands* and *Luxembourg*, where the supremacy of international treaty provisions over national legislation was accepted prior to the entry into force of the EEC Treaty, either on the basis of a clear constitutional rule (in *the Netherlands*) or on the basis of the case-law of the supreme court (in *Luxembourg*). However according to the *Costa* v. *ENEL* ruling all EC law prevails over

---

4 ECJ 14 August 1962, Case 26/62 *Van Gend en Loos* [1963] *ECR* p. 3.

5 ECJ 14 January 1964, Case 6/64 *Costa* v. *ENEL* [1964] *ECR* p. 1203.

Dutch law, which is undoubtedly an important extension of the rule laid down in Article 94 of the Dutch Constitution which only gives priority over Dutch law to self-executing (or directly applicable) provisions of international law.[6] Although the *Belgian* Constitution was silent on the matter of the domestic effect of international or European law, the Supreme Court adopted the principle of primacy as it had been formulated in *Costa*, and based it on the nature of international law and (*a fortiori*) of EC law. The other Belgian courts soon followed the same line.

In *France*, on the contrary, despite the existence of a constitutional provision (Art. 55) clearly recognising the priority of international treaties even over later French laws, the courts were surprisingly slow to accept that this constitutional provision could actually be used as a conflict rule in real cases and controversies. The *Cour de Cassation*, taking the lead for the "ordinary" court system, decided to cross the Rubicon in the 1975 *Cafés Jacques Vabre* judgment.[7] The *Conseil d'Etat* (and the administrative courts subject to its authority) followed suit much later, with the *Nicolo* decision in 1989,[8] after what must have been a very painful revision of established truths. Yet, by emphasizing the distinction between EEC law and "ordinary" international law, the European Court had encouraged the *German* and *Italian* courts to find a specific solution ensuring the primacy of Community law without necessarily extending this primacy to other international treaties (unlike what happened in the four other countries). By the early 1990s, therefore, the necessary adjustments of constitutional doctrine allowing for the primacy of EC law over national acts of parliament had been accomplished in all six countries. Yet, this primacy of EC law was not expressly inscribed in any of the six Constitutions; *France* and *the Netherlands* had a written rule, but dating from the 1950s and applying to international treaties in general, whereas the four other Constitutions remained entirely silent on the important question of the domestic effect of EC law.

The Single European Act (1986), according to De Witte,[9] did not leave any traces in the constitutions of the Six, but the signature of the Treaty on European Union (1992) set in motion a constitutional amendment process in two countries. In Germany, the amendments were made on the government's and parliament's initiative, and received the reserved blessing of the Constitutional Court in its famous Maastricht judgment;[10] in France, the *Conseil Constitutionnel* first identified three points on which the new Treaty was incompatible with the

---

[6] C.A.J.M. Kortmann, *European Union Law and National Constitutions*, Report for the XXth Fide Congress (London, November 2000).

[7] Ch. mixte, 24 May 1975, *aff. sté. Jacques Vabre*, *Bull. civ.* C.M., No. 4, p. 6, D.1975.497.

[8] C.E. Ass., 20 October 1989, *Nicolo*, D. 1990.135; J.C.P. 1989 II 21371.

[9] De Witte, loc. cit. n. 3, at p. 71.

[10] BVerfG 12 October 1993, 89 BverfGE 155; [1994] 1 *CMLR* 57.

existing text of the Constitution, and the Constitution was then amended so as to remove the inconsistency. In both countries, this resulted in constitutional provisions that explicitly recognize the existence of the European Union whereas, as indicated before, the ECSC and the EEC had not been mentioned in any of the six Constitutions. Article 23 of the German Basic Law, which now applies alongside the general international cooperation clause of Article 24, gives express support to the creation of the European Union and entrenches the participation rights of the *Länder* in the European integration process; it also entrenches substantive conditions for participation of Germany in the European integration process. Articles 88-1 to 88-4 of the French Constitution, while giving specific constitutional approval to the clauses of the Maastricht Treaty which the *Conseil Constitutionnel* had found to be contrary to the Constitution as it stood, also refer in general terms, and for the first time, to the existence of the EC and EU:

> "Art. 88-1: La République participe aux Communautés européennes et à l'Union européenne, constituées d'Etats qui ont choisi librement, en vertu des traités qui les ont instituées, d'exercer en commun certaines de leurs compétences.
>
> Art. 88-2 :Sous réserve de réciprocité et selon les modalités prévues par le Traité sur l'Union européenne signé le 7 février 1992, la France consent aux transferts de compétences nécessaires à l'établissement de l'Union économique et monétaire européenne."

Several legal writers both in the Netherlands and in Italy argued that the Maastricht Treaty contained such far-reaching provisions, particularly in the monetary field, that constitutional amendments were required, as was the case in France. The post-Maastricht phase of constitutional reform was thus limited to two countries only, and was short-lived. When, some years later, the Treaty of Amsterdam was adopted, the prevailing attitude was, again, that of minimising the constitutional implications of this further deepening of the integration process. This Treaty led to a small constitutional amendment in only one of the six countries, namely France, where, after a decision of the *Conseil Constitutionnel* finding the new immigration powers of the EC to be incompatible with existing constitutional law,[11] a special clause was added to the Constitution in order to cure this incompatibility.

---

[11] Conseil constitutionnel, Décision n° 92-308 DC du 9 avril 1992, *Maastricht I*, Recueil, p. 55; RJC, p. I-496 - Journal officiel du 11avril 1992, p. 5354.

6.2 Denmark, Ireland and the United Kingdom

The States joining the Communities in 1973 were in a different position from the founding Member States, according to Francis Jacobs.[12] The primacy of Community law, and the consequent impact on national sovereignty, albeit within limited fields, were now well known, and it was therefore possible to make both political and constitutional arrangements beforehand. In some cases and in some respects, however, a minimalist solution was adopted. The three new states responded to the challenge in very different ways.

In *Denmark*, where amendments to the Constitution are difficult to attain, reliance was placed on a 1953 amendment to the Constitution (Section 20) which was similar to the very general provisions contained in the Constitutions of several of the founding Member States and according to which: "Powers vested in the authorities of the Realm under this Constitution may, by statute and to a specified extent, be delegated to international authorities set up by mutual agreement with other States for the promotion of international rules of law and cooperation". Thus, it was not considered necessary or desirable (or perhaps feasible) to introduce a specific amendment to make provision for accession to the Communities or to recognize the primacy of Community law.

In *Ireland*, by contrast, a very specific amendment was made to the Constitution in 1972 to provide a basis for Irish membership of the Community (Art. 29 para. 4 (3)): "The State may become a member of the [ECSC, EEC and Euratom]. No provision of this Constitution invalidates laws enacted, acts done or measures adopted by the State necessitated by the obligations of membership of the Communities or prevents laws enacted, acts done or measures adopted by the Communities, or institutions thereof, from having the force of law in the State." That amendment, which was followed by the European Communities Act of 1972, seemed well designed to allow for the constitutional and legal requirements of membership and it is not therefore surprising to learn that it has been considered as a possible model by at least one of the applicant countries.

In the *United Kingdom*, in the absence of a formal constitution, only an enabling Act of Parliament could be used; and because of the principle of Parliamentary sovereignty, which implied that no Parliament could bind its successor, it seemed impossible to provide for the primacy of Community law in relation to a subsequent Act of Parliament. The main instruction is contained in Section 2 (1) of the European Communities Act (ECA), which provides: "All such rights, powers, liabilities, obligations and restrictions from time to time

12 Francis G. Jacobs, 'The Constitutional Impact of the Forthcoming Enlargement of the EU: What can be learnt from the experience of the existing Member States?', in Kellermann et al., op. cit. n. 1, at pp. 183-191.

created or arising by or under the Treaties, and all such remedies and procedures from time to time provided for by or under the Treaties, as in accordance with the Treaties are without further enactment to be given legal effect or used in the United Kingdom shall be recognized and available in law, and be enforced, allowed and followed accordingly; and the expression 'enforceable Community right' and similar expressions shall be read as referring to one to which this subsection applies."

That provision achieves a great deal with very few words. It directs that the legal consequences flowing from the Treaties, which the latter themselves require to be produced automatically in the United Kingdom, by virtue merely of their existence within the Community order, shall be so produced. The rights, etc. to which the provision relates are to be recognized and available in law, while retaining their Community character: this is not a marriage of legal systems but a co-habitation within the same British house. The whole stock of directly applicable and directly effective Community law was thus placed at the disposal of the courts of the United Kingdom, alongside the common law and statutes. The provision applies, moreover, to all Community rights, etc. "from time to time created or arising"; in other words, to those subsisting at the time of accession and those which have come into existence subsequently.

The second relevant provision of the ECA is tucked away in Section 2(4). It consists of the wording: "... any enactment passed or to be passed, other than one contained in this Part of this Act, shall be construed and have effect subject to the foregoing provisions of this section ...". Parliament is here saying, in effect, that all existing and future statutes are to be so read, and to have such legal force, as not to derogate from the earlier provisions of Section 2, and especially subsection (1). At the very least, solid protection is thereby given against the implied qualification or repeal of Community provisions applicable in the United Kingdom pursuant to the subsection. The third provision deserving mention is section 3(1), which states: "For the purposes of all legal proceedings any questions as to the meaning or effect of any of the Treaties, or as to the validity, meaning or effect of any Community instrument, shall be treated as a question of law (and, if not referred to the European Court, be for determination as such in accordance with the principles laid down by any relevant decision of the European Court)."

That the Act did have the effect of ensuring the primacy of Community law over subsequent United Kingdom legislation was recognized unequivocally by the House of Lords, sitting as the highest United Kingdom Court, in the *Factortame* litigation.[13]

---

[13] House of Lords 19 May 1989, *R* v. *Secretary of State for Transport ex parte Factortame Ltd* [1989] 2 *CMLR* 353 (Divisonal Court/CA); [1990] 2 AC 85, [1989] 2 *All ER* 692 (HL judgment). See also ECJ 19 June 1990, Case C-213/89 *Factortame I* [1990] *ECR* I-2433.

6.3 Greece

The relevant provision of the Greek Constitution (of 1975) is Article 28 which reads as follows:

> "1. The generally recognized rules of international law, as well as international conventions after they have been sanctioned by law and after they enter into force according to their respective terms, shall form an integral part of internal Greek law and shall prevail over any contrary provision of law.
> 2. To serve an important national interest and to promote co-operation with other States, competences provided for in the Constitution may be recognized by treaty or agreement to agencies of international organizations. A majority of three-fifths of the total number of Members of Parliament shall be required for the enactment of the law, which sanctions the treaty or agreement.
> 3. Greece shall freely proceed by law passed by the absolute majority of the total number of Members of Parliament to limitations of the exercise of national sovereignty, insofar as this is dictated by an important national interest, does not infringe human rights and the foundations of democratic government and is effected on the basis of the principle of equality and under the condition of reciprocity."

There is, however, disagreement over whether accession to the Community was based upon the second or third paragraph of the Article, or on both paragraphs. The voting requirements of both paragraphs were fulfilled. It is suggested that there is in any event no doubt concerning the prevalence of Community law over conflicting Greek law, whether prior or subsequent.

6.4 Spain and Portugal

In *Spain*, Article 93 of the Constitution is regarded as providing the basis for Spain's accession to the Communities. It provides as follows: "Authorization may be granted by an organic act for concluding treaties by which the exercise of powers derived from the Constitution shall be transferred to an international organization or institution. It is incumbent on the *Cortes Generales* [Parliament] or the Government, as the case may be, to ensure compliance with these treaties and with resolutions originating in the international and supranational organizations to which such powers have been so transferred."

It is also of interest to note the view of the Spanish Constitutional Court, as recorded in the Spanish report, to the effect that conflicts between Community law and Spanish law are not a matter for the Constitutional Court. That view could result in a position consistent with the position taken by the ECJ, notably in the *Simmenthal* Case, that it is for the ordinary courts to give effect to Community rights and to set aside, where necessary, any conflicting provisions of national law, and that such conflicts should not be reserved to a constitutional court or to any other special procedure which would prevent the ordinary courts from giving immediate effect to Community law.[14]

In *Portugal*, successive amendments to the Constitution in 1982, 1989 and (to take account of the Treaty on European Union) 1992 provided the foundations for the adaptation of the Portuguese legal order to the European Treaties. As in Spain, the possible non-conformity of Portuguese legislation with Community law is dealt with by the ordinary courts, without the intervention of the Constitutional Court.

6.5 Austria, Finland and Sweden

Austria, almost uniquely, adopted a constitutional law expressly and specifically providing for accession to the European Union (Arts. 23 a-f). That law did not, however, directly regulate the relationship between Community law and national law. The Austrian Constitutional Court has taken the position that a violation of Community rights is not a violation of constitutional rights. As with Spain and Portugal, therefore, the outcome should be that it is open to the ordinary courts to set aside provisions of national law which conflict with Community law.

In *Finland*, we are informed that the Constitution permits derogations, which need not be formally incorporated in the text of the Constitution: in the case of treaties, such derogations can be approved by a two-thirds majority of the votes cast in Parliament. In the case of the Treaty of Accession, that was done after a scrutiny of the Treaty by the Constitutional Law Committee of Parliament. The Implementation Act, which was adopted under the above procedure, contains the necessary substantive provisions, which are very brief: the Act states Finland's membership of the EU and provides for EC and EU law to have the force of law in Finland under the conditions laid down by the *acquis communautaire*.

In *Sweden*, in contrast, the Constitution was amended to provide for accession to the EU: more precisely, one provision of part of the Constitution, the "Instrument of Government" (*Regeringsformen*) – the characteristic provision dealing with transfer of powers to international organizations – was amended to provide that the Swedish Parliament may transfer decision-making powers to the EC "as long as they provide for protection of fundamental rights and freedoms equivalent to that guaranteed by this instrument and by the European Convention on Human Rights".

---

[14] ECJ 9 March 1978, Case C-106/77 *Amministrazione delle Finanze dello Stato* v. *Simmenthal* [1978] *ECR* 629.

6.6 The European deficit of national constitutional texts

The way in which the constitutional texts of some EU Member States deal with the European integration process is rather disappointing, particularly in view of the political support which their governments and parliaments (and, indeed, their populations) have constantly given to that process. Today still, there is for example not a single hint in the Dutch and Italian Constitutions to the fact that the country is a Member State of the European Union; the constitutional basis for membership, and for the application of EC law, is still to be found in old provisions dating from the late 1940s and early 1950s. A few years ago, Italy came close to inserting new provisions in its Constitution dealing with the European integration process. The provisions were part of a general draft for the revision of the Constitution, and failed to be enacted because the political agreement on the whole draft collapsed in the summer of 1998. In the Netherlands, the fact that the general constitutional framework does not put any obstacles in the way of the European integration process is taken as a justification for leaving things as they are, although some writers occasionally point to the odd situation that the text of the Constitution contains many rather trivial rules but fails to acknowledge one of the central constitutional realities of the country, namely its membership of the European Union, with all the legal consequences deriving there from. However, on 5 December 2000 in the Dutch Senate a proposal from Jurgens et al. was accepted to mention EU Membership in the Dutch Constitution.[15]

6.7 Constitutional limits to the primacy of European law

In the view of the European Court of Justice, any directly effective rule of EC law should prevail over any conflicting rule of national law whatever its rank in the domestic hierarchy of norms. However, according to De Witte[16] this "absolute supremacy" even over national constitutional rules is not easily accepted by the courts in the Member States, including the courts of a number of the founding Member States.

The Italian Constitutional Court has consistently held, ever since its *Frontini* judgment of 1973,[17] that EC law may derogate from "ordinary" rules of constitutional law, but not from certain fundamental principles or inalienable rights of persons. The latter are, in Italian legal parlance, "counter-limits" (*controlimiti*) to the limitations of sovereignty allowed by Article 11 of the Constitution: when

---

[15] Motion of MP Jurgens a.o. (Kamerstukken I 2000/01, 26 200 VI, no. 37, replaced by no. 37b).

[16] De Witte, loc. cit. n. 3, at p. 73.

[17] Constitutional Court judgment No.183/73 *Frontini/Ministero delle Finanze*, [1973], Giurisprudenza cost. 2401; [1974] 2 *CMLR* 372.

state institutions exercise sovereign powers, they must respect the fundamental values and principles of the Constitution, and these values and principles must continue to be respected when state powers are attributed to the *European* institutions.

On this point, the German *Solange-II* judgment[18] specified that the Constitutional Court would refrain from controlling whether individual EC acts respected fundamental rights (this being a matter left to the ECJ), but that it could control whether the general regime of fundamental rights protection in the EC continued to be equivalent to the German constitutional standard. In the *Bananenmarktordnung* judgment of 7 June 2000 the Court later confirmed this position.[19] The "constitutional identity" referred to in *Solange-II* is broader than the fundamental rights question. Article 23 of the Basic Law, adopted in 1992 (that is, after *Solange-II*) has spelled this out by requiring the European Union to respect "democratic, rule-of-law, social and federal principles as well as the principle of subsidiarity", and the Constitutional Court added to this, in the Maastricht judgment of 1993,[20] that it would control whether the EU institutions remain within the limits of their attributed powers. The exact significance of this 1993 judgment has been the object of considerable controversy in Germany and abroad; the judgment has also been attacked by many scholars, but so far the abstract hypothesis of an *ultra vires* act of the EU has not materialized in the Karlsruhe case law. Thus, the constitutional clauses concerning limitation of sovereignty have received a largely similar interpretation from the Italian and German constitutional courts. These clauses have been used in a double capacity. On the one hand, they allow for the smooth integration of EC law into the national legal system, discarding dualist doctrine for the exclusive benefit of EC law and ensuring the direct effect and primacy of EC law in all "normal" situations. On the other hand, the sovereignty clauses allow the constitutional courts of these two countries to protect what they consider to be the core of the Constitution against EU encroachments.

The position in French law is not fundamentally different. Although the *Conseil Constitutionnel* does not directly control the constitutionality of EC legislative acts, the ordinary and administrative courts still consider the Constitution as the highest norm, and will not enforce the primacy of international treaty law (including EU law) when such enforcement would run counter to a constitutional norm. Even in Belgium, the exemplary attitude of the *Cour de Cassation* in

---

[18] BVerfG 22 October 1986, 73 BVerfGE 339; [1987] 3 *CMLR* 225 - *re the application of Wünsche Handelsgesellschaft.*

[19] BVerfG 7 June 2000, 102 BVerfGE 147.

[20] BVerfG 12 October 1993, 89 BverfGE 155; [1994] 1 *CMLR* 57.

Le Ski[21] is now overshadowed by the ambiguous position adopted by the *Cour d'Arbitrage*, the quasi-constitutional court created in 1980, which declared itself competent to review the constitutionality of international treaties even after their entry into force although it has never, as yet, exercised this power in relation to EC law.[22]

The cause of all these reservations against an absolute primacy of EC law is the fact that constitutional courts, quite understandably, cannot accept that any source of law might prevail over the national Constitution itself, which after all is the source of their own existence. If the Constitution is seen as the basis for recognizing the primacy of Community law, then absolute primacy of the type postulated by the European Court in *Internationale Handelsgesellschaft*[23] is only possible by way of an "auto-limitation" clause in the Constitution. The Netherlands offers a solitary example of such a clause. Article 120 of the Dutch Constitution prohibits national courts from reviewing the constitutionality of treaty provisions and of decisions of international organizations, and thereby ensures the absolute supremacy of treaties once they have been properly ratified. Accordingly, the Dutch courts have never hinted at the existence of constitutional limits to EC law.

6.8 The tension between constitutional traditions and the reality of European integration

The constitutional connection between the (old) principle of popular sovereignty and the (new) attribution of powers to international organizations is particularly clearly illustrated by the Belgian Constitution. The restricted nature of this qualification is denoted by the fact that only the *exercise* of powers can be transferred to the international institution (which implies that they can return to the institutions of the state upon termination of the treaty or some other event in the future) and that the powers should be *delimited* (which presumably means that a substantial amount of powers should remain at the national level). The idea that European integration is nothing but the common exercise of sovereign powers of the nations is also clearly expressed in Article 88-1 of the French Constitution. It continues to command widespread support among constitutional authors in Germany, France and Italy. From the perspective of the *joint exercise of sovereignty*, the institutions of the European Union are, as it were, acting on behalf of the various sovereign peoples of the Member States. Yet, and this remained firmly established in constitutional

---

21 *Belgium* v. *S.A. Fromagerie Franco-Suisse Le Ski:* Cass., 27 mai 1971, Journal des tribunaux, 1971, 460.

22 CA n° 12/94, 3 February 1994, Moniteur Belge 1994, pp. 6137-6147.

23 ECJ 17 December 1970, Case C-11/70, *Internationale Handelsgesellschaft mbH* v. *Einfuhr- und Vorratsstelle für Getreide und Futtermittel* [1970] *ECR* 1125.

doctrine, nothing has changed in the basic rule that *sovereignty itself continues to reside in the people* and may therefore not be *alienated.*

This brief analysis suggests, according to Francis Jacobs,[24] that it may be helpful to outline the main categories of potential conflict between national constitutions and European law.

(1) A first case concerns the exercise by the European institutions of transferred powers: where, under the Constitution, powers have been transferred to the EC/EU, who is to adjudicate on whether powers have been exercised going beyond the scope of those transferred? From a European perspective it may seem inherently anomalous that such adjudication should be left to the national courts of each of the Member States. However, the perspective of the national courts, and particularly that of a national constitutional court, may be different. The dilemma seems intractable. The following sub-category may, however, provide some reassurance that solutions are nonetheless possible.

(2) A sub-category is the case where it is alleged that the exercise of powers by the EC/EU conflicts with fundamental rights protected by the Constitution. This is the most debated aspect of the subject, and is of great interest from a doctrinal point of view, perhaps because at a theoretical level it is one of those wonderful problems which admit of no possible solution. No doubt a Constitution cannot provide, explicitly or implicitly, that powers may be exercised by an international body even where they infringe fundamental rights protected by the Constitution. In practice, however, the ECJ itself has sought to overcome this difficulty by developing its own case law requiring the Community to observe fundamental rights recognized by the national constitutions; and this case law is now also enshrined in the Treaty. This solution has hitherto been broadly acceptable in the legal systems of the Member States, and it does indeed seem the only practical solution. Since what is at issue is the validity of a Community measure, it does not seem sensible to leave the decision to each national system.

(3) A third category is the more general case where the Constitution does not make adequate provision for the primacy of Community law. These difficulties have generally been overcome (if sometimes only after periods of uncertainty) by the national courts themselves, which have progressively recognized that the primacy of Community law, even if not explicitly provided for by the national Constitution, is inherent in the very nature of the Community system. Nonetheless such a pragmatic solution cannot, once again, provide any guarantee that difficulties will not recur.

---

24 Jacobs, loc. cit. n. 12, at p. 189.

(4) A fourth category is that of specific constitutional provisions which transpired to be in conflict with the Treaty as interpreted by the ECJ. For example, constitutional provisions in several Member States reserving posts in the public service to a state's own nationals have been found to conflict with the Treaty provisions on the free movement of workers and on freedom of establishment as interpreted by the ECJ.

Such specific conflicts cannot always be readily resolved by constitutional amendment: the amendment procedures may (as, for example, in Denmark) be extremely laborious. An alternative solution may be found in other ways: interpreting the constitutional provisions in the light of the more general provisions designed to give effect to Community law; or, if that is not possible, a "sympathetic" interpretation of the specific provision – so that, in the example taken above, "public service" is interpreted as restrictively in the Constitution as it is by the ECJ in the Treaty. Such interpretations may be encouraged by the realization that specific provisions of this kind are not inherently of a constitutional nature: the restriction of posts in the public service to a state's nationals is not a matter universally regulated at the constitutional level; it may be regulated at the level of ordinary legislation, over which Community law can more easily be held to prevail.

7. WHAT CAN BE LEARNT FROM THE EXPERIENCES OF THE NEW EU MEMBER STATES AND THE (PRE-)CANDIDATE COUNTRIES?

What is the impact that EU accession is likely to have on the national legal orders of the new EU Member States and (pre-)candidate countries? General concluding answers will be given in the contributions by Jenö Czuczai (as regards the judiciary), Anneli Albi (as regards the national Constitutions and Parliaments) and Steven Blockmans (as regards the executive) in Part II of this book. The fifteen country reports included in parts I and III further contain more specific and elaborate answers to the questions contained in the questionnaire for the six Matra Multi-Country countries and nine new EU Member States respectively.

8. CONCLUDING REMARKS

The impact of EU accession on the national legal orders of the new EU Member States and (pre-)candidate countries has been analysed for four different national legal powers and institutions: the national Constitutions, the national judiciary, the national executive and the national Parliament. In this introduction we have discussed the general impact of EU accession on the text and application of national Constitutions.

Through the comparative analyses of 15 countries (new EU Member States and (pre-) candidate countries) in the multi-country project all the participants were able to learn from each other's experiences in the adaptation of their national legal orders to the Community *acquis*. The drafting of constitutional amendments would be greatly simplified after the development of common guidelines or models for those parts of the national Constitutions dealing with the EU.

The role of national Constitutions is often underestimated by politicians at the EU level, but it is also often overestimated at the national level. The Irish referendum on the Treaty of Nice on 7 June 2001 was one example of different constitutional requirements and their impact on ratification. Although the Nice Treaty had been concluded by the EU Member States by common accord, the negative outcome of the Irish referendum made ratification for the moment impossible.

In any case, hopes and fears concerning further EU integration are not limited to the new EU Member States and (pre-)candidate countries alone, but are shared by the old Member States, as the negative outcome of the recent referenda in France and the Netherlands on the European Constitution have shown.

One may wonder whether we will still need national Constitutions once we have a European Constitution. National Constitutions are rigid instruments and often stand in the way of dynamic European integration. Could we not confine ourselves to organic Acts for the states, which could be more flexible?

At the constitutional level we have seen that in some Member States, constitutional provisions were not sufficiently adapted to facilitate the full effect of Community law. In some cases this was the result of difficulties posed by the national Constitution itself. The United Kingdom is a rather extreme example.

It is true that many of the difficulties have been overcome, in a very remarkable way, by judicial ingenuity, by constructive dialogue between the ECJ and national courts, and perhaps above all by a creative and pragmatic approach of the national supreme courts. But this does not seem a wholly satisfactory recipe for the future.[25]

In the first place, there are, as we have seen, continuing problems in the existing Member States. Several national supreme courts still hesitate to recognize unconditionally the primacy of Community law, and find no adequate basis in the national Constitution to do so. The situation therefore remains precarious.

Secondly, if solutions to conflicts have largely proved possible to date (in a relatively favourable legal and judicial climate) there can be no guarantee that this

---

25 Jacobs, loc. cit. n. 12, at p. 191.

will continue. The path of further constitutional amendment after accession may not always be available. In the context of enlargement, it would seem paradoxical if close attention is paid to the detailed transposition of the entire corpus of Community legislation by the candidate states, while little interest is shown in the constitutional provisions needed to make them effective.

EU accession urges all 15 countries to make fundamental constitutional changes. The impact of EU accession on the various Constitutions will mainly concern the following topics:

a. The principle of the transfer of the exercise of certain state powers to the EU deriving from national state sovereignty;
b. The relationship between Community law and national law: supremacy, primacy, direct applicability and direct effect in the national legal order;
c. Compliance with specific provisions of the EU and EC Treaty (European citizenship, voting rights, etc.);
d. Adapting specific provisions in national Constitutions which contradict the *acquis communautaire*, such as the acquisition of land and property by non-residents, extradition of own nationals, etc.

Adaptation of national Constitutions is necessary before and after accession. The content of national Constitutions should be continuously monitored. In this respect, the situation in the EU Member States may, after all, not be so different from that in the candidate countries, which are also faced with the question of whether their constitutions, despite their recent origin, may need to be changed so as to facilitate adaptation to the European Union legal order. In four old EU Member States, for example, no mention at all is made of EU or EC Membership in the wording of the Constitution.

Not only is it necessary from a legal point of view to make the necessary changes to the Constitution in advance, it is also socially and politically desirable to already confront the constitutional implications of membership of the EU before, not after accession. The constitutional *acquis* should be added to the screening process, the aim of which is to help the countries concerned increase their understanding of the rules that underpin the EU and identify more clearly which issues they need to address as they adopt and implement the *acquis communautaire*. The relevant sectors are identified, but not the constitutional *acquis*. A chapter on the constitutional *acquis* should be added and included.[26] A post-screening meeting should be held for candidate countries to explain what the constitutional requirements involved in the accession process are.

---

[26] Jenö Czuczai, 'Practical Implementation by the Acceding Candidate Countries of the Constitutional Acquis of the EU. Problems and Challenges', in Kellermann, et al., op. cit. n. 1, at pp. 411-422.

After accession changes may still on occasion be required. As the *acquis communautaire* is dynamic in nature, the adaptation of national Constitutions will be a continuing process. The Nice Treaty, the Charter of Fundamental Rights and any future Constitutional Treaty for Europe (will), when ratified and approved, have an impact at the EU and national level.

Ideas and suggestions for the future

Developing more or less identical texts for national constitutional provisions which focus especially on (i) the transfer of state powers to an international organization, and (ii) the relationship between the European Community legal order and the national and sub-national legal orders of the EU Member States and candidate countries would increase transparency. References in national constitutional texts to the finally approved European Constitution could be a starting-point for a confederation. Identical or at least very similar procedures for amendment and ratification in the national Constitutions could be very helpful for further integration. We therefore suggest the introduction of some kind of "European model" for describing the relationship between the Community legal order and the national legal order as well as one for the regulation of the transfer of state powers to the EC institutions. Such common guidelines or models would have to take into account the continuing developments in the Community legal order and its case law and help the candidate countries adjust their Constitutions with a view to joining the EU.

Another question which needs to be addressed is whether EU Member States, as happened for instance in Ireland, may invoke their constitutional provisions in order to justify the negative result of a referendum and thereby postpone ratification, especially considering that in other Member States there might not be such a constitutional obligation to hold a referendum as a condition for ratification.[27]

Another suggestion is to include in the national Constitution a provision that is similar to a provision in the Canadian Constitution of 1982 which would state that "the European Union Constitutional Law includes the Constitutions of all Member States as interpreted by their highest courts". This would guarantee constitutional integration as well as constitutional and legal pluralism.[28] Such an adaptation of national Constitutions, the bottom-up approach as it were, could render Europe more effective and bring it closer to the citizens.

---

[27] Alfred E. Kellermann, 'Postscriptum', in Kellermann, et al., op. cit. n. 1, at pp. 499 and 501: "A Member State cannot rely upon provisions of its Constitution for the purpose of justifying a failure to comply with obligations and time-limits resulting from directives" (ECJ, Case 100/77 *Commission* v. *Italy* [1978] *ECR* 887 para. 21).

[28] Europe 2004, Le Grand Debat, Setting the Agenda and Outlining the Options, Brussels, 15 and 16 October 2001, European Commission, Action Jean Monnet, Antonio-Carlos Pereira-Menaut, p. 77.

Part I

Matra Project Countries

BULGARIA

Evgeni Tanchev* and Jenia Peteva**

Broadly speaking, constitutionalism in the EU is the process of the gradual transformation of the Founding Treaties into a body of supreme and fundamental law that penetrates the national legal orders and has priority over the national legal systems of the EU Member States, including their Constitutions. The case law of the European Court of Justice (hereinafter referred to as "ECJ") has affirmed the fundamental characteristics of the constitutional order of the EC – the autonomy of the EC legal order, the principle of the rule of law, equality before the law, the supremacy, direct, immediate and universal effect of EC law,[1] the doctrine of implied powers of the Community institutions, pre-emption in the areas defined by the Founding Treaties, and protection of human rights.[2]

Gradually the Founding Treaties acquired the same status of higher law or supremacy that was always an undisputed feature of national Constitutions.[3] The constitutional nature of EC primary law has caused it to go beyond the classical public international law principle of "*pacta sunt servanda*". From international law which is given supremacy it has turned into supranational law within a supranational legal order and now shares some formal characteristics with national constitutional law.[4] The process of the constitutionalization of the

* Jean Monnet Professor New Bulgarian University, Professor and Head of Chair "Constitutional Law", Sofia University "St. Kl. Ohridski".

** LLM University of Leiden, Assistant Professor in Constitutional Law, Sofia University "St. Kl. Ohridski", Lecturer in EU Law, EC Law and Human Rights New Bulgarian University.

1 These widely recognized features of EC law were formulated by the Court during the 1960s; see cases *N.V. Algemene Transport- en Expeditie Onderneming van Gend & Loos* v. *Netherlands Fiscal Administration*, Case 26/62; *Costa* v. *ENEL*, Case 6/64.

2 See E. Stein, 'Lawyers, Judges and the Making of a Transnational Constitution', 75 *American Journal of International Law* (1981) pp. 1-27; P. Pescatore, 'The Doctrine of Direct Effect', 8 *European Law Review* (1983) pp. 155-157; J.H.H. Weiler, 'The Community System: the Dual Character of Supranationalism', 1 *Yearbook of European Law* (1981); A. Easson, *Legal Approaches to European Integration in Constitutional Law of the European Union* (Florence, F. Snyder, EUI 1994-1995).

3 For the meaning ascribed to higher law over the centuries, see I. Cappelletti in *Judicial Review in the Contemporary World* (Indianapolis, Bobbs-Merrill 1971) pp. 25-32 and his *Comparative Constitutional Law* (Indianapolis, Bobbs-Merrill 1979) pp. 5-11.

4 For the distinction between the supremacy of international norms and the direct effect of EC law, see J.H.H. Weiler, 'The Transformation of Europe', 100 *Yale Law Journal* (1990) p. 2403, in *The Constitution of Europe* (Cambridge, Cambridge University Press) pp. 41-42.

Founding Treaties has been given expression in ECJ case law in the qualification of EC primary law as a "constitutional charter" of the European Communities.[5]

For the countries that are applying for EU membership, EU constitutionalism implies that they must adapt their national Constitutions and their legal systems prior to accession. In addition, the way in which law is enforced in these states must be able to guarantee the proper functioning of the EU legal system.

The impact of EU accession upon the Bulgarian legal order is complex and dynamic. Adaptation of the national legal order to EU requirements has set in motion an economic, legal and social transformation process whose outcome is to ensure the effective functioning of the multi-dimensional EU legal system. The complexity of the process is largely the result of the changing role of the state on the one hand and the development of the EU into an organization with constitutional dimensions on the other. This development will most likely result in a conceptual transformation of the EU system. The unpredicted speed of this constitutional development has revealed the need for Bulgaria to provide a flexible legal framework with the potential to anticipate and absorb diverse and specific future developments in European integration.

1. THE ADAPTATION OF THE NATIONAL CONSTITUTION

The unwritten constitution[6] of the EU comprises provisions related to the values and principles of EC law that are contained in the Founding Treaties and in those

---

[5] Case 294/83 [1986] *ECR* 1339. The Opinion of the European Court of Justice on the Draft Agreement on the European Economic Area, delivered in December 1991, has been characterized as a zenith of the description of the Founding Treaties as a constitution. The EEC Treaty, albeit concluded in the form of an international agreement, nonetheless constitutes the Constitutional Charter of the Community, based on the rule of law. As the Court of Justice has consistently held, the Community Treaties established a new legal order for the benefit of which the states have limited their sovereign rights, in ever wider fields, and the subjects of which comprise not only Member States but also their nationals. The essential characteristics of the Community legal order which has been established are, in particular, its primacy over the law of the Member States and the direct effect of a whole series of provisions which are applicable to their nationals and to the Member States themselves". See also S. Weatherill, *Law and Integration in the European Union* (Oxford, Clarendon Press 1995) pp. 184-185; See also Opinion 1/91, 14 December 1991. See for more details D. Curtin, 'The Constitutional Structure of the Union: A Europe of Bits and Pieces', 30 *CMLR* (1993) pp. 17-69.

[6] At the time of writing, the Draft Constitution for Europe has not yet been adopted by the Intergovernmental Conference of the Member States. Therefore, the authors proceed from the law of the EU as in force until 15 August 2003. Throughout history, the term "Constitution" has had at least two meanings. Actual Constitutions have existed since ancient times and are still present in most states and even in organizations and corporations. These Constitutions are functional and regulate the institutional structure of different groups and how they function within the collective and what their relationship with the members of the collective should be. From this perspective, the European Union undoubtedly has an actual Constitution, regulating the structure and functioning of its institutions and their relationship with the Member States and the citizen. In the term Constitution's second meaning,

decisions of the ECJ that have had a constitutionalizing effect. It reflects a relatively high level of independence of the Communities from the Member States and establishes an elaborate structure of regulated competences and an institutional framework which exists independently from the Member States. The nationals of the Member States have EU citizenship. The constitutional principles and norms of EU law meet most of the formal requirements that are commonly imposed on the norms contained in the Constitutions of nation states as the body of higher law or law of the land.[7]

The unwritten EU constitution interacts with the national Constitutions, predetermining their regulation of the structure of the Community's institutional framework and the legal system, on the one hand, and influencing the internal legal order and the functioning of political institutions of the Member States, on the other. As opposed to in a federal system, where all the states' constitutions are automatically subordinated to the federal constitution, the Constitutions of the EU Member States have to be adapted to the Founding Treaties accompanied by only a limited transfer of sovereignty and preserving in this way the national identity and the historical peculiarities of the constitutional systems of the individual Member States.

In this contribution, the authors will start from the *status quo* on the understanding that the Draft Constitution for Europe as presented by the Convention on the Future of Europe does not invalidate, but rather consolidates and strengthens the fundamental aspects of the constitutional order of the EU.

1.1 Implementation of international law and transfer of legislative powers

The Bulgarian Constitution of 13 July 1991[8] was the first completely new constitution to be adopted in all the emerging democracies in Central and Eastern Europe. Article 5(4) of this Constitution establishes the democratic principle of the *primacy* of international law over any conflicting domestic legislation. The principle of the primacy of international law is considered to form an integral part of the supremacy of law as defined in the classic German doctrine of "*Rechtstaat*"

EU primary law (the Founding Treaties, especially after the Treaty of Amsterdam) is often considered as the EU's unwritten Constitution, by which is meant a set of legal instruments that contain fundamental rules of law.

[7] For the evolution of the concept of higher law throughout history, and especially in the aftermath of the drafting of the written Constitutions, see M. Cappelletti and W. Cohen, *Comparative Constitutional Law* (Charlottesville, Bobbs-Merrill 1979) pp. 5-11; C.J. Friedrich, *The Philosophy of Law in Historical Perspective*, 2nd edn. (Chicago, University of Chicago Press 1963) pp. 12-26.

[8] Constitution of the Republic of Bulgaria, promulgated in State Gazette No. 56 of 13 July 1991, in force since 13 July 1991.

or the principle of the Rule of Law as developed in the Anglo-Saxon legal tradition.

The Constitution adopts a *monist* approach to the incorporation of international norms into the national legal system. By virtue of Article 5(4), international treaties which have been ratified in accordance with constitutional requirements, have been promulgated, and have entered into force for the Republic of Bulgaria are part of the domestic legal order and no further national legislation is required for their enforcement. Article 5(4) further expressly provides that norms of international law which have thus become part of domestic legislation prevail over any conflicting provisions of domestic law. This means that the self-executing provisions of international treaties are directly applicable. International treaties supersede any contravening provisions of national legislation.[9]

By virtue of Article 149(1)(4) of the Constitution, the Constitutional Court shall rule on rule on the compatibility between the Constitution and the international instruments concluded by the Republic of Bulgaria prior to their ratification, and on the compatibility of domestic laws with the universally recognized norms of international law and the international instruments to which Bulgaria is a party.

According to the constitutional provisions concerning the implementation of international law in the domestic legal order, the provisions of international treaties thus prevail over the provisions of any Act, Decree, Order or Regulations within the legislative hierarchy of national law.[10] This conclusion may be reached based on a comparative analysis of the Constitutions in states that also maintain a monist approach where the legal status of norms of international law is either lower or by way of an exception, equal to, the provisions of the Constitution.

According to the interpretation given by the Bulgarian Constitutional Court to Article 5(4) of the Constitution, international treaties that are already part of the domestic legal system "acquire the status and force of laws" and "[as with] all the laws in the state, these ratified international treaties should be subject to constitutional control under Article 149(1)(2) of the Constitution".[11] The primacy of

---

[9] See Annotation to Article 5(4) of the Constitution of Bulgaria by Evgeni Tanchev in *Constitution of the Republic of Bulgaria – commentary* (in Bulgarian) (Ciela Publishing House 1999) pp. 41-45 at pp. 42-43. The Constitutional Court of the Republic of Bulgaria, Decision No. 7 of 2 July 1992, constitutional file No. 6/92, promulgated in State Gazette No. 56 of 10 July 1992. See also Constantin Economides, *The Relationship between International and Domestic Law*, European Commission for Democracy through Law, Collection "Science and Technique of Democracy" No. 6 (Strasbourg, Council of Europe Press 1994).

[10] See E. Танчев, "Източниците на правото в Сравнителното конституционно право" в Съвременно право 1995, кн. 1 и 3; A. Pizzorusso, ed., *Law in the Making* (Berlin/Heidelberg/New York/London/Paris/Tokyo, Springer 1988); G. Winter, ed., *Sources and Categories of European Union Law* (Baden-Baden, Nomos 1996); L.M. Díez-Picazo, *Sources of Law in Spain: An Outline*, EUI Working Paper No. 94/10 (San Domenico (Fl), European University Institute 1994).

[11] Decision No. 9 of 16 June 1999, file No. 8/99, promulgated in State Gazette No. 57 of 1999.

international law over any conflicting domestic legislation obviously means that international treaties occupy a higher hierarchical position. The ruling of the Constitutional Court has to be interpreted in the context of the determination of its particular constitutional powers.

Given the above, the principles implicit in Articles 5(4), 85(3) and 149(1)(4), and the analogy with some of the legal systems of other European countries places the provisions of international treaties on a par with or above Acts of Parliament, but below the Constitution of the Republic of Bulgaria. Any assumption of the opposite would go against the Constitution. If international treaties would rank alongside or above the Constitution, Articles 85(3) and 149(4) would be redundant. If treaty provisions ranked alongside the provisions of the Constitution, they would, from the moment of signing and ratification, automatically become part of the constitutional text and there would be no need to amend the Constitution before concluding "conflicting" international treaties or to review it to secure compliance with the international treaty prior to ratification. Furthermore, in this scenario, constitutional provisions would already be overridden and amended by the mere act of signing and ratifying "conflicting" international treaties. In effect, the primacy of international law over the national Constitution would mean that treaty makers would have a degree of Constituent power which completely disregards the fundamental principle of recognizing national sovereignty in public international law.

According to well-established case law of the Bulgarian Constitutional Court, "international treaties" in the meaning of Article 5(4) of the Constitution refer strictly to the respective instruments of public international law. They are "… by their nature bilateral and multilateral agreements that are concluded among states with the participation of the Republic of Bulgaria and that are regulated by public international law…".[12] The Bulgarian Constitution does not provide any legal basis for a transfer of legislative powers to international organizations, nor can this be achieved by any possible interpretation of the provisions of the Constitution in force.

1.2 Amendments

As was the case with the current Member States of the EU, the key issue in Bulgaria's accession to the EU is the constitutional recognition of the supremacy of EC law and the competences of the EU institutions.

The EC Treaty lays down the fundamental principles of EC law and regulates the key areas of European integration. It includes the notion of EU citizenship,

12 Decision No. 7 of 2 July 1992, file No. 6/92, promulgated in State Gazette No. 56 of 1992; Decision No. 9 of 16 June 1999, file No. 8/99, promulgated in State Gazette No. 57 of 1999.

following the amendments introduced by the Treaty of Maastricht, and it regulates the status of the Community institutions, which are simultaneously also the institutions of the EU and of the Euratom Treaty. The Maastricht Treaty supplemented the Community Pillar with two intergovernmental Pillars: Common Foreign and Security Policy and Justice and Home Affairs (which, after the Amsterdam Treaty became the Area of Police and Judicial Co-operation in Criminal Matters). An important part of the legal system of the EU has been the gradual strengthening of the protection of human rights, especially under Articles 6 and 7 of the TEU. Article 6(2) of the TEU rendered the standard of protection of human rights, developed in the law and practice of the European Convention of Human Rights and Fundamental Freedoms (hereinafter referred to as "ECHR") that was adopted under the auspices of the Council of Europe, a part of the *acquis communautaire*. This standard also forms part of the political criteria for accession under the 1993 Copenhagen Criteria for EU membership. Furthermore, the ratification of the Convention is a *de facto* condition for membership of the European Union.[13] Article 7 of the TEU further strengthens the protection of human rights by introducing a new constitutional rule that involves significant sanctions for serious violations of human rights in the EU Member States.

A constitutional foundation that would allow for the signing and ratification of the EC and EU Treaties could be created in several ways. There are two possibilities. The first is to adopt a general clause that would allow for the transfer of sovereign powers, or rather enable the "*pooling of sovereignties*", and for the recognition of the competences of the European institutions.[14] As far as the latter is concerned, this would involve the establishment of special bodies and the elaboration of constitutional procedures for the appointment of Bulgarian representatives to the European institutions.

It would further involve cooperation between the national authorities and the European agencies, as well as cooperation of certain specific bodies with the European Commission. A special position in this respect is accorded to the relationship between the DG Competition of the European Commission and the national competition authorities of the Member States. The latter have to cooperate with the

---

13 According to Section 6(1) of the Treaty on the European Union, the Union is founded on the principles of liberty, democracy, respect for human rights and fundamental freedoms and the rule of law. The European Court of Justice in its established case law has stated that fundamental rights form an integral part of the general principles of law, the observance of which it ensures. The ECHR is the major source of such fundamental principles and therefore its standards are of a primary importance. Case 4/73, *Nold* v. *Commission*, [1974] *ECR* 491, para. 13 (1974); Case 36/75, *Rutili* v. *Minister for the Interior*, [1975] *ECR* 1219, para. 32 (1975). See also R.A. Lawson and H.G. Schermers, 'A Bird's-Eye View of the European Convention', in R.A. Lawson and H.G. Schermers, *Leading Cases of the European Court of Human Rights* (Nijmegen, Ars Aequi Libri 1997) pp. xv-xl at p. xix.

14 The general term "European institutions" takes into account the fact that since the 1965 Merger Treaty the Communities have a common institutional framework.

Commission, and the Commission has investigative powers and jurisdiction in issues of cross-border competition in the EU.

As for the Euratom Treaty, the goals and effect of the nuclear energy policy have changed significantly over the years and must nowadays be considered in the light of the overall energy policy of the Community. This entails the establishment of a single energy market for electricity, free movement of goods with regard to gas transmission, price transparency, non-discrimination and equal treatment (only to be derogated from on the ground of national security), uniform safety standards concerning the common market for nuclear energy equipment and the adequate supply of nuclear energy, ensuring that nuclear energy will not be used for unlawful purposes, etc. Compliance with these standards, as with most areas of EC law, requires the adoption of laws that implement the Directives in Bulgarian legislation and compliance with the relevant international instruments to which the Community is a party. Of these, the most important is the Energy Charter. The requirements set out above are duly listed under Articles 79 and 80 of the Association Agreement between the Republic of Bulgaria on the one hand, and the European Communities and their Member States on the other.[15] The institutional framework of the Euratom Treaty includes, in addition to the basic European institutions, the Supply Agency that approves contracts between the producers of ores and nuclear fuels and the producers of nuclear energy. The Agency became operative in 1960 and is supervised by the European Commission. For this reason, the simple recognition of the competence of the European Commission will most likely be sufficient to ensure the recognition of the powers of the Agency with regard to the production of nuclear energy in Bulgaria.

There are no constitutional obstacles to the creation of a proper institutional framework for cooperation between the institutions established by the Bulgarian Constitution and the EU institutions. EU constitutionalism respects the constitutional structure of the Member States and the principle of national procedural autonomy. There are no requirements for an institutional set-up with regard to EC law. As for Police and Judicial Co-operation, participation of Bulgaria in Eurojust and Europol does not require any constitutional amendments insofar as these systems are based on intergovernmental cooperation rather than supranational arrangements. Moreover, the establishment of the Association Council under Article 105 of the Association Agreement and its powers to adopt binding decisions, as well as the establishment of the Parliamentary Association Committee under Article 111 of the Association Agreement, with advisory functions, support the view that the Bulgarian Constitution has a flexible framework for

---

[15] Europe Agreement for Association between the European Communities and their Member States, on the one hand, and the Republic of Bulgaria, on the other hand, ratified by law on 15 April 1993, State Gazette No. 33 of 20 April 1993, in force since 1 February 1995.

creating supplementary institutional arrangements within or in addition to the system of the constituted powers. Furthermore, in its Decision No. 3 of 2003,[16] the Constitutional Court expressly held that integration in the EU would require granting some of the constitutionally established institutions new functions, but that this would not require the amendment of the Constitution to the extent that the main principles of the Constitution are respected.

Nevertheless, there are some practical problems. Some of them concern the constitutional provisions and constitutional practice. The first problem concerns the wording of Article 5(4) of the Constitution, which does not allow for transfer of sovereignty to an international or supranational organization. Another issue is the scope of application and the content of the key constitutional principles that raise doubts about their viability in terms of ensuring a systematic application of EU law. Finally, the judicial system has been criticised for its inefficiency and weak capacity in terms of ensuring the enforcement of EU law. Upon a recent official visit of the Commissioner for Enlargement, Bulgaria was given a strict warning that a failure to amend its Constitution with regard to the part concerning the judiciary by September 2003 would be fatal for the successful ending of the membership negotiations within the mandate of the then EU Commission. This makes it necessary to amend the Constitution so as to overcome any potential deficiencies in the enforcement of EU law.

The procedures for amendment of the Constitution were influenced by the context in which the Constitution was adopted. One could say that the Constitution was drafted in reaction to this context. Furthermore, constitutional practice throughout the world has shown that the constitutional infrastructure is built during the first decade after a constitution's adoption; the living constitution is shaped by the decisions of the constitutional courts, by political agreement, and by influence brought to bear by heads of state.[17] During this process, any discourse on amending the Constitution may, on occasion, be premature. Anticipating problems of this kind and in an attempt to prevent the restoration of any kind of dictatorship by way of a formal amendment of the Constitution, the Founding Fathers created an *extremely rigid* constitution. Chapter IX of the 1991 Bulgarian Constitution establishes a dual (hybrid) regime of exercising constituent power. Following the traditions and the legacy of the 1879 Turnovo Constitution, the most important amendments of the Constitution must be drafted

---

[16] Decision No. 3 of 10 April 2003 on constitutional case No. 22 of 2002, promulgated in State Gazette No. 36 of 18 April 2003.

[17] The 1958 Constitution of the Fifth French Republic is probably the best example. In the words of De Gaulle, in his 1946 Bayeux speech, the Constitution needed some time to adapt to the political reality. "In the fifth year of its life, the Fifth Republic was established on the foundation I had laid down", C. de Gaulle, *Memoirs of Hope: Renewal and Endeavor*, Vol. 3 (London, Weidenfeld and Nicolson 1971) p. 338.

by a Grand National Assembly of 400 members, elected *ad hoc* for this purpose. The exclusive prerogatives of this classic, though somewhat outdated, repository of constituent power are the following: the adoption of a new Constitution, decisions regarding any changes related to the territory of the Republic and ratification of any international instruments envisaging such problems, decisions on changes in the polity of the state (unitary, federal, confederal, or granting of autonomy), and decisions on the form of government, the direct applicability of the Constitution, supremacy of international law and certain human rights guarantees and the amendment of constitutional amendment procedures.

The Constitutional Court has given a broad interpretation of the term "form of government" (Art. 158(3) of the Constitution). In its interpretative ruling in Decision No. 3 of 2003,[18] it held that this includes not only the main characteristics of the state, but also the system of constituted powers which currently comprise the National Assembly, the President of the Republic of Bulgaria, the Vice President, the Council of Ministers, the Constitutional Court and the organs, structure and organization of the judiciary as well as the conditions for membership, appointment and term of office of individual magistrates. The "form of government" thus includes the acts and powers of the constituted institutions, insofar as any amendment to the Constitution would change the *balance* between them. This balance complies further with the fundamental constitutional principles of state sovereignty, political pluralism, supremacy of the Constitution, a state based on the rule of law and the independence of the judiciary. In particular, the "form of government" includes any changes in the structure of the judiciary, such as transferring the investigative authorities to the scope of authority of the Ministry of the Interior. Amendments that concern the fundamental powers of any of the constitutional institutions, such as the presidential power of veto, also require the convoking of the Grand National Assembly.[19]

According to the broad interpretation given to Article 158(3) by the Constitutional Court, all other constitutional amendments, apart from those that are listed under Article 158 of the Constitution and are reserved for the Grand National Assembly, may be made either by the Grand National Assembly or the Parliament. Thus, the Founding Fathers also provided a rationalized model of constituent power vested in the National Assembly. Though designed in line with the trends in the modern, fourth-generation rules for constitutional amendment, the Bulgarian model for constitutional revision has so far proved, on the one hand, to be an effective barrier against quick, authoritarian and not well thought-out constitutional amendments, but, on the other hand, it has also been an ineffective mechanism in terms of flexibility of a constitution in transition.

---

[18] *Supra* n. 16.

[19] Ibid.

The constitutional amendment by the National Assembly requires an extremely high level of consensus, as the constitutional amendments have to be passed by special super-majorities. Amendments are to be initiated by the President or one-fourth of the Members of Parliament. The amendments become part of the Constitution if they are supported by a three-fourths majority of Parliament, on three separate parliamentary readings. There is a possibility for proceeding with a two-thirds majority if the Bill on the constitutional amendment has been supported in the first and second ballot by less than a three-fourths majority, but it has received more than a two-thirds support of the Members of Parliament.[20] In elections, super-majorities serve the purpose of ensuring a wide support to a single candidate in a pluralistic representative assembly. In the context of liberal constitutionalism and constitutionally responsible governance, the requirement of super-majorities in the constitutional amendment process serves the purpose of generating a consensus behind the proposed revision. This protects the opposition and the parliamentary minority against unilateral and authoritarian decisions of the parties in power, and prevents potential encroachments on human rights. In a pluralistic, highly fragmented Parliament such as the Bulgarian one, with coalitions sometimes too fragile to mobilize such majorities, it has been nearly impossible to reach the required majorities.

Bearing the above considerations in mind, we will outline the potential amendments that have been circulating in the public discourse, although these have not yet acquired the status of official proposals.

Most of the proposals for constitutional amendment refer to the enhancement of both institutional and functional constitutional safeguards for individual rights. One such proposal concerns the establishment of the institution of ombudsman. This proposal was an integral part of several draft constitutions, and it is important given that the institution of ombudsman exists in most of the EU Member States and some of the associated new democracies, as well as in the European Union. At the time of writing, the relevant Bill was pending in Parliament and was expected to be passed in the autumn of 2003. The establishment of an ombudsman, however, does not necessarily require the amendment of the Constitution. The Constitutional Court has also noted that "the form of government shall not be changed by the establishment of a new constitutional organ, if it is not a fundamental one and if its constitution will not affect the balance of powers between the rest of the constitutional institutions or the fundamental constitutional principles". This statement refers particularly to the institution of the ombudsman.[21]

---

[20] This model of voting bears some resemblance to the two-thirds majorities in the first and second ballot and the possibility for electing the President of the Greek Republic in the third ballot with a three-fifths majority of the Members of Parliament (Art. 32(3) of the 1975 Constitution of Greece).

[21] Ibid.

Another proposed amendment concerns the need to improve the functioning of the *judicial system*, by separating the prosecuting authorities from the judiciary, transferring the prosecution service to the executive power and introducing a limited term of office for judges. The reform of the judiciary has started by a proposal drafted by a parliamentary committee for the amendment of the Constitution.

In addition to the above amendment proposals, controversial opinions have been put forward to stipulate in the Constitution the right to bring *individual complaints to the Constitutional Court*, which would mean that citizens could become parties to constitutional proceedings to defend their rights where these are infringed by unconstitutional laws.[22] Currently, citizens can voice their concern about the protection of their human rights only by way of petitions to the parliamentary committee on human rights protection. The introduction of individual references to the Constitutional Court will undoubtedly extend the institutional guarantees for human rights. However, as practice in other states has shown, the number of petitions to constitutional courts is so high that it is practically impossible to address them in due course. As a result, the overall efficiency of the court may be significantly reduced. The introduction of individual petitions before the Constitutional Court can be effected by an amendment to the Constitution by Parliament.[23]

Proposals for a constitutional change have also been made in the field of institutions. Such proposals are aimed at increasing the efficiency of a constitutionally limited government, based on the principle of the rule of law. It has to be pointed out that this group of constitutional amendments is a result of sometimes hectic political debates, in which the arguments of the actors change depending on their political status in terms of control over political power, as well as on the prevailing political interests of the moment. As has been pointed out above, the Constitutional Court has found that only the Grand National Assembly can carry out this type of Constitutional amendments.

---

22 See Evgeni Tanchev, 'Constitutional Amendments Due to Bulgarian Full EU Membership', in A.E. Kellermann, et al., eds., *EU Enlargement: The Constitutional Impact at EU and National Level* (The Hague, T.M.C. Asser Press 2001) pp. 301-310. The Constitutional Court in its Ruling No. 1 of 1 July 1997 and Constitutional Decision No. 5 of 1997 took a radical step towards the indirect right of individual petition by giving the Supreme Court and the Supreme Administrative Court the power to suspend the hearing of a case to refer matters involving the constitutionality of certain acts to the Constitutional Court. Parties to cases involving possibly unconstitutional acts may ask the Court in question that the matter be so referred. (S.G., No. 54, 8 July 1997). This is, of course, the ultimate power of the Constitutional Court in respect of compliance with the constitutional provisions in force, which the Court is not allowed to change.

23 Decision No. 3 of 10 April 2003 on constitutional case No. 22 of 2002, promulgated in State Gazette No. 36 of 18 April 2003.

The main amendment proposals regarding the institutional setting concern the consolidation of the *institution of the President*. This would take place by means of the following changes: the possibility of overruling the Presidential veto by a qualified majority vote; strengthening of the functions of the President in respect of his position as a political arbiter by eliminating the restrictions imposed on Parliament; the dissolution of the government and wider discretion for the President in the procedure for the establishment of the government; granting the President the power to consult the people by referendum; and conferring on the President the right of legislative initiative (although this last proposal has not been thoroughly considered). It is beyond the scope of this paper to give an exact analysis of the substance of these constitutional amendment proposals, but suffice it to note here that introducing all the above amendments would mean transforming the parliamentary system of government into a semi-presidential or a presidential system. Therefore, a Grand National Assembly should be convened for adopting such amendments, in accordance with the constitutional amendment procedure provided in Chapter IX of the Constitution.

The remaining proposals concerning the institutions deal with streamlining the procedure for the establishment of a new government and the clarifying the status and powers of interim governments. In addition, certain proposals have been made which have exceptionally low chances for success. Such proposals include the regulation of delegated legislation as an effective instrument of modern parliamentary democracy, the creation of a Second Chamber to Parliament, and the restoration of the monarchy.

Amongst this relatively wide range of proposals for constitutional amendments, only those issues that concern the requirements for *EU accession* and the amendments to the constitutional provision on the *judiciary* have secured sufficient political consensus. As outlined above, only two bodies may undertake the amendment of the Constitution, depending on the material scope of the amendment. Thus, by virtue of Article 158(4) of the Constitution, the amendment of Article 5(4) of the Constitution to establish the supremacy of EC law and allowing for the transfer of competences to the EU requires the convening of the Grand National Assembly, whereas the current National Assembly (Parliament) can amend constitutional provisions concerning the judiciary, such as the magistrates' mandate and their irremovability.

On 23 April 2003, the National Assembly set up a Temporary Commission for preparing amendment proposals. The Commission limited its work to the reform of the judiciary and the membership of the EU. It recently presented proposals concerning the status of magistrates. As explained in the explanatory memorandum to the Bill, "the changes in the judiciary are imminent and a priority as they directly concern the effective and impartial functioning of the judiciary". The proposed amendments are well balanced and found unanimous support within the

Commission. They are a step forward towards improving the efficiency of the judiciary that protects fundamental rights. The proposed amendments concern three issues regarding the constitutional status of magistrates: their immunity, irremovability and the fixed term of office for top-level magistrates.

The amendments to Article 132 of the Constitution are based on the concept of "functional" immunity, which has two components. The first is the exemption from civil and criminal responsibility for acts performed while in office and for cases decided as a member of the judicial body, save in cases of general crimes of intent. The second is the required permission from the Supreme Judicial Council for the indictment of magistrates at an advanced stage of the criminal proceedings. The aim of functional immunity is to secure the independence of magistrates when they are acting within the scope of the powers assigned to them during their term of office, so that they should act only on the basis of their convictions regarding the facts and the law and remain free from any undue pressure. This functional immunity, however, is limited in scope. As a procedural impediment to the indictment of a magistrate at an advanced stage of the criminal proceedings it can only apply when there is sufficient evidence. Currently, the existence of "sufficient evidence" is not enough for the Supreme Judicial Council to form a clear idea and to rule in favour of or against the lifting of immunity. As a measure intended to protect the reputation of judges they cannot be detained without the permission of the Supreme Judiciary Council. Immunity may be lifted in such cases by the Chief Prosecutor or, to guarantee the normal course of the proceedings and to correct possible passiveness on the part of the Prosecutor, by one-fifth of the Council. The proposal indicates that the procedure needs further elaboration in legislation.

The difference with the rules currently in force is that judges would enjoy limited functional immunity, but not the general immunity as enjoyed by members of the National Assembly. Magistrates may further incur general criminal and civil liability for acts committed out of office. Immunity would thus be limited to the degree necessary to ensure the fundamental constitutional guarantees given with respect to the judiciary. It would not make them untouchable, though, as for their out-of-office activities they would bear the same responsibility as any Bulgarian citizen. The disciplinary responsibility of magistrates remains in place for any infringements of discipline at work under the labour legislation currently in force. This legislation refers to the obligations of magistrates as public servants, and they are not excluded from the scope of Article 132 in the envisaged amendments. By these rules, the organization of functional immunity complies with the recommendations of authoritative international institutions, now that it was based on, among others, the Regular Report of the European Commission on the progress of Bulgaria in the process of accession to the EU, the report for Bulgaria by the group of states against corruption (GRECO), both issued in 2002, the report for Bulgaria of the working group of the OSCE on corruption issues, issued in 2003, the memorandum for the reform of the judiciary by the Venice Commission, the UN Fundamental Principles for the Independence of the Judiciary, Recommendation N R (94) 12 of the Committee of Ministers of the Council of Europe on the independence, efficiency and the role of judges, etc. Similar rules can be found in the Constitutions of other countries of Central and Eastern Europe, such as the Czech Republic, Slovakia, Latvia and Slovenia.

Irremovability from office has always been part of Article 129(3) of the Constitution. After three years of membership of the judiciary, judges can no longer be removed, unless four exhaustive conditions are fulfilled. Irremovability is closely connected with the independence of the judiciary and of each individual magistrate.

In the proposed amendments to Article 129(3), conditions are tightened by increasing the required period of membership of the judiciary from three to five years and adding that during this period the magistrate in question must have conducted himself properly. A proposed new ground for revoking irremovability is that the magistrate concerned "systematically failed to perform his duties or by his actions damaged the prestige of the judiciary". Similar wording is also advocated by several international instruments, such as the UN Fundamental Principles for the Independence of the Judiciary and Recommendation N R (94) 12 of the Committee of Ministers of the Council of Europe on the independence, efficiency and the role of judges, which name the grounds of incapacity, serious infringement and unfitness. With this proposal, the Bulgarian parliamentary committee seeks to increase the responsibility of judges, following the example of the Constitutions of Sweden, Ireland, Lithuania, Slovakia, Greece and Malta. Further, the age limit of 65 years would replace the present ground for retirement, following the example of the Constitutions of Greece, Austria, Germany, Slovakia, Slovenia, Lithuania, Latvia, Malta, Poland, Estonia and Belgium. Finally, an amendment has been proposed according to which the legislator is obliged to pass, within six months, the necessary legislative amendments to regulate the transitional phase before full effect is accorded to each of the new rules proposed.

These draft amendments formally satisfy the urgent requirements of the European Commission. At the time of writing, thanks to broad political consensus, the amendments were expected to be passed after the exhaustion of the mandatory stages of the amendment procedure under Articles 154, 155 and 156 of the Constitution so as to enter into force at the end of September 2003.

1.3 Provisions contrary to the *acquis communautaire*

The amendments to the Constitution of the Republic of Bulgaria will be analysed from three perspectives. Firstly, we will attempt to establish which discrepancies will need to be eliminated from the Constitution prior to accession to the EU. Secondly, we will consider comparatively the constitutional amendments of the EU Member States, both those that were made ahead of ratifying the Founding Treaties, as well as those which were made in the countries that became full members of the EU following the enlargements that have taken place since 1993. Thirdly, we will also look at the trends in the development of the EU's unwritten 'constitution', which will impact on the amendments of the Bulgarian Constitution upon accession to the European Union.

Despite the fact that there is broad political and social consensus with regard to the amendments which need to be introduced in the Bulgarian Constitution in connection with the expected EU membership, no political decisions have yet been taken either on the way in which the amendments will be effected, or on which model deriving from the experiences of the current Member States will be followed. As a matter of fact, notwithstanding the peculiarities at the national level in all of the Member States, institutional modifications can be and have been performed without any amendments to the relevant Constitutions. However, some issues relate directly to the way in which the constitutional system is organized. These issues can be divided into three categories: (a) issues relating to the representation of the Member States in the Community institutions; (b) issues relating to the available mechanisms for shaping the national position on Community policies and functioning; and (c) issues relating to the designation of the national authorities which will be authorized to apply Community law.

At first glance, the issue of amending the Constitutions in the associated states does not appear to be at the top of the priority list, in comparison with the approximation of the national law with EU law. The constitutional amendments should be discussed by the public, so as to generate the necessary consensus for the content of the constitutional changes. However, certain provisions of the 1991 Constitution should be brought into conformity already as early as during the preparation period for full membership.[24] As has been pointed out by the European Commission in its Opinion on Bulgaria's accession application, such amendments would improve the efficiency of the institutions, so that Bulgaria could put into effect the recommendations regarding the political criteria for membership. Certain amendments are necessary in the field of fundamental rights of citizens and directly relate to full membership, such as Article 22 of the Constitution; other amendments affect the accession in an indirect way, with their purpose being to reinforce the principle of the rule of law (which constitutes one of the political criteria for accession). Overall, the amendments would not only bring the Constitution in conformity with the fundamental principles of European

---

[24] Commission Opinion on Bulgaria's Application for Membership of the European Union, Doc/97/11, Brussels, 15 July 1997. See also Tanchev, loc. cit. n. 22.

integration and with the requirements of the Founding Treaties, but they would also bring our legal system into compliance with European and universal standards. They would also favourably affect other fields beyond the approximation of legislation, as far as they favour the country's economic development, consequently creating the conditions for the preparation of the Republic of Bulgaria for full membership of the European Union.

One controversial issue has concerned the mode of eliminating the ban on the acquisition of land by foreign citizens, contained in Article 22 of the Constitution.[25] It would be insufficient to simply permit the acquisition of land by way of a legislative change, as this would hardly encourage foreign investors. In a rule-of-law-based state, it is impermissible to overrule a constitutional ban by way of a legislative regulation, and thereby circumvent the Constitution. Furthermore, the constitutional ban contained in Article 22 could be enforced by virtue of the supremacy and the direct effect of the Constitution under Article 5 of the Constitution. Altogether, keeping Article 22 unmodified would mean a complete discrepancy with the requirements of EU membership, as the Article contains a discriminatory barrier to the fundamental freedoms under EC law.

Amongst the amendments to the body of constitutional law which do not necessarily require the amendment of the Constitution itself is the issue of parliamentary control over matters of European integration. The participation of the national parliaments of the EU Member States in the process of decision making is a result of the need to increase the legitimacy of EU law, as well as to compensate for the democratic deficit in the work of its institutions. Because of an increasing transfer of powers to the European Union and the importance of the principle of subsidiarity, there is a need for the national parliaments to control the positions presented by the executive power to the Council of Ministers in the EU's decision-making process. On the one hand, the constitutional amendments should guarantee a fuller and a more detailed expression of the state's interests and, on the other hand, they should strengthen the principle of representative government, as well as implement the principle of transparency. In this way, the amendments would remedy the democratic deficit in the functioning of the institutions of the EU. In general, there is a trend for an increased role for the national parliaments in the EU's legislative process. This involves setting up new structures, such as the permanent commissions on European affairs, and developing the functions of the parliaments. Although the Bulgarian Constitutional Court has ruled that the existing institutions may be endowed with new functions and that new institutions could be established, the issues concerning the participation of the Bulgarian Parliament in the European system of governance need to be carefully considered.

---

[25] This ban is delicately referred to in the statement of the European Commission. See *supra* n. 24.

The standard of protection of human rights is another important issue in the debate about the necessary constitutional amendments. The jurisprudence of the European Court of Justice, in combination with Article 6(2) of the TEU, grants a special significance to the European Convention for the Protection of Human Rights and Fundamental Freedoms (hereinafter "ECHR"). The Convention was ratified by Bulgaria on 7 September 1992, but its provisions were taken into account already at the time of drafting the Constitution. However, the catalogue of rights under Part II of the Bulgarian Constitution does not fully overlap with the provisions of the ECHR. Even though the provisions of the Constitution reflect the principles of the ECHR and the catalogue of rights, as well as methods of interpretation, there are certain discrepancies. On the one hand, some of the rights are formulated in a broader way in accordance with other international legal instruments such as the International Covenant for Civil and Political Rights. On the other hand, however, there are certain grounds justifying restrictions that are not mentioned under the Convention. This reason, combined with the complexity of the transition process, calls for a more efficient system of remedies and a more coherent system of provisions in the substantive law.

Particular attention in this respect has to be paid to the principle of non-discrimination. The principle of equality and the prohibition of discrimination are recognized in all the democratic states governed by the rule of law. The Constitution of Bulgaria also provides for these fundamental principles. Article 6, which incorporates, in its first paragraph, the principle of equality, coincides in its wording with Article 1 of the Universal Declaration of Human Rights. The second paragraph prohibits discrimination on certain enumerated unjustifiable grounds. According to the Constitutional Court, any privileges based on any of the grounds mentioned in Article 6(2) shall infringe the principle of equality before the law.[26] On the one hand, unlike the prohibition of discrimination contained in Article 14 of the ECHR, which safeguards only the rights enshrined in the Convention,[27] the Bulgarian Constitution enshrines the principle of equality *per se* as a fundamental constitutional principle. As a matter of principle, equality and the prohibition of discrimination are inherent in the legal status and the protection of human rights. Article 6 of the Constitution is contained in Part I "Fundamental Principles"; there is no specific provision to that effect in the catalogue of human rights in Part II "Fundamental Rights and Obligations of the Citizens". Although the framers of the Constitution intended to introduce under Part II the minimum protection for fundamental rights as existing under the

---

26 Constitutional Court of the Republic of Bulgaria, Decision No. 14 of 10 November 1992, constitutional file No. 19/92, promulgated in State Gazette No. 93 of 17 November 1992.

27 Donna Gomien, David Harris, Leo Zwaak, *Law and Practice of the European Convention on Human Rights and the European Social Charter* (Strasbourg, Council of Europe Publishing and the Moscow Independent Institute of International Law 1998) (Russian version) pp. 450-452.

international human rights instruments,[28] the protection against inequality of treatment with regard to human rights is below the standard of protection granted under the ECHR. The Constitution does not explicitly mention colour, language, political or other opinion, and membership of a national minority, birth status – grounds explicitly provided for under Article 14 of the ECHR. Nevertheless, while Article 14 of the ECHR prohibits discrimination on any ground and gives a non-exhaustive list of grounds, the list under Article 6(2) is exhaustive, and this is also the established case law of the Bulgarian Constitutional Court.[29]

As a matter of fact, on 13 September 2002, the Council of Ministers approved a legislative Bill on the prevention of discrimination. This is a very positive step to ensure the efficiency of anti-discriminatory practices. The Bill extends the number of grounds on which discrimination is unlawful. Further, it prohibits both direct and indirect discrimination, introduces a number of rules against certain particular forms of discrimination, such as sexual harassment and discrimination at work, and establishes an independent institution for the prevention of, and control over, discrimination. The Bill implements EU Council Directives 2000/43[30] and 2000/78 EC,[31] as well as being based on a number of international instruments passed by the United Nations. If passed by Parliament, this Act could be an excellent ground for the systematic development and application of a coherent system of anti-discrimination law.

The subject matter of the constitutional revision determines which of the two amendment procedures provided in Chapter IX of the Constitution will have to be used. In case the amendments pertaining to the full membership of the EU will be introduced together with the amendments that fall under the exclusive competence of the Grand National Assembly by virtue of Article 158, the model of classic constituent power shall be applied. However, constitutional amendments concerning the model of state organization and the form of the state government would involve substantial complications. The change in the balance between the constitutional institutions through an increase or reduction of their powers constitutes by itself a "change in the form of government". Considering this, the amendments should be carried out in a way which would avoid the exceptionally difficult path of a constitutional revision by the Grand National Assembly. Because of this, preference should be given to those amendments that only include what is necessary for the ratification of the Accession Treaty between Bulgaria and the European Union. Such a rationalized procedure, where the

---

28 See Evgeni Tanchev, 'Constitutional Law Problems of the Compliance of the National Law with Directive 2000/43 EC of 29 June 2000 concerning the principles of racial and ethnic equality', in *Juridical World* 1/2001 pp. 145-153 at p. 147.

29 *Supra* n. 16.

30 *OJ* L 180, 19 July 2000, pp. 22-26.

31 *OJ* L 303, 2 December 2000, pp. 16-22.

amendments would be made by the National Assembly, could be used when a maximum degree of consensus exists among state institutions and political forces and within wider society in general concerning the purposes of the constitutional revision. An important role is played by the President of the Republic, who, according to the Constitution, symbolizes the unity of the nation and thereby has considerable possibilities to influence state policy and to facilitate the use of the National Assembly procedure.

It is clear that in the case of conclusion, ratification and entry into force of international treaties, the particular features of the relevant constitutional provisions must be considered alongside the particular features of the amendment procedure whereby the National Assembly introduces the amendment. Implementing Bulgaria's EU Accession Treaty cannot be done by a single act, but will require a procedure involving several stages, with each stage preparing the ground for the next. The stages would include the following: preparation of the Accession Treaty; preparation and submission to the National Assembly of a constitutional amendment Bill (under Art. 85(3) of the Constitution); adoption of the amendments under Chapter IX of the Constitution; the signing of the Agreement and arrangements regarding the time of ratification; reference to, and ruling by, the Constitutional Court under Article 149(1)(4) on the compatibility of the Accession Treaty with the Constitution (prior to ratification); passing of an Act of the National Assembly concerning the ratification of the Agreement.

By virtue of Article 85(3) of the Bulgarian Constitution, the EU Accession Treaty may be signed only after the Constitution has been amended. The negotiations on the preparation of the Agreement are normally conducted by the executive power, the Council of Ministers. Once the final draft has been prepared, it has to be determined which provisions of the Agreement would be incompatible with constitutional provisions at the moment of accession. Based on this, a legislative proposal for the amendment of the Constitution has to be drafted. Another more complicated option for the drafting and passing of such a Bill would be to have all the relevant steps carried out by the National Assembly. To this end, Parliament may decide to set up a special *ad hoc* Commission, made up entirely of lawyers and taking into account the principle of proportionate representation of the parties represented in Parliament. This Commission shall prepare and deliberate the Bill and the reasons for it in openness towards society. Once consensus has been reached among the Commission members the Bill is submitted to Parliament for signature. If one-fourth of Parliament signs, the Bill can be put on the agenda of the National Assembly (Art. 154(1) of the Constitution). From this moment onwards, the procedure under Chapter IX of the Constitution shall apply.

Parliament shall deliberate and vote on the Bill at first reading during a plenary session, taking into account the Commission's report. The members of Parliament shall express their opinion on the essence and purpose of the proposed amendment. After first reading, Parliament, through the President of the Commission, may submit written proposals concerning the amendments. The Commission shall then submit to the National Assembly a reasoned report, containing the written proposals of Parliament and its own position. Following this, the National Assembly shall deliberate and vote on the Bill, proposal for proposal, at second reading. Proposals going against the essence of the Bill as it was passed after first reading shall not be considered. After a reasonable period set aside for Parliament to determine its final position, the Bill will be voted on at third reading. If passed, the definitive text will be signed by Speaker and will be promulgated in the Official Gazette within seven days. Acts usually take effect on the day of their promulgation. Following the amendments to the Constitution, the Accession Treaty can be ratified and enter into force.

Prior to sending the ratification Bill to Parliament, the President of the Republic has to refer it to the Constitutional Court to obtain a decision on the compatibility of the Agreement with the Constitution after amendment (Art. 149(1)(4)). Parties to this case before the Constitutional Court are the President, the Government and Parliament. If the Constitutional Court finds the Agreement compatible, the Council of Ministers may submit the ratification Bill to Parliament. Parliament will then use the ordinary legislative procedure under the Rules of Procedure of Parliament to deliberate, vote on and pass the Bill. Once it has been passed, the Act shall be promulgated in the Official Gazette at which date it will also enter into force.

In sum, it may be concluded from the above that the complicated procedure for implementing the EU Accession Treaty would require Bulgaria's political elite and state institutions to achieve rapid consensus based on a modern political discourse.

1.4 Supremacy and direct effect

The issue of the compatibility of the Constitutions of the acceding states with EU law not only involves the introduction of international provisions into the national legal order and the legal effect of these provisions, but also the subordination of these Constitutions under a quasi-federal system. At present, European integration goes beyond the level of integration achieved by any other regional international organization and EC law has given rise to a new transnational legal order which, if not a federal legal entity in the classical sense, still strongly resembles one. For this reason, the issue of compatibility of the national Constitutions with the requirements of EU primary law is not so much one of the supremacy of international law over domestic law, but rather resembles the interdependence of constitutional frameworks on the national and international level. Making national constitutional law compatible with EU law is also quite different from the ordinary process of approximation of legislation, now that Constitutions are by nature different from ordinary legislation and their effects are felt throughout the territories of the Member States.

As has already been explained above, Article 5(4) of the Constitution of Bulgaria provides for the supremacy of international law over national legislation. However, this does not mean that the Constitution automatically guarantees the supremacy and direct effect of EC law.

The constitutional *acquis communautaire* is the degree of compatibility of the Constitutions of the EU Member States with EC primary law. Most EU Member States have had to amend their Constitutions to bring them into line with the body of primary law, especially following the Treaty on European Union. The frequency and scope of such amendments depend on the envisaged degree of transfer of sovereignty or delegation of powers to supranational institutions by new treaties. The newly accepted EU members will have to adopt the primary law in full and bring their Constitutions into line with its requirements upon accession. There is a discernable trend by which each subsequent accession will require a wider range of constitutional amendments as continuing developments in the European integration process widen the gap between EC primary law and the Constitutions of non-member states (but also of existing Member States!). At its present stage, however, the *acquis communautaire* does not require any extensive changes, such as changes in the form of government or in the organization of the different powers (legislative, executive and judiciary). However, countries that have applied for EU membership will have to adapt their Constitutions to the Founding Treaties, approximate their legislation, and prepare their judiciary, civil service and lawyers for the application and enforcement of EU law.

2. ROLE OF THE JUDICIARY (NATIONAL COURTS)

2.1 **Europe Agreement**

The main objective of the European Association Agreement with Bulgaria is to establish cooperation between the European Communities and Bulgaria in order to facilitate the country's accession to the EU. Association Agreements are international agreements. They fall in the category of mixed agreements, concluded between the Communities and third countries. Association Agreements set up an institutional framework consisting of three bodies. The first of these is the Association Council, which is a high-level political body comprised of the representatives of the Council of Ministers of the European Union and the European Commission on the one hand, and representatives of the associated state on the other. The Association Council decides on key issues of mutual interest, interprets the Association Agreement, settles disputes between the parties and, where necessary, sets up additional bodies for particular sectors of cooperation. The second body is the Association Committee, which supports and assists the work of the Association Council. It is composed of the representatives and members of the Council of Ministers of the EU and the European Commission, and representatives of the associated state at the level of the highest echelons of the civil service. The Association Council may delegate certain tasks to the Association Committee. The third body is the Parliamentary Association Committee. Composed of the representatives of the European Parliament and the Bulgarian Parliament, it is a consultative body that may make recommendations to the Association Council.

The Association Agreement with Bulgaria has been ratified by the Bulgarian Parliament. Decisions of the Association Council are passed by the Bulgarian Council of Ministers.[32] The decisions are applied on the same basis as provisions of international treaties to which Bulgaria is a party, also by the courts. The Supreme Administrative Court in its Decision No. 3420 of 9 April 2002[33] specifically ruled that the decision in question of the Association Council had become part of Bulgarian legislation and had to be complied with.

One of the main instruments for the adaptation of Bulgaria's economy prior to accession to the EU is the gradual establishment of a free trade zone with the accompanying rules for preferential origin and preferential customs duties. Some of the provisions concerning customs valuation and the levying of customs duties and VAT are self-executing by nature. In some cases traders have challenged the application of the provisions of the Association Agreement, first in administrative procedures and later before courts. Below, some decisions of the Supreme Administrative Court in which the Association Agreement was applied will be outlined.

In Decision No. 248 of 11 January 2002, the Supreme Administrative Court[34] confirmed the ruling of a district court which had held that tariff preferences are established on the ground of Article 35 of the Association Agreement and Protocol No 4 concerning the definition of the term "goods of origin".

---

[32] In this way, for example, Protocol No. 4 to the Association Agreement between the European Communities and their Member States, on the one hand, and the Republic of Bulgaria, on the other hand has been passed by Decision No. 1 of 1997 of the Association Council and was subsequently passed by Decisions Nos. 440 and 884 of the Council of Ministers.

[33] Decision No. 3420 of 9 April 2002 of the Supreme Administrative Court in administrative case No. 7259/2001.

[34] Decision No. 248 of 11 January 2002 the Supreme Administrative Court in administrative case No. 3698/2001. The decision mainly concerned procedural issues.

In Decision No. 4089 of 24 April 2002,[35] the Supreme Administrative Court quashed a district court decision on procedural grounds. The customs authorities had been unable to prove that the certificate of origin EUR 2 as presented by the applicant was not authentic. For this reason the Court confirmed the application of tariff preferences.

In Court Decision No. 8503 of 25 September 2002,[36] the Supreme Administrative Court ruled on appeal against a district court decision which in the preceding administrative proceedings had rejected a claim against the decision of the director of the District Customs Directorate by virtue of which the applicant was obliged to pay additional customs duties for an imported car. As the ground for levying additional customs duties it was adduced that the car was not a good of proved origin from the European Community, and as such could not benefit from any preferences. The district court had found that the declaration of the exporter and the certificate EUR 1 issued on the basis of Article 16 of Protocol No. 4 to the Association Agreement were faulty and had declared Article 11(1) of the Association Agreement on customs duty exemption inapplicable. The Supreme Administrative Court examined the application of Article 68 of the Customs Law and Article 69 of the Association Agreement, and upheld the decision of the district court. The Supreme Administrative Court has applied Article 11(1) of the Association Agreement and Article 16 of Protocol No 4 in several other cases where the facts were similar.[37]

2.2 Supremacy and direct effect

The Association Agreement, the Protocols to it and the decisions of the Association Council are by their nature international agreements. As such, the Bulgarian courts apply these instruments where they establish rights and duties. This is not the case, however, with EU law. Because the appropriate constitutional framework is lacking, EU law cannot have supremacy and direct effect with regard to Bulgaria.

Nevertheless, there are two ways in which EU law influences legal practice. Firstly, EU law is regarded as offering "guidelines" for the interpretation and application of the provisions of harmonized legislation. Secondly, EU law can be

---

35 Decision No. 4089 of 24 April 20021 of the Supreme Administrative Court in administrative case No. 10501/2001.

36 Decision No. 4420 of 30 July 1999 of the Supreme Administrative Court in administrative case No. 2587/2002.

37 Decision No. 5450 of 10 July 2001 of the Supreme Administrative Court in administrative case No. 7366/2000; Decision No. 9310 of 18 October 2002 of the Supreme Administrative Court in administrative case No. 3720/2002; Decision No. 9242 of 17 October 2002 of the Supreme Administrative Court in administrative case No. 3407/2002; Decision No. 11255 of 11 December 2002 of the Supreme Administrative Court in administrative case No. 5402/2002; Decision No. 5932 of 19 June 2002 of the Supreme Administrative Court in administrative case No. 1683/2002.

applied by means of Association Council decisions. EU competition law as been incorporated in Bulgarian law through harmonization of legislation and is thus applied in a roundabout way whenever decisions of the Commission for the Protection of Competition (the Bulgarian competition authority) are appealed against. The Commission is an administrative organ and its decisions are subject to judicial control. In such cases, the courts apply EC competition law, including the case law of the European Court of Justice.

2.3 Indirect effect

As the previous section has shown, the Supreme Administrative Court takes EC law as its guideline when interpreting the provisions of harmonized legislation. For example, in Decision No. 4420 of 30 July 1999,[38] the Supreme Administrative Court defined the term "misleading advertisement" in accordance with Article 2(3) of Directive 84/450/EEC of 10 September 1984,[39] and the provisions of Directive 97/55/EC of the European Parliament and the Council of 6 October 1997, amending Directive 84/450/EEC,[40] and included in it the concept of "comparing advertisement". The Court could not apply EC law directly as prior to accession EC law it does not have direct effect, but instead applied the provisions of the Directives as "guidelines" which have to be followed because competition law has already been harmonized in Bulgaria. This approach is further considered in compliance with Articles 69 and 70 of the Association Agreement which establish the obligation to harmonize both legislation and administrative protection against unfair competition. However, it should be noted that not all courts in Bulgaria follow the same approach.

2.4 Cases

Most of the relevant cases have already been discussed in the previous sections. However, a case ruled by the Supreme Administrative Court in 2002 could be mentioned. In this case, the applicant challenged the imposition of obligatory contributions to a state fund under Article 19, paragraph 2, point 6 of the Tobacco Act.[41] The applicant claimed that this provision was contrary to Article 60(2) of the Bulgarian Constitution and Article 11(4) of the Association Agreement. The Court rejected the claim due to substantial differences in the scope of the relevant provision of the Tobacco Act and Article 11 of the Association Agreement.

---

[38] Decision No. 4420 of 30 July 1999 of the Supreme Administrative Court in administrative case No. 1257/99.

[39] *OJ* L 250/18 of 19 September 1984.

[40] *OJ* L 290/18 of 23 October 1997.

[41] Decision No. 11393 of 13 December 2002 of the Supreme Administrative Court in administrative case No. 5010/2002.

2.5 Structure, procedures and practice

EU law respects the national constitutional structures. The ECJ has consistently held that national procedural autonomy is one of the principles of EC law. Therefore, EC law does not require any changes in the structure and procedures of the national courts. Changes could, however, ensue from the need to comply with EC law in practice and might result from the expected increase in the judiciary's workload. It has already been explained above that the application of constitutional principles is not subject to clear testing as in the practice of the ECJ. References to EU law in judgments concerning harmonized legislation could increase legal certainty.

If we make a comparison with the application of the European Convention on Human Rights and Fundamental Freedoms by the ordinary courts, we may observe a clear increase in references to the decisions of the European Court of Human Rights (ECtHR) as a whole, although references to particular judgments of the ECtHR are still insufficient. The increase in the number of references to the Association Agreement in recent years leads to the assumption that this trend will continue. It is difficult to speculate on the degree in which the judiciary's workload will increase. Much depends on the investment climate and the economic growth rate.

Even before the accession, judges have been overwhelmed with work, and this has required changes in the organization of the courts. Establishing special departments that would deal with the type of cases that form the bulk of the caseload would be one solution. A number of steps for streamlining the procedure have already been introduced over the past five years. They include making more use of expedited proceedings, procedural claims against undue delay and measures guaranteeing certain rights such as broadening the material scope of claims. Bringing the investigative authorities under the authority of the Ministry of the Interior would not give rise to many changes, as many investigative functions are already performed within the Ministry's framework.

3. ROLE OF THE EXECUTIVE (GOVERNMENT AND ADMINISTRATION)

3.1 Europe Agreement

The Europe Agreement is implemented by the administration in accordance with the powers delegated to the respective government departments. Within each Ministry there is a Directorate of European Integration to coordinate matters with other Ministries and to ensure the full compliance of the activities of the Ministry in question with the Association Agreement.

The Europe Agreement is applied in concrete cases whenever its provisions give rise to rights and obligations for individual parties. This is particularly true for the customs authorities, as has become clear from Supreme Administrative Court cases cited above. The Association Agreement is also consistently applied by the Commission for the Protection of Competition by means of the decisions of the Association Council on the application of EC competition law and practice and through the exchange of information between the Bulgarian Commission and the European Commission.

3.2 Preparation and implementation of EC/EU law

The institutional structure of the executive where compliance with the obligations under the Association Agreement and pre-accession activity is concerned is currently regulated by Regulation No. 33/11/02.2002 of the Council of Ministers.[42] According to this Regulation, the Council of Ministers shall determine and carry out Bulgaria's policy with respect to EU matters, the preparations for membership and the negotiations towards accession. To this end, the Council of Ministers has the following powers: to decide on the political issues involved in integration into the EU; to approve the mandate for negotiations by the Bulgarian representatives in the Association Council and the Association Committee; to approve documents concerning the Association Agreement, the position of Bulgaria in the negotiations and the financial memorandums for the successful use of EU subsidies. One important function of the Council of Ministers with respect to the preparations for membership is the approval of the national programme for the reception of EC law. The legislative initiatives put forward under this programme and in the negotiating positions are part of the legislative agenda of the Council of Ministers.

Unfortunately, one provision that was contained in a previous regulation obliging the Council of Ministers to submit the documents approved by it to the National Assembly and the President has been omitted from Regulation No. 33. Although this lack of information is made up for by other control mechanisms, an express obligation in this respect would contribute to better cooperation between the institutions.

The Minister of the Foreign Affairs is the leader of the Bulgarian delegation conducting the negotiations. A special position is held by the Chief Negotiator who has specific powers for the purpose of the accession negotiations and

[42] Regulation No. 33 of 11 February 2002 of the Council of Ministers for the organization and co-ordination of the preparation of the Republic of Bulgaria for accession to the European Union and conducting the association negotiations, promulgated in State Gazette No. 86 of 19 February 2002 as amended and supplemented State Gazette No. 85 of 5 September 2002, amended State Gazette No. 86 of 10 September 2002.

informs the Council of Ministers and the National Assembly about the negotiation process. The negotiation delegation also includes the President of the Bulgarian Mission at the EU, the Director of the Directorate "European Integration and Relations with the International Financial Institutions" at the Council of Ministers, the Vice-Ministers on European Integration and leading experts in foreign affairs, finance, economics, justice, home affairs and other areas of European integration.

The Chief Negotiator is mainly involved in the negotiation process and maintaining the dialogue with EU institutions. He/she represents Bulgaria and presents its positions at the Inter-Governmental Conference, at the level of vice-president of the delegation. He/she also leads the negotiation team at the Bulgarian Mission at the European Communities in Brussels. The Chief Negotiator formulates and puts forth concrete issues that may have emerged with respect to the negotiations and which have to be resolved by the necessary activities of the competent units that are responsible for the preparation of Bulgaria's accession. He/she also has coordinating functions towards a unified policy of Bulgaria on all issues regarding the EU. The Chief Negotiator must inform the Council of Ministers and the committees at the National Assembly of the negotiations' progress and possible problems which may have emerged that require action by these respective bodies and institutions.

In 2002, the position of Minister for European Affairs was created. The position of Chief Negotiator still exists, but is currently held by the Minister for European Affairs. In addition, the Minister for European Affairs took over some of the functions of the Minister of Foreign Affairs concerned with the coordination of the dialogue between the Bulgarian institutions and the European institutions. The Minister for European Affairs has the following powers: he/she coordinates the performance of the agreed terms in the course of the negotiations; monitors, coordinates and harmonizes the activity of the Directorates of European Integration within the Ministries and other institutions; approves the chiefs of the delegations in particular sectors for the dialogue with EU institutions; prepares the project for the National Programme on the implementation of the *acquis communautaire* in particular fields; and submits the project to the Council of European Integration. The Minister also informs the National Assembly.

For purposes of improved coordination and control, the Council of Ministers is assisted by the Vice-Prime Ministers who coordinate the preparations for membership of the EU and NATO. These newly created structures and positions show that for Bulgaria EU accession is a clear priority.

Another institution that is directly involved in the process of preparing Bulgaria for EU membership is the Council of European Integration at the Council of Ministers. The Council is presided over by the Prime Minister and includes the Ministers for the respective areas involved in the process of negotiations. The basic powers of the Council of European Integration are the following: considering Bulgaria's positions and mandates in the accession negotiations; nominating the members of the negotiation delegation (who are subsequently approved by the Prime Minister); proposing action plans and referring any problems with regard to European integration to the Council of Ministers to be decided; proposing priority activities on issues of European integration to the Council of Ministers; tendering and receiving evaluations of the effect of the implementation of EU legislation on particular sectors; approving the final list of project ideas for financing under the PHARE programme, which are subsequently proposed by Bulgaria to the programme management for approval and inclusion in the relevant financial memorandum.

The Council of European Integration ensures a unified and consolidated approach to the resolution of specific problems in the process of negotiations with the EU. Its coordinating functions are of crucial importance given the wide range of sub-processes following from the accession process as a whole. A sub-council of the Council of European Integration is the Coordination Council. Its main tasks are to provide the broad outlines of the activities of the working groups for the various negotiation chapters and to systematically monitor and evaluate the fulfilment of Bulgaria's obligations during the negotiation process as well as the implementation of the national programme on the implementation of the *acquis communautaire* and the regular updating of this programme. The enlarged negotiation team includes working groups. The relevant Minister or the head of the relevant institution, with the approval of possible other Ministers concerned and the Minister for European Affairs, appoints the members of the working groups. The head of each working group is appointed by the Prime Minister upon the proposal of the Minister for European Affairs. In the course of their work, the working groups may consult representatives of non-governmental organizations.

The Minister of Finance is in charge of the national coordination of EU financial aid and the coordination of the joint mechanism for monitoring the performance of the programmes financed under the pre-accession instruments. The Minister organizes and coordinates the elaboration of a national plan for economic development 2000-2006 and a national plan for development having regard to the requirements of EU law in the various areas involved. The Minister of Finance organizes the effective and lawful management of funding from the EU's Cohesion and Structural Funds, in compliance with the policy for Bulgaria's accession to the EU. The Minister also performs the function of National ISPA coordinator.

In addition, specialized structures for European integration have been set up in the public administration as well as in units that manage the financial aid under the pre-accession programmes. The main structures amongst these are the European Integration Directorate at the Ministry of Foreign Affairs, the Directorate on

European Integration and Relations at the International Financial Institutions, and the National Funds Directorate at the Ministry of Finance.

3.3 Impact of EU accession on the organization and practice of (a) central government and administration and (b) the decentralized authorities

So far, the preparations for EU accession have led to expansion of the administration. The number of civil servants has increased and recruitment of a further 479 servants is imminent. The administration was restructured with the establishment of special directorates for European integration and functional units for implementing new legal obligations assumed in the process of preparation for accession. New independent institutions have been established within the system of the administration. These are the Commission for the Protection of Competition and a number of independent agencies. Upon the passing of the Ombudsman Act and the Anti-Discrimination Act, two new institutions will be established, namely the ombudsman and an independent equal treatment commission. The preparations for accession have also resulted in expansion of the administration at the local level, with one example being the creation of units dealing with the use of regional aid and regional administering of the EU funds assigned under the PHARE and ISPA programmes.

We expect that in future the administration and decentralized authorities will feel the impact of the emerging need for optimising work processes within the administration and the trend for decentralization emerging in EU policies. The implementation of EU law requirements will increase the administration's workload and compel it to deal with ever more complex issues. Stricter requirements for administrative discretion are absolutely necessary to increase the administration's efficiency and ensure the proper enforcement of the law.

The relationship between national and EU institutions will further influence the work of the administration. A particular example is the Commission for the Protection of Competition. So far, the Constitutional Court[43] has been reluctant to exempt any of its decisions from judicial control by the Bulgarian Supreme Administrative Court, but this issue will have to be reconsidered once Bulgaria becomes an EU member, due to the authority of the EU Commission and the jurisdiction of the European Court of Justice.

---

[43] See Decision No. 22 of 24 September 1998 in constitutional case No. 18/98, promulgated in State Gazette No. 112 of 28 September 1998.

4. ROLE OF THE NATIONAL PARLIAMENT

4.1 Preparedness for legal approximation

The work of the National Assembly with regard to the preparation of Bulgaria for full membership of the EU is mainly performed in three areas: approximation of the legislation, amendments to the Constitution, and the formation of structures and elaboration of procedures by which the national parliament may control the acts prepared within the EU institutions and particularly the Council of Ministers.

The approximation of legislation is a part of the legislative process in Parliament that starts with the submission of Bills to the National Assembly and ends with their passing, on second reading, by the National Assembly. However, most of the work involved in the approximation process is carried out by the administration, insofar as the Council of Ministers holds the main initiative to submit Bills. As the amount of legislation that has been harmonized increases, the work of the Ministry of Justice and law enforcement by the courts will undoubtedly become easier.

The main specialized body within the National Assembly is the Commission on European Integration. It is composed of 24 members of Parliament. The seats are distributed in accordance with the number of seats which each political party occupies in the National Assembly. The organization and functioning of the Commission is regulated in the Regulations on the Organization and Functions of the National Assembly and the internal rules of procedure of the Commission, passed on the basis of Article 21(1) of the Regulation. Decision making takes place by unanimity of the represented political parties. This method is specific for the Commission on European Integration, reflecting the necessity for consensus and the priority of European integration.

The Commission on European Integration participates in the formation and implementation of Bulgaria's policies with regard to the accession to the EU. The powers of the Commission are as follows: deliberation of the legislative proposals under the National Programme for the Implementation of the *acquis communautaire* as well as relevant decisions, declarations and addresses, and passing reports, recommendations and proposals on the Bills; monitoring the work of the Council of European Integration at the Council of Ministers and the Coordination Council for the preparation of the Republic of Bulgaria for accession to the EU, as well as hearing reports by the Chief Negotiator on the course of the negotiations for accession and other reports of the Council of Ministers; issuing opinions on the legislative priorities according to the National Programme for the Implementation of the *acquis communautaire*; periodically debating issues concerning the preparations for accession, either jointly with other commissions or independently; presenting the necessary information to the Coordination Council for the work of the National Assembly on issues of European integration.

The main functions of the Commission on European Integration are its legislative activity and exercising parliamentary control over the Minister for European Affairs and the Chief Negotiator, as well as over the Ministers in charge of relevant subject areas.

As part of its legislative activity, the Commission on European Integration gives opinions concerning the compatibility with the *acquis communautaire* of all Bills submitted to the National Assembly. It considers these Bills in its role as "supporting commission".

The Commission on European Integration issues its opinions before the first ballot in the National Assembly. In them the Commission refers to the need for compliance of the Bill in question with Bulgaria's positions in the negotiation process. The Commission further refers to the negotiation chapter relevant to the negotiation process and the particular subject matter, examines the compatibility with the *acquis communautaire* and where necessary issues specific recommendations for improvement.

The opinions of the Commission on European Integration are submitted to Parliament on the Bill's first reading. If there are any discrepancies with the *acquis communautaire*, the members of Parliament are duly informed of this so that they may eliminate such discrepancies before the second ballot in the plenary session.

The Regulations on the Organization and Functioning of the National Assembly provide for an "expedited" procedure for passing laws. This means that if the Commission on European Integration has issued an opinion concerning a particular Bill only one representative of each parliamentary party may take the floor to speak for a maximum of ten minutes. This procedure is applied upon the express decision of the Commission on European Integration. The fact that the Commission has issued an opinion on the Bill is not by itself sufficient ground for application of the expedited procedure. In case of such an express decision of the Commission, the time permitted for amendment of the proposals is seven days.

In addition, the Commission on European Integration maintains contacts with the European Parliament, the European Commission, representatives of the other EU institutions, deputies of the national parliaments of the EU Member States and the European Commission Delegation in Bulgaria, as well as the EU Member States' ambassadors in Bulgaria.

4.2 Control over decisions taken by ministers in the Council of the European Union

This issue has not yet been the subject of debate. No special procedures other than general parliamentary control have been discussed.

5. CONCLUSIONS

During the period preceding accession, the countries preparing for full membership of the EU face the problem of approximating their legislation, whilst not yet having provided for the supremacy and direct, universal and immediate effect of European law in their territory. In other words, in these countries European law does not have the full juridical effect that it has in respect of the Member States of the EU. Approximation of legislation for one part resembles a transplant of certain foreign standards into Bulgarian legislation and for another part the introduction of international law in the domestic legal order under a dualist system.

There are certain issues that merit special critical attention. One of these concerns the way in which the approximation of laws has been effected. The rapid progress in recent years has been accompanied by the risk of passing inefficient regulation. Some regulations are inherently inapplicable because of insufficient institutional capacity. In other instances, unreasonable expenses have been incurred, with negatively impacts the competitive position. These problems are largely caused by an insufficient and unsystematic evaluation of the impact of the legislation in the early phases of the legislative process. This holds true in particular for the financial aspects and for seeking ways to optimise the current administrative capacity. This problem could be solved by a pragmatic constitutional or legal provision that would require a financial assessment of the effect of any proposed legislation. Although this is not an imperative requirement in the process of EU integration, it would have an overall positive outcome.

The influence of any new regulation on public finances is an important issue. The approximation of the legislation with EU law requires the creation of new bodies and an increase in the volume and number of tasks in the existing ones. Furthermore, changes in the rules, rights and obligations of citizens and economic actors also make for changes in the budget, not just at state level, but also at the level of public funds, municipalities, universities, etc. This is expected first to have an effect on the administration in the application of new rules (revenue from new taxes, but also an increase in expenses) and second on the economy due to changes in economic activity following the introduction of the new rules. These latter changes are difficult to predict, but they may include an increase in the rate of employment and in the related taxes and social security contributions, a decrease in the import of particular products and in VAT revenues, a decline in the number of small enterprises and craftsmanship, etc.

Besides the above issues, another major challenge at the current, advanced stage of the negotiations between Bulgaria and the European Communities lies in ensuring an effective judiciary and an administrative system that can guarantee the effective enforcement of EC law.

Addendum by the Editors

Since the completion of this chapter, the Constitution of Bulgaria has been twice amended in view of EU membership. In 2003, several provisions were modified in order to improve the independence and efficiency of the judiciary. In 2005, a relatively extensive package of amendments was introduced to create a constitutional basis for accession to the EU, and eliminate conflicts with EC law from the Constitution. The amended version of the Constitution can be found in English at the website of the Bulgarian National Assembly, at: <http://www.parliament.bg/?page=const&lng=en>.

The key amendments include the following:

Article 4(3)
The Republic of Bulgaria shall participate in the construction and development of the European Union.

Article 22[*]
(1) Foreigners and foreign legal persons may acquire property over land under the conditions ensuing from Bulgaria's accession to the European Union, or by virtue of an international treaty that has been ratified, published and entered into force for the Republic of Bulgaria, as well as through inheritance by operation of the law.
(2) The law ratifying the international treaty referred to in paragraph 1 shall be adopted by a majority of two thirds of all members of Parliament.
(3) The land regime shall be established by law.

Article 25(3)
No Bulgarian citizen may be surrendered to another state or to an international tribunal for the purposes of criminal prosecution, unless the opposite is provided for by international treaty that has been ratified, published and entered into force for the Republic of Bulgaria.

Article 42(3)
The elections for the European Parliament and the participation of European Union citizens in the elections for local authorities shall be regulated by law.

[*] This provision will take effect upon the entry into force of the Accession Treaty.

Article 85(1)

(1) The National Assembly shall ratify or denounce by law all international instruments which: ... confer to the European Union powers ensuing from this Constitution.

(2) The law ratifying the international treaty referred to in paragraph 1, point 9, shall be adopted by a majority of two thirds of all members of Parliament.

Article 105

(3) The Council of Ministers shall inform the National Assembly on issues concerning the obligations of the Republic of Bulgaria resulting from its membership in the European Union.

(4) When participating in the drafting and adoption of European Union instruments, the Council of Ministers shall inform the National Assembly in advance, and shall give detailed account for its actions.

Article 129

(3) Having completed a five-year term of office as a judge, prosecutor or investigating magistrate, and upon attestation, followed by a decision of the Supreme Judicial Council, the judges, prosecutors and investigating magistrates shall become irremovable. They, including the persons referred to in paragraph 2, shall be removed from office only upon:

1. completion of 65 years of age;
2. resignation;
3. entry into force of a final sentence imposing imprisonment for an intentional criminal offence;
4. permanent de facto inability to perform their duties for more than a year;
5. serious infringement or systematic neglect of their official duties, as well as actions undermining the prestige of the judiciary.

(4) In cases of removal from office under paragraph 3, point 2 and 4, the acquired irremovability shall be restored upon subsequent appointment to the office of a judge, prosecutor or investigating magistrate.

(5) The heads of the judicial bodies, except for those referred to in paragraph 2, shall be appointed for a period of 5 years and are eligible for a second mandate.

Article 131

Any resolution of the Supreme Judicial Council to appoint, promote, demote, transfer or remove a judge, prosecutor or investigating magistrate, for giving permission under Article 132, paragraphs 2 and 3, as well as the proposals under Article 129, paragraph 2, shall be passed by a secret ballot.

Article 132(1)

When exercising the judicial function, the judges, prosecutors and investigating magistrates shall bear no civil or criminal liability for their official actions or for the acts rendered by them, except where the act performed constitutes an indictable intentional criminal offence.

CROATIA

Tamara Ćapeta,* Dario Mihelin and Siniša Rodin*****

1. NATIONAL CONSTITUTION

1.1 Implementation of international law and transfer of legislative powers

1.1.1 *International law in the Croatian legal order*

In departure from the dualist constitutional practice prescribed by the Constitution of the former Yugoslavia, the Croatian Constitution of 1990 adopted a monist approach. As it was specified in the explanatory memorandum to the Croatian draft Constitution, "… a monist concept of the relationship between international and national law is introduced, according to which international treaties that have been signed and ratified in accordance with the Constitution and have been published become part of national law and in principle have priority over laws and must be applied by all state authorities within their respective jurisdiction."[1] This fundamental choice was made part of the Croatian Constitution in an attempt to put an end to the former practice according to which international human rights obligations were considered not directly applicable in the Yugoslav legal order, in accordance with the communist party doctrine of non-interference in internal affairs.

The Croatian Constitution of 1990 enabled the direct applicability of international treaties in the national legal order. According to the relevant constitutional provision, international treaties that are ratified and published form part of the Croatian internal legal order and take priority over ordinary laws.[2] This provision

---

* University of Zagreb, Faculty of Law.

** Ministry of European Integration.

*** University of Zagreb, Faculty of Law.

1 Vjesnik, 27 November 1990 at p. 6 (our translation).

2 Art. 140 (before constitutional amendment of 28 March 2001: Art. 134) of the Constitution. See *Narodne Novine* No. 41/2001 for consolidated text. The only amendment in this respect was making the application of international treaties conditional upon them being in force internationally. See Ustavni zakon o izmjenama i dopunama Ustava Republike Hrvatske, *Narodne novine* No. 135/1997.

has persisted up to today in almost unchanged form. In practice, the Constitutional Court has adopted a position according to which national laws can be scrutinized as to their compatibility with international treaties, and if necessary be declared invalid.[3] The Court explicitly mentioned international treaties as a source of law and confirmed their entrenched position in the hierarchy of legal rules.[4]

International treaties, being part of the national legal order pursuant to Article 140 of the Constitution, are to be applied by Croatian courts, and may, at least in theory, create individual rights. Despite the fact that the Constitution in Article 117 only mentions the Constitution and laws as sources of authority for the judiciary – which is contradictory to Article 140 – it does not seem that the Constitution intended to exclude international law as a source of legal authority. In support of this view, the Judiciary Act of 1994 may be cited under which Croatian courts, in addition to applying the Constitution and laws, can also apply international treaties as well as regulations enacted pursuant to the Constitution, international treaties or Croatian law.[5]

As far as other sources of international law are concerned, the Constitution refers to international law in four instances. Article 2(3) refers to territorial jurisdiction at sea "in accordance with international law", Article 31 refers to the principle of legality in respect of criminal offences by referring to international law, Article 33 regulates the right of asylum "in accordance with fundamental principles of international law", and finally, Article 138 provides for ratification of international treaties in accordance with rules of international law. However, there is no general constitutional provision referring to legal rules of international law similar to, for example, Article 25 of the German Basic Law,[6] and accordingly, no provision comparable to Article 100(2) of the Basic Law establishing

---

[3] The Constitutional Court took the position that the constitutional principle of the rule of law implies that laws have to comply with all entrenched legal rules, including international treaties. See Jasna Omejec, *Granice ovlasti Ustavnog suda u postupku ocjene suglasnosti zakona s Ustavom*, Zbornik Pravnog fakulteta u Zagrebu, Vol. 53, No. 6 (2003) pp. 1423 et seq.; Siniša Rodin, 'Main Accents in Practice of the Constitutional Court (1991-2001)', in Croatian Helsinki Committee for Human Rights and Netherlands Helsinki Committee, *Croatian Judiciary: Lessons and Perspectives* (Zagreb 2002) pp. 219-268.

[4] Decision of the Constitutional Court No. U-I-745/1999, of 8 November 2000: "The Constitution introduces another category of legal rules into the Croatian legal order: subject to Article 134 of the Constitution, international treaties which have been signed and ratified in accordance with the Constitution, and have been published, are part of the internal legal order and have priority over ordinary laws. Accordingly, the complete hierarchy of legal rules in the Croatian legal order as established by the Constitution comprises the Constitution, international treaties, laws and other regulations."

[5] Art 5(3) of the Judiciary Act, *Narodne novine* 3/1994 as amended *Narodne novine*, br. 3/94, 100/96, 131/97 and 129/2000. Article 5(3) remains unchanged.

[6] Constitution (Germany), Art. 25: "The general rules of public international law constitute an integral part of federal law. They take precedence over statutes and directly create rights and duties for the inhabitants of the federal territory."

jurisdiction for the Constitutional Court.[7] So far there has been no practice in Croatia concerning this issue.

Another reference to international law that is of constitutional importance can be found in the Constitutional Law on the Protection of National Minorities. Substantial amendments to this Law were adopted in December 2002[8] and its relevant provisions seem to have restricted the wording of the Law as it was framed back in 1991.[9] The 1991 Law provided for a non-exhaustive list of international instruments pursuant to which protection of fundamental rights in Croatia was guaranteed.[10] Under what has become Article 2 of the Constitutional Law, Croatia guarantees and protects fundamental rights guaranteed by international treaties, but only those specified in Article 1, so that the question concerning the effects of subsequently adopted international obligations or instruments which were not mentioned in Article 1, remains. Their effects are clearly covered by Article 140 of the Constitution that excludes possible restrictive effects of Article 2 mentioned above.

1.1.2 *Transfer of powers*

Plainly put, the Constitution provides that international treaties delegating constitutional powers to an international organization or alliance have to be ratified by a two-thirds parliamentary majority.[11] This provision has to be interpreted in the light of Article 2(1) of the Constitution defining Croatian sovereignty as inalienable, indivisible and intransferable. Seemingly, the intention was not to enable restrictions of national sovereignty, but to allow the exercise of constitutional powers at supranational level. In the absence of more concrete provisions or practice, there is little authority to assist in the interpretation of these constitutional provisions. However, the concept of sovereignty is sometimes used by conservative political actors to slow down political and economic reforms, or to promote particular political interests. In fact, forces opposed to closer integration with the EU are capitalizing on the fact that the pace of integration of associated states depends on the outcome of assessments of the economic and democratic progress in these states, which is sometimes understood as inadmissible intervention in the domestic affairs of the state. In a typical argument for their

---

[7] Constitution (Germany), Art. 100(2): "Where, in the course of litigation, doubt exists whether a rule of public international law is an integral part of federal law and whether such rule directly creates rights and duties for the individual (Article 25), the court obtains a decision from the Federal Constitutional Court."

[8] *Narodne novine* 155/2002.

[9] *Narodne novine* 61/1991.

[10] See Siniša Rodin, 'The Constitutional Court of the Republic of Croatia and International Law', 55 *ZaöRV* (1995) p. 783 at p. 795.

[11] Constitution (Croatia), Art. 139.

cause, advocates of national sovereignty exploit the fact that candidate countries are faced with a virtually non-negotiable deal, namely unconditional acceptance of the *acquis communautaire*, with very little or no room for bargaining left.[12] In Croatia, the argument of national sovereignty has also been repeatedly put forward in parliamentary and political debates related to the declaration of an exclusive fishing and ecological zone (EFEZ) under the terms of the Law of the Sea Convention.[13]

During the process of ratification of the Stabilization and Association Agreement[14] the question of whether regulatory powers have to be transferred to the Stabilization and Association Council arose. As a result of the political balance in the Croatian Parliament, the Agreement, although ratified by a majority, was not ratified by the two-thirds majority required for the delegation of regulatory powers to supranational bodies.[15] In response to the right-wing parties which claimed that the SAA was stripping Croatia of its national sovereignty, the Croatian Prime Minister and the Minister for European Integration decided to consider the Stabilization and Association Agreement as an ordinary international law treaty and refrained from pushing for the necessary two-thirds majority.[16] The way in which the Agreement had now been ratified gave rise to the question of whether the Stabilization and Association Council would have law-making authority. The Croatian Parliament, apparently under the impression that the Stabilization and Association Council could not, without further implementing measures, exercise constitutional regulatory powers, subsequently adopted the Law Implementing the Stabilization and Association Agreement.[17] Article 6 of this Law provides for a strictly dualist approach according to which decisions of the Association Council are subject to parliamentary ratification. This is a clear departure from the Constitutional mandate of monism provided by Article 140 of

---

12 See, e.g., Heather Grabbe and Kirsty Hughes, *Eastward Enlargement of the European Union* (London, The Royal Institute of International Affairs 1998) at p. 37. Anneli Albi, ' Europe Agreements in the Light of Sovereignty and Legitimacy: The Case of Estonia', in A.E. Kellermann, et al., eds., *EU Enlargement: The Constitutional Impact at EU and National Level* (The Hague, T.M.C. Asser Press 2001) pp. 195 et seq.

13 The zone was declared in 2003 to take effect in October 2004. The Parliament has excluded Member States of the European Union from enforcement of the EFEZ in June 2004 in order to facilitate the Council Decision on the Croatian candidacy for EU membership.

14 The Stabilization and Association Agreement with Croatia entered into force on 1 February 2005. See *OJ* 2005 L 26/3, and further Council Decision 2005/205/EC concerning the conclusion of the Enlargement Protocol to the SAA-Croatia, *OJ* 2005 L 68/30. For text of the Protocol, see *OJ* 2005 L 26/222.

15 Izvješća Hrvatskog Sabora, No. 315, 20 December 2001.

16 See, e.g., speech by Minister Neven Mimica in the Croatian Parliament on 24 October 2001 where it was claimed that no constitutional regulatory authority would be delegated to the Stabilization and Association Council. Source: <http://www.mei.hr>.

17 Zakon o provedbi sporazuma o stabilizaciji i pridruživanju, *Narodne novine*, International Međunarodni ugovori, No. 15/2001.

the Constitution which renders ratified international treaties part of national law. For this reason, it is questionable whether the Law is actually compatible with the Constitution.

To conclude, the Croatian Constitution makes provision for the transfer of legislative powers to supranational organizations, although this has not been confirmed by constitutional practice so far. However, the question remains whether it might not be better to introduce into the Constitution a specific legal basis for membership of the EU, which would provide for transfer of powers to the Community institutions, and at the same time make clear that legal norms adopted by these institutions have direct effect in the Croatian legal order and take precedence over national law.

1.2 Amendments

There are no provisions in the Croatian Constitution which are openly, *prima facie*, inconsistent with EU membership. Therefore, the EC/Euratom Treaties can be ratified without any formal amendments to the Constitution. However, certain constitutional provisions are so broadly worded that they do not preclude interpretations that may create obstacles to EC/Euratom membership. It would, therefore, be useful to amend these provisions in order to exclude any interpretation of them that would run contrary to Community law.

Some of these changes are necessary immediately, as part of the implementation of the Stabilization and Association Agreement,[18] and some are necessary in view of future full EU membership. Croatia can best express its genuine desire for full membership of the EU by meeting the constitutional requirements for membership. The suggested constitutional amendments refer to the following constitutional provisions:

(a) provisions that provide the legal basis for EU membership, including a definition of the method of exercising state sovereignty;

The Croatian Constitution defines national sovereignty as being "inalienable, indivisible and intransferable."[19] Such a constitutional definition of state sovereignty is ill-adapted to the requirements of membership of the EU. In this respect the Constitution should provide for the shared exercise of the state sovereignty in EU institutions. An amendment along these lines should be based on an understanding of sovereignty not as *summa potestas*, but as a place at the table.

---

[18] In anticipation of full ratification of the SAA, the provisions concerning trade already became applicable via an interim agreement which entered into force on 1 March 2002. See *OJ* 2001 L 330/3.

[19] Constitution (Croatia), Article 2(1).

Changing the definition of state sovereignty may prove to be politically difficult. The major political issues, for the time being, are related to fisheries and agricultural subsidies, both issues of key importance to one of opposition parties (Croatian Farmers' Party – HSS). Political support for the government will in this respect depend on the government's ability to negotiate favourable terms during the membership negotiations.

However, the most important task in the shaping of the political landscape will be to create a favourable public discourse. A discursive shift in understanding from the "traditional" to the "new" concept of sovereignty may even make the issue of amending Article 2(1) of the Constitution moot.

There is, at present, no provision in the Constitution which expressly provides for Croatia's membership of the EU. Article 141 regulates the possibility and the procedure for creating associations with other states. For this a two-thirds majority in Parliament is required and a referendum. The outcome of the referendum is considered to be positive if the majority of all persons eligible to vote are in favour, which may cause problems in case of a low turnout. Nevertheless, it would be possible for Croatia to join the EU on the basis of this provision. However, bearing in mind the importance of this step, and the specific nature of the EU, it may be useful to introduce into the Constitution a specific legal basis enabling membership of the EU. Such a provision would have to establish a procedure for ratification of the EU/EC Founding Treaties or EU Constitution, whatever the form or name by the time of Croatia's accession.

(b) provisions that define in closer detail the legal status of international law and of European primary and secondary law within the Croatian legal system;

At present, the legal status of Community law, both primary and secondary, within the Croatian legal system is not defined. There is no differentiation between rules of international law and rules of Community law, which at this stage is understandable, as Croatia is presently not a member of the EU. Also, the Constitution ignores the concept of self-executing treaties, although self-executing effect can be inferred from the fact that international treaties are considered an integral part of the Croatian legal order pursuant to Article 140 of the Constitution. There is a clear need for making rules of Community law an integral part of national law as well, and for their differentiation from international treaties and general rules of international law. Certainly, such a differentiation should recognize the specific legal nature of Community law, and does not necessarily have to change the position of international law in the Croatian legal order. In other words, rules of Community law, both primary and secondary, should be explicitly provided with legal force and their supremacy and the possibility of direct effect should be explicitly mentioned. This could be regulated either in the same provision that would provide the legal basis for EU membership (see under a. above), or in a separate provision regulating sources of law.

(c) provisions relating to the constitutional structure, more particularly to the relationship between the legislative and the executive;

Although the relationship between the legislative and the executive is not of any direct concern with respect to Croatia's membership of the EU, a proper allocation of powers may significantly influence the efficiency of the fulfilment of Croatia's commitments and obligations. The Croatian executive will need a more widely defined authority to act within the Council of Ministers, and Parliament will need broader and more efficient supervisory powers and a more clearly defined role in supranational decision making. Currently, under Article 112(4) of the Constitution, the government is authorized to pass subregulation in order to implement acts of Parliament. However, the need for the government to take part in the decision making at EU level calls for a change. It is desirable to provide for direct constitutional authority that would give the government the constitutional basis for making such decisions, and for implementing them in national law, where required by Community law. This would preferably be accompanied by a simultaneous obligation to inform Parliament regularly about such regulatory activities.

At present, the regulatory powers of the Government are to a large extent exercised subject to delegated powers as provided for by Article 87 of the Constitution. Pursuant to this Article, Parliament can authorize the Government to pass regulations during a one-year term and subject to subsequent parliamentary ratification. The same Article defines the exclusive regulatory powers of the Parliament (*Gesetzesvorbehalt*). These are the regulation of constitutional rights and liberties, ethnic rights, the electoral system, organization, jurisdiction and methods of work of state authorities and local self-government. These powers can therefore not be delegated to the Government.

As decisions of the Government, when exercising delegated powers, are subject to the parliamentary mandate and subsequent approval, discretion of the Government in Community affairs will strongly depend on the parliamentary definition of the mandate and Parliament's readiness to approve the measures adopted by the Government. This can potentially make the Government's role in implementing Community law more difficult, which is, however, rather an issue of constitutional practice than of constitutional drafting.

So far, two different attitudes towards delegation of powers can be identified. The practice of extending authority for delegated regulation in matters of internal policy has been very generous. Laws delegating regulatory authority use broad language such as "regulation of commerce." The Constitutional Court has warned

Parliament to be more specific when delegating regulatory powers to the Government.[20]

On the other hand, the consensus among the Croatian political parties seems to be that the Government should be under strict parliamentary supervision when foreign or European policy is at stake. This belief has led the opposition to ask for the re-negotiation of trade quotas in view of the recent accession of the 10 new Member States. Although this request was not granted, it is still an indication that the Government is considered to be subject to parliamentary control, even in cases where the government has direct constitutional authority.

Generally speaking, Parliament leaves the Government more discretion to pursue national policy than international policy, as it seems to supervise foreign affairs more closely. As Government involvement in European affairs becomes more frequent and substantial, turning formerly external affairs into domestic, the need for re-definition of Parliamentary supervision will become more pressing. As involvement of national parliaments in EU affairs is a matter for every Member State to decide on its own, and approaches in Member States differ, Croatia is would benefit from a public debate on this issue, within framework of the constitutional adjustment for membership.

(d) provisions governing procedure and jurisdiction of the Constitutional Court.

Issues of constitutional jurisdiction in relation to European Union membership are not unique to the Croatian legal system. Here, it is possible to build on the experiences of comparable legal systems, such as Germany or Italy.

As far as the jurisdiction of the Constitutional Court is concerned, the Court should be given clear constitutional authority to decide *ex ante* on the compatibility of international treaties with the Constitution. This type of jurisdiction is lacking under the present Constitution. The consequence of a declaration of compatibility will be a presumption of the conformity of the treaty with the Constitution, which would render future constitutional litigation on the point moot. To bring this in effect it will be necessary to amend the Constitutional Act on the Constitutional Court. In respect of membership of the EU, possible *ex ante* constitutional review of the accession treaty would make future objections as to the constitutionality of Croatia's membership of the EU more difficult.

Second, EU membership will require the amendment of the Constitutional Court's rules of procedure in order to bring them into line with the *Simmenthal* requirements, thus providing ordinary courts with recourse to the *exceptio illegalitatis* in case of incompatibility of national laws and implementing regulations

[20] Decision of the Constitutional Court U-II-66/1994 of 25 February 1994, *Narodne novine* No. 16/1994; see also Jadranko Crnić, Vladavina Ustava, *Informator* (Zagreb 1994) at p. 20.

with legal rules of Community law. Subject to the present Article 37 of the Constitutional Act on the Constitutional Court[21] ordinary courts faced with an issue of compatibility of a law with the Constitution have to ask the Constitutional Court to give a preliminary ruling on the point. In the event that the law in question is incompatible with Community law, the court must, under the Simmenthal rule, refrain from applying this law without it being necessary that the law is set aside first. In other words Community law requires ordinary courts to by-pass the concrete constitutional review procedure required by Article 37 of the Constitutional Act. In the Croatian legal system, the *exceptio illegalitatis* is applicable in cases of non-conformity of regulations with laws and the Constitution. However, in practice it is rarely applied. Compliance with the requirement to leave aside national law and apply the Community rule instead will necessitate not only legislative amendments, but also a radical departure from the existing judicial practice of ordinary courts.

1.3 Provisions contrary to the *acquis communautaire*

There are several provisions of the Croatian Constitution that will have to be amended in order to comply with requirements of the *acquis*. Also there are a number of other provisions that are not contrary to the *acquis* as such, but need to be amended for other reasons, ranging from inclarity to doctrinal imperfection. For purpose of this analysis we can identify two different categories of constitutional provisions that are actually or potentially incompatible with the requirements of EU membership:

(a) Constitutional provisions that are directly incompatible with the *acquis*;
(b) Constitutional provisions that are not directly incompatible with the *acquis* but are encumbering compliance with Community law because they are confusing, incomplete, unclear, or may potentially lead to interpretation that is incompatible with the *acquis*.

(a) *Constitutional provisions directly incompatible with the acquis*

i. Suffrage of EU citizens

Article 1 of the Constitution defines the fundamental concepts of the Croatian state. It introduces the concept of democracy and specifies that it is exercised by the people, being all Croatian nationals (*državljani*). Power is exercised by representation and direct democracy. Furthermore, Article 45 of the Constitution

[21] Ustavni zakon o Ustavnom sudu Republike Hrvatske, *Narodne novine* No. 49/2002.

guarantees the right to vote to Croatian nationals. Although the Constitution is silent on this point, it does not explicitly exclude the possibility of giving non-nationals the right to vote. In addition to this, Article 132 guarantees the right to local and regional self-government to citizens (*građani*). It is exercised by local and regional representative bodies elected on the basis of direct, equal and general suffrage. Croatian citizens have a right to run local affairs. Again, the wording of this provision does not expressly exclude EU citizens from the right to vote, however, as far as requirements of EU membership are concerned, the right to vote in local elections, being a participatory right, has to be guaranteed to all EU citizens *expressis verbis*.

These constitutional provisions are not broad enough to fulfil the requirements of Article 19 of the EC Treaty under which "Every citizen of the Union residing in a Member State of which he is not a national shall have the right to vote and to stand as a candidate at municipal elections in the Member State in which he resides, under the same conditions as nationals of that State."

Amendment of the relevant constitutional provisions should make direct universal suffrage in Croatian local elections of EU citizens residing in Croatia possible. In addition, Article 45 should also be amended to include the right of EU citizens residing in Croatia to vote in European Parliament elections.

ii. Access to the civil service

According to Article 44 of the Constitution, equal access to the civil service is granted to Croatian citizens only. This provision should be amended to include EU citizens in the areas required by Community law.

(b) *Constitutional provisions encumbering compliance with the acquis*

i. Definition and understanding of national sovereignty

One of the most serious constitutional issues that will have to be solved is that of national sovereignty. According to the present definition, national sovereignty is inalienable, indivisible and intransferable, as has already been explained above. Here, suffice it to say that this provision will have to be relaxed in order to reconcile it with Article 139 and to permit the transfer of regulatory powers to the Community institutions. While a more dynamic definition of national sovereignty would be welcome, it cannot be said that the present provision, as such, constitutes an absolute barrier to EU membership. Indeed, the compatibility of this provision with the requirements of EU membership depends entirely on its interpretation. After all, the fact that Article 139 makes the transfer of regulatory powers possible at all means it will allow for a more flexible interpretation.

Another problem may be posed by subsection 5 of Article 139 according to which Croatia retains the right to withdraw from international alliances with other states and to "autonomously decide on the exercise of transferred powers." While the first part is not manifestly contrary to membership of the EU, especially with the possible future entry into force of the Constitutional Treaty and its withdrawal clause in mind, the second part is clearly incompatible with the system of allocation of competences and the principle of subsidiarity, as defined in Community law in that it is clear that, once transferred, competences have to be judged in the light of Community criteria and not independently by individual states.

ii. Definition and understanding of the rule of law

A constitutional definition of the concept of the rule of law and widespread understanding of the concept among legal professionals and citizens at large is of paramount importance for Croatia's membership of the EU. The Constitution deals with this issue in the following provisions: Article 5 which contains the general provision referring to the principle of legality, Article 117 which specifies that the Courts adjudicate on the basis of the Constitution and statutory laws, and Article 118 which deals with the Supreme Court and specifies that it is responsible for the uniform application of laws and equal protection of citizens.

The main objection to these provisions is their formalistic approach that is also reflected in Croatian legal culture. While there is nothing wrong with the normative statement that laws should conform to the Constitution (Art. 5), the Constitution itself is often not considered as part of that law, but rather as a political document. Accordingly, courts are reluctant to apply the Constitution and rather refer to implementing legislation.[22] The same can be said of Article 117 of the Constitution. In our experience, therefore, courts have difficulties solving disputes that require direct recourse to the Constitution. This formalistic approach that has become an element of Croatian legal culture may make recourse to certain legal sources and interpretative techniques difficult, and may indirectly affect the application of Community law. Instead of referring to "laws" in the sense of Acts of Parliament, relevant constitutional provisions should refer to "law" (*Recht*, *droit*), which is a much broader, substantive concept which would encourage judges to consider a wider range of legal sources, both normative and informative, including the principle of justice as an inextricable element of the rule of law. Providing that courts are to settle disputes in accordance with the law

---

[22] The situation seems to be similar in Romania. As Gabriel Andreescu has emphasized, Romanian judges are reluctant to apply the Constitution: "(…) In the absence of an express article allowing the rights provided for by the Constitution to be directly enforced, the Romanian courts are extremely reluctant to consider them as such and have always asked for ordinary laws to include and develop such provisions with procedural terms." Gabriel Andreescu, *Right-Wing Extremism in Romania* (Cluj 2003) at p. 56.

would also open the door for direct application of sources of Community law, and maybe even more importantly, sources of soft law that inform judges in their decision making. To be sure, achieving the necessary epistemological shift in the understanding of what law is, is not a task for constitutional drafters, but for legal scholars and practitioners who shape the legal culture.

1.4 Supremacy and direct effect

As we have mentioned earlier, ratified and published international treaties that are in force form part of the national legal order and have precedence over ordinary laws. However, the hierarchy is as closely defined as it seems given the multitude of different legal sources that exist in the Croatian legal order. In addition to ordinary laws that are enacted by simple majority, the Croatian Constitution also envisages two kinds of organic laws. Under Article 82, provisions concerning the rights of ethnic minorities have to be passed by a two-thirds majority and provisions concerning fundamental rights, the electoral system, institutional arrangements and local self-government by a majority of all members of Parliament. Furthermore, under Article 131, the Constitutional Act on the Constitutional Court can only be amended by means of the procedure established for amendments of the Constitution itself. In the absence of constitutional practice concerning Article 140 of the Constitution as discussed above, Article 140 can be interpreted in two ways. If the words "precedence over laws" is interpreted in the sense of ordinary laws only, then international treaties could still be overruled by organic laws and constitutional laws. If the phrase is taken in a broader meaning as extending to all Acts of Parliament, then the supremacy of international treaties would be safeguarded. A clearer constitutional provision in this respect would be welcome. Additionally, as we have already mentioned above, we are of the opinion that an express reference to the effect and status of EU law in the Croatian legal order should be included in the Constitution together with an express legal basis for EU membership.

2. ROLE OF THE JUDICIARY (NATIONAL COURTS)

2.1 Introductory explanation and some facts and figures

Before answering the questions under point II, it might be useful to give a brief explanation of the organization of the judiciary in Croatia.[23] There are 114

[23] All the figures mentioned in this report are in accordance with the answers to the Questionnaire of the European Commission which the Croatian Government gave in the summer of 2003. The Questionnaire was issued in order to enable the Commission to prepare its opinion ("*avis*") on the

municipal courts that have first instance jurisdiction in civil and criminal cases. Appeals against their decisions are heard by the County Courts, and there are at present 21 such Courts. Apart from having appellate jurisdiction, the County Courts are also the courts of first instance for trying certain categories of criminal offences. Appeals against first instance decisions by the County Courts are heard by the Supreme Court. Criminal cases are initiated by the Public Prosecutor's Office which has branches at the municipal, county and central state level. There are at present 513 public prosecutors and deputy prosecutors in Croatia. Jurisdiction over commercial disputes lies with some 13 commercial courts, against whose decisions there is a possibility of appeal to the High Commercial Court. There are also 114 Misdemeanours Courts, whose decisions can be appealed against to the High Misdemeanours Court. Finally, there is a separate Administrative Court. At the top of the hierarchy of courts is the Supreme Court which has the task of ensuring the uniformity of law. Some 1868 judges and 6734 supporting staff work in the courts. The judges are elected by an independent body called the State Judiciary Council and are appointed for life with an initial probationary period of five years. Life tenure is considered a guarantee of judicial independence as laid down in the Constitution and the Courts Act. Judges are not allowed to be members of political parties or to engage in any activity which is incompatible with their independence.

Apart from the regular court structure, Croatia also has a separate Constitutional Court. It performs a judicial review of statutory law, both abstract and concrete, if so requested by a regular court for the purposes of deciding a particular case. The reason for this is that ordinary courts are not allowed to set aside a provision of law which they deem to be unconstitutional. In such cases, they are required to submit the matter to the Constitutional Court. Decisions on constitutionality taken by the Constitutional Court have effects *erga omnes*. Ordinary courts are, however, competent to review the constitutionality of non-statutory acts, although they use this power is rarely, if at all, in practice. Citizens also have access to the Constitutional Court to which they can make a constitutional complaint. The Constitutional Court then determines whether any fundamental rights which the Constitution guarantees to the citizen have been violated. The jurisdiction of the Constitutional Court in this procedure depends on the exhaustion of other remedies.

Croatian request for Membership of the Union, which in fact marked the beginning of the procedure leading to Croatia's EU membership. The answers given to this Questionnaire may be found online at the web pages of the Croatian Government: <http://www.vlada.hr>. On 17-18 June 2004, the European Council decided to follow up on the Commission's positive *avis* on Croatia's application for membership and granted the country candidate status, thereby opening it up to increased financial and technical assistance. See COM(2004) 257 final, Brussels, 20 April 2004 for the *avis* and *Bull. EU* 6-2004, point I.7.31 for the decision by the European Council.

The judicial culture in the Croatian courts can best be described as taking a positivist and formalistic approach to the law,[24] a situation that is not uncommon in other former communist countries,[25] some of which are now Members of the EU. The interpretation of the law is mostly textual, and dependent on legal dogmas, representing a world of their own, not necessarily matching the reality. The social context is rarely taken into account in the judgments, and even more rarely mentioned. Although expressly empowered by the Constitution to do so, judges rarely apply the Constitution directly when deciding cases. Even the Constitutional Court gives a very narrow and formalistic interpretation to the Constitution.[26]

The larges shortcoming within the Croatian judicial system and indeed in the Croatian legal system as a whole is the lack of any tradition of publishing case law. Based on the belief that judges have nothing to do with law creation, that 'the law' is written in the statutes and that case law is therefore irrelevant court decisions have never been regularly published. Only occasionally judgments would be published, and even then not in their entirety, but only those excerpts which whoever prepared the publication deemed to be relevant. The situation has started to improve only recently. As of the first half of 2004, the Supreme Court has a new website,[27] on which all of the new and many of the old judgments of that Court are published in their entirety. The High Commercial Court is now also instituting such a database. Decisions of the Constitutional Court are regularly published in their entirety in the Official Journal, called *Narodne novine*, including dissenting opinions, if any, and may also be downloaded from the Court's website.[28]

---

[24] Considering the law to be no more than a set of written rules is not only common among Croatian judges, but among lawyers more generally, and even among the general public. A good example is the way in which the word 'law' is usually translated in the media (both TV and newspapers), namely as 'zakon', meaning statute, and not as 'pravo', meaning law.

[25] Zdenek Kühn, 'Application of European law in Central European candidate countries', 28 *ELR* (2003) pp. 551-560.

[26] One extreme example of this formalism is the interpretation of the Constitutional Court according to which the right to a fair trial within a reasonable time did not exist in Croatia until Croatia ratified the European Convention on Human Rights and Fundamental Freedoms in 1997. The Constitution was amended on 9 November 2000, and Article 29 today expressly provides the reasonable time requirement. Before this Constitutional amendment, the right to a fair trial was guaranteed without explicit reference to the reasonable time requirement. The Constitutional Court has held that the reasonable time requirement only became applicable when the Convention entered into force for Croatia. In other words, it is not inferred from the general constitutional framework, or even from the explicit right to a fair trial which has been guaranteed by the Constitution in Art. 29 since 1990. This is a very clear example of narrow textual interpretation. See, for example, decisions of the Constitutional Court U-III A/2933/2002 and U-III/A2303/2003.

[27] Available at: <http://www.vsrh.hr>.

[28] Available at: <http://www.usud.hr>.

However, despite the fact that case law is finally becoming available, there are still many shortcomings in the system. One is the result of the prevailing consensus among the legal profession that only final (*endgültige*) judgments are publishable. Given that cases may be heard in several instances, it could therefore be years before the decision is finally published and then when it is, it will only consist of the judgment in the final instance. These decisions provide only very basic information concerning the facts that informed the court in making its decision. Thus, important statements of fact and even law may be lost. The lack of an opportunity to match the facts to the outcome of the case prevents a public discourse concerning the quality of judicial work and the development of law by interpretation.

Due to all this, a body of case law has never developed. The lack of published decisions has also prevented a discourse between the judiciary and the academic community from developing, which is an important element in shaping the legal order in other European countries and within the EU itself.

Another result of judgments remaining unpublished was not only that the living law was not known outside the judiciary, but that the judges themselves did not know other judges' positions on different aspects of law either. The uniformity of the law, the protection of which is the most important task of the Supreme Court, therefore had to be ensured in some other way. This was and still is done at sessions of the judges of Supreme Court where they adopt joint positions concerning the 'correct interpretation' of the law. Positions adopted at the meetings of the Chambers, bind all judges who belong to that Chamber. The positions are also transmitted to judges in the lower courts. They are not binding on them, but according to information that we have acquired through interviews with judges, the lower court judges do usually follow them, even if they do not agree, as this is 'easier' than seeking a confrontation with the highest judicial authority. The interpretation of law thus happens separately from the application of law.

Another significant problem of the Croatian judicial system is the slowness of the judicial process and the backlog of cases awaiting decision[29] (figures made public speak of some 1,500,000 pending cases). This has already created a record number of suits against Croatia before the European Court of Human Rights for breach of Article 6 of the European Convention on Human Rights and Fundamental Freedoms. For this reason alone, a reform of the Croatian judiciary is urgently needed, quite apart from the reasons related to the process of European integration.

Bearing in mind all the above, as a preliminary remark before any answers can be given to the questions concerning the role of the judiciary, it must be recalled

---

[29] See A. Uzelac, 'The Rule of Law and the judicial system: court delays as a barrier to accession', in Katarina Ott, ed., *Croatian Accession to the European Union. Institutional Challenges* (Zagreb, Institute of Public Finance 2004) p. 105.

that the sources of information concerning the judicial application of the law are very limited. Apart from the Internet sources mentioned above, the Rapporteurs have also relied on information which they have collected privately and directly from the judges. For this reason it is possible that the answers that follow are not entirely accurate. It is possible that the courts apply more Community law (or Community law principles) than reported, but information about this has not reached the rapporteurs.

2.2 Europe Agreement or Stabilization and Association Agreement

At the time of preparation of this report, the Stabilization and Association Agreement (SAA) was not yet in force, as some Member States had not yet ratified.[30] However, as was the case in countries that had signed Europe Agreements, in anticipation of the SAA's entry into force the Interim Agreement was signed with Croatia in order to put into effect those parts of the SAA for which the European Community is competent. The Interim Agreement applies as of 1 January 2002 and entered into force on 1 March 2002.[31] It mainly gave effect to the parts of the SAA regulating trade issues.

Thus the courts could not apply the SAA directly, but could nevertheless take it into consideration when interpreting Croatian law, and refer to it as an interpretive tool. However, cases in which this occurred were not reported in the existing law reports. At the time of writing, however, the Interim Agreement had already been in force for more than two years. This means that disputes could have arisen under it which could be brought before the Croatian courts. The courts would have been able to apply the Interim Agreement both directly and/or indirectly. However, we have no information of any Croatian court referring to the Interim Agreement. The Ministry of European Integration is not aware of any dispute either. The possible failure of the courts to refer to the Agreement may be the result of two factors: first, that no disputes involving the Agreement arose in practice or reached the courts, or second, that disputes did reach the courts, but that they were resolved without applying the Agreement.

2.3 Supremacy and direct effect

As Croatia is not a member of the EU, European law as such does not apply (except for the SAA/Interim Agreement). In this sense, it is impossible to answer

---

[30] While the majority of the Member States ratified the Agreement within the usual timeframes, the Netherlands, the UK and Italy for a long time withheld (notification of) ratification, because of their negative perception of Croatia's willingness to cooperate with the ICTY over the extradition of Ante Gotovina.

[31] See *supra* n. 18.

the question. However, we may rephrase it (as the ECJ often rephrases the questions of national courts in preliminary ruling procedure) as follows: are there indications from which it is possible to conclude which attitude the courts will take in relation to the principles of supremacy and direct effect once Croatia becomes a member?

In the pre-accession stage, it is possible to ask whether courts apply these principles in relation to the SAA/Interim Agreement and whether they distinguish between the SAA itself on the one hand and the decisions of the Stabilization and Association Council as secondary association law on the other. However, as has already been remarked in response to the previous question, there have been no cases of either direct or indirect judicial application of the SAA, the Interim Agreement or secondary association law so far.

An indication of the possible attitude towards supremacy and direct effect of, at least primary EU law, which the courts may be expected to adopt can be inferred from the judicial application of the European Convention of Human Rights and Fundamental Freedoms (further: European Convention), to which Croatia is a party as of 1997. The Constitutional Court has developed a practice of application of the European Convention where it uses the Convention in the abstract judicial review procedure as a basis to invalidate Croatian laws which go against Convention provisions[32] and where it uses it as an interpretative tool whereby it has sometimes quoted the case law of the European Court of Human Rights.[33] The supremacy of the European Convention in relation to Croatian laws did not prove problematic, as the Constitution expressly envisages the supremacy of international treaties in relation to ordinary laws in Article 140 (see in that respect the answer to the first question). The Constitutional Court has now developed well-established case law to the effect that non-conformity of Croatian laws with an international treaty constitutes a breach of the principle of the rule of law and is contrary to the Constitution.

However, as far as the ordinary courts are concerned, we have not found any evidence of their willingness to apply the European Convention directly. While it has been used as an interpretative tool (see the answer to the next question), no cases have been reported which were solved directly on the basis of the Convention. It is questionable to what extent the favourable attitude of the Constitutional Court towards the application of international law and its acceptance of international law's supremacy will influence ordinary courts. One example that makes this doubtful is the view expressed by the Civil Division of the Supreme Court on 2 October 1995 when it did not consider itself bound by legal opinions of the Constitutional Court expressed in decisions following a constitutional complaint

32 See, for example, decision of the Constitutional Court U-I/745/1999.

33 See, for example, decisions of the Constitutional Court U-I/745/1999; or U-III/2962/2002.

procedure.[34] It is difficult to assess the impact of this on the practice of the lower courts. However, as some judges who were asked this specific question have stated, this position of the Supreme Court is now considered obsolete.

Although there are no reported cases of direct application of the European Convention by ordinary courts, there are a few examples of direct application of some other international treaties by ordinary courts, such as the Vienna Convention on the International Sale of Goods,[35] and some international maritime conventions.[36] The cases in question, however, did not concern any direct conflict between a Croatian law and an international treaty, and no case in which such a conflict did occur has been reported.

However, as has already been explained, the Croatian constitutional order envisages a system of centralized judicial review of laws. Ordinary courts are not competent to leave aside laws which they consider unconstitutional. Rather, if they wish not to apply certain statute law in a case pending before them, they are obliged to stay the proceedings and refer the question of constitutionality to the Constitutional Court. Like the Italian Constitutional Court, the Croatian Constitutional Court has put the judicial review of the conformity of domestic legislation with international treaties on a par with the judicial review of legislation with the Constitution. It considered that any law that is contrary to the international commitments must also be in breach of the Croatian Constitution (principle of the rule of law).[37]

Under the law as it presently stands, Croatian courts may not leave aside Croatian laws which are contrary to Community law, even if the review of conformity with international treaties is equated to the review of conformity with the Constitution and EU/EC law is considered international treaty law for this purpose. As this would be contrary to the principles of direct effect and supremacy as interpreted by the ECJ, the status of European law in the Croatian legal order must be distinguished from the status of international law in general.[38]

Although after accession the courts will be empowered by Community law itself to leave aside national law, a better solution would be to enable courts to follow the *Simmenthal* rule by means of national law as well. This would make EU obligations more transparent to Croatian judges, and could result in a more effective application of Community law in practice.

On the other hand, the judicial review of non-legislative acts is decentralized. Thus, any ordinary court may leave aside a non-legislative act and apply the

---

[34] Select Decisions of the Supreme Court of the Republic of Croatia, 2 (1995) pp. 156, 157.

[35] See decision of the Croatian Supreme Court, VSRH II Rev – 61/99-2.

[36] See decision of the Croatian Supreme Court, VSRH Gzz 8/1992-2.

[37] Decision of the Constitutional Court U-I-920/1995; U-I-950/1996 of 15 July 1998, *Narodne novine* 41/1998.

[38] Case 106/77 *Simmenthal* [1978] *ECR* 643.

European Convention or any other international legal provision directly and of its own accord. However, no such cases were reported either.

As far as the differentiation between primary and secondary EU law is concerned, there have been some developments which may lead the courts to start applying this distinction. As has already been mentioned above, the Croatian Parliament on the initiative of the Croatian Government has adopted a Law on the Implementation of the SAA and Interim Agreement.[39] In this Law a radical dualist approach was adopted which is possibly unconstitutional, but its constitutionality has not been tested yet. The Law leaves the courts no choice but to differentiate between primary and secondary association law[40] given that it provides that decisions of the Stabilization and Association Council have to be either ratified by the Parliament, or enacted as legislation, or transformed into an act of Government in order to have effect in Croatia. In other words, they are not directly applicable, although, based on the SAA itself, acts of the Association Council are published in the Croatian Official Journal. Courts may thus based on the Constitution apply the SAA (and Interim Agreement) directly, whereas the Law on the Implementation of the SAA instructs them not to apply decisions of the Association Council directly, but only indirectly through an act by which they were transferred into Croatian law.

This situation where secondary association law first has to be transformed into an act of internal law gives rise to several questions, such as: what if the competent authority does not transform the decision of the Association Council or transform it wrongly? Could, or even should, the courts then apply the decision of the Association Council directly, as they would Directives once Croatia becomes an EU member? It is our opinion that the SAA itself, if interpreted in the light of its object and purpose – which is closer integration with the EU and potentially membership of the EU – authorizes Croatian courts to apply directly such secondary association law that is capable of creating direct effect subject to the criteria developed by the ECJ. This is supported by the "higher law" status of the SAA in the Croatian legal order and the fact that secondary association law has to be published in the Croatian Official Journal. It is questionable whether Croatian courts will accept such an interpretation, however.

Even if courts will interpret the SAA as allowing the direct application of secondary association law, they may still not leave aside Croatian law (in this case the Law on the Implementation of the SAA) on their own initiative. According to the Constitutional Law on the Constitutional Court, and the Courts Act,

---

39 *Narodne novine*, Međunarodni ugovori, No. 15/2001.

40 There is, however, always possibility for the court to initiate the review procedure of constitutionality of the Law on the Implementation of the SAA in front of the Constitutional Court. If found unconstitutional, this would allow Croatian courts to apply secondary association law directly, as there is nothing in the Constitution itself that would prevent it.

they must stay the procedure, refer the question to the Constitutional Court, and await its decision. Thus, they may not apply the principle of direct effect as set out by the ECJ in the Simmenthal case[41] during the pre-accession phase.

The non-recognition of the direct effect of secondary association law, apart from being contrary to the constitutional choice for monism in Croatia, is not in line with the case law of the ECJ. The ECJ has recognized that acts enacted by the bodies set up by agreements to which the EC is a party do form part of the Community legal order, and may be directly applicable, providing that the conditions for direct effect are satisfied.[42] Although, as far as Community law is concerned, the different method of implementation of SAA commitments by Croatia does not in itself represent a breach of the SAA,[43] the decision not to admit direct effect of secondary association law is certainly not evidence of Croatia's readiness to embrace European law principles.

How the courts will interpret the provisions of the Law on the Implementation of the SAA remains to be seen. However, if the differentiation between primary and secondary association law in relation to its effects is maintained and continues to be applied in practice, there is a danger that the courts will adopt the same attitude in relation to primary and secondary Community law later on.

2.4 Indirect effect

It must first be repeated that it is not very often that Croatian courts apply international law, either directly or indirectly. As to indirect effect as a rule of judicial interpretation, there have been no express references to it in the available case law.

However, using the available research facilities on the Internet, we did find a few examples in which the Supreme Court did refer to international treaties in order to interpret internal legal norms. Thus, for example, it has referred to Article 6 of the European Convention on Human Rights and Fundamental Freedoms in order to interpret the Croatian Law on Expropriation,[44] or more precisely, provisions of that Law that were enacted in order to bring the Law in line with the Convention, after a decision of the Constitutional Court proclaiming incompatibility.[45] It has also referred to ILO Convention No. 131 in order to confirm its interpretation of the Croatian Law on Labour Relations.[46] The Constitutional

---

[41] Case 106/77 *Simmenthal* [1978] *ECR* 643.

[42] Case C-192/89 *Sevince* [1990] *ECR* I-3461.

[43] Case 104/81 *Kupferberg* [1982] *ECR* 3641.

[44] See decisions of the Croatian Supreme Court, VSRH Gr 1-562/02-2; Gr 1-602/02-2; Gr 1-607/02-2; and Gr 1-662/02-2.

[45] See decision of the Croatian Constitutional Court, U-I/745/1999.

[46] See decision of the Croatian Supreme Court, VSRH Rev-3928/1994-2.

Court has also used the European Convention as an interpretative tool, in which cases, it has, as already reported, sometimes quoted from the case law of the European Court of Human Rights.[47] There is no evidence that ordinary courts have quoted the case law of the European Court of Human Rights or of any other judicial body.

As has been reported above, there are only a few examples of ordinary courts taking into account international law when interpreting internal legal rules. All of them relate to international law which is part of the Croatian legal order (ratified Conventions). We have not been able find any cases in which the courts took account of Community law, either primary or secondary, when interpreting Croatian law. On the contrary, there are examples of judges refusing to refer to Community law (a Directive in a concrete example) as an interpretative tool. This example was given by a lawyer who had invoked a Directive for interpretative purposes before a court and had her intervention characterized as "extravagant."[48] This is not a welcome attitude today when the principle of indirect effect is becoming increasingly important, as Croatia has entered a new stage in its relations with the EU. After all, both the SAA and the conditions for joining the EU require that Croatia adjusts its law to the *acquis communautaire.* This adjustment is not accomplished by the mere adoption of compatible legal norms, but needs to be complemented by the application in practice of legal norms in conformity with EU law. Thus, interpreting Croatian laws and other acts in the light of the Community law to which Croatian law has just been adjusted can be considered as one of the obligations following from the SAA, an obligation, which binds the state in all its manifestations, including the courts. Thus, one possible interpretation could be that non-adherence to the principle of indirect effect in such a case represents a breach of the SAA by the courts. It is, therefore, imperative that the courts' attitude towards interpretation of law changes.

2.5 **Cases**

Such cases in which the Supreme Court and the Constitutional Court have applied international treaties directly and cases in which they have used them as an interpretative tool have already been cited above. There are no reported cases in which either the Constitutional or the Supreme Court expressly referred to the principle of indirect effect. There are no cases in which these Courts referred to Community law when interpreting internal law either. Likewise, up to today, no

---

[47] See, for example, decisions of the Croatian Constitutional Court U-I/745/1999; or U-III/2962/2002.

[48] This is not a reported case. The information was acquired in a conversation with the lawyer in question.

cases have been reported in which the Interim Agreement, which is the only part of Community law in force in Croatia at the time of writing, was applied directly.

2.6 Structure, procedures and practice

Membership of the EU will itself not cause any changes in the organization of the judiciary in Croatia. It is clear from the case law of the European Court[49] that EU law does not interfere with the organization of justice in the Member States, provided that there is always a competent court that can hear actions based on Community law, and provided that the judicial protection it is empowered to offer is effective according to European standards.

Although an organizational change will not be necessary, the requirement of the effectiveness of judicial protection will provoke changes both in the procedural sphere and in the practice of the courts. However, this pressure to make the judicial process more effective already exists without the requirements of Community law. International commitments (such as Art. 6 of the ECHR), but also and even more importantly, real life, especially business, demand the speedier and more effective resolution of disputes. Such pressures have already caused some changes in the judiciary and in procedural law (more particularly in the codes of criminal and civil procedure). For the time being, the length of the proceedings adversely affects not only the protection of individual rights, but also the development and consolidation of judicial practice. For example, due to lengthy proceedings and transitory provisions in some laws that allow for the application of previous legislation to pending cases, the Supreme Court is at times forced to decide a case by applying a law that is no longer in force. In such cases, the interpretation of law by the Supreme Court does not serve the development of law. Temporal effects of legislation will obviously have to be taken into consideration in the process of harmonization in order to enable the full application of the *acquis communautaire* as of the day of accession.

Also, the procedure of constitutional review will have to be brought in conformity with the *Simmenthal* principle. This change, when implemented, will significantly empower lower court judges. As we have seen from the Italian experience, lower instance individual judges may write history in the development of European law. The power to leave aside national law and in realistic terms, to bypass the national judicial hierarchy and the Supreme Court, will have important consequences for the Croatian legal system. It will erode the role of the Supreme Court in preserving the unity of the Croatian legal system as it is now,

---

[49] Case 13/68 *Salgoil* [1968] *ECR* 453; confirmed, for example, in Case C-54/96 *Dorsch Consult* [1997] *ECR* I-4961.

and create conditions for the merging of the national legal system with the legal system of the EU.

Some new procedures and practices will also have to be established for future participation in the judicial system of the EU enabling references for a preliminary ruling and possibly for participation in the third-pillar judicial cooperation.

However, as far as Community law is concerned, it appears that its impact will be, or should be, more on judicial culture and practice than on legislative changes in the procedural law (although here formal changes may also prove necessary). After all, the Community legislator has so far declined to regulate questions of procedure and/or remedies before national courts (there are only a few Directives that touch on these matters and only in the limited field of the substantive application of such Directives). By contrast, pending legislative action, the European Court has created a number of principles and rules under the umbrella of the principle of effective judicial protection, which do demand changes in the remedial and procedural rules in the Member States. Such changes are to be made directly by national courts. In other words, it is not necessary to wait for the national legislator to provide them in the national procedural rules first. When a case before a national court involves Community law, national courts are required by Community law to adjust their internal rules where necessary to ensure the effective judicial protection of Community rights. Thus, national courts may be asked to question their internal statutes of limitation[50] and, if necessary, change them. The same may happen in respect of rules on evidence,[51] standing,[52] etc. National courts may be asked to provide for remedies that do not exist under national law – such as interim injunctions,[53] damages against the state[54] even if it acted as legislator,[55] or to award interest together with damages, even though they are not allowed to do that under national law.[56] The application of this type of case law of the European Court demands two things of the national courts: firstly, they need to be familiar with the case law of the European Court and keep themselves informed, and secondly and equally importantly, they have to be prepared to play the creative role required from them by Community law.

As to the first requirement, to become truly 'European judges' national judges need to familiarise themselves with Community law, not just in the sense of a set of written rules, but including the case law interpreting these rules as well as the principles of Community law which relate to their application and interpretation.

---

50 E.g., Case 33/76 *Rewe* [1976] *ECR* 1989; Case C-231/96 *Edis* [1998] *ECR* I-4951.
51 E.g., Case 199/82 *San Giorgio* [1983] *ECR* 3595.
52 E.g., Joined Cases C-87-89/90 *Verholen* [1991] *ECR* I-3757.
53 Case C-213/89 *Factortame* [1990] *ECR* I-2433.
54 Joined Cases C-6 and 9/90 *Francovich* [1991] *ECR* I-5375.
55 Joined Cases C-46 and 48/93 *Brasserie/Factortame III* [1996] *ECR* I-1066.
56 Case C-271/91 *Marshall II* [1993] *ECR* I-4367.

For this to be achieved, it is necessary to train all judges – present and future – in Community law. Up to now, not many judges have received such training, but the education process is expected to speed up now that Croatia has the status of candidate country, and part of the CARDS programme is allocated for the education of judges. A recent institutional development that might help in this task was the establishment of the Academy for Judges at the Ministry of Justice, which has as its primary task the permanent education of judges.[57] However, the new institution will not make much difference if the judges are not motivated to learn and adjust. The present Courts Act already provides for the mandatory permanent education of judges.[58] However, judges have generally failed to develop a habit of systematical self-education and the excuse is very often lack of time and finances.[59] If, however, Croatia wants to participate successfully in the EU, all judges, not just a few exceptions, need to be familiar with EU law and principles. One of the solutions which may make judges more knowledgeable is to introduce a system of professional advancement of judges which considers education as an important factor.

In addition to the current members of the judiciary, future judges must also receive EU law training. This means that Law Faculties must begin to offer courses in at least the basic principles of Community law. At present, only the Law Faculty of Rijeka University offers a mandatory course in basic Community law, while the Law Faculty of Zagreb University offered such a course on an optional basis, but will start teaching EU law as a mandatory subject as of the academic year 2004/2005. Other Law Faculties do not yet offer Community law courses.

Croatian law is not isolated from other legal systems and it will experience even more 'outside influences' once Croatia becomes an EU Member. Therefore, in addition to acquiring basic knowledge, judges will have to start informing themselves regularly about the case law of the ECJ and the Court of First Instance, courts of other Member States, and other Croatian courts. As was explained in the introduction to this part of the chapter, Croatian judges are not traditionally used to following national case law, let alone foreign or international case law. Becoming part of the European judiciary will, therefore, represent a significant cultural change, and will demand much effort on the part of Croatian judges. There are a many barriers on the way to the successful conclusion of this task. Firstly, the judges do not necessarily speak foreign languages and European

---

57 More about this institution may be found at the website of the Ministry of Justice: <http://www.pravosudje.hr/centar/index.html>.

58 This new duty was introduced in the Courts Act by the Amendments of 22 December 2000, and included in Article 62 (*Narodne novine*, br. 129/2000).

59 See in that respect, A. Kovačić, 'Stalna stručna izobrazba i usavršavanje sudaca', Hrvatska pravna revija, prosinac 2001, p. 130 at p. 132.

case law is not, and will not for a significant time be translated into Croatian. Judges do not have access to and/or knowledge of how to use databases of case law that exist on the Internet. Most importantly, judges claim that they do not have the time, taking into consideration the backlog of cases they have to solve and the amount of new legislation enacted daily. The same problems, however, have existed and continue to exist in the new 2004 enlargement Member States. Their experience will be of great practical value for organizing the process of learning and cultural change within the Croatian judiciary.

Secondly, Croatian judges have to be willing and able to start acting as 'European judges'. This issue is partly connected with the previous one. It is possible that a readiness to apply Community law and principles will only be created once the judges learn more about it. However, as has already been explained, in Croatia the judicial process is weighed down by a strong sense of formalism. Judges follow procedural rules enacted by the legislator. They may not change or avoid the application of such rules. However, Community law sometimes demands exactly that. Croatian judges will have difficulty accepting that, in the name of Community law, they are not only allowed, but also required to question their procedural and remedial rules, not to mention adjust them if necessary. This requires a cultural shift from formalism to creativity and substantive analysis in the judicial process. A precondition for that is a different perception of the role of the judge. The public, but also judges themselves, will have to accept that judges must not only mechanically apply the written laws, but that creative interpretation which takes into consideration the social momentum and needs of society is part of the judicial role. There is always danger in this – judges must remain judges, even if creative ones, and must not trespass on the legislator's grounds. And this should also become part of the judicial culture – that judges are aware that there is a border line between interpretation and law making, which they should be able to recognize in each case they are asked to decide.

To conclude, actual EU membership, but also prospective EU membership, finally leads the Croatian legal system to the road that the legal systems of the EU Member States have been taking since the early 20th century. For them it involved a change in the traditional separation of powers doctrine in favour of the judiciary through the recognition (more or less silent) of the law-creating role of judges. All the aspects mentioned above will require a shift within the judicial culture in Croatia and will change the perception, including the self-perception, of judges. Therefore, the biggest change that EU Membership is expected to bring to the Croatian judiciary and to the Croatian legal system in general is cultural, rather than legislative, and thus substantive, rather than formal.

3. ROLE OF THE EXECUTIVE (GOVERNMENT AND ADMINISTRATION)

3.1 Europe Agreement or Stabilization and Association Agreement

The fulfilment of all the obligations stemming from the SAA represented the start of serious reforms in the public administration as well as changes in society as a whole in order to facilitate the adjustment to the political, economic and legal standards of the European Union. The process adjusting to the conditions for associated membership has from the very start been linked to the process of adjusting the overall legal system to the criteria for full membership. Croatia plans to implement these two sets of criteria in two parallel, albeit procedurally separated, phases along the road to Europe. It is crucial that each next step in the process of the implementation of these reforms is planned very carefully. This planning includes the effective coordination and monitoring of the implementation of all the obligations stemming from the SAA, the development of strategies and the investment of efforts by all the key factors in the process of European integration.

This approach became even more important after the European Council of 17-18 June 2004 decided that Croatia is a candidate country for membership and that the accession process could be launched. In its *avis* the European Commission concluded that Croatia is a functioning democracy with stable institutions which function properly and that there are no major problems over assuring the rule of law and respect for fundamental rights.[60] As far as the economic criteria are concerned, Croatia can be regarded as a functioning market economy that should be able to cope with competitive pressures and market forces within the EU in the medium term. As to the third criterion, the European Commission assessed that Croatia will be in a position to take on the other obligations of membership in the medium term as well, except for environment obligations where long-term efforts are necessary.

The overall assessment by the European Commission is that Croatia has made significant improvements in aligning its legislation with the *acquis*, especially in terms of the Internal Market and Trade *acquis*. Following this, it is the Commission's view that Croatia should not experience any major difficulties in applying the *acquis* in the medium term in the fields of EMU, statistics, industrial policy, SMEs, science and research, education and training, culture and audio-visual, external relations and CFSP. Further efforts to align and implement the legislation, will be needed in areas such as free movement of capital, company law, fisheries, transport, energy, consumer and health protection, customs union and

[60] See *supra* n. 23.

financial control. Considerable efforts, both in the legislative and the administrative sense, will be needed in the areas of technical legislation, taxation, environment, free movement of persons, services, JHA, and regional policy.

In order to create the preconditions necessary for the adjustment of Croatia's legislation to the *acquis communautaire* and the implementation of all measures necessary for further rapprochement with the EU, the Government of the Republic of Croatia passed a number of conclusions as early as February 2001. These conclusions expressed the wish that key progress in attaining the necessary level of readiness for membership of the EU should be achieved by the end of 2004, with a view to implementing the strategic objective that Croatia reaches the required level of readiness for attaining membership of the EU by the end of 2006.

Through these conclusions, all ministries and public authorities committed themselves to undertake without delay preparations to modify the legislation which the Republic of Croatia has to harmonize with the *acquis communautaire*, and to take into consideration in the preparation of new acts, to the greatest possible extent, the provisions of the *acquis communautaire* and to provide information concerning the level of harmonization in the explanation of the act.

Recognizing the importance of the implementation of the SAA for its further progress towards full membership of the EU, the Government of the Republic of Croatia was determined to be well prepared when it started to implement the SAA. Therefore, work on the implementation instruments and related mechanisms commenced as soon as the SAA negotiations entered the final phase. The Government of the Republic of Croatia adopted the Implementation Plan for the SAA just before the SAA was signed. The National Programme for the Integration of the Republic of Croatia into the European Union (NPIEU), adopted in December 2002, upgraded this SAA Implementation Plan.

(a) *Implementation Plan for the SAA*

The Implementation Plan[61] is an operative document consisting of measures necessary for the successful implementation of the commitments undertaken in the SAA. It is the pivotal point of a system designed to ensure timely and thorough implementation of a number of policies that encourage the reforms contained in the SAA. However, the Implementation Plan goes beyond the SAA and reflects Croatia's own development goals in order to accelerate the process of adjustments to European standards. Therefore, it provides an accelerated implementation agenda compared to the SAA deadlines.

---

61 See <http://www.mei.hr/default.asp?ru=314&akcija=>.

The Implementation Plan is the main planning, coordinating, monitoring and reporting instrument for the implementation of the SAA. It defines precisely what has to be done, by whom and by when. It currently consists of more than 450 analytical and institutional measures, as well as measures related to the preparation of technical assistance projects, for the period 2001-2006. The Implementation Plan used to contain legislative measures as well, but as of 2004 they are included only in the NPIEU.

The Implementation Plan is conceived as an "evolving" document. Since its adoption, the Ministry of European Integration (MEI), as a coordinating institution, in close cooperation with all the governmental bodies involved, has regularly updated the Implementation Plan with new measures.[62] Other necessary modifications have been made so that the Implementation Plan constantly defines the implementation tasks according to the actual status and needs of the implementation of the SAA. It has been amended on several occasions, one of them taking into consideration the recommendations of the European Commission from the Reports on the Stabilization and Association Process in the Republic of Croatia.[63]

The MEI has designed a computer database for storing data on the implementation of measures, and for monitoring and preparing reports and analyses for the Government. The system was improved by the addition of an interactive CD-ROM that made the entire database publicly available. The database was further upgraded to enable data management to be decentralized.

Reports on the realization of the Implementation Plan are created on a monthly and semi-annual basis and are presented to the Government for adoption. Full transparency is one of the very important characteristics of the implementation process and all reports are publicly available online.

(b) *National Programme for the Integration of the Republic of Croatia into the European Union*

The Republic of Croatia prepared its National Programme for the Integration of the Republic of Croatia into the EU taking into consideration the relevant experiences of candidate countries in the preparation of similar programmes (National Programmes for the Adoption of the Acquis – NPAAs).

The NPIEU 2004[64] was adopted at the Government session on 15 January 2004. It was forwarded to the Croatian Parliament to have its Annex – "Plan of

---

62 In the aftermath of the last round of elections, the MEI merged with the Ministry of Foreign Affairs, which was renamed the "Ministry of Foreign Affairs and European Integration". For ease of reference the old abbreviation 'MEI' is retained in this text.

63 E.g., Commission Staffworking Paper Croatia, Stabilization and Association Report [COM (2002) 163], Brussels, 4 April 2002 SEC (2002) 341.

64 NPIEU 2003 and NPIEU 2004 can be downloaded from the web site of the Ministry for European Integration, available at: <http://www.mei.hr>.

legislative harmonization – 2004" adopted. Parliament passed the NPIEU 2004 and adopted the legislative Annex at its session of 29 January 2004.

NPIEU is primarily aimed at fulfilling the obligations that have been undertaken and at the development of guidelines for the implementation of all the reforms that Croatia will need on the way. However, at the same time it serves as a roadmap by which the Government of the Republic of Croatia realistically assesses its capacities and the capacities of Croatian society as a whole to implement all that is included in adjustment to EU criteria. This document presents assessments, guidelines, and tasks, with the intention that all relevant activities may be conducted in a more dynamic manner, so that Croatia will be ready for full membership of the EU by the end of 2006.

Given that the National Programme represents the central steering mechanism of the Government of the Republic of Croatia in the area of European integration from one year to another, it is precisely its implementation that will be the subject of future reports on the evaluation of the Stabilization and Association Process for Croatia.

The National Programme reflects Croatia's readiness, through the implementation of concrete measures, to implement the short-term and medium-term priorities of the EU integration process, with an emphasis on 2004. It focuses on several challenging issues on the road to integration of Croatia into the EU:

- Meeting political criteria;
- Economic adjustments;
- Harmonization of Croatia's legislation addressing all the chapters of the *acquis*;
- Strengthening administrative capacity for the implementation of the reforms;
- Communication strategy for informing the Croatian public about the European integration of Croatia.

A novelty in the definition of priorities in the NPIEU 2004, which also serves as the basis for its forthcoming revision, is the inclusion of the short-term priorities set out in the European Partnership for the Republic of Croatia, published at the same time as the Commission's *avis* on Croatia's application for membership.[65] Following this, the aforementioned revision of the NPIEU 2004 has now been undertaken with the intention of including the same number of short-term recommendations and concrete sectoral activities by the end of 2004, provided that the budget allows for their fulfilment. Short-term recommendations as well as mid-term ones will be the primary basis for the preparation of the NPIEU 2005.

[65] See Council Decision 2004/648/EC on the principles, priorities and conditions contained in the European Partnership with Croatia, *OJ* 2004 L 297/19.

A total of 83 legislative measures were planned to be enacted in 2003 (55 laws and 28 bylaws) to harmonize legislation with the *acquis communautaire*. Only one of these failed to get implemented, making the NPIEU 2003 implementation rate 98.8%. NPIEU 2004 plans for 265 legislative measures (42 laws and 223 bylaws) to be adopted.

The number of bylaws anticipated for 2004 gives a clear indication that the main focus in the harmonization process is shifting to the implementation of the adopted legislation. In this respect, following legal approximation, several new institutions have been or are about to be established in order to ensure effective implementation.

Implementation of the National Programme depends on the quality of day-to-day coordination at the level of ministries and other government agencies involved in the process. Coordination at the level of each state administration body is entrusted to "European Coordinators" who are charged with organizing work related to European integration, and with coordinating and overseeing implementation. In respect of the National Programme, the Coordinator's duty is to see to it that the tasks specified in the National Programme are carried out in a timely manner within his or her state administration body, and to keep the MEI informed on all matters related to the National Programme. The European Coordinator is responsible for the regular collection of information on the implementation of the National Programme at the level of his or her state administration body, and for preparing reports on the progress made in carrying out those tasks envisaged by the National Programme which fall within his or her sphere of activity.

Responsibility for the monitoring and realization of the implementation of the National Programme has been entrusted to every state administration body in the area of its competence. The MEI coordinates the implementation of the National Programme at the level of the Government of the Republic of Croatia. Since this is a demanding document in terms of content, it is divided into individual responsibilities of the MEI civil servants in charge of specific sectors of the National Programme. In monitoring a specific sector, MEI civil servants are in charge of the regular monitoring of the implementation of the National Programme on an operational level, and they have regular contacts with the staff from the sector of the state administration body which they monitor. This system provides for the monitoring of the implementation from an operational aspect, both on an inter-sectoral level and on the level of each state administration body.

An interactive database (Management Reporting Information System – MRIS) was established at the MEI for the purpose of facilitating the technical monitoring of the implementation of the National Programme. In order to avoid written reporting, each state administration body was provided with access to the interactive database into which the European Coordinators enter data on a monthly basis on the implementation of the National Programme for their area of competence. Data entered into the MRIS database is controlled directly on an operational level by MEI civil servants.

The National Programme is monitored weekly by the Government.

3.2 Preparation and implementation of EC/EU law

(a) *Coordination mechanisms for the implementation of the SAA*[66]

In order to ensure the coordinated and timely implementation of the SAA, the following mechanisms for coordination, monitoring and reporting have been set up:

- Implementation Plan for the SAA;
- National Programme for the Integration of the Republic of Croatia into the EU;
- Government sessions;
- A network of European Integration Coordinators and Deputy Coordinators at all line ministries;
- European Integration units at the line ministries;
- Working groups for harmonization of legislation;
- Frequent meetings between the MEI and line ministries;
- Daily horizontal coordination and cooperation on an operational level.

The Government discusses European integration issues at its regular sessions and adopts reports on the realization of the Implementation Plan and NPIEU in its regular procedure. The Government also occasionally requires the MEI to prepare special reports or analyses on different aspects of the implementation.

In order to establish a closer connection between the different departments involved in the European integration process, Coordinators and Deputy Coordinators for European integration have been appointed at the level of State Secretaries or Assistant Ministers as coordinators responsible for the overall functioning of the Ministries in the process of adjustment to the EU, ensuring an uninterrupted horizontal flow of information. This provides an "early warning" system which indicates possible implementation difficulties that can be detected in time and notified to the Government through regular reports on the realization of the Implementation Plan and NPIEU or specific analyses. In this way, the Government is able to make the necessary decisions to resolve potential problems in a timely manner.

---

[66] See *supra* n. 62 and the accompanying main text.

European Integration Units have already been established in line Ministries and they are in the process of increasing their administrative capacity.

Meetings between the MEI and line Ministries are held in order to address potential problems in implementation prior to such problems being passed on to the Government. In addition, further improvements in daily cooperation on an operational level are discussed and new measures planned.

On an operational level, MEI and line Ministry civil servants exchange information on the ongoing implementation of measures and update the computer database (see above).

(b) *Mechanisms of legal harmonization*

The process of the harmonization of legislation which commenced on the day of the signing of the Agreement has been developing gradually over a transition period ending six years after the SAA's entry into force. The gradual nature of this process is reflected both in the time frame and in the approach. The first phase in the process of harmonization of legislation encompasses the basic elements of the internal market, trade and trade-related areas and, finally, other elements of the *acquis* referred to in the Agreement. It includes five priority areas: public procurement, competition and state aid, technical legislation, consumer protection and intellectual property, and industrial and commercial property.

The MEI acts as a coordinating body in the process of harmonizing national legislation with EU law and as part of the regular Government procedure assesses the degree of harmonization in proposed regulations with the relevant *acquis* of the EU. The role of the Ministry will be explored in more detail below.

Recognizing the importance of the process of harmonizing legislation, the Government has introduced a novelty in its Rules of Procedure of the Government of the Republic of Croatia[67] whereby the opinion of the MEI has to be attached to, *inter alia*, draft proposals for Acts of Parliament and other legislation. This amendment to the Rules of Procedure[68] includes that proposed legislation which is harmonized with EU law should be marked as such (P.Z.E. br…). At the request of the proposer, legislation which is harmonized with EU rules may be enacted in an expedited procedure which combines first and second reading of the Act. The Committee for European Integration of the Croatian Parliament has a key role in this legislative process.

In order for the harmonization of legislation to be carried out as effectively as possible, the Government of the Republic of Croatia on 19 July 2001 adopted a Decision on the Measures in the Procedure of Harmonization of the Legislation of

---

[67] *Narodne novine* No. 107/2000.

[68] *Narodne novine* No. 117/2001.

the Republic of Croatia with the *acquis communautaire*,[69] whose mandatory application commenced on 1 December 2001. Under this Decision, state administration bodies, in the preparation of legislative documents which harmonize the legislation of the Republic of Croatia with the *acquis communautaire* pursuant to Article 69 of the SAA, are obliged to submit together with the Bill a complete statement on the harmonization which it achieves and a review of the conformity of the provisions of the Bill with the provisions of the relevant legislation of the EU. Both instruments, together with the Bill, are the submitted to the MEI for verification and confirmation. Considering that this is a novelty in Government procedure, the MEI will assist the state administration bodies in fulfilling these requirements by providing all necessary technical and expert support.

(c) *Compatibility statement*

The Compatibility Statement contains essential information in respect of the compatibility of a draft legislative proposal with the relevant SAA provisions as well as with the relevant EU legislation. The Statement formally declares the level of harmonization attained by the (draft) Bill (completely harmonized, partially harmonized, not harmonized). Before it can be submitted for further legislative processing, the Compatibility Statement must be validated through the signatures of the public officials responsible for adjustment to EU legislation.

(d) *Table of concordance*

In order for the harmonization of legislation to be carried out as effectively as possible, in addition to the Compatibility Statement, administrative authorities fill out a Table of Concordance, which is in fact a parallel review of the conformity of the provisions of the (draft) Bill with the provisions of the relevant legislation of the EU. The Table of Concordance also shows the deadlines for achieving complete harmonization.

The MEI provides to public authorities all the necessary technical and expert support required for filling in these instruments. Moreover, the competent authorities are required to include the MEI from the beginning in the preparation of legislation harmonizing Croatian law with the *acquis*. This significantly facilitates the final evaluation of the degree of harmonization achieved and also enables an exchange of knowledge on the sectoral level and on the level of the MEI as the body in charge of coordinating the process of harmonizing the legislation.

---

69 Government Decision of 19 July 2001, not published.

(e) *Working groups*

On 19 September 2002 the Government of the Republic of Croatia passed a Decision on the Establishment of Working Groups for the Harmonization of the Legislation of the Republic of Croatia with the *acquis communautaire*.

Working Groups are to be established for the 31 chapters of the *acquis communautaire*. At this stage, 14 working groups have so far been established in all 13 priority areas in the obligatory harmonization of legislation: electronic commerce, competition and state aid, intellectual, industrial, and commercial property, public procurement, technical legislation, financial services, accounting law, company law, consumer protection, land transport, health and safety at work, equal opportunities and protection of databases, as well as the judiciary and internal affairs.

The work of the Working Groups is important in resolving numerous preliminary issues related to the harmonization of the legislation which so far do not surface until specific proposals have already reached the Government procedure. Based on the duties undertaken by the Republic of Croatia in the Agreement, and also on the experiences of the candidate countries for membership of the EU, the work of the Working Groups greatly contributes to the process of the harmonization of legislation, by formulating common standpoints in resolving essential issues, and considerably accelerates the legislative process at Government level.

(f) *Exchange of experts between administrative bodies*

In order to share experiences and knowledge on the level of state administration bodies, the MEI has launched a national twinning initiative – an exchange programme for lawyers in the state administration bodies and lawyers at the MEI. This approach allows for the exchange of knowledge among experts concerning specific sectors on the one hand, and experts on the European rules that are relevant for harmonization in those sectors on the other. Almost all staff at the Administration for the Harmonization of Legislation are participating or have participated in the work of other state administration bodies on legal issues in their area of competence: in the Ministry of Finance, the Ministry of Justice, the Administration and Local Self-Government, the Ministry of Environmental Protection and Physical Planning, the Ministry of the Economy, the Ministry of Maritime Affairs, Transport, and Communications, and the Ministry of Health.

3.3 Impact of EU accession on the organization and practice of (a) central government and administration and (b) decentralized authorities?

The Government of the Republic of Croatia has undertaken and is planning a number of activities aimed at strengthening administrative capacity with the public administration bodies to enable them to adapt to the EU.

(a) *Central government and administration*

The Government 2003-2007 Programme makes the reform of government and administration a priority. Points on the programme include the following:

- The responsible citizen who fulfils his or her obligations towards the state deserves responsible and efficient public administration and is entitled as a tax payer to quality services from the public administration at all levels in return for his or her contribution. The reform of public administration and local self-government is a precondition for economic progress.
- The Government will consider and propose a new organizational structure for the public administration in order to increase efficiency and savings, especially bearing in mind its basic function, i.e., high-quality and rapid service to the public.
- The composition of the Government and the number of Ministries and their competences have been determined in accordance with the strategic priorities contained in Government policy at this stage of Croatia's development. The Government will implement the full computerization of the entire system of public administration and ensure its public supervision and full transparency towards the citizen.
- A central system of financial monitoring will be introduced to supervise the use of budgetary resources by the state apparatus.
- The present territorial organization of Croatia with the existing number of counties will be preserved, and part of the state affairs will be delegated to towns with more than forty-five thousand inhabitants so as to allow them to have greater influence on and responsibility for their development. A new system of financing local and regional self-government will be established by means of changing the tax policy, determining original revenues, reallocation of income tax and corporate tax and the introduction of annuities and fees in accordance with the programmes and projects of the local population.
- A system of direct elections for municipal, town and county mayors will be introduced. A systematic approach will be taken towards the removal of bureaucratic obstacles and the speeding up of administrative procedures. All the reforms will be subject to the fundamental goal – the organization of up-to-

date and efficient public services and administration as a service to citizens and businesses.

In this respect, some changes that have already been introduced relate to:

- the restructuring of Ministries and state administration organizations, including reductions in their number (14 Ministries instead of 19);
- the formation of new central state administration bodies – central state offices of the Government of the Republic of Croatia (for Administration, for e-Croatia, for State Property Management, for Development Strategy);
- the introduction of the function of State Secretary at Ministries.

The primary task of the Government is to halt the expansion of central administration, which means avoiding the establishment of new government administration bodies and appointment of new civil servants. The process of horizontal decentralization will moreover be encouraged by which some of the current duties of central administration will be transferred to autonomous organizations outside the system of Government administration, such as trade unions, employers' associations, universities, citizens' associations, etc.

Improving knowledge of EU affairs in the administration is another important task. Thus, the MEI has set up a system of education over the past few years, with more than 1000 attendees each year. As a result, numerous consultants cooperating with the MEI have found that the knowledge and skills of the civil servants involved in the work related to European integration are now greater than what the average administrative capacities of their colleagues from the current candidate countries were when they began to approach the EU. One of the priorities in the 2000-2004 Action Plan is granting scholarships to young experts to study abroad as postgraduates and their subsequent employment in various Government administration bodies in Croatia.

By a decision of 7 November 2002, the former Government started preparations for the reform of the public administration. The Government's vice-president coordinated these preparations, guaranteeing the direct involvement and support of the core of the Government in the reform. The appointed project leader was assistant Minister of European integration. The members of the project team are MEI civil servants who also provide all the necessary logistical assistance. A Project Steering Committee (PSC) has been formed for the purpose of supervising and steering the project. The members of the PSC are representatives of the Government of the Republic of Croatia. In addition to the PSC, a Project Council was also to be formed to serve as a counselling and advisory body and comprising eminent experts in the field of public administration from expert associations, the University, trade unions, employers' associations, NGOs, etc.

The public administration in Croatia, as well as society as a whole, is facing two exceptional, principally complementary challenges: the finalization of the transition into the market economy system and the transformation of the public administration into a service provider to the citizens. Both should be considered with regard to the EU standards and practices of individual Member States.

According to the Government decision the main goals of the reform were:

- To achieve an efficient system of decision / policy making and implementing, with simultaneous de-politization of the public administration. The administration should assist politics in creating policies and decision, while politics should create conditions in which the decisions may be implemented in an efficient and legal manner;
- The public administration, its structure and methods of work should be adjusted to provide services to the users – citizens. The results should be measurable and verifiable;
- In addition to efficiency, the public administration should start to work in accordance with a project approach where possible, and introduce more coordination on reform issues within line Ministries and institutions;
- The public administration should serve as one of the sources of impetus for: the development of a society based on knowledge, the strengthening of market competition and the capability of economic entities, the development of society values such as solidarity, understanding and social security, the computerization of society and sustainable development;
- The reform should ensure the employment of the top-quality human resources, their further training, motivation and retention within the service. The state as an employer in the conditions of fast economic growth and elimination of unemployment should be ready for competition with the private sector in attracting and retaining human resources.

In the process so far, a fruitful cooperation has been established with the SIGMA, an OECD initiative principally financed by the EC.

The planned result of the first stage of the reform – the preparation stage – is a Policy Document, identifying the main intervention areas and providing an assessment of the existing situation and an analysis of the problems and opportunities for improvement, as well as recommendations (possible multiple scenarios) for further activities. The recommendations address three different levels:

- system level (recommendations that concern the whole system of state administration, primarily the number and functions of individual administrative organizations and their powers, matters relating to the civil service, training, etc);

- sector level (recommendations concerning the improvement of coordination and functioning within a wider area of activities and sectors that include several administrative organizations);
- individual institutions level (where it is possible and necessary, recommendations will be given for reforms within individual institutions, primarily in their relation to other institutions and their functions).

Currently, all these documents are analysed at the Central Office for Administration. Furthermore, in March 2004, the Government formed a special commission on alignment of the state administration with the European standards which was given the task of preparing an Alignment Programme in six months' time.

(b) *Decentralized government and administration*

The Action Plan of the Government for the period between 2000 and 2004 envisaged the beginning of the process of decentralization and the strengthening of local and regional self-government in such way as to enable the local self-government units to perform a much broader scope of work, and to grant them wider autonomy with regard to the central Government and administration. A prerequisite to the successful realization of autonomy of local bodies is building their financial capacity through redistribution of revenues from national taxes, providing new and more profuse sources of local revenues, and using various non-fiscal financing instruments (joint stock holdings, bonds, loans, etc.).

The adoption of the Act on Local and Regional Self-Government, and the amendments to the Act on Financing Units of Local and Regional Self-Government, and special Acts on primary and secondary schools, health care and social welfare, heralds the actual beginning of the decentralization process, i.e., a transfer of Government administration duties from the national level to the units of local and regional self-government followed by the transfer of financial capacity.

In order to achieve better coordination of the European integration process with units of local and regional self-government, the MEI initiated the establishment of County Offices for European Integration. The County Office comprises civil servants working in municipal administration and representatives of the business sector. Its task at the county level is to start initiatives, serve as information and referential point for European integration issues, stimulate and coordinate the participation of employees in units of local and regional self-government in various educational programmes concerning European integration and to gather information on projects for the development of economy, municipal services and infrastructure in order to compete for EU funds. The MEI finances the work of the County Offices for European Integration and allocated amounts depend on planned activities for the following year. Representatives of the County Offices for European Integration meet annually with MEI representatives whereby the County Offices submit annual reports concerning their activities in the field of European Integration.

4. ROLE OF THE NATIONAL PARLIAMENT

4.1 **Preparedness for legal approximation**

Changes in the internal structure and parliamentary procedure for the purpose of integration with the EU have been introduced since 2001. These changes are reflected in the parliamentary Rules of Procedure.[70]

In February 2001 the Croatian Parliament set up the European Integration Committee as one of 25 standing parliamentary committees. Articles 96 and 97 of the Rules of Procedure govern the competences and the composition of the Committee. Concerning its role in the legislative process, the European Integration Committee has competences equal to other standing committees in the Parliament; it has the right to initiate Bills or amendments or to express common positions.

The European Integration Committee shall:

- monitor the harmonization of the legal system of the Republic of Croatia with the legal system of the European Union;
- monitor the exercise of the rights and commitments of the Republic of Croatia that ensue from international treaties pertaining to the Council of Europe;
- monitor European Union aid and cooperation programmes;
- cooperate and exchange experiences with bodies in the European Integration processes.

The Committee has a key role in the legislative process. The approximation of national legislation with Community law has to be regarded in the light of intensive legislative activity in Parliament with a large number of legislative Bills still in the pipeline. Given the Parliament's workload, there is often little time for substantial debate on the Bills and the purpose of harmonization of a Bill can be used as a reason to follow the expedited procedure pursuant to Article 159 of the Rules of Procedure in which first and second reading of the Bill are combined at the request of the proposer of the Bill. As another result of the amendments of the Rules of Procedure as mentioned above harmonization Bills are now marked "P.Z.E. br…".

---

[70] *Narodne novine* No. 6/2002, consolidated text.

4.2 Control over decisions taken by ministers in the Council of the European Union

The Croatian Parliament takes a strong stance on parliamentary control over the Government's actions in the framework of the implementation of the SAA and the Interim Agreement. As already explained above, this position is reflected in the Law on the Implementation of the Stabilization and Association Agreement and of the Interim Agreement on trade and trade related matters between the Republic of Croatia and the European Community. It regulates the procedure for determining the positions of the Republic of Croatia to be advocated by its representatives in the Stabilization and Association Council and the Interim Committee during their decision making and the forming of recommendations, as well as during the procedure for the implementation of the decisions and recommendations of the Stabilization and Association Council and the Interim Committee in the Republic of Croatia.

Article 1 of the Law stipulates that the Law in particular regulates the supervision by the Croatian Parliament over the implementation of the SAA, and of the Interim Agreement, as well as the supervision by the Croatian Parliament over the procedure of concluding bilateral conventions on regional cooperation.

As the SAA has a separate title on regional cooperation there is a special provision in the Law addressing this issue. Accordingly, in the course of negotiations aimed at concluding bilateral conventions on regional cooperation, the Government has to submit reports to the Croatian Parliament. Prior to the signing of a bilateral convention on regional cooperation, the Government shall forward its proposal for such conventions to the Croatian Parliament for its conclusions.

The supervisory powers of Parliament under the Law can be exercised both *ex ante* and *ex post*.

According to Article 4 of the Law, the Government is obliged to forward to the Parliament every proposal for a decision and proposals for a position to be advocated by its representatives in the Stabilization and Association Council (or the Interim Committee) prior to their adopting. The Law does not define the legal effects of the Parliament's opinion on the Government's proposal. Thus it is not clear whether a negative position of the Parliament would bind the Government or whether it would be merely advisory.

Ex post supervision is regulated by a procedure according to which the decisions of the Stabilization and Association Council and the Interim Committee that contain substantive amendments to the SAA and the Interim Agreement have to be implemented according to the treaty ratification procedure. Decisions by the Stabilization and Association Council and the Interim Committee that require that new laws are passed or that existing ones are amended have to be implemented according to the ordinary legislative procedure. This also applies to decisions of the Stabilization and Association Committee in such where the Stabilization and Association Council has delegated to it some of its powers.

The possible unconstitutionality of the described procedure of implementation of the SAA/Interim Agreement was already discussed above.

Whether constitutionally valid or not, it is, however, possible to conclude from the system which was put in place under the Law on Implementation of the SAA that there is sufficient political will to grant Parliament considerable powers in EU affairs. If the solutions adopted by the Law are translated into the situation of membership of Croatia in the EU, this would mean that the Croatian Parliament will have at least advisory influence over the Government's position in the Council. However, whether this is a good solution or a poor one has not actually been discussed in political or expert circles. On the other hand, the issue of a proper parliamentary role in EU affair is of huge importance for democracy in the country, but also for Croatia's efficient membership of the EU. Thus, as has already been remarked, a public debate on the role of Parliament and the relationship between Parliament and the Government in EU affairs is urgently needed. This could be made part of the debate on the possible constitutional changes necessitated by membership of the EU.

5. EUROPEAN CONSTITUTION

This chapter deals, in brief, with three issues: whether the EU's Constitutional Treaty[71] will strengthen the Community legal order,[72] whether it may represent an obstacle for Croatia's accession, and whether there are any obstacles in the Croatian Constitution or national legal order to ratification of the European Constitution.

5.1 Constitutional Treaty and strengthening of the Community legal order

As to the first question, the main issue, in our opinion, is that of citizen loyalty. While the level of loyalty varies from one Member State to another, and is ultimately a matter of individual choice, the European Court of Justice has long ago established that individuals form a constituent part of the Community legal order.[73] This position has been implemented in both the political and legal dimension.

---

[71] *OJ* 2004 C 310.

[72] For backgrounds and legal analyses on both general and specific aspects of the Constitutional Treaty, see D. Curtin, A.E. Kellermann and S. Blockmans, eds., *The EU Constitution: The Best Way Forward?* (The Hague, T.M.C. Asser Press 2005).

[73] Case 26/62, *Van Gend en Loos* [1963] *ECR* 1.

As far as the political dimension is concerned, the introduction of direct universal suffrage for the European Parliament and the gradual development of its powers have created a basis to attract the political loyalty of citizens, their involvement in European political parties and their participation in European policy making. The emergence and development of European citizenship has also contributed to this goal. These and other similar developments have been recognized by independent actors, such as the European Court of Human Rights that defined the European Parliament as the legislature of individual Member States.[74]

Another generator of European loyalty is the European Court of Justice which, by the development of the doctrines of supremacy and direct effect of Community law, created a system of protection of individual rights which competes with national legal protection and arguably creates added value to already existing levels of protection in national legal orders.

With this in mind, the Constitutional Treaty once in force has the potential of consolidating and making more transparent both the political participation and legal protection of individual rights.

Political and normative components of the European legal order have now been laid down in the single constitutional instrument the very name of which creates expectations comparable to those that are required from any national constitution.

However, there are some important caveats that have to be kept in mind where former communist countries are concerned. A first issue concerns the normativity of the EU Constitution. Whereas the constitutional traditions of "old" Member States take normative effects of the Constitution for granted,[75] the perception of the concept of constitution as mainly a political document still persists in post-communist legal culture. This is exemplified by a reluctance of the courts in those states to apply the Constitution directly. A side effect of this view is that even where the European Constitution grants additional individual rights to those existing in national legal orders, there is a little or no awareness at all of those rights in the Member States.

---

[74] See, e.g., Case of *Matthews* v. *The United Kingdom*, Application no. 24833/94, judgment of 18 February 1999, at pt. 54: "The Court thus finds that the European Parliament is sufficiently involved in the specific legislative processes leading to the passage of legislation under Articles 189b and 189c of the EC Treaty, and is sufficiently involved in the general democratic supervision of the activities of the European Community, to constitute part of the "legislature" of Gibraltar for the purposes of Article 3 of Protocol No. 1."

[75] The very name of the German Constitution, *Grundgesetz*, implies its normative dimension. It is a fundamental law, a law of fundamental character.

5.2 Impact of the EU Constitution on accession

Croatia became a candidate country on 18 June 2004, after a more-than-a-decade long "expression of interest." A public expectation of membership of the EU was one of the driving forces that contributed to the independence movement which considered socialist Yugoslavia and its totalitarian rule an obstacle to accession. Ultimately, independence was achieved under the terms of the Yugoslav Constitution that granted constituent republics a right to secede.[76] Since then, the secession clause has come to be understood as one of the central guarantees of national sovereignty, enshrined in at least two constitutional provisions: one defining national sovereignty as inalienable, indivisible and intransferable,[77] and the other providing for a right to withdraw from international structures, such as the European Union.[78]

While the right to withdraw from the European Union is not explicit under the present Treaty framework, Article I-59 introduces the possibility of withdrawal from the Union, subject to the national constitutional requirements of a withdrawing state. While the practical importance of this provision remains to be seen, its psychological impact will most probably facilitate the national political securing of Croatia's membership of the EU.

On the other hand, the word "Constitution" in Croatia still bears centralist connotations and may create political misunderstanding concerning the nature of the union Croatia is about to enter into.

On the positive side, however, it can be said that as certain fundamental concepts of the Community legal order, such as the supremacy and direct effect of Community law, will become constitutionalized,[79] the Croatian courts as well as other institutional actors will find it easier to accept and apply them. Express reference to the constitutional text will also make the application of rights based in European law more transparent.

5.3 Constitutional obstacles to ratification

Possible conflicts of the Croatian legal order with the legal order of the EU have been discussed above. However, it is not likely that the Croatian Constitution will pose any additional obstacles to ratification. It is likely that Croatia will accede to

---

76 This right was also confirmed by the Badinter Arbitration Committee, see *The Opinions of the Badinter Arbitration Committee: A Second Breath for the Self-Determination of Peoples*, available at: <http://www.ejil.org/journal/Vol3/No1/art13.html>.

77 Constitution (Croatia), Art. 2(1).

78 Constitution (Croatia), Art. 2(5).

79 See, e.g., the supremacy clause in Art. I-5a of the Draft Constitutional Treaty, Provisional consolidated version of the draft Treaty establishing a Constitution for Europe, Brussels, 25 June 2004, CIG 86/04.

the EU under the terms of the Constitutional Treaty, i.e., following its entry into force, and the adjustment of its constitutional and legal framework should be directed at that target. Constitutional requirements for accession will remain the same, and the most problematic constitutional provision that will possibly have to be amended remains the one requiring the absolute majority of the entire electorate in a referendum as a requirement for accession.

ROMANIA

Victor Duculescu* and Ruxandra Adam**

Accession to the European Union (EU) is one of the main objectives of Romanian foreign policy. All Romanian political groups endorsed this goal through the Snagov Statement in 1995. As was pointed out in the Programme of Governance for 2005-2008: "for 15 years, accession to the EU has represented the main political objective of all governing parties… With the closing of the accession negotiations, Romania will enter a new phase in which the process of European integration should, on the one hand, consolidate the institutions and the legislative work (through the transposition of the Community *acquis*) and, on the other hand, allow the Romanian society to safeguard its national identity and cultural heritage".[1]

Over the years, Romania's aspirations of becoming a member of the EU have been marked by a wealth of political actions and economic reforms, undertaken to ensure compliance with the EU's requirements. This process entailed complex, laborious legislative work, with a large number of legal experts being involved.[2] One of the essential accession prerequisites was the compliance of the Romanian constitutional system with the principles and legal order of the EU. To this end, various debates have been organized and studies have been written, and consultations on the potential constitutional amendments have been held with international organizations, such as the Venice Commission on Law and Democracy, and distinguished experts from the main democratic countries. In addition, political movements and academic institutions have conducted an extensive information campaign in order to find the best solutions for amending the Constitution. Valuable insights into the constitutional reform have also been obtained by the participation of the Romanian specialists in the MATRA project

* Professor Victor Duculescu, Ph.D., Member of the Association of European Recognised Experts (AEXEA).

** Ruxandra Adam, LL.M., Legal adviser, Ministry of European Integration, Romania.

[1] The Romanian Official Journal, No. 1265, Part I, Laws, Decrees, Decisions and other Bills, 29 December 2004 (translated by the authors).

[2] The authors of relevant academic studies and specialized papers include Ion Filipescu, Tudor Popescu, Corneliu Bârsan, Renate Weber, Adrian Năstase, Andrei Popescu, Antonie Iorgovan, Adrian Severin, Constanţa Călinoiu, Victor Duculescu, Simina Tănăsescu, Cristian Ionescu and Genoveva Vrabie.

lead by the prestigious Asser Institute in the Netherlands, which offered an opportunity to analyse the needs of the Romanian constitutional reform in a comparative context, and thereby learn from the experiences in different European countries. Undoubtedly, the case of Romania has certain special dimensions, not only from a strictly constitutional point of view, but also in terms of the complex challenges posed by the process of democratization. In the past, Romania had one of the most centralized economies in the former socialist block. Despite the difficulties encountered in restoring the national economy after 1990, several positive economic developments have taken place. Alongside economic growth – which reached 5.9 per cent in the first semester of 2005 – important measures have been adopted to accelerate the process of privatization and strengthen the rule of law. These elements are vital for Romania's accession process and for its future EU membership.

1. THE CONSTITUTIONAL REFORM IN ROMANIA

The Romanian Constitution, adopted in 1991, at the time was a progressive document in comparison to the totalitarian constitutions that had been in place since 1948. It established a democratic legal framework, protecting human rights and civil and political freedoms. However, despite being drafted with due consideration to the experiences in the main democratic countries (especially in France), it only reflected the situation at the time of its adoption and did not anticipate the future developments in a rapidly evolving European Union.

In 2003, a constitutional reform took place, which represented a major step towards adapting the domestic constitutional system and establishing an adequate constitutional framework and the legal basis for Romania's Euro-Atlantic integration. Constitutional provisions were harmonized with important EU requirements and with the principles of the *acquis communautaire*. The main amendments included provisions regarding the supremacy of EU law, the applicability of the EC treaties and of other EU legal instruments in the domestic legal order, the right of the Romanian citizens to vote in the elections of the European Parliament and to be elected to it, and the removal of certain restrictions on ownership rights. In addition, the newly amended Romanian Constitution explicitly came to state the principle of the separation and balance of powers within the state. It also introduced new rights, such as the right to culture and the right to a safe environment, and clarified certain rights that were already enshrined. Equal opportunities for men and women as regards access to public posts were also guaranteed. In addition, property is now guaranteed and protected irrespective of ownership, while nationalization and any other measures of forced transfer of assets to public property, based on political, social, ethnic or religious grounds, are forbidden. New rights have been conferred to young persons and national minorities, including the right of the Romanian citizens belonging to national minorities to use their mother tongue before the Romanian courts.

The constitutional reform in Romania has been accompanied by much complex harmonizing legislative activity with a view to bringing national legislation in line with the Community *acquis*. Following the constitutional reform, 198 laws were adopted in 2003, with a further 602 adopted in 2004 and 225 in the first half of 2005.[3] Meanwhile, the number of Government Emergency Ordinances (GEO) decreased significantly, in line with the 2003 constitutional amendment that allowed the adoption of GEOs only in exceptional situations. Among the legal measures and programmes having a direct impact on the accession criteria, it is important to mention the Legislative Programme for European Integration, the Strategy for the Acceleration of the Reform of the Public Administration, the laws on the judiciary, the Statute of Magistrates and the Supreme Council of Magistrates, the new Criminal Code, the strengthening of the National Anti-corruption Prosecution Office and the adoption of legal measures in the fight against corruption.

Romania's accession to the EU required the compatibility of the Romanian Constitution with manifold aspects of the EC Treaties and the elimination of discrepancies and strengthening of the content of some of the most important civil rights and freedoms in the light of the Charter of the Fundamental Rights of the EU proclaimed at the Nice Summit. Altogether some 79 amendments were introduced in 2003, all of which, according to a relevant study, either directly or indirectly addressed issues that concerned Romania's accession to the EU.[4] As far as compliance with the *acquis communautaire* is concerned, the main results of the constitutional reform were the following:

1. *As a principle, the constitutional reform created an adequate constitutional framework and the legal basis for Romania's accession to the EU and NATO.* The main provisions in this respect addressed the application of the EC Treaty and of other EU legal instruments, the right of the Romanian citizens to vote in the elections of the European Parliament, and to be elected to it, and the new rights relating to private property.
2. *The Constitution secured a number of basic principles*, such as checks and balances, political pluralism, free initiative, the unity of the state and civil solidarity.

---

3 Information updated as of July 2005.

4 Andrei Popescu, 'The Constitutional Amendment: an Essential Step towards Romania's Accession to the EU', speech delivered at the Scientific Session of the Hyperion University, Bucharest, November 2003 (in Romanian).

3. *The constitutional reform also introduced some important novelties*, either through the introduction of new rights, such as access to culture and the right to a healthy, well-preserved and balanced environment, or through the consolidation of rights already enshrined. As mentioned above, equal opportunities where granted to men and women as regards appointment to public posts, and private property is now granted and protected, regardless of ownership. Nationalization or any other measures of forced transfer of assets to public property based on political, social, ethnic or religious grounds are forbidden. The state grants social assistance to children and young people from disadvantaged families and to those who have been placed in orphanages. The reform has also created the prerequisites for the future elimination of compulsory conscription and its replacement with other forms of civil service.
4. *The guarantee of civil freedoms has been strengthened.* The new constitutional provisions provide the right of parties to an impartial and equitable trial within a reasonable period of time. Only a judge can order preventive detention during a criminal trial, for a maximum term of 30 days. This detention period may be extended by a maximum of 30 days each time, and it may not exceed 180 days altogether. Some amendments concern the institution of the Ombudsman: its mandate has been extended from 4 to 5 years, and s/he will have the right to directly address the Constitutional Court on the unconstitutionality of laws.
5. *Consolidation of the rule of law.* The constitutional reform anticipates the transformation of the Supreme Court of Justice into the High Court of Appeal and Justice, according to the tradition of the Romanian judicial system. The state has been made responsible for judicial errors while individual judges have been made responsible for bad faith or grave negligence. The powers and status of the Supreme Council of Magistrates have also been increased. This institution ensures the independence of justice and is comprised of magistrates and representatives of the civil society. Criminal investigations by the Judiciary Police have been brought within the scope of authority of the offices of the Public Prosecution which are attached to the courts of law. Romanian citizens belonging to national minorities have been granted the right to express themselves in their mother tongue during trials. This right can be exercised in such a way as not to hinder the proper administration of justice and not to involve additional expenses for any interested parties.
6. *A better division of the legislative powers of the two chambers of Parliament has been accomplished*, with the aim of accelerating the legislative process and eliminating the procedures of mediation and divergence. The number of citizens required for the exercise of the right to legislative initiative has been brought down from 250,000 to 100,000. Parliamentary immunity has been limited to the voting process and the political opinions expressed during the

mandate. The age threshold for senatorial elections has been reduced to 33 years. Most importantly, the possibility for the Executive to adopt Emergency Ordinances has been restricted to exceptional situations, the regulation of which cannot be postponed. Emergency status always has to be justified.

7. *The mandate of the President of Romania* has been extended to 5 years, and he is granted the right to refer to the Constitutional Court any legal conflicts of a constitutional nature between public authorities.
8. *The powers of the Constitutional Court* have been extended, with this institution being defined as "the guarantor of the supremacy of the Constitution". Its new powers include the resolution of legal conflicts of a constitutional nature between public authorities, upon request by the President of Romania, or one of the presidents of the two Chambers, or at least 50 deputies or 25 senators. The Constitutional Court also has the competence to examine the constitutionality of treaties and other international agreements, upon request by one of the presidents of the two Chambers or at least 50 deputies or 25 senators. Former provisions that allowed Parliament to annul, by a majority of two thirds of the votes cast, rulings of the Constitutional Court on the unconstitutionality of certain acts, have been eliminated. The full supremacy and binding nature of rulings of the Constitutional Court has thus been guaranteed.

The above examination of the Romanian constitutional reform allows us to conclude that the amendments are a remarkable event for Romania, with a strong emphasis on the country's will to accede to the EU, alongside other countries with which Romania traditionally has friendly and economic relations.[5]

However, the constitutional reform has not entirely resolved the issues related to Romania's accession to the EU. In some cases, the new constitutional provisions require, in the short term, the adoption of subsequent organic laws, such as the provisions regarding the elimination of conscription and its replacement by alternative civil service. The pertinent act has not yet been adopted. The lack of consensus between the main political forces has left unresolved the delicate problem of reforming the electoral system and the partial shift to the uninominal voting system. In addition, some specialists have criticized the new legislative procedure, which aims to accelerate the speed with which laws are adopted by dividing the powers of the Chambers on a 'debate and decision' basis.[6] A re-examination of certain problems will be necessary in a second phase of the

[5] See in more detail Victor Duculescu, 'La réforme constitutionnelle en Roumanie et les exigences de l'intégration européenne', *Revue Internationale de Droit Comparé*, 1/2004, p. 193.

[6] Tudor Drăganu, 'Some Critical Considerations on the Bicameral System Instituted by the Revision Law adopted by the Chamber of Deputies and the Senate', *Public Law Review* 4/2003, p. 63 (in Romanian); Ion Deleanu, 'The Main Themes of the Constitutional Revision', *Public Law Review* 2/2003, pp. 45-46 (in Romanian).

amendment process, which is expected to take place in 2007, in the light of the experiences and practices of other European states.

2. SOVEREIGNTY AND EUROPEAN INTEGRATION

2.1 The position of the Constitutional Court of Romania

The principle of sovereignty, as it was linked to the creation of European nations and nation states in Europe, is part of a long-standing tradition in Romania. Over the years, the principle of sovereignty has been enshrined in many bilateral and multilateral treaties, as a reconfirmation of its legal meaning, besides its moral and political connotations. There have been situations where this principle was invoked with the purpose of contesting foreign interventions that ultimately aimed to defeat the state organization and the Romanian people.

In the aftermath of the Revolution of December 1989, the doctrine of sovereignty has been considerably revised. The old approach, which considered sovereignty as a "shield" against foreign interventions, has been replaced by a modern, much more subtle vision, in accordance with modern international debate and the latest evolutions of the concept. In fact, two Romanian authors, Cristina Iliescu and Ruxandra Ionescu, have called for the abolition of the classical concept of sovereignty, and for its redefinition, in their study entitled "*Adapting the concept of sovereignty in the light of European integration*". They argue that "national sovereignty will only disappear once the nation does" and that "the European Union does not have and will never have its own sovereignty; it does not possess the 'competence of the competences' which is the essence of sovereignty". The authors maintain, however, that accession to the EU necessarily implies the adoption of constitutional provisions allowing the voluntary "renunciation by the States of the exclusive exercise of certain competences". They are of the view that "in respect to the exercise of sovereignty through representation … the powers of the national Parliament will decline … since the EU institutions will adopt a large number of legal acts directly applicable in the Member States".[7]

We should also mention a different point of view, which has been expressed by two other Romanian authors, Dorina Năstase and Mihai Mătieş. According to them, "[n]either European integration, nor the institutionalization of regionalism will be able to limit Romania's sovereignty. Both processes imply a certain transfer of powers from the state, but the purpose of the transfer lies with the accomplishment of public tasks, which, in the context of globalization, can no

---

[7] Cristina Iliescu and Ruxandra Ionescu, 'Adapting the concept of sovereignty in the light of European integration', available at: <http://www.colegejuridique.ro/files/c/2/ref> (in Romanian).

longer be fulfilled by the state alone. The general role of the state thus has to be reconsidered. Regionalization and European integration are the result of this reconsideration. We believe that Romania will not form an exception".[8]

On 16 April 2003, the Constitutional Court pronounced in its Decision No. 148 on the constitutionality of the legislative proposal for the amendment of the Romanian Constitution (the proposal was adopted on the basis of a national referendum, following extended parliamentary debate, with the involvement of the civil society).[9] This decision may provide a realistic appraisal of the new dimensions acquired by the principle of sovereignty in the context of the process of deeper integration. It comprises interesting elements of theoretical analysis concerning Romania's sovereignty and the country's accession to the European Union.[10]

This Decision, which essentially supports the proposed amendment of the Constitution and deems it compatible with the general principles and provisions of the 1991 Constitution, contains a series of observations, which have proved useful in the subsequent adoption of the constitutional acts. Romania has maintained and will maintain its status as an independent state subject of public

[8] Dorina Năstase and Mihai Mătieş, The future of Romania's national sovereignty in the light of European integration in 'Romania's Sovereignty in view of EU Accession', "Romania in the world", *Buletin informativ*, available at: <http://www.romaniainlume.ro/buletininformativ/html> (in Romanian).

[9] Decision No. 148 of 16 April 2003 of the Constitutional Court of Romania, the Official Journal of Romania 171 Part I, No. 317, 12 May 2003.

[10] The decision reads as follows: "As regards the transfer of certain competences of Romania to the Community institutions, the Constitutional Court takes note of the fact that the text of Article 145(1) (now Article 148) refers to the exercise of Romania's sovereign will to ratify the Founding Treaties of the European Union, by a law the adoption of which requires a qualified two-thirds majority. The Treaty of Accession has a double consequence, namely the transfer of powers to the Community institutions, on the one hand, and the common exercise, together with the other Member States, of the competences provided for in the treaties, on the other hand. As far as the first consequence is concerned, the Court holds that the mere participation of a state in an international treaty leads to this state's competences being limited, to the extent provided for in the international agreement. From this point of view, Romania's participation in the United Nations, the Council of Europe, the Central European Free Trade Agreement, and so forth, and the fact that it is a party to the Convention for the Protection of Human Rights and Fundamental Freedoms and to other international treaties implies a restraint of competences of the state authorities, acting as a 'relativization' of the national sovereignty. However, this consequence has to be understood in connection with the second one, which is brought about by Romania's integration in the European Union. In this regard, the Constitutional Court holds that the act of integration signifies, among other things, the sharing of the exercise of these sovereign attributes with the other states, which are members of the international organization. Therefore, the Constitutional Court finds that the transfer of certain competences to the structures of the EU does not confer on the latter a 'competence over competence', i.e., its own sovereignty. The Member States of the European Union have in fact decided to jointly exercise some attributes traditionally attached to national sovereignty. We have to bear in mind that world issues are nowadays treated in a global way, while inter-state developments and inter-individual communication occur at a worldwide scale. In this global context, the concept of national sovereignty can no longer be conceived as absolute and indivisible, without taking the risk of acknowledging an unacceptably isolated position".

international law (see, in this respect, the provisions of Article 1(1) of the Constitution). The accession negotiations were carried out between the European Union and Romania as a sovereign state which in 1993 concluded the Association Agreement. Upon becoming an EU member, Romania will have representatives on the Council and enjoy the membership rights granted by the Treaty establishing a Constitution for Europe (hereinafter, Constitutional Treaty) (provided that it will be ratified by the Member States) and the Accession Treaty. The following remarks should also be made with regard to retaining sovereignty.

Firstly, the Constitutional Treaty itself contains, in the general part, provisions on respect for the political and constitutional structures of the Member States (Art. I-5/1). The challenge for the future will not be that of "reforming" the constitutional structures embodying the national identity and the democratic options for the people, but that of synchronizing the prerogatives of various national institutions with the structures and mechanisms provided for in the Constitutional Treaty. Secondly, we believe that the drafting and adoption of laws by the Parliament, in its role as a "sovereign representative of the nation", will be affected only in part.

Secondly, the Constitutional Treaty enshrines several categories of competences: the exclusive competences of the Union, the shared competences and the competences of the Member States (Title V of Part 1). It is clear that as far as the last two categories are concerned, Parliament will only carry out its legislative activity in accordance with the provisions of the Constitutional Treaty. For the exclusive competences, however, Parliament's role will be a different one – that of supervising the way in which the Government enforces Community regulations. While it is true, on the one hand, that the classical prerogatives of the national parliament might be weakened, we witness, on the other hand, a redefinition of its role, which, from now on, has to take into account relations with the EU bodies. The functions of the national parliament would not become obsolete, but a review of Parliament's role appears nonetheless logical, given that various areas of state competence will be transferred to the EU by an act of will of the sovereign nation state. Parliament expresses its consent to the transfer of such competences by ratifying the Accession Treaty.

Thirdly, the sovereign state preserves the right to conclude international treaties (*jus tractatum*). Clearly, this right will be exercised with due regard to Article 307 of the EC Treaty (if the Constitutional Treaty enters into force, Art. III-341). The rights and obligations arising from the treaties that have been previously concluded with third countries shall not be affected in principle, but whenever inconsistencies with the Treaty appear, they shall be removed. On the other hand, the EU Member States cannot conclude future agreements that contravene the provisions of the Treaty. The sovereign competences of the Member States over *"jus tractatum"* are retained within these limits.

Fourthly, the state also to a large extent retains its economic sovereignty. During the accession negotiations, Romania requested several transitional periods or supplementary measures in certain negotiation chapters. This was done (for example in the area of agriculture) with the purpose of avoiding inconsistencies between Romanian and EC law.

Last but not least, special reference must be made to the chapter on human rights. This is a field where the constitutional reform brought novelties and clarifications. It enhanced the guarantees for citizens belonging to national minorities to use their mother tongue before courts and bodies of public administration. In the same vein, the role of the Supreme Council of Magistrates was strengthened, with a view to guaranteeing the independence of the judiciary, and measures were taken to increase the efficiency of the National Anti-corruption Prosecution Office. Whilst the precedence of international regulations in the field of human rights has been explicitly recognized since 1991, this area continues to develop. The acceptance of the case law of the European Court of Human Rights in Strasbourg is undisputable evidence that Romania has entirely abandoned the old view whereby human rights issues were perceived as an "exclusively internal problem".

It has been shown that the constitutional changes in Romania reflect the modern dimension of sovereignty. The concept of sovereignty is no longer understood in a classically rigid way, but involves new and more flexible dimensions. Like a new "Proteus", sovereignty has a modern image, which is fundamentally distinct from the one presented by Grotius and Vattel.

3. THE INCORPORATION OF THE *ACQUIS COMMUNAUTAIRE*

In the process of bringing the Romanian legal system into conformity with the EU legal order, the incorporation of the *acquis communautaire* has played a key part. Romania's accession to the EU involves more than providing constitutional principles regarding the applicability of the EU legal order; it involves extensive legislative work, the adoption of specific laws and the removal of all national norms conflicting with European ones. The obligation of harmonization dates back to 1993, when the Agreement establishing an association between the European Communities and their Member States, on the one part, and Romania, on the other part (commonly known as the "Europe Agreement") was signed. Article 69 of the Agreement expressly referred to the approximation of domestic legislation with Community regulations: "The Parties recognize that an important condition for Romania's economic integration into the Community is the approximation of Romania's existing and future legislation to that of the Community. Romania shall endeavour to ensure that its legislation will be gradually made compatible with that of the Community". Article 70 states that "[t]he approximation of laws shall extend to the following areas in particular: customs law, company law, banking law, company accounts and taxes, intellectual property, protection of workers at the workplace, social security, financial services, rules on competition, protection of health and life of humans, animals and plants, consumer protection, indirect taxation, technical rules and standards, nuclear law and regulation, transport and the environment". Until the accession, the Europe Agreement forms, together with the subsequent agreements and protocols deriving from it, the main legal basis for relations between Romania and the European Community. The Agreement was signed in Brussels on 1 February 1993; it has been ratified by the Romanian Parliament by Law No. 20/1993, and it entered into force two years later, on 1 February 1995. From this moment, Romania's accession to the European Community became a structured process. The Agreement set up the methods and the institutional framework for a permanent political dialogue, as well as the general principles, the objectives and the conditions for the free movement of goods, services, capital and persons, together with the gradual harmonization of the national legislation. The Europe Agreement became the basic instrument in preparing Romania's economy for accession, allowing the economic sectors to become acquainted with the rules on the functioning of the Single Market. In the preamble, the Agreement states that the final objective of this association is that Romania would become a Member of the European Union.

As regards the political dialogue, an institutional mechanism of bilateral dialogue was created, following the entry into force of the Agreement, both at the parliamentary level (through the setting up of the Romania-EU Parliamentary Association Committee) and at the executive level (through the establishment of structures ensuring the continuity and the coherence of relations between Romania and the EU). The main body is the Association Council, which comprises members appointed by the Romanian Government, on the one hand, and members of the Council of Ministers of the European Union and the European Commission, on the other hand. The Association Council monitors the implementation of the Association Agreement and has the competence to resolve any disputes between the parties, as regards the implementation or the interpretation of the Europe Agreement.

The Association Council is assisted by the Association Committee in fulfilling its responsibilities, with the Association Subcommittees selectively analyzing the areas provided for in the Association Agreement. The Association Committee deals with the issues related to the transposition of the *acquis communautaire* into national legislation, institutional development and relations between Romania and the EU deriving from the implementation of the Europe Agreement. Several annual meetings of the Romania-EU Association Council have taken place, alongside various meetings of the Association Committee and Association Subcommittees, which have analyzed the implementation of the Agreement and the progress recorded during the preparations for accession. The implementation of the Europe Agreement included, according to Article 7, a transition period of 10 years, divided into two five-year stages, with the first stage ending on 1 February 2000.

In terms of the progress of the legal approximation process, a study has shown the following:

> Starting with 2001 – and parallel to the speeding up of the negotiation process – the process of legislative approximation has been substantially accelerated. For instance, during 2003, a total of 780 laws relevant to the EU were adopted, 390 of which directly transpose the provisions of European legal texts. The Legislative Approximation Programme for 2002-2005 (which is part of the National EU Accession Programme) has been complemented with other working instruments to increase the efficiency of this process: the Legislative Accession Sustaining Programme and the Priority Legislative Programme (Acts of Parliament only) for Romania's Accession to the EU. The objectives for the first semester of 2004 are ambitious, as the Priority Legislative Programme comprises 82 legislative proposals reported as essential for the completion of the negotiation process.[11]

The absorption of the *acquis communautaire* includes much more than the mere adoption of legal provisions. It is an elaborate process, aiming at a fair implementation of EU law. This process takes place at the level of the state institutions enforcing EU regulations, transposed EU Directives and other European acts, but also at the level of the judiciary, which enforces European law in the light of the rich case law of the European Court of Justice and the experiences of other Member States.

The implementation of European law entails a solid system guaranteeing civil freedoms. In particular, a more efficient administration of justice is needed, in a way which constantly upholds its independence in relation to the other authorities, accompanied by the fight against negative phenomena within Romanian society, such as corruption or the outbreak of new forms of violence.

A special role is played in this context by the legal experts controlling the legality of the use of the EU pre-accession funds. As is well-known, there are three financial pre-accession instruments to assist the candidate countries: the PHARE, ISPA and SAPARD Programmes. They concentrate on the financial help corresponding to the priorities established in the Accession Partnership, with

---

[11] Adrian Năstase, 'Some Considerations on Romania's Accession to the EU Process', *Romanian Review of Community Law* 1/2004, p. 16 (in Romanian).

a view to helping the candidate countries to meet the EU membership criteria.[12] The PHARE Programme supports Romania by offering consolidated financial assistance for institutional development and the enhancement of structures ensuring consistency with the *acquis* and by contributing to the investments directed at improving social and economic cohesion. The ISPA Programme provides important financial aid targeting the rehabilitation and modernization of the environmental and transport infrastructures, as well as the development of a convergence between Romanian policies and those of the EU. The SAPARD Programme is a pre-accession financial instrument for agriculture and rural development. Its main objective is to speed up the implementation of the *acquis* and to consolidate the sustainable development of the agricultural sector and the rural areas, in order to gradually adjust the intervention mechanisms to the principles of the Community Agricultural Policy. All these Programmes are run by means of the establishment of concrete projects. Their aim is to ensure better distribution of the funds, and to address real development needs, using strict control mechanisms which involve legal and economic experts.

4. REFORMS CONCERNING ROMANIA'S JUDICIARY

Following the constitutional amendments, which included significant changes regarding the functioning of the judiciary, especially in terms of strengthening its role and increasing its independence from the other state powers, a legislative package on the reform of the judiciary was adopted. It consists of three laws: the Law on the Supreme Council of Magistrates, the Law on the Statute of Magistrates and the Law on the Judiciary. Significant changes have also been brought about by the following changes: the creation of specialized courts (juvenile, family, administrative-fiscal, labour and commercial courts, etc.) and of the leading Colleges of the Courts and Prosecutor's Offices; the random distribution of the files through the IT system; the reintroduction of the collegiality principle for the courts of first instance; the setting up of the information and public relations offices in the courts; the elimination of those prerogatives of the Minister of Justice that are related to the career of magistrates; the increasing role of the Supreme Council of Magistrates in respect of the selection, the promotion or sanctioning of the magistrates and the functioning of the courts.

This legislative package received a positive assessment from the Council of Europe. The former Minister of Justice emphasized that by adopting it, "the principles of the separation of state powers and the independence of justice are established by law and not by statements... [D]rawing on these new laws, several

12 Government of Romania, Ministry of the European Integration, Info 2001, p. 30.

strategies of implementation have been devised, comprising the measures to be enforced in the next period, the timetables and the financial allocations”.[13]

In June 2004, Mr Günter Verheugen, the European Commissioner for Enlargement at the time, paid tribute to the substantial progress Romania has made in the reform of the justice system. He underlined that the reform of the judicial system is influencing not only the evolution of the judiciary itself, but also has a positive effect on the harmonious development of the social, economic and political environment in Romania. Mr Verheugen also welcomed the visible efforts that have been made in adopting measures in the fight against corruption. However, he pointed out that it is not sufficient to punish individual acts of corruption – a deeper analysis of the phenomenon is necessary in order to identify the roots of corruption and establish measures to prevent it. The Anti-corruption Strategy elaborated by the Executive has been considered a first efficient tool in this respect, but it needs to be accompanied by in-depth research into the problem. The phenomenon of corruption is common to all European states in transition, including the ones that recently joined the EU. However, failing to find a timely resolution to the problems generated by corruption could result in major political costs.

The Programme of Governance for 2005-2008, which was approved by the Romanian Parliament on 28 December 2004, focuses on the problems connected with the reform of the justice system. The main objectives laid down in this Programme include the following: to guarantee the true independence of the judiciary, to ensure the effective access of citizens to the courts by improving the functioning of the judicial system as a public service, and to develop the institutional framework. A constitutional amendment was suggested to the effect of transforming the judicial authority into a “judicial power”, in accordance with the Romanian historical traditions and experiences of other democratic states.

Based on the guidelines established by the abovementioned paper, the Government drafted a Law concerning reform in the fields of property and justice. Taking into consideration the importance of such bills, the Government decided to take full responsibility for this legislative package before Parliament. The package of laws on the reform of justice, the area of property and related measures contained 17 legal acts, altogether containing over a 1000 articles. According to the Romanian legal system, the Government can take full responsibility before Parliament by means of a simplified parliamentary procedure, which allows the laws in question to be adopted immediately without debating specific articles. However, if at least a quarter of the Members of Parliament disagrees with either the Government taking full responsibility or with the content of the laws in

---

13 The ‘*Adevărul*’ Newspaper No. 4352, 30 June 2004 (translated by the authors).

question, Parliament is able to table a motion of censure, which, if passed (by the majority of deputies and senators) dissolves the Government.

The package of laws submitted to Parliament in June 2005 was of utmost importance. The reform in the field of property was aimed at guaranteeing private property as a fundamental institution in the market economy, while the reform in the area of justice envisaged the creation of an independent, reliable, impartial and effective judicial system, in accordance with Romania's commitments to the EU.

The first part of the package concerned the reform in the field of property. Its central provisions addressed the restitution of immovable property that had been incorrectly acquired during the Communist regime. The new legal framework states, as a governing principle, that properties which were incorrectly acquired will be returned in kind. This draft law repealed the exemptions to this principle, which concerned buildings that served as headquarters for political parties and embassies and public institutions. It has also provided for the acceleration of the restitution of immovable property belonging to religious denominations and national minorities, and for a simplification of the administrative procedures for granting equivalent compensation where restitution in kind was not available. As far as land is concerned, the intention was to give effect to the principle of *restitutio in integrum*, and to regulate in detail the procedure of retrocession of ownership rights regarding land intended for agricultural and forestry use. Several provisions concerned the legal circulation of land, with a view to simplifying the transfer of property. Finally, contracts for life annuity have been introduced, which means that owners of agricultural lands aged beyond 62 years may cede or lease out their land in exchange for a life annuity.

The provisions related to the reform of justice sought to establish an independent, impartial, reliable and effective judicial system, based on the Strategy for the Reform of the Judiciary 2005-2007 and the accompanying Action Plan. The main aspects dealt with the careers of judges and prosecutors, their appointment and promotion on the basis of professional criteria and reduction of the required length of experience for appointment to top judicial posts. The Law established in a clearer manner the situations leading to the disciplinary liability of judges and prosecutors, including, *inter alia*, non-observance of the provisions on the random distribution of cases. The law provides for the organization of open competitions for appointments to all top posts in the judiciary. The principle of specialization of judges is implemented through the mandatory creation of specialized sections or panels. Budgetary autonomy is also increased. Several important provisions concern the activity of the Supreme Council of Magistrates (SCM). The Law prohibits simultaneous membership in the SCM and holding a leading position at a court or prosecutors' offices, and it specifies the conditions for dissolution of the SCM. The law requires the SCM to reason its decisions, both those adopted in plenary and by the individual sections, and obliges it to submit an annual report of its activities to the united Chambers of Parliament before 15 February of the following year. Judges are appointed by the President of Romania, on the proposal of the SCM. The General Prosecutor and the Chief Prosecutor of the National Anti-corruption Prosecution Office (NAPO) are also appointed by the President, but on the proposal of the Ministry of Justice, with an opinion attached from the SCM.

The Members of Parliament for the Social Democrats tabled a motion of censure against this package of laws, but the motion was rejected 265 votes to 185 and the Bill was consequently considered adopted. Nevertheless, a group of 39 senators and 101 deputies from the Social Democratic Party, together with 25 senators from the Greater Romania Party and the High Court of Appeal and Justice, notified the Constitutional Court, alleging that several provisions of the package were contrary to the Constitution.

In its Decision No. 375 of 6 July 2005,[14] the Constitutional Court ruled that the following provisions were unconstitutional: the provision prohibiting judges and prosecutors elected as SCM members to continue their activity as judges and prosecutors; the provision bringing an end to the current terms of offices of top judges and prosecutors (who had been elected into such posts), so that such leading posts would be filled by an open competition; the provision requiring SCM members to choose within 15 days between the top post and SCM membership; the prohibition to accumulate both an employment pension and income resulting from activity as a judge or a prosecutor; the prohibition of allowing judges and prosecutors who have reached the legal age of retirement under Law 19/2000 on Public Pensions Schemes to retain their appointment.

Following this ruling by the Constitutional Court, the Laws on the reform of justice and property, as well as related measures, could not be promulgated by the President, who referred the Bill back to Parliament, which convened in a common assembly. When a law is found to be unconstitutional before its promulgation, Parliament, under Article 147(2) of the Constitution, must reconsider the relevant provisions so as to bring them into conformity with the Constitutional Court's decision. Following the parliamentary debate, which took account of the initial common Report of 11 July 2005 and the additional Report of 13 July 2005 that had been adopted by the Legal Commissions of the two Chambers, Parliament voted on and finally passed an amended version of the texts which were now in conformity with the Constitution. Thus, on 13 July, the Parliament approved the Report of the two Legal Commissions, by 403 votes to 38 (from the Greater Romania Party) and 1 abstention. Two of the provisions declared unconstitutional were rejected by the Legal Commissions, with the other two having been

---

14 The Official Journal of Romania, No. 591/2005.

amended. Consequently, only the President and Vice-President of the CSM cannot also be judges or prosecutors, and will consequently suspend such activities during their mandate in the CSM. Judges and prosecutors who receive a pension are now allowed in addition to earn income from professional activities; the former prohibition in this respect was abolished. The pension is no longer calculated according to the common provisions of Law 19/2000, but is based on the special provisions relating to magistrates. We have to mention, however, that the views of the political parties represented in Parliament differed with regard to the final versions of the provisions in question. Whilst representatives of the Social Democratic Party, Conservative Party and Democratic Union of Hungarians in Romania all gave their assent, Members of Parliament belonging to the governing alliance of Justice and Truth, although it voted in favour of the law as a whole, nevertheless emphasized that the version as it was finally adopted no longer corresponded to its initial purpose, and that for this reason they were prepared to block the justice reform. In these circumstances, Prime Minister Călin Popescu Tăriceanu intended to tender his Government's resignation and call early elections by October 2005 in order to ensure stronger support for the necessary reforms. This idea was given up, however, in the face of the immediate priority of the Government to reconstruct the country following the unprecedented floods that affected Romania in July 2005. The Prime Minister took responsibility before Parliament for a political statement related to the country's reconstruction (in the aftermath of the floods) and to the process of European integration and the reform of the judiciary.

The National Anti-corruption Prosecution Office (NAPO)[15] is an important state institution, directly connected to the enforcement of justice. The NAPO presented a Report which was discussed during a meeting organized by the Ministry of Justice. NAPO public servants are mobilized and effectively involved in fulfilling NAPO's duties of preventing crimes of corruption, crimes equivalent to crimes of corruption and crimes in connection withcorruption. The NAPO has investigated several complex cases where the accused used to hold important positions in public institutions or business. During 2003, the prosecutors, officers of the judiciary police and NAPO specialists brought 2229 cases of corruption, of which 951 have been resolved and 563 were dismissed for lack of competence or joined with another case. Some 48 cases have reached the stage of prosecution, and in 24 cases (representing 3 per cent of the overall number) proceedings have since started. On a total of 951 resolved cases, indictments have followed in 146 (15 per cent) while no charges were pressed in the remaining 805 (in 52 cases of

[15] Established by GEO No. 42/2002, approved by Law No. 503/2002 and amended by Law No. 161/2003.

acquittal Article 18(1) of the Criminal Code was applied).[16] Of a total of 548 defendants sued by the NAPO during 2003, 352 persons (approximately five times the number of 2000-2001 and 13 times that of 2002) held a post of leadership or control or another important position.[17]

The NAPO has proposed that GEO No. 43/2002 and the Law on the Judiciary be amended in order to increase the NAPO's autonomy. These proposals regulated the NAPO's financial independence and the appointment of judicial police officers and specialists and the adoption of rules on the organization and functioning of the NAPO both by an order of the NAPO General Prosecutor. Finally, it has been proposed that the annual report presented by the General Prosecutor of the NAPO should not be submitted to Parliament, but to the SCM instead, in a meeting that could be chaired by the President of Romania.

On 17 March 2005, the Ministry of Justice made public the results of the Freedom House Report on the fight against corruption in Romania. The Report stressed that the NAPO received too little support from the other competent authorities, and exposed that the NAPO itself during the electoral year 2004 had not shown sufficient neutrality towards persons considered "untouchable". The Report recommended the creation of a special department for data collection and joint operations with other bodies involved in the fight against corruption.[18]

As regards judicial rulings, a number of judgments delivered by the Constitutional Court and the ordinary courts are worth mentioning with regard to compliance with the rule of law and the guarantee of civil rights and freedoms, even though the Romanian courts do not yet apply EU law. By way of an example, in its Decision No. 73 of 4 June 1996, the Constitutional Court stated for the first time that the principle of separation of state powers, although not expressly laid down in the 1991 Romanian Constitution because it was considered superfluous or at least implicitly provided for in other parts of the Constitution, "can be derived from the entirety of the constitutional provisions and in particular from the ones concerning the functioning of public authorities and their relationships".[19] The Constitutional Court by expressing this important view secured the

---

16 Article 18(1) states that an act provided for in the Criminal Code shall not be considered to represent a crime, if, considering its minor violation of the social value protected by the law, and its concrete content, being obviously unimportant, it does not have the degree of social danger of a crime.

17 Including 1 former minister, 2 counsellors at the Government's General Secretary, 1 director of the SAPARD Agency, 1 prosecutor, 1 judge (president of the Court), 1 city mayor, 42 directors and inspectors, 26 chiefs of the credit departments and other banking servants, 6 civil servants within the general directorates of public finances, 136 police employees and gendarmes, 10 customs officers, 2 accounting experts, 5 legal advisors, 5 financial guard commissioners, 20 officers and non-missioned officers from the Ministry of National Defence, 1 lawyer and 90 businessmen.

18 Alexandru Stancu, 'The Freedom House Report criticizes the National Anticorruption Strategy', *Gardianul*, 18 March 2005, available at: <http://www.gardianul.ro>.

19 Official Journal of Romania, Part I, No. 255, 22 October 1996.

legal approach to the issue of the separation of powers in Romania. The solution adopted by the Constitutional Court is of utmost significance, as it guides the activities of public bodies in a spirit of strict observance of their competences thus ensuring the mutually fully independent functioning of each of the state powers.

In the practice of the Constitutional Court, one issue has attracted particular interest – the opposability and direct effect of the decisions of the Constitutional Court. On certain occasions, the Supreme Court of Justice has taken positions that conflict with those of the Constitutional Court. In its Decisions No. 486/1997 and 186/1999, the Constitutional Court has underlined the importance of complying with the rule of law in such situations. In the first decision,[20] the Constitutional Court established that based on Article 21 of the Constitution, the provisions of Article 278 of the Code of Penal Procedure were unconstitutional as they barred complainants from direct recourse to the courts. Article 278 of the Code of Penal Procedure reads as follows: "The complaint against measures taken or actions carried out by the prosecutor or following his instructions shall be solved by the chief prosecutor of the unit. When measures are taken and actions are carried out by the chief prosecutor or following his instructions, the complaint shall be resolved by the hierarchical superior prosecutor…". The Constitutional Court ruled that these provisions conflicted with Article 21 of the Constitution, which provides that "[e]very person is entitled to bring cases before the courts for the defence of his legitimate rights, liberties and interests", and that "[t]he exercise of this right may not be restricted by any law". Despite the fact that this Decision was published in the Official Journal of Romania, the Supreme Court of Justice refused to accept it (Decision No. 2531 of 17 June 1999). The Supreme Court of Justice stated that decisions of the Constitutional Court, by which the latter establishes the unconstitutionality of a certain law, could not be invoked by individuals other than the litigating parties; such decisions could eventually be binding for the Parliament, but not for the courts.

In the second Decision on the matter (Decision No. 186 of 18 November 1999), the Constitutional Court repeated its earlier findings. The decisions of the Constitutional Court establishing the unconstitutionality of a legal provision (contained in a law or a Government Ordinance) are binding and may be invoked *erga omnes*. The courts are therefore obliged to respect such decisions. According to the Constitutional Court, the binding nature of such decisions for the courts derives from the principle contained in Article 51 of the Romanian Constitution, which provides that "[t]he observance of the Constitution, of its supremacy and of the laws is binding". The arguments of the Supreme Court of Justice according to which judges must simply apply the law, and that justice is done in the name of

---

[20] Decision No. 486/1997 of the Constitutional Court, Official Journal of Romania, Part I, No. 105, 6 March 1998.

law, are indeed correct, but one should not ignore the fact that the observance of the Constitution is a fundamental duty for all judges. As shown in a study by judge Constantin Doldur published in the second issue of the Constitutional Court Bulletin, the Constitutional Court, which has been confronted in concrete cases with the divergent positions of the lower courts as regards the possibility of relying on decisions adopted by the Constitutional Court, established that "… decisions delivered by the Constitutional Court in cases where the defence of unconstitutionality was raised produce not only relative, *inter partes* effects in the particular case, but also absolute, *erga omnes* effects". This point of view was later confirmed by the 2003 constitutional reform, which introduced a new paragraph to Article 147(4), stating that "[t]he decisions of the Constitutional Court … shall be generally binding and effective for the future".

Another decision of major importance was the Constitutional Court's judgment on the Law on the legal status of property (both movable and immovable) that was confiscated by the Romanian state during the previous regime (from 6 March 1945 until 22 December 1989).[21] This Law, which was discussed at length in Parliament, provides that that such property shall be returned upon request, where possible in kind. If restitution in kind is not possible, restitution of an equivalent nature or compensation will be provided. The definition of abusively nationalized property is broad, covering various categories: buildings nationalized under Law No. 119/1948; buildings appropriated under court orders as punishment for political offences; buildings donated to the state under certain special regulations adopted from 6 March 1945 to 22 December 1989; buildings appropriated in compensation for unpaid taxes (through no fault of the owners); buildings appropriated because they were considered abandoned; buildings nationalized under unpublished laws and regulations; buildings nationalized under Law No. 119/1948 on requisitions which were never returned, and similar situations. After the adoption of the Law by the two Chambers of the Parliament, a group of Members of Parliament brought a complaint to the Constitutional Court, claiming that the concept included in the Law of "building that has been abusively nationalized" was much broader than its natural meaning. They criticized the inclusion of donations to the state in this category, as well as the provision requiring the return of equipment and installations together with the building itself. By Decision No. 43 of 7 February 2001,[22] the Constitutional Court of Romania dismissed these claims and found the Law compatible with the constitutional principles.

The Members of Parliament who referred the Law to the Constitutional Court more specifically considered the provisions of Article 2(b) contrary to Articles

---

21 Law No. 10/2001, Official Journal of Romania, Part I, No. 75, 14 February 2001.

22 Ibid.

16(2) and 41(8) of the Constitution. According to Article 2(b), the concept of 'buildings that has been abusively nationalized' also includes the category of buildings appropriated through estate confiscation pursuant to a conviction for political crimes pronounced in a court decision. The Members concerned argued that the Law failed to specify both the offences in question and that such offences should no longer be provided for undercriminal law. These omissions would open up the possibility of annulment of sentences of estate confiscation imposed by courts for offences *currently* provided for in criminal legislation, thus allowing some criminals to be placed above the law.[23]

5. THE ROLE OF THE EXECUTIVE (GOVERNMENT AND PUBLIC ADMINISTRATION)

The Romanian Government is the executive body that ensures, according to Article 102(1) of the Constitution, the implementation of domestic and foreign policy and acts as the general management of the public administration. Consequently, it plays a primary role in the process of EU integration.

In this respect, several important regulations at the Government level may be mentioned: GEO No. 11/2004 on the reorganization of the public central administration, GEO No. 24/2004 on the transparency of the activities of public institutions, and Government Decisions (GD) No. 402 of 23 March 2004 on the organization and functioning of the Ministry of European Integration (MEI). According to the Programme of Governance, the MEI ensures the coherence and coordination of the accession process. It is a special body of the central public administration, set up at the beginning of 2001. It directs the accession negotiations and coordinates the whole process of accession. The MEI has been an active coordinator and integrator of internal measures for the alignment of national law to EU legal norms, and it has ensured dynamic interaction with the Community institutions, in particular with the European Commission.

---

[23] The Court held that: "... It is obvious that the Law is directed against the additional punishment of estate confiscation, which, following the entry into force of the 1991 Constitution, can no longer be imposed. The parties claiming the unconstitutionality of these provisions argue that the Law by failing to specify both the offences to which they refer and that such offences should no longer be provided for under criminal legislation presently in force creates a possibility that some persons who have been convicted for offences under current legislation could be placed 'above the law', which would be contrary to Article 16(2) of the Constitution. However, the Court would observe that, as far as convictions accompanied by the imposition of the additional punishment of estate confiscation are concerned, the Law does determine the acts giving rise to these measures, namely '... offences of a political nature, provided for by the penal law, which have been committed as an act of opposition to the totalitarian communist regime'. Establishing whether a concrete act should be included in the category of offences envisaged by the law, is not a matter of constitutionality, but one that concerns the implementation of the law".

In order to facilitate the harmonization of laws, the Government has appointed within each Ministry a Secretary of State responsible for European integration. These persons are in charge of all relevant issues regarding EU integration which are specific to their institutions and ensure the direct relationship with the MEI. The establishment of the National Delegation facilitated the coordination of the entire process of the negotiations for Romania's accession to the EU. It is an inter-institutional body composed of representatives of all institutions (approximately 50 institutions) involved in the adoption and implementation of the *acquis*. It has played a significant role in preparing for the negotiations and assessing Romania's readiness to open each negotiation chapter. At the same time, it also scrutinizes the fulfilment of Romania's commitments undertaken during the negotiations.

The efforts made during the accession negotiations, the strict fulfilment of the ensuing obligations and the follow-up of the priority measures led to the completion of the negotiations by the end of 2004, creating the prerequisites for Romania's accession to the EU by 2007. During the period 2001-2004, the executive focused on an extensive process of internal cooperation and communication with the parliamentary political parties, the social partners and representatives of employers' associations and civil society and from academic circles. Externally, these efforts were backed by a strategy of cooperation with the EU Member States and the candidate countries. The cooperation with the European institutions has improved over the last period and the technical consultations with the European Commission have always been extremely helpful. The wide range of preparations and actions that are part of this process include numerous bilateral assistance projects, the setting up of joint working groups at sectoral level, weekly reporting on the developments regarding the negotiations, on-site meetings, and cooperation with the academia and various experts from the EU Member States.

The MEI has coordinated the drafting and updating of the programmatic documents pertaining to Romania's accession. The National Programme for the Accession of Romania to the EU (NPAR) was drafted with the contribution of all Ministries and institutions involved in the integration process. After a prior financial assessment, the NPAR presented a four-year strategic programme of necessary measures to fulfil the political and economic criteria, to transpose and implement the *acquis communautaire* and to reform the public administration. It was supplemented by the Action Plan for strengthening the capacity of the public administration and of the judiciary and by the Priority Measures for the preparation for accession. The MEI has continuously monitored and assessed draft proposals for legislation which could potentially run contrary to Romania's commitments under the Europe Agreement and devised solutions to bring domestic legislation in line with the Agreement. The Legal Directorate of the

MEI provides independent legal opinions on all draft legislation relevant to the EU prior to their adoption.

One should also mention GD No. 4 of 8 January 2004 on the distribution within the Ministries of counsellors for integration and the approval of criteria for the increase of their salary. Graduate students from both Romanian and foreign universities who hold degrees in the fields connected to European integration can join the Body of Counsellors for Integration and work in specific Ministries and public institutions. They are not civil servants, but are employed under an individual employment contract. The basic salaries and other salary rights are, according to the law, the same as for the position of diplomatic counsellors. The basic salaries can be increased by up to 50 per cent, taking into consideration professional experience, postgraduate studies, scientific and academic titles and other criteria approved by the GD.

Finally, it is worth mentioning three important instruments related to Government functions, namely GD No. 37/2004 on the setting up, organization and functioning of the Consultative Council for the negotiation of Romania's accession to the EU, GD No. 404/2004 on the organization and functioning of the Government's Cabinet and GD No. 405 on the organization and functioning of the General Secretariat of the Government.

The annex to GD No. 30/2004 approving the Government's National Action Plan for 2004[24] envisages important measures for the reform of the public administration both at central and local level. They concern the strengthening of control within public institutions, the improvement of the awareness and the ability of the judiciary to incorporate and to apply the *acquis*, and enhancement of the administrative capacity of the local public authorities to fulfil their responsibilities in the framework of decentralization. Other measures are aimed at intensifying the fight against corruption, improving human resources policies, monitoring the activities for the training of civil servants, and guaranteeing the transparency of administrative documents and operative communication with citizens. One of the top priorities is the decentralization of public services, especially the transfer of state activities and budgetary resources to the local public authorities, so that they may be used tofinance public services provided in local communities. The intention is to achieve full compliance with the Law on the status of civil servants and to provide a more efficient relationship between central and local administrations. The envisaged measures include the drafting of an Administrative Code, a Guide for the simplification of regulations and the establishment of a special fund for the reform of the public administration.

---

[24] The Official Journal of Romania, Part I, No. 83 bis, 30 January 2004.

6. THE ROLE OF THE NATIONAL PARLIAMENT

The Romanian Parliament has expressed its view of the significance of the accession process on a number of occasions. For instance, in its Declaration on Europe Day,[25] the Romanian Parliament acclaimed the eastward enlargement of the EU as part of a generous and visionary project of European construction, which offers an opportunity to build a Union in diversity and to devise a viable strategy for European peace. Parliament announced its willingness to contribute in its capacity as legislator to the fulfilment of Romania's commitments towards the EU.

In the legislative process, Parliament has granted priority to the deliberations on the Bills transposing EU legislation. The Rules of Procedure of Parliament have been amended to enable the use of the expedited procedure for dealing with Bills that harmonize Romanian legislation with EU requirements, as well as with Government ordinances based on Article 114(4) of the Constitution. Amongst the important laws that have been adopted in the last few years, those dealing with the following issues merit particular mention: acceleration of privatization, protection of classified information, the status of policemen, the organization and functioning of the Romanian police, the promotion of direct investments with a major impact on the economy, the regime governing aliens, equal opportunities and gender equality, electronic commerce, local public finances, and political parties. The most recent Bills which have been adopted since the end of 2004 and during 2005 include the Law on the prevention and combat of terrorism, the Law on administrative disputes, the Law on the organization and functioning of cooperative companies, the Law on the Romanian Integrated Custom Tariff, the Law implementing certain international sanctions, and the Law on agricultural cooperation.

In general, the Romanian Parliament has been very active since the constitutional reform. The reform proposal itself was a parliamentary initiative in the first place: the proposal for amending the Constitution was signed by 233 deputies and 94 senators who agreed with the text elaborated by the parliamentary commission that had been set up to this end in 2002. The Romanian Parliament has been increasingly active and the number of Emergency Ordinances has dropped significantly. Following the completion of the constitutional reform, 198 laws were adopted by Parliament in 2003 and at least 265 laws in 2004.[26] The number of Government Ordinances was 26 in 2003 and 48 in 2004. Some important laws from this period include the Code of Taxation and the Code of Fiscal Procedure, Code of Conduct for Civil Servants, Romania's accession to NATO, ratification

---

[25] Published in the Official Journal of Romania, Part I, No. 234, 9 May 2001.

[26] Prior to completing this contribution.

of a Treaty with the Russian Federation, the specifications of the prerogatives of the National Anti-corruption Prosecutor's Office, anti-discrimination laws, laws providing for support to single parent families, laws on local public administration, laws on the protection of disabled persons, a suspension of international adoptions, and the adoption of new international provisions such as those concerning the punishment of terrorist attacks and concerning children's rights. Emergency Ordinances have been adopted only in special cases, where urgent measures form the state authorities were required. These included ordinances pertaining to the support of young people, family benefits, unemployment benefits, the prohibition of international adoptions (on which new legislation is to be adopted later), the transparency of public institutions, and acceleration of privatization. Finally, as has been mentioned above, the regulations concerning the functioning of the two Chambers of Parliament have been modified in order to increase the efficiency of the legislative process and grant a higher priority to deliberations on the Bills relevant for Romania's accession to the EU.[27]

The parliamentary Commission on European Integration plays a special role in this process and until the accession will have the same status as the permanent commissions of the two Chambers. It contributes to the proper implementation of the Europe Association Agreement and examines on a regular basis the way in which the Government integrates into its policies the critical assessments contained in the European Commission's Reports on Romania. The members of the parliamentary commission took part in the meetings of the inter-ministerial committees where they presented opinions on Romania's progress in the incorporation of the *acquis communautaire* and the fulfilment of the Copenhagen Criteria. Members of the Romanian Parliament have participated in the meetings of the COSAC (Conference of Specialized Bodies in Community Affairs) together with members of parliament from the other candidate countries, expressing Romania's viewpoints and carrying out joint bilateral activities with the representatives of parliamentary commissions for European affairs from the other European countries.

As regards parliamentary control over the measures adopted by the Council of Ministers of the European Union, the procedure of questions and interpellations is used. It is a specific parliamentary method under which deputies, senators and parliamentary groups can address the executive, including the Prime Minister, requiring explanations and supplementary information, submitting opinions and suggestions, as well as making what are termed "political statements" whereby

[27] See Decision No. 23 of the Chamber of Deputies, 11 November 2003 (Romanian Official Journal No. 798, 12 November 2003) and Decision No. 20 of the Senate, 18 November 2003 (Romanian Official Journal No. 834, 24 November 2003).

standpoints are expressed with regard to the mechanism and outcomes of the integration process.

The Romanian Parliament has also taken part in the Debate on the Future of the Union, a central issue of which has been the strengthening of the Union's democratic dimension. The discussions have ranged from theoretical issues (delimitation of competences, information flow, etc.) to more practical problems regarding the concrete forms of exercising national control. The Romanian representatives in the Convention on the Future of Europe emphasized the strong correlation between the EU's democratic legitimacy and involvement of the national parliaments in EU activities. They called for more control by the national parliaments over the positions adopted by the governments within the Council, as well as for the strengthening of the institutional framework of cooperation between the national parliaments on the one hand, and between these and the European Parliament on the other hand.

The Romanian Parliament has expressed particular support to the reform of the COSAC, with the aim of improving the efficiency of this institution. The COSAC is an interparliamentary body that was set up in 1989 on the initiative of the former chairman of the French National Assembly, Laurent Fabius. It is undergoing a process of reassessment, following the proposals submitted by several countries, including the United Kingdom, Italy and the Netherlands, with a project for reforming the COSAC having also been drafted during the Dutch Presidency.[28] The Romanian Parliament finds that the COSAC has made an important contribution to the promotion of the parliamentary dialogue and the creation of a sustainable relationship between the national parliaments and the European Parliament. In the framework of the Debate on the Future of the Union, the following proposals have been made by Romanian Members of Parliament with regard to the COSAC. Deputy Puiu Haşotti is of the view that "[t]he COSAC experience should be extended to other committees in charge of sectoral policies in order to ultimately establish a European network of similar committees. At the same time, a more efficient COSAC requires a closer relationship between the European Parliament and the national parliaments".[29] Senator Liviu Maior has called for reinforcing the COSAC, which could become one of the main platforms for direct relations between the national parliaments and the European Parliament. According to him, the COSAC is "the best and the most coherent interparliamentary formula which could be enshrined under the Treaties". In his view, the COSAC would also offer "the most adequate forum to address the issue of an Agreement of Interparliamentary Cooperation".[30]

---

28 Skriv nava/adrese/land og tryk FM, 10 January 2003, Ref. No. EU_Presidency-COSAC.

29 The Convention on the Future of Europe. Contributions of Romania's representatives, a work published by the Ministry of European Integration, February-August 2002.

30 Ibid., p. 33.

As regards the option of creating a second chamber to the European Parliament, the idea has not found much support in Romania. Mr Puiu Hasotti among others claimed to oppose such a proposal, as it "would inevitably result in additional complication of an already complex institutional framework". He would prefer it if the European Parliament were put on an equal footing with the Council as co-legislators. This would enhance legitimacy as well as efficiency, resulting in a classic bicameral legislative body, where EU citizens would be represented in the European Parliament and the Member States in the Council. Creating instead a chamber composed of the members of the national parliaments would, in effect, denote the creation of "a third Chamber", which would significantly reduce efficiency. The Romanian Members of Parliament also contemplated the idea of setting up *ad hoc* parliamentary conventions comprised of both European and national parliamentarians in charge of specific tasks, such as reviewing the constitutional arrangements of the European Union or deciding about the direct financing of the Union.[31] Finally, it should be noted that the Romanian Members of Parliament took part in the activities of the Convention's Working Group on "The role of the national Parliaments in the present architecture of the Union". They supported the strengthening of the communication channels with all EU institutions, and the use of the COSAC as a consultative mechanism at sectoral levels.

The issues related to the involvement of the national parliaments and their control over Community institutions were also addressed in numerous national debates and projects. These were predominantly organized by the non-governmental organizations operating in the field, in cooperation with the Ministry of European Integration, the Romanian Parliament and the European Institute. The European Institute additionally organized debates with experts from the EU and the candidate countries.[32] The main conclusions that were reached at these various seminars on the Future of Europe in Romania underlined that the key requirements for the legitimacy of the European project and for the reduction of the democratic deficit are a greater degree of involvement of the national parliaments and enhancement of the role of the European Parliament.[33]

7. THE EUROPEAN CONSTITUTION

From the very beginning, Romania has welcomed and supported the idea of drafting a Constitution for Europe, by actively taking part in the debates that took

---

31 Ibid., p. 35.
32 Ibid., p. 84.
33 Ibid., p. 85.

place in the Convention for the Future of Europe. Meetings have been organized in 2002 and 2003 by the Ministry of European Integration and by different research institutes (such as the European Institute, universities and institutions of higher education). The topics concerned the objectives of the European Constitution, relations between the European and national institutions, respect for the principle of subsidiarity, and practical ways of synchronizing the objectives of the Treaty with the programmes for internal development. The view has been expressed that the emergence and the consolidation of European constitutional law[34] will certainly lead to the generalization of democratic and organizational principles which will prove beneficial for Romania's democratic and economic development.

The compatibility of some of the Romanian constitutional provisions with the Treaty establishing a Constitution for Europe has been discussed in several symposiums, especially with respect to the competences which will fall under the responsibility of the national parliaments and the division of the competences between the national and the EU institutions in this respect. The majority of Romanian lawyers represent the view that the new Article 148 (on Romania's accession to the EU and the supremacy of Community law) is compatible with other relevant provisions of the Romanian Constitution. These include, in particular, Article 1(1) ("Romania is a national, sovereign and independent, united and indivisible State"), Article 2, according to which the national sovereignty belongs to the Romanian people, and Article 61(1) which provides that the Romanian Parliament is "the representative, supreme body of the Romanian people and the only legislative authority of the State". In line with the Decision of the Romanian Constitutional Court of 16 April 2003, the principle of sovereignty is not affected, but will be exercised in new and more flexible terms, which allow for certain competences to be transferred to the EU institutions. This point of view seems to be widely recognized in the Romanian legal literature today. However, as has already been mentioned above, it is expected that the Constitution will undergo a second stage of reform in 2007, after Romania's accession to the EU, in order to ensure its complete and correct synchronization with the provisions of the Treaty establishing a Constitution for Europe. The future amendments will, *inter alia*, have to refer to the powers of the Parliament and the Government in the context of the adoption of the European Constitution. In the task of synchronizing the national provisions with those of the EU a balance must also be found between European values and Romanian interests. This also means that Romania still needs a certain measure of political education in the spirit of

---

34 Constanţa Călinoiu and Victor Duculescu, *Constitutional Law and Political Institutions* (Bucharest, Lumina Lex Publishing House 2003) Part XI The European Dimension of Constitutional Law, p. 265.

these European values. In any event, the anticipated future amendments are expected to put an end to any potential problems of compatibility.

8. CONCLUSIONS

For Romania, the last few years have been a period of intense legal preparations for meeting the accession criteria. The country has undertaken a host of activities and adopted numerous legal measures in order to adapt its constitutional framework to the fundamental principles of the EU and bring its internal legal system into conformity with the specific provisions of the *acquis communautaire*. This has been acknowledged by the European institutions, along with some realistic and objective suggestions that have been taken into account by the domestic authorities and which are currently being enforced. The accession negotiations, which were brought to a successful conclusion in the last months of 2004, represented a complex process aiming to ensure optimal conditions for Romania's accession to the EU and balancing a continuous and harmonious economical development with the challenges to the country's economy. The results of the negotiations show a considerable understanding of Romania's specific problems: altogether 50 transition periods were granted, which is more than was given to any other country from amongst the new Member States. As regards the chapters on Competition and Justice and Home Affairs, a safeguard clause has been inserted allowing a one-year delay to Romania's accession (2008 instead of 2007) if specific commitments are not respected in these areas. The European Commission thoroughly monitors the strict observance by Romania of its commitments and the adoption of the required legal and implementing measures. In order to avoid the activation of the safeguard clauses, Romania must endeavour to secure the borders, continue the reform of the judicial system, combat corruption and organized crime and maintain police cooperation.

It should be noted that there is a strong public consensus on the EU accession. Public surveys have continuously confirmed the support of the Romanians to the accession process and show the strong will of the Romanians to become members of the European family, to which they belong through their history, traditions, cultural affinities and language; more than 80 per cent are in favour of EU accession. Indeed, Romania's integration in the EU is perceived as the top national priority. As far as the issue of whether a special referendum should be held on accession is concerned, such a proposal has been advanced by one political party, but the Government has dismissed a referendum as superfluous.

Referring to the title of this volume – Hopes and Fears of the New Member States and (Pre-)Candidate Countries – it therefore appears that in Romanian civil society no significant concerns in relation to the integration process have been voiced. Nonetheless, certain difficulties, especially as regards the speeding up of the implementation of the *acquis*, have been encountered in the integration process. The EU has also drawn attention to the need to improve the functioning of Romania's state institutions and increase the quality of governance, especially within the public administration, and improve certain provisions regarding the protection of human rights. The fight against corruption also remains a vital issue.

To conclude, we would like to refer to the ideas of two eminent Romanian authors. Nicolae Titulescu, a famous Romanian politician and diplomat, who has been Minister of Foreign Affairs and the President of the League of Nations, once called for the "spiritualization of the borders" considering that "one man cannot be a stranger to other man just because a border is imposed between them".[35] George Ciorănescu, an eminent lawyer of Romanian origin who lived in France and was elected to the first European Parliament, in his work "The Romanians and the federal idea"[36] remarked that "[t]he nation I come from has always favoured Europe. It possesses the full maturity and the entire political and historical information to support the creation of a free, united and democratic Europe".

---

35 Nicolae Titulescu, ed., *Reflections* (Bucharest, Albatros 1985) p. 250.

36 Quoted by Gavril Iosif Chiuzbaian, *The exercise of power*, Continent XXI Ed. (Bucharest, Lumina Lex Ed. 2000) p. 157 (translated by the authors).

SERBIA AND MONTENEGRO

Slobodan Samardžić and Duško Lopandić*

Introductory explanations

Without a brief explanation of the nature of the newly emerged constitutional structure in the heart of the Balkans, the presentation and analysis of the constitutional characteristics of Serbia and Montenegro would leave much to be desired, particularly in view of its strategic orientation towards European integration. The purpose and meaning of the positive law constitutional provisions, which make up the normative framework of this specific polity, are difficult to understand if they are examined outside the overall political context and the goals of the new polity. The constitutional norms, which we will look into later, and the corresponding institutions mirror the nature of the "state union", the specific character of which makes it a very interesting topic for analysis.

What does the "specific character" of the state union of Serbia and Montenegro actually entail? The constitutional provision that defines the "state union" indicates that it is not simply a state. The very term "state union" suggests that it is not a specific form of state either, a federation for instance, as a type of compound state. While the term "compound state" consists of an adjective and a noun, the adjective imputing a special quality to the noun (state), in the phrase "state union" it is a noun (state) that describes a special quality of another noun (union).[1] A closer look into the basic provisions of the Constitutional Charter of Serbia and Montenegro and the rules pertaining to its institutions will help to explain why the drafters of the Constitution insisted on this linguistic nuance.[2]

---

* Dr Slobodan Samardžić, Professor of the Faculty of Political Science, Belgrade University (Introduction, parts 1 and 2). Dr Duško Lopandić, Director for European Union, Ministry of Foreign Affairs (parts 3 and 4).

[1] It is very difficult to translate the Serbian phrase "državna zajednica" into English. The English noun "state" is used as a modifier in the "state union" compound, which is not the exact translation of "državna zajednica". Even though it is not commonly used in the professional vocabulary, a literal translation into German – staatliche Gemeinschaft – might help the Western reader understand the semantics of the expression.

[2] The Constitutional Charter of the State Union of Serbia and Montenegro, Official Gazette of Serbia and Montenegro, No. 1 Year 1, 2003.

The "specific character" we are talking about is of no particular interest to us from the angle of the general theory of state, because modern history and the theory of state have already offered a wide variety of systems of government – unions, leagues, confederations, condominiums, associated states – which cannot be classified as typical state-like systems. From this broader point of view, the state union of Serbia and Montenegro is no historic novelty. Such or similar systems already exist, and are likely to persevere in contemporary history and in years to come.

The distinctive nature of Serbia and Montenegro is interesting in the context of the European integration process and the state union's participation in the Stabilization and Association Process (SAP) as a prerequisite for entry into the European Union (EU).[3] As far as the European Union is concerned, however, the main treaty actors are states, regardless of whether membership or the association process is at issue. What makes things easier, at least on the surface, is the fact that the Constitutional Charter has defined Serbia and Montenegro as a single subject of international law,[4] authorizing it to enter into international treaties and international organizations. However, even if discussed strictly from the angle of its international status, the position of the state union as a state is untypical – the more so the more extensive and complex the content of an international treaty is. The Stabilization and Association Agreement is an excellent example of an extensive and complex treaty, requiring from a signatory that aspires to the status of EU-associated member a long string of tasks to be fulfilled.[5] In this regard, the institutional mechanism of Serbia and Montenegro (the mechanism of permanent internal negotiations) is so complex that it is indeed questionable whether it can meet the requirements such an agreement entails.

Having said this, we have arrived at the very core of the state union's untypical constitutional structure. In order to clarify it briefly, we will set out its fundamental constitutional features:

(1) Within the state union, sovereign power, constitution-making power and every other effective power remains undivided in the hands of two constituents – the Member States of Serbia and Montenegro. The Constitutional

---

[3] Conclusions of the 24 November 2000 EU-Western Balkans Summit in Zagreb on the Stabilization and Association Process, *Bull. EU* 11-2000, point I.6.57; and Conclusions of the 21 June 2003 EU-Western Balkans Summit in Thessaloniki on the Stabilization and Association Process and 'The Thessaloniki Agenda for the Western Balkans: Moving towards European Integration', *Bull. EU* 6-2003, point 1.6.70.

[4] Art. 14, para. 1 of the Constitutional Charter says: "Serbia and Montenegro shall be a single international-law subject and a member of international global and regional organizations whose membership requires international subjectivity."

[5] See C. Pippan, 'The Rocky Road to Europe: The EU's Stabilisation and Association Process for the Western Balkans and the Principle of Conditionality', 9 *EFA Rev.* (2004) pp. 219-245.

Charter does not mention the issue of sovereignty explicitly, but its basic provisions and concrete institutional solutions (see other characteristics) make it clear that the Member States (as defined by the Constitutional Charter) have maintained all the prerogatives of sovereign power.

(2) The citizens of Serbia and Montenegro are neither constituents nor direct actors in the public life of the state union. They enjoy such constitutional status only in their respective Member States. A citizen of a Member State is also a citizen of the state union, but he/she can acquire state union citizenship solely through the citizenship of a Member State (Art. 7, para. 1).

(3) The state union only has transferred powers which have been entrusted to it by either the Charter (Art. 17, para. 1) or directly by the Member States (Art. 17, para. 2).

(4) The Constitutional Charter proceeds from two different and separated economic systems of the Member States, merely listing the establishment of a common market as one of the goals (Art. 3, sixth sentence). It is the Member States that are responsible for the establishment and smooth operation of the common market (Art. 12, para. 2). The parliament of Serbia and Montenegro is not allowed to pass any economic laws or decisions.

(5) The state union has no own income. The exercise of powers that have been transferred to the state union is funded by the Member States (Art. 18).

(6) In terms of their mode of election, the decision-making process and the powers they are given, the bodies of the state union are effectively the common bodies of the Member States at the level of the state union, rather than the actual bodies of the state union itself:

(a) The President of the state union is elected by the Parliament of Serbia and Montenegro to a four-year term of office. Once this term expires, a new president is elected from the other Member State. The President of Serbia and Montenegro is the head of the Council of Ministers.

(b) In its first two-year term of office, the Parliament of Serbia and Montenegro consists of delegations elected by the assemblies of the former Republics of Serbia and Montenegro. After that, new Members of Parliament will be elected by direct vote in accordance with the election laws of the Member States. Parity is not part of the make-up of Parliament (Serbia has 91 seats, and Montenegro has 35), but parliamentary decisions require the majority of votes within both delegations (i.e., at least 46 votes on the Serbian side and 18 on the Montenegrin side). Most of the decisions made by Parliament also still have to be passed by the individual parliaments of the Member States.

(c) The parity principle has been applied to the Council of Ministers, which, including its chairman, who is also the President of the state union, consists of six (3 + 3) members. Members of the Council are elected by the Parliament of Serbia and Montenegro. Within five constitutional departments (foreign policy, defence, internal economic relations, foreign economic relations and human rights) the Ministries coordinate the policies of the Member States. The Ministers of Defence and Foreign Affairs are assisted by deputies from the other Member State and will exchange office with them after two years. In diplomatic and consular offices of the state union the principle of parity and rotation also applies.

(d) The Court of Serbia and Montenegro has eight members (4 + 4), elected by the Parliament of Serbia and Montenegro. The Court independently exercises the functions of constitutional court and administrative court and may only act in regard of the regulations and powers of the bodies of the state union. The Court does not have superior jurisdiction.

(7) The Constitutional Charter (Art. 60) allows the Member States to withdraw from the state union after three years. Consequently, the Charter also allows for the dissolution of the state union.

These critical features of the constitutional system of the state union lead to the conclusion that it is a union of two independent states that operate as a single entity in international relations.[6] Regardless of the fact that the states that constitute the state union are not independent in how the conduct their international relations,[7] the underlying issue is to what extent their internal independence affects the implementation of a single foreign policy devised by the state union. Barely more than one year and a half after the birth of the state union (the Constitutional Charter was adopted on 4 February 2003), the relationship with the European Union already sparked serious dilemmas over the efficient implementation of foreign policy. We would like to illustrate this by the following example.

In order for negotiations on the Stabilization and Association Agreement to commence, Serbia and Montenegro first had to establish an Action Plan for the

---

[6] Whatever the name we may give to this polity (a union, a confederation) it is certainly not a federation. Not only the Constitutional Charter has carefully avoided the term, but the aforementioned constitutional features do not allow for the classification of Serbia and Montenegro as a federal state either. The same conclusion would be reached by reasoning *a contrario*, using a recent study on comparative federalism (Ronald L. Watts, *Comparing Federal Systems* (Montreal and Kingston, Queen's University 1999) p. 7), in which the author has analysed a host of contemporary federal systems and set out their general characteristics: 1) there is no mutual subjugation between federal and constitutive levels; 2) both have sovereign powers arising from the constitution; 3) both are authorised to cooperate with citizens directly in exercising their legislative, executive and taxation powers; and 4) both are directly elected by citizens. If we compare the basic characteristics of the state union of Serbia and Montenegro with those of contemporary federations, we can only conclude that Serbia and Montenegro is not a federation.

[7] This holds true only in the context of powers transferred to the state union. The Constitutional Charter expressly provides that the Member States can maintain international relations in their own spheres of competence, whenever international subjectivity is not required. (See Art. 14, para. 2 and Art. 15, para. 2).

Harmonization of the Economic Systems of the Member States. This document has to define the modes of and procedure for the establishment of a common market for Serbia and Montenegro that would allow for the free movement of people, goods, services and capital, and to determine the pace at which this is to be developed. The Action Plan, which was finally adopted by the Parliament of Serbia and Montenegro at the end of August 2003, only covered part of the overall process of internal economic harmonization (common customs and foreign trade policy). The plan indicates that full harmonization can be expected to have been achieved in three to five years.[8] The Action Plan is the result of direct talks between the counterpart ministries of the Member States, and the entire process, including the adoption procedure, took 15 months. Before the Parliament of Serbia and Montenegro adopted it, the document had already been passed by the parliaments of the two Member States. The Action Plan was one of the tests gauging the state union's readiness to sign the Stabilization and Association Agreement, the results of which are published in the European Commission's feasibility study.[9]

This example has already revealed a series of difficulties surrounding Serbia and Montenegro's united appearance on the international stage, let alone those that will inevitably emerge in the process of actual integration with Europe. The difficulties have arisen from the very nature of the state union as projected by the Constitutional Charter. It is definitely a union of the states, rather than a compound state that would enjoy the full capacity of international representation of its citizens and constituent units in the negotiations with the European Union. The question is whether the European Union will be ready to accept the constitutional reality of Serbia and Montenegro.

Before we can answer this question, we have to go back to the Belgrade agreement (full title: Proceeding Points for the Restructuring of Relations between Serbia and Montenegro), signed in March 2002.[10] This is a political document whose principles the Constitutional Charter rests on. EU High Representative for Common Foreign and Security Policy Javier Solana signed the Belgrade agreement as a witness. The drafting of the Constitutional Charter was monitored closely not only by experts, but also by EU senior officials. After the Charter was promulgated and its implementation could actually begin, politicians

---

8 See Action Plan for Harmonization of Economic Systems of Member States of the State Union of Serbia and Montenegro; Survey – Serbia and Montenegro, No. 2, 2003.

9 The European Commission has published its feasibility study on Serbia and Montenegro, in which it confirmed sufficient progress to open negotiations on a Stabilization and Association Agreement. See Press Release IP/05/421, Brussels, 12 April 2005. The text of the study is available at: <http://www.seio.sr.gov.yu/code/navigate.asp?Id=20>.

10 The text of the agreement is available at: <http://www.venice.coe.int/site/main/Texts/Serbia_and_Montenegro.htm>.

of Serbia and Montenegro asked for a special EU opinion on this particular case. In the meantime, the European Union incorporated new elements in its policy towards the Western Balkans, better known as the Partnership for European Integration, which it adopted at a summit in Thessaloniki in June 2003. One of the preparatory documents for the Thessaloniki declaration says: "The preparation of the countries of the Western Balkans for integration into European structures is a major priority of the European Union. The unification of Europe will not be complete until these countries join the European Union."[11] But no distinction was made between Serbia and Montenegro on the one hand and the other countries of the Western Balkans on the other, despite their different internal structures. Quite the contrary, the document held the same message for all: "The one major challenge common to all countries of the region remains the building of strong, *fully functioning states* [emphasis added], capable of delivering on the needs of their citizens, of ensuring effective regional cooperation and of more advanced relations with the Union."[12]

It goes without saying that the European Union will not adopt a special attitude towards Serbia and Montenegro due to its specific internal system. When it comes to treaty relations, the Union will simply treat Serbia and Montenegro as it treats any other country with which it maintains relations or which is an accession candidate. This is at least what has become clear from the third annual report of the European Commission on the stabilization and association process with Serbia and Montenegro.[13] In short, the EU considers the state union as a normal state of which it requires the fulfilment of the association conditions – in this case the start of negotiations on an SAA – in the same way as it has required this of the other pre-candidate countries. The fact that other public and private actors, including different regions within EU Member States,[14] also have a place in the complex operative system of the European Community and the European Union, does not mean that the Union adopts a special position towards these actors in the sense of concluding agreements with them.[15] Their share in state power is

---

[11] See *supra* n. 3.

[12] See Communication from the Commission to the Council and the European Parliament, The Western Balkans and the Challenge of Enlargement, Brussels, 21 May 2003.

[13] See Commission of the EC, Serbia and Montenegro, Stabilization and Association Report 2004, esp. pp. 2-3 (functionality of the institutions) and p. 30 (internal market and trade).

[14] The word "region" should be understood in its broadest meaning, as a self-governing territorial unit within a state, regardless of the level of constitutional autonomy.

[15] In terms of negotiating such agreements, there are, however, differences with other countries. Internal disputes surrounding the endorsement of the Internal Market and Trade Action Plan by the State Assembly of Serbia and Montenegro initially led the European Commission to stall the feasibility study for an SAA. It took full endorsement of the EU's so-called "twin-track" approach by political leaders of both Serbia and Montenegro to re-launch the feasibility study in October 2004. The twin-track approach to SAA negotiations means that the EU deals with the two republics on policies which they conduct separately, notably trade, economic and sectoral policies, while it

regarded as an exclusive matter of the internal constitutional order of the country in question.

1. NATIONAL CONSTITUTION

Pursuant to Article 3 of the Constitutional Charter, three of the six goals of the state union are related to European integration: to integrate with European structures, the European Union in particular (third sentence); to harmonize regulations and practices with European and international standards (fourth sentence) and to establish and ensure the unhindered operation of the common market on its territory, through coordination and harmonization of economic systems of the Member States, in line with the principles of the European Union (sixth sentence).

The fact that European integration has been placed so high up in the hierarchy of constitutional values and goals of Serbia and Montenegro reflects the commitment of the state union to the new strategic orientation after the political changes in Montenegro (1998) and Serbia (2000). The question now is whether this new commitment has produced the most suitable constitutional framework for its fulfilment? We will try to answer this question in accordance with the guidelines set out for the Project.

1.1 Implementation of international law and transfer of competences

According to Article 16 of the Constitutional Charter, "the ratified international treaties and generally accepted rules of international law shall have primacy over the laws of Serbia and Montenegro and of the Member States." Based on the explicit use of the term "primacy" to define the precedence of international treaties and the rules of international law over domestic line, it might be concluded that the drafters of the Constitution intended to opt for a monistic approach to the relationship between international and national law. After its acceptance into the domestic legal order international law is valid by itself and is directly enforceable before the national courts.

Article 10 of the Constitutional Charter, which governs the application of a special category of international law, supports this point of view: "Provisions of international treaties on human and minority rights and civil liberties that are in force in the territory of Serbia and Montenegro shall be applied directly." This "direct applicability" reflects how closely connected Serbia and Montenegro's

continues to work with the State Union where it is the competent authority, for example on international political obligations and human rights, in particular full cooperation with the ICTY.

approach is to the contemporary practice of incorporating international law in internal legal systems. Moreover, it is in line with the doctrine and practice under EC law as developed within the European Communities.

The issue of the constitutional room for manoeuvre that is permitted to the state union has a direct impact on its capacity to act independently in maintaining international relations, and on its efficiency in concluding and applying international treaties. This is a matter of utmost importance for a union of states such as Serbia and Montenegro. We have already mentioned that (1) the Charter has defined the state union as a single subject of international law and a member of international global and regional organizations (Art. 14, para. 1). As such (2), Serbia and Montenegro can "establish international relations with other states and international organizations, and conclude international treaties and agreements." The Parliament of Serbia and Montenegro (3) is in charge of the ratification of international treaties and agreements (Art. 19, ninth sentence).

Judging by these three constitutional provisions, the state union has at its disposal the common constitutional mechanisms that shape the international activity it performs as a "single subject of international law." However, when it comes to membership of international organizations, there is a constitutional provision which, if not exactly derogates, then certainly dilutes the capacity of the state union as a single subject of international law. Article 19, fifth sentence, stipulates that the Parliament of Serbia and Montenegro decides on Serbia and Montenegro's membership of international organizations, as well as the rights and obligations arising from such membership, but only with the prior consent of the competent bodies of the Member States. This not only makes the Member States important factors in internal decision making, but also makes them the actual decision makers in this sphere of international functions which are ultimately carried out by the state union. It is hard to deny that this will complicate the process of Serbia and Montenegro's integration with international structures and the application of international law, but this solution was a logic and systemic consequence of the nature of the state union.

The same systemic logic has determined the powers of other state bodies – the Council of Ministers and the Court of Serbia and Montenegro – in defining and carrying out foreign policy and in implementing international law. The issue of the Court and the judiciary in general will be discussed separately. For now, we will only examine the issue of the Council of Ministers.

Article 33, second sentence of the Constitutional Charter prescribes that the Council of Ministers "shall chart and carry out the policy of Serbia and Montenegro in compliance with the common policy and interests of the Member States." This provision concerns both internal and foreign policy, as subsequent decisions have confirmed. Our focus is now on the constitutional powers of three (out of the five) Ministries that participate in the implementation of Serbia and Montenegro's foreign policy.

Article 40, paragraph 2, provides that "the Minister of Foreign Affairs shall coordinate the drafting of foreign policy together with the competent bodies of Serbia and Montenegro." Article 43 of the Constitutional Charter is even more important for the policy of European integration: "The Minister for Foreign Economic Relations is responsible for the negotiation and coordination of the implementation of international treaties, including agreements with the European Union and the coordination of relations with international economic and financial institutions, following consultations with the competent Ministries of the Member States." Finally, the duties and responsibilities of the Minister of Human Rights have been specified in Article 45: "The Minister of Human Rights shall monitor the exercise of human and minority rights and, in collaboration with the competent bodies of the Member States, coordinate activities aimed at the implementation of and compliance with the international conventions governing the protection of human and minority rights."

On the face of it, these three provisions advocate the shared responsibility of the Ministries of the state union on the one hand and the corresponding bodies of the Member States on the other in carrying out international functions. In truth, however, it is the bodies of the Member States that have the main say, now that the Ministries of the state union merely coordinate their policies and act as their joint organs at the state union level.

In the light of these constitutional provisions we are now able to answer the question of the transfer of competences to international organizations. Two different positions have emerged from the practical experiences of existing EU members and the case law developed by the European Court of Justice: delegation of competences on the one hand and transfer of sovereignty on the other.[16] The EU Member States are more inclined towards delegation, particularly countries that take a dualistic approach to the incorporation of international law in the national legal order (the United Kingdom is a typical example). On the other hand, they must also comply with the position adopted by the European Court of Justice, which was set out for the first time in the 1962 *Van Gend en Loos* case. The Court held that the bodies of the Community "are granted sovereign rights, the exercise of which affects the Member States and, consequently, their citizens." According to this interpretation, the Member States have "restricted their sovereign rights, albeit in limited areas", and the aim of European Community law is to provide the citizens with rights, "which are becoming part of their legal heritage."[17]

---

16 See T.C. Hartley, *Osnovi prava Evropske zajednice* [The Foundations of European Community Law] (Beograd, Beogradski centar za ljudska prava 1998) p. 180.

17 Ibid., pp. 180-181.

The two approaches mentioned and the practice of the transfer of competences in the European Union proceed from the same starting point, namely that the Member State may freely dispose of its sovereign rights (competences) and use the sovereign power to exercise them. This, however, does not hold true in the case of Serbia and Montenegro. We have already noted that the Member States retain full sovereignty, while the state union is given transferred powers only (Art. 17). The state union is therefore restricted not only in disposing of its competences, but also in the manner in which they are carried out, because bodies of the Member States participate directly in the implementation of certain powers of the state union.

Since it cannot dispose of its powers of its own accord, the state union is not authorized to transfer these powers to international organizations either. Pursuant to the Constitutional Charter, this would fall within the jurisdiction of the Member States. Given the fact, however, that they have not yet adjusted their constitutions to the Constitutional Charter, concrete constitutional solutions to govern the transfer of competences to international organizations have yet to be found.[18]

1.2 Supremacy and direct effect

The Constitutional Charter does not contain any explicit provisions that expressly establish the supremacy of international law over national laws, or its direct effect. The Charter speaks of the precedence of international law over domestic legislation, but this is still far removed from the effective principle of supremacy and direct effect, particularly in the light of the European Court of Justice case law that developed these principles. If Serbia and Montenegro makes progress in its policy of integration, it will have to introduce corresponding constitutional changes and make these principles very explicit in the Constitutional Charter. After all, the current EU members and the states that have entered the Union in 2004 have had to do the same.

---

[18] Under the Constitutional Charter (Art. 65), the Member States are required to bring their constitutions in line with the Constitutional Charter within six months of the promulgation of the Constitutional Charter. This time limit expired on 4 August 2003. Serbia intends to adopt a completely new constitution, but this will certainly take time, at least until the end of 2004. Montenegro intends to introduce the appropriate adjustments in the existing constitution, but this process has not yet begun due to political controversy over the question of whether the current procedure for amending the constitution should be amended or used as it stands. There are many legal voids in both Member States, since the constitutions of the former republics, Serbia and Montenegro, are still in force, but many provisions cannot be applied because they are contrary to the Constitutional Charter. In its Report mentioned above, the Commission strongly stressed the need for adjustment and accordingly criticized the failure of the republics to fulfill their constitutional obligations (see above cited Document, pp. 3-4).

Considering that the Constitutional Charter recognizes both primacy (of international treaties in general) and direct applicability (of international treaties on human and minority rights in particular) the question arises why the drafters of the Constitution failed to introduce a provision on direct applicability in the general rule concerning incorporation (Art. 16), under which the incorporation of international standards of human and minority rights and civil liberties (Art. 10) falls. It is possible that the expression "primacy of international law" implies its "direct applicability", but this is not necessarily the case. International law can also have primacy over national laws after it has been incorporated by the enactment of additional implementing legislation, but this was obviously not the intention of the Constitutional Charter. On the other hand, the doctrine of direct applicability of international law eliminates any dualism in the relationship between international and domestic law. The practice of the international legal protection of human rights within national legal systems is clear evidence of this. Only EU law, however, has drawn the doctrine of direct applicability (of Community acts) to its logical and systemic conclusion by making it a principle of internal (domestic) law which is widely implemented within the EU Member States.

Bearing all that in mind, one can accept the good reasons of the drafters of the Constitution for insisting on a differentiation between "primacy" and "direct applicability" in concrete situations. Serbia and Montenegro is still not a member of the EU; hence, it cannot follow specific EU law principles such as the principle of supremacy, direct applicability and direct effect. For its future EU agreements the constitutional guarantee inserted in Article 16 of the Constitutional Charter seems to be sufficient in terms of their implementation. The problem, however, does not lie in this respect. The main problem concerns the constitutional capacity of the state union bodies to conclude, enforce and implement, i.e., to control the implementation, of such international agreements like the Stabilization and Association agreement.

1.3 Amendments

Since this question is one concerning the membership of international organizations, the ratification of the treaties mentioned would have to be dealt with by the cumulative application of two provisions of the Constitutional Charter, namely Article 19, ninth sentence, on the ratification of international treaties and agreements by the Parliament of Serbia and Montenegro, and Article 19, fifth sentence, governing Serbia and Montenegro's membership of international organizations which requires the prior consent of competent organs of the Member States. This requirement, however, still awaits further definition, as the two Member States have not yet adjusted their constitutions accordingly.

In the case of Serbia and Montenegro, the question posed above is mainly hypothetical since the country is still far removed from full membership of the European Union in terms of time, legal, systemic and economic requirements. There is still a long string of conditions Serbia and Montenegro has to fulfil before even talks on the Stabilization and Association Agreement could begin. The basic purpose of the Constitutional Charter is to provide a framework for the closer economic, legal and institutional integration of the two Member States, which should go hand in hand with their efforts to meet the 1993 Copenhagen Criteria and the conditions laid down in the feasibility study.[19] During the process, which also has a definite time dimension, several partial reviews of the Constitutional Charter might have to be carried out to simplify the legal and institutional mechanisms for the operation of the state union. This positive scenario which in no way runs counter to the goals of the state union as set out by the Constitutional Charter depends on whether the joint efforts to meet the EU requirements turn out to be successful, which would also boost the integration process. To be honest, however, the Constitutional Charter also offers a negative scenario, which would come into play if one Member State, or both of them, decided to make use of the option to break away from the state union three years after its creation (Art. 60). In that case, the state union would automatically cease to exist.[20]

These uncertainties, stemming not only from the actual circumstances, but also from the political strategies advocated by the two Member States and by Montenegro in particular where independence is still the instrumental concept for the ruling coalition, have made it impossible for political actors to concentrate completely on optimal internal adjustments to the requirements of the European integration process.[21]

1.4 Provisions contrary to the *acquis communautaire*

Not even a very careful reader of the Constitutional Charter would be able to find in it a provision that is contrary to the *acquis communautaire*. After all, this would be in sharp contrast with the goals of the state union, one of which refers directly to its integration into European structures, the European Union in particular (Art. 3, third sentence).

---

19 See *supra* n. 9.

20 Art. 60 of the Constitutional Charter also deals with the consequences of withdrawal by one or both Member States. If one Member States withdraws from the state union, the other will inherit the international legal personality of the state union. This provision (para. 5) is rather alarming, particularly in the light of the achievements the country has already made, such as, for example, its entry into the Council of Europe in February 2003.

21 The government of Montenegro has insisted on more than one occasion that it will hold a referendum on independence in 2006. See <http://www.vlada.cg.yu>.

The major problem is not so much in the wording as in the spirit of the Constitutional Charter, or, as we have noted earlier, in the nature and character of the state union. This type of internal system is unknown in recent European history. The last examples were the Swiss confederation until 1848, the German union until 1870 and the Austro-Hungarian dual monarchy (a real union) until 1918. However strong political reasons might have been for the system of government defined by the Constitutional Charter, it is essentially obsolete if viewed in the European context. The European Community/Union outgrew this level of internal organization a long time ago, perhaps as far back as 1951, when in its Treaty Establishing the European Steel and Coal Community it established the competences of the High Authority and the Court of Justice. The very existence of the *acquis communautaire* makes it crystal clear that a union of states is an outdated model for contemporary Europe.

On the other hand, Serbia and Montenegro are European states (both were internationally recognized at the 1878 Berlin Congress), which have coexisted within the borders of one state ever since 1918. Their peoples have never come into the kind of conflicts typical of Cyprus or Bosnia and Herzegovina. In principle, it seems very difficult to establish an optimal federal balance between Serbia and Montenegro bearing in mind the huge difference in size between them, but this is not necessarily an insurmountable obstacle if there is the political will to overcome it. The *acquis communautaire*, the result of a successful historical experiment, can be an outside catalyst for a sustainable institutional system of the state union. In the practical integration of these values in the internal system of the state union, the assistance of the European Union is indispensable.

1.5 Procedures to adapt the national constitution to the *acquis communautaire*

Any change to the Constitutional Charter is subject to the constitutional amendment procedure, which the Constitutional Charter has addressed with one single sentence: "The Constitutional Charter shall be amended under the same procedure and in the same manner as those applying to the adoption of the Constitutional Charter." (Art. 62). Article 61 equally briefly regulates the adoption of the Constitutional Charter: "The Constitutional Charter shall be adopted in identical wording by the People's Assembly of the Republic of Serbia and the Assembly of the Republic of Montenegro, and shall enter into force when the identical text of the Constitutional Charter is adopted and promulgated by the Federal Parliament."

Without going into the legal and technical ambiguities and contextual vagueness of these provisions, it is certain that the consent of the parliaments of the Member States is critical for the amendment procedure. This is entirely consonant with the nature of the state union, in which the Member States are the holders of highest authority (sovereignty). Consequently, it is their supreme representative bodies that can decide on changes to the Constitution.

However, if the *acquis* is to gain acceptance in the system of regulations and institutions of the state union, the process is unlikely to involve constitutional changes, but rather a number of action plans, like the one stipulating the harmonization of the two economic systems, which will regulate individual fields of the common policy and produce additional institutions (or change the role of the existing ones) to implement these plans. These factual systemic changes can be effected in the state union of Serbia and Montenegro only under the authority of the European Union, and within the Stabilization and Association Process. In that case, constitutional changes would simply follow the actual changes in the key policy areas of European integration. This is the most realistic way for the *acquis communautaire* to enter the legal, political and economic system of the state union.

2. ROLE OF THE JUDICIARY

The state union and the Member States have just begun to reform their judicial systems. A better organization of the courts is just one objective, the ultimate goal being the establishment of an efficient system to protect basic rights and freedoms, including internationally guaranteed rights and freedoms. In this regard, the judicial system viewed as inclusive of the state union and the Member States, is part of the overall system of government that we have classified as a union of states, as provided by the corresponding provisions of three relevant documents – the Constitutional Charter, the Charter of Human and Minority Rights and Civil Liberties and the Law on the Court of Serbia and Montenegro.[22]

We have already discussed the constitutional provision that allows for the direct applicability of international agreements on human and minority rights. This rule has been virtually repeated in Article 7 of the Charter of Human and Minority Rights. Together with the catalogue of rights and freedoms as set out by the Charter of Human and Minority Rights, Serbia and Montenegro has a model list of rights recognized and promoted at the international level.

---

[22] The Charter of Human and Minority Rights and Civil Liberties (Official Gazette of Serbia and Montenegro, No. 6, 2003) was adopted by the Parliament of Serbia and Montenegro on 28 February 2003 as an integral part of the Constitutional Charter (Art. 8 of the Constitutional Charter). The Law on the Court of Serbia and Montenegro (Official Gazette of Serbia and Montenegro, No. 26, 2003) was passed on 18 June 2003, as the last of a series of laws governing the operation of bodies of the state union.

The question is how to provide efficient protection of these rights. It is important to note that this protection is just subsidiary at the state union level. Pursuant to Article 9 of the Constitutional Charter, the state union ensures the protection of these rights only if the Member States do not provide for such protection. In other words, it is the courts of the Member States that are in charge of complete protection, save certain exceptions. The jurisdiction of the Court of Serbia and Montenegro also makes this obvious – it can rule on appeals filed by citizens, but only if the institutions of the Member States have threatened their guaranteed constitutional rights and freedoms, and only if no other form of constitutional protection has been provided for (Art. 46, third sentence, of the Constitutional Charter and Art. 9, para. 2 of the Charter of Human and Minority Rights).

The constitutional rule prescribing the direct application of international treaties on human and minority rights has been materialized in the Charter of Human and Minority Rights by the obligation of carrying out international court rulings by either the state union or the Member States, depending on whose institution has violated the given right (Art. 9, para. 3). Another relevant provision is Article 10 of the Charter of Human and Minority Rights, stating that guaranteed rights are to be interpreted in accordance with the applicable international guarantees for human and minority rights and the practice of international bodies supervising their implementation.

Likewise, in all the provisions governing the harmonization of the legislation of the Member States and the state union with the Constitutional Charter through court rulings, ratified international treaties are regularly cited immediately after the Constitutional Charter, with which the laws are to be harmonized.[23] In the hierarchy of legal acts, they are clearly superior to the laws of the Member States and the state union.

This is the general constitutional framework for basic rights and their protection in Serbia and Montenegro. This is not enough, however, to provide a complete answer to the question of the role of the courts in the implementation of the Stabilization and Association Agreement, or to the question concerning the application of principles of supremacy and direct effect, or to the issue of priority of primary and secondary EC legislation, or to be able to cite individual cases before the Court of Serbia and Montenegro and before the supreme and constitutional courts of the Member States. Serbia and Montenegro has simply not yet reached the accession level that would throw up these issues. In order to be able to come to grips with these problems some day, Serbia and Montenegro will have to prepare regulation not only from a legal point of view, but also from an

[23] See The Law on the Court of Serbia and Montenegro, Art. 34, Items 2 and 3, Art. 60, Items 2 and 3, Art. 103, Art. 118, paras. 1, 2 and 3. In some cases, not only ratified international treaties are cited, but also general international rules.

institutional one, which would have to be reflected in the first place in the adequate organization of the court system. Countries aspiring to full membership of the European Union have to be aware that the European Court of Justice demands sole jurisdiction over issues related to the application of European Community law by national courts, as well as over possible conflicts between Community and national law.[24] In order to meet this challenge, the national court system must not only be prepared, but also extremely effective. For now, however, suffice it that we set out the main elements of Serbia and Montenegro's current judicial structure.

The Court of Serbia and Montenegro combines the functions of a constitutional court and an administrative court with jurisdiction over the regulation and powers of the state union bodies only. When it decides on whether the constitutions and laws of the Member States are in conformity with the Constitutional Charter and laws of the state union, and when it decides on a conflict of jurisdiction between bodies of the Member States and bodies of the state union, the Court is doing so together with members of the constitutional courts of the Member States (Art. 49, paras. 1 and 2 of the Constitutional Charter). For this purpose, a so-called joint court session is convened, which must be attended by the majority of members of all competent courts. A court ruling requires a double majority (Art. 35, para. 1 of the Law on the Court of Serbia and Montenegro).

There is some systemic logic in this solution, since we are talking about judicial power within a union of states. For that reason, the court of the union cannot be a supreme court and, as such, a court of the last instance, save in the exceptional case of a citizen's appeal, with all its limitations. The Belgrade Agreement stipulates that the Court of Serbia and Montenegro does not have superior jurisdiction. As a separate and independent court, it is in charge of the affairs of the union only. The Constitutional Charter does not provide for a hierarchy of legal norms in the system as a whole (the state union and the Member States).[25] This is quite understandable, since the Member States have integral sovereign power, meaning that their constitutions are effectively the supreme legal acts.[26] As

[24] See Hartley, op. cit. n. 16, at p. 218.

[25] Art. 51 of the Constitutional Charter indirectly addresses this issue: "The Constitutional Charter, laws and competences of Serbia and Montenegro and the constitutions, laws and competences of the Member States must be adjusted." The provision does not define a hierarchy between the levels of constitutions, laws and competences. In other words, the order of legal superiority is rather vague.

[26] The Belgrade Agreement provides that the Constitutional Charter is the supreme legal act of the state union of Serbia and Montenegro, but the normative development of this rule through the Constitutional Charter and the Law on the Court of Serbia and Montenegro has made it clear that the Charter does not have that impact throughout the system (the state union plus the Member States). This provision is either a mere declaration, or it allows for the interpretation that the Constitutional Charter is the supreme legal act within a limited framework of regulations and institutions of the state union.

such, they are not subject to independent constitutional review by the Court of Serbia and Montenegro. If they are to be adjusted to the Constitutional Charter, this will require a joint action by the Court on the one hand and the constitutional courts of the Member States on the other. The entire adjustment procedure is thus subject to the preferences of any one of the Member State as the members of their constitutional courts cannot be outvoted in a joint session with the Court of Serbia and Montenegro. This principle, mutatis mutandis, also goes for the adjustment of laws of a Member State to the Constitutional Charter and state union laws and for the decision-making process in a conflict of jurisdiction between different levels of government.

In order to get a complete picture of the specific court system of Serbia and Montenegro, it is necessary to look into the legal effect of a ruling by the Court of Serbia and Montenegro, as specified by the Law on the Court. The Law has made a difference between the legal effect of a ruling that the Court has made independently, i.e., within the framework of the laws endorsed by the state union, and the legal effect of a ruling the Court has made together with the constitutional courts of the Member States. In the first case, any decision that a law is in breach of the Constitutional Charter enters into force automatically on the day that it is published in the Official Gazette of Serbia and Montenegro (Art. 118, para. 1). In the second case, any decision that the constitution of a Member State is not compatible with the Constitutional Charter, or that a law of a Member State is not in conformity with the Constitutional Charter or a law of the state union, has to be implemented by the parliament of the Member State concerned within six or three months (Art. 118, para. 3). The Law offers no solution if the Member State's parliament refuses to carry out the decision delivered at the joint court session; it is simply treated as a supreme authority in this case. It is important to note that this goes beyond the mere assessment of the compatibility of a Member State's constitutions and laws to the corresponding legislation of the state union – it also concerns the compatibility of a Member State's laws to ratified and published international treaties and agreements.

The question is how effective a non-hierarchical court system can be within the framework of the international obligations which Serbia and Montenegro have assumed under the Constitutional Charter. Or more specifically, how will this system respond to the EU judicial system, in which the supreme court, the European Court of Justice, insists on the supremacy of not only the law of the Community, but also of its own role in implementing this law. If the courts of the Member States of Serbia and Montenegro are not ready to accept the authority of the state union court (in normative rather than practical terms), how will they ever accept the supremacy of the European Court of Justice, let alone its direct administration of justice over the citizens and other legal entities that live and work on their sovereign territories?

Neither the standardized court system of Serbia and Montenegro nor the practice of its courts have so far been able to answer these questions.[27] In this regard, the most relevant question for Serbia and Montenegro is: *What impact do you expect EU accession to have on the structure, (rules of) procedure and practice (including workload) of the national courts?* In our particular case, the question should be re-phrased by replacing the word "accession" with "association".

The association process would have to introduce different rules in this area, too. Just like other institutional changes, these new rules should be introduced alongside with and, in a way, outside the existing constitutional and legal framework, but not necessarily contrary to it. Within the court system, it is essential that the Court of Serbia and Montenegro is able to develop independent case law. In the application of national and international law, its rulings would have to be based on the creative interpretation of positive law, general rules of international law, and the principles developed by the European Court of Justice. These decisions would have to form legitimate sources of national law, equal in rank to the Constitution and national legislation. This practice would give the Court the required judicial authority; an authority that would be supported by the European institutions. The existing network of courts in the Member States would gradually have to adapt to this independent court practice.

The entire process might begin, and even gain decisive importance, with the active use by the Court of Serbia and Montenegro of its constitutional competence. The Court is authorized to issue legal opinions for the purpose of promoting the uniform application of the Constitutional Charter, ratified international treaties and agreements, generally accepted rules of international law and of the laws and generally binding regulations of Serbia and Montenegro by the courts.[28] By actively advocating its standpoints, the Court should develop these opinions into generally binding decisions for the unification of court practice in the Member States. One this practice becomes commonly and habitually accepted, the citizens and legal persons of Serbia and Montenegro will gain access to better protection of their rights and the possibility of gradual harmonization of the national legal order with that of the European Union. This institutional adaptation would also have a positive impact on the reform of the rest of the institutional system of the state union.

---

27 As a matter of fact the Court of Serbia and Montenegro was established as late as June 2004 through the Assembly's election of the last judge. Hence, it is still not possible to examine the Court's practice as so far it has not heard a single case. This is why it is not possible to provide an answer to question No. 4.

28 This competence of the Court of Serbia and Montenegro is based on Art. 46, para. 2, of the Constitutional Charter, and has been elaborated in terms of procedure by Article 103 of the Law on the Court of Serbia and Montenegro.

2.1 Relationship between international and domestic law[29]

Where the enforcement of international law in domestic courts is concerned, the responsibility rests solely on the courts of the Member States of the state union. In this sense, we should use the term "enforcement" rather than direct applicability or direct effect, because of the nature of various international legal acts that are not self-executable and require the enactment of domestic laws. It is necessary to look at the issue of reliance on provisions of international law in order to assess the potential of Serbia-Montenegrin courts to apply Community law in the hopefully near rather than distant future. Although the factual obstacles are various, it can safely be said that there are no legal obstacles in that sense. There are no procedural rules providing criteria for dealing with domestic cases under international law, regardless of their nature and scope, and regardless of whether the case is being heard by a lower courts (such as a municipal or district court) or by the Supreme or Constitutional Court.

Bearing in mind that Serbia and Montenegro takes the monistic approach to the relationship between international and domestic law, we could say that it is up to the parties rather than to the courts to invoke provisions of ratified international legal instruments for the protection of individual rights. However, the practice is such that parties very rarely invoke such provisions, although there have been some encouraging signs in that direction lately.

Ever since the democratic changes of 2000, the Supreme Court of Serbia has been very receptive to the direct application of international conventions such as the International Convention on the Elimination of All Forms of Racial Discrimination and the International Covenant on Civil and Political Rights.[30]

The Supreme Court has held that "the protection of fundamental human rights is constitutionally guaranteed and is subject to judicial review."

Given that ratified international conventions are part of the internal legal system, the Supreme Court has on occasion directly applied Article 5 of the Convention on the Elimination of All Forms of Racial Discrimination, as well as Article 26 of the International Covenant on Civil and Political Rights. In it s judgment the Court has also held that the actions of the accused amounted to a violation of domestic law as well as ratified international legal instruments without distinguishing between the two, as both were part of the domestic legal system.

---

[29] We are grateful to Mr. Vladimir Todoric (Head of Unit, Office for European Integration of Serbia) for his contribution to this section.

[30] Judgment of the Supreme Court of Serbia Rev. 229/04 from 21 April 2004. In this case, three Roma were barred from the Sabac municipal swimming pool purely on the basis of their ethnic origin.

The Constitutional Court of Serbia regularly uses international legal instruments and applies the principles of international law in the course of interpreting the Constitution. For example, in a decision of 13 February 2003,[31] the Constitutional Court declared the national Judiciary Act void and unconstitutional by applying the provisions of the 1998 European Charter on the Statute for Judges and also has taken into account the 1985 UN Basic Principles on the Independence of the Judiciary.

Similarly, the Law on Aid to the Hague Indictees was declared unconstitutional on the basis of anti-discrimination provisions under the International Covenant on Civil and Political Rights.[32]

The factual obstacles to the application of domestic law in conformity with ratified international conventions are of a systematic nature. In this sense what is needed is the further education of judges, the elimination of certain problematic domestic provisions[33] and progressive legislative action.

Although the Serbian Constitution does not provide for the possibility of transfer of sovereign competences and is silent on the issue of joining international organizations,[34] we may still maintain that international law has primacy over domestic law. This is the case because constitutional law[35] so provides, and not because of the nature of any specific international legal regime. This is an important point to keep in mind when assessing future relations between Serbia-Montenegrin and Community law in terms of the primacy of the *acquis communautaire.* However, many issues in this respect will have to be re-evaluated after the constitutional changes in both the EU and Serbia Montenegro have taken effect.

3. ROLE OF THE EXECUTIVE (GOVERNMENT AND ADMINISTRATION)

3.1 Stabilization and Association Agreement

When it comes to the role of the executive of Serbia and Montenegro in the Stabilization and Association Process, there are two important facts worth noting:

1. As a union of states, that is, a state union, Serbia and Montenegro has a complex administrative structure;

---

31 Case IU 122/2002.

32 IU 152/2004.

33 For example, as a result of obligations following from Council of Europe membership, slander and defamation may no longer be prosecuted as crimes.

34 Although we do not consider the European Communities an international organization in the context of international law.

35 In this case the Constitutional Charter of Serbia and Montenegro, Art. 17.

2. Serbia and Montenegro has yet to conclude the Stabilization and Association Agreement (SAA) with the European Union. On the other hand, the country has been involved in the Stabilization and Association Process (SAP) for three years already, which includes certain institutional aspects that pave the way towards negotiations on the SAA itself.[36]

3.1.1 *Government and administration*

Serbia and Montenegro is a highly decentralized state union composed of two republics – the Republic of Serbia and the Republic of Montenegro. One of the goals of the state union, as provided expressly by Article 3 of the Constitutional Charter, is to "integrate with European structures, the European Union in particular," and to "harmonize national regulations and practices with European and international standards."

The Constitutional Charter also provides for the Office of President of Serbia and Montenegro and the Council of Ministers. Among other things, the President of Serbia and Montenegro represents the country at home and abroad, chairs the Council of Ministers and administers its work. The President also proposes to the Parliament of Serbia and Montenegro nominees for the Council of Ministers and relief of duty of its members (Art. 26 of the Constitutional Charter). In other words, the President of Serbia and Montenegro acts in the simultaneous capacity of head of state and head of government (prime-minister).

The Council of Ministers charts and pursues the policy of Serbia and Montenegro, coordinates the work of the Ministries and proposes to the Parliament of Serbia and Montenegro laws and regulations. Besides the President of Serbia and Montenegro, who chairs the Council, the Council has a further five members who are the Ministers of foreign affairs, defence, international economic relations, internal economic relations and human and minority rights.

The Constitutional Charter explicitly provides that "the Minister for International Economic Relations shall negotiate and coordinate the implementation of international treaties, including contractual relations with the European Union … following consultations with the competent Ministries of the Member States." (Art. 43) This article implies that the Minister has a duty to consult with representatives of the Member States when it comes to the development of relations with the European Union. Apart from this particular Minister, the Ministers in charge of foreign affairs and internal economic relations have been given a more or less

---

[36] Like on other topics of reform, short- and mid-term priorities are listed in the European Partnership with Serbia and Montenegro. See Council Regulation (EC) No. 533/2004 on the establishment of European Partnerships in the framework of the SAP, *OJ* 2004 L 86/1 and Council Decision 2004/520/EC on the principles, priorities and conditions contained in the European Partnerships with Serbia and Montenegro, *OJ* 2004 L 227/21.

direct obligation to address issues in connection with the promotion of cooperation with the European Union.

The Office of Serbia and Montenegro for Association with the European Union was established within the General Secretariat of the Council of Ministers. Article 17 of the Decree on the Internal Structure of Ministries, Organizations and Services of the Council of Ministers authorizes the Office to:

- follow, collect and provide information on EU regulations,
- monitor the implementation of reform in the association process,
- monitor the implementation of the EU financial aid programmes,
- coordinate the preparation and signing of the Stabilization and Association Agreement.[37]

Bearing in mind that most of the state union's institutions have been formed only recently, the allocation of competences in the field of international relations to the different Ministries has not yet been precisely defined, nor have the individual bodies responsible for cooperation with the Union been given a clear-cut mandate yet. For instance, the distribution of competences between the Ministry of Foreign Affairs, the Ministry of International Economic Relations and the Office for Association with the European Union is not as straightforward as it could have been.

Cooperation with the European Union, and the harmonization of certain regulations in particular, falls within the competence of not only the Ministries, but also of other bodies of the state union, especially those whose operations are closely linked with customs and trade policies and the functioning of the market, such as the Standardization Office, the Accreditation Office, the Office for Intellectual Property, the Statistics Office, and so forth. It is noteworthy that the Law for Implementation of the Constitutional Charter of the State Union of Serbia and Montenegro has failed to define conclusively the position of these former federal bodies.[38] Instead, they are to "continue to perform their duties" until their final status is prescribed (Art. 15). On the other hand, some important administrative bodies, such as the Federal Customs Administrations, sanitary, veterinarian and phyto-sanitary inspectorates, the central bank, a foreign exchange inspectorate, and so forth, have become institutions of the Republic of Serbia.

It should be pointed out that the adoption of the Constitutional Charter was followed up by an Action Plan for harmonization of the economic systems of Serbia and Montenegro (see below).

---

37 Official Gazette of Serbia and Montenegro No. 25 of 13 June 2003.

38 Official Gazette of Serbia and Montenegro No. 1 of 4 February 2003.

A number of bodies and organs to coordinate cooperation with the European Union were also formed in the individual Member States, Serbia and Montenegro. Their activities are also described here, given the structure of the state union and the fact that their independent powers have been stipulated on the level of the Member States.

The Ministry for Economic Relations with Foreign Countries was established within the Government of the Republic of Serbia. The responsibilities of the Ministry are, *inter alia*, to "devise a strategy for, coordinate and monitor the EU accession process."

The Department for European Integration (DEI) was first established within the Ministry for Economic Relations with Foreign Countries. The DEI was the central department of the Government of the Republic of Serbia concerning the coordination and monitoring of and reporting on activities related to the accession process, and a main driving force in areas such as studies and analyses, training, the organization of information flows, translations, and so forth.

The changes in the Serbian Government at the beginning of 2004 have brought into existence the *European Integration Office*.[39] The Office continues the work of the former European Integration Department of the Serbian Ministry for International Economic Relations. The establishment of the Office is yet another sign of the determination of this Government to speed up the preparations for EU integration. It was also established out of a need for a strong authority, tasked with the coordination of the association process on the principles of efficiency and low operating costs.

The main tasks of the Office are the following: coordinating, initiating, monitoring and reporting on the process of harmonization of Serbian legislation with the EU regulations; planning, monitoring and promotion of institutional capacities of the Republic of Serbia starting from the needs resulting from the EU association in cooperation with the relevant public administration bodies and organizations; coordination of the training process for civil servants on EU matters, and initiating, coordinating and monitoring public relations and promotion of activities relating to the EU association process. In addition to this, the Office provides technical support and organizes meetings of the Serbian Council for European Integration, manages the work of the Committee for the Coordination of the EU Association Process, liaises with the Office for European Integration of Serbia and Montenegro and corresponding institutions in Montenegro, and provides logistical support to the EI Committee of the Serbian Parliament.

---

[39] Decision of the Government of the Republic of Serbia of 8 March 2004, published in the Official Journal No. 25/04.

In Montenegro, a Ministry for Economic Relations with Foreign Countries and European Integration was formed to coordinate cooperation with the European Union and maintain contacts with central organs in charge of relations with the Union. The Ministry's responsibilities include:

- To coordinate all activities and cooperation with EU institutions at all levels, particularly with regard to the harmonization of the legislation with the regulations and standards of the EU, and to coordinate all activities relating to the Stabilization and Association process; and
- To cooperate with other regional and international economic organizations, institutions and initiatives.

In respect of the negotiations with the European Union and the future accession processes, it is important to note that the state union of Serbia and Montenegro is very specific insofar as it possesses almost no original and exclusive powers in economic matters, including customs and the free movement of goods, services, capital and labour. Article 12 of the Constitutional Charter stipulates that Serbia and Montenegro "shall have a single market," while Article 13 calls for "the free movement of people, goods, services and capital."

To this end, the Governments of Serbia and Montenegro in July 2003 adopted the "Action Plan for Harmonization of the Economic Systems of the Member States of the State Union of Serbia and Montenegro."[40] The Parliament of Serbia and Montenegro ratified the document at the end of August 2003. The Action Plan provides for harmonization in the areas of the "four freedoms" (free movement of people, goods, services and capital). In the context of the capacity of the state union to conclude agreements and negotiate with the European Union, the most important and the most delicate part of the Action Plan is that related to the free movement of goods. It is important to stress that the customs union of Serbia and Montenegro has not yet been completed and that customs rates for certain products and services will be harmonized within 18 to 24 months (after the adoption of the Action Plan), while for certain agricultural products full harmonization is to be expected in three to five years.

As a direct consequence of the Action Plan, several new joint bodies have been formed at the level of the state union. They include the Office of Serbian and Montenegrin Customs Administration and the Office for Veterinary and Phytosanitary controls. A competition authority has also been proposed.

The European Commission, which after the adoption of the Action Plan (July-August 2003) announced a feasibility study for talks on a Stabilization and Association Agreement between the European Union and Serbia and Montenegro,

---

40 Available at: <http://www.seio.sr.gov.yu/code/navigate.asp?Id=20>.

has already objected to certain deviations from the original aims of Action Plan. The Commission insisted on effective implementation of the plan, particularly in the establishment and effective operation of joint working bodies in charge of trade policy measures (such as a joint customs office, a joint office for veterinary and phyto-sanitary inspection, different inspectorates, etc.).

3.1.2 *Institutional relations and harmonization*

As for institutional relations with the European Union and harmonization with EU rules, two instruments have been applied ahead of the SAA. The so-called Consultative Task Force was formed in July 2001 by the FRY government administration and the EU Commission. The Consultative Task Force consisted of representatives of the Federal Government and its bodies, representatives of the administrations of the Republics of Serbia and Montenegro and UNMIK delegates on behalf of Kosovo on the one hand, and representatives of the EU Commission and EU Member States, acting on behalf of the European Union, on the other. This was a flexible institutional link between the Union and the then Federal Republic of Yugoslavia that allowed for the process of adaptation to begin even before formal talks on the conclusion of a Stabilization and Association Agreement. The ultimate goal of the task force was to open the process of consultation and adaptation of the system of Serbia and Montenegro to the Union's. The Consultative Task Force met five times from July 2001 to July 2002. At each meeting "Joint Recommendations" were adopted as instructions for the further steps in the reform of the Serbian and Montenegrin national system, or more precisely, in its adaptation to the EU rules.

The Consultative Task Force discussed the following matters:

- Permanent topics: democratization, respect for human and minority rights, the rule of law, economic reform and the fulfilment of international obligations;
- The 1st meeting (July 2001) – banking, trade, statistics, fiscal policy;
- The 2nd meeting (November 2001) – transportation, energy, telecommunications, customs, judiciary and internal affairs;
- The 3rd meeting (February 2002) – industry, competition, companies, intellectual property, social policy and employment;
- The 4th meeting (May 2002) – the "four freedoms" (free movement of goods, capital, labour and services);
- The 5th meeting (July 2002) – agriculture, veterinary and phyto-sanitary issues, the environment, fishery, consumer protection, audio-visual sectors, culture, education, research and development.

During the preparations for the transformation of the then Federal Republic of Yugoslavia into the state union of Serbia and Montenegro, the meetings of the Consultative Task Force were suspended.

After a one-year break, when the bodies of the state union were finally in place, a similar body was established – the *Enhanced Permanent Dialogue*. So far sessions of this technical working group have focused on political conditionality, justice and home affairs, economic and structural issues, especially the establishment of a single market, and infrastructure issues. The EPD now serves as a useful tool to monitor and deepen sectoral reforms in an EU integration context.

The EU Commission introduced a special communication mechanism for Kosovo entitled "SAP Tracking Mechanism for Kosovo" that does not include Belgrade representatives.

The second instrument providing support to the process of reform and harmonization in Serbia were the Reports on the Stabilization and Association Process, which the EU Commission submits every year. The reports cover each and every state of the Western Balkans, offering recommendations for individual areas and sectors of importance for the development of cooperation and association with the European Union. Accordingly, these reports offer non-compulsory instructions and benchmarks for the countries that have entered the Stabilization and Association Process.

The first report by the EU Commission on the Federal Republic of Yugoslavia covered the political and economic situation in the country and the development of the SAP process.[41] Each chapter offered recommendations for "priority areas" that should be focused on in the next twelve months – twelve recommendations for political reform and democratization, four recommendations for economic reform and twenty-one recommendations for sectoral harmonization in the context of stabilization and association.

The Commission's second report on Serbia and Montenegro was structured in much the same manner. Twenty-three recommendations were given for political reform (including the situation in Kosovo), seven for economic reform and thirty-one for sectoral reforms in the SAP process.

The inescapable conclusion is that the number of recommendations grew between the two reports.

In a chapter on Kosovo, the Commission pointed to a much-needed reform of the local judiciary, also advocating a better position of minorities, the use of minority languages in local areas and intensification of the efforts aimed at the return of displaced persons.

As part of the Stabilization and Association Process, the institutions of Serbia and Montenegro have drafted documents on the condition of legal institutions,

41 COM 2002 163.

which form the "input" for the EU Commission reports. These documents were prepared by the Office for EU Accession at the Council of Ministers. After a description of the institution-building process, Serbia and Montenegro emphasized in its reports the promulgation and implementation of the Constitutional Charter, which was adopted together with the Charter of Human and Minority Rights and Civil Liberties, the country's accession to the Council of Europe (April 2003), a reform in the defence sector and the reform of the judiciary, home affairs and the media. Serbia and Montenegro also adopted a Law on the Protection of Rights and Freedoms of National Minorities.

A very significant step in the process of further integration of Serbia and Montenegro in the EU was taken in the aftermath of the EU-Western Balkans Thessaloniki Summit, organized in June 2003 and in the context of the Third Annual Report on Stabilization and Association for 2004. In the Thessaloniki Agenda, it was concluded that the "*European Partnerships will be established for each of the SAP countries, inspired by the Accession Partnerships for candidate countries, and adapted to the specificities of the SAP. These Partnerships ... will identify priorities for action in supporting efforts to move closer to the EU*". On 14 June 2004, the EU Council adopted a Decision on the "principles, priorities and conditions contained in the European partnership with Serbia and Montenegro, including Kosovo as defined by UN SC Res. 1244 of 10 June 1999".[42] The European Partnership includes some 60 short-term and 45 medium-term priorities for Serbia and Montenegro. They include political conditions (democracy and rule of law, human rights and regional cooperation), economic conditions and EU standards.

Following the adoption of the European Partnership by the EU Council of Ministers, Serbia and Montenegro implemented the document in the Action Plan on implementation of the European Partnership.[43]

The new Serbian Government has reaffirmed the importance of the partnership with the EU as a strategic priority. Work on the implementation of the *European Partnership* began before it was formally adopted by the EU Council. First, a concise version of the Action Plan on the Implementation of the European Partnership was drawn up and adopted by the Government of the Republic of Serbia in April 2004. The Action Plan identifies and lists the required actions, the institutions responsible for implementation and the person(s) responsible for the drafting of the necessary laws and includes a time frame for implementation. Up to June 2004, nine draft laws were adopted by the Government and four out of these nine have already been passed by the National Assembly of the Republic of Serbia.

---

42 See *supra* n. 36.

43 Available at: <http://www.seio.sr.gov.yu/code/navigate.asp?Id=20>.

In the meantime, the Action Plan was reviewed through inter-ministerial coordination, as well as through meetings with Montenegrin authorities as regards some outstanding issues related to the Plan for the Harmonization of the Internal Market.

The Government of Serbia adopted a separate *Action Plan on Legislative Alignment* that lists 52 laws in the area covered by the *EU White Paper* that needed to be passed by the end of 2004. The Action Plan takes the form of a matrix schedule which lists the following: reason for legal action, responsible Ministries, framework deadlines for completion of the task; person(s) directly responsible for drafting the particular legislation. *The Action Plan marks the beginning of organized harmonization of legislation in Serbia with the acquis.*

Within the framework of communication concerning the SAP, together with the representatives of the EU Member States and the representatives of the European Commission Delegation in Serbia and Montenegro, the Serbian Government has launched a broad communication campaign in order to introduce the European Partnership to the various segments of society (NGOs, representatives of local self-government, representatives of the business community and the media). Activities mentioned above will ensure the "ownership" of all relevant stakeholders in order to achieve the best possible result of the European Partnership.

3.1.3 *Fulfilment of the political criteria of Copenhagen/Thessaloniki*

Major political criteria mentioned in the European Partnership for Serbia and Montenegro concern constitutional issues (see parts 1 and 2 above), army reform, public administration reform, judicial reform, property rights, the question of refugees, and Council of Europe obligations (including the introduction of an Ombudsman).

In the first year of its membership of the Council of Europe, Serbia and Montenegro managed to honour the majority of its commitments due to a general political consensus towards reforms. This positive and irreversible trend has continued following the Serbian parliamentary elections of 28 December 2003 and the confirmation of the mandates of the newly elected members. Already during the first session of the Assembly of Serbia, a number of legislative changes were adopted, thus harmonizing the existing legislation with the Council of Europe standards, most notably in terms of electoral law and voting procedures. A further 46 draft laws are in parliamentary procedure and are about to be subjected to parliamentary scrutiny in due course. The pending adoption of these laws will further contribute to a system of capacity building that will facilitate the efforts of the country on its path to Europe.

Serbia and Montenegro has ratified the European Convention on Human Rights and the European Convention for the Prevention of Torture and Inhuman or Degrading Treatment or Punishment, both as amended by the Protocols. The process of accession has been completed by the act of depositing the ratification instruments with the Council of Europe Secretary General, on 3 March 2004. The implementation of these two Conventions will bring a significant advance in respect of human rights and will present a challenge on a society-wide scale.

Major steps have also been undertaken in the fields of army reform, electoral reform in Serbia and judicial reform. However, Serbia and Montenegro was still facing difficulties in the middle of 2004 in achieving full cooperation with the International Criminal Tribunal in The Hague, which has had some consequences for the process of cooperation with the EU. After intense pressure from the EU's High Representative for Common Foreign and Security Policy and the Commission to extradite alleged war criminals in order to finalize the feasibility report in April 2005, serious headway was made with the arrest, in the first three months of 2005, of half a dozen suspects.

3.2 Preparation and implementation of EC/EU law

Apart from the administrative bodies listed above, the Council for European Integration was established at the state union level as a coordinating body. In principle, the Council's main role is political coordination covering the European integration process at all levels. It is to identify any incompatibility or incoherence that may arise in the operations of the state union and the republics alike. The Council consists of the President of Serbia and Montenegro, the Minister of Foreign Affairs and the Minister for Economic Relations with Foreign Countries of Serbia and Montenegro, the Serbian and Montenegrin Prime Ministers and four Ministers appointed by the Member States (two each).

In July 2002, the Republic of Serbia established the Council for European Integration.[44] The Prime Minister of Serbia is also ex officio the chair of the Council. The other members of the Council are the Deputy Prime Minister, the Government's Secretary-General and Ministers expected to take the most active role in the EU accession process. The Council offers strategic guidelines and political support to the process.

In addition to the Council, the Government of the Republic of Serbia on 17 October 2002 established the Commission for the Coordination of EU Accession. The Commission is chaired by the head of the Sector for European Integration. Members of the Commission are representatives of all relevant Ministries of the Government of the Republic of Serbia (Ministers, their deputies or, usually, their

---

44 Official Gazette of the Republic of Serbia No. 14/2002.

assistants). The Commission proposes measures for developing cooperation between republican bodies. This cooperation is to take place in organizations in charge of endorsing and implementing strategies that are of relevance to the EU accession process. The Commission also identifies the priorities in the process, as well as the best ways for harmonizing local regulations with EU standards. It also supervises the implementation of measures it has suggested. In other words, the Commission is an operative inter-Ministerial body that implements elementary instructions agreed upon by the Council for European Integration. The Serbian Government adopted a Conclusion in which it stated that each relevant Ministry should establish a special section for European integration. The process is under way.

The Republic of Montenegro has formed a similar structure to realize the policy of integration with Europe. Yet Montenegro has a smaller administration and fewer Ministries, which means that the Government, i.e., a competent Ministry, can act as coordinating body. The Montenegrin Government implements the activities for the purpose of the European integration process through the Ministry for International Economic Relations and European Integration (MIEREI) and the new Commission for the Coordination of the Process of Accession to the EU. The Department for European Integration within the Ministry is an organizational unit that is responsible for coordinating activities and preparing different strategic documents, especially the plan of harmonization of Montenegrin legislation with the *acquis*; the communication strategy; a document on training, information and documentation intended to elaborate and implement the strategy, planning, organization and coordination of the training programme; and the advanced training of personnel concerning the various aspects of the European integration process.

3.3 Impact of EU accession/association on the organization and practice of (a) central government and administration and (b) the decentralized authorities

A relatively small staff deals with the process of integration into the European Union in the administration of the state union and the two republics alike. It is beyond doubt that the further association process, including the negotiations with the Union, will emphasize the need for re-allocation of staff in the administration at large. As to the Serbian administration, all Ministries should establish their own respective "units for European integration", each employing a staff of ten. Presently, the number of Government employees in charge of EU integration issues is about 50. At the level of the state union, this number is around 40. The Montenegrin administration has some ten people dealing with EU accession. There is no doubt that these figures will go up in the months and years to come.

One of the fundamental long-term questions is the training and education of civil servants, including a proper personnel policy and a system of incentives for young, educated civil servants. Neither Serbia nor Montenegro handled these issues properly in the past.

Tangible procedures for cooperation with the European Union are bound to increase the responsiveness of the administration to the harmonization of national legislation with the Union's. Only a few steps have been made in that direction so far. For instance, the Government of the Republic of Serbia has already prepared amendments to its Rules of Procedure which imply the obligation of taking into account EU regulations when submitting draft laws for adoption (termed the Statement of Harmonization). The Statement is made by the administrative organ that was in charge of drafting the law or regulations in question assessing the level of harmonization of the draft rules with EU rules.

As part of the Stabilization and Association Process, a technical mechanism has been established to monitor the development of the legislative reform (the matrix schedule referred to above which offers an overview of the condition of the legislation).

The Republic of Serbia has also adopted a special Action Plan for Harmonization of Laws of the Republic of Serbia with EU law.[45] Even though Serbia and Montenegro does not have a legal obligation towards the European Union to harmonize local regulations with EU rules (as the relevant bilateral agreement has not yet been concluded), the desire for speedy integration in the Union also implies speedy legal harmonization. The Action Plan of the Republic of Serbia (which is not directly connected with the Action Plan for the Harmonization of the Economic Systems of Serbia and Montenegro) calls for fast-tracked adoption or amendment of 50 priority laws in the spheres falling within the competence of the republic. It has also specified deadlines, institutions and persons in charge of the realization of the Plan. These laws largely cover the sector of economy, that is, the EU internal market (investment funds, companies, anti-monopoly regulations, foreign trade, occupational safety, agriculture, veterinary service, fishery, phyto-sanitary protection, railways, postal service, road and air transportation, broadcasting, value added tax, consumer protection, environmental protection, data protection, insurance, bankruptcy proceedings, accountancy, contracts and torts, energy, etc.).

3.3.1 *Reform of the administration*

In order to initiate the process of public administration reform, the Serbian Government formed a Council for Public Administration Reform as its representative

[45] Decision by the Government of the Republic of Serbia of 31 July 2003.

advisory body. The Council (whose members are the Prime Minister, Deputy Prime Minister and all the Ministers involved in the process of public sector reform) has been set the task of establishing a Public Administration Reform Strategy. The strategy will form the basis for numerous laws necessary for the reform. It will cover all the relevant aspects of the reform, ensuring efficiency, openness, coherence, professionalism and administrative impartiality. Special attention will be paid to the mechanisms controlling administration and its relation with the citizens. The modernization and rationalization of working processes within the administration and the use of new technologies will be among the main objectives.

In the Republic of Serbia a Public Administration Reform Strategy was prepared in cooperation with international donors. The Strategy includes a precise schedule of activities (Action Plan). Furthermore, in cooperation with the World Bank, a major project is being realized towards the reform of the civil service salary system.

The reform is being carried out by the Ministry which is responsible for public administration matters.

In accordance with the basic principles included in the Public Administration Reform Strategy, preparations have begun for a Law on Government and a Law on Public Administration.

In March 2003, the Government of the Republic of Montenegro adopted the Public Administration Reform Strategy for Montenegro 2002-2009. The Strategy establishes the basic policy direction, overriding objectives, and measures in the reform process in areas that include state administration, local self-government and public services, and concerning functional elements of the administrative system, such as legal protection of citizens in their relations with the administration.

According to the Strategy, there are two basic reasons for administrative reform in Montenegro:

- To increase internal efficiency in the functioning of the state administration system; and
- To provide external stimulation and impetus for change in the administration for the purpose of its inclusion into broader social and socio-political systems.

The introduction of changes into the administrative system of Montenegro is a complex process and may best be regarded as a road to be travelled rather than a destination. We are of the opinion that the changes should not be too comprehensive and too radical, but also that they should not only be of a cosmetic and superficial nature. Basic activities relate to:

- the harmonization of current regulations and the adoption of new ones;
- the introduction of new functions;
- the reorganization or change of the overall administrative system's organizational structure, which also means "institutionalization" and abolition of unnecessary administrative institutions and establishment of new ones; and
- the training and advanced training of civil servants and of all public employees regarding the new way in which the administrative system is to function.

4. ROLE OF THE LEGISLATIVE (PARLIAMENT)

As in the case of the executive, the national legislative is also of a highly specific nature as a result of the special structure of the state union. Among other things, the Parliament of Serbia and Montenegro "shall decide on membership of international organizations and the rights and duties arising from that membership, with the prior consent of the competent bodies of the Member States," according to Article 19, fifth sentence, of the Constitutional Charter. However, when it comes to the ratification of international treaties, the Constitutional Charter does not prescribe such prior approval by the Member States.

The unicameral Parliament of Serbia and Montenegro is made up of 126 deputies – 91 from Serbia and 35 from Montenegro. According to Article 20 of the Constitutional Charter, Members of Parliament are elected by the Assemblies of Serbia and Montenegro in the first two years following the promulgation of the Charter and by direct vote afterwards.

It is noteworthy that the former FRY Parliament had established a special committee on European Integration which had several meetings. Formal cooperation was established between Serbia and Montenegro and the European Parliament, whose representatives met a few times.

One of the committees established within the Parliament of Serbia and Montenegro is the European Integration Committee. This Committee considers proposed legislation in the area of political relations and cooperation with the European institutions. It deals with questions related to the monitoring of the implementation of programmes and the dynamic of the cooperation. It also considers the compatibility of proposed legislation in Serbia and Montenegro with European rules, and controls the work of the Council of Ministers in these issues. The European Integration Committee is chaired by the President and has 13 members.

There is also a non-governmental initiative that the three parliaments operating in Serbia and Montenegro should adopt a special declaration on the goals of the European integration process, which would reflect a broader political and social consensus to support the national strategy for joining the European Union.

The Assemblies of the Republic of Serbia and the Republic of Montenegro have also established special committees for the purpose of European integration.

In May 2003, a Committee for European Integration was established in the National Assembly of the Republic of Serbia. Among its first activities was the adoption of a draft Resolution on European integration for discussion and adoption by Parliament.

On 21 October 2003, during its first meeting of the second ordinary session, the Parliament of Montenegro decided to establish a Committee for European integration for the purpose of strengthening the parliamentary dimension of the European integration process. The Committee was established as a working group of the Parliament of the Republic of Montenegro and is composed of the President and twelve members. The Committee for European Integrations monitors the legislative activities which are the result of the obligations assumed after the accession of Serbia and Montenegro to the Council of Europe of the need to harmonize legislation with EU rules, mainly the forthcoming Stabilization and Association Process.

5. EUROPEAN CONSTITUTION

5.1 Impact of the EU Constitution on the Community legal order and accession

We consider the Treaty establishing a Constitution for Europe (TCE) as a positive step in the process of European integration. It is intended to strengthen and clarify the present EU legal system. However, it is not impossible that the adoption and implementation of the TCE will provide grounds for the additional mobilization of "euro-sceptics". Once adopted, the TCE will represent a turning point in the development of EU law, as a new set of legal instruments will emerge (i.e., European laws, etc.), while some of the basic principles of EC law now contained in the case law of the European Court of Justice will become part of Treaty/Constitutional provisions.

However, the new system will probably further complicate the understanding and introduction of EU law for the administrations of candidate and pre-accession countries, if there will in fact be two parallel legal systems (the "old" and the "new") allowing for nuances and possible exceptions for some Member States in some sectors. In addition, the increase in the number of Member States (25 with a possibility of 27 or 28 in the near future) will complicate the overall system, especially where the decision-making procedure is concerned. We may therefore expect that the process of future EU enlargements will be anything but simple. It will probably be even more complicated than the last enlargement, both from the point of view of procedure as well as in view of the *acquis* which will be imposed on new applicant countries.

5.2 Obstacles to ratification

From the point of view of the Constitutional Charter as such there are no obstacles for ratification of the EU Constitution. The problem lies, however, in the national legal order, which is completely unprepared for the association and accession process. Unlike conventional legal orders, the Serbian Montenegrin legal order lacks internal legal unification and a hierarchy now that it consists of two mutually independent legal systems, which should be harmonized through the activity of their common legal instruments and institutions. This complicated legal construction would not be capable of adopting and implementing legal obligations arising under EU legislation or from ECJ case law.

Generally speaking three scenarios are conceivable for adjusting the present national legal order to EU law: 1) The system might be simplified into some form of federal legal order with the accompanying harmonized two-level legal system with both levels retaining internal autonomy; 2) The system might be dissolved into two individual and independent legal orders, which would separately adjust to EU law; 3) The EU might develop a special legal approach to the specific legal order of Serbia and Montenegro whereby it respects its untypical construction at least during the period of association.

We expect that future developments will lead in the direction of the first or second option once Serbia and Montenegro is ready to be included in the process of European integration.

SLOVENIA

Miha Pogačnik*, Marko Starman and Primož Vehar*****

1. THE CONSTITUTION OF THE REPUBLIC OF SLOVENIA[1]

1.1 Implementation of international law and transfer of legislative powers

The Constitution of the Republic of Slovenia was enacted by the National Assembly on 23 December 1991 and entered into force the same day. Since its adoption three amendments have been made regarding: (1) ownership rights of foreigners[2] in July 1997, (2) elections to the National Assembly[3] in July 2000 and (3) the EU clause[4] in March 2003. Due to the first amendment in 1997, Slovenia was the only candidate country that allowed EU Member States citizens to obtain real estate before its accession into the EU. This amendment was needed to make ratification of the Europe Agreement,[5] especially its Annex XIII,[6] possible.

* Dr Miha Pogačnik, European Law Institute.

** Mag. Marko Starman, Ministry of Justice of the RS.

*** Primož Vehar, Dipl. iur., Adviser to the Government of the RS, Office for Legislation.

[1] Regarding the Constitution of the Republic of Slovenia and its relation towards the Europe Agreement and implementation of international law, see also P. Vehar, 'Constitutional Problems in the Period of Pre-Accession in the Republic of Slovenia', in A.E. Kellermann, J.W. de Zwaan and J. Czuczai, *EU Enlargement, The Constitutional Impact at EU and National Level* (The Hague, T.M.C. Asser Press 2001) pp. 369-374 and P. Vehar and T. Ilešič, 'International Agreements in the Legal Orders of the Candidate Countries – Slovenia', in A. Ott and K. Inglis, *Handbook on European Enlargement – A Commentary on the Enlargement Process* (The Hague, T.M.C. Asser Press 2002) pp. 331-339.

[2] The Constitution, Art. 68: "... Foreigners may not acquire title to land...", was amended to: "Foreigners may acquire ownership rights to real estate under conditions provided by law or if so provided by a treaty ratified by the National Assembly, under the condition of reciprocity. Such law and treaty from the preceding paragraph shall be adopted by the National Assembly by a two-thirds majority vote of all deputies."

[3] Amending Art. 80 concerning the election system.

[4] The new Art. 3a concerning the transfer of the exercise of part of Slovenian sovereign rights and the relation parliament – government in EU matters, amended Art. 47 regarding extradition of Slovene citizens and Art. 68 regarding ownership of real estate.

[5] Europe Agreement Establishing an Association between the European Communities and their Member States, acting within the framework of the European Union, of the one part, and the Republic of Slovenia, of the other part, signed on 10 June 1996, entered into force on 1 February 1999.

[6] In Annex XIII the Government committed itself to take the necessary measures to allow the citizens of the EU Member States, on a reciprocal and non-discriminatory basis, the right to purchase

In the relation between international law and internal law in Slovenia, where only the Constitution is hierarchically above ratified and promulgated international treaties, on the basis of the Constitution (Art. 8) international treaties have precedence over all legal acts adopted by the National Assembly.

The fact that an international treaty has been ratified and promulgated in the Official Gazette (Uradni list) and acquires the character of internal law[7] does not mean it also has a direct effect in the sense of establishing rights and obligations for subjects.[8] This effect belonging to the so-called "self executive treaties" could only be decided before the national court, as it is a question of internal law.

The Slovenian Constitution in its Article 8 states:

> Laws and regulations must comply with generally accepted principles of international law and with treaties that are binding on Slovenia. Ratified and promulgated treaties shall be applied directly.

Although the Constitution of the Republic of Slovenia does not directly deal with the question of the relation between international and internal law the authors are of the opinion that the dualist approach in its mild form prevails in the Slovenian constitutional system. Apart from purely personal arguments the Constitutional Court has also dealt with the question. The Court in its opinion which dealt with the conformity of the Europe Agreement provisions with the Constitution of the Republic of Slovenia,[9] concerning the relation between international law and internal law stated that:

> The fulfilment of an international agreement can be realized already by the fact that its provisions pass directly into internal legal system of the State at the time of the coming into force of such agreement. Such fulfilment takes place in the case if an international agreement has been ratified in accordance with the internal legal system of the Republic of Slovenia...

and also

---

property in Slovenia by the end of the fourth year from the entry into force of the Europe Agreement and to grant to the citizens of the EU Member States, having permanently resided on the present territory of the Republic of Slovenia for a period of three years, on a reciprocal basis the right to purchase property from the entry into force of the Europe Agreement.

7 The Constitution, Art. 8.

8 A Treaty provision: "... Slovenia shall endeavour to ensure that..." is, in the authors' opinion, an example of a non self-executive provision.

9 Opinion of the Constitutional Court of 5 June 1997, Case RM 1/97, Uradni list RS (Official Gazette) No. 40/97, para. 20, available at: <http://www.us-rs.si>.

> provisions of an international agreement are integrated in the internal legal order of the Republic of Slovenia with the coming into force of such agreement on condition that they have been ratified in accordance with the internal law of the Republic of Slovenia.

The Constitutional Court's decision is not perfectly clear. It might wrongly lead to an understanding that an international agreement becomes an integral part of Slovenian legal order and shall therefore bind individuals by its enforcement on the international level. It should be noted that this is only true when the agreement has been ratified (and published) beforehand.

In practice an Act of Parliament that is usually titled "act on ratification" would give internal effects to an international treaty by simply incorporating the full text of the treaty in one of the provisions of the Act. However, it is only after entry into force of this act that the international agreement becomes a part of internal legal order, providing that the agreement is already in force at the international level.

Some case law exists that unfortunately can not confirm either a monist or dualist perception of the relationship between the international and the Slovenian legal order. The Constitutional court has examined both perspectives,[10] but has not come to a determined conclusion. However, there are some facts that show characteristics of the dualist system which have been confirmed by some scholars.[11] It is rather difficult to justify a pure version of either of the two concepts. Nevertheless, according to commentators the difference between the monist and the dualist doctrine is less and less clear.

In the Slovenian constitutional system international treaties rank above statutory provisions in the hierarchy of legal acts. According to Article 8 of the Constitution, statutes and other legislative measures shall accord with international treaties that are binding on Slovenia. Laws must be in conformity with generally accepted principles of international law and with valid treaties ratified by parliament, whereas national regulations and other general legal acts must also be in conformity with other ratified treaties.[12]

---

10 Opinion of the Constitutional Court, Case RM 1/97, Case RM 1/99, available at: <http://www.us-rs.si>.

11 See M. Pogačnik, Validity of International Agreements in the Republic of Slovenia (Veljavnost mednarodnih pogodb v Republiki Sloveniji), Pravnik, Ljubljana, 6-8/1996, M. Pogačnik, Direct Applicability of International Treaties (Neposredna uporaba mednarodnih pogodb), Podjetje in delo, 6-7/2000, M. Ilešič, The Europe Agreement and its legal effects in the internal legal order (Pridružitveni sporazum in njegovi učinki v notranjem pravnem redu), Podjetje in delo, 8/1997.

12 Art. 153(2) of the Slovenian Constitution, also Decision of the Constitutional Court of 24 October 1996, No. U-I-103/95, para. 4, available at: <http://www.us-rs.si>.

The Law on Foreign Affairs[13] regulates this constitutional subject by its provision determining which Treaties are ratified by the National Assembly and which of them by the Government.

Article 75, paragraph 3 states: "International treaties are ratified by the National Assembly except treaties which the Government ratifies in accordance to paragraph 5 of that Article."

To ensure such conformity the Constitution provides for the jurisdiction of the Constitutional Court to decide upon the conformity of laws, regulations and bylaws with international treaties adopted by the State.

So, in the hierarchy of the legal acts in Slovenia, international treaties ratified by Parliament rank above all legislative acts except the Constitution or Constitutional laws so the Slovenian legal system does not recognise the primacy of international law over the constitutional provisions.[14]

To sum up, in the Slovenian constitutional order the Constitution is the highest legal act followed by international agreements ratified by parliament. Ratified and promulgated international agreements prevail over internal Slovenian laws.

In case of conflict between the Constitution and an international treaty it is the Constitutional Court of the Republic of Slovenia that is empowered to decide upon the conformity of an act of ratification[15] of an international agreement with the Constitution. Should the Constitutional Court in the process of such assessment find that a provision of an international treaty is in conflict with the constitutional provisions it may abrogate the act of ratification. However, such a decision of the Constitutional Court only has effect for the internal legal system and certainly not for the obligation of the State under international law. The aim is to prevent the conclusion of an international agreement that would, through ratification, introduce unconstitutional norms in the internal legal order.

Transfer of competencies to international organisations is now allowed due to the new Article 3a which in paragraph 1 states:

> Pursuant to a treaty ratified by the National Assembly by a two-thirds majority vote of all deputies, Slovenia may transfer the exercise of part of its sovereign rights to international organisations which are based on respect for human rights and fundamental freedoms, democracy and the principles of the rule of law and may enter into a defensive alliance with states which are based on respect for these values.

---

[13] Art. 75 of the Law on Foreign Affairs (ZZZ-1), Uradni list RS (Official Gazette) No. 45-2549/2001.

[14] See Decision of the Constitutional Court of the Republic of Slovenia of 30 November 1995, No. U-I-147/94, at para. 8, available at: <http://www.us-rs.si>.

[15] Art. 160(1) of the Constitution of the Republic of Slovenia.

1.2 Amendments

The accession to a supranational organisation was not admitted by Slovenian constitutional order until March 2003. This was due to the fact that the transfer of sovereign rights implied by an accession was not foreseen and not allowed by the Constitution.[16]

This situation was overcome by the amendment of the Constitution that was based on Article 3 and its provision that all powers are derived from the nation and are executed by the national institutions.

This was in opposition to the supranational character of EC Treaty where some legislative, executive and also judicial powers are given to EC institutions, and where a single Member State has no control over these powers. Due to the direct application (where it is possible) in the case of a conflict of legal norms, the national courts and other institutions, moreover, have to give precedence to EC law over the national constitution and of course, also over any other national legal norms. The principles of direct effect and primacy of Community law cannot be found in the Treaties. They were developed by ECJ judgements in the 1960s, formulating a part of Community law for all EU Member States.

These facts were and still are hardly understood and believed by many traditionally oriented lawyers and politicians who insist on the position that the Constitution is hierarchically the highest legal act and that all state authorities, no matter if they are from the legislative, executive or judicial branch, have to ensure this hierarchy and respect it.

The 2003 accession of Slovenia also showed some other constitutional aspects, apart from the hierarchy of legal acts and transfer of exercise of part of sovereign rights, especially in respect to the relation Government – Parliament in EU matters.

The Constitution was amended in March 2004 with a new Article 3a and amending Articles 47 and 68 and reads as follows:

Article 3a

Pursuant to a treaty ratified by the National Assembly by a two-thirds majority vote of all deputies, Slovenia may transfer the exercise of part of its sovereign rights to international organisations which are based on respect for human rights and fundamental freedoms, democracy and the principles of the rule of law and may enter into a defensive alliance with states which are based on respect for these values.

---

[16] The Constitution, Art. 3 para. (2): "In Slovenia supreme power is vested to the people. Citizens exercise that power directly at elections, and consistently with the principle of the separation of legislative, executive and judicial powers".

Before ratifying an international treaty referred to in the preceding paragraph, the National Assembly may call a referendum. A proposal shall pass at the referendum if a majority of voters who have cast valid votes vote in favour of such. The National Assembly is bound by the result of such referendum. If such referendum has been held, a referendum regarding the law on the ratification of the treaty concerned may not be called.

Legal acts and decisions adopted within international organisations to which Slovenia has transferred the exercise of part of its sovereign rights shall be applied in Slovenia in accordance with the legal regulation of these organisations.[17]

In procedures for the adoption of legal acts and decisions in international organisations to which Slovenia has transferred the exercise of part of its sovereign rights, the Government shall promptly inform the National Assembly of proposals for such acts and decisions as well as of its own activities. The National Assembly may adopt positions thereon, which the Government shall take into consideration in its activities. The relationship between the National Assembly and the Government arising from this paragraph shall be regulated in detail by a law adopted by a two-thirds majority vote of deputies present.

Article 47

No citizen of Slovenia may be extradited or surrendered unless such obligation to extradite or surrender arises from a treaty by which, in accordance with the provisions of the first paragraph of Article 3a, Slovenia has transferred the exercise of part of its sovereign rights to an international organisation.

Article 68

Aliens may acquire ownership rights to real estate under conditions provided by law or a treaty ratified by the National Assembly.

1.3 Provisions contrary to the *acquis communautaire*

Since March 2003 there are no constitution provisions contrary to the *acquis communautaire*.

[17] That is an exemption of principle on ratification of treaties and that is why the authors are of the opinion that such a provision should not be a part of Art 3a. It would be better if written into Art. 8 of the Constitution of the Republic of Slovenia, which the Government proposed from the very beginning.

1.4 Supremacy and direct effect

As stated above, in the hierarchy of legal acts in Slovenia, international treaties ratified by Parliament rank above all legislative acts except the Constitution or Constitutional laws, however, the Slovenian legal system does not recognise the primacy of international law over the constitutional provisions. The new provision of Article 3a, paragraph 3 states:

> Legal acts and decisions adopted within international organisations to which Slovenia has transferred the exercise of part of its sovereign rights shall be applied in Slovenia in accordance with the legal regulation of these organisations.

Thanks to that provision there is no doubt regarding the supremacy and direct effect of EU law.

1.5 Procedures to be followed to adapt to the *acquis communautaire*

The Procedure for amending the Constitution[18] consists of two stages and starts by a proposal by at least twenty deputies of the National Assembly, by the Government or by no less than thirty thousand voters. Such a proposal shall only be proceeded upon the vote of a two-third majority of the present deputies of the National Assembly.[19] The National Assembly may then enact an act to amend the Constitution upon the vote of a two-third majority of all elected deputies.

There is also a possibility for the people to take part in the amending procedure if such is demanded by no less than thirty of the National Assembly deputies. An amendment could then be adopted by referendum if a majority of all voters, eligible to vote, voted at the referendum and a majority of those who were voting, voted for the amendment.

There were some expectations that when amending the Constitution and transferring a part of sovereign rights, the confirmation of such a parliamentary decision would be requested by way of a referendum, however, there has only been a (successful) referendum on joining the EU.

Slovenia has already amended its Constitution including recognizing the supremacy of the EU legal order in the Republic of Slovenia as from May 2004, when it became one of the EU Member States. Constitutional amendment was of special importance not only because of the transfer of part of sovereign rights and

---

[18] The Constitution, Arts. 168-171.

[19] The National Assembly consists of ninety deputies.

the recognition of the supremacy of EU law, but also because of the settling the relation between Parliament and Government in EU matters.[20]

2. ROLE OF THE JUDICIARY

2.1 Europe Agreement or Stabilisation and Association Agreement; supremacy and direct effect; indirect effect; cases; impact of EU accession on structure, procedures and practice

There were few cases dealing with the legal issues brought to our legal system by the "European Association Agreement" (EAA). All of them were dealt with by the Constitutional Court. One was already mentioned: the ruling about the constitutionality of the EAA.[21] The opinion was delivered on the proposal of the Government in the process of ratification of the above-mentioned agreement. The opinion as the main issue deals with the constitutionality of the obligation adopted by law on ratification to change the Constitution in the period set up by the international agreement. The Constitutional Court stated in 1997 that such an obligation is unconstitutional. This issue is now a moot topic because the Constitution was later changed and more recently changed again.

What is even more interesting about the opinion is that the justices in their concurring opinions, even though it was not raised by the applicant, touched upon the concept of incorporation of the acquis in the field of antitrust law, even before full membership. In the obiter dicta, one of the judges stated that the EAA is transferring sovereignty from the Slovenian authorities by forcing the courts to apply the law and legal principles of the European Communities including case law of the ECJ. It goes on by saying that this would include the law adopted after the EAA entered into force. Such incorporation would in his opinion mean legally already being in the same position as Member States but only on the "passive side" and this would be unconstitutional. In legal theory this concept was shared and even advocated.[22] So far there is no case law of lower courts that applied EC law directly.

---

20 A constitutional provision regarding the role of the national parliament in EU matters can also be found in those of Germany, France, Austria, Sweden, Finland and Hungary.

21 Opinion of the Constitutional Court of 5 June 1997, Case RM 1/97, Uradni list RS (Official Gazette) No. 40/97, para. 20, available at: <http://www.us-rs.si>.

22 Pridružitveni sporazum in njegovi učinki v notranjepravnem redu; M. Ilešič, GV, 10 December 1997.

The Constitutional Court in a more recent opinion,[23] however, spoke about the nature of the obligations imposed by the EAA. The Central Bank asked the Constitutional Court to repeal some clauses of the "Law on saving scheme for houses", because it interferes with its duties to set up a monetary policy. One of the legal grounds stated by the applicant was the EAA which imposed the obligation to the authorities in Slovenia to align all its legislation and practices with EU law step by step but not later than by the time of accession. The applicant also held that the law was contrary to the acquis in this area. The Constitutional court brushed aside this argument by saying that the clause in the EAA is not of such a nature that it can produce direct effect.

The Constitutional court stops there, but we can argue *a contrario* that other clauses can have direct effect and produce rights for individuals before national courts.

During the pre-accession era the question of how full membership would affect the judicial system in Slovenia has often been raised. We have been experiencing some of these effects, but the majority of them can only be imagined with some difficulty. We will try to examine some of the effects that, in our opinion, will significantly determine the future of the third branch of power.

The indirect effects are those that might be referred to as "market" effects in the broader sense of the word, which will flood over both the "private sector", and to a certain degree the public institutional sector of the judiciary. By the private sector of the judiciary we primarily mean attorney and notary services. Competition will lead to changes in these professions, perhaps not immediately, but inevitably. Competition in the area of university law studies will also have an effect on the judiciary, and not least of all the adoption of the fundamental principle (under the new Constitution) of mutual recognition of all judicial decisions. The inefficient judicial system itself will experience competition and cases will move to countries where justice is more efficient. At the same time the pressure to unify standards of efficiency in the judicial system will remain the same or will even increase.

These effects are of an indirect nature, more could be cited. The question is how we can specifically prepare for this. It is hard to define such effects with a plus or minus. Allow us to mention another: for a number of years the European Union has organized forms of informal and semi-formal links, a network of representatives of the judiciary in various countries, meetings, joint education and even formal working links. It is beyond dispute that these activities are aimed at building an awareness of belonging to a European judicial elite.

---

[23] Opinion of the Constitutional Court of 21 November 2000, Case U-I-283/00, Uradni list RS (Official Gazette) No. 86/2000, available at: <http://www.us-rs.si>.

"Direct effect" is working in a new legal and institutional framework. All elements of the judicial system will have a stake in this process. When speaking about the judicial branch we mean firstly the courts, the prosecutor's office, the Attorney General's office, attorneys and notaries.

The judiciary was only really making preparations for accession via education and training. According to the Judicial Education Center, which is the umbrella organization for the education of judges and prosecutors, all judges have encountered at least one of the three forms of education about European law. During the first phase they received short lectures at judicial colleges reviewing the acquis communautaire, sources of law and methods of interpretation. This primarily had the intention of awakening sufficient early interest in this area on the part of judges and prosecutors and raising an awareness European law will be an unavoidable part of their everyday work. Building on this education there were more specific, high-intensity seminars of several days' duration, at which the law regulating the free flow of goods, labour, and capital services, monetary union, competition law and so forth were discussed. In addition the role of national courts in the functioning of European Community courts and legal remedies were highlighted. The next European experience that judges were able to participate in were the professional excursions. These were carried out with the primary aim of examining the specific work of colleagues in the European environment and, not least of all, establishing direct contacts. Some of the judges and prosecutors even had the opportunity, albeit as observers, to participate in the work of European institutions such as the European Judicial Network, Eurojust and the European Judicial Training Network.

The members of the judiciary are becoming aware that the law will be harder to find, and interpretation will be more demanding. European Community issues two types of acts, viz. those that must be directly applied and those that commit the Member State to incorporating them in its legal system. Judges will apply both of them. The acts that must be applied directly are regulations. Any legislative intervention that would execute or interpret regulations would entail a breach of the fundamental principles of European law. Judges must therefore apply such law autonomously and are obliged themselves to find any judicial practice on the part of the European Court of Justice regarding individual questions.[24] Due to the efficient and uniform functioning of the acquis communautaire regulations take precedence over domestic norms. This means that in each case judges have to assess the accordance between the national norm and the regulation, and also

---

24 The question of good translations of the European law already in force (that we will inherit in full) and the problem of translations of judgements by the European Court of Justice remain important, and continue to be of relevance after accession. The process of translation and expert editing of the judgments of ECJ has just started.

refrain from applying national regulations if they feel that they contravene European regulations.

For judges this is, to put it mildly, an unusual operation. Even though Article 8 of the Constitution expressly enacted the precedence of ratified international treaties over domestic legal norms, courts have practically made no use of these powers. They have actually applied certain international treaties directly, but have adopted the doctrine not to apply national law if it contravened the international treaty.

All law of the European Communities can come before national courts in one form or another. *De facto* supervision by the judicial branch of power of the implementation of European obligations by the legislative and executive branches has been established.

We should mention here the court's right and obligation to request interpretation of European law by the European Court of Justice. The preliminary rulings procedure is to a certain degree similar to the procedure for requesting an abstract assessment of constitutionality that any Slovenian court may initiate before the constitutional court if it feels that an act of law applied in a specific case contravenes the constitution. Courts have infrequently made use of this possibility: from 1990 to 2000 there were just 37 such requests.[25] We believe that the courts will use the preliminary ruling procedure more often than the recourse to the Constitutional Court: firstly, because the parties are going to propose such a recourse especially in important cases and, secondly, because the courts will probably seek the opportunity to get a legal opinion of the highest authority. The Ministry of Justice developed a proposal to have at least one specialist judge at every high court level in EU law to assist his/her colleagues at the high and district courts in these matters.

In Member States, prosecution services have felt the acquis less directly than judges. The reason is that prosecutors apply EU law through domestic law. They have been somewhat more involved in operational co-operation in the area of criminal proceedings between Member States. They are already involved as representatives of acceding countries in the work of EJN, which includes direct exchange of information and co-operation in transborder cases. The prosecutor service is involved only as observer in the work of Eurojust and OLAF.

By law the Attorney General's Office is the sole state body representing Slovenia's interests before international and national courts. Irrespective of whether the European Court of Justice is deemed a national or an international court, it is the Attorney General's office that will represent Slovenia's interests before this

---

[25] A more precise date shows the same pattern, viz. in the period between 1 January 1996 and 22 October 2002 there have been 26 requests from regular courts to the Constitutional court: Supreme court issued 7, high courts 7, district courts 3, county courts 3, misdemeanour courts 4, labour courts 2.

court. What we consider to be even more important is that in all disputes before the European Court of Justice in which preliminary rulings are decided upon, any Member State can appear with its legal position. In other words the Attorney General's office will represent Slovenia's interests before the European Court of Justice when it is dealing with a request for a preliminary ruling not only from Slovenia, but also from any other country. Will the Attorney General's office do this itself? Will a special department be established for this purpose, or will domestic or foreign attorneys be engaged? These are questions to which we do not have the answers yet.

The attorney profession will on the one hand face competition from their colleagues in European countries, and on the other will have to adapt to the requirements of the new legal environment. Experience of cases before the European Court of Human Rights shows that Slovenian attorneys (like the Attorney General's office) were very slow in adapting to and training for such cases. It is only very recently that they have been capable of appearing before the European Court of Human Rights with the necessary level of skill. We believe that the situation in connection with European Community law will be somewhat different, primarily because the financial interests in these cases are more significant. Usually where there is a chance to earn more, there is greater flexibility.

3. ROLE OF THE EXECUTIVE

3.1 Europe Agreement or Stabilisation and Association Agreement; co-ordination mechanisms; impact of EU accession on the organization and practice of (a) central government and administration and (b) decentralized authorities

At its session of 20 February 2003 the Slovenian Government adopted a programme of co-ordination of European affairs in collaboration with the Office of the Secretary-General of the Government as follows:

- First Pillar: Government Office for European Affairs (SVEZ)
- Second Pillar: Ministry of Foreign Affairs (MZZ)
- Third Pillar: SVEZ and MZZ

SVEZ is responsible for co-ordinating affairs falling within the Third Pillar, where the Ministry of Justice and Ministry of the Interior enjoy a high level of autonomy, while the Ministry of Foreign Affairs plays an important intervention role. The Ministry of Foreign Affairs will, when necessary, within the limits of its jurisdiction and in agreement with the Government Office for European Affairs, also assume the co-ordination of individual affairs within the framework of the Third Pillar.

The ministries and government offices will retain jurisdiction and responsibility for preparing a standpoint on participation in the formulation of EU legislation. The central authority does not prepare any substantive standpoints.

All authorities contain an appropriate internal organisational unit, which is responsible for co-ordination within an individual ministry/authority concerning European Union affairs, and which at the same time functions as a contact point for co-ordination authorities.

The co-ordination of standpoints on the first level of harmonisation is carried out within the framework of European affairs working groups, following the model of negotiation working groups, which consist of representatives of the ministries, constituent authorities, government offices and SVEZ for the First and Third Pillars, and MZZ for the Second Pillar, and if necessary for the Third Pillar. The contents (defined by the Council working groups) that fall within individual jurisdictions are specified for each working group separately. An individual working group is run by the ministry responsible for the major part of the working group's tasks. Every working group has a leader, deputy leader, and secretary and deputy secretary from the ministry in charge. The working groups must assume the standpoint of the Government regarding individual materials, and propose a Slovenian representative to represent the relevant standpoint in the EU (representative of the Mission, relevant ministry or authority). Depending on the nature of the material, this standpoint can be final or can function merely as a proposal to be discussed by the Government.

The so-called "European portal" for documents is accessible to all those participating in the adoption of decisions on individual affairs. SVEZ (First and Third Pillars), and in particular cases also MZZ for the Third Pillar, will for each document separately appoint the ministry in charge, which will formulate a draft standpoint to the relevant material, notify authorities of the material, set a time limit for reaching a co-ordinated standpoint and determine the method of endorsement of standpoints (to be endorsed only by the ministry or working group, or also by the Government and/or the National Assembly – NA).

4. ROLE OF THE NATIONAL PARLIAMENT

4.1 Preparedness for legal approximation

The Slovenian Parliament (the National Assembly) had and still has a strong role in the accession process. In the negotiation process, its Committee for Foreign

Policy confirmed all governmental positions for negotiations, which gave the negotiating process a clear democratic legitimacy.

Although the heaviest burden of approximation of legislation was on the Government, the National Assembly not only ratified the Europe Agreement, and changed the constitution, but also made all processes more transparent and open to the public by harmonising legislation.

A specialised working body is the Commission for European Affairs, set up by the National Assembly in 1996 with tasks to:

- discuss general affairs concerning European integration,
- co-ordinate the work of the parent working bodies in connection with European integration and provide them with opinions, recommendations and warnings,
- analyse the consequences of the integration strategy on Slovenia and prepare overall reports,
- monitor the accession strategy of the Republic of Slovenia to the European Union and its implementation,
- monitor the implementation of the harmonization of Slovene legislation with the *acquis communautaire*,
- co-operate with the institutions in Slovenia, European Union institutions and other countries in connection with integration issues,
- organize presentations of public opinion on integration issues,
- compile and stores EU related information,
- monitor the use of EU funds,
- perform other tasks related to European affairs which do not fall within the competence of other working bodies.

The Commission for European Affairs was quite successful in performing its tasks. We should also mention a great engagement in work of EU Convention[26] and COSAC.[27] We can also find some shortcomings such as: 10 members only, a weak role of specialised committees in scrutiny, not a permanent Committee but a Commission, no clear division of competencies with the Committee for Foreign Policy, a separate Joint Parliamentary Committee… Some of these shortcomings resulted from the fact that the opposition held the Commission for European Affairs.

---

26 A chairman of the Commission for European Affairs was invited to the EU Convention presidium.

27 Conférence des organes spécialisés dans les affaires communautaires.

4.2 Control over decisions taken by ministers in the Council of the EU

Slovenia has become a member of the EU in May 2004 and the National Assembly is preparing to play its role in the EU. There is an awareness of a democratic deficit in the EU, namely that governments have, through the Council, a legislative role in the EU legislative procedure where national parliaments are not present. The only way to influence legislative processes for national parliaments is by scrutinising of and co-operating with their governments.

The National Assembly sees its role not only in the scrutiny of Government work, but also in the control of the principle of solidarity in the EU, and in co-operation with other national parliaments and European Parliament.

To fulfil these tasks some organising changes will be needed. The first step was changing the Constitution. Constitutional provisions in Germany, France, Austria, Finland, Sweden, Hungary, and also in the Constitution of the Republic of Slovenia deal with the role of a National Parliament in the EU and with the relation parliament – government in EU matters.

Article 3a, paragraph 4 namely states:

> In procedures for the adoption of legal acts and decisions in international organisations to which Slovenia has transferred the exercise of part of its sovereign rights, the Government shall promptly inform the National Assembly of proposals for such acts and decisions as well as of its own activities. The National Assembly may adopt positions thereon, which the Government shall take into consideration in its activities. The relationship between the National Assembly and the Government arising from this paragraph shall be regulated in detail by a law adopted by a two-thirds majority vote of deputies present.

Thanks to that provision a law regulating relations between the legislative and the executive has to be adopted. A small group of experts in the National Assembly prepared a draft for this law, which during the summer of 2003 was in consideration by political parties and the Government. This law deals with very sensitive constitutional relations between Parliament and Government.

When this draft was adopted in the autumn of 2003, Slovenia went in a similar direction as Finland and Sweden – with a strong parliamentary role in EU matters.[28]

The idea being to define "EU affairs" first and then to clarify the division of competencies in EU affairs between Parliament and Government. Parliament should only be dealing with matters that would fall under its competence and

---

[28] But not as strong as in Denmark and Austria where decisions of parliament are legally binding for their governments.

Government should keep autonomy performing an executive function as well as being responsible to Parliament for the policy and decisions taken.

The main role should include the parliamentary Committees for EU Affairs and for Foreign Policy which should adopt decisions on behalf of the plenary, taking into account standpoints of specialised committees. The government will promptly inform the National Assembly of proposals for EU acts and decisions and send them to Parliament immediately after receiving them, together with an impact assessment.[29] The National Assembly may adopt positions thereon that the Government will have to take into consideration in its activities. In cases that the Government acts differently, Parliament should immediately be informed, together with reasons for its steps.

The National Assembly should discuss EU matters also in plenary session in the case of amendments to the EU Treaties and before each European Council; the prime minister and ministers should then be present.

The National Assembly thus faces a great challenge.

29 Concerning economy, public sector, environment, state budget and legislation.

TURKEY

Kemal Başlar* and Erdoğan İshakoğlu**

1. NATIONAL CONSTITUTION

1.1 Implementation of international law and transfer of legislative powers

The question can be divided into four distinct parts, each of which merits individual attention:

(a) The incorporation and implementation of international law in the Turkish national legal order
(b) The rank and status of international law in Turkey
(c) Direct applicability of treaties under Turkish laws
(d) Transfer of competences to international organizations

(a) The incorporation and implementation of international law in the Turkish national legal order

As Turkey adopts a monist approach to international law, there is no need for an international treaty to be transformed into national law once the procedure of ratification is completed. That is to say, in order to regard an international treaty as part of the law of the land, a formal process of ratification is the only criterion. Article 90 of the 1982 Constitution lays down the basic principles concerning the ratification of treaties. As far as Article 90(1) is concerned, the ratification of treaties is subject to adoption by the Turkish Grand National Assembly by a law approving of the ratification.[1] This principle has two derogations which are spelled out in Article 90(2-3) of the Constitution.

* Kemal Başlar, LL.M., Ph.D., Law Clerk at the Constitutional Court.

** Erdoğan İshakoğlu, LL.M., Judge at the Ministry of Justice.

[1] For more information regarding international law in Turkey, see Aslan Gündüz, 'Eroding Concept of National Sovereignty: The Turkish Example', *Avrupa Araştırmaları Dergisi* [Marmara Journal of European Studies], Marmara Üniversitesi Avrupa Topluluğu Enstitüsü, Vol. 1/1-2 (1991) pp. 99-154; Murat Sen, 'International Agreements in the National Legal Orders of the Candidate Countries: Turkey', in Andrea Ott and Kirstyn Inglis, eds., *Handbook on European Enlargement: A*

> Treaties regulating economic, commercial, and technical relations, and covering a period of no more than one year, may be put into effect through promulgation, provided they do not entail any financial commitment by the state, and provided they do not infringe upon the status of individuals or upon the property rights of Turkish citizens abroad. In such cases, these treaties must be brought to the knowledge of the Turkish Grand National Assembly within two months of their promulgation.
>
> Treaties in connection with the implementation of an international treaty, and economic, commercial, technical, or administrative agreements which are concluded depending on an authorization given by law shall not require approval by the Turkish Grand National Assembly. However, treaties concluded under the provision of this paragraph and affecting the economic or commercial relations and private rights of individuals shall not be put into effect unless promulgated.

These derogations are so widely interpreted in practice that it is at the disposal of the Council of Minister to decide whether a treaty falls within the ambit of the second or third paragraphs or not. Never has this discretion of governments been challenged in the past before the Council of State (*Danistay*) on the grounds that governments trespassed the domain exclusively reserved for Parliament. Should the Council of Ministers, in some cases, mistakenly issue a decree in order to incorporate a treaty into municipal law instead of seeking the approval of Parliament, the judicial review of this governmental discretion has not been questioned before *Danistay*. All the same, Article 90(4) of the Constitution ensures that Parliamentary approval is required provided that treaties, falling in the second and third paragraphs, result in amendments to Turkish laws.

After a treaty is approved either by Parliament or the Council of Ministers, as far as Article 104 of the Constitution is concerned, it is the President that shall ratify and promulgate the law concerning the ratification of international treaties. Albeit not mentioned in the Constitution, there is an internal ratification process which empowers the Government in all ratification processes. This is enunciated in the Law on Conclusion, Entry into Force and Promulgation of International Agreements (Act No. 244), according to which all treaties, notwithstanding that they need any prior enabling act of Parliament to become binding, are to be approved by a decree of the Council of Ministers. Without this decree, treaties do not duly enter into force, even if Parliament gives its consent. In the light of the

---

Commentary on the Enlargement Process (The Hague, T.M.C. Asser Press 2002); Vahit Biçak and Zühtü Aslan, *Constitutional Law: Supplement 55 Turkey*, International Encylopedia of Laws, André Alen, ed., (The Hague, Kluwer Law International 2004) esp. pp. 47-51; Kemal Başlar, 'The Implementation of International Law in Turkish Municipal Law', *Annales de la Faculté de Droit D'Istanbul*, Vol. 34/51 (2002) pp. 53-114.

fact that no appeal can be made against the decisions and orders signed by the President on his own initiative, he shares this power with the Council of Ministers through a decree of the Council of Ministers (Art. 105 of the Constitution and Art. 3(1) of Act No. 244).

An international treaty approved by the President must, in principle, be published in the Official Gazette. The text of the treaty and its Turkish translation are also published together with the governmental decree ratifying the treaty concerned. However, if a treaty falls within the ambit of exceptions laid down in Article 90(3), and is related with technical and administrative treaties and treaties concluded in connection with the implementation of an international treaty then it enters into force without publication.

(b) The rank and status of international treaties in Turkey

The 1982 Constitution makes three references to the term "international law". In the articles laid down below, all sources of international law contravening national legislation are given priority.

To begin with, on the suspension of the exercise of fundamental rights and freedoms, Article 15(1) touches upon issues of international concern:

> In times of war, mobilisation, martial law, or state of emergency the exercise of fundamental rights and freedoms can be partially or entirely suspended, or measures may be taken, to the extent required by the exigencies of the situation, which derogate the guarantees embodied in the Constitution, provided that obligations under *international law* are not violated. [emphasis added]

Secondly, on the status of aliens, Article 16 says;

> The fundamental rights and freedoms of aliens may be restricted by law in a manner consistent with *international law*. [emphasis added]

Finally, on the declaration of state of war and authorisation to permit the use of armed forces, Article 92(1) reads

> The power to authorise the declaration of the state of war in cases deemed legitimate by *international law*, and, except where required by international treaties to which Turkey is a party or by the rules of international courtesy, to send Turkish Armed Forces to foreign countries, and to allow foreign armed forces to be stationed in Turkey is vested in the Turkish Grand National Assembly.[2] [emphasis added]

---

[2] This provision is a result of the legal lacuna seen the 1924 Constitution which was in force until the 1961 Constitution superseded it. In sending troops to the Korean War in 1950, many lessons

Apart from these provisions, there are two provisions which give superiority – but only to "international treaties". The first provision, enunciated in Article 42, makes a specific reference to international treaties. Article 42 reads:

> No language other than Turkish shall be taught as mother tongue to Turkish citizens at any institutions of training or education. Foreign languages to be taught in institutions of training and education and the rules to be followed by schools conducting training and education in a foreign language shall be determined by law. The provisions of *international treaties* are reserved. [emphasis added]

This derogation stems from the rights of (non-Muslim) minorities recognised by some international treaties. For example, Article 37 of the Lausanne Peace Treaty of 1923 stipulates that

> Turkey undertakes that the stipulations contained in Articles 38 to 44 [on the protection of minorities] shall be recognised as fundamental laws, and that no law, no regulation, nor official action shall conflict or interfere with these stipulations, nor shall any law, regulation, nor official action prevail over them.

Last but not least, Article 90(5) of the Constitution, as a cardinal provision entertaining the status of international treaties, deserves a special place in this regard. The final sentence of the fifth paragraph of Article 90 provides that

> In case of contradiction between international agreements regarding basic rights and freedoms approved through proper procedure and domestic laws, due to different provisions on the same issue, the provisions of international agreements shall be considered.

This sentence was added on 7 May 2004[3] as a result of an attempt to harmonize Turkish law with EU law. The original intention of the Government was to place all treaties over national laws. A few weeks before the constitutional amendment was introduced, the supremacy of treaties was confined only to treaties on fundamental rights and duties. With the introduction of the new amendment, the Constitution has differentiated human rights treaties from all other treaties including EU/EC treaties, the Association Agreement and the *acquis communautaire*.

---

were drawn. Ever since 1961, this article was used on three occasions: in the Gulf Crises and the Agile Force, in the Restoration for Hope Operation in Somalia and in sending troops to Kosovo.

[3] Act No. 5170 (Official Gazette, 22 May 2004 – No. 25469).

Article 90(5), which reads "International treaties duly put into effect have the force of law", does not provide a clear answer as to whether treaties including the Association Agreement, hierarchically speaking, have equal footing with laws or whether it manifests the monist doctrine and therefore does not refer to the rank of treaties. In view of the fact that there is no other reference indicating the rank and status of international treaties, ever since the adoption of the 1961 Constitution, which contained the same sentence, the legal status of treaties has been contingent upon the interpretation of the phrase "having the force of law".

Even though the last paragraph proclaims that international treaties are part of our domestic law, doctrinal discussions are not unambiguous. There are three approaches as to the meaning of *having the force of law*. The first group of academics are of the conviction that treaties have equal standing as that of ordinary domestic legislation, in that the Constitution explicitly acknowledges that international treaties have the force of law. They, therefore, hold the view that the fact that juridical review of the constitutionality of treaties is hampered, this does not elevate treaties to supra-constitutional status. Had the laymen wished to grant treaties superior position in comparison to national legislation, they would have expressed this in unequivocal terms, just as many European Constitutions did. The corollary of this standpoint is that treaties can be amended by a law by dint of *lex posterior derogat prior* principle. That is to say, they can be amended, abolished or abrogated by a law or a Decree-Law (*Kanun Hükmünde Kararname*) after duly being put into effect.

This viewpoint has been entrenched with the reasoning of the Act No. 244. According to the *travaux préparatoires* of the Act, "The Constitution has not empowered treaties so as to surpass laws; it has only given the power of laws. Hence, it is probable to enact a law that is contrary to a treaty. In this case, there are two separate issues: Inapplicability of a treaty in Turkish law is one thing; due to this, the emergence of international responsibility of Turkey is another thing. What the Constitution did was only to block the course to review the constitutionality of international treaties".

The second group of writers argue that literal interpretation of the last paragraph of Article 90 is obscure and void. The connotation of the denial of judicial review by the Constitutional Court paves the way to the conclusion that international treaties are superior to national laws. As a result, in the case of conflict between international provisions and national ones; international treaties do prevail. Even in cases where international obligations contravene constitutional norms, the first should take precedence. Therefore, under no circumstances can the *lex posterior* principle come to the fore.

All in all, theoretical and doctrinal disputes on the meaning of "having the force of law" have often had a largely verbal character and frequently no practical significance. On the way to becoming an equal partner of the international community per se and a member of regional organisations in particular, Turkish positive law needs some serious amendments in relation to incorporation of international and regional treaties.

(c) Direct applicability of treaties under Turkish laws

It is apt to mention that the "having the force of law" phrase might mislead the reader inasmuch as it appears that no act of transformation is necessary for the transfer of treaty provisions into the national legal system. However, this is only the case for treaties containing self-executive provisions or creating abstract and objective rights and obligations. In the case of the implementation of policies and programs of action that contain unclear, vague, equivocal language, or treaties of an explanatory or declaratory nature, or treaties that create subjective rights and obligations, the treaty provisions need to be laid down in a national act for their implementation. To put it differently, the fact that Article 90(5) places treaties on an equal footing with parliamentary acts should not be construed to mean that all treaties have direct effect in domestic law. On the contrary, if treaty provisions do not contain self-executing clauses, they have to be enforced through an enabling act of Parliament to be directly applicable.

In view of the fact that there is no explicit provision on the issue of direct effect (save only four articles, namely, Arts. 15, 16, 42 and 92), the determination of directly applicable provisions in practice has been at the disposal of the Judiciary. For example, the case law of *Danistay* indicates that treaties obliging the authorities to refrain from taking certain measures against citizens, treaties directly granting certain rights to citizens, treaties governing the necessary conditions for granting certain rights to citizens, treaties creating a state of affairs or establishing the necessary conditions under which citizens have a certain legal status, treaties governing conditions related to the responsibilities of the authorities, and treaties related to the acquisition of citizenship and minority rights, are regarded as directly applicable.[4]

(d) Transfer of competences to international organizations

The transfer of legislative, executive and judicial powers to international organizations is not allowed under the Constitution.

To begin with, Article 6(1) proclaims that "Sovereignty is vested fully and unconditionally in the nation". Article 6(2) it reads: "The Turkish Nation shall

---

4 M. Sen, 'International Agreements in the Legal Orders of the Candidate Countries', in Andrea Ott and Kirstyn Inglis, eds., *Handbook on European Enlargement: A Commentary on the Enlargement Process* (The Hague, T.M.C. Asser Press 2002) pp. 341-346 at p. 345.

exercise its sovereignty through the authorised organs as prescribed by the principles laid down in the Constitution". The third and final paragraph of the same article is a bulwark against the transfer of sovereignty to international organizations that lays down the principle that "The right to exercise sovereignty shall not be delegated to *any individual, group or class.* No *person* or agency shall exercise any state authority which does not emanate from the Constitution".

Secondly, Article 7 provides for no leeway as to the transfer of legislative power inasmuch as "legislative power is vested in the Turkish Grand National Assembly on behalf of the Turkish Nation. *This power cannot be delegated.*"

Article 8 allows no room for EU institutions in the use of governmental authorities: The Article says "Executive power and function shall be exercised and carried out by the President of the Republic and the Council of Ministers in conformity with the Constitution and the law".

The same applies to the use of judicial power. Article 9 says "Judicial power shall be exercised by independent courts on behalf of the Turkish Nation". This provision does not vest jurisdiction in the ECJ's case law for Turkish judges.

Accordingly, the Constitution surely requires amendments on the way to full EU membership. No attempt has been made so far with regard to the delegation of sovereign authority to international organizations. In light of the supremacy and direct effect principles as well as supranational powers of EU institutions, amendments to the Constitution are inevitable. Otherwise, the ratification of EU treaties would amount to serious breaches of constitutional provisions.

As to the manner of transmitting legislative, executive and judicial powers to the EC, there are two approaches in this regard. The first one is the modification of Articles 6, 7, 8 and 9 one by one. As far as the experience of other EU members is concerned, this is not a plausible way. A much better approach would be the introduction of a general clause authorising transfers to the Community institutions.

The best place for such an introduction appears to be in Article 6. When, and if, Turkey is given a date for the commencement of negotiations for full membership, it will be incumbent upon Parliament to add a new clause (i.e., a new paragraph) to Article 6. The last and fourth paragraph of Article 6 would be like:

> The Republic of Turkey may transfer legislative, administrative and/or judicial prerogatives to/with/in favour of an international/regional organisation or institution by/pursuant to a treaty.

1.2 Supremacy and direct effect

As noted above, Articles 15, 16, 42 and 92 of the Constitution recognise the supremacy of international law/treaties. According to Article 90(5) treaties on fundamental human rights and freedoms have supremacy over conflicting national legislation. Although one can scrutinise what is meant by "fundamental" or "basic" rights and freedoms, as they are not listed down in the Constitution, such a scrutiny will be of no or little avail to the discussion on the supremacy and direct effect of European law.

It is appreciated that the supremacy and direct effect of European law should find itself a legal abode in the Constitution. To this end, several attempts were made in the past. Given that Article 90(5) of the Constitution is a stumbling block towards entering into the EU, pro-European Members of Parliament tried to amend the last paragraph of the Constitution in 2001 during which 37 provisions of the Constitution were changed as a follow-up to the Copenhagen Criteria. However, Euro-sceptics, including the President, managed to prevent the amendment from being passed.

In April 2004, an attempt was made once again to change Article 90(5) of the Constitution in such a way as to accept the supremacy of all international treaties over national law. Although the crux of the amendment bill was EU affairs, the provision did not directly refer to the EU. Upon fear of the loss of sovereignty being raised by some quarters, the supremacy of treaties was finally confined only to human rights treaties. Hence, the amendment failed to satisfy the prerequisites of EU membership.

Needless to say, Article 90(5) of the Constitution does not guarantee the twin pillars of the EC law: namely, the supremacy and direct effect principles. By no means does it or will it provide the necessary wording should Turkey be given a definite date.

1.3 Amendments

As the legal status of the EU/EC and Euratom Treaties are not, taken literally, different from other international treaties, it appears, at first glance, that the ratification process would not require an amendment. All the same, this is not the case in that Article 6 vests sovereignty fully and unconditionally in the nation. The corollary of which is that, it is the nation that should decide whether legislative power can be delegated or not. One wonders whether Parliament is entitled to transfer its power to a supranational organization through an ordinary ratification process envisaged for ordinary treaties. One must acknowledge that the issue as to how Parliament is to ratify the EU/EC treaties is, so to speak, at Parliament's discretion. No serious academic research has been carried out so far to allow us to know how Parliament will respond.

If and when Turkey is given a date to start negotiations for full membership, this issue will come to the fore. It is likely that a new method will be devised for the ratification of the said treaties, which might include approval through weighted (e.g., two-thirds) majority and calling a referendum.

If the ratification of the European Treaty is carried out after constitutional amendment, the Constitutional Court is not entitled to interfere with the amendment of the Constitution. According to Article 148 of the Constitution, the Constitutional Court shall examine the constitutionality of amendments of the Constitution only in respect to form; that is to say, the verification of constitutional amendments is restricted to a consideration of whether the requisite majorities were obtained for the proposal and in the ballot, and whether the prohibition on debates under urgent procedure was complied with. Therefore, the Court is not entitled to say, e.g., that the transfer of sovereignty is against the Constitution. Whether the Court should have a say when it comes to EU accession could be subject to debate.

If the ratification procedure, hypothetically speaking, is carried out without necessary constitutional changes then the Constitutional Court may interfere with the ratification process. When the act of approval is challenged before the Constitutional Court, by reviewing the constitutionality of the Accession Treaty it may render a decision that the law of approval leading to ratification is contrary or incompatible with the Constitution.

1.4 Provisions contrary to the *acquis communautaire*

It was not until a couple of years ago that the answer to this question was very comprehensive and page-filling.[5] In order for Turkish law to be in complete harmony with the Copenhagen criteria of 1993, several provisions of the Constitution have been amended in recent years. As to date, there have been eight reform packages adopted by Parliament. Thanks to these, most legal stumbling blocks have been done away with in a few years time.

Despite these efforts, there are still some provisions that are contrary to the dynamics of European integration. In the last reform package, adopted on 7 May 2004, ten articles of the Constitution were changed.[6] Two articles in the said

---

[5] See, for example, Christian Rumpf, '*Turkish Constitutional Law and the European Union from a European Point of View*', Constitutional Implications of Accession to the European Union, European Commission for Democracy through Law, Council of Europe Publishing, Science and Technique of Democracy, No. 31 (Strasbourg, 2002) pp. 61-108.

[6] (1) The statement "State organs and administrative authorities shall act in compliance with the principle of equality before the law in all their proceedings" was added to Article 10; (2) "The execution of capital punishment" statement was removed from Article 15; (3) A passage in Article 17 mentioning capital punishment was removed, together with the statement "during implementation of the directives of executive powers in times of emergency rule"; (4) Article 30 was re-written: "A printing house, its annexes and press equipment duly established as a press enterprise under law shall not be seized, confiscated, or barred from operation on the grounds of being an instrument of crime";

reform package were watered down and rendered meaningless, as far as their rationale is concerned. The first one is the fifth paragraph of Article 90. The aim was to amend this article so as to specify that "all" international agreements have superiority over the Turkish law in the event of a conflict. Within the last 10 days before the package came before the General Assembly of the Parliament, the term "international agreements" was confined only to "human rights treaties".[7] The original wording of this amendment was as follows:

> In case of contradiction between international agreements regarding basic rights and freedoms approved through proper procedure and domestic laws, due to different provisions on the same issue, the provisions of international agreements shall be considered.

This change is against the spirit (and *ratio legis*) of the reform package, which aimed to harmonize Turkish law with the Copenhagen Criteria.

The second unsuccessful attempt is the last paragraph of Article 38. The wording of the paragraph is "No citizen shall be extradited to a foreign country on account of an offence *except the obligations resulting from being a party to the International Criminal Court.*" This formulation does not fully conform to the *acquis communautaire*, i.e. the Convention regarding the simplified extradition among Member States (1995) and the decision creating the European arrest warrant replacing the current extradition system (based on the 1957 Convention and its Protocols). The introduced paragraph does not provide the possibility for any judge of a Member State to deliver an arrest warrant whose effects are to be recognised in other Member States. The wording of Article 38(12) should have been: "No citizen shall be extradited to a foreign country on account of an offence except for the obligations arising out of a ratified international commitment on the basis of reciprocity".

---

(5) In Article 38, the sentence "no one can be sentenced to the death penalty" and "No citizen shall be extradited to a foreign country on account of an offence except the obligations resulting from being a party to the International Criminal Court" were added; (6) Parliament's authority to approve death sentences was annulled, as outlined in Article 87; (7) Article 90 was changed, allowing domestic laws to become subordinate to international laws approved through the proper procedure, in the event that they conflict; (8) The Office of Chief of General Staff's right to appoint a member of the YOK was removed from Article 131; (9) Article 143, which outlines the foundation and operation of the DGMs, was removed; (10) The State Audit Department's (Sayıştay) authority, set in Article 160, was expanded and the sentence that calls for secret inquiries into the military's expenses was removed.

[7] In 2001, Article 90(5) of the Constitution was among the projected changes. However, at the last minute, the Members of Parliament voted against a provision which was to replace the so-called "equality clause". In other words, the then-new proposal suggested that international organizations' (i.e., the EU) legislation should take precedence over national law.

There are other provisions of the Constitution that are contrary to the *acquis*. The first group of articles are sovereignty-related ones. As previously mentioned, Articles 6, 7, 8 and 9 should either be taken one by one or a wholesome formulation be made so as to delegate international organizations legislative and administrative powers.

There are other problematic provisions. To begin with, in the Constitution, there are two words towards which special attention should be drawn. These are namely "alien" and "everyone". Legally speaking, alien means all foreigners who do not enjoy Turkish nationality and "everyone" denotes every Turkish citizen. This kind of legal interpretation of these two words is highly problematic in some cases. For example, Article 16 says that "the fundamental rights and freedoms of aliens may be restricted by law in a manner consistent with international law". There is likelihood, albeit only to a certain degree, that the concept of "aliens" might be interpreted in practice so as to include EU citizens. But this may not be the case. To prevent any future controversy, an explanation should be added to the said Article so that EU citizens should not be treated differently from non-EU citizens of other nations.

As for Article 35, it reads "everyone has the right to own and inherit property". It is subject to debate whether aliens can own real estate in Turkey. By analogy, it could be said that this right has been endowed only to Turkish citizens and foreigners are not allowed to purchase real estate. Taken literally, however, the word "everyone" might be said to include aliens as well. Article 35 of the Land Law (No. 2644) was amended and Article 87 of the Village Law was abolished in 2003 (by Law No. 4916) to be in conformity with the *acquis*. The constitutionality of acquisition of property by aliens is subject to debate. At the time of writing, an application has been lodged at the Constitutional Court demanding that Article 35 of the Land Law be declared unconstitutional. Should this be the case after the decision of the Constitutional Court, then a specific provision is needed so that aliens may enjoy the right to property under conditions provided by law. For EU nationals, acquiring the right to property and land is an outcome of the free movement of capital and freedom of establishment. It has yet to be seen whether the Constitutional Court will read the word "everyone" broadly so that EU nationals might be categorised within this term or not.

Article 23 acknowledges that "everyone has the right to freedom of residence and movement". So long as this article is interpreted in parallel with Article 16 of the Constitution, it does not require amendment. Otherwise, it can be against the free movement of persons and right to residence for EU citizens.

Article 70 says that "every Turk has the right to enter public service". This provision should be restricted so that EU citizens are given the chance of being employed at certain public services. Otherwise, the presence of this provision is against the free movement of persons within the Union, which includes the right to go to another Member State to seek employment and work as an employer, employee, or free-lancer, etc. The right to take a job in another Member States is essential for workers and jobseekers to make use of a larger labour market offering greater choice and opportunity.

According to Article 67, "... citizens have the right to vote, to be elected, and to engage in political activities independently or in a political party, and to take part in a referendum". This provision should be changed in such a way that EU citizens residing in Turkey be able to take part in local elections and vote in the European Parliament elections. Otherwise, the right to vote, which is one of four rights of EU citizenship, will be hampered. The right to vote includes "the right to be voted". In other words, in local elections the right to stand as a candidate for an EU national residing in a Member States is a part of participatory rights. Although it is not a matter for constitutional provisions, the details of the right to vote for the European Parliament need adaptations in the national legislations.

The natural outcomes of the right to vote and stand as a candidate, are the recognition of the participation in political activities by non-nationals. At present, Article 68 reserves the right to form political parties and, in accordance with the established procedure, to join and withdraw from them, to citizens. As the EU law forbids any discrimination on the basis of nationality, any obstacle to the political activity of Union citizens should be removed.

The title of Article 71 is "the right of petition" according to which "Citizens and foreigners resident considering the principle of reciprocity have the right to apply in writing to the competent authorities and to the Turkish Grand National Assembly with regard to the requests and complaints concerning themselves or the public". This article should be elaborated in order that the right to access to information and the right to have recourse to an ombudsman be furnished under this heading.

Last but not least, as far as Article 73 is concerned, "taxes, fees, duties, and other such financial impositions shall be imposed, amended, or revoked by law". Prior to full membership, this provision should be changed so as to allow Community institutions to levy taxes and other fiscal measures.

1.5 Procedures to be followed to adapt the national constitution to the *acquis communautaire*

As there is no explicit provision with regard to the ratification of regional treaties *per se* and the EU/EC treaties in particular, general principles of the amendment procedure are likely to govern the accession to the EU. In other words, the approximation of the constitutional provisions to the *acquis* will be made through an ordinary amendment procedure laid down in Article 175 of the Constitution:

> The constitutional amendment shall be proposed in writing by at least one-third of the total number of members of the Turkish Grand National Assembly. Proposals to amend the Constitution shall be debated twice in the Plenary Session. The adoption of a proposal for an amendment shall require a three-fifths majority of the total number of members of the Assembly by secret ballot.
>
> The consideration and adopting of proposals for the amendment of the Constitution shall be subject to the provisions governing the consideration and adoption of legislation, with the exception of the conditions set forth in this article.
>
> The President of the Republic may refer the laws related to the Constitutional amendments for further consideration. If the Assembly adopts the draft law referred by the President by a two-thirds majority, the President may submit the law to referendum.
>
> If a law is adopted by a three-fifths or less than two-thirds majority of the total number of votes of the Assembly and is not referred by the President for further consideration, it shall be published in the Official Gazette and shall be submitted to referendum.
>
> A law on the Constitutional amendment adopted by a two-thirds majority of the total number of members of the Turkish Grand National Assembly directly or if referred back by the President for further consideration, or its articles as considered necessary may be submitted to a referendum by the President. Laws or related articles of the Constitutional amendment not submitted to referendum shall be published in the Official Gazette.
>
> Laws related to Constitutional amendment which are submitted to referendum, shall require the approval of more than half of the valid votes cast.
>
> The Turkish Grand National Assembly, in adopting the laws related to the Constitutional amendment, shall also decide on which provisions shall be submitted to referendum together and which shall be submitted individually.
>
> Every measure including fines shall be taken to secure participation in referenda, general elections, by-elections and local elections.

As EU/EC treaties are meant to transfer/delegate/co-share some part of sovereign powers, the above-mentioned procedure might be set aside, and a new procedure may be devised when the time comes. The constitutional recognition of supremacy and direct effect of EU law as well as transfer of sovereign powers may necessitate direct referendum. This is important because, at present, the current ruling party, namely, AKP (Justice and Development Party) has had more than 2/3 of the Parliament with 36 per cent vote in the general elections. In other words, AKP, with 369 out of 550 MPs, representing more than 66 per cent of Parliament, is entitled to delegate legislative powers to EU organs. Should this be the case, then democratic legitimacy of the constitutional amendment may result in heated debates on this very delicate issue. To prevent such a political morass, the AKP Government may opt for holding a referendum to resolve the situation.

2. ROLE OF THE JUDICIARY (NATIONAL COURTS, INCLUDING ADMINISTRATIVE BODIES WITH ADJUCATING POWERS)

It is pertinent at the outset to cast light on the Turkish judiciary to better assess the role of the judges in the implementation of EC law.

2.1 The courts in Turkey

I. Justice courts

Justice courts are divided into three categories:[8]

1. Civil and criminal courts of first instance: Civil courts fall into three categories: small-claims courts (*Sulh Hukuk Mahkemeleri*), High/District Courts (*Asliye Hukuk Mahkemeleri*) and Specialized Tribunals (e.g., Commercial Courts, Labour Tribunals, Family Courts, Juvenile Courts, Maritime Courts). Criminal courts are divided into four sections: the Penal Peace Courts (*Sulh Ceza Mahkemeleri*), the Penal Courts of General Jurisdiction (*Asliye Ceza Mahkemeleri*), the Penal Courts of Assize (*Ağır Ceza Mahkemeleri*) and Specialized Tribunals established by law.[9]

2. Intermediate (regional) courts of appeal: These are divided into civil and criminal chambers. Each regional court of appeal must have at least three civil and two criminal chambers.

3. Court of cassation (*Yargıtay*): The Court of Appeal is composed of thirty-three chambers: twenty-one of them are civil chambers and eleven are penal chambers.[10]

---

[8] The three-tiered structure is the result of improving the efficiency of the judiciary on the way to EU membership. The Law on Establishing the Intermediate Courts of Appeal (No. 5235) was approved by the National Assembly on 26 September 2004. It came into force on 1 April 2005. There are 4063 courts at all levels. Among them, 204 are the Penal Courts of Assize, 51 are Commercial Court, 655 are the Penal Courts of General Jurisdiction, 85 are Family Courts, 487 are the Penal Courts of the Peace, 640 are High/District Courts, 491 are small-claims courts, 328 are Single-Judge High/District Courts, 719 are Land Courts, 80 are Labour Courts, 3 are Traffic Courts, 138 are Execution Investigation Authorities (Enforcement Courts), 16 are Juvenile Courts, 9 Consumer Courts, 3 are Intellectual Property Courts, 10 are Executive Judges, 26 are Regional Administrative Courts, 62 are Administrative Courts, and 48 are Tax Courts.

[9] Much-debated the State Security Courts (*Devlet Güvenlik Mahkemeleri*) were abolished through the eight reform packages on 7 May 2004 with the Law No. 5170, Art. 9.

[10] With the introduction of the regional courts of appeal, the workload of the Court of Cassation will decrease significantly. As a result of this restructuring mechanism, the number of chambers will be cut down on gradually.

II. Administrative courts

Administrative courts consist of three divisions:

1. Administrative and tax courts (*İdare ve Vergi Mahkemeleri*)

2. Regional Administrative Courts (*Bölge İdare Mahkemeleri*): Judgements of single-judge courts are reviewed by Regional Administrative Courts.

3. The Council of State (*Danıştay*): It is a court of appeal for the decisions given by subordinate administrative courts. In addition to being a court, it is also a consultative body providing the government with expertise and advice, especially in legal matters. The Court is also competent to hear more specialized suits relating to the rulings of financial courts, the decisions of professional associations and independent administrative authorities/boards. It has 13 chambers.

III. Military courts

The first instance courts are military courts and military disciplinary courts. They have jurisdiction to try non-military persons for military offences and for offences committed against military personnel in military areas. The Military Court of Appeal (*Askeri Yargıtay*) is the last instance for reviewing the decisions and judgements given by the military judicial organs.

With regard to administrative issues, the Supreme Military Administrative Court (*Askeri Yüksek İdare Mahkemesi*) has jurisdiction in cases arising from administrative acts and actions by military authorities and also cases arising from administrative acts and actions by civilian authorities but involving military personnel and related to military service.

IV. Constitutional Court (*Anayasa Mahkemesi*)

The Constitutional Court was established by the 1961 Constitution. The 1982 Constitution slightly modified the composition and organization of the Court. The Court has no chambers. The 1982 Constitution lays down access to the Constitutional Court in two channels: Abstract control of norms (action for annulment, principal proceedings) and concrete control of norms (constitutional objection, incidental proceedings).

V. Court of Auditors (*Sayıştay*)

The Court of Auditors is independent of both the legislature and the executive.

VI. Court of Jurisdictional Disputes (*Uyuşmazlık Mahkemesi*)

The Court of Jurisdictional Disputes is empowered to deliver final judgements in disputes between courts of justice, and administrative and military courts concerning their jurisdiction and decisions.

2.2 Appointment and election of judges

In Turkey, the judicial profession is a career job. As an exception, practising lawyers and academics have the chance of being appointed under certain conditions (e.g., success, experience, etc.). Career judges are selected through nationwide examinations.[11] In order to take part in the examinations, judges of justice courts should hold a bachelor of law degree (LL.B). This requirement is not sought for administrative court judges. To train candidate judges efficiently, the Justice Academy has been in operation since July 2003. After two-year-in-service-training, the judges, with the approval of the Supreme Council of Judges and Public Prosecutors, are appointed, by secret ballot, by the Ministry of Justice.[12]

According to Article 139 of the Constitution, judges and public prosecutors shall not be dismissed, or retired before 65 (the age prescribed by the Constitution); nor shall they be deprived of their salaries, allowances or other rights relating to their status, even as a result of the abolition of court or post. The Minister of Justice is empowered to appoint judges and public prosecutors with their consent, to temporary or permanent functions in the central offices of the Ministry of Justice. The Minister of Justice may, in cases where delay is deemed prejudicial, confer temporary powers on judges or public prosecutors to prevent the disruption of services, subject to the approval of the Supreme Council of Judges and Public Prosecutors at its first meeting thereafter (Art. 159).

The career system of judge and prosecutors has been set out in the Law of Judges and Prosecutors (No. 2802). According to Article 15 of the Law, there are four professional stages. These degrees are third class, second class, first class and first plus class. In order to become a Supreme Court judge, one has to be at the first class degree. When a judge is eligible for membership in the Court of Cassation and the Council of State and spends six years at the first class degree, he/she is promoted to first plus class degree.

---

[11] There are 30 law faculties in Turkey. As part of improving the quality of jurists on the way to full EU membership, the duration of education in law faculties will increase from 4 to 6 years. Each year almost 4000 students graduate. Almost 5000 graduates apply for the entrance examinations. In recent years, less then 5 per cent have the chance of being a judge/prosecutor.

[12] The appointment of judges is regulated in the Judges and Public Prosecutors Law (No. 2802) (Arts. 7-12 on candidacy, Art. 13 on appointment).

The Constitutional Court is composed of eleven regular and four substitute members. The President of the Republic shall appoint two regular and two substitute members from the High Court of Appeals, two regular and one substitute member from the Council of State, and one member each from the Military High Court of Appeals, the High Military Administrative Court and the Audit Court, three candidates being nominated for each vacant office by the Plenary Assemblies of each court from among their respective presidents and members, by an absolute majority of the total number of members; the President of the Republic shall also appoint one member from a list of three candidates nominated by the Higher Education Council from among members of the teaching staff of institutions of higher education who are not members of the Council, and three members and one substitute member from among senior administrative officers and lawyers (Art. 146). The rapporteur-judges (law clerks) are appointed by the President.

As to the Council of State, three-fourths of the members (councillors) of the Council of State are appointed by the Supreme Council of Judges and Public Prosecutors from among the first category administrative judges and public prosecutors, or those considered to be of this profession; and the remaining quarter by the President of the Republic from among officials meeting the requirements designated by law. The president, chief public prosecutor, deputy president, and heads of division of the Council of State are elected by the Plenary Assembly of the Council of State from among its own members for a term of four years by secret ballot and by an absolute majority of the total number of members. They may be re-elected at the end of their term of office (Art. 155).

Members of the Military Court of Appeals are appointed by the President of the Republic from among three candidates nominated for each vacant office by the Plenary Assembly of the Military High Court of Appeals from among military judges of the first category, by secret ballot and by an absolute majority of the total number of members. The president, chief public prosecutor, vice-presidents and heads of division of the Military High Court of Appeals are appointed according to rank and seniority from among the members of the Military High Court of Appeals (Art. 156).

Members of the Supreme Military Administrative Court of Appeals who are military judges may be appointed by the President of the Republic from a list of three candidates nominated for each vacant office by the president and members of the Court, who are also military judges, by secret ballot and by an absolute majority of the total number of such members, from among military judges of the first category; members who are not military judges may be appointed by the President of the Republic from a list of three candidates nominated for each vacant office by the Chief of the General Staff from among officers holding the rank and qualifications prescribed by law. The term of office of members who are not military judges cannot exceed four years. The president, chief public prosecutor and head of division of the Court may be appointed from among military judges according to rank and seniority. The organization and functioning of the High Military Administrative Court, its procedure, disciplinary affairs and other matters relating to the status of its members are regulated by law in accordance with the principles of the independence of the courts and the security of tenure of judges within the requirements of military service (Art. 167).

In Turkey, there are 5972 judges (4282 of them are men, 1690 are women) and 3211 public prosecutors (3077 are men, 134 are women). Out of 9183 judges and prosecutors in total, 8118 of them are in Civil and Criminal Courts; 500 judges are in the administrative courts. 263 judges are at the Ministry of Justice, 573 of them are at the Court of Cassation and 221 are at the Council of State serving as law clerk.

2.3 Independence of the courts

According to Article 138 of the Constitution, judges are independent in the discharge of their duties; they shall render their decisions in accordance with the Constitution, law, and their personal conviction conforming to the law. According to Article 140 of the Constitution, judges shall discharge their duties in accordance with the principles of the independence of the courts and the security of tenure of judges. No organ, authority, office or individual may give orders or instructions to courts or judges relating to the exercise of judicial power, send them circulars, or make recommendations or suggestions. No questions can be asked, debates held, or statements made in the Legislative Assembly relating to the exercise of judicial power concerning a case under trial.

The qualifications, appointment, rights and duties, salaries and allowances of judges and public prosecutors, their promotion, temporary or permanent change in their duties or posts, the initiation of disciplinary proceedings against them and the subsequent imposition of disciplinary penalties, the conduct of investigation concerning them and the subsequent decision to prosecute them on account of offences committed in connection with, or in the course of, their duties, the conviction for offences or instances of incompetence requiring their dismissal from the profession, their in-service training and other matters relating to their personnel status are regulated by law.

The independence of the judiciary is protected above all by the existence of the Supreme Council for the Judiciary. Nevertheless, judges and public prosecutors are attached to the Ministry of Justice as far as administrative functions are concerned. The Supreme Council of Judges and Public Prosecutors, whose president is the Minister of Justice, deals with the admission of judges and public prosecutors of courts of justice and of administrative courts into the profession, appointments, transfers to other posts, the delegation of temporary powers, promotion, and promotion to the first category, the allocation of posts, decisions concerning those whose continuation in the profession is found to be unsuitable, the imposition of disciplinary penalties and removal from office. It takes final decisions on proposals by the Ministry of Justice concerning the abolition of a court or an office of judge or public prosecutor, or changes in the jurisdiction of a court.

It is said that the principle of the independence of the judiciary is, to a certain extent, undermined by the fact that judges and prosecutors are attached to the Ministry of Justice which is the head of the Supreme Council of Judges and Prosecutors which takes decision on the careers of all judges and prosecutors. It is feared that the possibility of removal and transfer to remote regions of Turkey by the Supreme Council may have negative effects on judges' attitudes and decisions.

The budget of the Ministry of Justice is within the General Budget of the State. The budget of Military Courts is listed in the budget of the Armed Forces. The Constitutional Court and the Court of Jurisdictional Disputes have separate budgets. They are all classified within the General Budget.[13] It is at the disposal of Parliament to decide how much money will be allocated to the Courts. The Government has no role to play in this regard. Neither can it reduce the allocated amount within a fiscal year.

The percentage of the budget of the Ministry of Justice is less than 0.01 per cent of the State Budget. Therefore, salaries of judges could be said to threaten their independence. A candidate judge receives €525 per month; a judge with ten years of experience earns €750 per month. There are 4700 judges who are in these two categories. Their salaries range from €525 to €750 per month. Judges, whose service in the judiciary is more than 10 years, are paid around €900-1000 per month. The highest salary is given to those who have attained the first plus degree. Supreme Court judges' salaries are not different from other judges at the first plus degree. They all receive some €1450 per month.

2.4 Other aspects of the judiciary

According to Article 36 of the Constitution, everyone has the right of litigation either as plaintiff or defendant and the right to a fair trial before the courts through lawful means and procedures. No court may refuse to hear a case within its jurisdiction. Hence, the right to appeal to the Justice Courts is open to every legal and real person, including aliens. As to the Constitutional Court, individuals can claim the constitutionality of a given provision only before a court *a quo*.

---

[13] I.e., they are not put into consolidated budget.

Individual complaint procedure is not recognized in the Constitution. In the very near future, the Government is planning to change the Constitution so as to pave the way to individual application to the Constitutional Court.

According to Article 125 of the Constitution, recourse to judicial review is available against all actions and acts of administration. National or international arbitration may be suggested to settle the disputes which arise from conditions and contracts under which concessions are granted concerning public services. Only those disputes involving foreign elements can be solved by international arbitration.

However, the acts of the President on his own competence, and the decisions of the Supreme Military Council are outside the scope of judicial review (Art. 125). Moreover, no appeal to any judicial instance against the decisions of the Supreme Council of Judges and Public Prosecutors is allowed under the Constitution (Art. 159).

Turkey has made progress since 1999 in relation to the execution of judgements of the European Court of Human Rights (ECtHR), particularly over the last year. The Law Amending Various Laws (No. 4793) adopted on 23 December 2003, added two new provisions to both civil and criminal procedure laws. According to this, a new 11th paragraph has been added to Article 445 of the Law on Civil Procedure (No. 1086) and 6th paragraph to Article 327 of the Law of Criminal Proceedings (No. 1412). Through these changes it has become possible to seek the right to retrial on the basis of a decision of the European Court of Human Rights declaring that there has been a violation of the European Convention for the Protection of Human Rights and Fundamental Freedoms (ECHR) and its protocols. This allowed for the re-trial of Leyla Zana and the other former DEP parliamentarians. Furthermore, the payment of just satisfaction awarded by the Court in 1998 was made in the *Loizidou* case in December 2003.[14]

In the last few years, judges and prosecutors have applied the ECHR and the case-law of the ECtHR in hundreds of cases which resulted mainly in acquittals. Especially, after the constitutional affirmation of the supremacy of international human rights treaties in Article 90(5) of the Constitution, more and more judges now rely on the ECHR provisions. Suffice it to give one recent example: The İzmir 7th District Court ruled on 28 September 2004 that the dissolution of the Human Rights Agenda Association for failing to comply with the conditions laid out in Article 8 of the Associations Law violated Article 11 of the ECHR.[15]

The Constitutional Court also refers to the case law of the ECtHR. For example, when the Court declared in 2003 the unconstitutionality of *de facto*

---

[14] Case of *Loizidou* v. *Turkey* (Application No. 15318/89).

[15] E. 2004/150, K. 2004/488.

expropriation, it cited three decisions of the EctHR to strengthen its decision.[16] There are other parallel examples.

The Court of Cassation has delivered important judgements applying the reform packages concerning the use of the Kurdish language,[17] re-trial,[18] torture, and freedom of expression.[19]

The Justice Academy provides training for Ministry of Justice personnel, lawyers and notaries. The training covers the European Convention on Human Rights and EC Law. Furthermore, young and successful judges are sent to European universities for postgraduate degrees in EC law. During 2003-2004, all judges and prosecutors received training on the European Convention for the Protection of Human Rights and Fundamental Freedoms (ECHR) and the case law of the European Court of Human Rights (ECtHR). Moreover, seminars were organised all over the country for judges and prosecutors on, *inter alia*, EU law, judicial cooperation, intellectual property rights, juvenile criminal justice and organised crime. The Ministry of Justice distributed to courts throughout Turkey a manual on the case-law of the European Court of Human Rights and seven handbooks on human rights, including the right to a fair trial and the prohibition of torture. The legal changes introduced by the seven reform packages were compiled and distributed to judges, public prosecutors and law enforcement officials.

With regard to the training of attorneys, notaries and prosecutors, 2600 judges, prosecutors and lawyers have been trained on the third pillar with particular emphasis on EC law in 115 activities (conferences, seminars, and workshop) held within the past three years.

The Ministry of Justice and the EU Commission agreed on a project dubbed "the Modernization of the Judiciary and the Penal Reform". The budget of the project is 11 million Euros, almost all of which will be funded by the EU. According to the target of the three-year-project, hundreds of judges and other judicial staff will be trained, and new prison standards will be introduced. One important aim of the project is to reform penitentiaries so as to meet EU standards.

---

[16] E. 2002/112, K. 2003/33 (Date of Decision 10 April 2003) (Official Gazette 4 November 2003). The cited decisions of the ECtHR are *Papamichalopoulos-Greece* (No. 14556/89) *Carbonara & Venture-Italy* (No. 24638/94) and *Belvedere Alberghiera S.R.L.-Italy* (No. 31524/96).

[17] The Court of Cassation, on 22 December 2003 overruled the judgement of the Van Criminal Court of Peace of 10 December 2003. In another case, the Court of Cassation on 17 July 2004 overruled the judgement of the Şanliurfa Criminal Court of 2002.

[18] The Court of Cassation on 14 July 2004 overruled the judgement of the State Security Court of 30 March 2004 in the case *Zana and her mates*.

[19] Judgement of the Court of Cassation of 15 July 2004 in the *Erdal Taş* case overruling the judgement of a lower court which had convicted a journalist on the basis of Art. 312 of the Penal Code. In its judgement, the Court held the principle that freedom of expression entails the right to criticize.

Before answering the following questions, one must finally mention the possibility of accessing the case law of European Courts. To begin with, important decisions of the ECtHR are being translated by the Directorate General for Multilateral Political Affairs (International Political Organisations, Council of Europe and Human Rights) and distributed to public agencies. The Police Academy publishes a journal called "The Journal of Decisions of European Court of Justice" where related cases are translated. The Ankara Bar Association also publishes summaries of the ECtHR cases in its bimonthly journal. As for the case law of the ECJ, there has been no systematic attempt to translate the decisions of the Luxembourg Court.

Almost all cases of the ECtHR wherein Turkey is a party are translated into Turkish and published on the homepage of the Ministry of Justice. In addition to this, they are also published in printed form at the Bulletin of Judiciary and distributed nationwide. The most important decisions of the ECtHR have been compiled into a single volume of 914 pages and presented to all judges and prosecutors.

With regard to the case law of the ECJ, 32 important rulings of the Court (relating mainly to Turkish migrants) have been translated into Turkish. The Ministry of Justice got a 507-page book published in 2002 with a view to educating the judges. In this book the EC legislation and the case law of the ECJ are presented. Out of 92,000 pages of secondary legislation of the EC/EU, 12,000 pages (which amount to 1100 regulations and directives) have been translated into Turkish. A small percentage of them have been published.

2.5 European Association Agreement

There have been 24 cases decided by the European Court of Justice[20] and a number of cases ruled on by other national courts of Member States with regard to the 1963 EC-Turkey Association Agreement, the Additional Protocol, and Association Council Decisions. The ECJ treats the decisions in the same way as the Association Agreement and regards these documents as an integral part of the Community legal order and as enjoying primacy over all domestic law of the EU Member States, as well as over conflicting secondary law of the EU Member States.[21] As the question is related to the application of the Associate Agreement

---

[20] The latest decision is the *Öztürk* Case delivered on 28 April 2004, Case C-373/02. nyr. These decisions are available at: <http://europa.eu.int/eur-lex/en/search/search_case.html>.

[21] For the legal status of EC-Turkey Association Council Decisions, see Nikolaos Lavranos, 'Legal Interaction between Decisions of International Organizations and European Law', University of Amsterdam, June 2004, pp. 61-75 at p. 63. Also published in Groningen, Europa Law Publishing 2004.

in Turkish courts, the case law of German, Dutch and French courts on the rights of Turkish migrant workers will not be mentioned here.[22]

In order to answer this question, it is necessary to point out initially the legal status of the Association Agreement and the Association Council decisions in domestic law. The Association Agreement (the Ankara Agreement, for short) of 1963, which entered into force on 1 December 1964, is the legal basis of the association between Turkey and the EU. An Additional Protocol was signed in 1970. Both are international agreements duly ratified. These treaties are not directly applicable in Turkish municipal law. Neither can it be said that they are superior over national law in the light of Article 90(5) of the Constitution. As a result of this, it is not compulsory for national courts to refer to and apply the Association Agreement.

The difference between EC-Turkey Association Agreement and other Europe Agreements is that the Association Council established under the Agreement, unlike its contemporaries, has been vested with too much power. According to Article 22(3) of the Ankara Agreement:

> Once the transitional stage has been embarked on, the Council of Association shall adopt appropriate decisions where, in the course of implementation of the Association arrangements, attainment of an objective of this Agreement calls for joint action by the Contracting Parties but the requisite powers are not granted in this Agreement.

With this power, the EC-Turkey Association Council adopted the Decision 1/95 on Customs Union. This Decision, concerned *entirely* with the free movement of goods and related issues, composed of 66 articles, entered into force on 1 January 1995.[23]

In relation to the Customs Union, Article 66 of the 1/95 Decision of the Association Council says that

> The provisions of this Decision, in so far as they are identical in substance to the corresponding provisions of the Treaty establishing the European Community *shall be interpreted* for the purposes of their implementation and application to products covered by the Customs Union, in conformity *with the relevant decisions of the Court of Justice of the European Communities.*

22 See the application of Associate Council Decision at national level in EU Members, ibid., pp. 65 et seq.

23 See Steve Peers, 'Living in Sin: Legal Integration under the EC-Turkey Customs Union', 7 *European Journal of International Law* (1996) pp. 411-430, available at: <http://www.ejil.org/journal/Vol7/No3/art3-01.html#TopOfPage>.

As the article points out it is incumbent upon Turkish judges to take into account the jurisprudence of the ECJ in order to give meaning to the provisions of the 1/95 Decision. Although no case has been found in this regard, as the Customs Union gets deeper, the Courts will have to refer to the decision of the ECJ as part of the dictum *pacta sund servanda.*

As no candidate country has entered into this kind of close cooperation with the EU other than Turkey, there are some references of national courts with regard to the provisions of the Customs Union Decision. Turkey is especially under the obligation to adopt a detailed list of EC legislation and international conventions on intellectual property rights (IPRs) and implement most rules of the TRIPS (Trade-Related Aspects of Intellectual Property Rights) agreement. Turkey is also obliged to adopt the EC's competition and state aid rules. For example, the Turkish legislation on the protection of patent rights has been prepared according to EC norms. The Decree-Law on Trademarks (No. 556) was issued in 1995 to adopt national legislation, *inter alia*, to comply with the Customs Union provisions.[24]

Article 4 of the Decree-Law says that

> Where the provisions of International Agreements which have entered into force as provided by the Laws of the Turkish Republic afford preferable provisions than this Decree-Law, persons referred in Article 2 may request treatment according to the preferable provisions.

For example, the Court of Cassation ruled in 1988 that the 1883 Paris Convention for the Protection of Industrial Property, to which Turkey acceded in 1925, prevails over the Intellectual Property Act No. 551.[25] In this case, the plaintiff who possesses "Davidoff", as a trademark, wanted it to be protected in Turkey. The District Court refused the application on the grounds that the 6-month and 3-year prescription periods, laid down in Article 15 of the Decree-Law No. 551, had elapsed. According to Article 6bis(2) of the Paris Convention, the prescription period is at least five years.[26] Paragraph 3 of the same article says that "no time limit shall be fixed for requesting the cancellation or the prohibition of the use of marks registered or used in bad faith." In the end, the Court settled the matter by relying on the provision of the Paris Convention and upheld the claim of the

---

24 Decree-Law No. 556 Pertaining to the Protection of Trademarks (in force as from 27 June 1995).

25 The Court of Cassation, 11th Civil Chamber, E.1988/1918, K.1988/3940, (1988) 15/5 Yargıtay Kararları Dergisi, 680.

26 "A period of at least five years from the date of registration shall be allowed for requesting the cancellation of such a mark. The countries of the Union may provide for a period within which the prohibition of use must be requested."

plaintiff who registered the "Davidoff" trade mark long before the accused party, holding that there was resulting unjust competition.

Three years later, the Court of Cassation once again had to deal with the time-bar set for the protection of trademarks,[27] although the Court has said that perpetual protection of trademark is against the *ratio legis* and the spirit of the Intellectual Property Act and of the 89/104 Directive[28] adopted in accordance with Article 189 of the EC Treaty (laying down a five-year time period). As a result, the Court settled the case in accordance with the Paris Convention.

In another case, the Court of Cassation had to deal with the meaning of Article 10(2) of Annex 8 of the 1/95 Decision which says that "This decision does not imply exhaustion of intellectual, industrial and commercial property rights applied in the trade relations between the two Parties under this Decision" (the so-called parallel import principle).[29]

As to the Council of State, one can find some cross referrals to the EC law in its decisions. For example, when dealing with the legality of the pecuniary penalty given by the Competition Board, the Council upheld the decision of the Board and mentioned that the criteria used for the imposition of pecuniary penalty are consistent with the practice of the EU Commission and the case-law of the ECJ and the standards provided for the Guidelines on the Implementation of Pecuniary Penalties in the EU Competition Law.[30] In another case, the Council of State referred to Articles 13 and 14 of the 1/95 Decision (on the adjustment of custom tariffs).[31]

2.6 Supremacy and direct effect

Since Turkey is not a full member of the EU, national courts have not yet had the chance to pronounce upon the principles of supremacy and direct effect of EU/EC law in their decisions. However, as the Association Agreement, the 1970 Protocol and the Decisions of the Association Council contain provisions having the impact of natural and legal persons especially in the fields of competition and intellectual law. Therefore, in these areas, albeit limited, EC law is taken into account to determine the legal position of the parties. All the same, this is not tantamount to embracing the supremacy and direct effect principles.

---

[27] The Court of Cassation, 11th Chamber, E.2001/10860, K.2002/3275, 8 April 2002.

[28] First Directive 89/104/EEC of the Council, of 21 December 1988, to Approximate the Laws of the Member States Relating to Trade Marks (*OJ* L 40 of 11 February 1989, p. 1).

[29] E.g., the Court of Cassation, 11th Chamber, E. 1999/2086, K. 1999/4505, 26 May 1999 (on *LANCOME Et Beaute et Cie*).There are a lot of other cases.

[30] The Council of State, 10th Chamber, 18 November 2003, E. 2001/1441, K. 2003/4468.

[31] The Council of State, 1st Chamber, E. 1997/136, K. 1997/195, 24 December 1997 (on Council of Ministers Decree on Import Regime).

It is worth mentioning that the implementation of the European Convention of Human Rights has been a litmus test for the Turkish judiciary. Before 22 May 2004, Article 90 of the Constitution did not contain a clause on the supremacy of human rights treaties, the case law of Supreme Courts recognising the supremacy of human rights treaties is a good omen as it has parallels with EC law. The case law of the Constitutional Court,[32] the Council of State[33] and the Court of Cassation[34] lead one to conclude that in the future the recognition of the supremacy and direct effect of Community law will not present problems.

There is another point worth mentioning. International law relies primarily for its effectiveness on the implementation by national judiciaries in that when state officials do not want to apply an international rule they take refuge in the non self executing shield; it is only the duty of the legislator to make it executable. To this end, Article 138 of the Constitution provides that "Judges ... shall give judgment in accordance with the Constitution, law, and their personal conviction conforming with the law". As the implementation of the direct effect and supremacy principles hinges, to a large extent, on the willingness of the judiciary to accept them, it is necessary that judges be encouraged to apply Community law. Hence, Article 138 might be paraphrased so as to cover Community law. Alternatively, the wording "in accordance with ... law" may be interpreted in such a way as to take into account Community law with a certain rank of priority. Otherwise, recourse to the preliminary review procedure, furnished in Article 234 of the EC Treaty, may be limited.

Article 11(2) of the Constitution says that "Laws shall not be in conflict with the Constitution". It might be useful to add a phrase to this sentence so that the obligations arising from the EC law are not ignored. The sequel of the sentence might be "Laws *and laws of supranational nature* shall not be in conflict with the Constitution".

In this light, the harmonization and translation of the *acquis* should go hand in hand with recruiting judges, changing the syllabi of the curricula of law schools making EC law a compulsory course, and in-service training of existing judges. Efforts continue to develop sustainable training programmes on the *acquis* and its implementation especially in the field of Justice and Home Affairs with a view to

---

[32] The Constitutional Court, E.1987/1, K.1987/18, 11 September 1987, AMKD, 23, 305: E.1990/15, K.1991/5, 28 February 1991 (Official Gazette, 27 March 1992, No. 21184): E.1996/15, K.1996/34, 23 September 1996 (Official Gazette, 27 December 1996): E.199/25, K.1991/1, 10 January 1991, (Official Gazette, 5 March 1992, No. 21162) and in E.1996/6, K.1991/20, 3 July 1991, (Official Gazette 8 March 1992, No. 21165).

[33] The Council of State, Joint Decision of the General Board of Supreme Council of State, E.1988/6, K.1989/4, 7 December 1989) (Official Gazette 9 February 1990, No. 20428).

[34] The Supreme Council of the Court of Cassation, 24 May 1995, 4-367/550, July 1995, YKD, 1013-1027: The Court of Cassation, 11th Civil Chamber, E.1988/1918, K.1988/3940, (1988) 15/5 YKD 680.

increasing the knowledge of judges and public prosecutors on the basic principles of Community law.

2.7 Indirect effect

As stated above, EC law is not superior and directly applicable. Therefore, judges are to take into account the positive law of Turkey. As there are a few cases that are indirectly referring to the EC legislation, it is hard to speculate how the judiciary will adopt a consistent attitude.

Generally speaking, Articles 26 and 27 of the 1969 Vienna Convention on the Law of Treaties say that "Every treaty in force is binding upon the parties to it and must be performed by them in good faith" and "A party may not invoke the provisions of its internal law as justification for its failure to perform a treaty". Thanks to the legal acumen of judges, in most cases, treaties are taken seriously by adhering to the *pacta sund servanda* principle. Despite the fact that international treaties, except the ones on human rights, are regarded at the same level as laws, judges in most cases are not inclined to apply *lex specialis* and *lex posterior* principles.

2.8 Cases

The Constitutional Court has not so far dealt with the Community Law directly. Nevertheless, the Constitutional Court, every now and then, faces unconstitutionality of laws enacted for the adoption of the *acquis*. For example, on 3 August 2002, Law No. 4771, dubbed as the EU Harmonisation Law, was passed by Parliament, making a number of amendments in various laws to remove obstacles in Turkish positive law on the way to EU membership. The Nationalist Movement Party (MHP), which was then a part of the three-pronged coalition, filed a lawsuit at the Constitutional Court requesting the annulment of six articles of the Law No. 4771. Despite some quarters forming a fierce front against the reforms,[35] the Constitutional Court on 27 December 2002 dismissed the claims.[36] As mentioned earlier in this report, Article 35 of the Land Law (on the acquisition of

---

[35] Namely, abolition of the death penalty, the recognition of cultural rights of non-Muslim minorities, allowing religious and minority institutions to buy and sell property; broadcasting television programmes in languages other than Turkish; teaching in languages other than Turkish provided they do not compromise constitutional principles; that no punishment be applied to written, vocal or pictorial criticism of the military, state institutions, parliament, the government, justice system or Turkish identity; the right to re-trial if the European Court of Human Rights finds a violation of rights guaranteed by the Convention.

[36] E.2002/146, K.2002/201, 27 December 2002, Official Gazette, 11 December 2003, No. 25313.

land by foreigners) is challenged before the Constitutional Court. It is expected that by early 2005, a decision will be given in this regard.

As to the Council of State, one can allude to three interesting decisions on the Customs Union and candidacy period.

The first decision is on the legal status of the 1/95 Decision of the Association Council. The background of the case is as follows: In March 1995, the Association Council adopted the 1/95 Decision on Customs Union, the EC's first substantial customs union with a third state. It is concerned *entirely* with the free movement of goods and related issues. Although the Decision put Turkey under obligation to adopt legislation, to reach agreements and to apply Treaty articles equivalent to provisions adopted by the EC, it was not regarded as an agreement (i.e., treaty). The Customs Union required not just abolition of tariffs and quotas between the parties, but a common customs[37] and common trade policy.[38] These require changes in national legislation. However, the Association Council Decisions are neither sent to Parliament for approval, nor promulgated by a Governmental Decree nor ratified by the President, nor are they published in the Official Gazette. This is against the practice of other candidate countries which regard Association Council decisions as a form of treaty, or quasi-treaty and publish them in Official Gazettes/Law Collections.[39]

Although, the way the 1/95 Decision was adopted is blatantly against Article 90(4) of the Constitution, the Council of State did pretend not to see the fact that the Council decisions are out of the scope of the judicial review of the Constitutional Court.[40]

---

37 Article 13: "Upon the date of entry into force of this Decision, Turkey shall, in relation to countries which are not members of the Community, align itself on the Common Customs Tariff.

38 With a view to harmonizing its commercial policy with that of the Community, Turkey shall align itself progressively with the preferential customs regime of the Community within five years as from the date of entry into force of this Decision. This alignment will concern both the autonomous regimes and preferential agreements with third countries.

39 See, national reports of candidate countries in Ott and Inglis, op. cit. n. 1. See especially Wolfgang Weiß, 'EC Agreements in the Member States', ibid., at pp. 201-204; Frank Hoffmeister, 'International Agreements in the Legal Orders of the Candidate Countries', ibid., at pp. 209-220; For Bulgaria, E. Evtimov, ibid., at p. 223 and the National Report of Bulgaria, at pp. 33-34; For Czech Republic, V. Týč, ibid., at p. 230; For Cyprus, N. Emiliou, ibid., at p. 241; For Estonia, E. Pärn, ibid., at p. 253; For Hungary, O. Várhelyi, ibid., at p. 259; For Latvia, D. Luters-Thümmel, ibid., at p. 276; For, Lithuania, V. Vadapalas and I. Jarukaitis, ibid., at p. 285; for the Slovak Republic, B. Boháčik, ibid., at p. 337.

40 Moreover, Turkey has to accept decisions taken within EU committees without having the right to take part in this decision-making process. According to Articles 16, and 52 to 64 of the Customs Union Decision, Turkey undertakes the same obligations as the EU members. This amounts to *de facto* transfer of legislative power. For general information see Zuhal Yeşilyurt Gündüz, 'Turkey's Approach towards the EU: Views from Within, Perceptions': *Journal of International Affairs*, 8/3, September-November 2003, available at: <http://www.mfa.gov.tr/grupa/percept/VIII-3/ZuhalYesilyurtGunduz.htm>.

When the first case came to the Council of State in 1996, the plaintiff argued that the Decision which was signed by the Minister of Foreign Affairs be declared invalid. The Council of State, after citing the ruling of the Administrative Court which deemed the Decision to be a resolution for an international organisation, stated that the plaintiff had no *locus standi* to initiate the proceeding and thereby quashed the appeal.[41]

The Court was faced with another claim in 2001 regarding the invalidity of the National Programme for the Adoption of the *Acquis* (NPAA) and the Decree of the Council of Ministers on Approval and Implementation of the National Programme. The Court again struck down the application on the grounds that the National Programme is not an enforceable act of Government.[42]

The third and last case is very recent. In January 2004, the Council of State faced the question as to the legal validity of the 1/95 Association Council Decision. The Chairman of the Chamber of Commerce of Ankara lodged an application demanding that the Decision be declared null and void on the ground that the Decision was put into force contrary to the provisions of Articles 87 and 90 of the Constitution. The plaintiff argued that the procedure envisaged in the Constitution was not followed for the Decision even though the Decision is an agreement in practice. The plaintiff was of the conviction that the Decision is very much different from other decisions of the Association Council in view of the fact that it contains provisions similar to treaties.

The Court got around these arguments cunningly and held that declaring an act as "null and void" has not been enumerated among the tasks of the Council of State and therefore, the Court is not entitled to hear the case.[43]

In all these cases, the 10th Chamber did not even take into account the merits of the case. By taking a diplomatically skilful approach, the Court did not want to intervene in one of the problematic issues of high politics.

2.9 Structure, procedure and practice

In view of the fact that the population of Turkey is slightly lower than the total population of all new Member States (approx 71[44] to 73 million respectively), there are a good many reasons to conclude that Turkey's efforts to reform the judiciary should be far more complicated than those of other states.

---

41 Danıştay (The Council of State) 10th Chamber, E.1996/1908, K.1998/759, 23 February 1998.

42 Danıştay (The Council of State) 10th Chamber, E.2001/1633, K.2001/2722, 26 June 2001.

43 Danıştay (The Council of State) 10th Chamber, E.2003/6017 K.2004/12, Decision Date 12 January 2004.

44 Turkey's population is 68 million. With over three million Turkish workers living in Europe, who constitute by far the largest group of third-country nationals legally residing within the EU, the population of Turks reaches over 71 million.

This conviction stems from the fact that when Turkey recognised the individual application procedure for the European Commission on Human Rights in 1987 and for the European Court of Human Rights in 1990, thousands of applications have been lodged to the registries of the ECHR. For many years, Turkey was in the forefront of countries regarding the number of applications made against the Member States. At present, Turkey has been surpassed by other countries. This illustrates that when Turkey becomes a full member, the number of applications made to national courts and the ECJ might be much higher than expected. For example, in February 2004, the Court of First Instance of the European Court of Justice approved a lawsuit for damages filed by YEDAŞ, a Turkish automotive-parts producing company, which claims that it has incurred losses due to Turkey's membership in the Customs Union and that it has sustained quantifiable and significant losses due to omissions by a European Community institution, and has brought an action for damages before the Court of First Instance.[45] The Company aroused great interest and cleared the path for other firms. The case is still pending. There are a number of firms that are in the queue. This example shows that in the future not only the case law of the ECJ and CFI, but also national courts will increase in the field of competition law.

Before restructuring the judiciary in the face of a massive flow of incoming applications, the education of judges should be given priority.

To begin with, the teaching of the EC law could be a compulsory subject in 30 law faculties. Secondly, teaching English should be compulsory for law schools. The fact that the complete translation of the *acquis* is an insurmountable task for the near future, means that judges should be able to read and understand at least the relevant case law of the ECJ.

In-service training is important for the possibility to make preliminary references to the European Court of Justice under Article 234 of the EC Treaty. Thanks to the efforts of the Undersecretariat of the EU of the Ministry of Justice, there are intensive seminars conducted to raise awareness.

All courts should be equipped with speedy and free internet access. There must be a database through which judges can get access to the relevant case law of European courts as well as Turkish courts. One a project being carried out at the moment has each judge being given a notebook computer. An intranet system, called UYAP, has recently become operational. It is expected that the interconnection of courts to each other will significantly speed up trials.

---

[45] Turkey is the only country that became a party to the Customs Union without receiving membership status from the EU.

3. ROLE OF THE EXECUTIVE (GOVERNMENT AND ADMINISTRATION)

3.1 Europe Agreement or Stabilization and Association Agreement

Turkey signed the Association Agreement with the European Economic Community more than four decades ago.[46] The EEC's response to Turkey's application in 1959 was to suggest the establishment of an association until Turkey's circumstances permitted its accession. The ensuing negotiations resulted in the signature of the Agreement Establishing an Association between the Republic of Turkey and the EEC (known as the Ankara Agreement of 1963) and the Additional Protocol of 1970.[47]

As the Ankara Agreement is a framework treaty, its implementation has been provided through the protocols and the decisions of the Turkey-E(E)C Association Council. Suffice it to mention herewith the most important protocol, namely, the Additional Protocol of 1970 and the 1/95 Customs Union Decision, the most important decision of the Association Council.

The Additional Protocol provided that Turkey would abolish tariff and quantitative barriers to its imports from EEC in accordance with a timetable containing two calendars set for 12 and 22 years and called for the harmonisation of Turkish legislation with that of the EU in economic matters. Turkey complied, on the whole, with the terms of the Protocol. But, the Additional Protocol which envisaged the free circulation of persons between the Parties in the next 12 to 22 years has not been put into force by the E(E)C. Had this been done, the free circulation of goods and services and the harmonisation of Turkish legislation with that of the EEC in a multitude of areas would have been achieved at the end of the 22 year timetable, or, to be more precise, after 1995.

At the end of the 22 year time table, the Council of Association adopted Decision 1/95 on the completion of the Customs Union between Turkey and the EC in industrial and processed agricultural goods on 6 March 1995.[48] Accordingly, the association regime entered its final stage with the introduction of the customs union on 1 January 1996 between Turkey and the EC. At the same meeting, another resolution on accompanying measures was adopted and the EU made a

---

46 Turkey applied to be associate member to the European Economic Community (EEC) on 31 July 1959 according to Article 238 of the Treaty of Rome, nineteen months after the enforcement of the Treaty of Rome.

47 Ankara Agreement was signed at Ankara, on 12 September 1963. It entered into force on 1 December 1964. The Additional Protocol was signed at Brussels on 23 November 1970. It entered into force on 1 January 1973.

48 Turkey is the only candidate country that started to implement customs union before becoming a full member of the EC/EU.

declaration on financial cooperation with Turkey as part of the Customs Union "package".

Since the enforcement of a Customs Union as from January 1996, Turkey has made great progress in adopting EU legislation and forming similar structures like those in the Community. Turkey has fulfilled a large part of its obligations defined in Association Council Decision No. 1/95 and concluded customs union by 2001. To be more specific, after entry into force of the Customs Union Decision, Turkey abolished all duties and charges having equivalent effect imposed on imports of industrial products of EC and EFTA origin.[49] Furthermore, Turkey commenced the implementation of Common Customs Tariff, applied by the EC, to industrial products originating from third countries. To this end, Turkey harmonized its tariffs and equivalent charges on the import of industrial goods from "third countries" and progressively adopted EU commercial policy and preferential tariff policies within 5 years. For certain specifically-identified "sensitive" products, Turkey would maintain rates of protection above those specified in the Common Customs Tariff for imports originating in third countries for up to five years. These products include mainly ceramic products, motor vehicles and footwear.

As a result of these measures, Turkey's weighted rates of protection for imports of industrial products have fallen from 5.9 per cent to 0 per cent for products originating in the EU and EFTA and from 10.8 per cent to 6 per cent for products originating in third countries. These rates will drop further to 3.5 per cent after the fulfilment by the EU of its commitment under the Uruguay Round. Although agricultural products are excluded from the Customs Union Decision, Turkey is progressively adopting many aspects of the Common Agricultural Policy. However, in return the EU is under the obligation of taking as much account as possible of Turkish agricultural interests when developing its agricultural policy. Progressive improvement, on a mutually advantageous basis, of the preferential arrangements for the trade in agricultural products is also envisaged.[50]

As the Customs Union requires Turkey to harmonise its commercial and competition policies, including intellectual property laws, with those of the Union, and extends most of the EU's trade and competition rules to the Turkish economy, harmonization work with the EU's commercial policy includes monitoring and safeguarding measures on imports both from the EU and third countries, the management of quantitative restrictions and tariff quotas and the prevention of dumped and subsidized imports.

---

[49] Turkish Customs Law, being in force since early 2000, has been completely revised and reinforced.

[50] See 'Relations between Turkey and the European Union', available at: <http://www.mfa.gov.tr/MFA/ForeignPolicy/MainIssues/TurkeyAndEU/EUHistory.htm>.

The Customs Union that was meant to be applied between the Parties went much further than the abolition of tariff and quantitative barriers to trade between the Parties and the application of a Common External Tariff to imports from third countries, and envisaged "harmonization with" E(E)C policies in virtually every field relating to the internal market, and most importantly by adopting common commercial policy *vis-à-vis* to third countries.

According to the preferential trade regimes, Turkey has already concluded bilateral free trade agreements with EFTA, Israel and all Central and Eastern European Countries (CEECs), which have been granted preferential market access. Negotiations are in progress with Croatia, Tunisia, Egypt, Morocco and Palestine. Additionally, a free trade agreement has been concluded as to products covered by the European Coal and Steel Community (ECSC). There is now effective co-operation between Turkey and the EU in the fields of standardisation, calibration, quality, accreditation, testing and certification. New rules parallel to EU's industrial standards and conformity assessments have been enacted, and an accreditation institute was set up in 2000 to oversee the implementation.[51]

Turkey has adopted EC rules and legislation on competition. Subsidies through State resources in any form whatsoever which distort or threaten to distort competition are banned. However assistance to promote economic development in Turkey's less-developed regions and assistance intended to promote cultural heritage conservation and which does not adversely affect competition will be allowed. On the other hand, Turkey is progressively adjusting any state monopoly of a commercial character so as to ensure that no discrimination exists in the conditions under which goods are produced or marketed between nationals of EU member countries and Turkey. The co-operation between Turkey and the EC in the fields of standardization, calibration, quality, accreditation, testing and certification is ever-developing. Turkey has aligned its legislation on intellectual and industrial property rights to EC standards and has implemented laws covering consumer protection, and the protection of competition. Both sides are banned from using internal taxes as indirect protection mechanisms and from using tax rebates as export subsidies.

In sum, the Turkish Governments of recent years have amended laws to conform to EC legislation eliminating technical barriers to trade. EU related reforms and their implementation have been a stock-in-trade item on the weekly agenda of the Council of Ministers since December 2003. A Deputy Prime Minister has been commissioned to provide a brief account to the Council on progress in implementing the National Programme for Adoption of the *Acquis*. The Ministers have also received regular briefings about the state of play of the implementation of the reforms.

---

[51] Ercan Atak, 'Harmonization of Turkish Legislation and Practice with that of the European Union', available at: <http://www.tbmm.gov.tr/ul_kom/kpk/pre1.doc>.

3.2 Preparation and implementation of EC/EU law

Coordination mechanisms for the preparation and implementation of EC/EU law can be classified into two groups. These are, namely, (a) Coordination mechanisms established between/within Turkish Ministries and public institutions; (b) Coordination mechanisms composed both of the representatives of EC/EU and Turkish sides.

3.2.1 *Coordination mechanisms between/within Turkish ministries and public institutions*

In order to ensure coordination between Turkish Ministries/public institutions, there are three main coordination mechanisms which have been envisaged for the preparation and implementation of EC/EU Law. These are as follows:

A. Inter-ministerial Monitoring Group for the EU Reforms

A High-profile Monitoring Group for the EU Reforms was established in September 2003 with a view to ensuring effective implementation of the reforms made within the framework of the harmonization process. The Monitoring Group is responsible for determination of the problems arising from the implementation of the reforms and for solution to these problems.

The Reform Monitoring Group is composed of the Ministers of Foreign Affairs, Justice and the Interior and high-level bureaucrats, namely the Secretary General for the EU Affairs, the Head for Human Rights of the Prime Ministry and the Head of the Advisory Committee for Human Rights. The Monitoring Group is chaired by the Minister of Foreign Affairs and Vice-Prime Minister.

The implementation of the reforms continues to be a permanent item on the agenda of the Council of Ministers. In addition, the Council of Ministers decided to designate a Deputy Prime Minister to report to the Council on a weekly basis on the situation of draft legislation pertaining to the commitments under the Turkish National Programme.

B. Secretariat General for the EU Affairs

A "Secretariat General for the EU Affairs" under the Prime Ministry was set up in 2000 to co-ordinate all of Turkey's policies related to the pre-accession process.[52]

[52] The Law No. 4587 on the organization and functions of the General Secretariat for the EU adopted by the Turkish Grand National Assembly on 27 June 2000 and published in the Official Gazette No. 24099 on 4 July 2000.

The General Secretariat was connected to the Minister of Foreign Affairs in 2003. According to Article 2 of the Law No. 4587 establishing the Secretariat, the General Secretariat for the EU Affairs is assigned coordinating, in conformity with plans and programmes, internal efforts of harmonization to be carried out by the Turkish public organizations and agencies, providing secretarial services to the boards and committees which shall be established with a view to preparing Turkey for membership to the EU, and guiding the implementation of the decisions of the said boards and committees, conducting required research and studies in line with the decisions of the Government and the boards and committees to be established, awarding, by contract and in areas of its competence, to natural and legal persons both within Turkey and abroad, the tasks of making studies, research and translations, issuing, through the Prime Ministry, regulations, communications, circulars and other similar regulatory instruments concerning the services that it is responsible to render.

Besides taking into consideration the process of alignment of Turkish legislation to *acquis communautaire*, the government adopted a novel approach in its legislation procedure whereby the opinion of the Secretariat General for EU Affairs has to be given and attached, *inter alia*, to the draft proposals before it is sent to the Prime Ministry.

C. EU Departments of the ministries and public institutions

Following the Decree-Law No. 367,[53] issued by the Council of Ministers on 14 April 1989 and calling for the establishment of EC affairs units/agencies within the ministries, public institutions and dependent organizations attached to the Prime Ministry, the European Community/Union Coordination Departments have been established in almost all ministries. These departments provide coordination on issues concerning the European Community within the framework of their ministries respective functions.

After the Helsinki Summit in December 1999 where Turkey was accepted as a candidate country, EU departments of the ministries and public institutions have greatly expanded both in administrative terms and in terms of number of staff employed.

A prominent example is the General Directorate of Relations with the European Union, established under the State Planning Organisation whose functions are to conduct studies and research on the targets and policies to be determined by

[53] Decree-Law on the establishment of the units that deal with the European Community affairs in the ministries and public institutions and on making amendment in the chart which is appendix of the Decree-Law No. 190. It was published in the Official Gazette No. 20158 on 4 May 1989.

the Government within the scope of relations with the European Union comprising economic, social, legal and other subjects and to make recommendations.[54]

3.2.2 *Coordination mechanisms composed of the representatives of both the EC/EU side and the Turkish side*

The bodies established in order to provide continuity of relationship between Turkey and the Community and to create the grounds for the solution of problems between the two parties are as follows:

- *A* ***Council of Association (Turkey-EC Association Council)*** has been established pursuant to Article 6 of the Ankara Agreement to ensure the implementation and the progressive development of the Association. The Council of Association which is the most important body of Turkey-EC Association has the power to take decisions. The decisions of the Council of Associations are part of the *acquis communautaire* and legally binding.
- *A* ***Turkey-EC Joint Parliamentary Commission*** has been established pursuant to European Parliament's decision on 14 May 1965, Turkish Grand National Assembly's decision on 22 June 1965 and decision of Turkey E(E)C Association Council on 27 July 1965. The Commission is composed of an equal number of members from the Turkish Grand National Assembly and European Parliament. The Commission is responsible for the evaluation of issues stemming from the Ankara Agreement with particular emphasis on the annual reports submitted by Association Council to the Office of Speaker of the Turkish Grand National Assembly and the European Parliament.
- *A* ***Turkey-EC Association Committee*** has been established by the Decision number 3/64 of the Council of Association. The Committee prepares the agenda of the Council of Association, and evaluates the technical problems arising from Partnership Relations. The Committee is composed of technicians from both sides.
- *A* ***Customs Cooperation Committee*** has been established in accordance with Article 6 of the Ankara Agreement and under the Decision of the Council of Association number 2/69 to ensure the implementation and development of the association common regime.
- *A* ***Turkey-EU Joint Consultative Committee*** has been established pursuant to the Decision of Turkey-EC Association Council number 1/95 with a view to ensuring cooperation on a systematic and regular basis.

---

[54] Article 15 of the Decree-Law No. 540 (Reorganization of the State Planning Organization; decided by the Council of Ministers on 19 June 1994 based on the authority accorded by the Law No. 4004, dated 16 June 1994).

The Helsinki European Council of 1999 called on the Commission to draw up an Accession Partnership for Turkey and to set up appropriate monitoring mechanisms. It also invited the Commission to prepare of analytical examination of the Community's *acquis*. In line with the Helsinki European Council Conclusions, on 11 April 2000 with the decision of the EC-Turkey Association Council, 8 sub-committees were established to carry out an analytical examination of the level of alignment of the Turkish legislation with the *acquis communautaire.*[55] These subcommittees are working in the following fields: 1. Agriculture and Fisheries; 2. Transport, Environment and Energy; 3. Internal Market and Competition; 4. Innovation, Education and Cooperation Programmes; 5. Regional Development, Employment and Social Policy; 6. Trade, Industry and ECSC Products; 7. Economics and Monetary Issues, Capital Movements and Statistics; and 8. Customs, Taxation, Drug Trafficking and Money Laundering.

The sub-committees work under the authority of the Association Committee,[56] to which they shall report after each of their meetings, as they do not have decision-making capacity. Between June 2000 and July 2001, they completed two rounds of meetings in Brussels and Ankara/Istanbul on a rotating basis. The third round was initiated in March 2002 and completed in July 2002. The fourth round of meetings was held in October 2003.

3.3 Impact of EU accession on the organization and practice of central government and administration and the decentralized authorities

The Turkish Government announced its own National Programme for the Adoption of the EU *Acquis* (NPAA) on 19 March 2001. It was updated and published in the Official Gazette in 2003.[57] With this document, Turkey heralded a new beginning in her efforts in the fields of democratization, human rights and liberal economic policies. The NPAA also requires a wide range of harmonization efforts in many fields including the political system. In the NPAA, there are special chapters in all parts called "Necessary Institutional Changes". In these chapters, Turkey's commitments aiming at strengthening the administrative capacity have been indicated. These commitments include:

- The establishment of new institutions, units, departments, boards etc.,
- Training of the personnel of both central and decentralized authorities,

---

[55] Decision No. 3/2000 of the EC-Turkey Association Council of 11 April 2000 on the establishment of subcommittees of the Association Committee (2000/378/EC).

[56] The EC-Turkey Association Committee has been established by the decision number 3/64 of the Association Council. The Committee prepares the agenda of Association Council, and evaluates the technical problems arising from Partnership relations. The Committee is composed of technicians from both sides.

[57] Official Gazette, No. 25178 on 24 July 2003.

- Revision and re-organization of central and decentralized authorities,
- Expansion of these authorities.

These kinds of legislative and administrative changes have been made to strengthen the administrative capacity both in the central government and the decentralized authorities since the adoption of the first NPAA.[58]

These initiatives on strengthening the administrative capacity have had a very important effect on the organization and practice of central government and administration and the decentralized authorities. The initiatives on strengthening the administrative capacity require:

- Effective operation of the central government and administration and the decentralized authorities,
- Transparency of the government and decentralized authorities.

With regard to the transparency of the government and decentralized authorities, "The Law on the Right to Information" (No. 4982) was enacted in 2003. This act requires any central or local public institutions to reply to a request from natural persons or legal persons, whether citizen or foreigner, for access to official information or documents within 15 working days. This will undoubtedly help to improve relations between citizens and public authorities; to combat corruption and to achieve good administration.

The current government has launched a comprehensive preparation for public administration reform and drawn up a series of draft laws. In the context of public administration reform, various current duties of the central government will be transferred to local administrations and decentralization of the administration will be accomplished. This draft aims at decentralization for strengthening of the local government in such way as to enable the local self-government units to perform a much broader scope of work and to grant them a higher and wider level of autonomy from the central government.

The EU *acquis communautaire* does not contain provisions governing the functioning, structure, responsibilities or management of Municipalities, Metropolitan Municipalities or Provincial Local Administrations. Nevertheless, the draft Public Administration Law[59] is a framework law regulating the governing principles as regards central and local administrations. The said framework law envisages the removal of branches of certain ministries by delegating their

---

[58] The first NPAA was adopted on 19 March 2001 and published in the Official Gazette No. 24352 on 24 March 2001.

[59] This draft law, named the Law on Basic Principles and Restructuring of Public Administration, was accepted by Turkish Grand National Assembly on 15 July 2004. However, the President, by means of a veto, did not approve this law. The government still intends to enact this law.

competences and mandates to the local administrations. Thus, central and local public administration will have to make adjustments itself accordingly in the transitional period.

In fact, the Public Administration Reform, apart from this framework law, is a bundle of various laws such as the draft Law on Municipalities, draft Law on Metropolitan Municipalities and draft Law on Provincial Local Administrations and the Court of Audit Law. The principles of subsidiarity, partnership, transparency, accountability, as highlighted in the Commission's White Paper on Governance, have been reflected in several mechanisms in these draft laws, such as the inclusion of NGO representatives in Municipality Assemblies, City Councils, as well as in the auditing of municipalities, etc.

The European Charter of Local Self Government, signed by 41 states including certain EU member states, is the only international document that defines a common framework of understanding in the area of local governance. The Charter has also been taken into consideration during the preparation of the abovementioned draft laws. The draft laws will harmonize Turkish legislation with the Charter to a large degree.

A comparison of the Council of Europe Monitoring Committee Report dated 29 May 2003 and the three draft laws shows that these laws comprise major steps towards harmonization with the Charter.

There is no doubt that the initiatives on strengthening of the administrative capacity will be kept up during and after the negotiations regarding the accession of Turkey to the EU.

4. ROLE OF THE NATIONAL PARLIAMENT

4.1 Preparedness for legal approximation

With the contribution of the Turkish Grand National Assembly, Turkey is going through a dynamic process of legal, political and economic reforms on the road to European Union membership. After the Helsinki Summit of 1999, and especially, after the Turkish National Programme for the Adoption of the European Union *Acquis* of 24 March 2001, Turkey has undeniably made unprecedented efforts to honour the undertakings the National Programme for the Adoption of the *Acquis*. Between January 2000 and December 2004, the Turkish Grand National Assembly adopted a total of 774 new laws.[60] The rationale for the rapid legislation process was to a great extent to harmonize Turkish legislation with EU Law.

[60] Law No. 4501 was adopted on 21 January 2000; the final law (No. 5275 on Law on Execution of Punishment and Measures) was adopted on 13 December 2004). This figure covers approval of ratification of international treaties.

In order to advise the Parliament about the conformity of relevant laws with the *acquis*, the EU Harmonization Committee was established within the Turkish Grand National Assembly (TGNA), in April 2003 to work as a consultative body in the pre-accession process. The "European Union Harmonisation (Alignment) Committee", a specialized body, was set up in April 2003. As one of 17 permanent Parliamentary Committees, it is a supportive committee composed of 17 parliamentarians who know English or French very well.[61]

The main tasks and duties of this Committee are as follows:

(a) to monitor and discuss developments related to the process of accession of Turkey to the European Union,
(b) to monitor developments in the European Union and to give information to the Turkish Grand National Assembly on these developments,
(c) at the request of a Parliament speaker or *ex officio*, to review the compatibility of draft bills prepared by government or individual deputies, with the legislation or standards of the European Union and to submit opinions on these subjects to the principal Parliamentary committees, such as Constitutional Committee, Justice Committee or Foreign Affairs Committee,
(d) to draw up an evaluation report on developments related to the process of accession of Turkey to the European Union and its own annual activities and to give information on this report to the Turkish Grand National Assembly and the government,
(e) to conduct relations with Parliaments of Member States of the EU, of other candidate countries and institutions of the EU,
(f) to carry out activities for raising awareness of public opinion on accession to the European Union.

This Committee has the right to demand and gather information related to its tasks from ministries, public institutions, local authorities, universities and private institutions. The annual activity and evaluation report of the Committee can be put on the agenda of the plenary session of the Turkish Grand National Assembly in which this report is read and discussed. This report of the Committee is also sent to the Prime Ministry and relevant Ministries. The Committee has given its opinion on numerous pieces of legislation. The Committee invited representatives of the European Commission and of the Council of Europe to some of its discussions, such as on the draft Turkish Penal Code and the Local Administration Law.

As a starting point, the preamble and 33 articles of the Constitution, more than one-fifth of the Constitution composed of 177 articles, were amended on 3

---

[61] The organization and functioning of this permanent Committee is regulated by the Law numbered 4847 and internal rules of procedure of the Turkish Grand National Assembly.

October 2001. The package of constitutional amendments covers a wide range of issues, such as improving human rights, strengthening the rule of law and restructuring democratic institutions. This was only the initial step of a deep political reform process that Turkey initiated, which was soon followed by complementary and administrative measures to ensure their implementation. Turkey has also achieved comprehensive legislative reforms that reinforce and safeguard fundamental rights and freedoms, democracy, the rule of law and the protection of and respect for minorities. In this context, the Turkish Grand National Assembly has enacted nine "harmonization laws" packages which have introduced many radical changes.

In this vein, major laws that have been amended or enacted within the last three years are: Penal Code, Code of Penal Procedure, Law on Regional Courts of Appeal, Anti-Terror Law, Law on Establishment and Proceedings of State Security Courts, Civil Code, Law on Associations, Law on Foundations, Press Law, Criminal Record Law, Political Parties Law, Assembly and Demonstration Marches Law, Law on the Census, Law on National Security Council, Law on Establishment and Broadcasting of Radio and Television, Forensic Medicine Law; Formation, Competence and Proceedings of Family Courts, Law on Judicial Academy, Law on Execution of Punishment and Measures.

With these laws, the advisory role of the National Security Council has been redefined, the number of civilian members of the Council has been increased and the competence of the Council has been narrowed. Comprehensive legislative measures against torture and maltreatment have been put into force. The Death penalty has been abolished. The right to retrial in the light of the decisions of the European Court of Human Rights has been introduced to the Criminal Procedural Law, Civil Procedural Law and Administrative Procedural Law. Rules concerning conditions in prisons and detention houses have been brought in line with the norms of the European Convention of Human Rights and recommendations of the European Committee for the Prevention of Torture. The state of emergency has been lifted in all provinces of Turkey. The contents of freedom of thought and expression, freedom of the press, freedom of assembly and demonstration marches have been broadened. Provisions concerning associations and foundations have been improved. A new Civil Code has been enacted especially to reinforce gender equality. Much legislation has been amended to protect and improve cultural diversity, and to guarantee cultural rights and to enhance the right to learn and broadcast in different languages and dialects. Legislation concerning non-Muslim communities and foreigners has been improved. In the first stage, the military judge who had been one of the three judges of State Security Court was removed from the Court. The competence of State Security Court has been narrowed; the persons who are investigated or tried in State Security Courts have gained almost the same rights as persons who are investigated or tried in ordinary criminal courts. And finally, on May 2004, the State Security Courts were abolished and removed from the Turkish Court Structure. In addition, several international conventions in the context of the Council of Europe, and the United Nations relating to political criteria have been signed or ratified by TGNA.

In addition, the recent Law on the Amendment of Some Articles of the Constitution of the Republic of Turkey (No. 5170), entered into force 22 May 2004. Within the context of these constitutional amendments: gender equality has been further reinforced; the supremacy of human rights treaties has been recognized; the death penalty has been abolished in all circumstances, including in time of war or imminent threat of war; the freedom of press has been further strengthened; the necessary constitutional change has been made with a view to becoming party to the Statute of the International Criminal Court; the member of the High Education Council selected by the Army General Staff has been removed; the constitutional basis of State Security Courts has been abolished; and transparency in auditing state property in possession of the Armed Forces has been ensured.

With these legislative works (legislative packages for harmonization), the Turkish Grand National Assembly has been able to harmonize a good many laws in order to fulfil the political criteria which were the prerequisites to the opening of accession negotiations. However, the ultimate aim is to renew basic laws individually in the middle term through an integrated approach.[62]

Turkey has acceded to/signed/ratified a significant number of international human rights instruments since the Helsinki Summit of 1999, both within the UN framework and within the framework of the Council of Europe.[63] Acceding to or ratifying all international treaties[64] to which EU Member States are party is on the agenda of Turkish Grand National Assembly.

---

[62] Basic laws that are to be changed radically are as follows: Law of Obligations, Commercial Code; Law on the Establishment, Duties and Jurisdiction of the Arbitration; Law on Personal Data Protection, Law on the Union of Judges and Prosecutor of Turkey, Law on Ombudsman, Law Amending Law of Civil Procedure, Acts increasing the number and diversity of the specialised courts.

[63] The UN Covenant on Civil and Political Rights and the UN International Covenant on Social and Economic Rights (although with reservations); Protocol No. 6 to the European Convention for the Protection of Human Rights and Fundamental Freedoms (ECHR) on the abolition of the death penalty; UN Convention on the Elimination of All Forms of Racial Discrimination; the European Convention on the Exercise of Children's Rights and the Optional Protocol to the UN Convention on the Elimination of Discrimination against Women. Turkey has signed the UN Convention against corruption and ratified the Council of Europe Criminal Law Convention on Corruption. In January 2004, Turkey joined the Group of States against Corruption (GRECO). In April 2004 Turkey signed the Second Optional Protocol on the abolition of the death penalty. Turkey ratified the Optional Protocol to the Convention on the Rights of the Child on the Involvement of Children in Armed Conflict in October 2003.

[64] Turkey has not yet signed the Framework Convention for the Protection of National Minorities or the Revised European Social Charter and the Rome Statute of the International Criminal Court.

All in all, as the Turkish Grand National Assembly regards EU membership as a new step forward, a milestone confirming the founding philosophy of Turkey, in recent years it has taken a very active roll in the process of European integration by enacting various laws containing reforms in political, economic and social arenas that have been anticipated for decades. The TGNA has proved itself to be in the vanguard on the way to the legal approximation of national legislation with EC/EU law.

4.2 Control over decisions taken by ministers in the Council of the European Union

Possibly because of the fact that Turkey is a candidate country that has not started accession negotiations with the European Union yet, this issue has not been considered and discussed in Turkey hitherto. No special procedures except for general parliamentary control have been debated as of yet. As a general rule, the Turkish Grand National Assembly can have recourse to "question, interpellation, parliamentary investigation and vote of no confidence" as general parliamentary control mechanisms to keep control over decisions taken by ministers in the Council of the European Union.

As a candidate country, Turkey is aware of a democratic deficit in the EU, where governments play a legislative role in the EU. Turkey will evaluate the possibility of specific *ex ante* and *ex post* parliamentary control over the positions, decisions and actions of the Turkish Government in the Council of the European Union, in the case of membership of Turkey. Turkey intends to examine closely existent and proposed systems on this subject and the COSAC system for adopting efficient *ex ante* and *ex post* mechanisms and ensuring parliamentary control over decisions taken by ministers in the Council of European Union by taking into consideration the democratic deficit in the EU.

5. EUROPEAN CONSTITUTION

5.1 Impact of European Constitution on the Community legal order and accession

There are positive and negative aspects of the Treaty establishing a Constitution for Europe. On the positive side, there is a strong sense in Turkey that the draft European Constitution will strengthen the Union's legal order. To begin with, Turkey supported the idea that the Union should have a single legal personality,[65]

---

65 See State Minister and Deputy Prime Minister Mesut Yılmaz's address, available at: <http://www.euturkey.org.tr/abportal/uploads/files/EKİM-%20M%20Yilmaz.doc>.

replacing the existing legal personalities including that of the European Community. Turkey also subscribed to the abolishing of the pillar structure. Turkey favoured extending the judicial review by the Court of Justice and consultation with the European Parliament to the agreements to be concluded in the framework of second pillar.

The Treaty establishing a Constitution for Europe, *inter alia,* simplifies and consolidates the existent patchwork European Union legal order and brings to the EU legal order some new positive achievements. With regard to the positive side, this draft European Constitution brings citizens closer to the European Institutions and European design; delicately sets out how the EU institutions will work together, fills the democratic deficit considerably by enhancing the powers and roles of the European Parliament and National Parliaments of the Member States; allows national parliaments to challenge proposals for new EU laws, brings about better division of the European Union and Member States competences, entrenches decision making in the enlarged EU by extending "majority voting" to more areas, thus removing each country's veto power; increases transparency, level of respect for human rights and democracy, efficiency, and legitimacy of the Union by incorporating the Charter of Fundamental Rights into Constitution and giving it legally binding status, by abandoning the three pillars design and by mergering founding treaties and by attributing legal personality to the Union.

On the other hand, regarding the negative side, the Constitution does not give European citizens a greater say. In other words, it does not address how citizens relate to EU institutions. Citizens will find it hard to influence policies on justice and home affairs at the EU level because Members of European Parliament appear still to be not well-qualified when it comes to regulations and law-making. With regard to the enhanced role of national parliaments, it can be said that it is futile to debate laws if national parliaments have no powers to block them. National Parliaments will not be able to veto unacceptable laws in key areas such as trade, immigration or asylum. This is important when one considers that the EU Constitution accelerates the extension of EU powers to 15 new areas, including national employment, justice and home affairs policies.

Although all these criticisms have been voiced about the draft of the European Constitution, the general conviction in Turkey is that it is step forward and cannot be perceived as an impediment for accession of new states to the European Union, since the legal criteria for accession of new states to the European Union are not affected in any way.

5.2 Obstacles for ratification of the European Constitution

As long as due amendments are made to the 1982 Constitution, the ratification of the EU Constitution will not present problems. However, referral to two ancillary points would be useful.

According to Article 4 of the Constitution, "the provision of Article 1 of the Constitution establishing the form of the state as a Republic, the provisions in Article 2[66] on the characteristics of the Republic, and the provision of Article 3[67] shall not be amended, nor shall their amendment be proposed." If the European Constitution contained a provision contrary to the principles enunciated in Articles 1-3 of the Constitution, then its ratification would encounter serious obstacles.

As Turkey is sensitive to this issue, the Turkish Government played an active role in having the Christianity clause in the Constitution removed. As Turkish authorities are very diligent about preserving the secular identity of Turkey, any reference to religious preferences in the future might bring about legal arguments.

The EU Constitution is a historic milestone for all Member States. Therefore, its ratification process may be said to be different from other treaties. Recent discussions about how to ratify the Constitution have borne this out. In view of the fact that at least eight countries have already committed to holding a referendum over the EU Constitution, and more may follow suit, the Turkish Constitution might be changed so as to provide a provisional article on the ratification of the EU Constitution. However, as it is uncertain when the accession will finally take place, the issue of a referendum is not on the national agenda for the time being.

66 "The Republic of Turkey is a democratic, secular and social state governed by the rule of law; bearing in mind the concepts of public peace, national solidarity and justice; respecting human rights; loyal to the nationalism of Atatürk, and based on the fundamental tenets set forth in the Preamble".

67 "The Turkish state, with its territory and nation, is an indivisible entity. Its language is Turkish. Its flag, the form of which is prescribed by the relevant law, is composed of a white crescent and star on a red background. Its national anthem is the "Independence March". Its capital is Ankara."

Part II

Comparative Analyses

IMPACT OF EUROPEAN INTEGRATION ON NATIONAL CONSTITUTIONS AND PARLIAMENTS

Anneli Albi*

1. THE IMPACT OF (FUTURE) ACCESSION ON THE NATIONAL CONSTITUTIONS

1.1 The background to the amending of the Constitutions for the purpose of European integration

The Constitutions of five out of the six MATRA project countries studied in part I of this book are new: Bulgaria and Romania adopted their Constitutions in 1991 after the regime change, and Croatia and Slovenia did so in 1990 and 1991 respectively, as a result of gaining independence from the Yugoslav Federation. The Constitutional Charter of Serbia and Montenegro was adopted in February 2003, while Turkey's Constitution dates back to 1982. Similarly to the other Constitutions of Central and Eastern Europe, these Constitutions set forth complex provisions and safeguards for the protection of sovereignty and independence and, notably, most of them did not initially contain provisions concerning the delegation of powers to international organisations.[1] The Constitution of Croatia, and the recently adopted Constitutional Charter of Serbia and Montenegro, form exceptions in this respect. In the former, Articles 139 and 141 establish the procedure for ratification of "international agreements which grant international organizations or alliances powers derived from the Constitution". At the same time, it should be noted that the Croatian Constitution prohibits accession to alliances that may involve a renewal of "any Balkan state form of any kind" (Art. 141). In this respect, it is interesting to note that a similar mechanism, reconciling Western integration with a sensitive historical background, has been used in the Constitution of Lithuania: Lithuania was the only country, amongst the CEE accession countries, whose Constitution from the beginning contained a constitutional basis for the country's participation in international organisations.

* Dr Anneli Albi, Ph.D (European University Institute, Florence); Lecturer in EU law, University of Kent (UK).

[1] See in more detail A. Albi, *EU Enlargement and the Constitutions of Central and Eastern Europe* (Cambridge, Cambridge University Press 2005) pp. 24 et seq.

At the same time, however, it expressly prohibited participation in organizations based on the former USSR.

Amongst the reasons for the (initial) absence of a constitutional basis with regard to the delegation of powers to international organisations, the following could be pointed out. In Romania, as the contributors note, the Constitution "reflected the historical moment of the time of adoption".[2] Although it was, at the time, a progressive document, establishing a democratic framework and protection of fundamental rights, it failed to provide mechanisms that could accommodate European integration. Whilst this explanation probably also applies in part to the other countries, the silence with regard to international organisations seems to have been additionally caused by the sensitivity of the question of sovereignty after the change of the regime. In addition, the Constitutions of the Communist period did not deal with any aspects of international law, and it may be that because of this, the countries considered it their priority to establish mechanisms for the application and supremacy of international law, but remained cautious towards going a step further and creating a basis for delegation of powers to international organisations.

The absence of the provisions on transfer of powers to international organisations, with the exception of the Constitution of Croatia and that of Serbia and Montenegro, appears to be the primary reason why the contributors deem it necessary to amend the Constitutions for EU membership. Although the Constitutions do contain provisions on the application of international law (see section 1.3), these provisions were not considered to be sufficient to authorize membership in the EU. The Croatian contributors find that Croatia's accession could take place on the basis of the existing Articles 139 and 141; however, they nonetheless recommend complementing the Constitution with a special EU clause because of the EU's particular supranational character, and the definition of Croatia's sovereignty as inalienable, indivisible and untransferable in Article 2(1) of the Constitution.[3]

The second main reason for amending the Constitutions, as pointed out by the contributors, is the supremacy of the Constitutions. This is established expressly in Article 153(1) of the Constitution of Slovenia, Article 5 of the Constitution of Bulgaria, Article 5 of the Constitution of Croatia and Article 11(2) of the Constitution of Turkey. In addition, in Slovenia (Art. 160) and Bulgaria (Art. 149(1)), the Constitutions establish a procedure for preliminary constitutional review of treaties and treaties that are found to conflict with the Constitution may only be ratified after a prior constitutional amendment.[4] Some constitutional courts have

[2] V. Dudulescu and R. Adam, Romania, in this volume.

[3] T. Capeta, D. Mihelin and S. Rodin, Croatia, in this volume.

[4] In Romania, such a review was introduced by the amendments of 2003; see section 1.3.

reaffirmed the supremacy of the Constitutions over international treaties.[5] Amongst other reasons for amending the Constitutions for the purpose of membership of the EU, the contributors have mentioned the need to eliminate potential obstacles to integration and thereby demonstrate the country's readiness for accession, and that the amendments would also signal a genuine desire for full membership.

1.2 (Draft) amendments relating to the transfer of powers to the EU

The countries addressed in the framework of the MATRA project are at different stages of European integration, and this is also reflected in the situation regarding the amendment of their Constitutions for EU membership.

Slovenia, as a first-wave accession country, completed the amendments on 3 March 2003. The basis for delegating powers to the EU is created in the new Article 3a para. 1, which provides as follows:

> Pursuant to a treaty ratified by the National Assembly by a two-thirds majority vote of all deputies, Slovenia may transfer the exercise of part of its sovereign rights to international organisations which are based on respect for human rights and fundamental freedoms, democracy and the principles of the rule of law and may enter into a defence alliance with states which are based on respect for these values.

The second paragraph further regulates the accession procedure, which will be addressed later in section 2. The remaining amendments will be considered below in sections 1.3, 1.4 and 4.2.

In Romania, the Parliament in September 2003 adopted a remarkably extensive package of altogether seventy-nine amendments, which was subsequently approved by the people in a referendum held on 18-19 October. The core of the amendments lies in five paragraphs of Article 148, located in the new Section VI, which is entitled 'Euro-Atlantic Integration'.[6] The first paragraph lays down the basis for the transfer of powers to the EU: "Romania's accession to the constituent treaties of the European Union, with a view to transferring certain powers to Community institutions, as well as to exercising in common with the other Member States the abilities stipulated in such treaties, shall be carried out by

[5] Constitutional Court of Slovenia, Decision of 5 June 1997 on Europe Agreement, available at: <http://www.us-rs.si/en/index.html>, para. 12; Constitutional Court of Bulgaria, Decision No. 7 of 2 July 1992, published in *Durzhaven Vestnik* 56/92.

[6] Initially, the new provision was numbered as 145^1, but the Romanian Constitution was renumbered as a result of EU amendments. The new numbering will be used throughout this contribution, unless stated otherwise.

means of a law adopted in the joint session of the Chamber of Deputies and the Senate, with a majority of two-thirds of the number of deputies and senators". There was previously no clear basis for a transfer of powers. Furthermore, EU entry without such a provision would have been controversial under Article 1 of the Constitution, according to which Romania is "a sovereign, independent, unitary and indivisible National State".

In 2005, Bulgaria introduced a package of EU amendments that is also relatively extensive. Article 4(1) provides that the "Republic of Bulgaria shall participate in the construction and development of the European Union". According to Article 85, "[t]he National Assembly shall ratify or denounce by law all international instruments which … confer to the European Union powers ensuing from this Constitution", by a majority of two-thirds of all Members of Parliament. In the course of the debates, the question arose as to whether the EU amendments can be carried out by parliamentary procedure, or would require recourse to a rather difficult mechanism – the convening of the Grand National Assembly (see section 2 for the details of these amendment procedures). In July 2004, the Constitutional Court ruled that the first mode of amendment could be used. The Court's justification was that the Bulgarian Constitution is open to the international legal orders for the pursuance of aims and values under Article 24(2) of the Constitution, regarding the achievement of a "fair international order". Therefore, Bulgaria can transfer powers for the purpose of building a united Europe, and exercise part of its powers together with the other Member States of the EU. The Constitutional Court further ruled that the accession treaty would not change the balance of the constituted powers and the form of the state because Bulgaria will participate in the composition of the EU institutions and in the passing of their acts. The Court's view appears to demonstrate the sensitivities surrounding the rather difficult amendment procedure, given that in the contemporary world, the EU is regarded as one of the most highly integrated organizations, with far-reaching effects upon sovereign governance and the division of powers within its Member States. Such tensions with regard to the rigid procedures were also present in a number of 2004 accession countries, especially in the Baltic States, where a somewhat liberal interpretation of the procedural requirements had to be used.[7]

In the other countries, the EU amendments are still in the phase of theoretical debates. In Croatia, which officially became a candidate country on 18 June 2004, the contributors recommend the introduction of amendments that would create a legal basis for EU membership, and would include provisions defining how sovereignty will be exercised in the EU as well as providing the procedure for ratifying the Founding Treaties.

---

[7] See in more detail Albi, op. cit. n. 1, chapter 5.

In the case of Serbia and Montenegro, the question of amending the Constitutional Charter with regard to entry into the EU is, according to the contributors, very hypothetical since the country's full membership of the European Union is a matter of a distant future. In terms of delegation of powers, however, the Constitutional Charter is remarkably open towards European integration. Indeed, Article 3 of the Constitutional Charter, which sets out six goals for the "state union", contains three goals that are connected to European integration: to integrate with European structures and the EU in particular (third sentence), to harmonize regulations and practices with European and international standards (fourth sentence), and to establish and ensure an unhindered operation of the common market on its territory, through coordination and harmonization of the economic systems of the two constituent states, in line with the principles of the European Union (sixth sentence). The main obstacle to integration in constitutional terms is the fact that the "state union" between Serbia and Montenegro is of a rather specific and unusual character. They are, according to the contributors, two independent states which perform as a single entity in international relations. The main problem therefore lies in the constitutional capacity of the bodies of the "state union" to conclude, enforce and implement international agreements, such as the Stabilization and Association Agreement. Since the "state union" does not dispose of its powers on its own, it is not authorized to transfer them to international organizations; this would fall within the jurisdiction of the two respective states. Therefore, concrete constitutional solutions will have to be introduced in future with regard to the transfer of competences to international organisations.

In Turkey, a series of amendments regarding human rights have been passed in recent years in order to meet the Copenhagen Criteria, but a direct basis for EU entry is yet to be created. Currently, the Constitution does not allow for the transfer of powers to international organisations. For instance, Article 6(1) proclaims that "[s]overeignty is vested fully and unconditionally in the nation". Article 6(2) reads that "[t]he Turkish Nation shall exercise its sovereignty through the authorised organs as prescribed by the principles laid down in the Constitution". Article 7 provides that "legislative power is vested in the Turkish Grand National Assembly on behalf of the Turkish Nation. This power cannot be delegated". Similar provisions are contained in the Constitution with regard to the exercise of the executive and judicial powers.

Before concluding this section on the transfer of powers, it is interesting to note that in Croatia, the contributors have pointed out that there were calls to introduce certain constitutional amendments already at the time of implementing the Stabilization and Association Agreement (SAA). They report that during the ratification of the SAA, the question arose of whether regulatory powers and law-making authority should be transferred to the Stabilization and Association Council. Since political support in the Croatian Parliament fell short of the two-thirds majority which would have been required by the Constitution in case of delegating regulatory powers the Agreement was ratified by a qualified majority. In response to the right-wing parties claiming that the SAA is stripping Croatia of its national sovereignty, the Prime Minister and Minister for European Integration declared that the SAA is simply an ordinary international treaty and, therefore, they did not push for ratification by a two-thirds majority. The Croatian Parliament subsequently adopted the Law Implementing the Stabilization and Association Agreement, which provided that the decisions of the Association Council are subject to parliamentary ratification.

1.3 The position of treaties and EC law in the national legal orders

Besides the question of transfer of powers, the constitutional amendments for EU membership also focus on the question of whether a separate constitutional basis is required for the application of EC law in national legal orders. Unlike the cautious approach with regard to international organisations, most of the Constitutions in question establish, to some extent, the direct applicability and precedence of ratified international treaties. This is also the case with the other CEE countries, which have been characterised as having an 'international law-friendly character' in comparison with many Western European Constitutions.[8] This is partly in reaction to the dualist tradition of the Communist regime. As explained by the Croatian national contributors, the monist approach was chosen "in an attempt to put an end to former practice according to which international human rights obligations were considered not directly applicable in [the] Yugoslav legal order according to the [C]ommunist party doctrine of non-interference with internal affairs".

However, the contributors in all of the MATRA project countries have found that the current regulation concerning the application of treaties does not in a sufficient manner secure the application of EC primary and secondary law, and, therefore, they advocate amendments in this respect (amendments have already been adopted in Slovenia and Romania, with Bulgaria having opted for staying with the existing rules on this matter). The relevant constitutional provisions and case law in the individual countries are as follows.

In Slovenia, the application of international law was, prior to the amendments, based on Article 8 which provides that: "Laws and regulations must comply with generally accepted principles of international law and with treaties that are

[8] K. Korkelia, 'New Trends Regarding the Relationship between International and National Law (with a special view towards the states of Eastern Europe)', *Review of Central and East European Law*, 3/4 (1997) at p. 227; V. Vereshchetin, 'Some Reflections on the Relationship between International Law and National Law in the Light of New Constitutions', in R. Müllerson, M. Fitzmaurize and M. Andenas, eds., *Constitutional Reform and International Law in Central and Eastern Europe* (The Hague: Kluwer Law International 1998) pp. 5-14.

binding on Slovenia. Ratified and promulgated treaties shall be applied directly". Further, according to Article 153, legislative measures must, *inter alia*, conform to the generally accepted principles of international law, to the international agreements currently in force and adopted by the National Assembly, and to other ratified international agreements. The Constitutional Court has confirmed that international agreements "rank above statutory provisions in the hierarchy of legal acts"; they "are integrated in the internal legal system … with the coming into force of such agreement on condition that they have been ratified in accordance with the internal law of the Republic of Slovenia". In the case of ratified self-executing treaties, they can create rights and obligations also for natural and legal persons in the country.[9] However, considering the particular needs of the application of EC law, the Constitution was supplemented with a new Article 3a para. 3. It provides that "Legal acts and decisions adopted within international organisations to which Slovenia has transferred the exercise of part of its sovereign rights shall be applied in Slovenia in accordance with the legal regulation of these organisations".

In Romania, the 2003 amendments made the following changes. Paragraph 2 of Article 148 establishes that after accession, the provisions of the Treaties and of mandatory Community regulations "shall take precedence over the opposite provisions of the national laws, in compliance with the provisions of the accession act". This provision is also applied to the acts that revise the EU's Founding Treaties (para. 3). These provisions are reinforced by paragraph 4, which obliges the Parliament, the President, the Government and the judicial authorities to guarantee the implementation of the obligations arising from the accession act and acts mentioned in para. 2. These provisions are significant because, unlike the other countries in question, Romania is considered to be a partially dualist country, where precedence was previously granted only to human rights treaties. As before, Article 11 of the Constitution provides that the state pledges to fulfil in good faith its obligations deriving from the treaties to which it is a party, and that ratified treaties are part of national law. Article 20 adds that the constitutional provisions concerning human rights are interpreted and enforced in conformity with the Universal Declaration of Human Rights and other treaties to which Romania is a party, and that human rights treaties take precedence in case of inconsistencies with internal law. It is interesting to note that with the exception of the regime applied to EC law and human rights treaties, Romania continues to be a dualist country. As a matter of fact, a limit to the priority of international law was added in the second paragraph of Article 20, which now provides that "where any inconsistencies exist between the covenants and treaties on fundamental

[9] Decision No. RM-1/97, 5 June 1997. *Uradni list RS* [Official Gazette], No. 40/97, paras. 12, 18 and 20.

human rights Romania is a party of, and the national laws, the international regulations shall take precedence, *unless the Constitution or national laws comprise more favourable provisions* [emphasis added]". Finally, the supremacy of the Constitution is reaffirmed in the new Article 1(5), which provides that "the observance of the Constitution, its supremacy and the laws shall be mandatory".[10]

In Bulgaria, Article 5(4) provides that the ratified and promulgated international instruments, which have come into force with respect to Bulgaria, are to be considered as part of the domestic legislation of the country and that they shall supersede any domestic legislation stipulating otherwise. Based on this, the self-executing provisions of international treaties are immediately enforceable. The Constitutional Court has confirmed that Article 5(4) provides for the immediate and direct inclusion of the provisions of international agreements as an integral part of the internal law of Bulgaria. The direct effect is subject to the conditions that the treaty is ratified, published and entered into force. Non-ratified treaties need transformation by legislative means.[11] Even though the Bulgarian contributors found that Article 5(4) would not be sufficient to guarantee supremacy and direct effect of EC law, no amendments were introduced in this respect as part of Bulgaria's 2005 EU package.

In Croatia, the Constitution of 1990 took a monist approach to the application of international law. Article 140 provides that "[i]nternational agreements concluded and ratified in accordance with the Constitution and made public, and which are in force, shall be part of the internal legal order" and "shall be above laws in terms of legal effects". Their provisions may be changed or repealed only under the conditions and in a way specified in them, or in accordance with the general rules of international law. International treaties, being part of the national legal order pursuant to this Article, are to be applied directly by the Croatian courts, and may create individual rights. However, the Croatian contributors recommend a constitutional amendment, in order to differentiate EC law from international law, by granting direct effect to the primary and secondary sources of EC law.

In Serbia and Montenegro, the Constitutional Charter has also taken a monist approach to international treaties. According to Article 16, "the ratified international treaties and generally accepted rules of international law shall have primacy over the laws of Serbia and Montenegro and of the Member States". But only human rights treaties are expressly accorded direct applicability: "[p]rovisions of international treaties on human and minority rights and civil liberties that are in

---

[10] In parallel, a similar provision was repealed from Art. 51.

[11] Constitutional Court Decision No. 7, 2 July 1992, published in *Durzhaven Vestnik* 56/92, as reported in E. Konstantinov, 'The Implementation of International Treaty Obligations in the National Legal Order – the Answer of the Bulgarian Constitution', *Journal of Constitutional Law in Eastern and Central Europe*, 1/1995, at pp. 66, 69-70.

force in the territory of Serbia and Montenegro shall be applied directly" (Art. 10). The national contributors are of the view that these provisions do not meet the doctrines of supremacy and direct effect as established in EC law, and therefore corresponding constitutional changes have to be made once the country makes sufficient progress in the process of European integration.

In Turkey, Article 90 paragraph 5 provides that "[i]nternational treaties duly put into effect have the force of law. No appeal to the Constitutional Court can be made with regard to these treaties, on the ground that they are unconstitutional". In May 2004, a new sentence was added to this provision, providing that "[i]n case of a conflict between the laws and international agreements duly put into effect in the field of fundamental rights and freedoms due to difference in provisions on the same matter, the provisions of the international agreements shall prevail". The last sentence thus grants a privileged status to human rights treaties. In the course of the amendments in 2001 and 2004, several attempts were made by pro-European Members of Parliament to introduce a provision into Article 90(5) that would secure the supremacy of all international treaties over national law. However, Euro-sceptics, including the President, managed to prevent the amendment from being passed. Because of fears concerning a loss of sovereignty that were raised in some circles, the supremacy of treaties was eventually granted only to human rights treaties. The contributors, however, represent the view that the current constitutional provisions do not cover supremacy and direct effect of EC law, and thus need an amendment once Turkey is given a date for accession.

1.4 Other amendments

In this section, we will briefly consider the issues which have been raised besides those already mentioned earlier (transfer of powers and application of EC law). It should be noted at the outset that the amendments regarding the control of national parliaments over the governments in EU affairs will be addressed separately in section 4.2, and some general remarks from a comparative perspective will be made in section 5.

In Slovenia, the remaining constitutional amendments were as follows. Article 47 was amended with a view to the European Arrest Warrant: "No citizen of Slovenia may be extradited or surrendered unless such obligation to extradite or surrender arises from a treaty by which, in accordance with the provisions of the first paragraph of Article 3a, Slovenia has transferred the exercise of part of its sovereign rights to an international organisation". Article 68 on the sale of real estate to foreigners, which had already been amended in 1997 with a view to the Europe Agreement, was reworded to abolish the condition of reciprocity: "Aliens may acquire ownership rights to real estate under conditions provided by law or a treaty ratified by the National Assembly". It is important to point out that Slovenia also authorized accession to NATO, by means of a reference to "defence alliances" in Article 3a para. 1.

In Romania, the amendments adopted in 2003 include a large number of EU-related provisions, besides the ones already mentioned. Several provisions deal with the position of citizens in relation to EU issues. EU citizens are accorded the right to elect and be elected in the local elections (Art. 16(4)). Romanian citizens, after the country's accession to the EU, explicitly have the right to elect and be elected to the European Parliament (Art. 38). Article 19(1) introduces the possibility of extraditing Romanian citizens in accordance with international agreements. Article 44(2) introduces the possibility for foreigners to acquire land "under the terms resulting from Romania's accession to the European Union and other international treaties which Romania is a party to, on a mutual basis, as well as a result of lawful inheritance". Further, the possibility for adopting a common currency is opened in Article 137(2), which previously provided that the national currency is the *Leu*, with its subdivision, the *Ban*. Several provisions deal with the membership of NATO. Finally, a significant part of the amendments regulate various aspects concerning the judiciary, following the European Commission's request presented in the Regular Reports where the country's compliance with the Copenhagen Criteria was assessed. Altogether, Romania's EU amendments appear to be the most comprehensive amongst the Central and Eastern European countries, and even go far beyond those introduced in most of the 'old' Member States.

In Bulgaria, the remainder of the amendments pertaining to the EU concern the following: the removal of the ban on the acquisition of land by foreigners (Art. 22); the extradition of Bulgarian nationals to a foreign state or international criminal tribunal for the purposes of criminal proceedings (Art. 25); and the election of the European Parliament and the electoral rights of EU citizens (Art. 42) In addition, an important set of amendments was introduced in 2003 to improve the independence and efficiency of the judiciary (Arts. 129-132).

In Croatia, the contributors mention that the treaty on accession to the EU could be ratified without a formal amendment, since none of the provisions are openly inconsistent with EU membership. However, they nevertheless recommend the introduction of certain amendments, in order to exclude potential interpretation contrary to Community law. The amendments should, according to the contributors, include the recognition of the electoral rights of the EU citizens, which currently is not secured by Articles 45 and 132 of the Constitution. The amendments should also modify Article 44, in order to provide equal access to the public service to EU citizens in areas required by EC law. In addition, the contributors find that the Government should be authorized by the Constitution to act within the Council of Ministers and implement EC law in national law with a wider margin of discretion, considering that under the current Article 112(4), the Government's powers are restricted to passing sub-regulations to implement the

Acts of Parliament. The Constitutional Court should be given a clear authority for preliminary review of treaties. Further, the procedural rules of the Constitutional Court may need modification, to establish the recourse of ordinary courts to *exceptio illegalitatis* in case national laws are incompatible with EC law. The contributors also raise a more general issue of changing the current culture of a formalistic interpretation of law, which may obstruct recourse to certain legal sources and interpretative techniques used in Community law, and thus indirectly affect its application.

In Serbia and Montenegro, as mentioned, there are no debates yet about preparing the Constitution for EU entry. The contributors have pointed out that the provisions of the Constitutional Charter are not contrary to EC law, given that the Charter declares on several occasions that EU integration is the country's main goal. The challenges rather lie in the "state union" character of the association between Serbia and Montenegro, with ensuing difficulties in determining their relationships with the EU.

In Turkey, as already mentioned, the Constitution has been amended on several occasions in respect of human rights, in order to meet the Copenhagen Criteria. One such revision took place on 3 October 2001, when the Preamble and 33 articles of the Constitution were amended to improve human rights, strengthen the rule of law and restructure democratic institutions. On 5 May 2004, another package of amendments entered into force, which, as seen, gave precedence to international human rights treaties. Additionally, in result of this reform, gender equality was reinforced, the death penalty was abolished in all circumstances, the freedom of press was strengthened, and a number of other aspects of human rights were improved. However, amongst the issues that may raise doubts about compatibility with EC law, the contributors have pointed out the following. Article 39, which currently allows extradition only under the obligations arising from membership of the International Criminal Court, may contradict the system of the European Arrest Warrant. Further, Article 16 allows the restriction of rights of foreigners, which may jeopardize the equal treatment rights of EU citizens. Article 70 reserves the right to work in the public service only to Turkish citizens; this provision may need a revision so that EU citizens would be granted the right to be employed at certain public posts. Articles 67 and 68 respectively reserve to Turkish citizens voting rights and the right to form political parties, which appears to potentially undermine the voting rights of EU citizens.

2. PROCEDURAL ISSUES AND ACCESSION REFERENDUMS

In procedural terms, the accession process involves ratification of the accession treaty, a referendum (depending on the rules in the individual country), and, central to this contribution, amendment of the national Constitution. It is interesting to note that the constitutional amendment procedures in CEE countries are often rather rigid, especially as concerns the provisions regarding fundamental principles and sovereignty. By way of example, all amendments in Romania require a referendum and some fundamental provisions may not be amended. In Bulgaria, a special constitutive body has to be elected in order to amend the fundamental provisions. The Bulgarian contributors have pointed out that the decision to establish a rigid constitutional amendment procedure was influenced by the context of adopting the Constitution, and "its character [as] a reactive Constitution"; the aim was to avert possibilities of restoring any kind of dictatorship and to secure a broad consensus for amendments. However, in a highly fragmented Parliament, it has previously been nearly impossible to mobilize the required super-majorities.

In Romania, the main elements of the amendment procedure are the following. To begin with, it is prohibited to amend provisions that concern the following issues: the national, independent, unitary, and indivisible character of the Romanian State; the republican form of government; territorial integrity; independence of the judiciary; and political pluralism and official language (Art. 152). A draft amendment has to be adopted by the Chamber of Deputies and the Senate by at least a two-thirds majority of all members in both Chambers (Art. 151(1)). If no agreement is reached, the draft may be adopted by a mediation procedure, where both Chambers shall decide in a joint session by at least a three-fourths majority of all deputies and senators (Art. 151(2)). All constitutional amendments also have to be approved by the people in a referendum (Art. 151(3)). As regards the procedure of joining the EU, the 2003 amendments provide that accession shall take place by means of a law adopted in a joint session of the Chamber of Deputies and the Senate by a majority of two-thirds of the number of deputies and senators (Art. 148). Since the amending of the Constitution took place by a referendum, central to which were the EU amendments, that referendum has also been regarded as one legitimising the EU accession. In the referendum, 91 per cent of the people voted in favour of the amendments, with a turnout of 56 per cent. The 2003 amendments additionally introduced the preliminary review of the constitutionality of treaties (Art. 11(3)). If a treaty is found to be unconstitutional, it cannot be ratified. Once a treaty has been found constitutional, it "cannot be the subject of an objection of unconstitutionality" (Art. 147(3)). Earlier, the Constitutional Court's review was only possible on the constitutionality of the domestic laws which ratify international treaties, prior to their promulgation (Art. 144 (in the former numbering)).

In Bulgaria, constitutional amendments have to be carried out by a specially elected Grand National Assembly (GNA) in case the amendments concern fundamental issues. The GNA consists of 400 members (Art. 157), who are elected by the procedure for parliamentary elections. In order to amend the Constitution, a two-thirds majority of all GNA members is required, in three ballots on three different days (Art. 161). Other amendments fall under the competence of Parliament (Art. 153). The passing of the amendment requires an extremely high level of consensus: a thre-fourths majority of all deputies on three ballots on three different days (Art. 155(1)). A Bill which has received less than a three-fourths but more than a two-thirds majority of all deputies is eligible for re-introduction no earlier than two and no later than five months, with a majority of two-thirds of all deputies (Art. 155(2)). The list of fundamental issues for which the election of the GNA is required is as follows: the adoption of a new Constitution; changes related to Bulgaria's territory and ratification of any international instruments concerning such issues; changes in the form of state or the form of government; direct applicability of the Constitution or application of ratified international treaties; irrevocability of fundamental rights; and the amendments concerning the constitutional amendment procedure (Art. 158). The Constitutional Court has interpreted the expression "form of government" (Art. 158(3)) broadly: this includes not only the main characteristics of the state but also the system of constituted powers (National Assembly, President, Vice President, Council of Ministers, Constitutional Court and the organs of the judiciary), their structure, as well as their acts and powers to the extent that the balance among them would be changed. According to the Constitutional Court, this list also includes the fundamental constitutional principles of state sovereignty, political pluralism, supremacy of the Constitution, state of the rule of law and the independence of the judiciary.[12] However, as seen above in section 1.2, the Constitutional Court, perhaps somewhat strikingly, did not find that the transfer of powers to the EU would require the convening of the GNA.

The procedure for EU accession was regulated separately in the 2005 amendments: the law ratifying the treaty regarding EU accession has to be adopted by a majority of two-thirds of all Members of Parliament (Art. 85(1-2)). Article 85(4) provides that the conclusion of an international treaty which requires an amendment to the Constitution shall be preceded by the passage of such an amendment. Referendums may be held on issues which fall under the Parliament's competence (Art. 84(5)). The pertinent decision has to be taken by Parliament, on the proposal of a quarter of all deputies or the Council of Ministers. A valid referendum requires the approval of a majority, with a 50 per cent turnout. No referendums are allowed on amending the Constitution. Article 149 establishes the constitutional review of treaties prior to ratification, which may be initiated by one-fith of all deputies, the President, the Council of Ministers, the Supreme

12 Interpretative ruling in Decision No. 3 of 2003.

Cassation Court, the Supreme Administrative Court and the Chief Prosecutor (Art. 150).

In Slovenia, the National Assembly adopts the acts amending the Constitution by a two-thirds majority vote of all deputies.[13] If required by at least 30 deputies, the constitutional amendment proposal may be submitted to a referendum; a valid referendum requires a minimum turnout of 50 per cent. The Constitutional Court has warned against the hidden modification of the Constitution by means of ratifying international treaties.[14] The ratification of the treaty on transfer of competences to international organisations requires a two-thirds majority vote of all deputies, and the National Assembly may also call a referendum, as provided in the first and second paragraphs of the amended Article 3a. Slovenia held the EU accession referendum on 23 March 2003; a convincing majority of 90 per cent voted in favour of accession, with a turnout of 60 per cent. In the process of ratifying a treaty, the Constitutional Court, on the proposal of the President, the Government or a third of the deputies of the National Assembly, issues an opinion on the conformity of such a treaty with the Constitution.

In Croatia, the decision to amend the Constitution requires a two-thirds majority of all Members of Parliament.[15] The existing Article 139 provides that international agreements which grant to international organizations or alliances the powers derived from the Constitution, shall be subject to ratification by Parliament by a two-thirds majority vote of all Members of Parliament. Article 141 provides that the procedure for association may be instituted by at least a third of the Members of Parliament, the President or the Government, and the final decision has to be subject to a referendum. As mentioned, the contributors have recommended a special procedure for joining the EU. A referendum is required for joining an association of states (Art. 141). In addition, a referendum may be called by Parliament on a proposal for amending the Constitution, on a Bill, or on any other issue within its competence (Art. 86(1)). The President may call a referendum, at the proposal of the Government and with the countersignature of the Prime Minster, on a proposal for amending the Constitution or any other issue which he considers to be important for the independence, unity and existence of the state (Art. 86(2)). In both cases, Parliament has to call a referendum if so required by 10 per cent of all voters. Valid referendums require a minimum turnout of 50 per cent and the result is binding. The Croatian Constitution does not provide for preliminary constitutional review of treaties.

In Serbia and Montenegro, the Constitutional Charter can only be amended by the same procedure which was envisaged for its adoption (Art. 62). The adoption

13 See for details Part 9 of the Constitution.

14 Decision of 5 June 1997, *supra* n. 5, paras. 35-38.

15 See for details Chapter VIII of the Constitution.

required the approval of an identical text by the People's Assembly of the Republic of Serbia and the Assembly of the Republic of Montenegro, and it entered into force when the identical text was adopted and promulgated by the Federal Parliament (Art. 61). Article 14(2) of the Constitutional Charter provides that Serbia and Montenegro can "establish international relations with other states and international organizations, and conclude international treaties and agreements". However, the decision on membership of international organizations, as well as the rights and obligations arising from such membership, is subject to the prior consent of the competent bodies of the respective Republics (Art. 19(5)). The Parliament of Serbia and Montenegro is in charge of the ratification of international treaties and agreements (Art. 19(9)).

In Turkey, the adoption of a constitutional amendment proposal requires a three-fifths majority of the total number of members of the Grand National Assembly by secret ballot.[16] The amendment process involves a referendum, should the Assembly adopt an amendment which the President has reserved for further consideration. A referendum is also required in cases where certain majorities are not met by the Assembly. The ratification of treaties concluded with foreign states and international organizations is subject to adoption, by the Turkish Grand National Assembly, of a law approving the ratification (Art. 90(1)). The contributors are of the view that once a date for full membership is given to Turkey, it is likely that a new method will be devised for the ratification of such treaties, which might include approval through a weighted majority and a referendum.

3. THE IMPACT OF THE EUROPEAN CONSTITUTION

The contributions with regard to the MATRA project countries (part I of this book), in general, consider the adoption of the European Constitution as a positive development. In particular, it is found that the new document makes the Union's legal order more coherent and transparent by consolidating the previously scattered treaty provisions. The contributions also find that it will increase the democratic legitimacy of the Union and make the Union's functioning more efficient. In terms of the nature of the new document, the national contributions mostly appear to be of the view that it constitutes a treaty rather than a constitution, as it does not bring about revolutionary changes, and it has to be approved by each and every Member State under their national ratification procedures.

As regards the question of whether the ratification of the European Constitution would involve national constitutional obstacles, most of the contributors

16 For details see Art. 175 of the Constitution.

share the view that the European Constitutional Treaty does not bring about any changes to the conditions of membership compared to the time of accession, and thus no additional constitutional amendments are required, apart from those necessary for EU membership. Indeed, Slovenia ratified the document in a parliamentary procedure in February 2005. However, the Croatian contributors point out that the word "Constitution" in Croatia bears a statist connotation, and may thereby create a political misunderstanding about the nature of the union Croatia is about to join. This view is probably also present elsewhere, given that Constitutions, under traditional constitutional law, have been inextricably associated with states. On the other hand, a revision of traditional constitutional views, alongside with a post-national approach to constitutionalism which is emerging in European scholarly circles,[17] can be seen in Bulgaria, where contributors have made the following comment:

> For the first time in history a written constitution is adopted by a non-statal entity which means that constitutionalism has expanded to new horizons going beyond the nation state. ... It does not mean that by adopting a Constitution, the EU is transformed into a state or a full[y] fledged federation. It also does not mean that the EU Constitution and the emerging beginnings of global constitutionalism mark the process of the withering of nation states. Instead, the EU and global constitutionalism will exist hand in hand with the Constitutions of the nation states... Moreover, the nation states will be the main actors in the evolving constitutional pluralism...[18]

The existence of a wider discussion on the impact of the European Constitution upon the national Constitution has only been reported in Romania. Some lawyers in Romania have found that the new document may pose challenges to certain constitutional provisions, especially Article 1 of the Constitution which declares Romania to be a national, sovereign and independent, united and indivisible state. However, following the Romanian Constitutional Court's decision of April 2003, a large part of Romanian legal literature seems to be of the view that the principle of sovereignty will not be affected, since it will be exercised in a new, more flexible manner, allowing for the transfer of some competences to European institutions. Nonetheless, a second stage of constitutional reform is scheduled for 2007, and it is likely to include a better "synchronisation" of the provisions of the Romanian Constitution with those of

---

17 See for a discussion A. Albi and P. Van Elsuwege, 'EU Constitution, National Constitutions and Sovereignty: An Assessment of a 'European Constitutional Order'', *European Law Review* (2004) pp. 741-765.

18 Evgeni Tanchev and Jenia Peteva, Bulgaria, in this volume.

the European Constitution, in order to put an end to any potential claims of incompatibility.

4. THE ROLE OF THE NATIONAL PARLIAMENTS

4.1 **Parliamentary participation in the pre-accession adaptations**

The relationships between the CEE applicant/candidate countries and the EU fall, as foreign relations, under the competence of the Governments, due to which the balances of powers have shifted considerably in favour of the executive branch. Therefore, it is important to examine how the parliaments control this process. In the Europe Agreement spheres (in Croatia the Stabilisation and Association Agreement (SAA); Slovenia is now a Member State of the EU), the political decision-making and supervisory powers belong to the Association Councils, which are composed of the foreign Ministers of the EU and the respective CEE countries. Executive and technical functions are assigned to the Association Committees, which may establish special committees. In Slovenia, Bulgaria and Romania, the Governments were also the main actors in the process of accession negotiations.

Democratic involvement in the pre-accession process takes place by the following mechanisms. Firstly, the parliaments are involved in the approximation by way of usual parliamentary deliberation and adoption of laws. In fact, a number of countries have provided for the possibility of using the expedited procedure to deliberate matters of EU law. For instance, in Croatia, Article 159 of the Rules of Procedure permits to merge into a single reading an act which is being harmonized with EU law. The parliaments are also involved by way of ratification of the Europe Agreements/SAA, as well as by adopting the constitutional amendments for EU membership. Democratic control also takes place through the parliaments' plenary sessions devoted to deliberating EU issues.[19]

Secondly, the crux of democratic involvement lies in the commissions of European affairs, established within the national parliaments. For instance, in Romania, this Commission was established in 1995, in Slovenia in 1996, in Croatia in 2001 and in Turkey in April 2003 (in Turkey, this Commission is called "European Union Harmonisation Committee"). In Serbia and Montenegro, there is a European Integration Committee within the Parliament of the "state

[19] For comparative information about the role of parliaments in the 2004 accession countries, see Z. Mansfeldová and M. Klíma, eds., *The Role of the Central European Parliaments in the Process of European Integration. International Conference in Prague, 12-14.09.1997* (Prague, Institute of Sociology, Academy of Sciences 1998).

union", as well as separately within the respective national parliamentary assemblies of both Serbia (as of May 2003) and Montenegro (as of October 2003).

These commissions, as a rule, include representatives from all political parties represented in the parliament. Depending on the stage of integration of the given country and the relevant treaty (Europe Agreement/SAA), the tasks of the parliamentary commissions of European affairs involve a wide range of activities. For instance, these commissions monitor the approximation and accession strategy; elaborate and harmonise national legislation with EU law; debate and issue declarations or opinions on legislative Bills involving approximation; cooperate with, and issue recommendations to the Governments and hear reports by the Ministers and negotiators; examine the annual Reports of the European Commission; examine the economic and social aspects of integration; maintain contacts with committees and parliaments of the EU Member States, European Parliament and other EU institutions as well as the COSAC; contribute on a parliamentary level to the achievement of the Europe Agreement purposes and ensure implementation of the Europe Agreements/SAA; and organise information campaigns.

Thirdly, these commissions of European affairs usually form the candidate country's part in the Association Parliamentary Committees. These are the bodies of democratic control in the Europe Agreement/SAA areas; they may request from the Association Council information regarding the implementation of the Agreement, and issue non-binding recommendations.

As regards the degree of involvement of the national parliaments, the Slovenian and Croatian contributors have pointed out that their countries' parliaments have had a strong role in the integration process. For instance, in Slovenia before accession, the Parliament's Committee for Foreign Policy had to confirm all governmental positions for negotiations. In Croatia, the Government is obliged to forward to Parliament every proposal for a decision and the proposals for a position to be advocated by its representatives in the Stabilisation and Association Council prior to taking the decision.

Although the contributors consider parliamentary control over EU integration to be strong and effective, it may be instructive also to mention some weaknesses which have been pointed out with regard to the democratic control in the 2004 accession countries, and may be present also in the group of countries in question. For instance, it has been suggested that the parliamentary debates have remained rather general and little specialist knowledge was provided on various implications of approximation. With regard to Slovenia, Drago Zajc has reported that the Euro-capacity of the Parliament was for many years insufficient because of the lack of foreign relations specialists working in the Parliament compared to the Government, and particularly because the deputies themselves were not motivated enough to deal with the complicated European issues. The European matters were viewed in Parliament as international in the classic way, i.e., as something 'foreign'.[20] A study by Heather Grabbe and Kirsty Hughes has pointed out that there was strikingly little debate over EU conditionality within the CEE parliaments, media and within governments, and that this is one of the reasons why the CEE countries did not make effective use of bargaining in the accession negotiations.[21] Further, it has been pointed out that harmonisation took place at a rather fast speed, which left insufficient time for normal deliberation between the coalition and opposition, or interest groups and society. In fact, the Bulgarian contributors have also pointed out that the rapid progress in approximation involves the risk of passing inefficient regulation, and the risk of inherent inapplicability due to insufficient institutional capacity and unreasonable expenses. Further, it has been pointed out with regard to the 2004 accession countries that the margin of manoeuvre for the parliaments was relatively limited, as the laws had previously been controlled in the Ministries with regard to their compatibility with EU law. In order to improve democratic control, it is therefore perhaps advisable for the current applicant and candidate countries to establish clear procedures for involvement of the parliament as well as the wider society and interest groups.

4.2 The role of the parliaments in the EU decision-making process

As regards the national parliaments' control over the governments in the EU decision-making process, relevant constitutional amendments have been adopted in Slovenia, Romania and Bulgaria, with the contributors of the other countries recommending similar provisions.

In Slovenia, paragraph 4 of the new Article 3a provides as follows:

> In procedures for the adoption of legal acts and decisions in international organisations to which Slovenia has transferred the exercise of part of its sovereign rights, the Government shall promptly inform the National Assembly of proposals for such acts and decisions as well as of its own activities. The National Assembly may adopt positions thereon, which the Government shall take into consideration in its activities. The relationship between the National Assembly and the Government arising from this paragraph shall be regulated in detail by a law adopted by a two-thirds majority vote of deputies present.

---

20 D. Zajc, 'The Responsibilities of a Central European Parliament in the Process of European Integration – the Case of the Parliament of Slovenia and its Commission for European Affairs', in Mansfeldová and Klíma, op. cit. n. 19, at p. 98.

21 H. Grabbe, 'A Partnership for Accession? The Implications of EU Conditionality for the Central and East European Applicants', European University Institute, Robert Schuman Center, Working Paper No. 99/12 (Florence, EUI 1999) at p. 34, with reference to H. Grabbe and K. Hughes, *Eastward Enlargement of the European Union* (London, The Royal Institute of International Affairs 1998).

Based on a new Law on Cooperation between the Parliament and Government in EU matters, a new Committee of EU affairs was established in May 2004, which has greater competences and a stronger role of scrutiny. The leading role is played by the Committee of EU Affairs (in matters pertaining to the First and the Third Pillar) and the Committee for Foreign Policy (in Second Pillar matters). Both Committees adopt decisions on EU affairs on the basis of positions of the relevant standing committees, although under certain circumstances, an individual EU matter can also be discussed in the plenary sessions. While the meetings of the above committees are closed to the public, the materials used are publicly available. In case the Government cannot follow the position of the respective parliamentary committee, it has to inform the National Assembly and explain the circumstances. At least once a year, the National Assembly is to hold a plenary session on European issues. The Parliament has also opened an office in the European Parliament in March 2004, to better cooperate with EU institutions. Overall, Slovenia has chosen a medium solution in the degree of involvement of the national parliament: its positions bind the government only in a political sense.

In Romania, the new Article 148(5), introduced as part of the 2003 amendments, provides that "[t]he Government shall send to the two Chambers of the Parliament the draft mandatory acts before they are submitted to the European Union institutions for approval." A more detailed regulation is to be established as the country gets closer to the accession date.

In Bulgaria, Article 105 provides as follows: "[t]he Council of Ministers shall inform the National Assembly on issues concerning the obligations of the Republic of Bulgaria resulting from its membership in the European Union" (para. 3). Paragraph 4 further provides that "[w]hen participating in the drafting and adoption of European Union instruments, the Council of Ministers shall inform the National Assembly in advance, and shall give detailed account for its actions".

In Croatia, the parliament's role in the EU decision-making process has not yet been considered, but the contributors find pertinent constitutional amendments necessary. In the light of the current experience, the contributors predict that the Croatian Parliament will have a strong control over the Government's actions in the future accession negotiations, as well as in the framework of future membership.

In Turkey and Serbia and Montenegro, the amendments concerning the role of the parliament have not yet been considered.

It should be noted that several country contributions mention the importance of strengthening the role of the national parliaments in the EU's decision-making process. This is seen as vital for reducing the democratic deficit in the EU and the famous gap between the EU and its citizens.

5. CONCLUDING REMARKS: WHAT CAN BE LEARNT FROM THE EXPERIENCES OF THE (PRE-)CANDIDATE COUNTRIES AND NEW MEMBER STATES?

By way of concluding remarks, it would be fitting to consider how the constitutional amendments and relevant draft proposals in the six countries of the MATRA multi-country project compare with those in the new and old Member States of the EU, especially given that this volume also contains reports concerning constitutional developments in the new accession countries.

It should be noted at the outset that the experience in the Member States in terms of adapting their Constitutions for European integration is rather diverse. Amongst the Constitutions of the "old" Member States, perhaps three broader models could be distinguished. The first group consists of Constitutions that contain explicit provisions on the delegation or transfer of powers to the European Union (e.g., the Constitutions of France, Germany, Portugal, Ireland, Austria, Sweden and, due to reforms adopted in 2001, Greece). Besides these general clauses, most Constitutions in this group contain further provisions dealing with specific aspects of EU membership. Of these, the following issues have led to an amendment in several countries: the control of the national parliaments over the Governments in the EU decision-making process; the active and passive voting rights of EU citizens in the elections of local municipalities and of the European Parliament; and issues related to Monetary Union.[22] The second and the third group are formed by those Constitutions where European integration has been accommodated under a general clause on international organizations, the difference being that in the second group, the Constitutions contain some amendments pertaining to specific aspects of EU membership. The Spanish, Finnish and Belgian Constitutions and, since 2001, the Italian Constitution fall into the second group. The third group of Constitutions contain no express references at all to any aspects of EU membership (notably, the Constitutions of Denmark, Luxembourg and the Netherlands).

Those Constitutions that mention EU membership in a minimal manner have rightly been criticised for a 'European deficit', in that their provisions are becoming obsolete with regard to the actual exercise of powers, which is increasingly influenced by the EU.[23] It is by now well established that the EU has a

[22] For details, see Albi, op. cit. n. 1, chapter 2.

[23] B. De Witte, 'Constitutional Aspects of European Union Membership in the Original Six Member States: Model Solutions for the Applicant Countries?', in Alfred E. Kellermann, Jaap W. de Zwaan, Jenö Czuczai, eds., *EU Enlargement. The Constitutional Impact at EU and National Level* (The Hague, T.M.C. Asser Press 2001) at p. 73. In addition, Andras Sajo has referred in a similar context to a strategy of what Stephen Holmes has called the "gag rules", i.e., 'a strategic decision to remain silent on a particular issue'. Whilst on the one hand, according to Sajo, this strategy is not

particular supranational character, and its effects upon the Member States' sovereignty are far-reaching in comparison with the ordinary international organisations. Although the adaptation of national Constitutions for EU membership is not expressly required by EU *acquis*, the above line of thought offers a valuable perspective for assessing the national constitutional amendments.

In the 2004 accession countries from Central and Eastern Europe, the experts and scholars initially raised a number of issues which needed an amendment in view of EU membership. However, the final solutions remained in several countries relatively minimal. This was mainly caused by difficult amendment procedures and high levels of euro-scepticism ahead of the accession referendums in a number of countries, as well as the need to find last-minute political compromises, to make accession constitutionally possible. As a result, a number of CEE accession countries opted for the "international organisation" approach (Poland, the Czech Republic, Lithuania, Latvia, Slovenia), kept the amendments to a minimum (with the exception of Slovakia, Slovenia and the Czech Republic), and/or interpreted the procedural requirements in a rather liberal manner (Baltic countries).[24] Indeed, several CEE accession countries introduced some additional amendments after accession, or are contemplating doing so.

As a matter of fact, the issue of incompatibility of a national constitutional provision with EU law recently led to a controversial decision in Poland. The Polish Constitutional Tribunal found that a provision of the Code of Criminal Procedure, which implemented the European Arrest Warrant by allowing the extradition of Polish citizens, was incompatible with Article 55 of the Polish Constitution, which explicitly prohibits the extradition of Polish citizens.[25] Ahead of EU accession, the need to amend this constitutional provision had been pointed out by several scholars, but to no avail. Even though the Tribunal gave an 18-month period for implementing its decision, there has been a degree of divergence in the practice of the ordinary courts, with some of them refusing to adjudicate on the extradition of Polish citizens. The European Arrest Warrant has also triggered debates on the constitutionally correct way of implementing it in the Czech Republic.[26]

---

unreasonable given that it is still unclear how the European system is going to develop, it entails, on the other hand, the risk of undermining the functionality and social relevance of national constitutions. See A. Sajo, 'Accession's Impact on Constitutionalism in the New Member States', in G.A. Bermann and K. Pistor, eds., *Law and Governance in an Enlarged European Union* (Oxford, Hart 2004) p 427.

[24] See the chapters on new EU Member States in this volume; for a comparative analysis see Albi, op. cit. n. 1, chapter 5, and A. Albi, '"Europe" Articles in the Constitutions of the Central and Eastern European Countries', 42 *Common Market Law Review* (2005) p. 399.

[25] See the chapter on Poland by S. Biernat in this volume.

[26] See the chapter on the Czech Republic by J. Zemanek in this volume.

The Polish Constitutional Tribunal's decision demonstrates the need for the legislators to eliminate potential conflicts with EU law from the national Constitutions prior to accession, and shows that there are limits to interpretation by the constitutional courts. In fact, constitutional courts have often been left in the process of European integration with an unduly hard burden of finding *a posteriori* constitutional justifications for fundamental transfers of powers. It should also be noted that adequate amendment of the national Constitutions would provide a higher legitimacy to the delegation of competences from national to the EU level. Furthermore, a clear constitutional recognition of the EU's powers would increase transparency and legal certainty, and bring the Union a step closer to the citizens.[27]

Against this background, the constitutional amendments which have been adopted or are being drafted in the MATRA project countries, described in part I of this book, appear to be relatively extensive and favourably disposed towards European integration, eliminating a number of direct or indirect constitutional conflicts with EC law rather than attempting to resolve these by way of constitutional interpretation. The amendments were remarkably comprehensive in Romania and Bulgaria, which might indicate that it might be better to adjust the Constitutions at an earlier stage of European integration. Such amendments are likely to ensure an efficient application of EC law as well as legitimacy of the integration process. Slovenian amendments were also relatively extensive, but a setback appears to be that the amendments were addressed to international organisations in general rather than introducing a direct reference to EU membership. For the reasons considered in this section, is to be hoped that the remainder of the candidate and pre-candidate countries will follow the model of those new and old Member States and candidate countries which have opted for a more comprehensive adaptation of national Constitutions with EU law. In addition, should the European Constitution be ratified and enter into force regardless of the obstacles that have emerged in the ratification process, it might also be worthwhile considering the introduction of a reference to the European Constitution in the national Constitutions.

27 See for a further discussion on the importance of amending constitutions adequately with regard to European integration, especially in the countries of Central and Eastern Europe, Albi, op. cit. n. 1, at pp. 114 et seq.

IMPACT OF EUROPEAN INTEGRATION ON THE ROLE AND FUNCTIONING OF THE NATIONAL JUDICIARY

Jenő Czuczai*

1. GENERAL OBSERVATIONS

1. It seems necessary to devote much more attention in the future to the issue of the impact of European integration on the role and functioning of the national judiciary in national reporting, especially because the European Commission as well as the Member States appear determined to attach more and more importance to the problems and issues relating to the proper functioning of the judiciaries in the candidate countries of the second and third waves of EU Eastward Enlargement. Evidence of this is, for example, that institution-building and enforcement-related aspects are increasingly focused on and developed by the EU and are therefore an important element in the forthcoming preparations for accession.[1]

2. Another more general observation is that it should be made absolutely clear what the term 'national judicial system' should be understood to mean. Does it only cover the court system of a specific candidate country or should it be taken to include prosecutors (examining magistrates) as well as attorneys and notaries, as they are also part of the legal profession and as such significant elements of the judicial system?[2] We believe that the broader meaning is the correct one, especially if we take into account the rapid developments in the Third Pillar EU *acquis* and the recent developments in the field of judicial cooperation within the EU, not only in the context of cooperation among the courts of the Member States in civil and commercial matters, but also in terms of the fight against international organized crime, etc. In this context, one could also think of the European Judicial Area or Eurojust, or UCLAF, or the Green Paper on a European Prosecu-

---

* Dr Jenő Czuczai, Vice-President of the European Law Academy, Budapest.

[1] See Communication from the Commission to the Council and the European Parliament on the Roadmaps for Bulgaria and Romania, COM (2002) 624 final, p. 3. point 2, pp. 6-7 point 2, pp. 19-20, p. 25 and pp. 39-40. Similarly, see the recent Accession Partnerships for Romania and Bulgaria, issued in March 2003 in this context. Reference should also be made to the Copenhagen Membership criteria, see in more detail Marise Cremona, ed., *The Enlargement of the EU* (Oxford, Oxford University Press 2003), especially M. Maresceau, 'Pre-accession', at pp. 9-40.

[2] As was touched upon in the chapter on Slovenia.

tor, as well as of related provisions in the new Constitutional Treaty under ratification.

3. Very little information can be found in the national contributions as far as institutional, legal and practical guarantees are concerned in terms of assuring the effective independence of the judiciary.[3]

4. A better understanding (or a more focused conceptualisation) of the notion of "*accession Union acquis*" is needed.

5. Special emphasis has recently been put on the elaboration of a Code of Ethics in the (pre-) candidate countries.

In the remainder of this contribution, the six Matra project countries will be focused on (sections 2-7). As this book also includes contributions based on the same questionnaire from nine new EU Member States that joined the EU on 1 May 2004, this contribution will also pay attention to some of the main experiences of the national judiciaries in these countries as far as the first application of EU laws and the newly-developed practice of judicial dialogue with the ECJ are concerned (section 8).

2. DO THE NATIONAL COURTS REFER TO AND APPLY THE EUROPEAN ASSOCIATION AGREEMENT?

Preliminary observation

It should be noted that it was not always possible to answer this question, for example in the case of Serbia and Montenegro where a Stabilisation and Association Agreement was not even being negotiated yet, or in the case of Croatia where the Stabilisation and Association Agreement has only recently fully entered into force (on 1 February 2005). In such countries, no court practice has as yet developed on the subject, apart from constitutional court practice in some countries, such as Slovenia, or Supreme Administrative Court practice as in Bulgaria, or issues concerning the customs union under the Turkish-EU Association Council Decision No. 1/1995 in Turkey.

[3] This issue should be considered in the context of the first Copenhagen membership criterion, namely "an applicant state shall assure the stability of guaranteeing the democracy, rule of law, respect for human rights, respect for and protection of minority rights". It is beyond doubt that one of these institutions is the judiciary whose stability (including their effective independence) must be guaranteed by all means.

Slovenia

So far, there has been no case law of ordinary courts in which EC law was applied directly. However, there is one famous Constitutional Court (CC) opinion (Case RM 1/97, No. 40/97) which dealt with the EU-Slovenian Europe Agreement (before it was ratified). The opinion concerned the constitutionality of an obligation which had been undertaken by Slovenia in the EA to the effect that Slovenia would change its Constitution within a certain period determined in the EA. Although the Constitutional Court found this provision to be unconstitutional, the Slovenian Constitution was amended regardless to comply with the disputed obligation (which concerned property, more specifically land). The opinion of the CC is also important because of the reason behind it which was another question raised, namely that of the rules on competition in the EA and their possible direct effect. A similar constitutional issue was raised in Hungary in 1996.[4] The CC – similarly to Hungary – refused as a possible conceptual approach (or as a possible interpretation of the EA) the unilateral acceptance of "*pre-Member State legal status*". In another CC ruling the direct effect of the EA provision on the approximation of laws was also denied (examination of the Law on savings schemes for houses in 2000).

Romania

So far, the national courts in Romania have not referred directly to the provisions of the 1993 Europe Agreement with Romania.

Bulgaria

Bulgarian courts both refer to and apply the Europe Agreement in two ways. First, they directly apply decisions of the Association Council and second, the provisions in the EA on the levying of customs duties (e.g., the right to for tariff preference), on the origin of goods and on VAT issues (Arts. 11, 35 and 69 of the EA and Protocol No. IV, in particular Art. 16) have direct effect. The contribution lists several decisions of the Supreme Administrative Court in this respect.

Croatia

As the SAA with Croatia only entered into force a few months ago, the courts have not been able to apply it directly so far. For this reason, no cases referring to the SAA (or to the Interim Agreement that applies as of 1 January 2003) have yet been reported.

---

[4] See in more detail Allan F. Tatham, 'Constitutional judiciary in Central Europe and the Europe Agreement: Decision 30/1998 (VI.25) AB of the Hungarian Constitutional Court', 48 *International and Comparative Law Quarterly* (1999) pp. 913-920.

Serbia and Montenegro

As was mentioned above, no relevant case law is expected from Serbia and Montenegro yet, as it has not yet concluded a Stabilisation and Association Agreement.

Turkey

Though no direct reference has yet been made to the Association Agreement of 1963 (Ankara Agreement) by the Turkish courts, nonetheless, in terms of the on-going approximation of the legislation, it may well be reflected in the application of provisions stemming from the *acquis* (although concrete examples are not provided). Furthermore, there have been some 30 cases before the ECJ which were somehow related to the EC-Turkey Association Agreement. Another interesting development is the *YEDAS* case (YEDAS is a Turkish car manufacturing company) which was brought before the Court of First Instance in February 2004.[5] In this case, the company claims damages for losses allegedly suffered by it due to the entry into force of the EU-Turkey Customs Union.

3. HAS THE JUDICIARY ALREADY PRONOUNCED ITSELF ON THE PRINCIPLES OF SUPREMACY AND DIRECT EFFECT?

Preliminary observation

Based on the answers to this question which were given in the national reports, it can be concluded that the question has proved slightly premature now that all the participating Matra project countries referred to the fact that they were not yet EU Member States (apart from Slovenia).

Slovenia

The national report observes that it is an important question whether or not the Slovenian Constitution has now in practice been made subject to EC primary law following the constitutional amendment of early 2003. The judiciary has not yet pronounced itself on this issue.

Another interesting development in Slovenia concerns a recent Constitutional Court ruling on the direct effect and applicability of the Council Decision of 28 February 2002 establishing Eurojust, in particular as regards the provisions on the nomination of members of the Eurojust Joint Supervisory Body.[6] The facts of the case are, in brief, as follows. Slovenia has a Code on the Nomination of Slovenian

---

[5] CFI, Case T-367/03 *Yedas Tarim ve Otomotiv Sanayi ve Ticaret A.S.*, *OJ* 2004 C 59/36.

[6] Decision No. U-I-120/04-14, Official Gazette RS, No. 82/2004.

Candidates for Judicial Posts on International Tribunals.[7] This national law sets the minimum age for potential candidates at 40. One of the applicants for Slovenian membership of the Eurojust Joint Supervisory Board was not yet 40 at the time of his application. For this reason, the Minister of Justice rejected the application. The applicant challenged this administrative decision before the Slovenian Constitutional Court by submitting the following arguments: (i) the Council Decision on Eurojust which after accession has supremacy over Slovenian law in accordance with Article 3a of the Slovenian Constitution does not mention any kind of age limit. This means that the national law is contrary to the decision and may therefore not be applied; (ii) the age limit as such goes against the provisions of the Founding Treaty where it establishes the principle of non-discrimination on grounds of age. The Slovenian Constitutional Court, however, dismissed the application holding that the relevant Council Decision, where it provides that: "In order to set up the Joint Supervisory Board, each Member State, acting in accordance with its legal system, shall appoint a judge….", allows for national law to apply in respect of the eligibility criteria to be observed. A similar problem concerning age requirements occurred in the Slovenian nomination of a judge for the CFI.

Romania

In Romania, courts have not yet considered the supremacy and direct effect of EC law either. Nevertheless, it should be noted that in the 2003 amendment of the Romanian Constitution of 1991 the following provisions were introduced on these issues: (i) the new Article 145 (Integration into the EU) under the new Title V on 'Euro-Atlantic Integration', more specifically subsection 2: "As a result of the accession, the provisions of the constituent Treaties of the EU, as well as other mandatory community regulations shall take precedence over the opposite, in compliance with the provisions of the accession act", and (ii) subsection 4 of the same Article: "The Parliament, the President of Romania, the Government, and the judicial authority[8] shall guarantee that the obligations resulting from the accession act and the provisions of para. (2) are implemented". What does this mean, however, especially in the light of the new Article 140(1) of the Romanian Constitution stating that: "The constitutional court shall be the guarantor of the supremacy of the Constitution", taken together with Article 1(5):[9] "The observance of the Constitution, of its supremacy and of the laws is binding" and taking into account the new Article 11(3)): "If a treaty to which Romania is to become a

---

[7] Official Gazette RS, Nos. 64/2001 and 59/2002.

[8] It must be noted that the original draft text of this paragraph in the chapter on Romania did not yet include the words "judicial authority"!

[9] See the recent amendment of 2003 to the 1991 Constitution of Romania, point 29.

party comprises provisions contrary to the Constitution, its ratification shall only take place after the revision of the Constitution"?[10] The issue is then, which law will have supremacy in Romania after accession: the Constitution or the EU legal acts mentioned under the new Article 145(2)? A further question is what in Romania the constitutional term "national laws" is understood to mean: is the Constitution one of these national laws? What will happen if the situation described in Article 11(3) of the Constitution occurs in the sense that the Constitution is found to contain provisions that are contrary to the Founding Treaties of the EU (or the new Constitutional Treaty) and the compulsory constitutional revision before ratification fails for some reason? Would that mean that Romania cannot join the EU or has to exclude itself from the EU as the case may be, due to a lack of national ratification?

Bulgaria

Due to the fact that the appropriate constitutional framework is not yet in force in Bulgaria, EU law cannot have supremacy and direct effect in this country yet.

Croatia

As Croatia is not yet a member of the EU, the question concerning the supremacy and direct effect of EU law is rather premature. It should also be mentioned that decisions of the Association Council (based on the Law on the implementation of the SAA and the Interim Agreement, published *Narodne Novine* No. 15/2001) "have to be either ratified by the Parliament, or enacted as internal legislation (Act of Parliament) or transformed into an act of the Government in order to have effect in Croatia" and are therefore not directly applicable (which constitutes a radical dualist approach in terms of "secondary association law"). Consequently, while the courts can directly apply the SAA itself (based on the Constitution), they are barred from doing so in terms of secondary association law. This situation raises the question of what should follow if the Croatian legislator fails to transpose a decision of the Association Council into the national legal order? What legal and/or political consequences would that entail, especially taking into account the relevant ECJ practice on such matters (*Sevince* case)? In Croatia, the direct effect of certain provisions of the ECHR has been acknowledged by the Constitutional Court.[11]

---

[10] See also Decision of the Romanian Constitutional Court No. 186/November 18, 1999.

[11] E.g., of Art. 6 in Decision U-IIIA-740/2002, *Narodne Novine* No. 9/2003.

Serbia and Montenegro

The doctrines of supremacy and direct effect are not addressed in the national report of Serbia and Montenegro except in the context of human rights and fundamental freedoms. In this respect the state union's Constitution – in accordance with monist principles – paves the way for the direct effect of the European Convention on Human Rights, and sets out as an important objective the direct applicability of ECtHR established case law (Arts. 9-10 of the Charter of Human and Minority Rights and Civil Liberties.[12] No case law has, however, emerged yet, although the members of the Court of Serbia and Montenegro at state union level have now been appointed. Here mention should be made of the encouraging experience of the Supreme Court of Serbia in terms of direct application and supremacy of international law. Several cases have been examined in the national report, for example, a 2004 judgment of the Supreme Court of Serbia in which the Court made direct reference to Article 5 of the Convention on the Elimination of all Forms of Racial Discrimination and to Article 26 of the International Covenant on Civil and Political Rights. The case concerned three Roma who had been barred from the municipal pool in Sabac based on their ethnic origin. From an EU law point of view, this kind of judicial practice is remarkable taking into account aspects of supremacy and direct effect. In another case which the Serbian Constitutional Court decided in 2002 the Judiciary Act was annulled by the direct application of and reference to the 1998 European Charter on the Statute for Judges and the 1985 UN Basic Principles on the Independence of the Judiciary.

Turkey

Since Turkey is not yet a full member of the EU, national courts have not yet pronounced themselves on the principles of supremacy and direct effect of EU law. In order to ensure the application of these principles, however, further constitutional changes are needed, apart from the famous 2001 and 2004 amendments. However, the direct effect of international agreements and treaties (or more generally, 'self-executing' international law) is recognized by the Turkish Council of State and these instruments even take precedence over national law (monist approach) according to the Council's permanent case law. Problems have at times been encountered, however, in respect of the transformation of the decisions of the Association Council into national law, which to some extent resembles the situation in Croatia.

---

12 The Charter is an integral part of the Constitutional Charter of Serbia and Montenegro (Art. 8, see also Art. 46, third sentence). Official Gazette of Serbia and Montenegro, No. 6 of 2003, adopted on 28 February 2003.

4. PRINCIPLE OF INDIRECT EFFECT

Slovenia

For the time being, Slovenia's judiciary cannot be said to recognize the principle of indirect effect. Nevertheless, the Slovenian Report makes an interesting comparison in respect of the future preliminary ruling procedure in the country with the current possibility for judges to turn to the Constitutional Court if they consider that the applicable national law is contrary to the Constitution. The statistics in Slovenia show that from 1990 until 2000 a total of 37 such requests were addressed to the CC and a total of 26 from 1996 until 2002, which reveals a certain reluctance on the part of the national courts to make use of this legal tool. A similar concern was voiced in the Croatian Report where the statistics are even more disappointing. It is therefore difficult to anticipate at this point how active the courts in these two countries will be in applying Article 234 TEC after accession. So far during the last 16 months in post-accession Slovenia, not one preliminary request from this new Member State has yet reached the ECJ.

Romania

Romania does not recognize indirect effect.

Bulgaria

Bulgaria recognizes indirect effect in, for example, the field of competition. The national competition authority and the competent courts must already take into account the relevant EC competition *acquis* (including ECJ case law). Unfortunately no concrete cases are mentioned in the report. A concrete example is, however, given in the field of consumer protection, where the Supreme Administrative Court when interpreting national Bulgarian law on misleading advertisements in a 1999 case took into account concrete provision of Directive 84/450/EEC as amended. According to the national rapporteur this case might prove rather exceptional, however.

Croatia

As to indirect effects as a rule of interpretation, there is no express reference in the available Croatian case law. In fact, it is not very often that Croatian courts apply international law or international case law at all, either directly or indirectly, although the principle of *favor conventionis* or *Völkerrechtfreundliche Auslegung* is known and acknowledged by Croatian courts.

Serbia and Montenegro

The question of indirect effect is at this stage too premature for Serbia and Montenegro to answer.

Turkey

The Turkish report does not address the issue of indirect effect in an EC law dimension, but was only discussed in general terms for a general international law perspective. Nevertheless, the report significantly states that: "At present, however, secondary Community legislation cannot be relied upon before the national courts, nor can they be used as sources of interpretation". In a later update of the report, the rapporteurs have already referred to some cases that are relevant to the question, such as, for instance, the *Davidoff* case.

5. CASES

Slovenia

The Slovenian report mentions no further cases besides the ones already examined.

Romania

In the practice of the Constitutional Court and of the Supreme Court in Romania (or of the ordinary courts for that matter) no issues have yet been encountered that are directly connected to the interpretation and direct application of Community law. As far as the implementation of the established case law of the ECtHR is concerned, only the Constitutional Court has referred to rulings of the ECtHR (for example, in its decisions Nos. 183/2003, 342/2003, 350/2003, 360/2003, 6/2004, 94/2004, 100/2004, 151/2004). No evidence of this was found, however, at the level of the ordinary courts. Mention should also be made here of the recent Constitutional Court ruling No. 591/2005 on the constitutionality of the new reform package on justice, which was adopted in June 2005 and based on the Government Strategy for the reform of the judiciary 2005-2007 (Official Journal of Romania, Decision 375 (6 July 2005) p. 16). This Strategy was elaborated in the light of the EU requirements concerning especially the independence of the judiciary and the transparency of the judicial process. The Constitutional Court found certain provisions in the package (*inter alia*, on the incompatibility rules concerning membership of the Supreme Council of Magistrates, or on open competition for leading posts in the judiciary) to be unconstitutional, thus blocking the reform for a while. This CC decision serves to demonstrate from an academic point of view the difficulties and controversies that may arise in the process of legal transition and the Europeanisation of national judiciaries.

Bulgaria

No further cases apart from the ones mentioned above are referred to in the Bulgarian report.

Croatia

According to the Croatian rapporteurs, “It may be that judges apply more Community law (or Community law principles) than reported, but information about this is lacking” and they conclude that “Croatian courts do not make use of the principle of indirect effects as an interpretative tool”. In their latest update the Croatian national rapporteurs mentioned that some developments had recently taken place in terms of ensuring more transparency of and better access to court judgments, especially concerning rulings of the Croatian Supreme Court and Constitutional Court. Another interesting point is that since October 1995 it is the general practice of the Croatian ordinary courts to consider themselves “not bound by legal opinions of the Constitutional Court expressed in its decisions in the framework of the constitutional complaints procedure”. According to the Croatian Judiciary Act, regular courts are not competent to leave aside Acts of Parliament which they consider unconstitutional. If they have doubts concerning the constitutionality of provisions which they should normally apply in a given case pending before them, they have to stay the proceedings and refer the question of unconstitutionality to the Constitutional Court. It is, however, not common practice for judges to do this. Another issue is that if a national law is contrary to an international treaty, the Constitutional Court will also declare that law to be contrary to the Constitution. This creates the danger that the forthcoming Acts of Accession, which will be treated as international treaties and the secondary EC law following from these Acts may be treated similarly by Croatian judges, i.e., they will believe that they should refer such matters to the Constitutional Court, which is clearly in breach of EC law.

Serbia and Montenegro

No case law has yet emerged, given that the Law on the Court of Serbia and Montenegro (Official Gazette of Serbia and Montenegro, No. 26, 2003) was only passed on 18 June 2003 as the last of a series of laws governing the operation of bodies of the state union. The implementation of the Law has yet to start. The national report accordingly and significantly states that: “The state union and the Member States have just begun to reform their judicial systems. A better organization of the courts is only one objective, the ultimate goal being the establishment of an efficient system to protect basic rights and freedoms, including internationally guaranteed rights and freedoms.” The report also states that: “The Court of Serbia and Montenegro combines the functions of a constitutional court and an administrative court with jurisdiction over the regulation and powers of the state union bodies only”. Moreover, the Belgrade Agreement stipulates that the Court of Serbia and Montenegro does not have any superior jurisdiction and cannot interpret or apply the national Constitutions of either Serbia or Montenegro.

This means that there is no judicially relevant hierarchy between the Court of Serbia and Montenegro and the national judiciaries of the two composite republics. In legal terms, therefore, Serbia and Montenegro is not a federal state. Consequently, as far as the jurisdiction of the Court of Serbia and Montenegro is concerned, it may be summarised as follows: the Court of Serbia and Montenegro can only rule on appeals by citizens (of the respective republics), but only if the institutions of the republics have threatened their guaranteed (at state union level) constitutional rights and freedoms and only if no other form of constitutional protection has been provided for at national level. According to the national rapporteurs, no relevant cases in this respect have yet been heard. Finally, it should be mentioned that the key judicial body in Serbia and Montenegro will be the Joint Session of the Court of Serbia and Montenegro. If the state union Court is called upon to decide whether the Constitutions or the laws of the composite republics are in conformity with the Constitutional Charter or with laws of the state union, or when it has to decide conflicts of jurisdiction between bodies of the state union and of the two republics, the Joint Session of the Court of Serbia and Montenegro must be convened. It consists of the members of the Constitutional Courts of the two and the judges sitting on the state union Court. The Session may only proceed if a majority of the members of each of the three courts are present. The state union Court's ruling requires a double majority, which means that the majority of members of the Court of Serbia and Montenegro must vote in favour and a majority of the Constitutional Court of the republic concerned. When the state union Court has delivered its judgment it is the task of the national Parliament of the republic concerned with the ruling to implement it within six months. The Law on the Court of Serbia and Montenegro does not provide for the situation that the national Parliament fails to carry out the decision. In any event, it emerges clearly from this description that only the actual practice can and will reveal how the Court system will operate on a daily basis at state union level.

Turkey

Although the high courts of Turkey (Constitutional Court, Court of Cassation, Council of State) have not so far encountered matters directly related to Community law, they have in many judgments referred to international treaties and general principles of international law. In 1987 Turkey recognised the competence of the European Commission on Human Rights to receive individual petitions and went on to recognise the compulsory jurisdiction of the Court in 1990. The Turkish contributors in the latest update of their chapter described how the overall number of directly implemented relevant ECtHR judgments in this context is steadily increasing and includes the famous and politically very important and sensitive *Zane* case and, for instance, the *Loizidou* case from 1998 which is a promising trend.[13] The Turkish chapter also contains a very interesting analysis on the practice of the highest courts where the implementation of the European Convention of Human Rights in Turkey is concerned. The conclusion is that in Turkey the direct applicability of the Convention is already ensured in many fields (such as, for instance, non-discrimination, inhuman and degrading treatment and punishment, Art. 11, the right to marry of a police officer, the right to leave the country (Protocol No. 4 to the Convention), freedom of religion, etc.), which shows how much the Convention is already part of the national legal order as compared to the situation in the other project countries.

6. IMPACT OF EU ACCESSION ON THE STRUCTURE, (RULES OF) PROCEDURE AND PRACTICE (INCLUDING WORKLOAD) OF THE NATIONAL COURTS

Slovenia

Slovenia is a relatively small country (as compared to the other participating countries in the project), which is probably why there are only 772 judges and 2201 other judicial technical and advisory staff. Slovenia has established a Judicial Training Centre which means that the training of judges, prosecutors and other law practitioners in EU law is a regular feature of the education of the judiciary. More attention still needs to be devoted to the translation of the EU *acquis*, however, including the rulings of the ECJ. There is also a strong need for an increased systemised collection of translated ECJ rulings that have been published before May 2004. In the chapter on Slovenia, an important feature that is mentioned concerning the impact of accession on the national judicial system in broader terms is how to solve the issue concerning the future representation of the country before the ECJ (depending on the type of pleading). Such matters are, however, part of the general homework which many countries wishing to join the EU still have to do. In Slovenia, the Ministry of Justice is the key actor in this process, as is also the case in Hungary for example. Finally, the report describes the national regulatory framework for the preliminary ruling procedure, which is also a matter most pre-accession countries and indeed some accession countries have to deal with.

Romania

The contribution addressed this issue in some detail. First of all, it should be noted that the 1991 Romanian Constitution was recently amended (in the light of

[13] See The 2004 Regular Report on Turkey's progress towards accession, Brussels, 6 October 2004, COM (2004) 656 final, pp. 11 et seq. and pp. 23-27, in particular pp. 16-18 and pp. 26-27.

the recent NATO and imminent EU accession) by the Law on the revision of the Constitution of Romania.[14] This Law modified Articles 124-125 (High Court of Cassation and Justice), Article 130 and Articles 132-133 (Supreme Council of Magistrates) and Article 151 (on the establishment of a special court to hear disputes arising out of the activities of the Court of Audit). Following this constitutional amendment, the Romanian Parliament enacted an important legislative package on the reform of the judiciary in the light of the preparations for EU accession. Three major laws from this package were adopted in mid-2004: (i) Law No. 304/2004 on the organization of courts (Judiciary Act), (ii) Law No. 303/2004 on the status of magistrates, and (iii) Law No. 317/2004 on the Supreme Council of Magistrates. The main aims of the reform were: (a) to increase the transparency of the functioning of the judiciary, (b) to establish more efficient legal and institutional guarantees for securing the true independence of the courts, by, first of all, eliminating the prevailing prerogatives of the Ministry of Justice in the administration of the courts, especially concerning the careers of judges and thus eliminating the potential for possible political influence on the administration of justice.

Taking into account all these constitutional and legislative reforms in the field of justice, the current state of play can be briefly summed up as follows: (1) The judicial system in Romania is quite complex. There are a total of 243 courts, and approximately 3700 judges (of which around 70 per cent are women). There are five types of specialised courts, including juvenile courts. (2) The judiciary's administration is headed by the Supreme Council of Magistrates, which for the time being seems to be a body that is semi-independent from the executive, given that the judiciary's annual budget (apart from the funding of the High Court of Cassation and Justice) is established and administered by the Ministry of Justice. If the Supreme Council of Magistrates were completely independent, it would be competent to submit its own proposal on the judiciary's annual budget directly to Parliament and defend it directly before the National Assembly, as is the case in, for example, Hungary and Poland. (3) Judges are appointed (and can be removed from office) by the President on the proposal of the Supreme Council of Magistrates. One problem concerning the pension system for retired magistrates is that the pensions are very low. For this reason, retired judges may under certain circumstances be reinstated. The Supreme Council of Magistrates is obliged to submit an annual report to Parliament. The rules on the composition of the Supreme Council have recently been tightened by the introduction of stricter rules on incompatibilities. (4) Like, for example, France, Romania has a National Institute for Magistrates which deals with the training of judges and prosecutors

[14] Published in the Official Gazette of Romania No. 669 of 22 September 2003 and approved by a nation-wide referendum on 19 October 2003.

in, among other things, EU law. Between 550 and 600 judges per year receive training in EU law. Romania has begun the task of translating ECJ rulings into Romanian, but no special manual has yet been issued on ECtHR or ECJ established case law. (5) The national report makes a special note of the problem of corruption within the judiciary. To combat corruption a special body was established: the National Anti-corruption Prosecution Office (NAPO). The NAPO dealt with 2229 cases in 2003. The report also mentions some concrete examples of corruption cases, for example, when on 10 October 2004, the High Court of Cassation and Justice (which also acts as the judiciary's disciplinary authority) submitted to the Bucharest Tribunal the files of two judges who had been convicted in the *Nahor* case so that the Tribunal could issue the execution mandates and implement the convictions. One prosecutor and one attorney were also convicted. They were all found guilty of taking substantial amounts of money from the well-known cigarette and gun dealer, Shimon Nahor, in exchange for intervening for his release. In 2005, the legislator introduced a computerised random case allocation system which might help in further eliminating (even potential) corruption within the judiciary. Another positive development is the recent adoption of the Code of Ethics for Magistrates. (6) Finally, special attention should be devoted to the new Article 145(4) in terms of its impact on the Romanian judicial system (legal certainty versus the possibility for extraordinary appeal against unappealable court rulings, which is an instrument inherited from socialism).[15]

Bulgaria

The Bulgarian report did not provide much information on this matter, but did state that "references to individual judgments of the ECtHR are still insufficient in court rulings".

Croatia

In Croatia there are 249 courts and 1868 judges (of which around a third are women) and 6734 clerks. The number of judges is therefore high and judges can on average rely on the support of three to four clerks per judge. Croatia has a Judges' Academy falling within the competence of the Ministry of Justice. The Academy takes care of the training of judges in, among other things, EU law. The training of other legal professionals (e.g., prosecutors, attorneys, notaries, etc.) in

---

[15] The chapter on Romania does not mention to what extent Romanian courts make reference to ECtHR decisions in their judgments. This question becomes especially relevant in the light of one of the identified priorities for reforms in the Commission Roadmap for Romania where it says that: "*the system of extraordinary appeals against final judicial decisions should be revised in line with the European Convention of Human Rights and in order the reinforce the principle of legal certainty*". It would be interesting to see how Romania plans to realize this priority.

EU law has not yet been properly addressed. EU law is a brand-new discipline in Croatia in the curriculum of high education facilities as well. For example, EU law has only recently become a mandatory subject at the Law Faculty of Zagreb University.

As far as the judiciary is concerned, the greatest problem in Croatia is the enormous amount of cases pending before the courts and the resulting backlog which means that parties sometimes have to wait five to seven years before receiving a final judgment. At the moment, there are approximately one million cases pending, which explains the number of complaints against Croatia before the ECtHR concerning the violation of Article 6 of the Convention, especially the reasonable time requirement). This situation has to be improved before accession. Croatia also still has some problems concerning the transparency of the functioning of the judiciary. The case law of the Croatian courts is not regularly published (except for Constitutional Court rulings). Access to judicial decisions is restricted and only a selection of final decisions of the Supreme Court are made accessible through a recently established website. However, decisions are not published in full and the reasoning of the Court is omitted. This is another area where improvements are necessary before accession. The report further stresses the need for changes in the legal culture and in the judges' mentality. These changes could well result from (preparations) for EU accession and are therefore in that sense also an example of the accession's impact on the national judiciary.

Serbia and Montenegro

The question of the practical impact of EU accession on the national judiciary of Serbia and Montenegro can best be addressed at the level of the composite republics of the state union. At present, the relevant information is only available for Serbia. The main points concerning the Serbian judiciary are the following: (1) There are 187 courts in Serbia,[16] employing 2356 judges and 18168 supporting technical and advisory staff, which means five to six court employees per judge. The report did not state, however, whether this is also the situation in practice. Serbia seems to be experiencing some problems with the computerization of the courts and in this respect working conditions are poor. (2) Serbia has a separate system of commercial courts which play an important role. A unique feature of Serbia's court system as compared to the other countries under analysis is that Serbian judges once elected by the National Assembly on the proposal of the High Judicial Council are appointed for an indefinite period of time (although the retirement age is set at 60). This means that political factors cannot be excluded in the election. To our knowledge, this is an extreme model as far as the rest of Europe is concerned. The annual budget for the judiciary has increased over the

[16] See Law RS OG. No. 29/2004 on the Organization of the Courts.

last three years to approximately 75 million euro in 2004. The budget is established and administered by the Government. (3) One of the most striking pieces of information in the national report was that the average salary in the Republic of Serbia in July of 2004 was 200 euro per month, while the average salary of judges on municipal courts was 420 euro per month. This is obviously unacceptable. The Serbian Government attempted to solve this problem by drastically increasing court fees (by four to five times their amount in 2002) and by spending the resulting extra income on the reform of the judiciary. No statistics were provided on the practical implementation of this judicial reform, however. (4) Serbian judges do not refer to concrete judgments of the ECtHR. There is no official translation into Serbian of ECtHR or ECJ rulings. There are no manuals in Serbian on the most important cases of the ECJ or the most relevant EC secondary law. (5) It should be mentioned that in Serbia administrative judicial review of acts of the executive is not yet ensured in full. The first independent Administrative Court (at first instance) will be operational only from 1 January 2007. Therefore the area of (as yet non-existent) administrative justice will claim more attention in the years to come, as its development is evidently a pre-condition for fulfilling the political criteria for EU membership from a rule of law point of view. (6) The contributors summarize the current state of affairs with respect to the administration of the judiciary as follows: "In Serbia, the courts' administrative authorities (High Judicial Council, Grand Personnel Council and Supervisory Board) are not fully independent and the situation is therefore not entirely adjusted to the requirements of the European Charter on the Statute for Judges or the Recommendations of the Council of Ministers of the Council of Europe on the independence, efficiency and role of judges. The position of these authorities could be improved by defining their role in the Constitution". This may mean that the judicial reform in connection with Serbia's potential candidacy for EU membership has to start by making the necessary amendments to the Serbian Constitution as regards the judiciary. (7) Serbia established a Judicial Training Centre in 2001. It was founded by the Ministry of Justice and the Serbian Association of Judges. The Training Centre also trains judges in EU law and this training is to be extended to other legal professionals (prosecutors, attorneys at law, notaries, law enforcement personnel, etc.) in the near future.

Turkey

The main conclusions and statements from the Turkish national report are the following:

(i) Turkey has a three-tiered court system, consisting of firstly the civil, criminal and administrative courts of first instance, secondly the intermediate (regional) courts of appeal, and finally the Court of Cassation and the Council of State as the supreme courts. This system was introduced on 1 April 2005 by the Law on the Establishment of the Intermediate Courts of Appeal (Law No. 5235) and was the result of the accomplishment of Turkey's purpose to improve the efficiency of the national judiciary on the way to EU membership. In Turkey there are 4063 courts in all (with a high number of specialised courts among them), and around 9200 judges (including 3200 public prosecutors). Of the judges over 75 per cent are men and this figure is even higher among public prosecutors (approximately 95 per cent). These figures show that in size the judiciary in Turkey is huge with an incomparably high number of courts (for example, in Hungary there are only 163 courts for 10 million people whereas in Turkey there are more than 4000 courts for 75 million inhabitants), but it must be kept in mind that the number of judges in Turkey is relatively low (5972) as compared to the number of courts (in Hungary there are close to 3000 judges). Many of these Turkish courts are criminal courts (over 1400) and the number of military courts is also still remarkable, although in May 2004 the "state security courts" were abolished at the suggestion of the EU. Judges are appointed by the Ministry of Justice with the approval of the Supreme Council of Judges and Prosecutors and this system is unique in Europe. According to Article 139 of the Turkish Constitution, judges and public prosecutors shall not be dismissed, or retired before 65, nor shall they be deprived of their salaries … even as a result of the abolition of the court or of the post. Judges and public prosecutors are attached to the Ministry of Justice in administrative terms, and the President of the Supreme Council of Judges and Public Prosecutors (which administers the career advancement of judges based on proposals of the Ministry of Justice) is the Minister of Justice himself. Generally speaking, in Turkey the role of the Ministry and of the Minister of Justice in the administration of the courts is crucial, which at least in institutional terms and with regard to the EU accession process raises the question of the separation of powers in the light of the independence of the judiciary. The annual budget of the judiciary (apart from the funding of the Constitutional Court and the Court of Jurisdictional Disputes, which is directly submitted Parliament) is established and administered by the Government as part of the annual state budget allocated to the Ministry of Justice.

(ii) The percentage of the state budget which is reserved for the Ministry of Justice is less than 0.01 per cent, which is quite low. At present, candidate judges receive 525 euro per month, and judges with ten years' experience earn 750 euro per month. Some 4700 judges (of the total of 5970) belong to these two categories. Judges whose length of service in the judiciary is more than 10 years are paid between 900 and 1000 euro per month. Supreme Court judges receive around 1450 euro per month. In this respect the national rapporteur remarked that the salaries of judges could be said to form a threat to their independence.

(iii) Turkey has a Justice Academy which has been operational since July 2003. The Academy is responsible for the training of judges, public prosecutors and even notaries, also in the field of EU law (although at present the emphasis is on the established case law of the ECtHR). Over the last three years some 115 activities (conferences, seminars, etc.) have taken place involving a total of 2800 judges and a number of other lawyers who received training in EU Third-Pillar matters with special emphasis on EC law. Finally, it should be mentioned that there are 30 law faculties at Turkish universities, which is not a very high figure for such a large country (by comparison, Hungary has nine law faculties) and EU law is mostly an optional subject in higher legal education.

(iv) The translation of ECtHR rulings into Turkish is well underway. In Turkey there is, for example, a Journal of Decisions of the ECtHR and the Ankara Bar Association regularly publishes summaries of ECtHR decisions in its bi-monthly journal. There are also some manuals of selected ECJ decisions, for example a bi-lingual manual in Turkish and English of over 500 pages in which the for Turkey 32 most important ECJ cases (mainly relating to Turkish immigrants) have been included, ranging from the *Van Gend en Loos* case to the *Boeing MacDonnell* case of 1997 and even covering specific internal market aspects, such as the Customs Union, free movement of workers, etc. Concerning secondary law, of the 92000 pages of EU *acquis*, around 12000 have already been translated into Turkish.

(v) There is a project for the computerization of the Turkish judiciary in the context of pre-accession preparation, which is currently being implemented and aims to provide every judge with their own personal note-book computer and install an intranet system for the judiciary called UYAP. UYAP has already become operational.

(vi) The judicial review of all administrative acts (Art. 159 of the Turkish Constitution) is not yet fully ensured in Turkey. For example, there is not yet a right to appeal against the decisions of the Supreme Council of Judges and Public Prosecutors, despite the fact that this Council is the most important disciplinary authority for the judiciary and a disciplinary decision can substantially affect the legal position (rights and obligations) of a judge. According to the statistics cited by the national rapporteur on average 200 to 300 disciplinary proceedings are conducted per year against judges in Turkey. The right to appeal should therefore also be made available in these cases in accordance with Article 125 (1) of the Turkish Constitution.

7. CONCLUDING REMARKS AND SUGGESTIONS

For a second round in the context of the Matra project national rapporteurs could be requested to explore the following issues, now that the current contributions are not always fully comparable on these points:

1. A short description of the judicial system would be appreciated. Question in this regard could be: how many courts are there in your country (also giving information on the different levels)? Do you have specialised courts (e.g., a separate administrative court system)?

2. How many judges are currently in office? What is their average age? These questions should be answered for all available instances.

3. How are judges appointed and by whom? What is their term of office? How can they be removed from office?[17]

4. How are judges in the respective countries trained in EU law?[18] Is there a separate training centre for judges (magistrates)[19] or is this expected to be established in the foreseeable future? Are there national trainees in EU law? If so, how have these been selected and based on which criteria? Has a special bar exam in EU law for judges (or other law practitioners) been introduced in your country or will this be introduced?

5. How are decisions of the ECJ translated, if at all, into the national language of your country?[20] How many decisions of the ECJ have been translated so far? Are there priorities based on which ECJ decisions are selected for translation? Are specialised ECJ case law manuals being compiled for judges (or other law practitioners) in your respective countries or are such manuals planned for the future?

6. How does your country plan, if at all, to create a complementary[21] regulatory environment for the proper implementation and application of Article 234 TEC (and Art. 68 TEC and Art. 35 TEU), for example, on the issues of the compulsory

[17] A very good example of this is the Bulgarian report.

[18] See, for example, the Croatian report.

[19] In Hungary, for example, to this day no National Training Center for Judges where they could receive training in EU law has yet been set up.

[20] For example, in Slovenia a start on the translation of ECJ decisions was only made six months before accession.

[21] See the Turkish report for an example of the misunderstanding of EC law.

suspension of the pleadings, the right to appeal against the referring court decision, and the obligation of the referring court to inform the Ministry of Justice,[22] etc.)? Are there plans to modify your country's Codes of Civil and Criminal Procedure or have modifications already taken place? What is your view of the attitude of members of the judiciary towards this important judicial dialogue with the EU?

Most of the participating countries in the Matra project have provided valuable additional information on these points, especially Turkey, Romania and the composite republic of Serbia although others were largely silent on these matters. It is advisable in the future to devote more attention to these institutional and enforcement-related aspects of the EU-accession driven pre-accession preparation when examining the national judiciaries in candidate and pre-candidate countries.

8. ADDENDUM: THE FIRST EXPERIENCES OF THE COURTS IN THE 10 NEW EU MEMBER STATES IN THE APPLICATION AND IMPLEMENTATION OF EU LAW

This book does not only contain the chapters based on the national reports of the six Matra project countries, but also the chapters on the new countries that joined the EU on 1 May 2004, i.e., the former candidate states. Their chapters were written on the basis of the same questionnaire as was presented to the Matra project countries. Below, a brief summary will be given of the most important first experiences of the national judiciaries in the new Member States as far as the application of EU law and the newly-developed practice of the judicial dialogue with the ECJ are concerned. The summary will only stress the points that may be useful and instructive for current and future candidate countries. More detailed information can be found in the individual chapters on the new Member States in part III of this book.

1. The current new Member States when still candidate countries chose a "training the trainers" approach to prepare their judiciaries through educating their judges for the implementation and application of EU law. This has proven to be invaluable. Each new Member State now has numerous judges specialised in EU law in general or in specific areas of EU law, which as qualified judges are given positions at almost all important courts, thus allowing them to train and/or assist their colleagues on a permanent basis in EU law and practice. This approach to

---

22 Or, for example, in Slovenia, the General Attorney's Office.

training judges in EU law deserves to be followed by the current (pre-)candidate countries.

2. In the field of direct effect and direct applicability of EU law there are many lessons to be learnt from the recent practice of the judiciaries in the new Member States. First of all, more attention should be paid to the practice of the ECJ relating to the contemporary effect of EC law after accession. Many cases first arose before accession, but had to be decided by national courts after accession. One could think of the four cases analysed in the Hungarian national report in this respect which concerned a criminal case involving the immediate application of Council Regulation 2913/1992 on the EC Customs Code, a request for a preliminary ruling concerning the application and interpretation of Council Directive 93/13/EEC on unfair contract terms in relation to a consumer contract which had been concluded before accession, a decision by the Hungarian Supreme Court on the applicability of the EC competition *acquis* to a merger which had been initiated before accession (BH/2005/7/270), and, finally, a recent request for a preliminary ruling on the interpretation of Article 33 of the Council Directive 77/388/EEC on the common system of value-added tax, as in Hungary companies are obliged to pay a local industrial turn-over tax, which is very similar to the value-added tax, but the Directive allows only one type of value-added tax to be used in a Member State. In the latter case it can be pointed out that the EC never questioned the tax regime concerned before accession and that the relevant national laws all date from before accession. Similar cases are Case C-475/03 *Banca Popolare di Cremona* which is still pending before the ECJ and the sugar-stocking case mentioned in the Estonian Report.

With regard to the direct application of EC laws it has also emerged that there are priority areas where EU law must be applied immediately after accession. Based on the national reports of the new Member States, these priority areas are the following: the EC Customs Union (in view of the regulations, see the Hungarian Report), the EC Common Agricultural Policy (in view of direct action for direct payments, see the Polish and Lithuanian reports, and also the sugar-stocking cases reported by Hungary and Estonia), EC financial schemes (in view of the regulations on the structural funds and cohesion funds), the free movement of persons (e.g., regulations on the common visa policy), the non-discrimination *acquis*, etc. This means that the current candidate countries should also focus on these typically internal-market related areas, as the application of this part of the EC *acquis* has to be flawless immediately after accession.

3. Another interesting feature that has emerged in the first year of application of EU law in the new Member States is the new significance of the role of the Constitutional Courts in upholding the EU legal order and EU values after

accession, as can be concluded from the chapters on, for instance, Poland, Estonia and Hungary. This new role of the Constitutional Court is probably partly due internal political conflicts in the different new Member States concerned, mainly between euro-sceptics and supporters of the integration at national level. Another reason is the fact that the EU adaptation process of some national Constitutions resulted in the inclusion of direct reference in the national constitution to the EU Treaties (e.g., in Hungary, and to some extent in Estonia) or that provisions that were contrary to the EU constitutional *acquis* were allowed to remain part of the Constitution after accession (e.g., in Poland). This post-accession driven intensified role of the national Constitutional Courts in the EU context can be clearly observed for example in Poland, where three cases have already been decided by the Polish Constitutional Tribunal within one year, which is remarkable. The cases concerned constitutional issues related to the rules on the election of Polish members to the European Parliament (case K 15/2004; a more or less similar problem occurred in Estonia), the constitutionality of the Acts of Accession concluded with Poland (case K18/2004), and the constitutionality of the transposing national law for the framework decision on the European Arrest Warrant (case P1/05; similar proceedings on the European Arrest Warrant have also been initiated in the Czech Republic). In Hungary, the Constitutional Court in 2004 still dealt with the constitutionality of a national implementing act on sugar market-related Commission regulations (case 17/2004 AB). All these cases that are analysed in the national reports of the new Member States show that a new level of judicial dialogue will have to be established (or may even have been established already, perhaps informally), namely a dialogue between the ECJ and the national constitutional courts. It is an inevitable part of the process and the technicalities involved in this constitutional judicial dialogue may be instructive in many ways for the current candidate countries as well.

4. Concerning the application of the instrument of requesting preliminary rulings, the national reports show that most of the new Member States' judiciaries are quite cautious about it and reluctant to use it, apart from Hungary, which has already referred five questions.[23] It is unclear where this reluctance stems from. Perhaps the time involved in obtaining a preliminary ruling is considered too long (it may take more than two years) or judges might be insufficiently aware of the instrument or they may be too conservative and regard EU law as foreign law and would rather use national law to decide the case. The latter possibility seems the most realistic, i.e., that judges in the majority of the new Member States prefer to apply domestic law, as may be inferred from the Estonian Constitutional Cham-

[23] See *OJ* (2004) C 251/09, *OJ* (2004) C 262/27, *OJ* (2004) C 71/15, and two recent ones that have not yet been notified in the *OJ*.

ber decision mentioned above and the dissenting opinion of several judges in this case (who nevertheless formed a minority). Further reflections on this point might also be useful for the current candidates, such as for Romania and Bulgaria.

5. Finally, some new Member States have regulated a national procedure for the adoption of court decisions on referring questions for preliminary ruling to the ECJ, such as, for example, Slovenia, Hungary and Slovakia. It must be stressed, however, that such a national regulatory framework is not at all necessary, as the preliminary ruling procedure is directly regulated by the Treaties. Nonetheless, the solutions adopted in some of the new Member States seem to some extent understandable, as the underlying purpose was obviously to assist judges, especially those of the older generation who had more difficulty absorbing EU law training, to become more (easily) familiar with this important institution of EC law. However, as appears from some of the national reports, national rules on the preliminary ruling procedure do not always have the desired effect. This may be illustrated by an example from Hungary, in a case before the Budapest Regional Court of Appeal (case 2. Pkf. 25.201/2005/3) where the judges reasoned that if the procedure is regulated in, for example, the Code of Civil Procedure, this means that when it is used (or not used as the case may be) in a concrete case, the court in question does not apply EC law, but national law, which creates a real danger that EC law (including the relevant case law of the ECJ) is easily ignored. This is an unfortunate development, given that the preliminary ruling procedure is by origin expressly an EC law institution, which the (pre-)candidate countries are advised to bear in mind.

Another negative aspect of the national rules referred to above is that in some countries (such as Hungary) the referring court is obliged to send a copy of its decision – for information purposes only – to the Ministry of Justice at the same time that it sends the file to the ECJ. This requirement may well influence the court in its decision on whether to refer or not and thus potentially harms judicial independence. It is recommended therefore that these unnecessary and artificial obstacles to the effective implementation of the preliminary rulings procedure (which is the only real guarantee for a fruitful judicial dialogue between the ECJ and the national judiciaries in the new Member States) are revised shortly.

IMPACT OF EU ACCESSION ON THE ROLE OF (POTENTIAL) CANDIDATE COUNTRIES' EXECUTIVES

Steven Blockmans*

1. INTRODUCTION

The executives of the Member States are involved in both the legislative process of the European Union and the implementation of EU law at national level. Candidate and potential candidate countries have to prepare themselves for both functions. The Matra Multi Country project has emphasized the preparation of the different parts of the executive of (potential) candidate countries for their role as implementing bodies for EU law, as especially the attainment of this goal provokes substantial changes in the role, functioning, and workload of the Governments and national administrations.[1] In turn, these changes prompt an inevitable reorganization of the executives' services and a revision of the (potential) candidate countries' administrative laws.

With regard to the impact of EU accession on the role of the executive, this study has revolved around three main themes:

(i) the extent to which the Governments and national administrations of the countries participating in the project implement and/or apply the conditions laid down in the Europe Agreements or Stabilization and Association Agreements;
(ii) the coordination mechanisms which have been envisaged by the Governments and national administrations of these countries to implement EU law; and
(iii) the impact which (future) EU accession has on the organization and practice of these Governments and national administrations.

* Researcher on the law of the European Union, T.M.C. Asser Institute (The Hague).

[1] As to the role of the national administrations as implementing bodies for European legislation, it can be said that, when applying EU law, these bodies may be regarded as exercising a function within the EU system, and thus have the character of decentralized EU bodies. This is one aspect of what has been dubbed "dédoublement functionnel". For this reason, EU accession provokes substantial changes in the functioning of national administrations as well as in the material administrative law. Accession, and by the same token pre-accession, increases the workload of the entire national administration, thereby prompting an inevitable reorganization of its services.

It is not the intention of this chapter to give a detailed overview of the answers to the abovementioned questions provided in the national contributions, nor does it aim to pass judgment on the national Governments' and administrative authorities' past and present actions, abilities and capacities to adhere to the conditions set for future accession (or indeed membership in the case of Slovenia). The combined reading of the European Commission's annual progress reports, including those in the framework of the Stabilization and Association Process, and the national reports prepared in the framework of this project, which (after some further adaptation) feature as chapters in this book, provides ample information to draw one's own conclusions. In recognition of the evident limits of a comparative analysis on the changing role, organization and functioning of the executives of six countries which find themselves at different stages of the EU (pre-)accession process, this horizontal analysis will merely offer observations on the "bottlenecks" and "best practices" of (potential) candidate countries' efforts to adapt their executives for the implementation of EU law at national level.

2. ORGANIZATION AND PRACTICE OF THE EXECUTIVE

Most of the changes in the process of public administration reform present themselves as the consequence of obligations flowing from negotiations with the European Union. While today's environment is forcing Governments and administrations to adapt to their fast-changing societies anyway, i.e., also if there is no pressure from the Union, EU accession helps (potential) candidate countries to prepare and implement changes more quickly. Combining issues concerning the organization and practice of central Government and administration and decentralised authorities, a number of peculiar and innovative measures should be mentioned which were adopted to reform the public administration into a corruption-free service provider for the citizens, a process which in all of the project countries is a prerequisite for economic progress and culminates in most of these countries in the finalization of the transition into a market economy system.

2.1 Organization of the executive

Two kinds of institutional mechanisms exist for the preparation and implementation of EU law: coordination mechanisms between and/or within (potential) candidate countries' Ministries and coordination mechanisms consisting of the representatives of the EU and the (potential) candidate countries. As the institutional mechanisms for bilateral cooperation with the EU have already been exhaustively dealt with elsewhere,[2] attention will only be paid here to the former type of mechanism.

---

[2] For literature on the composition, tasks and powers of negotiation delegations, association councils, association committees and the like, see, e.g., A. Evans, 'Institutions', in A. Ott and K.

All six countries originally engaged in this project have emphasized the importance of the existence of central bodies for the coordination of the technical implementation of the process of *rapprochement*. In most cases, this task has been facilitated by the creation of (i) a high-level Council on European Integration (Bulgaria) and a Secretariat General for European Affairs (Turkey) under the umbrella of the Prime Minister's Office, or a 'synthesis' Ministry of European Integration (Romania, Croatia);[3] (ii) medium-level State Secretaries, coordinators and deputy coordinators, directorates or units for European integration in line Ministries; and (iii) lower-level working groups for the harmonization of legislation (usually modelled after the negotiation working groups). A peculiar division of high-level tasks exists in Slovenia, where different Ministries are responsible for the coordination of activities related to each of the three Pillars of the EU Treaty.[4] Serbia and Montenegro, a potential candidate and a decentralized state union composed of two republics, is a different story altogether: a number of bodies and organs similar to the ones mentioned above were set up in both Serbia and Montenegro, with powers stipulated at the level of the composite republics.[5]

In most of the countries involved in the project, the reorganization of public administration in view of future accession to the EU has led to a substantial and ongoing increase in the number of civil servants.[6] Noteworthy in this respect is the Action Plan 2003-2007 of the Government of Croatia. This plan envisages putting the brakes on further expansion of the administration and stimulates efforts to restructure Ministries and state administration organizations (including a reduction in their numbers), to avoid the creation of new governmental bodies and the appointment of new civil servants and employees. Also, the Action Plan encourages the process of horizontal decentralization whereby some of the current duties of the Government's administration will be transferred to autonomous

Inglis, eds., *Handbook on European Enlargement. A Commentary on the Enlargement Process* (The Hague, T.M.C. Asser Press 2002) pp. 1043-1078.

3 Both in Bulgaria and Turkey, a separate inter-ministerial mechanism was created at this level to monitor the implementation of the reforms in the framework of the harmonization process ('Coordination Council' resp. 'Monitoring Group for the EU Reforms'). In Croatia, like in other countries, the central Government also discusses European integration issues at its regular sessions and adopts reports on the realization of the National Programme and Implementation Plan. Recently, the Ministry of European Integration has been incorporated in the Ministry of Foreign Affairs.

4 The Government Office for European Affairs (SVEZ) is responsible for coordinating affairs falling within the scope of the First and Third Pillars of the EU Treaty, while the Ministry of Justice and the Ministry of the Interior enjoy a high level of autonomy in these domains. The Ministry of Foreign Affairs (MZZ) is responsible for Second Pillar affairs and plays an important interventionist role in the framework of the Third Pillar.

5 For more information, see the chapter on Serbia and Montenegro by D. Lopandić and S. Samardzić in this volume.

6 See, e.g., the chapters on Bulgaria, Turkey, and Serbia and Montenegro.

organizations *outside* the administration, such as trade unions, employers' associations, universities, etc.[7]

2.2 Administrative capacity-building

Most of the (potential) candidate countries are still coping with the legacy of a post-communist state administration with a highly centralized structure composed of a Minister at the top to develop policies and a passive state administration to implement the Minister's decrees. Administrative capacity-building and increasing political independence, efficiency and accountability of the administration are thus key priorities in the pre-accession process. In the six countries originally participating in this project the reform of the public administration has been undertaken through, *inter alia*, the adoption of laws regarding the status of civil servants, the introduction of transparent selection procedures and the organization of competitive *concours* for their recruitment, the reform of the salary system, the targeted training of civil servants by national institutes for public administration (specifically also in EU affairs), enabling greater flexibility in managing human resources and a higher level of workforce mobility between public administration bodies, the adoption of laws on access to information, the removal of administrative barriers,[8] computerization and the introduction of e-government,[9] the adoption of a code of ethics, the introduction of disciplinary procedures, and the creation of the post of Ombudsman.[10]

In the case of Romania the demilitarization of the police and the fight against corruption have been separate stumbling blocks. They were addressed by the entry into force of a new law on the statute of the police which explicitly states that policemen are non-military civil servants operating under the rule of law, and the setting up of a National Anti-corruption Prosecutor's Office as an autonomous structure within the Ministry of Public Administration. Also in Romania, the Prime Minister's Control Authority has been designated as OLAF's single interlocutor.

---

[7] See the chapter on Croatia.

[8] See the chapter on Slovenia.

[9] See *infra* section 2.3.

[10] For more detailed information on these reforms, see, e.g., the chapter on Bulgaria. In Serbia and Montenegro, the Governments of both republics have adopted public administration reform strategies, the implementation of which is monitored in Serbia by the Government's Council for Public Administration Reform. Reform of the public administration in Turkey is governed by the Government's own NPAA of 19 March 2001, which stipulates "Necessary Institutional Changes" in each of its chapters.

2.3 Coordination between (newly established and existing) executive bodies

Apart from the regular coordination, monitoring and reporting instruments such as "evolving" planning documents, national integration programmes, and meetings in inter-ministerial monitoring and/or working groups, the importance of working with interactive databases, CD-ROMs and portals on EU affairs to monitor the adoption and application of decisions implementing the *acquis* should also be underlined. In Slovenia, the construction of what is termed the "European portal" for access to relevant documents is underway. The portal will be accessible to all those participating in the adoption of decisions on individual affairs. SVEZ (First and Third Pillars), and in particular cases also MZZ for the Third Pillar, will, for each document, appoint the Ministry in charge (which will formulate a draft position on the relevant material), the authorities that must be notified of the material, the time limit for the adoption of a coordinated position and the method of approval of positions (either only by the Ministry or working group in question, or also by the Government and/or National Assembly).

Croatia will follow suit with the creation of an interactive database (Management Reporting Information System; MRIS) at the Ministry of Foreign Affairs and European Integration for the purpose of facilitating the technical monitoring of the implementation of the National Programme. In order to avoid written reporting, each state administration body will be provided with access to the MRIS into which the European Coordinators will enter data on a monthly basis on the implementation of the National Programme in their area of competence. Data entered into this database will also be controlled directly on an operational level by civil servants at the Ministry.

Special mention should also be made of a Croatian initiative for the horizontal exchange of knowledge and experiences on the level of state administration bodies. The Ministry of Foreign Affairs and European Integration in Zagreb has launched a national twinning initiative consisting of an exchange programme of lawyers in state administration bodies with lawyers employed by the Ministry. Almost all employees of the Administration for the Harmonization of Legislation participate or have participated in the work of other state administration bodies on legal issues in their area of competence: in the Ministry of Finance, the Ministry of Justice, Administration and Local Self-Government, the Ministry of Environmental Protection and Physical Planning, the Ministry of the Economy, etc.

2.4 Decentralization

With respect to decentralization, successfully realizing the autonomy of decentralized authorities and strengthening their local and regional self-government is more likely when they are not only enabled to perform a much broader scope of functions, but also when real powers are transferred (not just 'delegated') from central Government and when the local authorities' financial capacity is expanded by means such as the redistribution of revenues from national taxes or the use of non-fiscal financing instruments. In most of the countries involved, this process was given shape with the adoption of laws on local self-government and local administration.[11]

3. HARMONIZATION OF LEGISLATION

3.1 **General remarks**

All countries involved in this Matra-sponsored project have been and will continue to be engaged in the harmonization of their national legislation with the *acquis* of the Union. They are implementing EU law on the basis of either the conditions attached to membership of the EU and thus flowing from the Treaties (as in the case of Slovenia), or those laid down in a Europe Agreement (Bulgaria, Romania, Turkey)[12] or a Stabilization and Association Agreement (Croatia). Even if such a legal obligation did not formally rest upon Serbia and Montenegro at the time when the project was taking place, such a duty will hopefully soon be imposed.[13] On 10 October 2005, the EU launched SAA negotiations with Serbia and Montenegro, i.e., five days after the fifth anniversary of the democratic uprising in Belgrade which ousted Milosević from the President's seat. The EU warned that their conclusion is possible only if ICTY indictees Radovan Karadzić and Ratko Mladić are handed over to the Hague tribunal in the meantime. Be that as it may, a few steps have already been taken towards approximating the legislation, such as the adoption of a special Action Plan for the Harmonization of Laws of the *Republic of Serbia* with EU law, which calls for fast-track adoption

[11] In this context too, the situation in Serbia and Montenegro is somewhat special. See Lopandić and Samardzić in this volume.

[12] The obligation for Bulgaria and Romania now flows from the Treaty between the Kingdom of Belgium, the Czech Republic, the Kingdom of Denmark, the Federal Republic of Germany, the Republic of Estonia, the Hellenic Republic, the Kingdom of Spain, the French Republic, Ireland, the Italian Republic, the Republic of Cyprus, the Republic of Latvia, the Republic of Lithuania, the Grand Duchy of Luxembourg, the Republic of Hungary, the Republic of Malta, the Kingdom of the Netherlands, the Republic of Austria, the Republic of Poland, the Portuguese Republic, the Republic of Slovenia, the Slovak Republic, the Republic of Finland, the Kingdom of Sweden, the United Kingdom of Great Britain and Northern Ireland (Member States of the European Union) and the Republic of Bulgaria and Romania, concerning the accession of the Republic of Bulgaria and Romania to the European Union, *OJ* 2005 L 157/11.

[13] On 12 July 2005, the Commission put forward to the Council a mandate for negotiations with Serbia and Montenegro on an SAA. See Press Release IP/05/915, Brussels, 12 July 2005.

or amendment of 50 priority laws in the internal market sphere. The Government of the Republic of Serbia has also prepared amendments to its Rules of Procedure, which imply the obligation of taking EU law into account when submitting draft laws for adoption (known as the Statement of Harmonization). As part of the Stabilization and Association Process, a technical mechanism has been established to monitor the development of legislative reform (called the "matrix" which offers an overview of the condition of the legislation).

The fulfilment of all the obligations stemming from EU membership, or the EA or SAA, forms the starting point for serious reforms of the public administration of (pre-)accession and associate countries so as to facilitate adjustment to the political, economic and legal standards of the European Union. In all associate countries guidelines have been developed for the implementation of the reforms that these countries are expected to perform on their way to membership. Each country must lay down these guidelines in a National Programme for the Adoption of the *Acquis* (NPAA). These programmes are primarily aimed at fulfilling the obligations which were undertaken under the EA/SAA. At the same time, the NPAAs serve as a roadmap by which the Governments can realistically assess their capacities, and those of society as a whole, (i) to implement all measures and actions necessary for accession to the EU, (ii) to give direction to the political and economic criteria, (iii) to transpose and apply the *acquis*, and (iv) to reform the public administration. This roadmap is backed up by a financial quantification of the efforts towards alignment and integration over a specific period of time. The NPAA sets out assessments, guidelines and tasks, with the intention that all relevant activities will prepare the candidate for full membership by the projected date of entry into the Union.

In each of the participating countries, working groups for the harmonization of the national legislation with the *acquis* have been established pursuant to the 31 chapters under negotiation. The work of these working groups greatly contributes to the process of harmonization of legislation and the adoption of common standpoints to resolve essential issues, and considerably accelerates the legislative procedures at Government level. The harmonization process first involves legislation on the basic elements of the internal market, trade and trade-related areas (public procurement, competition and state aid, technical legislation, consumer protection and intellectual property, and industrial and commercial property), and later other elements of the *acquis* referred to in the EA/SAA.[14] The difficulties which (potential) candidate countries generally face in the translation of the *acquis* into their national legal orders have become apparent with the EU's big bang enlargement of May 2004. It is to be hoped that the five non-members

[14] The national rapporteurs for Turkey emphasize that Turkey is the only candidate country which started to implement a customs union with the EC before actual EU integration.

united in this project will draw lessons from the ten new Member States' more unfortunate experiences.[15]

3.2 Innovations in the initiation of national harmonization legislation

The Ministry of European Integration, or its equivalent, is the coordinating body in the process of the harmonization of laws and in regular Government procedure assesses the degree of harmonization of draft legislation with the relevant provisions of the *acquis*. Recognising the importance of the process of harmonizing the legislation, the Government of Croatia on the basis of its Rules of Procedure introduced a procedural novelty, whereby the opinion of the MEI has to be attached to draft Bills and proposals for other regulations. The Committee for European Integration of the Croatian Parliament also plays a key role in the legislative process. In keeping with the Decision on the Measures in the Procedure of Harmonizing the Legislation of the Republic of Croatia with the *Acquis*, state administration bodies, in the preparation of legislative documents which harmonize the legislation of Croatia with the *acquis* pursuant to Article 69 of the SAA, are obliged to submit together with the Bill a completed statement on the degree of harmonisation and a parallel review of the conformity of the provisions of the Bill with the provisions of the relevant legal acts of the EU (compatibility statement). Both instruments, together with the Bill, are then submitted to the MEI for verification and confirmation.[16]

3.3 Procedural limits

The Romanian Government's law-making practice to bring national legislation in line with that of the EU was, until recently, almost entirely based on Government emergency ordinances, a feat which has been bitterly criticized in the Commission's regular reports. These legislative instruments entered into force immediately and only required subsequent approval by Parliament. The Commission pointed out that this was cause for concern, as the legislation could be adopted before proper reference was sought. Transparency was thus seriously reduced and Parliament's prerogative to subsequently modify or reject the new legislation introduced by way of such emergency ordinances might have induced legislative instability. The application of such procedures should be limited to cases of an exceptional nature. Romania has since ceased this practice.

---

[15] For an indication of figures, see, e.g., the chapter on Romania.

[16] For further details, see the Croatian chapter.

3.4 Proliferation of semi-autonomous institutions

In addition to the creation of a string of central bodies for coordination, each of the countries involved in this project has witnessed the establishment of a whole series of independent or semi-autonomous institutions in order to ensure the effective implementation of the adopted legislation. One could think of national competition authorities, standardization bodies, data protection agencies, consumer protection councils, etc. Whether the proliferation of such institutions may serve to reverse the widening gap between the progress achieved in most of the project countries in the approximation of laws on the one hand and the ability of the administrations to implement and enforce the newly adopted legislation on the other, remains to be seen.

4. LOOKING AT THE FUTURE: THE INTEGRATION CHALLENGE POSED BY THE WESTERN BALKANS

The success of EU enlargement is one of the few unambiguously positive achievements of the post-Cold War world, indeed nothing short of a political miracle. In less than a decade, the prospect of EU membership succeeded in consolidating democratic and market reforms throughout Central and Eastern Europe. The accession process profoundly transformed societies as diverse as those of Slovenia, Bulgaria and Romania. There is widespread consensus that it can do the same for the Western Balkans. However, there is one critical difference: the EU lacks experience in the integration of weak states (e.g., the state union of Serbia and Montenegro, Bosnia-Herzegovina, Albania) and territories (e.g., Kosovo). Reversing the ancestral ways of nation-building in the Western Balkans and building functional Member States while integrating them into the European Union is the unique challenge which Brussels faces in the Western Balkans. The International Commission for the Balkans, in its March 2005 report, has advocated a so-called 'Member State-building strategy' which is quite distinct from the mechanisms deployed by the international community in other parts of the world and from the EU accession process as typified by the last wave of enlargement.[17] The objective of such a strategy is not simply to build stable, legitimate states whose own citizens will seek to strengthen and not destroy them, but rather the establishment of states that the European Union can accept as full members with absolute confidence.

---

[17] See International Commission on the Balkans, *The Balkans in Europe's Future* (Sofia, Centre for Liberal Strategies 2005) at p. 14.

A successful strategy for the integration of the countries of the Western Balkans will necessarily depend upon the development of functioning state administrations, using the instruments of the EU accession process. In the case of the Western Balkans, the European Commission will have to assume responsibility for some of the institutional choices that the applicants are forced to make. This will be tough on the EU, because, so far, it has been a reluctant nation-builder, unwilling to recommend specific institutional solutions to EU candidate countries.

The transformation of the EU accession process into one of Member State-building implies that the very negotiating process must be fine-tuned with a view to encouraging institution building in the applicant countries. Hitherto, accession negotiations with the EU have focused on the terms under which applicants will adopt, implement, and enforce the *acquis* and, notably, on the granting of possible transitional arrangements which are limited in scope and duration. From the most recent round of enlargement it has become clear that room for improvement largely lies in the process of implementation of the rules that make up the *acquis*. At the heart of the accession strategy for the Western Balkans should be the need to move on quickly from the formal adoption of legislation to the development of the capacity to implement it. The development of this policy capacity will be absolutely critical for the prospects of the weak states of the Western Balkans in their aspirations to join the EU. Therefore, the negotiating framework for each country of the Western Balkans needs to be enhanced so as to include capacity building as its principal and explicit objective. Also, the introduction of the "benchmark" concept in the negotiating framework for membership talks with Croatia is undoubtedly a step in the right direction.[18]

What the most recent round of enlargement has also made clear is that, while institutional issues – administrative capacity building and reform of the judiciary – were the most challenging, they were tackled last. It has been rightly suggested that instead of starting with the White Book on the Single Market, the countries of the Western Balkans would be much better served by a White Book on Freedom, Security, and Justice.[19] In practical terms this would mean that assisting future (potential) candidate countries in the field of justice and home affairs would be the overriding priority for the accession process and that the state of the rule of law would be the major criterion in evaluating the progress of (potential) candidate countries on their journey to the EU.

---

[18] Council Conclusions of 16 March 2005, Press Release No. 6969/05 (Presse 44).

[19] See International Commission on the Balkans, op. cit. n. 17.

Part III

New Member States

CYPRUS

Nicholas Emiliou*

1. NATIONAL CONSTITUTION

The foundation for the constitutional structure of the Republic of Cyprus,[1] which comprises the Constitution together with two Annexes (containing the Treaty of Guarantee and the Treaty of Alliance), was laid by the Zurich and London Agreements,[2] which were thought to provide the final settlement of the Cyprus problem. The Treaty of Guarantee[3] and the Treaty of Alliance[4] have been given constitutional force.[5] The Constitution of the Republic of Cyprus of 1960 is rigid, detailed and complex. The 1960 Constitution 'stands out as the centrepiece of an intricate network of international agreements and undertakings, delicately but inextricably interwoven with one another and with the Constitution itself…'.[6]

* Dr Nicholas Emiliou, Ambassador of the Republic of Cyprus, Permanent Representative of Cyprus to the European Union. The views expressed in this paper are personal and do not necessarily reflect the views of the Government of the Republic of Cyprus. This contribution is based on N. Emiliou, 'Impact of EU Accession on the National Legal Orders of New Member States: The Case of Cyprus', in J.W. de Zwaan, et al., eds., *The European Union: An Ongoing Process of Integration – Liber Amicorum Alfred E. Kellermann* (The Hague, T.M.C. Asser Press 2004) pp. 285-293.

[1] The Republic of Cyprus was set up by means of the Treaty of Establishment between Cyprus, Britain, Greece and Turkey. The Treaty provides that the Republic 'shall comprise the island of Cyprus … with the exception of two areas defined in Annex A of this Treaty, which areas shall remain under the sovereignty of the United Kingdom.' This secured British military bases on the island.

[2] The Zurich and London Agreements of 11 and 19 February 1959, respectively, declared Cyprus an independent republic, whose independence, constitutional order and territorial integrity were guaranteed by the United Kingdom, Greece and Turkey.

[3] The Treaty of Guarantee between Cyprus, on the one hand, and Britain, Greece and Turkey, on the other, aimed at the protection of the constitutional order created by the Zurich and London Agreements and the exclusion of political or economic union of the island with any State. The three guarantor powers guaranteed the continued existence and maintenance of the constitutional order as well as the independence and territorial integrity of Cyprus. By means of Article IV, each of the three guarantor powers reserved 'the right to take any action with the sole aim of re-establishing the state of affairs established by the present Treaty', provided that 'common or concerted action may not prove possible'.

[4] The Treaty of Alliance was concluded between Cyprus, Greece and Turkey and provided that military contingents of each State should be stationed in the territory of the Republic. This had the purpose of securing the parties' responsibility to resist any attack or act of aggression directed against the independence or territorial integrity of Cyprus.

[5] Art. 181 of the 1960 Constitution.

[6] S.A. de Smith, *The New Commonwealth and its Constitutions* (London, Stevens 1964) p. 285.

According to paragraph 21 of the Zurich Agreement, several of its provisions had to be included in the Constitution of the Republic of Cyprus as fundamental – basic articles, not subject to any revision or amendment. These basic articles, stipulated by the Constitution itself to be unalterable,[7] include all or parts of forty-eight separate articles out of a total of 199. On the other hand, according to Article 182(2) and (3) of the 1960 Constitution, any other provision of the Constitution (i.e., non-basic provisions) 'may be amended, whether by way of variation, addition or repeal' by a law passed by a majority vote comprising at least two-thirds of the total number of the Representatives belonging to the Greek community and at least two-thirds of the total number of the Representatives belonging to the Turkish community.

As a result of the deliberate withdrawal of the Turkish Cypriots and their refusal to participate in the state organs of the Republic since 1964, the Supreme Court of Cyprus, in its landmark judgment in *Attorney General of the Republic* v. *Ibrahim*,[8] adopted the doctrine of necessity. This doctrine has been further elaborated by case law as an integral part of the legal and constitutional order of the Republic, so much so, that it is possible to deviate temporarily from strict compliance with constitutional provisions. In other words, the doctrine has been applied in Cyprus to validate public acts facing procedural difficulties which are impossible to remedy because of the political boycott by the Turkish Cypriot leadership and, later, foreign invasion. Thus, pending the solution of the political problem, any necessary constitutional amendments of non-basic constitutional provisions may be adopted by a law passed by a majority of at least two-thirds of Greek Cypriot members of the House of Representatives.[9]

Article 169 of the 1960 Constitution deals with the means of ratification of treaties, conventions and international agreements as well as their effect on internal law. The Constitution of Cyprus vests the power to ratify in different authorities of the Republic, depending on the subject matter of the treaty, convention or international agreement. Cyprus is a monist country. In the Republic of Cyprus, a treaty negotiated or signed under a decision of the Council of Ministers and ratified by a law passed by the House of Representatives and published in the official Gazette of the Republic acquires superior force to any municipal law.[10] A ratifying law comes into operation on the date of its publication in the Gazette

---

[7] Art. 182(1) of the 1960 Constitution. A list of these basic articles of the Constitution is to be found in Annex III thereto.

[8] (1964) *CLR* 195.

[9] On this basis, there have been, since 1985, a number of amendments to non-basic provisions of the 1960 Constitution, such as Art. 111.

[10] See Art. 169(2) and (3) of the 1960 Constitution.

unless provided otherwise.[11] According to Article 169 of the Constitution, subject to the provisions of Article 50 and Article 57(3) of the Constitution,[12]

- all international treaties and agreements relating to commercial matters, economic co-operation (including payments and credit) and *modus vivendi* are concluded under a decision of the Council of Ministers;
- every other international treaty, convention or agreement, negotiated and signed under a decision of the Council of Ministers, is concluded and becomes operative when approved by a law made by the House of Representatives; and
- every treaty, convention and agreement (concluded in accordance with the above provisions) is published in the Official Gazette of the Republic and on its application has superior force to any municipal law, on condition that such treaty, convention or agreement is applied by the other party thereto.[13]

The 1960 Constitution contains no provisions providing for the transfer of competences to international organisations nor does it allude to any similar concepts.

The Constitution, under the terms of Article 179(1), is the supreme law of the Republic and is therefore not within the ambit of the definition of 'municipal law' within the meaning of Article 169(3), which covers any ordinary law prior or consequent to an international treaty.[14] Thus, the hierarchy of norms in the Cypriot legal order is (a) the Constitution, (b) international treaties and (c) ordinary laws.[15] A treaty is therefore inferior to the Constitution and the latter prevails in case of any inconsistency between constitutional provisions and the provisions of the treaty.[16]

On the other hand, it is clear that Community law – which is based on treaties between the EC Member States – forms a distinct legal system which is capable of creating directly effective rights for those subject to it. These Community rights are not only independent of national laws but are also to be regarded as superior to them. The acceptance by national courts of the supremacy of Community law is a prerequisite for its full reception into national law.

---

[11] See Art. 82 of the 1960 Constitution.

[12] Arts. 50 and 57(3) of the 1960 Constitution concern the right of veto of, respectively, the President and the Vice-President of the Republic.

[13] For a clear statement by the Supreme Court as to when such reciprocity is excluded, see the Supreme Court's judgment in *Malachtou* v. *Armefti* (1987) 1 *CLR* 207.

[14] For the definition of the term 'law', see Art. 186(1) of the 1960 Constitution. See also the Supreme Court's judgment in *Malachtou* v. *Armefti.*

[15] See, for example, *Eracleous* v. *The Municipality of Limassol* (Appeal No. 5793), judgment of the Supreme Court of 14 December 1993, which recalled the above hierarchy.

[16] See *Malachtou* v. *Armefti.*

In the Cypriot constitutional order, executive power is ensured by the President (and the Vice-President) of the Republic (Art. 46(1) of the 1960 Constitution) and it is exercised by the Council of Ministers (Art. 54(1) of the 1960 Constitution). The legislative power of the Republic is exercised by the House of Representatives 'in all matters' except those expressly reserved to the Communal Chambers under the Constitution (Art. 61 of the 1960 Constitution).[17] The Supreme Court exercises all the judicial power of the Republic, including constitutional matters, such as the constitutionality of laws, conflicts of competence between the organs of the Republic and electoral petitions.[18]

Under Article 179(1), the Constitution is the supreme law of the Republic. On the other hand, Community law by its own terms is supreme and takes precedence over all national law, including national constitutions. It should be noted, however, that Article 179 is not a basic provision of the Constitution and can therefore be amended under the procedure provided for by Article 182.

Moreover, membership of the European Union involves a partial loss or transfer of the exercise of sovereign powers in favour of the Union. This, *prima facie*, appears to sit uneasily with Article 61 of the 1960 Constitution, which provides that the House of Representatives exercises the legislative power of the Republic 'in all matters'. Article 61 is a basic article and is therefore unamendable.

A way of overcoming the above-mentioned difficulties would be to amend Article 169 of the 1960 Constitution (a non-basic provision), in accordance with the procedure prescribed in Article 182, by adding specific paragraphs reflecting, *mutatis mutandis*, the contents of Articles 29(4)(3), 29(4)(4), 29(4)(5) and 29(7) of the Irish Constitution.[19] The adoption of such an amendment would cover the

---

[17] The Communal Chambers were designed to serve as legislative, executive and economic authorities in religious, educational, teaching and cultural affairs of the two Cypriot communities, as well as issues of personal status. See Arts. 86-111 of the 1960 Constitution.

[18] See Arts. 133-164 of the 1960 Constitution. The jurisdiction of the Supreme Court is derived from Arts. 136 and 152 of the Constitution. See also Law 33/64.

[19] Art. 29 of the Irish Constitution provides, *inter alia*, as follows. Art. 29(4)(3): 'The State may become a member of the European Coal and Steel Community (established by Treaty signed at Paris on the 18th day of April, 1951), the European Economic Community (established by Treaty signed at Rome on the 25th day of March, 1957) and the European Atomic Energy Community (established by Treaty signed at Rome on the 25th day of March, 1957). The State may ratify the Single European Act (signed on behalf of the Member States of the Communities at Luxembourg on the 17th day of February 1986 and at The Hague on the 28th day of February 1986).' Art. 29(4)(4): 'The State may ratify the Treaty on European Union signed at Maastricht on the 7th day of February 1992 and may become a member of that Union.' Art. 29(4)(5): 'The State may ratify the Treaty of Amsterdam amending the Treaty on European Union, the Treaties establishing the European Communities and certain related Acts signed at Amsterdam on the 2nd day of October, 1997.' Art. 29(7): 'No provision of this Constitution invalidates laws enacted, acts done or measures adopted by the State which are necessitated by the obligations of membership of the European Union or of the Communities, or prevents laws enacted, acts done, or measures adopted by the European Union or by the Communities or by institutions thereof, or by bodies competent under the Treaties establishing the Communities, from having the force of law in the State.'

actual accession of the Republic to the Union as well as the transfer of the exercise of national executive, legislative, judicial and treaty-making powers to the EU institutions, thus pre-empting the potential problems posed by Articles 54(1), 61(1), 136, 152 and 169 of the 1960 Constitution.

Moreover, for reasons of clarity and legal certainty, Article 179(1) of the Constitution (also a non-basic provision) could be amended as follows: '*Subject to the provisions of Article 169* [t]his Constitution shall be the supreme law of the Republic.' Such an amendment would ensure that constitutional provisions do not affect the Treaty of Accession and Community law in any way and would safeguard their supremacy over the Constitution.

Any amendments to the 1960 Constitution necessitated by the accession of the Republic to the European Union will be enacted by the House of Representatives under Article 182(2) and (3) of the Constitution. The 1960 Constitution contains no provision concerning the possibility of holding a referendum, even though there is nothing in the Constitution precluding this possibility.

The House of Representatives ratified the Treaty of Accession on 14 July 2003,[20] on the basis of Article 169 of the Constitution, following an opinion by the Attorney General to the effect that no amendment of the Constitution was necessary prior to the ratification of the Treaty.

2. ROLE OF THE JUDICIARY

According to the Supreme Court's case law,[21] an international treaty, being inferior to the Constitution by virtue of Article 179(1), is subject to judicial review in the sense that the constitutional provisions prevail in case of any inconsistency between them and the provisions of the treaty. A treaty does not, *stricto sensu*, repeal municipal law but only has superior force to it, taking precedence in its application. Such a treaty retains its nature as part of international law. However, having regard to its nature and its connection with the international obligations of the Republic, it cannot be amended or repealed by any posterior law contrary to its provisions or the provisions of the Vienna Convention on the Law of Treaties.[22] According to the Supreme Court, a ratified treaty delineates not only the international obligations of the State, as defined therein, but also the internal law until the day that, under its own provisions or in accordance with the Vienna Convention on Treaties, it ceases to be operative.

20 See Ratifying Law N35(III)2003, published in the *Official Gazette* No. 3740 of 25 July 2003.

21 See *Malachtou* v. *Armefti*.

22 The Vienna Convention on the Law of Treaties was ratified under Art. 169 of the 1960 Constitution by Law 62/76.

Article 169 of the 1960 Constitution does not apply only to treaties affecting rights and obligations of the State but also covers all treaties, conventions and agreements ratified and concluded in conformity with paragraph 2 thereof, provided that all other requirements are satisfied.[23]

According to the Supreme Court case law, the requirement of reciprocity under Article 169(3) is waived in the case of:

> 'treaties whose nature, objective and function in the international relations and the international legal order exclude the condition of reciprocity. Such are multilateral conventions the object of which is not to create any subjective or reciprocal rights for the contracting parties themselves but their objective and their intent is to promote certain principles of law, moral and legal values and which a contracting party signs and ratifies only for the realisation of this objective. Examples are: Conventions for the protection of human rights and the improvements and formulation of common rules and the achievement of social justice.
>
> ...
>
> Where there is any international mechanism of control or supervision, the condition of reciprocity again cannot validly be raised.'[24]

Self-executing treaties are directly applicable:

> 'We agree ... that for a treaty to be applicable it must be self-executing... We need not in this case attempt to give a general definition of the term "self-executing treaty". Pious declarations and provisions relating to political and international relations in a convention are not self-executing provisions. Only such provisions of a Convention are self-executing which may be applied by the organs of the State and which can be enforced by the Courts and which create rights for the individuals; they govern or affect directly relations of the internal life between the individuals, and the individuals and the State or the public authorities. Provisions which do not create by themselves rights or obligations of persons or interests and which cannot be justiciable or do not refer to acts or omissions of State organs are not self-executing. International law is primarily a law between States and normally treaties have effect upon States only. As it has been pointed out by the Permanent Court of International Justice (Series B. No. 15), this rule can be altered by the express or implied terms of the treaty, in which case its provisions become self-executing. If treaties contain provisions with regard to rights and duties of the subjects or the contracting States, their courts, officials, and the like, these States

---

23 See *Malachtou* v. *Armefti*.

24 Ibid. See also *Shipowners Union* v. *The Registrar of Trademarks & Others* (1988) 3 *CLR* 457.

must take such steps as are necessary, according to their Municipal Law, to make these provisions binding upon their subjects, courts, officials and the like (Oppenheim's *International Law*).[25]

The question whether or not treaties are self-executing is influenced by the wording of the convention, its provisions and the relevant constitutional law in a given country ...'.[26]

In the same case, Pikis, J. observed:

'Ratification by the legislature incorporates the treaty or convention, as the case may be, into domestic law by virtue of the legislative power vested in the House of Representatives (Article 61 of the Constitution); and if its provisions are self-executing they acquire the force of law quite independently of paragraph 3 of Article 169 (of the Constitution) or its impact on domestic legislation. The point is exemplified by the decisions of the Supreme Court in *Mizrahi* v. *The Republic*[27] and *Kannas* v. *The Police*[28] in which the Court referred to the European Convention on Human Rights ratified by Law 39/62 as an integral part of our domestic legislation without at all inquiring into the question of reciprocity. A provision of a treaty or convention is self-executing if the rights vested or the obligations imposed thereby are comprehensively defined to the extent of making them, without further addition or modification, enforceable before a court of law...'.[29]

In respect of the question whether the courts in Cyprus recognise a rule of interpretation whereby national law must be interpreted in conformity with international obligations, there are indications, in the case law of the Supreme Court, that such a rule has been adopted, at least as far as treaties whose 'intent is the promotion of values and the protection of human rights' are concerned.

In its judgment in the *Shipowners Union* v. *The Registrar of Trademarks & Others* case,[30] the Supreme Court stated (per Stylianides J.):

'The aforesaid international instruments[31] are not only relevant, but should serve as a guide to the interpretation of our constitutional provisions...

---

25 L. Oppenheim, *International Law*, Vol. 1: Peace, 8th edn. (London, Longmans 1955) p. 924.

26 Per Stylianides J. in *Malachtou* v. *Armefti*.

27 (1968) 3 *CLR* 404.

28 (1968) 2 *CLR* 35.

29 See *Malachtou* v. *Armefti* at 234-236.

30 (1988) 3 *CLR* 457.

31 Author's note: For example, the European Convention on Human Rights, ILO Convention No. 87 concerning Freedom of Association and Protection of the Right to Organise, and the UN Covenant on Civil and Political Rights.

> Before concluding I would like to stress that it is the duty, not only of the Courts, but all authorities of the Republic, including executive, administrative and legislative, to secure within the limits of their respective competence the efficient application, both of the Part II of the Constitution – Fundamental Rights and Liberties – and the ratified International Conventions for the enjoyment of the rights and freedoms declared and safeguarded thereby…'.

Accession to the European Union is not expected to have a significant impact on the structure, rules of procedure, practice and workload of the courts of the Republic, at least in the short or medium term.

3. ROLE OF THE NATIONAL PARLIAMENT

The task of harmonising national legislation with the *acquis communautaire* has been successfully completed by the House of Representatives. This task was facilitated by the setting up of a special parliamentary fast-track system together with the establishment of a special Committee for European Affairs. This Committee examines all legislative instruments that are required for the approximation of national legislation to the *acquis*. All bills that were submitted to the House of Representatives in the context of the harmonisation process were examined directly by this Parliamentary Committee, irrespective of the specific topic they sought to regulate. Following the examination of those bills by the Committee, they were submitted to the plenary for adoption. The House made extensive use of this procedure and adopted the majority of *acquis*-related legislation in this way.

The possibility to approve framework laws by the House and allow for technical dispositions to be adopted through administrative regulations by Ministries (notably in the field of internal market legislation) also contributed positively to the harmonisation process.

The House of Representatives supervises the executive's ability to implement the various harmonisation bills once they have been enacted.

The extent to which the House will be able to exercise control over decisions taken by Ministers in the Council of the European Union is rather limited. This is due to the fact that the Republic Cyprus is organised on the basis of a presidential system of government[32] based on the doctrine of the separation of powers, which is applied in a rather more vigorous manner than elsewhere in the European Union, where the majority of Member States are parliamentary democracies.

---

32 Art. 1 of the 1960 Constitution.

Thus, in Cyprus, the Government is independent of the confidence of the House of Representatives.

4. TREATY ESTABLISHING A CONSTITUTION FOR EUROPE

The signing of the Treaty Establishing a Constitution for Europe by the Heads of State and Government forms a landmark in the process of advancing European integration. The eventual enactment of this constitutional text will strengthen the Community legal order, *inter alia*, in the following ways:

a. the Constitution as currently envisaged will substitute the multitude of existing constitutional texts for a single text thus promoting clarity and legal certainty;
b. the existing complicated pillar structure will disappear, but intergovernmentalism will be preserved where this is deemed necessary;
c. the European Union will acquire legal personality, while the European Community will cease to exist as a separate legal entity and will be totally absorbed into the European Union;
d. the Charter of Fundamental Rights will be integrated into the Constitution and will acquire legal value and status;
e. there will be a clear legal basis for the accession of the European Union to the European Convention on Human Rights;
f. there will be a clearer division of Union and national competences;
g. the Union's instruments of action will be simplified;
h. the decision-making procedures will also be simplified;
i. qualified majority voting, as modified, will be extended; and
j. a right of legislative initiative by citizens will be introduced.

There are no obstacles in the Cypriot legal order to the ratification of the European Constitution. Most probably, the European Constitution will be ratified by the Republic of Cyprus through action by the House of Representatives.

CZECH REPUBLIC

Jiří Zemánek*

1. NATIONAL CONSTITUTION

1.1 Implementation of international law and transfer of legal powers

The amendment of the Czech Constitution,[1] enacted after some hesitation by the Assembly of Deputies of Parliament[2] on 1 June 2002,[3] has substantially broadened the scope of relevance of international law within the Czech legal system (1) and enabled the transfer of certain competences to supranational entities (2).

To start with "the Czech Republic shall observe its obligations resulting from international law" (Art. 1, para. 2, of the Europe Clause). Rather than a simple constitutional recognition of the fundamental international law principle of *pacta sunt servanda* this declaration serves as a dual guideline for domestic authorities. First the legislator must seek *the legislative solutions compatible* with international obligations following from mandatory rules of customary law (*ius cogens*), binding international treaties,[4] acts of international institutions, unilateral legal acts, etc. Second, the public administration, the courts and other entities applying the law shall operate on the presumption that national law is in harmony with international obligations and shall always choose out of several possible interpretations within the scope of their discretion *the most international law friendly interpretation* of the national legal provision in question. So far, this provision has played a subsidiary role as compared to other constitutional rules governing law enforcement. It was, however, intended to counterbalance the existing basic characteristic of the Czech Republic as a sovereign state.[5]

The constitutional instruction to observe international obligations does not entail the material reception of *international customary rules*. The judiciary has always

---

* Jean Monnet Professor of European Law, Charles University, Prague.

1 Act no. 1/1993 Coll. ("Const."); for English translation see: <http://www.ecln.net>.

2 See for the opinions expressed during the general debate and the reasons for the hesitation J. Zemánek, 'The amendment of the Czech Constitution for the Accession to the European Union', in A.E. Kellermann, J.W. de Zwaan and J. Czuczai, eds., *EU Enlargement. The Constitutional Impact at EU and National Level* (The Hague, T.M.C. Asser Press 2001) pp. 423-433.

3 The Constitution as amended by the Const. Act no. 395/2001 Coll.

4 For the special regime with respect to some treaties see *infra.*

5 Art. 1, para. 1 Const.

rejected the direct application of non-incorporated international custom, whereas statutory references have been the exception.[6] Recently this situation has started to change,[7] which presents a new challenge for the ordinary courts which shall now on occasion have to identify the normative substance of international custom.

The status of *acts of international organizations* within the Czech legal order was derived from the way in which their founding treaties had been received in the Czech legal order (see *infra*) and used to be governed by measures (decrees, regulations) taken by the state administration.[8] Later, special laws were passed by Parliament on a case-by-case basis which made it impossible for the Czech Republic to respond promptly. A prompt response is important, for example, to implement effective international sanctions.[9] Recently, general statutory rules that enable the introduction of mandatory international sanctions at the national level (whereby Parliament retains the possibility to control the exercise of the relevant competences by the Government) have been established. These rules also formed the basis for a duty to implement sanctions that were adopted within the EU Common Foreign and Security Policy, even when these were not binding for the Czech Republic before accession.[10]

Rights protected under an international treaty which have been incorporated in the Czech legal order must be respected by the Czech authorities, including the interpretation these rights have been given by the respective international supervisory bodies. Therefore, the acts of incorporation already implicitly had to take into consideration the relevant *decisions of international judicial bodies* and the Constitutional Court has indeed referred to interpretative opinions in such decisions (mostly those of the European Court of Human Rights) in its judgments and reasoning. The Czech Government plays a key role in the implementation of international judgments by having to provide fair satisfaction to persons whose rights have been injured by a breach of international obligations and by initiating the amendment of provisions contrary to such obligations or – as the case may be – by asking the Constitutional Court to annul such provisions. Apart from this competence, the Constitutional Court is also competent to take any measures necessary to implement a binding decision of an international tribunal if this

---

6 I.e., within the sphere of Private International Law, see Act no. 97/1963 Coll., Art. 4.

7 Act no. 61/2000 Coll. on Maritime Navigation; Act no. 158/2000 Coll., on Investigation, Research and Exploitation of the Sea Bed outside the Jurisdiction of States; etc.

8 For instance, the Ministry of Foreign Trade was authorized by Art. 56 of Act no. 42/1980 Coll. on Foreign Economic Relations to restrict or prohibited certain commercial operations, meeting the requirements of the UN embargo; this flexible solution was criticized in the early 1990s for not being subject to regular parliamentary control.

9 Act no. 78/1997 Coll. on Measures Concerning Libya; Act no. 304/1999 Coll. on Measures Concerning Yugoslavia; Act no. 48/2000 Coll. on Measures Concerning the Taliban; etc.

10 Act no. 98/2000 Coll. on Implementation of International Sanctions for Keeping the Peace and Security.

cannot be implemented otherwise (by governmental or parliamentary action)[11] and to set aside any judgments going against international law. The narrow scope of incorporation of international treaties (only those on human rights and fundamental freedoms) in the Czech legal order "justified" a restrictive interpretation of the notion of "international tribunal" in the practice of the Constitutional Court.[12] It has not yet been clarified what kind of measure the Constitutional Court should take in case an international tribunal decided that a right that is internationally protected has been violated by a judgment of the Constitutional Court itself. In this respect, the introduction of an extraordinary remedy and accompanying procedural rules have been debated, but no legislation has followed from this.[13]

The Europe Clause has extended the range of *international treaties* having direct effect and taking precedence over statutes under national law. So far, this position was reserved to a very limited and important group of treaties. Now, however, according to Article 10 of the Europe Clause, all[14] "promulgated international treaties, to the ratification of which Parliament has given its consent and by which the Czech Republic is bound, form a part of the legal order; if a treaty provides otherwise than a statute, the treaty shall apply." This means a fundamental shift in the approach of national law to international treaties.[15] This was traditionally[16] based on the doctrine of extreme dualism, which entails the material adaptation of the relevant national laws to the obligations set out by the international treaty in question, rather than their merely formal transformation into national law by a legislative act. The method required as a result of the dualist approach was cumbersome for the legislator and could not guarantee the complete and consistent implementation of treaty obligations.[17] This situation was

---

[11] Art. 87, para. 1 i) Const.

[12] According to Art. 117 of Act no. 182/1993 Coll. on the Constitutional Court ("ConstCAct"), the jurisdiction of the Constitutional Court is limited to implementation measures exclusively concerning the decisions of international bodies on human rights and fundamental freedoms (not, as the case may be, on international crimes, etc.).

[13] Despite the lack of a special provision in the ConstCAct (due to the fact that a draft amendment was rejected in Parliament), the rules on extraordinary remedies under the Code on Civil Procedure (Act no. 99/1963 Coll.) could be applied subsidiarily.

[14] All "presidential" treaties, not only those concerning human rights and fundamental freedoms, as was the case under the previous constitutional *status quo*.

[15] The lack of any transitory provisions in the Europe Clause gave rise to some criticism of the legal uncertainty in respect of the effects of international treaties ratified prior to the entry into force of the Europe Clause. The prevailing opinion is that *ex tunc* effect should be accorded to all treaties to which the Czech Republic is a party, regardless of their date of ratification.

[16] A certain mistrust of international treaties is attributable to pre-WW II times when the ("First") Czechoslovak Republic withstood the pressure of the international community (the victorious powers) to give the core articles of the Treaty of St. Germain-en-Laye the force of constitutional provisions ("lois fondamentales").

[17] The most famous recent case concerned the unenforceability of the Europe Agreement on the Association of the Czech Republic with the European Communities against the Czech legislation on

only relieved by reception clauses in several laws which referred to international treaties as *lex specialis*. Although this practice was not authorized by the Constitution, it was not considered contrary to it either,[18] although it was subject to the consent of Parliament to the ratification of the treaty.[19] Treaties incorporated in this – *ad hoc* – way had priority over national law, but did not enjoy any special status in the hierarchy of sources of law. As a result, it was very difficult for individuals to claim their rights under international law.

The present general clause on the incorporation of international treaties introduced the *monistic doctrine* into the national legal order, providing treaties with internal effect without depriving them of their international status. The changed wording of the provision has clarified the position of international treaties: they are not only – from the international perspective – *directly applicable*, i.e., able to establish immediate individual rights and duties as "part of the legal order", but also – from the national perspective – (implicitly) self-executing, not requiring any act of incorporation and *taking precedence over statutes* (if not over the Constitution). The priority of international treaties is limited to cases where national provisions materially conflict with them and take precedence in terms of application to these specific cases, not in terms of the validity of the national provisions as such. Treaties also have priority over national laws that have been enacted later, i.e., the rule *lex posterior derogat legi priori* does not govern this relationship.[20]

The list of international treaties which require the consent of Parliament for their ratification by a simple majority of both Chambers, acting on an equal footing, has been extended.[21] The list now comprises: (a) all treaties stipulating rights and duties for individuals (no longer limited to treaties on human rights and fundamental freedoms), (b) alliances, peace treaties and other political treaties, (c) treaties establishing the membership of the Czech Republic of an international organization, (d) economic treaties of a general character and (e) treaties which require an implementing law.

The direct effect and priority of international treaties which form a part of the Czech legal order was consequently reflected in a *duty of the courts to apply* such treaties, making their decisions a binding source of law.[22] It remains important to

---

competition (Act no. 63/1991 Coll.); the political reasons for maintaining this practice before November 1989 need not to be extolled here.

18 J. Malenovský, *Poměr mezinárodního a vnitrostátního práva obecně a v českém právu zvláště* (Brno, Doplnek 2000) p. 72.

19 Nevertheless, the state administration sometimes gave priority to governmental or even ministerial agreements and set aside Acts of Parliament even though this was not in accordance with the Constitution.

20 A similar type of priority of international treaties can be identified in Spain, France and Greece, as well as – as the result of case law – in Belgium and Luxembourg.

21 Art. 49 Europe Clause.

22 Art. 95, para. 1 Europe Clause.

underline this self-evident duty, however, as the ordinary courts have still trouble with the direct (immediate) application of superior law.[23] Disregarding an international treaty entails a breach of the fundamental right to judicial protection.[24]

The "integration dimension" of the Czech European Clause provides the necessary constitutional authorization to accede to the European Union: "Certain powers of the Czech Republic authorities may be transferred by a treaty to an international organization or institution" (Art. 10a, para. 1, of the Europe Clause). It was obviously assumed that the Czech Republic would indeed join such international organizations or institutions. The general wording (institutions, organizations) was used for two reasons: the lack of any express statement concerning the legal personality of the European Union in the TEU[25] and the wider possibility of opening up the option to transfer sovereign powers to other supranational entities as well.[26] Whether the use of the term "international organization or institution" implies reluctance on the part of the Czech Republic concerning any future advancement of the European Union beyond the present level of federalization or its development into a quasi-state entity (political union) is doubtful. This view is supported by the following arguments.[27]

"Transfer" means the "cession" or "conferment" of the material substance of powers, implying their waiver at the national level, rather than their mere "exercise" by the EU. Transfer must be without any reservations and is irrevocable throughout the membership of the organization and cannot be withdrawn or derogated from unilaterally under any circumstances (*rebus sic stantibus, vis major*). Any re-nationalization of powers could occur only on the basis of an express authorization under European law or after the voluntary withdrawal of the Czech Republic from the EU (acts of Czech authorities implying otherwise are null and void for being *ultra vires*). Although the transfer is unconditional,[28] it cannot lead to "any change in the essential requirements for a democratic state governed by the rule of law", as such changes are "impermissible".[29]

---

[23] See Constitutional Court judge Pavel Holländer, *Ústavněpravní argumentace. Ohlédnutí po deseti letech Ústavního soudu* (Praha, Linde 2003) p. 85.

[24] Art. 36 of the Charter of Fundamental Rights and Basic Freedoms (Act no. 2/1993 Coll., "Charter").

[25] See the records of the deliberations in the Assembly of Deputies of the Czech Parliament on the draft Europe Clause (Doc. no. 884, 3rd period 2001).

[26] Such as to the International Criminal Tribunal under its Rome Statute (although paradoxically, this transfer has not yet taken place).

[27] These arguments reflect the constitutional experience of the "old" Member States; the Czech courts have not yet had occasion to test them.

[28] No implicit commitment concerning the execution of powers by the EU (loyalty to certain values and principles, reciprocity, etc.) can be deduced from Art. 10a, para. 1, of the Europe Clause.

[29] Art. 9, para. 2 Const.

The scope of the transfered powers is limited ("certain") by the European *acquis*, both its existing and future content as brought about through the pursuit of the objectives of the Union as they have been set out under the Treaties and agreed to by the Czech Republic through the conclusion of the Treaty on Accession. Any future extension of the objectives may only be undertaken by the conclusion of a revision Treaty, which – from the Czech perspective – would have the same status under the Europe Clause.[30] In this respect, the Europe Clause not only confers permission to conclude such a revision Treaty, but also urges the Czech authorities to aspire – within the limits of their discretion – to the full utilization of the potential deepening of the European integration for the fulfilment of the mission which has been entrusted to them by the Constitution. This constitutes an inherent reservation towards the competence of the European Union.[31]

The broad authorization to transfer sovereign powers in Article 10a, paragraph 1, of the Europe Clause therefore not only serves to facilitate accession to the existing Treaty establishing the Union as a supranational entity, but also the conclusion of any future revision Treaty implying a further transfer of competences.

1.2 Supremacy and direct effect

The Czech Constitution provides for direct effect and supremacy of international law over Czech law in broad terms. So far, it can serve as the basis for implementation of the inter-governmental part of the obligations resulting from EU membership (Second and Third Pillar). However, the position of the Community part of European law under Czech law is primarily governed by the respective Community law principles, not by national law.[32] It is one of the effects of the waiver of the respective legislative, executive and judicial rights agreed to by the Member States that they can no longer determine the effects of Community law at national level.[33] Therefore, any national constitutional definition or instruction in this respect would be not only superfluous, but – considering the dynamic

30 It excludes any transfer only "on the basis of such a treaty", through an act of the institutions established by the Treaty (see otherwise, e.g., Art. 7, para. 2, of the Constitution of the Slovak Republic), i.e., without prior parliamentary consent.

31 This must not be confused with the flexibility clause (Art. 308 TEC), which is already a part of the *acquis*.

32 In addition, Community law has an indirect effect on national law now that the national authorities must interpret national law in the light of the *acquis*.

33 Z. Kühn and J. Kysela, 'Na základě čeho bude působit komunitární právo v českém právním řádu?', *Právní rozhledy* 1/2004, p. 23; J. Zemánek, 'Ústavní zakotvení účinků práva Evropské unie v České republice', in České právo na prahu Evropské unie, Acta Universitatis Carolinae Iuridica 1-2/2004, p. 45.

approach of the European Court of Justice in this respect – untenable in the long term.[34]

The draft Europe Clause nevertheless attempted to regulate in the only possible way – namely in a very open way – how the Czech authorities should deal with Community law.[35] The reason that this draft provision was rejected was not the reason set out above, however. As the debate on the Europe Clause showed, there was much more confusion and lack of knowledge concerning the effects of Community law at the national level than expected. A minority contended that the Czech Constitution should provide institutions that apply the law with authoritative guidelines concerning the effects of Community law, which could only be done through an extensive interpretation of Article 10 of the Europe Clause (supremacy also over the Czech Constitutional order), supported by Article 1, paragraph 2 Europe Clause (direct effect and supremacy also of secondary Community law).[36] The lack of clarity concerning the autonomous position of European law within the Czech legal order as a result of a *minimalistic (implicit) approach* to the Europe Clause is expected to be lifted by the Constitutional Court (Supreme or Supreme Administrative) which will no doubt refer to the relevant established case law of the ECJ.

1.3 Amendments

The prominent position of both categories of international treaties within the Czech legal order, replacing in their application sources of law of national origin,[37] must not later be undermined by objections concerning the inconsistency of those treaties with the Constitution, as this could call into question the *bona fide* fulfilment of treaty obligations. For this reason, the Europe Clause introduced the *ex ante* review (i.e., prior to ratification) by the Constitutional Court of the conformity of international treaties with the constitutional order.[38] Such a review may be initiated by one of the Chambers of Parliament during the process of

---

[34] The constitutions of Poland (Art. 91, para. 3) and Slovakia (Art. 7, para. 2) regulate some of the effects.

[35] First alternative: "Constitutional laws, international treaties forming part of the legal order, statutes and other legal regulations cannot be interpreted and applied in a way incompatible with the obligations ensuing from the membership of the Czech Republic in the European Union." Second alternative: "Should it follow from the Treaty on Accession, the law of the European Union forms part of the legal order of the Czech Republic together with the effects stipulated by it."

[36] J. Malenovský, 'Mezinárodní smlouvy podle čl. 10a Ústavy ČR', *Právník* 9/2003, p. 841; J. Syllová, 'K "nadřazenosti" budoucího ústavního evropského práva', *Právní rozhledy* 9/2003, Supplement 'European Law', p. 14.

[37] Both the treaties under Art. 49 as well as the treaties on the transfer of powers to a supranational entity under Art. 10a of the Europe Clause could be reviewed.

[38] The constitutional order of the Czech Republic (Art. 112, para. 1 Const.) consists of the Constitution, the Charter and other constitutional acts.

approving the treaty, by a group of Members of Parliament or Senators after approval or by the President of the Republic after the treaty is submitted for ratification.[39] The object of the review includes international treaties forming part of the legal (not constitutional) order (simple Art. 49 Constitution treaties) and having priority over statutes under Article 10, and treaties on transfer of sovereign powers to a supranational entity under Article 10a of the Europe Clause but only in respect of their compliance with Article 9 paragraph 2 of the Constitution ("hard core" constitutional provision on the protection of essential requirements for a democratic state governed by the rule of law).[40] The scope of the review differs per category.[41] The treaty under review cannot be ratified before the issue of conformity has been decided[42] or, if the Constitutional Court finds the treaty unconstitutional, until the reason for its unconstitutionality has been removed.[43]

The compatibility of the Treaty on Accession (providing for accession to the Treaties establishing the European Community and the European Union)[44] with the Czech constitutional order was not tested before its ratification, despite criticism from the opposition parties. Therefore, harmony between the constitutional order and European law is to be presumed. Nevertheless, severe controversy arose recently among Czech authorities concerning the implementation of the framework decision on the European Arrest Warrant[45] (under the Third EU Pillar dealing with Police and Judicial Cooperation in Criminal Matters) by means of amendments to the Criminal Code and the Code of Criminal Procedure. The warrant was considered to be inconsistent with the constitutional order as well as with the international treaties under Article 10 such as the European Convention on Extradition and certain bilateral agreements. The possibility of extraditing Czech citizens as a result of the European Arrest Warrant was argued to go against the prohibition of forced expulsion of nationals from the country.[46] In this case, it was argued, constitutional amendment would always be necessary as the Constitution as the basic law may only be supplemented or modified – even

---

39 Act no. 182/1993 Coll. on the Constitutional Court of the Czech Republic, § 71a.

40 Art. 87 para. 2 Const.

41 The review of treaties under Art. 10a of the Europe Clause should focus only on compliance with the procedural conditions for the transfer of powers, whereas the material substance of the transfer, which is the single purpose of this category of international treaties, cannot in principle be unconstitutional and could be reviewed only in extreme circumstances when core constitutional values would be endangered by such a transfer ("the essential requirements" clause of Art. 9, para. 2 Const.).

42 Art. 87, para. 2, of the Europe Clause; the new competence of the Constitutional Court was also laid down by amending Act no. 48/2002 Coll. to the ConstCAct.

43 Art. 89, para. 3, of the Europe Clause.

44 *OJ* L 236 of 23 September 2003, p. 1.

45 Council framework decision 2002/584/JHA, *OJ* L 190 of 18 July 2002, p. 1.

46 Art. 14, para. 4, of the Charter.

where European law is concerned – *by constitutional acts*,[47] not by merely implied effects or by an interpretation, as this could jeopardize the democratic foundations of the state.[48] The implementation Act was passed by both Chambers of Parliament, but the President of the Czech Republic used his constitutional veto[49] to block the Act. This veto can only be overriden by unanimous second vote of all Deputies in the Assembly. Annulment proceedings at the Constitutional Court for testing the constitutionality of the Act can be initiated later.[50]

Ratifying a revision of the EC/EU Treaty by referendum would require a new constitutional Act.

1.4 Provisions contrary to the *acquis communautaire*

The following (non-exhaustive list of) constitutional provisions may be considered contrary to the *acquis communautaire* and need to be brought in line with it:

- under Article 4, paragraph 1, of the Charter it is provided that "Duties may be imposed upon persons only on the basis and within the limits of law (...)", which excludes, among other things, the imposition of duties by Community regulations; where this is the case, this provision *should not be applied*;
- under Article 21, paragraph 1, of the Charter it is provided that "(Czech) citizens have the right to participate in the administration of public affairs either directly or through the free election of their representatives", which contradicts Article 19 TEC on the equal treatment of all Union citizens in local elections to municipalities in which they reside; the legislative definition of "citizen"[51] *will have to be interpreted extensively in conformity with EU law* (i.e., 'citizen' equals 'citizen of the Union'); the relevant Act on local elections has already been adapted.

1.5 Procedures to adapt the national constitution to the *acquis communautaire*

The ratification of the treaty as regards the transfer of sovereign powers requires the consent of Parliament, unless the constitutional Act, passed by a three-fifths majority in both Chambers,[52] provides that such ratification requires the approval

---

47 Art. 9, para. 1 Const.

48 Art. 9, para. 3 Const.

49 Art. 62h Const.

50 Art. 87, para. 1 a Const.

51 Art. 42, para. 1, of the Charter reads as follows: "Whenever this Charter uses the term 'citizen', this is to be understood as a citizen of the Czech Republic".

52 Art. 39, para. 4, of the Europe Clause.

of the population as obtained by a referendum.[53] these strict requirements for the democratic legitimisation of the transfer of state authority, which after all "emanates from the people"[54] as a *pouvoir constituant*, is necessary due to the far-reaching implications which such transfer may have for the population. Parliament is competent to decide which procedure will be followed.

The political climate in the autumn of 2002 was such that no clear majority could be expected in Parliament and it was therefore decided to hold a nation-wide referendum. The referendum on accession of the Czech Republic to the European Union in June 2003 was based on the following principles:[55]

- voters were not obliged to take part in the referendum, i.e., no compulsory participation;
- there was no minimum threshold or quorum established for the validity of the referendum's outcome;
- a simple majority could decide;
- the question put required a simple "yes" or "no" on joining the EU on the basis of the Treaty on Accession;
- the result of the referendum would be binding and would take the place of consent by Parliament;
- the possible refusal by the President of the Czech Republic to call the referendum or to implement it in due course could be contested before the Constitutional Court;[56]
- in case of a no-vote, the referendum could be repeated after two years.

For any future public voting on the ratification of a revision EU Treaty a new constitutional Act (either a general Act or another *ad hoc* Act) would first have to be passed by Parliament[57] even though direct democracy is considered a constitutional principle.[58]

---

[53] Art. 10a, para. 2, of the Europe Clause.

[54] Art. 2, para. 1 Const.

[55] Const Act no. 515/2002 Coll.

[56] Art. 87, para. 1 l and m as supplemented by Const Act no. 515/2002 Coll.

[57] The opposition parties have rejected draft legislation establishing a general referendum many times, out of the apparent fear of frequent (populistic) recourse to this instrument by the Government in case of weak political support, which would frustrate due parliamentary process.

[58] "A constitutional Act can designate the conditions under which the people may excercise state authority directly", Art. 2, para. 2 Const.

2. ROLE OF THE JUDICIARY (NATIONAL COURTS, INCLUDING SPECIAL BODIES WITH JUDICIAL FUNCTIONS)

2.1 Europe Agreement

Before the enactment of the Europe Clause, the Europe Agreement[59] did not form a part of the Czech legal order, unless provisions on human rights and fundamental freedoms were concerned (e.g., non-discrimination of migrating EU workers in respect of employment conditions). Only the Agreement's provisions referred to in the incorporation clauses in several Acts were applied by the Czech *ordinary courts* and were given priority over other Acts. Since 1 June 2002 all self-executing provisions of the Europe Agreement (such as those on the removal of barriers to the cross-border performance of business, the free trade area, etc.) could be applied directly; but the 23-month period between then and 1 May 2004 (the date of the Czech accession) was too brief to develop specific case law.

Nevertheless, administrative courts as well as the Constitutional Court did make direct reference to Community law in their decisions. The *Constitutional Court* referring to Article 64(2) of the Europe Agreement[60] upheld an assessment by the Anti-Monopoly Office that there had been abuse of a dominant position under the Act on Protection of Economic Competition on the basis of criteria arising from the application of Article 82 TEC by the European Commission and the European Court of Justice.

2.2 Supremacy and direct effect

As has been explained above, there was no commitment of the Czech courts and administrative authorities to enforce the Community principles of supremacy and direct effect under the Europe Agreement. Cases evidencing their enforcement by ordinary courts since the accession have not yet been reported.

However, some – in this respect unfortunate – developments have occured in the case law of the Constitutional Court recently that could (indirectly) discourage the ordinary courts from fulfilling their European function. After the enactment of the Europe Clause which in Article 10 put an end to the privileged position of international treaties on human rights and fundamental freedoms as equal to constitutional Acts and as the only type of treaty able to lead to the annulment of contrary legislation, the Court however insisted on retaining the exclusive competence to decide such annulment procedures. This implies that ordinary courts will not be able of their own accord to leave aside such legislation based on

---

[59] No. 7/1995 Coll.

[60] *Škoda, a.s.*, III. ÚS 31/97, CollConstC, Vol. 8, p. 149 et seq.

the supremacy of the treaty under Article 10 of the Europe Clause.[61] The Court justified its decision in an *obiter dictum* by relying on the imperfect adjustment of the Codes on Civil Procedure and Criminal Procedure to the Europe Clause, now that these two Codes still oblige ordinary courts to stay the proceedings and refer questions of incompatibility to the Constitutional Court. This questionable case could undermine the *desired shift in judicial mentality* now that courts after accession face the challenge of deciding on the supremacy and direct effect of law which is not of domestic origin, immediately and independently at the judicial level to which the dispute in question was brought.[62]

2.3 Indirect effect

The Czech ordinary courts have relied mostly on the traditional methods of interpretation of law. In spite of their training in the application of European law, which has recently been intensified, judges can hardly be expected yet to be fully aware of their role in offering legal redress in cases of violation of European law through incorrect implementation of that law, in particular, through the incomplete or completely lacking transposition of a Community Directive. In the case of directives, after the time-limit for their transposition has expired, the courts have to enforce any directly effective individual rights granted by such directives[63] and interpret relevant provisions of Czech law in conformity with any non-directly effective provisions and with principles of primary European law (indirect effect).[64] The courts are further expected to decide on damages in the case of state liability for breach of obligations resulting from European law.[65]

Currently, it is being discussed whether the Czech Act on Compensation of Damages Arising from Unlawful Decisions or Incorrect Action by Public Authorities[66] provides an effective remedy in case of defective implementation of Community Directives by the legislator or whether the Act should be amended, or whether the resulting damages may be remedied under civil law.

2.4 Cases

In one case[67] the Constitutional Court justified its annulment of several provisions of the amendment Act on the Czech National Bank ("CNB")[68] by reasoning that

---

61 Case Pl. 36/2001 CollConstC, also published as no. 403/2002 Coll.
62 The Court reaffirmed its position in Case I. ÚS 752/2002 CollConstC, Vol. 30, p. 65 et seq.
63 Case 152/84 *Marshall* [1986] *ECR* 723, among others.
64 Case 106/89 *Marleasing* [1990] *ECR* 4135, among others.
65 Cases 6/90 *Francovich* and 9/90 *Bonifaci* [1991] *ECR* 5257, among others.
66 Act no. 82/1998 Coll.
67 Case Pl. ÚS 59/2000, CollConstC, Vol. 22, p. 249.
68 Act no. 6/1993 Coll.

they were inconsistent not only with the requirement of the independent status of the CNB guaranteed by the Czech Constitution, but also with Article 108 TEC, which provides for a similar status of all central banks of the Member States, even if there was no obligation in the Europe Agreement to harmonize Czech law in this respect. Another amended provision that was annulled concerned the primary purpose of the CNB[69] – to maintain "price stability" instead of the former "stability of the currency" – was justified by reasoning that a precondition for this provision was to amend the Constitution, as the Czech Republic – taking its application for admission into "the family of democracies in Europe"[70] seriously – must respect its own Constitution. On this occasion the Constitutional Court defined the requirement of *"conformity of the implementation of Community law with the Constitution"*, which also post-accession seems to provide guidance in procedures on the annulment of implementation laws when these are inconsistent with the Constitution.

In another case, after referring to the Charter of Fundamental Rights of the EU,[71] the Constitutional Court rejected a claim that Community law was not relevant for the Czech Republic pre-accession, when it was not a Member State of the EU.[72] The Court here followed the case law of the European Court of Justice on the *principle of proportionality* by reasoning that it already applied[73] this principle as one of the general principles of law common to the European legal culture and constitutional traditions. In this case the Court had to assess limitations imposed on the fundamental rights under the Czech Charter,[74] the essence and significance of which must be preserved.

2.5 Structure, procedure and practice

Amendments have been proposed to the Codes of Procedure[75] which are not intended to repeat the provisions on the preliminary ruling procedure before the ECJ under Article 234 TEC and Article 35 TEU, but are meant to make the judiciary aware of the possibility to use this European law instrument and of its effects within the Czech legal order. Doctrine, referring to the famous German

---

69 Art. 98, para. 1 Const.

70 Preamble of the Constitution.

71 Case Pl. ÚS 11/2000 CollConstC, Vol. 23, p. 105 et seq., also published as no. 322/2001 Coll on Free Choice of Occupation and on Data Protection.

72 Case Pl. ÚS 5/2001 CollConstC, Vol. 24, p. 79 et seq., also published as no. 410/2001 Coll on Production Quotas on Milk; Case Pl. ÚIS 39/2001 CollConstC, Vol. 28, p. 153 et seq., also published as no. 499/2002 Coll on Production Quotas on Sugar.

73 Case Pl. ÚS 33/1997 CollConstC.

74 Art. 4, para. 4, of the Charter.

75 Code of Civil Procedure no. 99/1963 Coll., Code of Administrative Judicial Procedure no. 150/2002 Coll., Code of Criminal Procedure no. 141/1963 Coll.

and Austrian judgment[76] urges the Constitutional Court to qualify[77] any failure of the court of last instance in a given case to refer to the ECJ as *a breach of the fundamental right to an effective remedy and a fair trial* under the Czech Charter,[78] as proclaimed by ECJ case law.[79] The Constitutional Court should not hesitate to invalidade the statute concerned or annul the court's final decision if these are contrary to European law, and should only refer to the European Court of Justice in case of doubts concerning the proper interpretation or suspected invalidity (*ultra vires*) of an act of European law. The legislation on the Constitutional Court[80] would have to be supplemented accordingly. The first "European" cases to arise before the Czech Supreme Administrative or Constitutional Court are expected to provide further guidance to general judicial practice.

As to the workload, the ordinary courts do not seem to be aware of their "European" mandate yet. They should avoid the idea that the interpretation of legal provisions of an external (international, European) origin is the same as the interpretation of similar provisions of domestic origin. It is expected that references to the European Court of Justice for a preliminary ruling will not be frequent, but not rare either during the years immediately following accession.

3. ROLE OF THE NATIONAL PARLIAMENT

3.1 **Preparation and implementation of EC/EU law**

No special legislative procedure on legal approximation was established before the accession. An attempt by the Czech Government to obtain from Parliament the constitutional authorization to issue regulations flexibly (which would have the same status in the hierarchy of laws as Acts) on the implementation of the Europe Agreement failed in the spring of 1999. The Government subsequently issued *guidelines for drafting* approximation legislation in respect of its compatibility with European law[81] and created a special department as part of the Government Office to supervise the process of approximation. The Government also agreed an expedited procedure with Parliament (Assembly of Deputies) for legal approximation. Parliamentary committees for European integration were created in both Chambers.

---

[76] Judgment of the German BVerfG no. 2300/95 of 11 December 1995; Judgment of the Austrian BVerfG no. 10369/99 of 9 January 2001.

[77] Within its jurisdiction to hear constitutional complaints under Art. 87, para. 1d Const.

[78] Arts. 36 and 38 of the Charter.

[79] Recently: ECJ, Case C-224/01 *Köbler* v. *Austria* [2003] *ECR* I-10239.

[80] Act no. 182/1993 Coll.

[81] Decree no. 1212/1999.

In May 2004 *the Government's Rules on Law-making* were adapted[82] to the requirements of the implementation of obligations following from the membership of the Czech Republic of the European Union, among other things by imposing the duty to grant the relevant public authority the powers and instruments it would need for the direct application of European legal acts (regulations), to respect the time-limits for the transposition of Community directives, to refer in the draft of the implementation Act to the European act in question as promulgated in the *OJ* L-series, and to use the appropriate legislative techniques. Despite all this, the Government cannot eliminate the major problem of the lack of feedback during the parliamentary phase of the legislative process, when the compatibility of governmental drafts with European law may be reduced by modifications submitted by Members of Parliament who do not previously have to test the compatibility of these modifications with EU law. When this occurs, the additional amendment Act must first be drafted and as a consequence the Czech legal order is becoming more intricate and confusing. In 2000, such repeated amendments made up 90 per cent of all promulgated Acts, with the average time between the date of publication of an Act in the Collection of Laws and the date of its enforcement only being 3 days.[83]

3.2 Control over decisions taken by ministers in the Council of the European Union

The Europe Clause obliged the Czech Government to "inform Parliament, regularly and in advance, on issues connected with obligations resulting from the Czech Republic's membership" of the EU.[84] This is a broad duty, in particular when having regard to the narrow time-limits in the law-making process at Union level.

"The Chambers of Parliament shall give their views on prepared decisions" of the Union "in the manner laid down by their Standing Orders".[85] The Chambers, acting on an equal footing, are obviously not obliged to do so. It is not quite clear, whether "the manner" of expression of the opinions can make them binding on the Government, now that the Standing Orders have the same legal force as Acts.[86] The exercise of this competence of the Chambers may be left "to a body

[82] Decree no. 506/2004.

[83] See the report of F. Cvrcek at the conference on "The position and the mission of the Law in the constinental legal culture: traditions, the present and future developments", organised in the Senate, 27-28 May 2004.

[84] Art. 10b, para. 1, of the Europe Clause.

[85] Art. 10b, para. 2, of the Europe Clause.

[86] Act no. 90/1995 Coll. on the Standing Order of the Assembly of Deputies; Act no. 107/1999 Coll. on the Standing Order of the Senate.

common to both Chambers" by means of "a statute governing the principles of dealings and relations between both Chambers, as well as externally",[87] i.e., to a joint committee for European integration.

Recently, both Standing Orders have been amended to enable effective parliamentary control of the Government's activities in the process of decision-making at Union level.

The Government shall immediately submit all draft Union acts, accompanied by the Government's preliminary opinions, to *the Assembly of Deputies* through its permanent Committee for European Affairs.[88] The Committee monitors and selects the documents, taking into consideration in particular their expected impact on the Czech legal order, and may invite other committees that are competent in the relevant field to give their opinion on the subject. The Committee in its resolution as well as the Government may ask the President of the Assembly to put the draft on the agenda of the next plenary session of the Assembly. If the draft is not tabled for plenary debate, the Committee's resolution is considered as the final standpoint of the Assembly. The Government is not permitted to formulate a final standpoint before this procedure has been completed, except in emergency cases. When the Assembly (in the plenary session or through the Committee) has passed a resolution, the Government "must have regard" to it in the position which it finally presents in the Union institutions.

The standing order of *the Senate*[89] lists some documents which the Government must not fail to submit to it for its attention. The Committee for European Union (or, as the case may be, any other authorized committee) monitors the documents so received, distributes them available among the Senators and selects those of special attention. The President of the Senate must put a Bill on the agenda of the next plenary session when so requested by the Committee or by a group representing at least one-fifth of all Senators. The special, flexible procedure applies in emergency cases. During a period of 35 days after the submission of the Bill, the Government cannot vote on a legislative act in the Council "without knowledge" of the Senate's standpoint on the subject.

The stricter control procedure in the Assembly of Deputies when it comes to Government policy in European affairs reflects Parliament's constitutional role of controlling at a fundamental level the actions of the Government which may even result in the adoption of a resolution of no confidence by the Assembly.

---

87 Art. 10b, para. 3, of the Europe Clause.

88 Amendment Act no. 282/2004 Coll.

89 Amendment Act no. 172/2004 Coll.

4. EUROPEAN CONSTITUTION

4.1 Impact of the EU Constitution on the Community legal order and accession

The broad public debate on the European Constitution has not yet started in the Czech Republic. Several issues have been discussed in public meetings organized by the Senate during and after the deliberations of the European Convention,[90] however, and these have also been assessed in expert analyses.[91]

Generally speaking, the *consolidation* of primary law (including the treaties on accession) and the *codification* of some of the practice of the EU institutions (including leading case law of the ECJ and granting legal personality to the Union) definitely strenghten the *enforceability* of European law within national legal orders. Also, the clearer division of competences between the Union and its Member States, the enhanced position of the European Parliament in the legislative process, the more instrumentalized access of the national parliaments to the subsidiarity principle, the imposition of conditions and limits on the delegation of implementing powers to the Commission, developed earlier as the practice of "comitology", the enforced protection of fundamental rights with direct effect under the binding Charter, full jurisdiction of the ECJ in the Third Pillar and so on and so forth are certainly improvements that are to be welcomed. On the other hand, the complexity of Part III of the European Constitution with the past evolution of its provisions can only be countered to a limited extent by simplified revision procedure.[92]

The majority of wishes expressed by the Czech authorities before the Intergovernmental Conference were motivated by *political rather than legal* considerations:[93] the representation of the Member States and their populations in the qualified majority voting by the Council; the passing to the qualified majority or the ordinary legislative procedure (in some policy areas in Part III) only by the

---

[90] For a record of the most recent discussion which took place on 4 June 2004, see 'Dopady prijeti Ustavni smlouvy EU na vnitrostatni ustavni poradek' [Impact of the Treaty on an EU Constitution on the National Constitutional Order]; see also: Senat no. 1/2004 (collection of articles on the Draft European Constitution).

[91] Among others, J. Zemánek, 'The Judicial System of the European Union in the Draft Constitutional Treaty', in I. Pernice and M.P. Maduro, eds., *A Constitution for the European Union: First Comments on the 2003-Draft of the European Convention* (Baden-Baden, Nomos 2004) p. 107 et seq.; J. Zemánek, L. Tichy, R. Kral, P. Svoboda and M. Tomasek, 'Posudek k návrhu Ústavy Evropské unie' [The Expertise on the Draft Constitution of the European Union], in *České právo na prahu Evropské unie* [Czech Law on the Threshold of the European Union], Acta Universitatis Carolinae – Iuridica 1-2/2004, p. 13 et seq.

[92] Arts. 444 and 445 of the Draft.

[93] Decision no. 105 (4th period) of the Committee for European Integration of the Senate of 30 September 2003 and the decisions of the Government on the mandate of its representative at the IGC.

decision of the European Council ("the passerelle clause"); the new concept of the presidency of the Council of Ministers; the number and status of members of the Commission; the scope of the flexibility clause; the accession of the EU to the European Convention for the Protection of Human Rights and Fundamental Freedoms; etc.

The eurosceptics rejected the Constitution in mostly general terms without bringing any well-founded arguments, and simply stated that instead of a more democratic process it brings intensified integration.

4.2 Obstacles to the ratification of the European Constitution

The European Constitution will of course be discussed in more detail in connection with the *expected political (parliamentary) decision on its ratification* by popular approval in a nationwide referendum.[94] It is at present very difficult to predict the outcome of such a referendum, given that the Czech population and authorities have only briefly had the opportunity yet to experience the operation of the existing EC/EU Treaties in practice. The timing of the abovementioned political decision should take into account the public opinion of the day and consider its possible development since the last referendum on accession. First, however, we must await the new constitutional enactment of the referendum (by an Act of Parliament requiring the consent of three-fifths of the Members of Parliament).

One obstacle to ratification could be a preliminary decision of the Constitutional Court on the European Constitution's (non-)conformity with the Czech constitutional order (see *supra* 1.1). However, despite arguments in Czech constitutional law doctrine to the contrary, the Court indicated that such a decision would not necessarily obstruct ratification, excluding an implicit waiver of the constitutional provisions in question, the application of which would be frustrated by the principle of supremacy of EU law.

---

[94] The Declaration on the Programme of the Government of the Czech Republic, August 2004, Chapter 3.

ESTONIA

Anneli Albi*

1. NATIONAL CONSTITUTION[1]

1.1 Implementation of international law and transfer of legislative powers

Amongst the Constitutions of Central and Eastern Europe, which generally accord a prominent position to the provisions of sovereignty and independence, the Constitution of Estonia could be characterized as one of the most protective of sovereignty. Its very first article declares that Estonia is an "independent and sovereign democratic republic, wherein the supreme power of state is vested in the people." Furthermore, "the independence and sovereignty of Estonia are eternal and inalienable" (Art. 1(2)). The amendment of these provisions is subject to the approval by the *pouvoir constituant*: Article 162 requires a referendum for the revision of the fundamental principles of the Constitution. Besides these safeguards to sovereignty and independence, there was no clear basis for delegating powers to international organizations in the Constitution. Although Article 121 authorizes Parliament to ratify, *inter alia*, treaties that concern membership in international organizations, this provision was originally intended for organizations of a more technical nature. The *travaux préparatoires* of the Constitution in the Constitutional Assembly of 1991 made it clear that on the basis of Article 1 of the Constitution, Estonia's entry into political, economic and military associations of states requires a prior constitutional amendment by means of a referendum.[2] In addition to the above, the Constitution prohibits the conclusion of unconstitutional treaties (Art. 123(1)). Due to these provisions and safeguards, the Estonian Constitution could be characterized as one of the most "souverainist" Constitutions.[3]

* Dr Anneli Albi, Lecturer in European Law, University of Kent (UK).

[1] The material in Part I draws upon the section 'Estonia' in A. Albi, *EU Enlargement and the Constitutions of Central and Eastern Europe* (Cambridge, Cambridge University Press 2005) pp. 88 et seq.

[2] *Põhiseadus ja Põhiseaduse Assamblee* [Constitution and Constitutional Assembly] (Tallinn, Õigusteabe AS Juura 1996) at p. 530.

[3] See on the "souverainist" character of CEE constitutions in general A. Albi, 'Post-modern versus Retrospective Sovereignty: Two Different Sovereignty Discourses in the EU and Candidate Countries?', in N. Walker, ed., *Sovereignty in Transition* (Oxford, Hart 2003) pp. 401 et seq.

At the same time, it should be noted that the Constitution is favourable towards international law: Article 3 of the Constitution declares that the "[u]niversally recognized principles and rules of international law are an inseparable part of the Estonian legal system." In addition, Article 123(2) provides that treaties ratified by Parliament are applied in case of a conflict with Estonian laws. Based on these two provisions, Estonia is deemed to be a monist country, where ratified treaties are applied directly and take precedence over conflicting domestic law.[4]

1.2 Supremacy and direct effect; amendments; procedures to be followed to adapt the national constitution to the *acquis communautaire*

In 1996, a comprehensive analysis of the Constitution was undertaken by the Constitutional Expert Commission, which was established by the Government from amongst leading lawyers and scholars, in order to determine areas where a revision may be necessary. The results, published in 1998, included a Report entitled "Potential Accession to the European Union and its Consequences for Estonian Constitutional Law."[5] In this Report, the Expert Commission concluded that because of the principles laid down in the aforementioned Articles 1 and 123(1), the Constitution does not permit Estonia's entry into the EU without prior constitutional amendments. It therefore offered several amendment proposals, which would have had to be approved by referendum, as required in Article 162 of the Constitution. Central to the proposed amendments was a new draft paragraph 1, to be added to Article 1, which would have provided that "Estonia may, on the basis of a referendum, participate in the European Union, which is an association of states created by its Member States on the basis of the Treaties." In addition, draft Article 123(1) would have specified the conditions for the delegation of powers. The Expert Commission also deemed it necessary to eliminate two manifest conflicts with EU law. The first concerned the Bank of Estonia's exclusive right to emit Estonia's currency (Art. 111), in view of the expected adoption of the common currency a few years after accession to the EU. The second conflict concerned Article 48, which allows only Estonian citizens to belong to political parties, and may thus hinder the effective exercise of the EU citizens' right to stand in the elections of local councils and the European Parliament. The Expert Commission also pointed out the need for constitutional

---

[4] R. Maruste, 'EIÕK staatus Eesti õigussüsteemis' [The status of the ECHR in the Estonian legal system], 9 *Juridica* (1996) at pp. 476-478.

[5] 'Võimalik liitumine Euroopa Liiduga ja selle õiguslik tähendus Eesti riigiõiguse seisukohalt' [Potential accession to the European Union and its consequences for Estonian constitutional law], Report of the Constitutional Amendment Expert Commission of Estonia, 1998, available in Estonian at: <http://www.just.ee/juridica2.html>.

provisions which would establish the Parliament's relations with the Government in EU affairs. Finally, it offered an optional clause on the direct applicability of EU law, given that Article 123 of the Constitution grants direct applicability and supremacy only to the treaties ratified by Parliament, and hence was not found to cover the supremacy of EU secondary legislation.

Until early 2002, the amendment discussions proceeded mainly from the Expert Commission's Report. Although the opinions concerning the issues and the extent of the constitutional amendments varied, most foreign experts and Estonian lawyers deemed it necessary to amend the Constitution in order to join the EU, and a relatively wide agreement could be discerned with regard to the need for amendments pertaining to a similar range of issues as those pointed out by the Expert Commission.[6] The main dispute revolved around the issue of whether the amendments should concern Article 1, and thus necessitate a constitutional amendment referendum, or whether they should rather be placed in Chapter IX on foreign relations, or in a new special EU Chapter.

However, in the wake of rising Euroscepticism, which peaked in May 2001 when the polling agencies recorded that 59 per cent of the voters were against joining the EU, the amendment of the Constitution became a political rather than a legal issue, and the question of amending Article 1 was increasingly exploited by the Eurosceptic movements. The sensitivity of the situation was exacerbated by the rather difficult constitutional amendment procedure, which is lengthy and requires a high political and popular consensus.[7] In this context, the then Prime Minister Mart Laar expressed uncertainty as to whether the Constitution needed to be amended at all,[8] and it was not clear until March 2001 whether a referendum would be held. For instance, the then President Lennart Meri recommended holding a referendum instead some years after EU membership, on whether the Estonians wanted to withdraw from the Union.[9]

---

6 Cf., also J. Laffranque, 'Constitution of the Republic of Estonia in the Light of Accession to the European Union', *Juridica International – Law Review of Tartu University* (2001) pp. 207-221.

7 Chapter XV of the Constitution provides three procedures for constitutional amendment. Firstly, although a referendum may be used for all amendments, its use is obligatory where the amendments concern Chapters I 'General Provisions', including sovereignty and independence, and Chapter XV 'Amendment of the Constitution'. Secondly, ordinary provisions may be amended by two successive memberships of the Parliament. In this case, the amendment Bill must be supported by a majority of all deputies and, in an unmodified form, by the succeeding Parliament in the first reading, with a three-fifths majority. The third option, which according to the *travaux préparatoires* of the Constitution is meant for technical issues of minor importance, is the procedure of urgency. In this case, a resolution to consider an amendment Bill requires a four-fifths majority of Parliament; the Amendment Act has to be passed by a two-thirds majority of all deputies. A rejected amendment may not be re-initiated within a year.

8 Speech by M. Laar at the session of Parliament on 18 January 2001, transcript available in Estonian at: <http://www.riigikogu.ee>.

9 H. Roonemaa, 'Meri: rahvas võiks aastate pärast hääletada euroliidust välja astumist' [Meri: the people could vote on secession from the EU after a few years], *Eesti Päevaleht*, 5 May 2001.

Against this backdrop, the Ministry of Justice, insisting on the time constraints and the difficulty of finding a consensus in Parliament, started to promote, in 2002, the idea of not amending the Constitution, but "supplementing" it instead with the so-called "Third Constitutional Act", which would exist beside the Constitution and the Implementing Act of the Constitution. After fast and relatively closed deliberations within an *ad hoc* commission, the Act on Supplementing the Constitution of Estonia was initiated in Parliament in May 2002. Article 1 of this laconic Act provides that "Estonia may belong to the European Union, proceeding from the founding principles of the Constitution of the Republic of Estonia." Article 2 continues that "[i]n case Estonia belongs to the European Union, the Constitution of the Republic of Estonia will be applied, taking into consideration the rights and obligations deriving from the Accession Treaty." The third article subjects the amendment of this Act to a referendum.

The Act had passed all three readings by 18 December 2002, and was opposed only by the People's Union Party, who insisted upon the inclusion of a clause concerning the people's right to decide on the ratification of those future treaties that might bring about fundamental changes to the character of the EU polity.[10] The Act was approved in a referendum on 14 September 2003, where two referendums – on accession and on the "supplementing" of the Constitution – were fused into one, following an amendment to the Referendum Act. Thus, the people were asked in a single question whether they approved the supplementing of the Constitution and the accession to the EU. Initially, two separate questions had been envisaged, but there was a risk of a constitutional deadlock should one be answered in the affirmative and the other in the negative. The referendum was successful: 67 per cent of the voters were in favour of accession.[11]

The "Third Constitutional Act" should inevitably be seen in the light of the high costs involved in potentially remaining outside the EU, especially those related to geopolitical concerns, and security and economy. Given Estonia's drastic history, the country could simply not afford to risk remaining outside the EU, in a geopolitical "grey area".

However, some questions have been raised concerning the correctness of such a solution. The procedural and substantive shortcomings of the Act attracted criticism from prominent lawyers such as Allar Jõks (Legal Chancellor)[12] and Rait Maruste (Judge at the European Court of Human Rights and the former President of the Supreme Court),[13] as well as from some lawyers who issued a joint public

10 'Rahvaliit põhiseaduse täiendamise vastu' [The People's Union is against the Supplementing of the Constitution], *ETA News*, reported in *Delfi news portal*, 28 May 2002.

11 Thirty-three per cent were against, with the turnout being 64 per cent.

12 A. Jõks, 'Põhiseadus muutuste künnisel' [Constitution at the doorstep of changes], *Postimees*, 17 April 2002.

13 R. Maruste, 'Põhiseadust tuleks siiski muuta' [The Constitution should still be amended], *Postimees*, 30 January 2002.

statement.[14] The criticism has revolved around the following issues. First, the Third Constitutional Act does not fit well into the Estonian legal order, unlike in some countries where constitutional laws possess a status equal to the Constitution and are amended in accordance with the constitutional amendment procedure (e.g., Austria, Sweden, the Czech Republic). The Estonian Constitution does not provide for such constitutional acts, and the legal position of the Implementing Act of the Constitution is not equal to the Constitution, given that it regulated an initial transitional period and has predominantly expired. Secondly, the three rigid amendment procedures do not include the possibility of adopting an act which would exist independently alongside the Constitution. Thirdly, in Central and Eastern Europe, the Constitutions tend to be regarded as legal rather than political documents, in contrast to the declaratory Constitutions of the Communist period. In this respect, the Third Constitutional Act poses the risk of obscuring and devaluating Estonia's clear, directly applicable and up-to-date Constitution, as it will be interpreted in the light of one general principle deriving from the Third Act, a document standing outside Estonia's traditional constitutional system. Fourthly, the content of the Third Act fails to reflect how the membership of the EU impacts upon the exercise of state powers, as well as to eliminate some manifest conflicts between the Constitution and EU law. Indeed, Justice Maruste has characterised this Act as "nihilism towards the constitutional state."[15]

The Constitutional Chamber of the Supreme Court also encountered some constitutional challenges in these respects. After the referendum, altogether nine cases were brought to the Constitutional Chamber of the National Court, challenging the mode of the constitutional revision and the fusion of the two types of referendums. One of the challenges was brought jointly by the Estonian Voters' Union and Ms Vilu, who claimed that the referendum question contained two mutually exclusive parts, given that it was impossible to simultaneously retain eternal and inalienable independence (Art. 1 of the Constitution) and transfer part of it to the European Union.[16] In addition, these claimants argued that under Articles 102, 161, 162 and 163 of the Constitution, the Constitution may only be "amended" and not "supplemented" by an independent act. Another major case was brought by Mr Kulbok, the leader of the Eurosceptic Movement, who asked the Court to review the compatibility of the Accession Treaty with the Constitution.[17] Referring to the aforementioned 1998 Opinion of the Constitutional Expert

---

14 A. Albi, M. Gallagher, I. Koolmeister, R. Maruste, L. Mälksoo and P. Roosma, 'Ühispöördumine seoses nn Põhiseaduse Kolmanda akti riigiõiguslike probleemidega' [Joint statement concerning the constitutional problems of the Third Constitutional Act], 5 *Juridica* (2002) at pp. 352-353.

15 Maruste, see *supra* n. 13.

16 Decision No. 3-4-1-11-03 of 24 September 2003, *Vilu and Estonian Voters Union*, available in Estonian at: <http://www.nc.ee>.

17 E.g., Decision No. 3-4-1-12-03 of 29 September 2003, *Kulbok*, available at: <http://www.nc.ee>.

Commission, where it had been found that entry into the EU required a prior amendment of Article 1 by means of a referendum, Kulbok argued that the Accession Treaty should not have been concluded until after such amendment. Kulbok also referred to an official communication by the then Legal Chancellor Mr Truuväli, who had held the same view as the Constitutional Expert Commission in this respect. Kulbok additionally challenged the legality of the fusion of the two types of referendums. According to him, the referendum question ("Do you support accession to the European Union and the adoption of the Law on Supplementing the Estonian Constitution") was a question composed of two parts, leaving voters in confusion as to which question was to be answered. Further, he argued that the "supplementing" of the Constitution was void because, on the one hand, the Referendum Law did not allow for the adoption of laws by means of a referendum on an "important national issue", and, on the other hand, the accession referendum could not be regarded as a mixture of a constitutional amendment referendum and a referendum on an "important national issue" either, because the referendum outcomes were to enter into force at different times under Article 63 of the Referendum Law. Most of the remaining seven complaints concerned the unclear formulation of the question, and alleged procedural breaches of the Referendum Law.

All cases were rejected by the Constitutional Chamber on procedural grounds; the substance of the challenges was not addressed. The Court stated that according to the Law on the Procedure of Constitutional Review 2002, constitutional review of treaties can only be initiated by courts and by the Legal Chancellor, not by individuals. Further, it found that the deadline for challenging the constitutionality of the Parliament's decision on "supplementing" the Constitution, and on fusing the two types of referendums, had expired long before the referendum.

Following these controversies, the debates on constitutional revision have been re-opened after the successful holding of the accession referendum.[18] As a matter of fact, the Reform Party has adopted a resolution calling on the Parliament to convene a Constituent Assembly, which would start work on a new Constitution, to be produced in a few years' time.[19] The EU-related issues that would be addressed in the new Constitution include participation in the EMU, collective defence in the framework of the EU and NATO, the government's role in Brussels and the appointment of judges to the EU courts. Such plans to adopt a new Constitution with a set of EU provisions should be welcomed. As the author

---

[18] E.g., R. Maruste, 'Eesti vajaks uut põhiseadust' [Estonia needs a new Constitution], *Eesti Päevaleht*, 26 March 2004; U. Reinsalu (Chairman of the Constitutional Affairs Commission of the Parliament), 'Eesti põhiseadus 21. sajandil' [Estonian Constitution in the 21st century], *Postimees*, 30 January 2004.

[19] 'Reformierakond käivitab töö uue põhiseaduse koostamiseks' [Reform Party launches work on the creation of a new Constitution], *Postimees*, 24 January 2004.

has discussed in more detail elsewhere, wider references to the EU within the Constitution would better allow the national Constitutions to meet the rationale of Constitutions in the process of European integration.[20]

2. THE JUDICIARY AND EU-RELATED CASE LAW

The Estonian judiciary has undergone extensive training in EC law, with relevant courses having been organized in the framework of various EU programmes and those of the governments of some Member States. In the first year of EU membership, EC law has been involved in a number of cases in the Estonian courts. From the perspective of the relationship between EU law and national constitutional law, three cases are of particular interest.

The first major case was already mentioned in the previous section: the Constitutional Chamber of the Supreme Court took a pragmatic approach towards European integration when dealing with the challenges to the legality of the accession referendum and the mode of constitutional revision.

The second case of a wider interest was decided by the General Chamber of the Supreme Court on 19 April 2005.[21] In this case, the Chancellor of Justice submitted a petition to review the constitutionality of certain provisions of the Political Parties Act. One of these concerned Article 5(1) of the Act, according to which Estonian citizens may become members of political parties. A similar provision is also contained in Article 48(1) of the Constitution. The Chancellor of Justice pointed out that this provision was in conflict with Article 19 of the EC Treaty and Directive 94/80/EC, according to which EU citizens have the right to vote and be elected in the elections of local councils, on the same conditions as national citizens. The Chancellor of Justice drew attention to Article 2 of the aforementioned Act Supplementing the Constitution, which provides that the Constitution will be interpreted in the light of the Accession Treaty. On the basis of this Article, he argued, Article 48(1) of the Constitution should be interpreted in a way which would allow EU citizens to belong to Estonian political parties for the purposes of municipal elections. This interpretation, in turn, makes it necessary to amend Article 5(1) of the Political Parties Act.

The General Chamber of the Supreme Court found that notwithstanding the references to the provisions of the Estonian Constitution, the Chancellor of Justice was challenging Article 5(1) of the Political Parties Act essentially on the

---

[20] See for a more detailed discussion A. Albi and P. Van Elsuwege, 'EU Constitution, National Constitutions and Sovereignty: An Assessment of a "European Constitutional Order"', 29 *ELR* (2004) pp. 741-765, and Albi, 'EU Enlargement', see *supra* n. 1.

[21] Decision No. 3-4-1-1-05, on the Constitutionality of the Political Parties Act, 19 April 2005, in English available at: <http://www.nc.ee>.

ground of compatibility with EU law. None of the relevant domestic Acts, however, confer on the Chancellor of Justice a competence to request from the Supreme Court an annulment of a law on the ground of incompatibility with EU law. Therefore, the National Court decided that it could not review the Chancellor of Justice's application regarding the compatibility of Article 5(1) of the Political Parties Act with EU law. Referring to the ECJ case *IN.CO.GE. '90*,[22] the Supreme Court held that in the event of a conflict between an Estonian Act and EU law, the national Act should simply be disapplied in that case. The Court also noted that it is up to the legislators to decide whether to introduce procedures for review in future. Incidentally, the Constitutional Affairs Committee of Parliament in January 2005 initiated the amendment of the contested provision, with a view to granting EU citizens the right to belong to political parties.

A Dissenting Opinion was attached to the Supreme Court's decision by Justice Julia Laffranque, with five other judges supporting it. Justice Laffranque disagreed with the decision not to review the Chancellor of Justice's petition. She argued that, even though there was no legal basis for reviewing the petition with regard to the compatibility with EU law, the Court should have reviewed it with regard to the compatibility with the Estonian Constitution, in combination with the Act Supplementing the Constitution. She regretted the fact that the Constitutional Chamber did not address the impact and meaning of the Act Supplementing the Constitution, and did not offer an interpretation of the Constitution in this new constitutional context, thereby leaving important questions concerning legal certainty unresolved. Justice Laffranque also pointed out that a preliminary ruling should have been asked from the European Court of Justice on the interpretation of Article 19 of the EC Treaty. By way of a comment, it might be that the Constitutional Chamber intentionally chose not to give a clear interpretation to the Act Supplementing the Constitution, given the controversies surrounding it (see section 1), and preferred instead to signal the need to resolve this issue by the legislator on a political level.

The third major case concerning the relationship between EU law and Estonian constitutional law is expected to come out of a group of what are known as "sugar fines" cases. Ahead of EU accession, there was a major sugar panic in Estonia. The sugar price was expected to increase significantly after accession, and people as well as companies bought large stocks. Meanwhile, an EU Regulation from January 2004[23] limited the amount of sugar allowed in the country on the date of accession, with fines being provided for stocks beyond that amount, to

---

[22] ECJ, Joined Cases C-10/97 and C-22/97 *Ministero delle Finanze* v. *IN.CO.GE. '90* [1998] *ECR* I-6307.

[23] Commission Regulation No. 60/2004 of 14 January 2004 laying down transitional measures in the sugar sector by reason of the accession of the Czech Republic, Estonia, Cyprus, Latvia, Lithuania, Hungary, Malta, Poland, Slovenia and Slovakia.

avoid the buying of sugar for speculative purposes. Estonia is expected to incur a very high fine of up to 31 billion euros. Shortly ahead of accession, the Government of Estonia attempted to deal with this issue, by adopting the so-called Excess Stocks Act. That Act was published on 27 April 2004, and took effect three days later, on 1 May 2004. Thus, the companies effectively had just three days to get rid of their sugar stocks. Under this Act, fines were imposed on those companies that held larger sugar stocks than permitted. At least 22 companies that were fined have contested this Act in the courts of first instance. They argue that the fines go against the Estonian Constitution, especially as concerns the right to property and the principles of non-retroactive legislation, legal certainty, legitimate expectations and proportionality. In addition, only published laws are binding in Estonia. It is very likely that these cases will go to the Constitutional Chamber of the Supreme Court, and, under the Estonian Constitution and in the light of the Supreme Court's previous case law regarding the principle of legal certainty, these companies have strong claims. However, since the case also concerns the implementation of EC law and its supremacy, the case is likely to prove controversial. In a case regarding similar excess stocks upon Austria's accession,[24] the European Court of Justice rejected the claims of breach of the principles of legitimate expectations and proportionality, on the ground that the European Commission enjoys a large measure of discretion in the field of Common Agricultural Policy, and diligent economic operators must have known about the transitional measures.

It might also be of interest to mention that the Constitutional Review Chamber of the National Court made a general reference to EU law already in the pre-accession stage, stating the need to consider the legal principles of the EU. According to it, "[i]n creating the general principles of law for Estonia[,] the general principles of law developed by the institutions of the Council of Europe and the European Union should be considered. These principles have their origin in the general principles of law of the highly developed legal systems of the member states."[25]

3. ROLE OF THE NATIONAL PARLIAMENT

Although the Constitutional Expert Commission recommended in its 1998 Report to introduce a constitutional amendment with regard to the role of Parliament in EU affairs, the final solution of "supplementing" the Constitution did not include

---

24 ECJ, Case C-179/00 *Gerald Weidacher*, decided on 15 January 2002.

25 Decision No. III-4/A-5/94, on the constitutionality of the Property Law Enforcement Act, 30 September 1994, available in English at: <http://www.nc.ee/english/>.

such provisions. Instead, Parliament's role was regulated by way of amending the Act on the Parliament's Procedural Matters[26] on 11 February 2004.

The New Chapter 18(1) of this Act is devoted to the parliamentary deliberation of matters pertaining to the European Union. According to the Act, the Government has to submit to Parliament any Bills the scope of application of which requires, according to the Constitution, the adoption, amendment or annulment of a law or a decision of Parliament, or Bills the adoption of which may have a significant economic or social impact. The Government may also submit other documents that are of significance. Bills shall be accompanied by an explanatory letter, indicating, *inter alia*, the Government's position and the impact of the Act. The Bills are deliberated by the European Affairs Commission or, if the Bill concerns the EU's Common Foreign and Security Policy, by the Foreign Affairs Commission. These Commissions take a position on behalf of Parliament. The Government is obliged to respect the Parliament's position. In case of taking a diverging position, the Government has to justify it to the respective Commission on the first opportunity. At least once a year, the Prime Minister presents to Parliament an overview of the Government's activities in EU matters.

4. EUROPEAN CONSTITUTION

In Estonia, the European Constitution is predominantly perceived as an international treaty rather than as a Constitution. In the words of the Chairman of the Constitutional Affairs Committee of Parliament, nothing will change in the Estonian legal order.[27] This view partly reflects the difficulties surrounding the holding of two referendums in a short period of time, especially given the drastically low turnout (26.7 per cent) in the elections of the European Parliament in June 2004. The above-mentioned sugar fine, which amounts to a significant percentage of the state budget at a time when there are more urgent priorities, such as education and healthcare, has also caused resentment amongst the people towards the EU.

Against this background, the Government has decided not to hold a referendum on the European Constitution. Although the final decision will be taken by the Parliament, the majority of MPs are against holding a referendum. The only state institution to encourage a wider debate and examination of the new document has

---

[26] Riigikogu Kodukorra Seadus (RT I 2003, 24, 148), amended 11 February 2004 (RT I 2004, 12, 77) 15 March 2004.

[27] E.g., U. Reinsalu, as quoted in the article 'Põhiseadus säilitab euroliidu tänase näo' [The Constitution preserves the European Union's current face], *Eesti Päevaleht*, 15 July 2003.

been the Chancellor of Justice, who has called upon the Government not to rush ahead with the parliamentary ratification.[28] According to the Chancellor, it would be regrettable if the Constitutional Chamber of the National Court might eventually have to give a judgment on the implications of the new document, if the case should be brought before it. Rather, Parliament should ascertain in advance that the Constitution does not require any amendments before proceeding with ratification. Subsequently, in February 2005, Parliament established an expert committee to undertake a more profound analysis of whether the European Constitution can be ratified without amending the Estonian Constitution. The committee's decision was expected by June, but it was postponed until autumn 2005, in the aftermath of the French and Dutch referendum results.

The view that there is no need for a referendum or a constitutional amendment appears to contrast, to some extent, the position expressed by the Expert Commission in the aforementioned 1998 Report. In that Report, it was found that Estonia may not be a member of the EU should the latter adopt a Constitution, since such a move would signal a transition towards a federal polity.

Even though the EU's new basic document is generally found not to amount to a fully-fledged Constitution, it certainly does go beyond what is normally associated with an international treaty, and constitutes another milestone in the process of integration as a "constitutional" treaty.[29] This, however, should not be regarded as a step closer to a potentially federal future: the EU rather is a novel "*sui generis*" political entity that combines intergovernmental and supranational elements, with nation-states remaining central to its construction. Nonetheless, the ratification of the "constitutional treaty" appears to call for wider references to the EU in the national Constitutions, in order to provide a higher legitimacy on the national level to the participation in the process of ever deeper integration.[30] This holds particularly true for the Constitution of Estonia, considering its "souverainist" character and its prominent role in the Estonian legal order. The ratification of the European Constitution equally calls for a revision of the traditional national constitutional theory, to accommodate the emergence of the notion of a Constitution in a non-state context, such as the EU as a new type of transnational polity.

---

28 K. Kalamees, 'Jõks kutsub üles eurodebatile' [Jõks calls for a Euro debate], *Eesti Päevaleht Online*, 19 October 2004, available at: <http://www.epl.ee>.

29 See in more detail Albi and Van Elsuwege, *supra* n. 20. See also K. Lenaerts and D. Gerard, 'The structure of the Union according to the Constitution for Europe: the Emperor is Getting Dressed', 29 *ELR* (2004) pp. 289-322.

30 See for further discussion Albi and Van Elsuwege, *supra* n. 20.

HUNGARY

Jenő Czuczai*

1. THE ADAPTATION OF THE NATIONAL CONSTITUTION IN THE LIGHT OF HUNGARY'S ACCESSION TO THE EU

1.1 Implementation of international law; conflicts; 'Europe-clause'; supremacy and direct effect of EC law

1.1.1 *The Hungarian approach (Act No. LXI of 2002)*[1]

The Hungarian model for constitutional adaptation to the EU constitutional *acquis* – with special regard to the so-called "integration (or Europe) clause" – may be summarized as follows:[2]

- On 17 December 2002, Parliament amended the Hungarian Constitution (Act No. XX of 1949 as amended several times) through Act No. LXI of 2002 (published in Magyar Közlöny on 23 December 2002) for the purpose of the forthcoming EU accession. A new Article 2/A was inserted to serve as what is termed the "integration clause". Many experts believe, however, that the Hungarian Constitution still displays a constitutional gap in that it does not address the question of what should follow if national law conflicts with international

* Dr Jenő Czuczai, Vice-President of the European Law Academy, Budapest.

1 Act No. LXI of 2002 was adopted by the Hungarian Parliament on 17 December 2002, and entered into force – with some exceptions – on 23 December 2002. See as background literature, for example, (in Hungarian): N. Chronowski and J. Petrétei, 'EU Csatlakozás és alkotmánymódositás: minimális konszenzus helyett politikai kompromisszum' [EU accession and modifying the Constitution: a political compromise instead of minimum consent], 8 *Magyar Jog* (2003) pp. 449-466, or A. Sajó, 'Az EU csatlakozás alkotmányosságra gyakorolt hatása az új tagállamokban' [The constitutional impact of EU accession on the new Member States], 2 *Fundamentum* (2003) pp. 14-26, or J. Czuczai, 'Kritikai elemzés az EU csatlakozást érintő magyar Alkotmánymódositásról' [A critical assessment on the EU accession-related amendments to the Hungarian Constitution], in J. Czuczai, ed., *Jogalkotás, jogalkalmazás hazánk EU csatlakozása küszöbén* [Law making and law enforcement in the light of Hungary's forthcoming accession to the EU] (Budapest, KJK-Kerszöv 2003) pp. 129-151.

2 This section of the national report has already been published in J. Czuczai, 'Constitutional preparation for EU accession in the new Central and Eastern European member states', in J.W. de Zwaan, et al., eds., *The European Union: An Ongoing Process of Integration – Liber Amicorum Alfred E. Kellermann* (The Hague, T.M.C. Asser Press 2004) pp. 269-293, in particular on pp. 278-283.

law (Art. 7(1)),[3] or in our situation, in case of possible future conflicts of Hungarian laws with EU law having direct effect and direct applicability. For this reason, it is highly likely that the Constitution will need to be amended again some time after accession.

- The Government did not submit the Bill on the amendment of the Constitution in the light of EU accession until 15 October 2002.[4] It should be mentioned that in Hungary the Constitution can be amended only with the support of a 2/3 majority of the 386 members of the unicameral Hungarian Parliament, which means that the adoption of an amendment to the Constitution requires a minimum of 255 votes in favour. No affirmative referendum is further required, however. At present, the 2/3 majority rule means that the Constitution can only be amended with the support of the largest of the opposition parties (the Alliance of Young Democrats – Fidesz), now that the Government coalition parties (the Hungarian Socialist Party and the Hungarian Liberal Party) only represent 198 votes in the House whereas the opposition parties represent 188 votes (of which the Fidesz has 165). Act No. LXI of 2002 was, however, passed almost unanimously on 17 December 2002.

- Hungary at present has a *dualist constitutional system* and wishes to maintain this approach in the future. This means that a special "integration clause" needed to be incorporated in the Constitution. The finally adopted new Article 2/A (1) reads as follows: "By virtue of treaty, the Republic of Hungary, in its capacity as a Member State of the European Union, may exercise certain constitutional powers jointly[5] with other Member States[6] to the extent necessary in

[3] The English translation of Art. 7 of the Hungarian Constitution reads as follows: "Art. 7(1) The legal system of the Republic of Hungary accepts the generally recognized rules of international law, and shall further ensure harmony between domestic law and the obligations assumed under international law."

[4] See Parliamentary Bill No. 1114/2002. Later on, however, the Government withdrew its previous Bill on the subject and resubmitted it on 5 November 2002. The new Bill was numbered No. 1270/2002 and this is the Bill that was finally passed by Parliament (with several amendments).

[5] The draft Bill (No. 1270/2002) still used the term "delegation" of state powers stemming from the Constitution (instead of "transfer" of certain state powers stemming from the sovereignty) because the drafters considered that the term "delegate" might indicate in the amended future Constitution that the "transfer of certain state powers" on the part of Hungary was not to be permanent, in other words that it was not done with the ultimate purpose of making this constitutional action irreversible. The wording that was finally adopted was "jointly exercise certain constitutional powers with other Member States."

[6] It should be mentioned that the finally adopted amendment to the Romanian Constitution of 1991 (with regard to the forthcoming EU accession) contains a similar solution, namely: "New title: Euro-Atlantic Integration", Art. 145(1) "Romania's accession to the constituent treaties of the European Union, with a view to transferring certain powers to Community institutions, as well as *to exercising the abilities in common with other Member States stipulated in such Treaties*, shall be

connection with the rights and obligations conferred by the treaties on the foundation of the European Union and the European Communities (hereinafter referred to as "European Union"); these powers may be exercised independently and by way of the institutions of the European Union.[7]

Subsection (2) of the new Article 2/A goes on to stipulate that: "The ratification and promulgation of the treaty referred to in Subsection (1) shall be subject to a two-thirds majority vote of the Parliament." Hungary is one of six new Member States (besides Slovakia, Estonia, Malta, Lithuania and Latvia) where the EU is specifically mentioned in the integration clause and does not just use the more general wording "international organization (or institution)". This is a positive aspect of the Hungarian amendment.

- In 2002, it was generally believed in Hungary that there was no "constitutional roadmap" for accession, such as model provisions to bridge the gap between the national legal orders of acceding candidate countries with the legal order of the EU. For this reason, Hungary followed its own way. It was further believed that the "integration clause" should be drawn up as flexibly and open-mindedly as possible. As historically proven by the present Member States' approach, legal accuracy (or dogmatic) are often quite unhelpful in this exercise.

---

carried out by means of a law adopted in the joint session of the Chamber of Deputies and the Senate, with a majority of two thirds of the number of deputies and senators", Art. 145(2) "As a result of the accession, the provisions of the constituent Treaties of the EU, as well as the other mandatory Community regulations *shall take precedence over the opposite provisions of the national laws*, in compliance with the provisions of the accession Acts", Art. 145(3) "The provisions of paragraphs (1) and (2) shall also apply accordingly for the accession to the Acts revising the constituent Treaties of the EU", Art. 145(4) "The Parliament, the President of Romania, the Government, and the judicial authority shall guarantee that the obligations resulting from the accession Acts and the provisions of paragraph (2) are implemented" (Art. 77 of the amending Constitutional Law, which law was approved by a valid nation-wide referendum in Romania on 19 October 2003). A similar solution can also be found in the Lithuanian "Europe clause" in Art. 146(1) of its Constitution.

[7] In fact, this joint exercise approach closely resembles the current French model: Art. 88-1 La République participe aux Communautés européennes et a L'Union européenne, constituées d'Etats qui ont choisi librement, en vertu des traites qui les ont instituées, d'exercer en commun certaines de leurs compétences. Art. 88-2 Sous réserve de réciprocité et selon les modalités prévues par le Traite sur l'Union européenne signe le 7 février 1992, la France consent aux transferts de compétences nécessaires à l'établissement de l'Union économique et monétaire européenne. [Art. 88-1: The Republic shall participate in the European Communities and in the European Union constituted by States that have freely chosen, by virtue of the treaties that established them, to exercise some of their powers in common. Art. 88-2: Subject to reciprocity and in accordance with the terms of the Treaty on European Union signed on 7 February 1992, France agrees to the transfer of powers necessary for the establishment of European economic and monetary union. Subject to the same reservation and in accordance with the terms of the Treaty establishing the European Community, as amended by the Treaty signed on 2 October 1997, the transfer of powers necessary for the determination of rules concerning freedom of movement for persons and related areas may be agreed. Statutes shall determine the rules relating to the European arrest warrant pursuant to acts adopted under the Treaty on European Union.].

- It is still necessary, however, that Hungary amends its Constitution further by a wider package of amending Bills[8] as at present a number of laws in force of constitutional significance may not be fully in line with the relevant EU *acquis* (such as, for example, Act No. XI of 1987 on law making) and due to the fact that some new questions have arisen in the context of Hungary's accession to the EU (such as, for example, the implications of joining the EMU (third stage)). The Hungarian Parliament has been given broad powers in the future formulation of EU-related integration policies at national level[9] (following Austria, Denmark and Finland in this respect).

- As was mentioned earlier, one important issue in the constitutional adaptation process in Central and Eastern Europe is whether the Constitution itself should be made subject to EU law or not. In Hungary the largest opposition party argues and regularly stresses in Parliament that the EU accession-related constitutional amendments should exclude forever the supremacy of EU law over the Hungarian Constitution. This means in political terms that the Constitution itself should be literally interpreted this way.[10] The Hungarian Constitutional Court has not yet taken position on this. From an academic point of view, it is less easy to embrace this political approach.

- In Hungary many scholars believe that the EU accession process will not touch upon the country's sovereignty. This is because it is now generally believed in Hungary that sovereignty is indivisible and a corollary of Hungaria's statehood and the independence of the country under public international law. It is also widely accepted among experts that sovereignty is not *per se* transferable, either partially or in full. This circle of experts believes, therefore, that after accession Hungary will remain a sovereign (independent) Member State of the EU. This does not mean that from an internal point of view, the exercise of certain constitutional powers, stemming from the Hungarian Constitution itself, has not been restricted by Hungary's accession to the EU, in the sense that after accession these constitutional powers can only be exercised jointly with other Member States by the competent and constitutionally authorized Hungarian state organs, obviously within the framework of the EU institutions.

---

[8] Such a package has now been submitted to Parliament, viz. Bill No. 4486 and attached draft Bills as currently under discussion in Parliament.

[9] See Act No. LIII of 2004, entered into force on 24 June 2004.

[10] Those who are in favour of this proposal argue that only two Constitutions in the old Member States allow textually that the "EC law supremacy doctrine" could also apply to the Constitution itself (Greece, Portugal). I do not agree, however.

- A compulsory referendum on EU accession took place in Hungary on 12 April 2003. The referendum can be said to have been successful with a participation rate of 46 per cent and around 84 per cent of participants voting in favour. Parliament subsequently authorized the Government to sign the Acts of Accession in Athens on 16 April 2003 (Parliamentary Resolution No. 37/2003 (IV.15)). These Acts were then unanimously ratified by the Hungarian Parliament (Parliamentary Resolution No. 133/2003 (XII.17), and published in the Hungarian Official Gazette No. 143/2003 by Act No. LXXX of 2004, which entered into force on 1 May 2004.

- Many experts in Hungary believe that more focus should be put in the coming years on training judges (including the judges on the Constitutional Court) in EU law as their approach to the EU constitutional *acquis* will be the true "proof of the pudding" in the process of how the *acquis foundationel de l'Union* and the general principles of EC law will be implemented in practice in Hungary after accession. It is beyond doubt that much work still has to be done in this respect. To facilitate the efficient application and interpretation of the EU *acquis* in practice, a clear-cut and well-formulated "Europe clause" in the national Constitution is essential. Such a clause would have to include clear guidance for judges and civil servants in cases where national law conflicts with directly applicable EC legal norms. It is also crucial for educative purposes and for changing the mentality and habits of at times quite conservative and orthodox judges[11] in Central and Eastern European countries in transition (including Hungary) and to better accustom them to the living practice of the constantly evolving EU *acquis* in the years and decades to come. This requirement is, therefore, *prima facie* a social and socio-political factor as well as a psychological guarantee for the success of the Eastward enlargement process and is only a legal or constitutional necessity in the second place.

- Hungary, by virtue of the finally adopted wording of its "Europe clause", may best pursue its national preferences in three ways. (i) First of all, the words "to the extent necessary" in Article 2/A of the Constitution can only be brought to life by interpretation by the Constitutional Court. This means that the role of the Hungarian Constitutional Court will be crucial after accession as far as the proper application and implementation of the EU *acquis* in Hungary is concerned. (ii) Secondly, Hungary has chosen what is known as the minimum

[11] In the former socialist/communist period, judges were accustomed to interpreting the law grammatically. However, the efficient application of the EU *acquis* would rather seem to require the use of the *interpretatio legis systematica* and *legis teleologica*. We should bear in mind that the majority of judges in the newly acceded EU Member States all received their legal education during the communist/socialist regime.

approach to EU constitutional adaptation. This means that the Europe clause is brief and flexible as well as "selfish" in the sense that it allows for different possible interpretations after accession. One can even say that although the adopted text – in terms of its wording – closely resembles the French Europe clause (Art. 88 of the French Constitution,[12] in practical terms the approach is more similar to the past Italian experience of bridging the gap between the national legal order and the EU legal order, as the Hungarian Europe clause does not regulate important EU-related topics such as the supremacy of EC law. This means that the role of the Hungarian Supreme Court (and generally of all ordinary courts) will also be very important after accession, especially in terms of how to fill the obvious constitutional gaps referred to above. (iii) Thirdly, the constitutional amendments of December 2002 failed to address the outstanding problem of Article 7(1) of the Hungarian Constitution, namely that it remains unregulated what is to be done when a conflict arises between Hungarian law (including the Constitution) and an EC legal norm having direct effect and direct applicability in a concrete legal dispute after accession? This question is highly topical since according to the Constitution of Hungary in force, all judges and courts are subject to the Hungarian Constitution and laws, and the courts and other state organs are bound by the Constitution (Arts. 50(3) and 77). In this respect it is to be hoped that the Hungarian judiciary will play a constructive role and be constructive in its approach after accession.

1.2 Provisions contrary to the *acquis communautaire*

Apart from the problems mentioned above in relation to Articles 2/A and 7(1), five more (non-exhaustive) examples may be given where further amendments to the Hungarian Constitution still seem necessary:

- Article 69(1) of the Constitution stipulates that a Hungarian national cannot be extradited (the Constitution uses the term "expulsion", but this is widely interpreted in case law to include extradition). This paragraph will probably need to be reconsidered in the light of the new EU framework decision on the European Arrest Warrant.[13]

---

[12] See *supra* n. 7.

[13] Similar constitutional problems occurred in Poland, see P1/2005 ruling of the Polish Constitutional Tribunal, available at: <summaries@trybunal.gov.pl>, and a constitutional scrutiny procedure on the same issue has also been initiated in the Czech Republic (not yet decided).

- Article 70(4) of the Constitution stipulates that all Hungarian nationals have the right to participate in public affairs. This should also be reconsidered after accession to include EU citizens.

- Article 70/E of the Constitution only entitles Hungarian nationals to social security benefits and allowances. This too should be revised after accession.

- Article 77(1) and (2) of the Constitution stipulates that: "The Constitution is the basic law of Hungary. The Constitution and laws established in accordance with this Constitution are binding on everybody in Hungary", but these provisions fail to address EU law with direct effect and direct applicability, and especially fail to provide for the possibility that a conflict arises between EU law, which is supreme, and the national Constitution. This provision should therefore also be reconsidered after accession.

- Article 32/D concerning the National Bank, must also be still amended with respect to the introduction of the euro before Hungary joins the EMU.[14]

2. JUDICIARY

2.1 Implementation of the Europe Agreement in the pre-accession preparation phase

The pre-accession implementation practice of the EU-Hungary Europe Agreement has already been analysed in great detail by one of Hungaria's Constitutional Court judges.[15] Since his report there have been no significant changes in this field. Hungarian courts before 1 May 2004 did not refer to any of the provisions of the Europe Agreement or to any secondary source of EC law in accordance with the strict dualistic approach explored by the Hungarian Constitutional Court in its famous ruling No. 30/1998 (VI.25) on the constitutionality of certain provisions of the EU-Hungary Europe Agreement.[16]

---

[14] See in more detail on this question, J. Czuczai, 'Az EU alkotmányi szerződésének hatása a magyar alkotmányfejlődésre' [The impact of the Treaty establishing a constitution for Europe] (Budapest 2005), 3 *Europai Jog* [Journal of European Law] (2005) pp. 3-16, in particular on pp. 7-9.

[15] See A. Harmathy, 'Constitutional questions of the preparation of Hungary for accession to the EU' in A.E. Kellermann, J. de Zwaan and J. Czuczai, eds., *EU Enlargement – The Constitutional Impact at EU and National Level* (The Hague, T.M.C. Asser Press 2001) pp. 315-327. For an update of this report see A. Harmathy, Hungarian report presented at the international conference on 'The position of constitutional courts following integration into the EU', held in October 2004 in Slovenia, available at: <http://www.us-rs.si/pcceu/index.php?sv_path=589,722>.

[16] See in more detail, A.F. Tatham, 'Constitutional judiciary in Central Europe and the Europe Agreement: Decision 30/1998 (VI.25) AB of the Hungarian Constitutional Court', 48 *International*

As far as the post-accession application and implementation of EU law in Hungary is concerned, the record after one year is extremely promising and the practice is dynamic.

2.2 The approach of the Hungarian Constitutional Court towards EU law after accession

The Hungarian Constitutional Court addressed the relationship between Hungarian law and EU law quite soon after accession. On 5 April 2004 the Hungarian Parliament adopted an Act on the agricultural surplus stocking in order to properly implement two related Commission regulations, namely Commission Regulation No. 1972/2003 and No. 60/2004. The Act related to sensitive agricultural products (like sugar) as far as their pre-accession driven manipulative stocking in Hungary was concerned and intended to identify market operators involved in speculative trade with a view to avoiding or preventing any unexpected undesirable dumping or distortive effect on competition in the EC internal market with regard to these products after accession. The adopted Act would have entered into force only three weeks after accession, but a number of provisions clearly had retroactive effect. The President of Hungary, however, did not sign the adopted Act but sent it, before promulgation, to the Constitutional Court for preliminary constitutional scrutiny.[17] The Constitutional Court found the Act unconstitutional, but based its reasoning purely on national constitutional grounds.[18] As a result, however, the Act could not enter into force.

From our point of view, the importance of this Constitutional Court ruling lies in the fact that under point III.5 of its decision the Court for the first time after accession addressed the relationship between EU law and Hungarian law in a post-accession constitutional dimension. The Court ruled as follows: (i) The adopted Act and its constitutionality can be examined without touching upon any kind of EU law issue. Consequently, Article 2/A(1) of the Hungarian Constitution shall not apply. This is possible, as the Constitutional Court only examines the constitutionality of adopted Hungarian Acts of Parliament and does not deal with either the validity, or the interpretation of the Commission regulations referred to

---

and Comparative Law Quarterly (1999) pp. 913-920. On the other hand, however, we should mention a concrete case before the ECJ in which the application of the EU-Hungary Europe Agreement was at issue, namely Case C-347/03 *Regione autonoma friuli-Venezia Giulia* v. *Ministero delle Politiche Agricole e Forestali*, decided on 12 May 2005, not yet reported, a case that concerned the use of the Tokai Aszú trademark (a famous Hungarian wine). Hungary won the case and will have the exclusive use of the "Tokai" trademark from 1 April 2007.

17 See for a detailed and critical analysis of the case, A. Sajó, 'Learning co-operative constitutionalism the hard way: The Hungarian Constitutional Court shying away from EU supremacy', Systemtransformation und 'Europaisierung' I, 3 *ZSE* (2004) pp. 351-371.

18 See Constitutional Court ruling No. 17/2004 (V.25).

above. It therefore only examines the constitutionality of implementing national legal measures without involving in the review process the Commission regulations themselves. (ii) The Hungarian Constitutional Court has jurisdiction over the constitutionality of the national laws even where these are the legislative result of implementing Commission regulations. This is possible now that the Hungarian law in question is not a simple translation of the EC regulations (although it does refer to the regulations in several places) and given that the Commission regulations in terms of rights and obligations address the Member States, not the citizens of the Union. Moreover, the regulations themselves allow the Member States to adopt further implementing national laws in order that the objectives of the regulations can be accomplished. Consequently, even after accession, on 25 May 2005, the Constitutional Court was able to declare the challenged Act unconstitutional without addressing any points of EU law in its ruling, such as, for example, the direct applicability of the regulations in Hungary according to Article 249 EC Treaty, or the implications of Article 10 EC Treaty, which is relevant for the question of how, when no national implementing legislation is in force on 1 May 2004, the two Commission regulations could still be given applicability in Hungary).

The approach of the Hungarian Constitutional Court towards EU law as explored above may be characterized as rather defensive in the sense that the Court already wished to defend its competences in the post-accession reality, and not very innovative in the sense that the court in this first ruling after accession did not refer to any of the relevant ECJ case law. In fact, the Constitutional Court in this ruling divided the legal order of the enlarged EU into an EU legal order on the hand and a separate Hungarian legal order on the other and as of 1 May 2004, erected a large constitutional wall between the two in terms of its own jurisdiction. From the constitutional point of view, the Court thus has no jurisdiction over EC legal acts (such as Commission regulations), but retains full jurisdiction over the review of the constitutionality of national implementing laws even after accession. This constitutional logic closely follows the logic of a previous Constitutional Court ruling No. 4/1997 (I.12) on whether the Court had ex-post jurisdiction over the constitutionality of the EU-Hungary Europe Agreement (which in 1996 was already fully in force). To this question the Court answered that it did not have jurisdiction over the international agreement itself, as this would violate the general *pacta sunt servanda* principle of public international law, but that it did have jurisdiction over the implementing national law.

2.3 Direct application of EC law after accession?

As far as the direct application of EC law by Hungarian courts after accession is concerned, two concrete judgments may be mentioned.

(a) The first case was decided by the Hungarian Supreme Court[19] and relates to the contemporary effect (or the immediate application) of EC law in a new Member State. In this case which concerned the authorization of a merger between two companies in the cement waste industry, the question of the application of the EC competition *acquis* was raised, essentially concerning a procedural issue, namely from when EC competition law could apply in Hungary. The merger took place in 1999. Following a complaint, the Hungarian competition authority initiated an investigation on 18 January 2001. The proceedings resulted in a final decision by the competition authority in a resolution dated 9 January 2002. These events all still took place before accession. A third company, which had not taken part in the transaction, but was concerned about its market-distorting effects, challenged the above decision of the competition authority before the competent administrative court in Hungary by making reference to several EC law sources (in fact wrongly, as it mentioned, for example, the *Plaumann* case[20] as a national competition case).

The court of first instance rejected the claim out of hand, without entering into the merits, for lack of *locus standi*, now that the claimant could not show a legal interest under Hungarian competition law. The Court of Appeal upheld this decision, but the claimant then turned to the Supreme Court arguing that the proceedings had been ongoing at the time of Hungary's accession to the EU and that therefore EC law applied, which did give the claimant a legal interest and thereby *locus standi*.

The claimant also requested the Supreme Court to refer the matter to the ECJ for a preliminary ruling on the question of whether relevant EC law should apply to proceedings ongoing at the time of accession. The Supreme Court, however, declined this request, indirectly[21] basing itself on the *Cilfit* doctrine of "acte clair" (although it made no concrete reference to any ECJ rulings), and upheld the previous court's rulings in substance. The Supreme Court took the position that under the given circumstances EC law could not apply as the competition authority has delivered its final decision in the matter on 9 January 2002. This decision was received by all the parties concerned on 20 February 2002. According to Article 327 of the Hungarian Code of Civil Procedure there were only 30 days counting from 20 February 2002 for all the parties concerned in the case to file an action with a court against this administrative decision. At the end of March 2002, therefore, the time-limit for filing an action had irrevocably lapsed.

---

19 See Judgment of the Hungarian Supreme Court, reported in the *Official Gazette of the Supreme Court* 2005/July/270th decision.

20 Case 25-62 *Plaumann* [1963] *ECR* English special edition 95.

21 See as the relevant permanent case law of the ECJ on this issue: Cases C-1/73 *Westzucker* [1973] *ECR* 723, C-258/81 *Metallurgiki Halyps* [1982] *ECR* 4261, C-43/95 *Data Delecta* [1996] *ECR* I-4661, C-122/96 *Saldanha* [1997] *ECR* I-5325.

Since Hungary only joined the EU on 1 May 2004, even the possibility of any application of EC law in this case was thus *per se* excluded. It is striking, however, that in the reasoning of its decision, the Supreme Court did not mention a single ECJ case or source of EC legislation. Otherwise, however, the Supreme Court's reasoning appears correct, as in terms of procedurial questions the principle of "immediate application of EC law" should be interpreted narrowly (*interpretatio legis restrictiva*).[22]

(b) The second case was a criminal case of which the facts were briefly as follows:[23] quite some time before 1 May 2004, certain products had been imported from Germany and Austria, on which the customs levies due under Hungarian law had not been paid. The import further involved some elements of corruption. The Public Prosecutor's Office initiated criminal proceedings against the persons concerned and indicted them for, among other things, smuggling. The criminal court of first instance found them guilty and sentenced them to a term in prison. However, on appeal before the criminal court of second instance, which heard the case after accession, the appellants were acquitted based on the following reasoning. The offence of which the appellants had previously been found guilty can only be committed in relation to products that are subject to customs duty according to the national law on customs in force. On 1 May 2004 when Hungary became a Member State of the EU, Council Regulation No. 2913/1992/EC on the Community Customs Code replaced the national law on customs previously in force. According to Article 4(8) of this Council Regulation, customs are only levied on products imported in the Community from third countries. In this case the products in question had been imported from Germany and Austria, which are EU Member States, which meant that based on directly applicable EC law the products could no longer be considered products subject to customs duty. The criminal court of second instance went on to consider that since Article 2 of the Hungarian Criminal Code stipulates that where a later law adopted during the course of a trial declares the behaviour under indictment as no longer punishable or if its application is more favourable for the accused, then this later law shall apply. Consequently, the court held that it had to apply the relevant Council Regulation and acquitted the appellant. In other cases, based on the same reasoning, the Public Prosecutor's Office decided not even to indict the suspects concerned and ended its investigations immediately after accession. Some academics criticized this interpretation of the law by arguing that it surely could not

---

22 See Saulius Lukas Kaleda, 'Immediate effect of Community law in the new Member States: is there a place for a consistent doctrine?', 10 *European Law Journal* (2004) pp. 102-122, in particular pp. 109 et seq.

23 See Final Judgment of the Hajdú Bihar County Court (a second instance criminal court), reported in the *Official Gazette of the Supreme Court* under No. 6 of the series January 2005.

have been the intention of the Community legislator when it enacted the Council Regulation in question that the prison gates be opened in new Member States.

2.4 Non-application of EC law after accession

There is one interesting case decided recently by the Hungarian Supreme Court in which relevant EC law was not applied.[24] The facts of the case are as follows: a student who was enrolled at the Faculty of Theology of the Károli Gáspár Protestant University in Budapest publicly confessed that he was gay. As a result, he was excluded from the Faculty and could not continue his studies. The Association of Gays and Lesbians then turned to the courts asking that the Faculty's decision be declared unlawful as contrary to the relevant Hungarian law on equal opportunities. In its pleadings, the Association also referred to several EC law sources, such as, for example, Articles 12 and 13 EC Treaty and Article 21 of the EU Charter of Fundamental Rights which both among other things deal with discrimination on grounds of sexual orientation. The case was finally heard by the Supreme Court, which completely ignored the EC law-based arguments, and did not even refer to them in its judgment. The Supreme Court finally rejected the Association's claim by holding that the Faculty of Theology of a Protestant University had the right to define specific moral and theological requirements which students of Theology have to fulfil as these students will automatically become members of the clergy of the protestant church after their graduation. This means that they are already subject to the rules of this church during their studies and one of the rules is that homosexuals are not allowed to preach in Hungary. Without commenting on the substance of this judgment, the claimant certainly made a mistake when it did not initiate the relevant procedure for requesting that the Supreme Courts refer the case to the ECJ for a preliminary ruling on whether EC law had to apply and if so, to what extent and how, and perhaps most importantly, why?

2.5 Indirect application of Directives by courts in Hungary after accession

Under this heading, a case under labour law might be mentioned,[25] which has however not yet been finally decided: it is currently being heard by the second

---

[24] See the case between *Association of Hungarian Homosexuals* v. *Károli Gáspár Protestant University*, the final judgment of the Supreme Court not yet reported in the *Official Gazette of the Supreme Court.*

[25] See Judgment No. 3.M.330/2004/14 of the Veszprém District Labour Court (Veszprém is a pretty historical town being very close to the lake of Balaton in Hungary), currently being under appeal procedure.

instance court. The case is also good example of the pragmatic post-accession consequences of the badly designed legislative products of the pre-accession approximation of law. The facts of the case can be summarized as follows: a doctor working in a hospital was required to be on call regularly which meant that he had to spend nights at the hospital so as to be on hand in emergency cases. According to the applicable Government Decree No. 233/2000 and Parliamentary Act No. LXXXIV of 2003 only a quarter of the time spent on call is considered working time and remunerated accordingly, while the remaining three-quarters are considered "resting time" for which no payment is due. The doctor instituted court proceedings in October 2004 (i.e., after accession) claiming that the "resting time" also had to considered part of his working hours for which he should receive payment. In his submissions, the claimant referred to Articles 2(1) and 3 of Council Directive 93/104/EC of 23 November 1993 concerning certain aspects of the organization of working time[26] and to the preliminary rulings of the ECJ which have so far interpreted these provisions (*SiMAP* and *Jaeger*).[27] The Directive as interpreted by the ECJ stipulates that the hours physically spent on call duty at the hospital, irrespective of how many of these were spent resting, in their totality have to be considered as working time and therefore paid out to the employee. The defendant asked the court to disregard the claimant's arguments based on EC law and reject the claim now that Hungarian law in force must apply. In its judgment, the court of first instance found in favour of the claimant on all counts, including all the arguments referring to ECJ cases and ordered the defendant to pay out the remaining three-quarters on-call working time spent at the hospital. The court of first instance reasoned that the national law in question had to be interpreted in the light and spirit of the applicable Directive and respecting the supremacy of EC law. If a Directive has been badly transposed into domestic law by the national legislator, then the EC law doctrine of indirect effect

---

[26] *OJ* 1993 L 307/18.

[27] See Case C-303/98 *Sindicato de Médicos de Asistencia Pública (SiMAP)* v. *Conselleria de Sanidad y Consumo de la Generalidad Valenciana* [2000] *ECR* I-7963, p. 13 and point 3. of the preliminary ruling which reads as follows: "3. Time spent on call by doctors in primary health care teams must be regarded in its entirety as working time, and where appropriate as overtime, within the meaning of Directive 93/104/EC if they are required to be at the health centre. If they must merely be contactable at all times on call, only time linked to the actual provision of primary health care services must be regarded as working time." The second case, Case C-151/2002 *Landeshauptstadt Kiel* v. *Norbert Jaeger* (not yet reported) was decided by the ECJ on 9 September 2003 and further developed (under point 1 of the preliminary ruling) the reasoning in SiMAP as follows: "1. Council Directive 93/104/EC of 23 November 1993 concerning certain aspects of the organization of working time must be interpreted as meaning that on-call duty performed by a doctor where he is required to be physically present in the hospital must be regarded as constituting in its totality working time for the purposes of that Directive even where the person concerned is permitted to rest at his place of work during the periods when his services are not required with the result that that Directive precludes legislation of a Member State which classifies as rest periods an employee's periods of inactivity in the context of such on-call duty."

of EC Directives has to apply, which means that the conflicting national law must be replaced by the Directive as appropriate. The defendant consequently appealed against this judgment arguing that the Directive does not have direct effect and cannot apply directly, as it is addressed to the Member States, not to Member State citizens, and that therefore national law in force cannot be ignored. It further argued that the indirect effect of a Directive is acknowledged only if the legal relationship concerned is vertical, which is not the case here, as the dispute is governed by national labour law, which is of a private law nature regulating horizontal relationships and thus precludes the Directive from having indirect effect. The case is presently pending before the court of second instance.

2.6 First experiences with the preliminary ruling procedure in Hungary[28]

In Hungary the first (in terms of when it was published) request for a preliminary ruling[29] was made by the Budapest Municipal Court in a criminal law case. The case was widely covered in the Hungarian press and is known as the *Red Star* case. In a nutshell, the facts are as follows: the Vice-President of the Labour Party (which is not represented in Parliamentary) had worn a red star on his pullover in the course of a demonstration held close to the building of Parliament. According to Article 269/B(1) of the Hungarian Criminal Code[30] this is an offence liable to punishment. The local criminal court found the accused guilty and duly sentenced

---

[28] So far there have been three requests for a preliminary ruling referred by Hungarian courts to the ECJ, and one case referred by a Greek court in which Hungary has an interest, namely: *OJ* 2004 C 251/09, *OJ* 2004 C 262/27, *OJ* 2004 C 71/15, and a fourth which is not yet notified in the *Official Journal*. Hungary is one of the new Member States where the procedure for requesting preliminary rulings is regulated in national legislation. See Act No. III of 1952 on the Code of Civil Procedure, Arts. 155/A and 249/A as well as Act No. XIX of 1998 on the Code of Criminal Procedure under Art. 266(1) point c. In addition to this, a quasi-judicial body has also been authorized to refer questions under Art. 234 EC Treaty, namely the "public procurement arbitration committees", see Art. 333 of Act No. CXXIX of 2003 on public procurement. The substance of all these provisions is that it is at the full discretion of the court in question to decide whether to refer questions concerning the content of EC law to the ECJ or not. However, the parties may request in a special procedure that the court does so. The court decision rejecting the claim for referral is not appealable at first instance, but decisions upholding the claim are. In the second instance, both decisions can be appealed against. Finally, if the court does decide to referring questions to the ECJ, a copy of this decision must at the same time be sent to the Ministry of Justice for information purposes.

[29] See Budapest Municipality Court of Justice 22.Bf.6645/2004/4 order, dated 24 June 2004. See also András Osztovits 'Az első magyar előzetes döntéshozatali eljárás iránti kérelem' [The first request for a preliminary ruling in Hungary), 5 *Európai Jog* [Journal of European Law] (2004) pp. 16-21.

[30] The provision of the Hungarian Criminal Code referred to reads as follows: "269/B (1) A person who uses or displays, in public, documents orimages describing the SS, the hammer and sickle or the symbol consisting of a five-pointed red star commits – if the conduct does not amount to a more serious criminal offence – a minor offence, and shall be punished by a fine."

him. On appeal, the second instance Budapest Municipal Court stayed the proceedings and turned to the ECJ for a preliminary ruling on the following issues: (i) The Municipal Court considered the relevant provision of the Hungarian Criminal Code to be contrary to the principle of non-discrimination based on nationality (Art. 12 EC Treaty), as in many other Member States of the EU the public use or display of a red star is not an offence (e.g., Italy, the Czech Republic and France, where Communist parties are or have been in the recent past in Government and the party symbol of these parties is in fact the red star). This means that the accused is being discriminated against on grounds of nationality, as identical behaviour is not penalized in other Member States. (ii) The Municipal Court further referred to Article 6 TEU, Council and European Parliament Directive 43/2003/EC[31] and Articles 10 to 12 of the EU Charter of Fundamental Rights. Based on the Charter, the Municipal Court considered that the relevant provisions of the Hungarian Criminal Code could be said to violate the fundamental freedom of expression of opinions and beliefs. If a person believes in the communist ideals and wishes to express this belief in public by wearing a red star such behaviour in a democratic society based on the principle of the rule of law cannot be penalized as long as it does not violate others peoples' rights.

As this request was the first submitted to it under Article 234 EC Treaty by a new Member State and taking into account that the ECJ wishes to develop a good and well-functioning working relationship with national courts in the new Member States, the ECJ found the request admissible.[32]

In our opinion, however, the ECJ should have found it inadmissible. First of all, in essence the request concerns the interpretation and application of a provision of the national Criminal Code (Art. 269/B(1)), not of any point of EC law. Neither Article 234 EC Treaty, nor Article 35 TEU allows that national courts refer preliminary questions in order that the ECJ interprets provisions of the national criminal code. Moreover, in the EU the substantive criminal law of the Member States is not today a subject for approximation of laws, especially in the field concerned (restrictions on the exercise of the fundamental freedom of expression), and consequently the question of how a Member State regulates this matter is at present the exclusive competence of the Member State in question (for example, no framework decisions have yet been taken on this issue in the EU). The argument based on non-discrimination is completely unfounded as the contested provision of the Hungarian Criminal Code applies to "Anyone who…", which means that any person residing in Hungary, regardless of nationality, who displays the conduct described would be liable to criminal prosecution based on this provision. Secondly the EU Charter, which was also referred to in the

31 See *OJ* L 180/22.

32 See pending case before the ECJ Case C-328/04 *Vajnai Attila*.

request, is not yet legally binding; it is only a political declaration and is applicable to Member States only when they implement EU law. But in the given field, as mentioned above, there is no EU law. Thirdly, Directive 43/2003/EC referred to in the request does not cover the issue at hand, which is clear even from its title, while Article 6(1) TEU cannot be interpreted by the ECJ now that Article 46 TEU *expressis verbis* excludes this.

Finally, it is possible that the Municipal Court's actual motives for referring to the ECJ was that it disagreed with Decision No. 14/2000 (V.12) of the Hungarian Constitutional Court, in which the Court had found that Article 269/B(1) of the Hungarian Criminal Code does not go against the constitutionally guaranteed fundamental freedom of expression in Hungary and is therefore constitutional and had thereby rejected a request for its annulment. National courts are bound by decisions of the Constitutional Court which also means, in my view, that the EC law-based instrument of the preliminary ruling cannot be used to escape this obligation.

The second request for a preliminary ruling request was submitted by the Szombathelyi local court in a civil law case concerning consumer protection.[33] The case gives another example of badly-designed pre-accession approximation laws. The facts of the case were as follows: a person wanted to sell a property and to this end turned to an estate agent. The estate agent used a standard contract in its dealings which included the standard term that if the sale negotiated by the estate agent between the seller and the buyer for whatever reasons was not concluded or failed otherwise, the seller was nevertheless required to pay the commission fee to the estate agent. In the case in question, the sale fell through and the estate agent based on the term described requested payment of its fee from the seller. The seller thereupon brought an action before the court asking it to declare the contract null and void. During the proceedings in first instance, the court *ex officio* recognized that the applicable provision of the Hungarian Civil Code (Art. 209) was in fact the result of a pre-accession legal approximation process. More specifically, the Civil Code provision in question had been intended to implement Council Directive 93/13/EEC on unfair contract terms[34] (specifically Arts. 3 and 6 of the Directive). The court in its analysis of the transposition of the Directive however discovered that Article 6(1) of the Directive and the corresponding national law were contradictory on two points. First of all, Article 6(1) of the Directive stipulates that an unfair contract term does not impose any obligation – *ipso facto* – on the consumer whatsoever, whereas the

---

[33] This request for a preliminary ruling is analyzed in more detail in *Lajos Vékás*, 'A Ptk. 209.§-ának megmérettetése az Európai Biróság előtt' [The testing of Article 209 of the Hungarian Civil Code before the ECJ], 6 *Európai Jog* [Journal of European Law] (2004) pp. 8-11.

[34] See *OJ* 1993 L 95/29.

corresponding Hungarian law requires the consumer to challenge the contested contractual term before the courts for invalidity. This means that the consumer can only enjoy the protection of the Directive depending on the discretion of the court and not *ex lege*. Secondly, the Directive under Article 6 provides that if the conditions for invalidity have been fulfilled the entire contract is invalid, whereas Article 234(1) of the Hungarian Civil Code allows the court to declare the contract partially invalide on the unilateral request of the service provider concerned. After having recognized these contradictions, and in order to overcome them, the court referred three questions to the ECJ for a preliminary ruling. The ECJ has since admitted the request.[35]

The third request for a preliminary ruling was in fact referred by the Athens administrative court of first instance prior to Hungary's accession to the EU (namely in January 2004). It relates to the manufacturing of Suzuki cars in Hungary and to selling activities in Greece and concerns the application of the relevant Protocol on the Euro 1. certificate attached to the EU-Hungary Europe Agreement. This case, which is now pending before the ECJ, will not be examined any further here, as it was not submitted by Hungary and was not submitted after Hungary's accession.[36]

Finally, the most recent request for a preliminary ruling submitted at the end of July 2005 by the Komárom-Esztergom County Court concerns the interpretation of Article 33 of Council Directive 77/388/EEC on the common system of value-added tax.[37] The case arose as in Hungary companies are obliged to pay to the local authorities what is known as local industrial turn-over tax, which is in fact another value-added tax, while the Council Directive provision referred to only allows one value-added tax levied once in the Member States, and in Hungary this is the VAT. On the other hand, Hungarian law currently in force requires companies to pay both. The Government has argued that the EC has been informed of the current situation during the accession negotiations and that the Commission did not object to it at the time. Moreover, all the related national laws were adopted before accession and entered into force before May 2004. Given the fact that the question was referred only very recently, there is no further information available on it yet.[38]

---

35 See pending case before the ECJ, Case C-302/04 *Ynos Ltd* v. *János Varga*.

36 See *OJ* 2004 C 71/15. Case C-23/04 *Sphakianakis AEBE* v. *The Hellenic Republic*.

37 *OJ* 1977 L 145/1.

38 It has not yet been notified in the *OJ*. Nonetheless, the legal problems raised by the Hungarian referring court seem very similar to those raised by another pending case before the ECJ, namely Case C-475/03 *Banca Popolare di Cremona* v. *Agenzia Entrate Ufficio Cremona*. The opinion of AG F. Jacobs in this case is already available on the ECJ web site.

3. THE ROLE OF THE NATIONAL PARLIAMENT

3.1 Preparedness for legal approximation; special instructions or committees for the implementation of EC/EU law

The Hungarian Parliament is sufficiently prepared to monitor the legal harmonization process in Hungary in a post-accession dimension. The Parliament's controlling and monitoring task is carried out by the standing parliamentary committee on EU integration affairs. Since May 2004 several new legal experts have been recruited by this Committee to deal with the enormous workload that the process of harmonization has already imposed on this Committee over the past one and a half years. The renumeration of Members of Parliament who are part of the committee was increased on 1 September 2004 by a 40 per cent extra allowance.[39] The Government already adopted the new mechanism for legal approximation before accession. This decision shifted the main responsibility for post-accession-related harmonization from the Ministry of Justice to the line Ministries that are competent in the respective regulatory fields. These Ministries are therefore primarily responsible for the further legal transposition and the institutional implementation process of the EU *acquis* as developing.[40] The main novelty of this regime is that which ever Ministry drafted the national position paper (for example, during the discussion of the draft EC legal measure in question within the framework of the different Council/Commission regulatory and/or advisory committees, or finally for the Coreper meetings),[41] that is to say was involved in it from the beginning of a given EC law-making process, must remain responsible in full for that Community act (e.g., a resulting Directive) and therefore continue to be in charge of its entire implementation process at national level afterwards (*one-shop, one-door system*). Nevertheless, the Ministry of Justice has remained generally responsible for the programming and monitoring of legal harmonization as well as for representing Hungary before the ECJ.[42]

The Inter-ministerial Committee for EU Integration Matters under the leadership of the Minister responsible for EU integration affairs has remained

---

39 See Act LIII of 2004 on the cooperation of the Parliament and the Government in EU affairs (hereinafter referred to as: Parliamentary Control Act) passed by Parliament on 17 May 2004, and entered into force on 24 June 2004. The relevant provisions are paras. (2)-(4) of Art. 10 of the Act.

40 See Government Resolution No. 1036/2004 (IV.27) on the determination of the tasks involved in the harmonization of laws arising from the legal status of EU membership of Hungary including the programming of these tasks and the monitoring of the implementation.

41 See also in detail Government Resolution No. 1023/2005 (III.10) on the representation of the Hungarian Government in the different formations of the Council of the EU and the responsibilities for the preparation of the Hungarian position papers for the Council meetings.

42 See Government Resolution No. 1084/2004 (VIII. 27) on the representation of Hungary before the European Court of Justice.

responsible for the overall coordination of tasks after accession.[43] The Committee is assisted by 49 expert groups depending on the subject-matter. The Minister responsible for EU integration affairs represents Hungary in the General Affairs Council, except where issues related to the Second Pillar or the humanitarian aid and development policy in general are concerned, when the Government is represented by the Minister of Foreign Affairs. In the Third Pillar Council, the Government is represented either by the Minister of Interior or by the Minister of Justice depending on the subject-matter. From the beginning of 2005, the Minister responsible for EU integration affairs is assisted by two independent Offices under his supervision, of which one is the Office for National Development (dealing with the programming and implementation of the EC aid scheme in Hungary), and the other is the Office for European Affairs (dealing with the management of EU affairs in Hungary in general). Both are headed by a titular secretary of state. Finally, as far as strategic questions in terms of EU matters are concerned a Government Cabinet for EU issues has been established in early 2005. It is headed by the Prime Minister and of which five other key Ministers are members of it.[44]

3.2 Control by the national parliament over decisions taken by Ministers in the Council of the EU

The Hungarian model as it was finally introduced can be considered a medium-strong solution. Our regime is similar to the Austrian, Finnish and Danish approach, although with some specific characteristics. As far as the new Member States are concerned, the Hungarian model is very similar to the Slovenian model and to some extent to the models in the Baltic States. The details can be summarized as follows.

As explored above, the Hungarian Parliament amended the national Constitution in December 2002 by passing Act No. LXI of 2002. Article 6(2) of the amending Act introduced a new provision into the Hungarian Constitution:

> Article 35/A (1) The detailed rules on the controlling powers of Parliament and its committees over the Government in European integration affairs, on the consultation

[43] See Government Decree No. 334/2004 (XII.23) on the competences and powers of the Minister responsible for EU coordination. It should be noted that regional planning and policy-making has been placed under the supervision of a new minister without portfolio at who is responsible for these issues at the Prime Minister's Office. Therefore, from the end of 2004 this sector no longer forms part of the horizontal coordination of EU matters in Hungary.

[44] See Government Resolution No. 1022/2005 (III.10) on the establishment of the Government Cabinet for EU matters. For further literature on these issues see Imre Forgács, 'Megoldott-e az európai ügyek kormányzati koordinációja' [Has the Government coordination of EU matters been solved?], 3 *Európai Jog* [Journal of European Law] (2005) pp. 33-39.

procedure between the Parliament and the Government, and on the obligations of the Government to provide information to the Parliament in this context shall be determined by an Act, for the adoption of which a two-thirds majority of the Members of Parliament present during the voting is required. (2) The Government shall send to Parliament all the proposals on the agenda in the decision-making procedures of the institutions of the EU in which the Member State governments participate.

Following the constitutional authorization referred to above, Parliament on 17 May 2004 passed Act No. LIII of 2004 on the cooperation of the Parliament and the Government in European Union affairs (hereinafter: Parliamentary Control Act). This Act entered into force on 24 June 2004 and can be summarized as follows.

First of all, it should be emphasized that there were neither constitutional traditions, nor public law roots available in Hungary prior to regulating on the subject-matter. Therefore it was important to consider the relevant experiences of the "old Member States", in particular of those Member States that were admitted to the EU in the framework of the previous (1995) enlargement process. Secondly, all the political parties represented in Parliament agreed that there was a political necessity to find the necessary compromise that finally led to the adoption of the Parliamentary Control Act, despite the fact that it was primarily in the interest of the opposition parties to have this regulatory scheme in place on time.

From an academic point of view, one of the most important parts of the Parliamentary Control Act is its Preamble which reads as follows:

By virtue of article 35/A of the Constitution, in order to promote cooperation between the Parliament and the Government in EU affairs and for the fulfilment of the interests of the Republic of Hungary – in line with the Protocol attached to the Treaty of Amsterdam on the role of the national Parliaments in the EU, and the efforts of the EU to ensure a larger role for national parliaments – Parliament hereby passes the following Act establishing detailed rules concerning the Parliament's authority to exercise control over European integration affairs, consultation with the Government, and the obligation of the Government to provide information.

This appears to be a clear message from the legislator that when enacting this Act it took into the consideration the relevant developments in the IGC elaborating the Treaty establishing a Constitution for Europe.[45]

---

[45] See Treaty establishing a Constitution for Europe, *OJ* 2004 C 310/3 (hereinafter referred to as: the new EU Constitution), in particular the following relevant parts of the Constitution: (i) Art. I-11 (fundamental principles), especially the following sentence: 3. The institutions of the Union shall apply the principle of subsidiarity as laid down in the Protocol on the application of the principles of subsidiarity and proportionality. National parliaments shall ensure compliance with that principle in

For the purposes of this contribution, the following provisions of the Parliamentary Control Act are considered relevant:

(a) Article 1(2) gives special decision-making powers to the standing parliamentary committee on EU affairs in the following manner: Unless provided otherwise in this Act, the parliamentary standing committee dealing with European Union affairs shall have the power to decide matters in the procedure concerning drafts of the EU specified in this Act. This means that the committee can make decisions on behalf of Parliament except in those cases where the Parliamentary Control Act *expressis verbis* requires a plenary session of the House. So far, no cases concerning the application of this provision have yet arisen.

(b) Article 2 of the Parliamentary Control Act is also crucial as it obliges the Government to send to Parliament all EU documents "immediately after receipt", "including any other document if and when requested by Parliament".

(c) Further, the Parliamentary Control Act obliges the Government to indicate all EU drafts which it considers to be of particular importance for Parliament, namely documents, (a) referring to a subject for which the Constitution required that implementing legislation be passed by a qualified majority of Parliament, (b) referring to the determination of the contents of fundamental rights and/or obligations laid down in the Constitution, or of the essential guarantees for their enforcement, (c) or including any provision clearly conflicting with Acts of Parliament in force (Art. 2(3)). The Government is also required to attach an explanatory note to such EU proposals – or indeed to any other documents for which Parliament so requests – indicating the draft position which it intends to present in the Council (the obligatory contents of such an explanatory note are described in Art. 3(3) and (4) of the Act). An important guarantee is that "The Government shall send its proposed position to Parliament at a date enabling consultations upon the merits considering the EU's agenda for decision-making".

(d) The consultation procedure is an optional instrument in the hands of Parliament (or rather of the standing parliamentary committee on EU affairs), and not compulsory in all cases (i.e., necessarily applying to all EU documents sent by the Government). The committee decides by a simple majority whether the consultation procedure shall be put in motion either on the proposal of its President or on the request of two-fifths of the committee's members, with the interesting

accordance with the procedure set out in the Protocol, (ii) the First Protocol attached to the Constitution on national parliaments, and (iii) Arts. III-257-277.

restriction, however, that the two-fifths can only initiate the procedure four times per year.[46]

(e) It should also be stressed that in the framework of a consultation procedure the committee must hear the Government's position *in camera* and all documents received by the committee in this respect must be kept confidential.[47] These rules seem to have been insufficiently considered from the point of view of the principles of transparency and of participation. What must the citizens of Hungary think if the standing parliamentary committee on EU affairs always sits *in camera* and ignores in its work the implementation of the principle of transparency? It should also be mentioned that the national Parliament (including parliamentary committees, etc.) is also a lobbying forum in terms of EU decision-making for the national interest groups and/or NGOs, trade unions, chambers of commerce and other organizations representing business, etc. Not to mention the new EU Constitution, which specifically stresses the transparency principle as regards the work of the Council.[48]

(f) The Parliament's position is not legally binding upon the Government, but Article 4 of the Parliamentary Control Act establishes a very strict controlling system, namely that: (i) Prior to the Council meeting deciding on the adoption of the EU draft measure, the responsible Minister or State Secretary shall appear before Parliament at the request of Parliament and shall expound the position which the Government intends to represent at the Council meeting (Art. 4(3)), and that (ii) The Government shall elaborate its position to be represented in the decision-making process of the EU taking into account the standpoint of Parliament as a starting point (Art. 4(4)), and (iii) If the draft of the EU covers a subject whose regulation requires a qualified majority vote of Parliament by virtue of the Constitution, the Government may deviate from the standpoint of Parliament only in justified cases (Art. 4(5)). Articles 5 to 7 of the Parliamentary Control Act further impose a permanent obligation on the Government to regularly inform Parliament concerning all developments that may occur in relation to the EU law-making processes.

(g) Another interesting provision is Article 8 of the Parliamentary Control Act providing that The Government shall make the proposal to the respective institutions of the EU concerning Hungarian nominees for the Commission, the

---

[46] See Art. 134/B (2)-(3) of the rules of procedures of the Hungarian Parliament as amended by Parliamentary Resolution No. 47/2004 (V.18), Art. 4, entered into force on 24 June 2004.

[47] See Art. 134/A(3) of the rules of procedures of Parliament referred to above.

[48] See in this context, for example, Art. I-24(6) of the new EU Constitution.

European Court of Justice, the Court of First Instance, the Court of Auditors and the Board of Directors of the European Investment Bank, respectively. Parliament may only hear the person proposed by the Government. This means that there is no competition at all among Hungarian candidates to be proposed for the highest posts in the most important EU institutions, which seems regrettable as the present system might make nominations fully dependent on internal decision-making within the political parties.

Finally, the implementation of the Parliamentary Control Act shows a mixed picture. The standing parliamentary committee on EU integration affairs does not meet very frequently and over the past one and a half years a mere 18 consultation procedures (or Art. 134/B procedures) have been initiated, resulting by and large, after less than heavy debate, in the full acceptance of the Government position.

4. EUROPEAN CONSTITUTION

4.1 Impact of the EU Constitution on the Community legal order and accession

According to the official Hungarian position,[49] Hungary welcomes the Treaty establishing a Constitution for Europe as signed by the Member States in Rome on 29 October 2004 and seems ready to implement it. In the official commentaries on the new EU Constitution, the experts underline the following elements of the new EU Constitution as extremely positive from a Hungarian point of view:[50]

- As is well known, one of the most important points to be addressed by the IGC as far as Hungary was concerned was the protection of minority rights. Hungary made several proposals in this respect to the IGC. Finally a compromise was agreed upon among the Member States resulting in the present wording of Article I-2 of the Constitution under the heading of "The Union's values". It reads as follows: The Union is founded on the values of respect for human dignity, freedom, democracy, equality, the rule of law and respect for

[49] See Györkös Péter, 'Politikai megállapodás az Alkotmányos Szerződésről-az Ír elnökség mérlege' [Political compromise on the EU Constitutional Treaty – the results achieved under the Irish Presidency], *Európai Tükör*, Budapest 2004/4-5 (July-August) pp. 166-170.

[50] This heading of the national report is explored in more detail in another article by the present author, 'Some Points Concerning the EU Constitution from a Hungarian Perspective', in A.E. Kellermann, et al., eds., *The EU Constitution: The best way forward?* (The Hague, T.M.C. Asser Press 2005).

human rights, including the rights of persons belonging to minorities. These values are common to the Member States in a society in which pluralism, non-discrimination, tolerance, solidarity and equality between women and man prevail. These words, although not completely satisfactory on the protection of minority rights, were under the given circumstances the maximum achievable result for the Hungarian delegation. It is clear, however, that the text rejects any collective rights approach by only speaking of "rights of persons belonging to minorities" and makes it insufficiently clear whether the provision in question concerns ethnic or national minorities or both, while this was in fact the main Hungarian concern. Instead, the provision merely uses the vague term "minorities" which could include any type of minority ranging from Muslims, to Roma, to groups with different sexual orientations. This was not the Hungarian aim in terms of its original proposals on this question, but nevertheless Article I-2 is more than nothing.

- Some Hungarian scholars also welcome Article I-5(1) in the new EU Constitution, which reads as follows: The Union shall respect the equality of Member States before the Constitution as well as their national identities, inherent in their fundamental structures, political and constitutional, inclusive of regional and local self-government. It shall respect their essential State functions, including ensuring the territorial integrity of the State, maintaining law and order and safeguarding national security. This is an important commitment to Hungary, as perhaps to most other new Member States, in the light of avoiding any possible scenario of what has been termed second-class membership, which is one of the main fears in the countries of Central and Eastern Europe.

- Also welcomed in Hungary is Article I-26(5) of the new EU Constitution which reads as follows: The first Commission appointed under the provisions of the Constitution (that means from 2009) shall consist of one national of each Member State, including its President and the Union Minister for Foreign Affairs who shall be one of its Vice-Presidents. This is a great victory for all smaller Member States, and we must not forget that out of the ten new Member States, nine are small, the only "large" one being Poland.

- Another very important provision is Article I-11.2, in particular where it reads as follows: Competences not conferred upon the Union in the Constitution remain with the Member States. It is the first time that this important principle is declared expressis verbis at primary law treaty level.

- Hungary may also welcome Chapter III of Part I of the new EU Constitution dealing with “enhanced cooperation”. It is particularly welcome that (i) Enhanced cooperation shall be open at any time to all Member States, in accordance with Article III-418 (Art. I-44(1), second indent), that (ii) Acts adopted in the framework of enhanced cooperation shall bind only participating States. They shall not be regarded as an acquis which has to be accepted by candidates for accession to the Union (Art. I-44(4)), and that (iii) The Commission and the Member States participating in enhanced cooperation shall ensure that they promote participation by as many Member States as possible (Art. III-418(1), second indent, and Articles III-416-423). This last element is brand new, but extremely important for the purpose of the principle of solidarity and of the “catching-up doctrine”.

Some critical observations concerning the new EU Constitution:

- First of all, the title of the new EU re-founding Treaty is somewhat unfortunate. The Treaty cannot be considered a “Constitution” primarily because the EU is not a state (or a federation), and secondly it is not useful from a sociological and/or psychological point of view to label a document a Constitution when it is not one. Another issue is that of the political, moral and legal grounds based on which this (re-)founding Treaty addresses “Europe” as a whole when the EU has only 25 Member States which could not aspire to regulating matters for the remaining countries of Europe (for example, there are currently 46 countries that are members of the Council of Europe).

- Another point of criticism is that the Treaty is in fact a constitutional cocktail. Essentially, only Parts I and II are of a constitutional nature and significance, whereas the Parts III and IV are of a founding Treaty character. It would have been better to make the first two Parts into a separate Constitutional Charter (perhaps annexed to the main Treaty as a Protocol), while Parts III-IV could have continued to form a multilateral founding Treaty.

- A further weakness of this Constitution is that it does not set out any definitions at the beginning. Finally, as far as Part III is concerned, its contents and wording are even more complex and sophisticated than those of the current EC Treaty, which means that in this respect the goal set out in the Laeken Declaration on the future of Europe, which was to make the new Treaty a simpler instrument in terms of language, style, etc., and make it better understandable for the citizens of Europe seems not to have realized.

4.2 Obstacles in the national constitution or national legal order to the ratification of the European Constitution

In Hungary, the Constitution did not call for a nationwide referendum which is why Parliament could rapidly, just shortly after Lithuania, ratify the new EU Constitution by a majority of over 95 per cent on 20 December 2004 (Parliamentary Resolution No. 133/2004 (XII. 23)).

LATVIA

Anita Ušacka*

The European Union (EU) represents a new model of supranational governance which is groundbreaking in its structure and in its impact on national sovereignty. On the one hand, the EU is a product of state sovereignty because each Member State voted for voluntary inclusion in the Union. On the other hand, the supranational institutions created by the EU can make decisions which supersede the power of the states in areas of traditional state autonomy. Some Member States have proceeded to EU membership without modifying governing legal texts which seem to contradict the legality of EU membership. However, the Latvian Government and judiciary were concerned to ensure that Latvia's founding document, the Constitution (*Satversme*) would reflect the jurisprudential idea of transfer of power to a supranational governing body, while maintaining its constitutional integrity.[1] This article describes the process, impact and effects of Latvia's EU accession on the structural imperatives and actual text of the Constitution.

1. CONSTITUTIONAL ORDER BEFORE ACCESSION TO THE EU

Numerous amendments, both minor and extensive, have been made to the Constitution of Latvia since its initial adoption. The Latvian Constitution was adopted by the Constitutional Convention of Latvia in 1922 but was suspended during the 50 years during which Latvia remained a *de facto* Soviet Republic. The Constitution was partly renewed in 1990 and fully renewed in 1993 to re-establish Latvia as an independent constitutional democracy. Unlike the other countries in Eastern Europe which were faced with the task of creating new modern Constitutions

* Professor Anita Ušacka, Ph.D., Judge of the International Criminal Court, former Judge of the Constitutional Court of the Republic of Latvia.

[1] See Anita Ušacka, 'The Impact of the European Integration Process on the Constitution of Latvia', in A.E. Kellermann, et al., eds., *EU Enlargement: The Constitutional Impact at EU and National Level* (The Hague, T.M.C. Asser Press 2001) at pp. 337-346. See also Anita Ušacka, 'Direct Democracy in Latvia. Country Report', in A. Auer and M. Bützer, eds., *Direct Democracy: The Eastern and Central European Experience* (Aldershot, Ashgate 2001) at pp. 94-108.

upon gaining independence from the Soviet Republic, Latvia was able to renew its 1922 Constitution, and subsequently apply changes to this document.

The Constitution is a short Constitution containing 116 articles composed of laconic language embodying the paradigm of democratic principles and legal traditions which emerged in the beginning of the 20th century. Between 1993 and 2003, there were four minor amendments to the Latvian Constitution and two substantial amendments. The most important amendments include the amendment creating the Constitutional Court in 1996 and the new Chapter VIII, "Fundamental Rights", added in 1998.[2] The 1998 amendment provides important political, constitutional, social, economic and cultural rights and enshrines human rights provisions within Latvia's Constitution.

On 4 May 1990, Latvia adopted the "Declaration of Restoration of Independence of the Republic of Latvia" restoring independence through a transition period[3] and on 21 August 1992, the Latvian Supreme Council adopted a Constitutional Law restoring full independence for the Republic of Latvia.[4] Latvia, like many of the former socialist states of Central and Eastern Europe, embarked upon a far-reaching transition programme to forge political and economic ties with Western Europe and to re-enter modern Europe as an independent state with respect for international human rights standards. Latvia joined the United Nations and the OSCE in 1991. Latvia joined the Council of Europe on 10 February 1995. In March 2004, Latvia became a member of NATO.

2. EU ACCESSION AND THE DEMAND FOR CONSTITUTIONAL REVISION

Latvia was among the first countries to declare its intent to join the European Union when the Union declared itself open to new members. EU accession negotiations began in February 2000 and were finished in 2002. On 16 April 2003 an accession treaty was signed and on 1 May 2004 Latvia became one of the newest Member States of the enlarged European Union.

[2] Ilona Ceica and Ligita Vasermane, 'Latvian Law Guide', 31 *Int'l J. Legal Info.* (2003) p. 20. Note that access to constitutional review serves a function specific to transitional democracies in allowing for the resolution of ambiguity in certain constitutional provisions, thus ideally avoiding constitutional crises.

[3] 1990. gada 4. maija Deklarācija par Latvijas Republikas neatkarības atjaunošanu // Cilvēka tiesības. Likumdošanas aktu un informatīvo materiālu krājums. Latvijas Republikas 6. Saeimas Cilvēktiesību un sabiedrisko lietu komisija, 1997.

[4] 1991. gada 10. decembra konstitucionālais likums "Cilvēka un pilsoņa tiesības un pienākumi" // Cilvēka tiesības. Likumdošanas aktu un informatīvo materiālu krājums. Latvijas Republikas 6. Saeimas Cilvēktiesību un sabiedrisko lietu komisija, 1997, 18.-21. lpp. (176 lpp.).

As early as 1995, Latvia agreed to certain obligations to ensure the approximation of the legislation of Latvia to the legislation of the European Union. The Europe Agreement, signed in 1995, established an association between the European Community (EC) and its Member States. Article 69 of the Europe Agreement signed between the EC and the Republic of Latvia[5] states:

> The Parties recognize that an important condition for Latvia's economic integration into the Community is the approximation of Latvia's existing and future legislation to that of the Community. Latvia shall endeavor to ensure that its legislation will be gradually made compatible with that of the Community.

Advancement of Latvia towards the European Union clearly demanded the approximation of Latvian legal principles and norms to those existing in the European Union. The first discussions on approximation revolved around necessary changes to Latvian legislation. Though the Europe Agreement was signed in 1995, real discussion on the required constitutional amendments did not start until 2000. In August 2000, the Latvian Prime Minister decreed the creation of a special working group, to work through 1 March 2001 drafting amendments to the Constitution relating to EU accession. The working group was composed of representatives from Parliament, the Ministries of Justice and Foreign Affairs, the European Integration Bureau, the State Chancellery and the Constitutional Court and was headed by the Minister of Justice. Once the working group began talking about constitutional changes, debate ensued regarding whether legal approximation under the Europe Agreement would require changes to the Constitution, and if Constitutional changes were necessary and how best to align Latvia's Constitution with the requirements of EU accession.

Of particular concern to the working group, and to all constitutional democracies facing EU accession, was the question of whether a general or specific constitutional basis existed regarding the possibility of accession to the European Union.[6] Renewal of the Constitution embodied a reaffirmation of the principle of Latvian national sovereignty, as expressly stated in Article 2 of the Constitution of Latvia which states that "The sovereign power of the State of Latvia is vested in the people of Latvia." It was the task of the working group to determine the extent to which language and structure of the Constitution would require amendment in order to properly adapt to the required transfer of competences to the EU.

---

[5] 'Europe Agreement establishing an association between the European Communities and their Member States, of the one part, and the Republic of Latvia, of the other part', signed 12 June 1995, *Latvijas Vestensis*, 12 June 1995, No. 138.

[6] See generally, Cardozo Law Review Symposium, 'Peaceful Transitions to Constitutional Democracy: Transcript of the Proceedings', 19 *Cardozo L. Rev.* (1998) p. 1953.

At the same time, the working group was responsible for preserving the democratic intent and principle embodied in the original text of the Constitution.[7]

The changing definition of sovereignty and the evolution through globalization of a form of shared sovereignty added to the controversy surrounding the transfer of competences from Member States to EU institutions. At issue in the context of EU accession are two principal concepts of sovereignty. On the one hand is sovereignty as legally and classically defined from the times of Roman law through the French Revolution, involving rights to be exercised only by the sovereign over his or her domain composed of the right to impose an expected solution within the sovereign's boundaries, or the right to have the last word in a conflict involving the sovereign's nation. On the other hand is a newly developing concept of shared or international sovereignty as framed within the EU Treaties. Sovereignty of the classical type involving unilateral and isolationist economic, political and social power[8] no longer exists in any of the EU Member States. The growing strength and size of the European Union represents a new mode of governance and a new form of sovereignty. EU law becomes part of internal mechanisms as national courts enforce EU law. At the same time, because EU law emanates from treaties enacted among sovereign states, it carries attributes of international law. EU law has even acquired constitutional status, even in the absence of a formal constitutional document, which the EU is currently drafting, as a number of Member States have amended their Constitutions to incorporate reference to the Union. This evolution represents a groundbreaking innovation wherein a form of constitutionalism has been created without a corresponding state and without a sole constitutional document. This "international sovereignty" creates limits on Member States' discretionary powers through the transfer of the common exercise of powers from individual states to EU institutions.

Constitutional powers which were previously exercised solely within each Member State are now functions of the EU. Among other powers, the EU holds the capacity to establish governing organs, protect private autonomy, provide for democratic participation and to operate with supremacy over other legal norms. Much has been written on the matters of supremacy and direct effect of EU law, as they pose a visible evolution in the transfer of sovereign powers to the EU. While EU law has been established as supreme over the laws of the Member States and has consistently been applied by national courts to strike down conflicting national legislation, the reverse does not hold true.

---

[7] See Anita Ušacka, 'The Impact of the European Integration Process on the Constitution of Latvia', in A.E. Kellermann, et al., eds., *EU Enlargement: the Constitutional Impact at EU and National Level* (The Hague, T.M.C. Asser Press 2001) at pp. 337-346.

[8] See generally, Joshua Bardavid, 'The Failure of the State-Centric Model of International Law and the International Criminal Court', 15 *N.Y. Int'l L. Rev.* (2002) p. 9.

The other Constitutions of the EU Member States embody a variety of approaches to the issue of transfer of power to the EU. For example, the Constitutions of Germany and Sweden[9] contain express limits regarding the transfer of national competences while the Constitution of Finland contained no constitutional permission for the transfer of sovereign power and required amendment.[10] The text of the Constitution in Article 68 simply stated that "All international agreements, which settle matters that may be decided by the legislative process, shall require ratification by the *Saeima*." Furthermore, Article 68 of the Constitution and Article 13 of the 1994 "Law on International Agreements of the Republic of Latvia" create a hierarchy of laws to be applied by the national courts wherein international norms are of a higher legal force than national ones, with the exception of the Constitution. Though the language of the Constitution provided a strong framework for the functioning of a traditional constitutional democracy, the original 1922 language was insufficient to incorporate the limitations on sovereignty imposed by EU accession and would require revision.

2.1 Main problems of the constitutional revision

Several means of constitutional revision were possible and much debate and discussion arose regarding which type of amendment would be best. When determining how to amend the Constitution to reflect Latvia's EU accession, two primary types of amendment were suggested – one extensive and one more minimalist. The extensive proposal involved amending several Articles of the Constitution as well as supplementing the Constitution with a new Chapter on membership of Latvia in the EU. An advantage of this proposal would be the possibility of incorporating Latvia's strong tradition of normative regulations. Had a new Chapter been added, it might have been placed after Chapter VIII and might have provided greater direction and regulation regarding the restrictions involved in the transfer of authority to EU institutions and the connections between the rights and principles of the EU and the Latvian legal system, among other vital issues.[11]

---

[9] See Rainer Arnold, 'National Sovereignty and the European Union', European Commission for Democracy Through Law (Venice Commission) Seminar on "The Implications of the New Century and Striving to Join European Structures for Constitutional Courts", 17-18 November 2000, Tartu, Estonia, at para. 2.

[10] Finland's entry into the Common Market in 1995 was effectuated on the basis of an international treaty whereby the transfer of sovereign powers was made possible for a State as a result of its sovereignty. The constitutional reform of 1 March 2000 introduced a provision into the Finnish Constitution which shows that the Constitution incorporates membership of the EU. Idem at para. 2.

[11] See *supra* n. 7.

A more minimalist path might have involved the addition of a short supplementary phrase or clause to the Constitution which would simply state that Latvia is a Member State of the European Union.[12] The advantage of this minimalist path would be the possibility of maintaining constitutional stability while retaining the precision and laconic language of the basic law.

Another alternative included the passing of constitutional laws, such as the "Law on the Rights of Persons" which had provided a human rights framework before the creation of Chapter VIII of the Constitution. The proposed adoption of a special constitutional law which would make amendments to the basic text of the Constitution redundant did not conform to any legal tradition in Latvia nor does the Constitution envisage such a measure. It was considered undesirable to implement such an important step as EU accession through the passing of a constitutional law – a method without a solid historical or constitutional basis in Latvia.

Another proposal involved the adoption of a new Constitution. Some believed that the Constitution, adopted more than 80 years ago, did not reflect the dramatic changes Latvia has undergone, for example, in its lack of a Chapter or Article dedicated to local authorities. The possibility of adopting a new Constitution was envisaged in Article 4 of the "Declaration on the Renewal of the Independence of the Republic of Latvia" of 4 May 1990. Though Article 4 of the Declaration was never formally repealed, it was never implemented either and finally, the 1922 Constitution was fully restored and cancelled this proposal. It was recognized that a new Constitution could not be created in such a short time. In the end, the proposal to adopt a new Constitution was never taken very seriously.

Interpretation offered another means of revision. After the restoration of independence, all branches of the Latvian Government started to study the field of interpretation. Under Soviet rule all norms were strictly regulated by a central authority, which catalogued all rights and prohibitions. This meant that the doctrine of interpretation had been taboo – legal practitioners could only interpret norms in the way condoned by the central authority and as legal interpretation was not taught in schools interpretation was effectively eradicated as a tool of legal analysis. During the post-independence period, the use of interpretation was increasingly applied through the analysis of case law of the European Court of Human Rights (ECtHR). The case law of the ECtHR was used by the Latvian Executive Branch in applying the law and by Latvian courts in analysing conflict of laws. Interpretation of constitutional language offers a means of changing legal norms without the implementation of literal changes to the text of the Constitution. Interpretation is required for all cases in which legal norms must be applied, however, to apply norms which change the structure of a Constitution through interpretation might have been seen as usurping democratic functions. Judicial

12 As suggested by Egils Levits, 'The Satversme and the European Union'.

interpretation is an effective method of bringing the Constitution into line with developing norms; however, it could not provide the full answer regarding Latvia's accession to the EU.

If a normative basis did not exist within the Constitutions of the EU Member States it has been created to allow for the transfer of internal competences from the Member State to the Community level. In the case of the Latvian Constitution, the first four Articles establish the independence and democratic integrity of Latvia in language which debatably did not allow for the transfer of designated powers to the EU. The fundamental constitutional norm of Latvia stated in Article 1 of the Constitution holds that "Latvia is an independent democratic republic." This Article contains two elements. The first is "independence"– an element directed outwards to the international legal sphere and maintaining that Latvia shall be an independent state. The second element is directed inwards towards the national constitutional legal sphere – holding that Latvia shall be a democratic state. Within this framework, Latvia would lose part of its defined independence within the meaning of Article 1 of the Constitution upon becoming an EU Member State. Upon joining the EU, Latvia transfers part of its competence to the Union, requiring a modification of the concept of "independence" within Article 1 of the Constitution.[13]

Article 2 of the Constitution states that "The sovereign power of the State of Latvia is vested in the people of Latvia." Varying views have been expressed on the necessity of amending Article 2 in anticipation of EU accession. Some argued that Article 2 must be amended to reflect the fact that upon accession, supreme power would no longer belong solely to the Latvian people but also to the institutions of the European Union.[14]

The process of preparing for EU membership demanded that Latvia address whether the Constitution contained the basis to allow for the transfer of certain agreed upon competences to the institutions of the EU. The question was posed whether it was necessary to amend the constitutional text of Articles 1 and 2 of the Constitution, a document with more than half a century of history, with language containing the very essence of the democratic structure of the Republic of Latvia.

2.1.1 *EU law and supremacy*

The EU is based upon international agreements between its members which remain separate states, but voluntarily subordinate themselves to the Union in certain spheres. The operative language creating the EU and its institutions does not demand that the Member States relinquish their independence. However, the

---

13 See *supra* n. 7.

14 'On Essential Amendments to our Satverseme' by Arnis Buka, student of the Faculty of Law of Latvian University. *Latvijas Vestnesis*, 2 March 2000, No. 71/72.

full functioning of the EU is dependent on the Member States voluntarily surrendering power in certain designated spheres. The normative order of the EU depends on a relationship with the legal orders of the Member States which is not coercive yet is hierarchical. As a result, Member States must divide powers once exercised solely by the sovereign nation. Naturally, this raises problems regarding the limits of power of the EU and the Member States. Through a string of seminal cases,[15] the Court of Justice has indicated the supremacy of EU law over Member State law and even over Member State Constitutions. The lack, heretofore, of a clear statement of the primacy of European Law in the Treaties underscores the importance of judicial interpretation in creating a legal order which grants supreme authority to EU institutions.[16]

In conjunction with the principle of supremacy, the doctrine of direct effect further diminishes traditional sovereignty within the EU Member States. The doctrine of direct effect confers the rights and obligations of EU law upon Member State nationals, not just upon the states, meaning that the legislation passed by the EU has the actual authority to effect change in Member States, and reigns supreme over the national acts of its Member States. In the pivotal *Van Gend en Loos* decision the Court proclaimed that:

> The conclusion to be drawn [...] is that the Community constitutes a new legal order of international law for the benefit of which the states have limited their sovereign rights, albeit within limited fields, and the subjects of which comprise not only Member States but also their nationals. Independently of the legislation of Member States, Community law therefore not only imposes obligations on individuals but is also intended to confer upon them rights which become part of their legal heritage.[17]

---

[15] See Case 11/70, *Internationale Handelsgesellschaft* [1972] *CMLR* 255 (1970) wherein the ECJ held that "the validity of a Community measure or its effect within a Member State cannot be affected by allegations that it runs counter to either fundamental rights as formulated by the Constitution of that State or the principles of a national constitutional structure." See also Case 6/64 *Costa* v. *Enel* [1964] *ECR* 1141: "The transfer by the states from their domestic legal systems to the Community legal system of the rights and obligations arising under the Treaty carries with it a permanent limitation of their sovereign rights, against which a subsequent unilateral act incompatible with the concept of the Community cannot prevail."

[16] The wording used to indicate the supremacy of an EU Constitution as currently contained in part I, Art. 10 of the Draft Constitution reads as follows: "The Constitution, and law adopted by the Union's Institutions in exercising competences conferred on it, shall have primacy over the law of the Member States." Draft Treaty establishing a Constitution for Europe, adopted by consensus by the European Convention on 13 June and 10 July 2003, submitted to the President of the European Council in Rome on 18 July 2003 (hereinafter Draft Treaty), available at: <http://europa.eu.int/futurum/constitution/index_en.htm>, pt. I, Art. 10. In case there was any remaining doubt, this statement asserts EU supremacy over Member States' law notwithstanding any provisions to the contrary in the Constitutions of the Member States.

[17] Case 26/62 *Van Gend en Loos* [1963] *CMLR* 105.

In its confirmation that the EU (at that time still the EEC) constitutes a "new legal order" the ECJ did more than to promulgate the doctrine of direct effect.[18] This judgment marked a shift in the language and interpretation of the EC/EU treaties from an international agreement among Governments to a *de facto* Constitution. A number of cases in the 1970s made it clear that citizens could rely on EC Regulations and partially on Directives as much as they relied on the Treaties.[19] The emergent power imbued in the Treaties and most EC/EU legislation has the same binding nature upon citizens and Governments as a Constitution and actually supersedes any Member State Constitution. Article 234 of the Treaty of Nice gives power to the Member State courts to refer issues of Community law to the ECJ for interpretation.[20] The combined effect of these statements, among other consequences, is that the Constitutional Court of the Republic of Latvia ceases to be the court of last instance since Latvia's joining the EU and the Latvian Constitution is no longer the final word on individual rights within Latvia.

The Constitutional Court of Latvia is currently hearing a case directly concerning the hierarchy of laws and Latvian legislative compliance with international law. In January 2004, the Constitutional Court agreed to hear a petition submitted by a judge of one of the courts of general jurisdiction concerning the perceived non-compliance of a provision of the Latvian Code of Administrative Violations and the United Nations Convention on Facilitation of International Maritime Traffic.[21] The official response of the Latvian Parliament, issued by procedural requirement to the Constitutional Court, disagreed with the position of the petitioning judge. The Latvian Parliament asserts, among other arguments, that the disputed Article of the Latvian Code of Administrative Violations conforms to an EU Directive on maritime traffic.[22] The case, which

---

[18] The term "direct effect" was coined in the Court's statement that, "It follows from the foregoing considerations that [Article 12 of] the Treaty [...] must be interpreted as producing direct effects and creating individual rights which national courts must protect." Idem. The court indicated that EU provisions should be given direct effect by national courts, having impact on private individuals as well as the state, provided that the provisions meet the following conditions: (i) the provision must be clear and unambiguous; (ii) it must be unconditional; (iii) it must be intended to be operational in Member States without further implementation. Idem.

[19] Art. 189 of the Treaties outlines the types of legislation used in the EU. A Regulation has binding force directly, as issued, in the Member States. A Regulation is not modified and/or "implemented" by Member State Governments. It is immediate law as passed by the EU governing bodies. A Directive, on the other hand, leaves the form and method of implementation of the law up to the discretion of the Member State Governments. This generally means that Member State Governments must formally pass the Directive into law.

[20] Treaty of Nice, *OJ* 2002 C 325/1, 127.

[21] United Nations Convention on Facilitation of International Maritime Traffic, London (9 April 1965) available at: <http://www.admiraltylawguide.com/conven/facilitation1965.html>.

[22] This case concerns Art. 114(2) of the Latvian Code of Administrative Violations which imposes a large fine on a transport company which, knowingly or unknowingly, provides transportation into Latvia for an individual travelling without valid border-crossing documents. The petitioner

will be decided in the coming year, highlights the growing importance of the new legal order and the complex questions of hierarchy of laws facing the Latvian judiciary.

2.1.2 *The principle of subsidiarity*

One substantive strategy to limit the central power of the EU has been through the concept of "subsidiarity"[23] which provides that when the EU does not have exclusive jurisdiction, the EU will act only if the Member States cannot achieve the objectives of a proposed action. According to one theorist the principle of subsidiarity was imposed within the EU legal order in an attempt to stop the "flow of centralisation that the dynamics of integration had imposed on the material division of powers between the Community and the Member States."[24] By this analysis, subsidiarity is meant to function as a countervailing influence to pervasive EU supremacy. In a more general sense, application of the principle of subsidiarity was meant to ensure that EU decisions were made at the most appropriate level.

The principle of subsidiarity offers a framework for arranging institutional hierarchy within the Community as well as a means of delimitation of competences between the European Communities and the Member States. Given the broad applicability of this principle, the definition and parameters of subsidiarity must be made more precise to enhance its practical application as a means to achieve a stable power dynamic between the EU and the Member States.

2.2 **The problem of referendum**

The first four Articles in the first Chapter of the Constitution form the basis for Latvian independence and democracy and establish the principle that Latvia is an independent state. The doctrine of supremacy and direct effect, even if partially limited by the application of subsidiarity, necessarily impinges upon state sovereignty, as traditionally defined. As strict adherence to these Articles, which delimit the sovereignty of the Republic of Latvia, has been crucial to the democratic

---

asserts that this Article of the Latvian Code of Administrative Violations conflicts with Arts. 5 and 8 of the United Nations Convention on Facilitation of International Maritime Traffic which requires that any Government party to the Convention will inform the UN Secretary-General should the Government bring its own formalities differing from the standards set forth in the Convention.

[23] Art. 3b of the EC Treaty defines the principle of subsidiarity. Treaty on European Union, 7 February 1992, *OJ* 1992 C 224/1, 191.

[24] Antonio Goucha Soares, 'Pre-emption, Conflicts of Powers and Subsidiarity', 23 *ELR* (1998) at p. 135. See also Christoph Henkel, 'The Allocation of Powers in the European Union: A Closer Look at the Principle of Subsidiarity', 20 *Berkeley J. Int'l L.* (2002) p. 359. See also *supra* n. 9, at para. 5.

operation of the state, amendments to these four Articles could only occur by referendum. The concept of public referendum, a political reform created in the early 20th century[25] and incorporated into the original language of the Constitution upon its adoption in 1922, allows for direct participation of citizens in their government, and in this respect reflects a fundamental concept of democracy. A referendum on accession to the EU is clearly mandatory under the provisions and the essence of the Constitution, as demonstrated by the language of Article 77 of the Latvian Constitution. Article 77 states that the *Saeima* must submit any amendments to the first, second, third, fourth, sixth, or seventy-seventh Articles of the Constitution to a national referendum. Prior to the 2003 amendments to the Constitution, there were only four types of popular referendum, none of which created a parliamentary or governmental right to formulate the issue of referendum regarding accession to the EU.[26]

The four types of referendum contained in the text of the Constitution before 2003 were as follows. First, as stated in Article 77 of the Constitution: "If the *Saeima* has amended the first, second, third, fourth, sixth or 77th Article of the Constitution, such amendments, in order to enter into force, shall be submitted to a national referendum." Pursuant to this Article, the *Saeima* must hold a popular vote to approve such amendments, thus this is called an obligatory referendum. Second, according to Articles 48 and 50 of the Constitution, if the President has initiated the dissolution of the *Saeima*, an obligatory referendum must follow to determine whether the *Saeima* shall be dissolved. Third, if, pursuant to Article 70, the President has suspended the promulgation of a law for a two-month period and the request of not less than one-tenth of the total electorate to submit the suspended law to a referendum was received during this period, then a national referendum may be held according to Article 74. This type of referendum is called the optional veto referendum. Finally, if the *Saeima* has not adopted the draft law or the draft amendments to the Constitution submitted by no less than one-tenth of the total electorate pursuant to Articles 78 and 79, a referendum will automatically occur upon the veto of the *Saeima*. None of these four instances allowed for the *Saeima* or the Government to submit a law to a referendum on their own initiative or to ask the electorate to answer a question formulated by the *Saeima* or Government through referendum. As a result, several proposed amendments to the Constitution were suggested to provide the electorate the right to vote upon EU accession and to address the question of how EU membership would affect Latvian sovereignty.

---

25 See Elizabeth Garrett, 'Issues in Implementing Referendums in Israel: a Comparative Study in Direct Democracy', 2 *Chi. J. Int'l L.* (2001) p. 159.

26 See *supra* n. 7.

One proposal involved the amendment of Article 73. Article 73 of the Constitution specifies which issues cannot be solved by a referendum, including agreements with other nations in its list of issues which may not be submitted for national referendum. Upon discussion, it was determined that the language of Article 73 did not require amendment as the membership in the EU did not constitute an agreement with foreign nations, as originally conceived in the drafting of Article 73, but rather an agreement with a supranational entity or an international organization.

An opposing opinion suggested that any amendment of the Constitution mentioning membership of Latvia in the European Union formally modifies the concept of "independence expressed in Article 1 and possibly the sense of sovereignty in Article 2 of the Constitution."[27] From this viewpoint, any such amendment should be submitted to a national referendum, as envisaged in Article 77 of the Constitution. It was suggested that if the constitutional amendments were formulated precisely, then two national referendums would not be necessary. Instead, it was proposed that as the people voted for or against the precisely formulated amendments to the Constitution, they would simultaneously vote on the issue of Latvia becoming a Member State of the European Union. Though this proposal was time efficient and well structured, it was not accepted as the means of amending the Latvian Constitution to envisage EU membership.

Several amendments proposed by opposition political parties would have substantially changed the status of a referendum vote in Latvia. Three primary amendments pertaining to referendum were proposed by opposition political parties but ultimately dismissed. One group supported the idea that Latvia's NATO membership should proceed along the same path as Latvia's EU accession, through a Latvian referendum on NATO membership and inclusion of the fact of Latvia's NATO membership in the Constitution. While proponents of this plan pointed out that Slovenia and Hungary both incorporated such changes upon joining NATO, the majority disagreed with the necessity of such measures. The majority was persuaded that considering the fundamental differences between joining the EU, a supranational organization with the power to promulgate and enforce legislation, versus joining NATO, an international organization with military goals which does not pass legal acts, NATO membership did not require a popular referendum or constitutional amendment. A second plan attempted to change the circumstances under which the people of Latvia could initiate a referendum with the intended goal of allowing citizens to initiate a referendum on EU accession. This plan was also not accepted as the majority was not persuaded that Constitutional Articles 1 and 2 require a public referendum on EU membership. A third suggested amendment to referendum laws would have allowed non-

[27] See *supra* n. 12.

citizens to participate in the referendum on EU accession. This proposal was dismissed as being contrary to the Constitution which gives citizens the voting power in a referendum. Though these changes were ultimately not incorporated in the Latvian concept of referendum, they exemplify the diversity of proposals and the rigorous debate which EU accession prompted in Latvia.

3. REVISION OF THE CONSTITUTION OF REPUBLIC OF LATVIA IN 2003

On 8 May 2003, the Parliament of Latvia approved amendments to the Constitution which came into force on 6 June 2003. These amendments secured the legal basis for transfer of state institution competences to international institutions and provided for a referendum on membership of Latvia in the EU.[28] Among the many proposed forms of amendment, the laconic proposal to amend only two Articles of the Constitution was accepted. It was agreed that amendment would proceed with changes to Article 68 and Article 79.

Article 68 retains the text of the 1922 Constitution stating that "All international agreements, which settle matters that may be decided by the legislative process, shall require ratification by the *Saeima*." The revisions of 2003 add 3 parts to Article 68 with the statements that:

> Upon entering into international agreement, Latvia, with the purpose of strengthening democracy, may delegate a part of its State institution competences to international institutions. International agreements in which part of the State institution competences are delegated to international institutions may be ratified by the *Saeima* in sittings in which at least two-thirds of the member of the *Saeima* participate, and a two-thirds majority vote of the members present is necessary for ratification.
>
> Membership of Latvia in the European Union shall be decided by a national referendum, which is proposed by the *Saeima*.
>
> Substantial changes in the terms regarding the membership of Latvia in the European Union shall be decided by a national referendum if such a referendum is requested by at least one-half of the members of the *Saeima*.

[28] Information and statistics from the Central Election Commission of Latvia web site, available at: <http://web.cvk.lv/pub/?doc_id=28427> (last visited 15 March 2004).

There are a number of primary characteristics to be noted in these amendments. The amendment to the Latvian Constitution in Article 68 states that "Latvia, with the purpose of strengthening democracy, may delegate a part of its State institution competences to international institutions." To delegate is defined as "to assign authority to another",[29] however authority is not so much wholly transferred as shared through the agreement to jointly determine economic, political and social matters throughout Europe. Given the great economic returns, not to mention the myriad other benefits of EU membership, the choice to retain formal national sovereignty by remaining outside of the Union does not compute. Instead, the Member States choose to exchange formal sovereignty for their place within a domain of "[s]hared, integrated and supra-nationalized sovereignty."[30]

The amendment within the first added part of Article 68 establishes that Latvia may enter into international agreements wherein state competences are delegated but only "with the purpose of strengthening democracy." Further, the transfer of state competences may only be to international institutions, not to foreign countries. This particular wording may be interpreted in part as a reaction to Latvia's decades under Soviet rule resulting in a determination not to transfer state power to another state or to transfer power if such transfer is not in furtherance of democratic principles. By increasing the ratification standards from a simple majority of the *Saeima* to a two-thirds majority, the drafters indicate the gravity and the need for a high threshold of approval for international agreements which will result in the transfer of state competences.

It has been noted that the word "delegate", which generally connotes a vertical assignment of power downwards, does not best reflect the action by which Latvia assigns certain competences to the EU, a supranational entity with areas of legal supremacy over the Member States. It would have been more accurate to state that Latvia, upon joining the EU, would "transfer" or "assign" certain competences to the EU. Unfortunately, those drafting the amendment chose to use a word with Latin roots – "delegate" – rather than using a word which might have held more contextual accuracy.

In part 2 of the amendment, the reality of the change proposed is made clear by the literal statement that it is membership in the EU which shall be addressed. Again, the seriousness of this step is affirmed by the requirement of a referendum, as a national vote is only required in limited and momentous cases. The context of the referendum is also stated clearly – that a referendum shall be held only when initiated by the *Saeima*.

---

29 *Merriam Webster Collegiate Dictionary of the English Language* (2003). See also *Bouviers Law Dictionary 1856 Edition*: "Delegation: The transfer of authority from one or more persons to one or more others."

30 See *supra* n. 9, at para. 3(c).

Finally, the use of the phrase "substantial changes in the terms regarding the membership of Latvia in the European Union" indicates that the drafters conceived of the entire spectrum of accession, from membership through withdrawal, as types of change which would require the vote by a national referendum, upon the request of at least one-half of the members of the *Saeima*. As cited in the Expert Paper by the Latvian Ministry of Justice, the language of the constitutional amendment incorporates the fact that both membership and withdrawal are at issue. While there are Treaty provisions concerning accession to the Union, and there are Treaty provisions relating to issues where a State is delinquent in its obligations arising under Union membership, there are no Treaty provisions concerning secession from the Union.[31] The absence of Treaty language regarding the issue of Member States' withdrawal indicates two possibilities: either the states accept that secession is not an option, or they assume that the power to withdraw is the ultimate power retained by each sovereign state. Under the latter view, joining the Union could in no way change or alter the state's fundamental right to withdraw. If the states retain the right to interrupt their state of "limited independence" by discontinuing their membership in the EU, they retain this aspect of their sovereignty. Under this interpretation, Latvian membership in the EU does not alter the literal meaning of Article 2 of the Constitution, if strictly because no Treaty language exists to controvert the language of Article 2 of the Constitution. The draft European Constitution permits a Member State to "decide to withdraw from the European Union in accordance with its own constitutional requirements" and may provide a specific process by which a Member State would leave: "A Member state which decides to withdraw shall notify the Council of its intention… The Union shall negotiate and conclude an agreement with that state, setting out the arrangements for its withdrawal."[32] However, though exit or withdrawal of a Member State from the EU is theoretically allowed, it is practically foreclosed as an option due to the very real political and economic losses which would be suffered by the withdrawing state.

While three new parts were added to Article 68, Article 79, by comparison, was only minimally amended with the addition of two clauses within the existing sentence. Amendments to Article 79 retained the original text declaring "An amendment to the Constitution submitted for national referendum shall be deemed adopted if at least half of the electorate has voted in favour." The very strict numerical demand in the original language of Article 79 was considered problematic, and there were calls to amend the language to envisage a smaller quorum only in the case of joining the EU. Additional text was added (new language in italics), which provides:

---

31 See Consolidated version of the Treaty on European Union, *OJ* 2002 C 325/5, 37 *ILM* 67.

32 The European Convention, Preliminary Draft Constitutional Treaty, CONV 369/02 (28 October 2002) Arts. 44 and 45.

> A draft law, *decision regarding membership of Latvia in the European Union or substantial changes in the terms regarding such membership* submitted for national referendum shall be deemed adopted if the number of voters is at least half of the number of electors as participated in the previous *Saeima* election and if the majority has voted in favour of the draft law, *membership of Latvia in the European Union or substantial changes in the terms regarding such membership.*

The additional clauses of Article 79 state that Latvia's EU membership was to be determined by a public referendum initiated by Parliament and that further substantial changes in the terms of Latvia's EU membership would be decided by a national referendum if a referendum were requested by at least half the members of the *Saeima*. To adopt EU membership, a number equalling at least one-half of the voters who took part in the prior parliamentary elections would have to vote, with the majority voting in favour of Latvia joining the EU. Elections took place in September 2003 and Latvian citizens turned out in strength to participate in the referendum. 71.49 per cent of the eligible voting population voted in the referendum with 66.97 per cent voting in favour of Latvian membership in the EU and 32 per cent voting against.[33] With the majority favouring accession, Latvia celebrated the May 1 decision by the European Commission.

4. CONCLUSION

The Latvian governing entities now look to EU legislation and case law as well as precedent of the European Court of Justice and legal norms established by other Member States' courts, to form national law. These non-domestic entities effectively exercise sovereignty within the state through their impact on domestic law, entrenching norms originating outside of the classical sources of sovereign power. Through their solid vote in favour of EU accession, the Latvian citizenry established that they distinguish between the involuntary loss of sovereignty through Soviet annexation which they voted to overcome, versus the enthusiastically embraced voluntary transfer of certain governmental powers to the EU. Only time and growing experience will determine the direction the Latvian courts will take and how well the courts will manage in their new role within the European Union. It remains to be seen whether the 2003 Constitutional amendments will be sufficient to address all matters of EU integration but the legal basis created was adequate for accession of Latvia into the Union. Now the law-making bodies of Latvia must simply gain experience and embrace the "legal heritage" which has become part of their inheritance as an EU Member State.

---

33 Results of the referendum of 11 November 2003 from the *Saeima* EU Information Centre, available at: <http://www.eiroinfo.lv/pages/SEUIC/content_list.jsp?category_id=210>.

LITHUANIA

Irmantas Jarukaitis*

1. NATIONAL CONSTITUTION

1.1 Implementation of international law and transfer of legislative powers

The Constitution of the Republic of Lithuania which was adopted by means of a referendum on 25 October 1992 establishes provisions both with regard to the relationship between international treaties and national law and concerning the transfer of competences to international organizations.

As regards the relationship between international and national law the Constitution[1] as well as the relevant case law of the Constitutional Court of Lithuania clearly show that Lithuania follows a monistic approach.[2] This means that once ratified by the Parliament provisions of international treaties as such are incorporated into the national legal system and may be applied directly in proceedings before the domestic courts (of course, only if their provisions are self-executing). One may note that Article 138 paragraph 3 mentions only *ratified* international agreements. Nonetheless, the Constitutional Court extended this provision to all international agreements of the Republic of Lithuania, irrespective of whether they have been ratified by the *Seimas* [the Parliament].[3] This position

* Irmantas Jarukaitis, Lecturer at Vilnius University, Faculty of Law and Deputy Director General of the European Law Department of the Ministry of Justice of Lithuania. Opinions expressed in this contribution are strictly those of the author.

1 Art. 138 para. 3 of the Constitution provides: "International agreements which are ratified by the Seimas of the Republic of Lithuania shall be a constituent part of the legal system of the Republic of Lithuania." For the English version of the Constitution of the Republic of Lithuania (incorporating later amendments) see the website of Parliament, available at: <http://www3.lrs.lt/cgi-bin/preps2?Condition1=239805&Condition2=>.

2 Opinion of the Constitutional Court in the case concerning the compatibility of Arts. 4, 5, 9 and 14, as well as of Art. 2 of Protocol No. 4 of the European Convention for the Protection of Human Rights and Fundamental Freedoms with the Constitution of the Republic of Lithuania of 24 January 1995. Rulings and Decisions of the Constitutional Court of the Republic of Lithuania, Vol. 4, 1998, p. 17.

3 See the Ruling of the Constitutional Court of 17 October 1995 on the compatibility of Part 4, Art. 7 and Art. 12 of the Law of the Republic of Lithuania on International Treaties of the Republic

of the Constitutional Court was later reflected in Article 11 paragraph 1 of the new Law on Treaties, adopted in 1999,[4] which refers to all international treaties concluded by Lithuania. It is worth mentioning that the Constitution does not expressly clarify the rank in the legal hierarchy of international treaties within the national legal order. Before the enactment of the Law on Treaties, international treaties were not given supremacy in all spheres of domestic regulation. However, this question has now been settled by Article 11 paragraph 2 of the Law on Treaties.[5] According to its provisions international treaties ratified by the *Seimas* have supremacy over national legal acts. However, this is only true for ratified treaties; treaties concluded by the Government, which do not require ratification, do not enjoy supremacy over laws passed by Parliament.[6] This is due to the conclusions of the Constitutional Court that to provide for supremacy of Government-concluded treaties would amount to conferring legislative power onto the Government, which according to the Constitution, it does not have.[7] On the other hand, one of the reasons to opt for parliamentary ratification of international treaties is when provisions of relevant treaties differ from those established by the national laws.[8] Through the procedure of ratification priority is thus given to the rules contained in such international treaties. However, the supremacy of ratified international treaties over national laws or other legal acts does not extend to supremacy over the Constitution itself, which has the highest

of Lithuania with the Constitution of the Republic of Lithuania, available at: <http://www.lrkt.lt/1995/n5a1017a.htm>.

4 *Valstybės žinios* [Official Journal], 9 July 1999. The English translation of the Law is available at: <http://www3.lrs.lt/cgi-bin/preps2?Condition1=197068&Condition2=>.

5 Art. 11 of the Law stipulates: "1. International treaties of the Republic of Lithuania shall be executed in the Republic of Lithuania. 2. If a ratified international treaty of the Republic of Lithuania stipulates other provisions than the laws or other acts of the Republic of Lithuania, irrespective of whether they are in force at the moment of the conclusion of the treaty or enter into force following the conclusion of the treaty, the provisions of the international treaty of the Republic of Lithuania shall apply. 3. If the execution of an international treaty of the Republic of Lithuania requires that a law or other legal act should be enacted, the Government of the Republic of Lithuania shall submit a draft law to the Seimas according to established procedures, or shall issue a decree, ensuring that other legal acts are adopted in accordance with its competence."

It should be added that Art. 11 para. 3 of the Law refers to the situation that the provisions of the relevant treaty are not self-executing. In this case the Government of the Republic of Lithuania, as the institution with the general obligation of ensuring the implementation of international treaties in Lithuania, is empowered and obliged, taking into account the nature of the treaty, to take all necessary steps in order to ensure the full functioning of the international treaty within the domestic legal system.

6 Parliament ratifies international treaty by passing ratification laws.

7 See the Ruling, *supra* n. 3.

8 See Art. 7 para. 1(8) of the Law on Treaties. Besides, Art. 138 para. 1 of the Constitution and Art. 7 of the Law on Treaties define categories of treaties which are subjected to ratification by the Parliament.

legal force in the hierarchy of the domestic legal order.[9] The Constitution cannot be amended through ratification of an international treaty and the Constitutional Court of Lithuania has the power to review the constitutionality of international treaties.[10] The Constitutional Court is competent to give non-binding opinions with respect to international treaties.[11] If the Court finds incompatibility, the Constitution would have to be amended accordingly in order to make ratification of such a treaty possible. The Constitutional Court is also competent to perform *ex post* reviews of the constitutionality of international treaties.[12] This would imply that the Constitutional Court is competent to review the legality of their ratification as well. However, the Constitutional Court when interpreting Article 7 of the Constitution has indicated that this provision "cannot invalidate the international Treaty [...], however, it requires that the provisions of the international treaty should not contradict the provisions of the Constitution, otherwise it would be questionable how to implement the Convention in the internal law of the Republic of Lithuania."[13] It seems that if such a case were to arise, Parliament would have two options: either to amend the Constitution in order to remove any contradictions, or to decide to withdraw from the international treaty.[14] So far, there has been no need to deal with such matters in

[9] Art. 7 of the Constitution provides: "Any law or other statute which contradicts the Constitution shall be invalid."

[10] To date, this power has been used only once when the President of the Republic of Lithuania asked the Constitutional Court to review the compatibility of certain provisions of the European Convention on Human Rights with those of the Constitution prior to its ratification. See the above-mentioned Opinion of the Constitutional Court in the case concerning the compatibility of Arts. 4, 5, 9 and 14, as well as of Art. 2 of Protocol No. 4 of the European Convention for the Protection of Human Rights and Fundamental Freedoms with the Constitution of the Republic of Lithuania of 24 January 1995. Rulings and Decisions of the Constitutional Court of the Republic of Lithuania, Vol. 4, 1998, p. 17. See also on the issue: V. Vadapalas, 'Opinion of the Constitutional Court of the Republic of Lithuania in the Case Concerning the Conformity of the European Convention on Human Rights with the Constitution of Lithuania', *Zeitschrift für ausländisches öffentliches Recht und Völkerrecht* 1995, Band 55, No. 4, pp. 1077-1094.

[11] Art. 107 para. 3 of the Constitution states: "[...] on the basis of the opinions of the Constitutional Court, the Seimas shall make the final decision [...]".

[12] Art. 73 para. 3 of the Law on the Constitutional Court provides that "the Constitutional Court shall deliver opinions on whether international treaties of the Republic of Lithuania contradict the Constitution. Opinions concerning international treaties may *also* [emphasis added] be asked prior to their ratification." *Valstybės žinios*, 1993, No. 6-120. The English translation of the Law, available at: <http://www3.lrs.lt/cgi-bin/preps2?Condition1=21936&Condition2=>.

[13] See the Opinion, *supra* n. 2.

[14] It is obvious that in such a case the state, when unable to fulfil its obligations under an international treaty, may not rely on its constitutional provisions. See Arts. 26, 27 and 46 of the Vienna Convention on the Law of Treaties. *UNTS*, 1151. See also Advisory Opinion of the Permanent Court of International Justice of 4 February 1932 in *Treatment of Polish Nationals and Other Persons of Polish Origin or Speech in the Danzig Territories* case. PCIJ (ser. A/B), 1932, No. 44, p. 24 and R. Jennings and A. Watts, eds., *Oppenheim's International Law*, 9th edn. (Burnt Mill, UK, Longman 1992) pp. 84-85.

practice as the Court has not yet had an opportunity to review the constitutionality of an international treaty after its ratification.[15] Finally, it should be noted that the Constitutional Court has ruled that it is also competent to review the compatibility of Governmental decrees with ratified international treaties.[16]

Several words should be said about the relationship between general international law (customary law) and Lithuanian national law. As opposed to the question of international treaties, this issue is not addressed directly in the Constitution of Lithuania. However, attention should be drawn to Article 135 of the Constitution which makes a reference to general international law, but this reference is made only with regard to Lithuania's foreign policy.[17] One may argue that when pursuing domestic policy the state should not base its actions on different principles than those used for purposes of foreign policy.[18] Nonetheless, this is only one argument in order to secure the direct effect of these principles on the national level, thus creating rights and duties for persons.[19] It remains to be seen, whether courts will be willing to extend the monistic approach to cover rules of general international law; to date at least they have not yet done so.[20]

Turning to the application of international treaties by ordinary Lithuanian courts several trends can be noted. First of all, most of the treaties applied in domestic proceedings are of an economic nature and are therefore applied in civil cases. One should also note that lower courts are still rather conservative and references to provisions of international treaties are not that frequent. This is due to the fact that during Soviet rule there was no tradition whatsoever of applying international law in domestic proceedings before national courts. The Supreme Court of Lithuania, however, has already developed a rather consistent practice of

---

15 See also on the subject: V. Vadapalas and I. Jarukaitis, 'Constitution of the Republic of Lithuania, International Law and Accession to the European Union', in F.F. Segado, ed., *The Spanish Constitution in the European Constitutional Context* (Madrid, Dykinson L.R. 2003) pp. 473-488.

16 See the Decision of the Constitutional Court of 25 April 2002, available at: <http://www.lrkt.lt/doc_links/main.htm>.

17 Art. 135: "In conducting foreign policy, the Republic of Lithuania shall pursue the universally recognized principles and norms of international law, shall strive to safeguard national security and independence as well as basic rights, freedoms and welfare of its citizens, and shall take part of sound international order based on law and justice."

18 Such a conclusion may be also drawn from the doctrine of the Constitutional Court. See Ruling of the Constitutional Court of 9 December 1998 on the compatibility of the death penalty provided as a sanction under Art. 105 of the Republic of Lithuania Criminal Code with the Constitution of the Republic of Lithuania, available at: <http://www.lrkt.lt/angdoc.htm>.

19 See also V. Vadapalas and I. Jarukaitis, *Tarptautinės humanitarinės teisės įgyvendinimas Lietuvos Respublikoje* (Vilnius, Eugrimas 2000) pp. 18-19.

20 It seems that at least theoretically there are grounds to invoke general international law in Lithuania. For example, in order to ensure the prosecution of war crimes under the Criminal Code, it would be necessary to rely on general international law because in some cases provisions of the Criminal Code refer directly to general international law (e.g., Arts. 101, 103-105, 111, 112 of the Criminal Code). *Valstybės žinios*, 2000, No. 89-2741.

application of international treaties, at least in civil proceedings.[21] In addition, by its case law the Supreme Court has extended the principle of priority of international treaties over national law to also cover non-ratified international agreements in civil cases. This is due to the fact that the Civil Code includes provisions declaring the principle of priority of international law over national law.[22] Still, the general trend of the increasing importance of international treaties is true only with regard to civil cases. So far, use of international treaties in criminal and administrative cases by ordinary courts has been sparing. This is especially evident in respect to the European Convention on Human Rights. For the most part the situation is the result of the above-mentioned Opinion of the Constitutional Court.[23] Although supporting the monistic doctrine the Court made one important reservation in that respect.[24] As was mentioned, the Opinion of the Court has the character of a recommendation and Parliament did not express any reservations concerning the application of the Convention in criminal cases after the Opinion had been delivered. Besides, the Constitutional Court developed quite a consistent practice of referring to the provisions of the ECHR and the case law of the European Court of Human Rights in its rulings. Some authors even suggest that the ECHR is a *de facto* source of constitutional law in Lithuania.[25] However, it appears that so far the ordinary courts are not eager to follow this approach and apply provisions of the Convention in criminal cases. There is no doubt that such an approach is already precluding the effective protection of human rights on a national level, as it also tends to avoid litigation before the European Court of Human Rights itself.

---

21 See V. Vadapalas and I. Jarukaitis, 'International Agreements in the Legal Order of the Candidate Countries: Lithuania', in A. Ott and K. Inglis, eds., *Handbook on European Enlargement. A Commentary on the Enlargement Process* (The Hague, T.M.C Asser Press 2002) pp. 281-289.

22 Art. 1.13 para. 1 of the Civil Code. *Valstybės žinios*, 6 September 2000, No. 74. See also Decree No. 28 of the Senate of the Supreme Court on the practice of the application of rules of international private law by courts of the Republic of Lithuania of 21 December 2000 and the review of such court practice, available at: <http://lat.litlex.lt/teismupr/teismu.htm>.

23 See the Opinion, *supra* n. 2.

24 The Court stated: "Civil law provides for direct applicability of international treaties by resolving their collision with the norms of the law of the Republic of Lithuania [...]. In criminal law such a method for resolving the collision of norms is not applied. In such cases the criminal law and laws of criminal procedure of the Republic of Lithuania are directly applicable, and international treaties are directly applicable only in cases provided for by such laws [...]. If in the application of criminal law doubts arise concerning the possibility of enforcing human rights guaranteed by the Convention, the question should be resolved by means of constitutional review in which it is asked whether or not the law contradicts the Constitution." It should be added that neither the Criminal Code, nor the Code of Criminal Procedure makes any reference to the Convention.

25 E. Kūris, 'The Constitutional Court and Interpretation of the Constitution', in E. Jarašiūnas, E. Kūris, K. Lapinskas, A. Normantas, V. Sinkevičius and S. Stačiokas, *Constitutional Justice in Lithuania* (Vilnius, 2003) pp. 272-273.

When speaking about the question of transfer of competences to international organizations attention should be drawn to Article 136 of the Constitution, which establishes that "the Republic of Lithuania shall participate in international organisations provided that this does not contradict the interests and independence of the State." As may be noted, the reference is only to international organizations, not to supra-national organizations. This is not surprising when we recall the historic circumstances at the time of the Constitution's drafting: it is difficult to imagine that the drafters were even contemplating Lithuania's membership in the EU. This constitutional provision served as the basis for Lithuania's participation in traditional international organizations, but, as we will see further on, was considered insufficient to form the basis for EU membership.

1.2 The Constitutional Act on Membership of the Republic of Lithuania in the EU and some remaining issues

Discussions concerning the constitutional basis for Lithuania's accession to the EU lasted for several years. The first expert group which was entrusted with the task of evaluating the relevant constitutional provisions and to submit recommendations on this issue was formed by the Board of the Parliament back in 1998. It concluded that the Constitution should be amended in order to provide for a clear constitutional basis for Lithuania's accession to the EU and drafted several proposals for amendments to the Constitution. However, opinion in academic and political circles concerning the necessity of amendments to the Constitution to enable EU membership was far from unanimous. Some argued that the above-mentioned provisions of Articles 136 and 138 of the Constitution were sufficient as the EU is not all that different from traditional international organizations and EU law should be treated as international law. It should be noted in this context that on 1 March 2001 a *Seimas* Commission on Constitutional Amendments was formed. One of the tasks of this Commission is to discuss proposed amendments to the Constitution and, where necessary, to submit draft amendments to Parliament. The Commission, after discussing the issue with constitutional lawyers who claimed that the EU is similar to ordinary international organizations, at the beginning of 2002 took the approach that no constitutional amendments were needed. However, after a more in-depth analysis of the EU-related questions the Commission decided to reopen the debate. Following this decision several other expert groups were formed, the last one being also involved in the wider discussion on the future of the EU and the draft Treaty Establishing a Constitution for Europe. When analysing the issue of transfer of competences to the EU several factors were taken into account. First of all, at least the formal provisions of the Constitution seem to be rather protective and closed with regard to external powers.[26] This is not a coincidence – one should remember that at the time when the Constitution was adopted the Soviet army was still in the country.[27] It is clear that the aim of these constitutional provisions was to emphasize the re-established independence of Lithuania. It should be noted in this regard that on 8 June 1992 the Constitutional Act on the Non-Alignment of the Republic of Lithuania with Post-Soviet Eastern Alliances was approved and that this Act later became part of the Constitution.[28] These protective provisions of the Constitution clearly fail to provide the whole picture, as ever since the re-establishment of its independence in 1990 Lithuania has been an active participant in international relations. Besides, the above-mentioned provisions of Articles 136 and 138 of the Constitution also support claims concerning the openness of the Lithuanian constitutional system.

On the other hand, the specific nature of the EU requires transfer of a vast array of legislative, executive and judicial powers traditionally exercised by state institutions and thus raises the question of whether Article 136 of the Constitution would be an appropriate constitutional basis for such a transfer? Attention should also be drawn to Articles 4 and 5 of the Constitution which are very straightforward as regards the exercise of public powers.[29] As has already been mentioned the main arguments for use of Article 136 as the constitutional basis for accession to the EU were based on the assumption that the EU is an ordinary international organization, which is simply not the case. As was explained above, it certainly was not drafted with EU membership in mind. Therefore, the final view was taken that Article 136 does not cover Lithuania's membership in the EU

---

26 Art. 1 of the Constitution declares that: "The State of Lithuania shall be an independent and democratic republic." Art. 2: "the State of Lithuania shall be created by the People. Sovereignty shall be vested in the People." More provisions on sovereignty may be found in the following articles: Art. 3: "no one may limit or restrict the sovereignty of the People or make claims to the sovereign powers of the People. The People and each citizen shall have the right to oppose anyone who encroaches on the independence, territorial integrity, or constitutional order of the State of Lithuania by force." Art. 4 of the Constitution: "the People shall exercise the supreme sovereign power vested in them either directly or through their democratically elected representatives."

27 The last Russian army troops left Lithuania on 31 August 1993.

28 The Act provides: "The Supreme Council of the Republic of Lithuania, [...] resolves: 1. To develop mutually advantageous relations with every state which was formerly a constituent part of the USSR, but to never and in no way join any new political, military, economic or any other state alliances or commonwealths formed on the basis of the former USSR. 2. That activities which seek to involve the State of Lithuania into state alliances or commonwealths as specified in Article 1 of this Constitutional Act shall be considered hostile to the independence of Lithuania and shall incur liability in accordance with the law. 3. That no military bases or army units of Russia, the Commonwealth of Independent States, or its constituent states may be located on the territory of the Republic of Lithuania."

29 Art. 4: *supra* n. 26; Art. 5 provides: "in Lithuania, the powers of the State shall be exercised by the Seimas, the President of the Republic and Government, and the Judiciary. The scope of powers shall be defined by the Constitution [...]".

and that to interpret Article 136 otherwise would imply a *de facto* amendment of the Constitution.

Besides the transfer of certain competences to the EU, the accession to this supranational organization also entailed changes in the balance of powers between the Parliament, the Government and the courts. Further, the provisions of Article 138 of the Constitution were considered to be not fully suitable for a smooth operation of EU law at national level, since they refer only to international treaties and thus leave unanswered questions as regards other sources of EU law (EU secondary law, ECJ case law, etc.). The experience of some of the "old" EU Member States showing that national courts have problems with the recognition of the special nature of EU law when this law derives from ECJ case law which provides no extra guidance on the subject at national level was also taken into account.[30]

As has already been noted above, various expert groups drafted several versions of constitutional amendments which mainly focused on the insertion of provisions concerning the transfer of competences to the EU, the relationship between EU law and national law and modes of involvement of the Parliament in EU matters in Articles 136 and 138 of the Constitution. However, the final approach adopted by the Commission on Constitutional Amendments was to include these provisions in a separate Constitutional Act, which would become an integral part of the Constitution. As required by the Constitution[31] Parliament voted twice on the provisions of the Constitutional Act. It was finally adopted on 13 July 2004 and came into force one month later. The Constitutional Act[32]

---

[30] See, for example, A.M. Slaughter, A.S. Sweet and J.H.H. Weiler, eds., *The European Court and National Courts – Doctrine and Jurisprudence. Legal Change in Its Social Context* (Oxford, Hart Publishing 1998). As regards Lithuania: I. Jarukaitis, *Constitutional Basis of Accession of the Republic of Lithuania to the European Union* (Teisė, Mokslo darbai 2003) No. 49.

[31] Art. 148 of the Constitution provides: "The provision of Article 1 of the Constitution 'the State of Lithuania is an independent democratic republic' may only be amended by referendum in which at least three-fourths of the electorate of Lithuania vote in favour of such an amendment. The provisions of Chapter I ('The State of Lithuania') and Chapter XIV ('Amendment of the Constitution') may be amended only by referendum. Amendments of other chapters of the Constitution must be discussed and twice put to a vote at the Seimas. There must be a break of at least three months between the votes. A draft law on amendment of the Constitution shall be deemed adopted by the Seimas if, during each of the votes, at least two-thirds of all the Members of the Seimas vote in favour of the law. An amendment of the Constitution which has been overruled may be submitted to the Seimas for reconsideration not earlier than after one year."

[32] The Constitutional Act on Membership of the Republic of Lithuania in the European Union: "The Seimas of the Republic of Lithuania, executing the will of the citizens of the Republic of Lithuania expressed during the referendum held on 10-11 of May 2003 on the membership of the Republic of Lithuania in the European Union; expressing its conviction that the European Union respects human rights and fundamental freedoms and that membership in the European Union will contribute to a more effective safeguarding of human rights and freedoms; noting that the European Union respects national identity and constitutional traditions of its Member States, seeking to ensure full participation of the Republic of Lithuania in European integration as well as the security of the

covers a broad range of issues: transfer of competences to the EU, the relationship between EU law and national law, the relationship between the Parliament and the Government in the EU decision-making process, as well as giving more flexibility to the Government when it comes to EU decision-making procedures.

Without any doubt the adoption of this Constitutional Act is to be assessed positively. It establishes a clear constitutional regulation of relevant issues and reflects the changed reality after Lithuania's accession to the EU.[33]

On the other hand some important questions remain unanswered. The first concerns the relationship between EU law and provisions of the Constitution of Lithuania. Although the ECJ is very clear in this regard, it should be noted that Article 7 paragraph 1 of the Constitution of Lithuania provides that "any law or

---

Republic of Lithuania and welfare of its citizens; on 16 September 2003 ratified the Treaty Between the Kingdom of Belgium, the Kingdom of Denmark, the Federal Republic of Germany, the Hellenic Republic, the Kingdom of Spain, the French Republic, Ireland, the Italian Republic the Grand Duchy of Luxemburg, the Kingdom of the Netherlands, the Republic of Austria, the Portuguese Republic, the Republic of Finland, the Kingdom of Sweden, the United Kingdom of Great Britain and Northern Ireland (Member States of the European Union) and the Czech Republic, the Republic of Estonia, the Republic of Cyprus, the Republic of Latvia, the Republic of Lithuania, the Republic of Hungary, the Republic of Malta, the Republic of Poland, the Republic of Slovenia and the Slovak Republic concerning the Accession of the Czech Republic, the Republic of Estonia, the Republic of Cyprus, the Republic of Latvia, the Republic of Lithuania, the Republic of Hungary, the Republic of Malta, the Republic of Poland, the Republic of Slovenia and the Slovak Republic to the European Union signed on 16 April 2003 in Athens; adopts and promulgates this Constitutional Act: 1. The Republic of Lithuania as a Member State of the European Union shall share with or entrust to the European Union competencies of its State institutions in the spheres provided for in the founding Treaties of the European Union and to the extent that, together with the other Member States of the European Union, it could jointly meet its commitments in those spheres and could also enjoy the rights accorded by membership. 2. The norms of the acquis of the European Union shall be an integral part of the legal order of the Republic of Lithuania. Where it follows from the founding Treaties of the European Union, the norms of the acquis shall apply directly, while in the event of a conflict between legal norms, the norms of the acquis shall prevail over the laws and other legal acts of the Republic of Lithuania. 3. The Government shall inform the Seimas about proposals to adopt legal acts of the European Union. As regards proposals to adopt the legal acts of the European Union regulating the spheres which, under the Constitution of the Republic of Lithuania, are related to the competences of the Seimas, the Government shall consult the Seimas. The Seimas may recommend to the Government a position of the Republic of Lithuania in respect of these proposals. The Seimas European Affairs Committee and the Foreign Affairs Committee, in accordance with the procedure set forth in the Statute of the Seimas, may submit to the Government the opinion of the Seimas concerning proposals concerning the adoption of legal acts of the European Union. The Government shall assess the recommendations or opinions submitted by the Seimas or its Committees and shall duly inform the Seimas about their execution following the procedure prescribed by legal acts. 4. The Government shall consider the proposals relating to the adoption of the legal acts of the European Union following the procedure prescribed by legal acts. The Government may adopt decisions or resolutions concerning those proposals and their adoption shall no be subject to the provisions of Article 95 of the Constitution." *Valstybės žinios*, 2004, No. 111-4123. The English version of the Act is available at: <http://www3.lrs.lt/cgi-bin/preps2?Condition1=237876&Condition2=>.

[33] This proposition is without prejudice to discussions on whether, taking into account the specific features of the EU, it is still appropriate to speak only of transfer of state institutions' competences to the EU.

other statute which is in conflict with the Constitution shall be invalid." The earlier rigid practice of the Constitutional Court emphasizing the paramount place of the Constitution within the national legal system and writings of constitutional lawyers do not remove doubts that this provision will not be applied to EU law.

Further, the earlier practice of the Constitutional Court as regards its jurisdiction to rule on the compatibility of governmental decrees with international treaties[34] will have to be modified as regards primary EU law, since according to the ECJ practice it is up to the ordinary courts to take decisions on this issue.[35] Of course, after adoption of the Constitutional Act the Constitutional Court will also have to take into account provisions of the Act when interpreting the Constitution as a whole, but as the case law of some constitutional courts of the "old" Member States shows, even the "integration" clauses are unable to provide answers to all questions concerning constitutional relations between the EU and national law. Besides, writings of constitutional lawyers pointing to earlier practices of the German Federal Constitutional Court and the Italian Constitutional Court sometimes hint at the possibility of constitutional review of EU secondary legislation by the Constitutional Court of Lithuania.

At least from one perspective the application of EU law in Lithuania is still problematic: Article 7 paragraph 2 of the Constitution provides that "only laws which are promulgated shall be valid." The Constitutional Court has stated several times that this provision forms part of the rule of law. However, so far, no official publications of secondary EU legislation adopted prior to Lithuania's accession to the EU exist in Lithuanian. This is especially problematic with regard to Regulations, which are acts of direct application and may therefore directly establish obligations for all legal subjects. Again, it is unclear what the outcome would be if this issue were to be raised before the Constitutional Court (or before the ECJ).

In addition, mention should be made of the unclear position taken by the Constitutional Court with regard to the preliminary rulings procedure under the EC Treaty. Already there are several cases pending before the Constitutional Court which among other things raise questions of interpretation of EU law.[36] The first question is whether the Constitutional Court may be regarded as a court or tribunal from the point of view of Article 234 of the EC Treaty. Attention should be drawn to the fact that the constitutional courts of the EU Member States are

---

34 See *supra* n. 16.

35 For example, the ECJ decision in Case C-106/77 *Amministrazione delle Finanze* v. *Simmenthal SpA* [1978] *ECR* 629.

36 For example, a request is currently pending before the Constitutional Court concerning the compatibility of the governmental decree establishing provisions on the liability of Internet service providers with the Constitution and the Law on the Provision of Information to the Public. The case involves both issues related to fundamental freedoms (i.e., freedom of expression) and the interpretation of the Electronic Commerce Directive.

not unanimous on this issue either, nor is academic doctrine. It is clear that the Constitutional Court is not an ordinary judicial body and at least where the Constitutional Court of Lithuania is concerned, proceedings before it are not directly *inter partes*.[37] On the other hand it is obvious that a ruling of the Constitutional Court may have an impact on the interpretation of EU law. In the author's opinion, referring questions from constitutional courts to the ECJ would open up the discussion concerning the connection and horizontal relations between national constitutional law and EU law. By referring various questions to the ECJ and thus having an opportunity to indicate their own views and reasoning on a particular subject the constitutional courts would have an opportunity to promote national constitutional values at the EU level. In any event, it will soon become clear what approach the Constitutional Court decides to take – either cope with these challenges independently or to refer questions to the ECJ. Attention should be drawn to the fact that differently from the Law on Courts[38] and the Law on Administrative Proceedings[39] (see further) the Law on the Constitutional Court of the Republic of Lithuania[40] was not supplemented with provisions as regards reference of questions to the ECJ by Lithuanian courts. Although in the author's opinion the lack of such provisions should not be regarded as an obstacle for references by the Constitutional Court to the ECJ, as the Constitutional Court could rely directly on the relevant provisions of the EC Treaty, this fact might play a role in defining relations between the Constitutional Court of Lithuania and the ECJ.

Finally, in the context of unresolved issues, attention should be drawn to the fact that the above-mentioned Constitutional Act was adopted and came into force only after Lithuania's accession to the EU (13 July and 13 August 2004 respectively). It is not entirely clear what reasons precluded the adoption of the Act before the accession. On the one hand, it is obvious that the adoption of such provisions is a politically sensitive process. On the other hand, the support of the general public for Lithuania's accession to the EU was constantly high.[41] Besides, the results in both ballots for the adoption of the Constitutional Act in Parliament

---

37 For criteria determining whether a particular body is a court or tribunal, see, for example, the ECJ decision in Case C-54/96 *Dorsch Consult Ingenieurgesellschaft mbH* v. *Bundesbaugesellschaft Berlin mbH* [1997] *ECR* I-4961.

38 *Valstybės žinios*, 1994, No. 46-841, the new edition of the Law is in force as of 1 May 2002; the English translation of the new edition (not incorporating later amendments) is available at: <http://www3.lrs.lt/cgi-bin/preps2?Condition1=187988&Condition2=>.

39 *Valstybės žinios*, 1999, No. 13-308. For the English version (not incorporating later amendments), available at: <http://www3.lrs.lt/cgi-bin/preps2?Condition1=91191&Condition2=>.

40 *Valstybės žinios*, 1993, No. 6-120.

41 For example, almost 90 per cent of those who participated in the referendum concerning Lithuania's accession to the EU (organized on 10-11 May 2003; over 63 per cent of citizens entitled to vote participated in the referendum) were in favour of Lithuania's accession to the EU. The latest opinion polls show that over 78 per cent of the population support Lithuania's membership of the EU.

show that political support was also high.[42] Be that as it may, however, the delay to some extent undermines the importance of the Constitutional Act, since it creates an impression that adoption of the Act was not indispensable for the clear establishment of the constitutional basis for Lithuania's accession to the EU. Besides, considered from a theoretical perspective, the Constitutional Court would have quite a difficult task if a question were put to it concerning the constitutionality of a transfer of competences and the constitutional basis for the application of EU law in the period between the accession of Lithuania to the EU and the entry into force of the Constitutional Act. The first solution would be to find some alternative constitutional basis (most probably, the above-mentioned Arts. 136 and 138 of the Constitution) justifying the accession. However, such a decision would undermine the importance of the Constitutional Act itself, since it would make the adoption of the Act redundant. On the other hand, if the Constitutional Court ruled that there was no constitutional basis to join the EU without the adoption of express provisions, this would have serious political and almost inconceivable legal consequences.

1.3 Amendments

Before the accession several constitutional provisions were identified as possibly incompatible with EU law. Two of these were amended taking into account Lithuania's accession to the EU. The first one relates to the right of EU citizens to participate in municipal elections in the Member State in which they reside, since the former version of Article 119 of the Constitution granted this right exclusively to Lithuanian citizens. Amendments to Article 119 of the Constitution were adopted in June 2002 and now provides that "citizens of the Republic of Lithuania and other permanent residents of an administrative unit shall be elected according to the law to local government Councils for a four-year term on the basis of universal, equal and direct suffrage by secret ballot by the citizens of the Republic of Lithuania and other residents of the administrative unit" thus removing the former inconsistencies with EU law.

Another sensitive issue was the purchase of land by foreigners. When the Constitution was adopted in 1992 Article 47 established the right to purchase land only for Lithuanian citizens (as regards agricultural land this right was not granted even to legal persons established in Lithuania). There were two rounds of amendments. The first one took place in 1996 when the purchase of non-agricultural land was to some extent liberalized.[43] The amended version of Article

---

[42] During the first voting 117 and during the second 115 out of 141 Members of Parliament voted in favour of the adoption of the Constitutional Act.

[43] After amendments made in 1996 Art. 47 of the Constitution provided: "1. Land, internal waters, forests, and parks may only belong to the citizens and the State of the Republic of Lithuania by the right of ownership. 2. Local governments (municipalities), other national entities as well as

47 established cumbersome and complicated regulations on these issues and did not liberalize the purchase of agricultural land by foreigners and legal persons. Article 47 was therefore amended a second time Article 47 in January 2003. The aim of these amendments was to ensure the full compatibility of the relevant constitutional provisions with EU law.[44]

In addition, some thought and discussion was devoted to the need to amend Article 13 paragraph 2 of the Constitution[45] taking into account the adoption of Framework Decision 2002/584/JHA of 13 June 2002, concerning the European arrest warrant and the surrender procedures between the Member States. However, it was decided that amendments were not needed, since the relevant requirements stem directly from the EU Treaty.

Further, Article 125 paragraph 2 of the Constitution provides that "the right of issue of currency shall belong exclusively to the Bank of Lithuania." On the one hand there is no doubt that the issue of currency is traditionally regarded as forming the core of the state's sovereign powers. On the other hand it was argued during the process of drafting of the constitutional amendments related to the accession that the currency provision of the Constitution covers only the emission of the national currency, the litas. Therefore it is without prejudice to the emission of the euro by the European Central Bank and thus amendments to the provision in question are not necessary, since the transfer of competences in this field is covered by the general clause on the transfer of competences to the EU.[46] Based on this assumption a decision was made not to amend the Constitution. However, in the recent Convergence Report the European Commission expressed its opinion that the above-mentioned provisions of the Constitution are not fully compatible with Article 109 of the EC Treaty and the Statute of the ECB (although the main issue is Art. 106(1) of the EC Treaty).[47] It therefore appears

---

those foreign entities conducting economic activities in Lithuania which are specified by the constitutional law in compliance with the criteria of European and Transatlantic integration which the Republic of Lithuania has embarked on may be permitted to acquire into their ownership non-agricultural land plots required for the construction and operation of buildings and facilities necessary for their direct activities. The land plot acquisition procedure, terms and conditions, as well as restrictions shall be established by the constitutional law."

[44] Currently Art. 47 para. 3 of the Constitution provides: "foreign entities may acquire ownership of land, internal waters and forests in the Republic of Lithuania in accordance with a constitutional law." The constitutional law basically specifies some procedural aspects and defines the legal subjects which are allowed to buy land.

[45] Art. 13 para. 2 of the Constitution provides: "It shall be prohibited to extradite a citizen of the Republic of Lithuania to another state unless an international agreement of the Republic of Lithuania establishes otherwise."

[46] A similar approach was adopted in the Netherlands, although the relevant provisions of the Dutch Constitution are less straightforward than those of the Constitution of Lithuania.

[47] Report from the Commission. Convergence Report 2004. Brussels, 20 October 2004, COM (2004) 690, p. 6, available at: <http://europa.eu.int/comm/economy_finance/publications/european_economy/2004/cr2004_en.pdf>.

that there is still a need to evaluate the necessity of constitutional amendments in this field.[48]

1.4 Procedures

Different proposals were put forward concerning procedures to be used for the adoption of the relevant constitutional amendments (later: the Constitutional Act). Theoretically, the Constitution allows two types of procedures for its amendment: by way of referendum (in some cases the Constitution stipulates that this procedure is compulsory) and by way of parliamentary voting. Besides, Article 9 paragraph 1 of the Constitution provides that "the most vital issues concerning the life of the State and the People shall be decided by referendum." Accession to the EU was without doubt one of the most important issues after the re-establishment of Lithuania's independence in 1990. However, taking into account the fact that the basic question of whether to become a member of the EU was answered in the affirmative by the referendum, it was still decided to adopt the Constitutional Act by means of the parliamentary voting procedure. As has already been noted[49] the Constitution establishes rigid procedures with regard to its amendment, namely two ballots in Parliament at least three months apart with at least 2/3 of the votes on both occasion having to be in favour of amendment.

Other constitutional amendments mentioned above in section 3 of this report were adopted using the same procedure that was used for the adoption of the Constitutional Act.

2. ROLE OF THE JUDICIARY IN THE PROCESS OF INTEGRATION

2.1 Europe Agreement; supremacy and direct and indirect effect

During the past few years, Lithuanian courts have become more familiar with international treaties and are relying on their provisions more frequently. However, although this may seem surprising, Lithuanian courts have never referred to the Europe Agreement in their decisions despite the monistic approach adopted by the Constitutional Court, the importance[50] of this Agreement and the

---

48 See also on the subject: A. Albi, 'Common Currency and National Constitutions', in F. Torres, A. Verdun, Ch. Zilioli and H. Zimmermann, eds., *Governing EMU. Economic, Political, Legal and Historical Perspectives* (European University Institute, European Central Bank, European Investment Bank 2004) pp. 63-80.

49 See *supra* n. 31.

50 Even leaving aside its political importance, the provisions of the Agreement defining economic relations between the parties were of particular importance taking into account that the main foreign trade partners of Lithuania were mostly EU Member States.

fact that it was in force for quite a long period of time.[51] This fact also illustrates the reluctance of Lithuanian courts to apply provisions of international treaties.[52]

As regards the application of EU law, during the several months after Lithuania's accession to the EU, no case law had yet been produced by the national courts where express confirmation was given of the principles of supremacy or direct effect of EU law. So far there has been one decision of the Supreme Court where the applicant tried to rely on provisions of a directive, but the Court simply held that in this particular case the provisions of the directive had not been violated.[53] On the other hand, the Supreme Court in one of its recent decisions relied on provisions of EU law[54] and even considered the necessity to refer the issue to the ECJ, as the applicant had requested. However, the Court pointed to earlier decisions in which it has referred to ECJ case law and considered that the relevant ECJ case law in this field was clear and decided not to ask for a preliminary ruling.[55]

As regards the principle of indirect effect of EU law it should be noted that the Supreme Court of Lithuania had already developed a consistent practice of referring to EU law even before accession.[56] Of course, in these cases provisions of EU law were used only as additional sources of interpretation by the Court, but it still demonstrates that the Court has a clear understanding of the consequences of Lithuania's integration in the EU and of the legislator's intention to approximate national laws with legal provisions of the EU. This principle is confirmed by the practice of Lithuanian courts as regards its application of international agreements as well as EU law. Already before accession there were some decisions both of the Supreme Court and the Supreme Administrative Court[57] where these courts confirmed the principle of indirect effect of EU law. In

---

[51] The Europe Agreement came into force on 1 February 1998 and applied until Lithuania's accession to the EU.

[52] See Vadapalas and Jarukaitis, *supra* n. 21.

[53] See the decision of the Supreme Court No. 3K-3-301/2004 m of 12 May 2004, available at: <http://ovada.tic.lt/lat/nutartis.aspx?id=25350>.

[54] Council Directive 89/104/EC, Council Regulation 40/94, the relevant case law of the ECJ and OHIM.

[55] See decision of the Supreme Court No. 3K-3-461/2004 of 27 September 2004, available at: <http://ovada.tic.lt/lat/nutartis.aspx?id=27003>.

[56] E.g., decisions of the Supreme Court in cases No. 3K-3-1288/2002 m; No. 3K-3-1288/2002 m; No. 3K-3-167/2003 m. Generally, these cases concerned trademarks, industrial design, etc.

[57] E.g., The Supreme Administrative Court in its decision of 11 June 2003 dealt with the issue of the application of EU law. In this case the Competition Council adopted a decision that Lietuvos telekomas (the incumbent telecom operator) abused its dominant position and when interpreting provisions of national laws took into account relevant provisions of EU law. The telecom operator on appeal claimed that the Competition Council could not legally directly apply EU law before accession. The Supreme Administrative Court rejected the appeal thus confirming the validity of the Competition Council decision. As regards the direct application of EU law the Court rightly pointed out that the Competition Council had not applied EU law directly, but had interpreted domestic law

recent decisions delivered after Lithuania's accession to the EU the Supreme Administrative Court when interpreting provisions of national tax law made numerous references to EU law.[58] The Court ruled that it is not in a position to apply EU law directly since the facts of the dispute arose before the accession when EU law was not yet part of the national legal system. However, the Court relied on EU law indirectly through the interpretation of national provisions which were already harmonized with the relevant provisions of *acquis*.[59]

As regards the Constitutional Court the above thesis concerning the use of EU law as a source of inspiration for interpretation of the national laws is to some extent applicable to the case law of the Court when it interprets the Constitution of Lithuania. If we look at the practice of the Court we find that the Court has referred to EU law in its rulings several times before Lithuania joined the EU. One of the first rulings where this occurred was delivered in December 1998, when the Court held that provisions allowing capital punishment under the Criminal Code were unconstitutional. Here the Court made a reference to the resolution adopted by the European Parliament in 1997 where the EP made a strong statement against the death penalty.[60] Further, in one of its rulings concerning the constitutionality of temporary exclusive rights granted by the law to one specific telecommunications operator the Constitutional Court extensively relied on EU law, including various directives and decisions adopted by the

---

in the light of EU law (indirect effect) taking into account that Parliament upon passing the Telecommunications Law had indicated its wish to harmonize its provisions with relevant EU requirements. See the decision of the Supreme Administrative Court No. A[5] – 530/2003 of 11 June 2003, available at: <http://www.lvat.lt/?item=nutart>.

58 Namely, Directives 67/227/EEC, *OJ* 071, 14 April 1967 p. 1301, and 77/388/EEC, *OJ* L 145, 13 June 1977 p. 1, and various ECJ decisions dealing with the principle of fiscal neutrality, e.g., decisions in Cases C-3/97 *Goodwin and Unstead* [1998] *ECR* I-3257, C-455/98 *Tullihallitus* [2000] *ECR* I-4993, etc.

59 See decisions of the Supreme Administrative Court in cases No. A7-745-04 11.3 of 21 September 2004 and No. A1-355/2004 11.2; 11.3 of 27 October 2004, available at: <http://www.lvat.lt/?item=nutart>.

60 Ruling of the Constitutional Court of 9 December 1998 on the compatibility of the death penalty provided as a sanction under Art. 105 of the Criminal Code of the Republic of Lithuania with the Constitution of the Republic of Lithuania; Ruling of the Constitutional Court of 11 November 1998 on the compatibility of Part 4 of Art. 38 of the Law of the Republic of Lithuania on Elections to the *Seimas* and Part 4 of Art. 36 of the Law of the Republic of Lithuania on Elections to Local Government Councils with the Constitution of the Republic of Lithuania; Ruling of the Constitutional Court of 14 March 2002 on the compatibility of para. 2 of Art. 11 of the Law of the Republic of Lithuania on Pharmaceutical Activities with the Constitution of the Republic of Lithuania; Ruling of the Constitutional Court of 23 October 2002 on the compatibility of Art. 8 and para. 3 of Art. 14 of the Law of the Republic of Lithuania on the Provision of Information to the Public with the Constitution of the Republic of Lithuania; Ruling of the Constitutional Court of 26 January 2004 on the Law of the Republic of Lithuania on Alcohol Control and the Rules for Licensing the Production of Alcohol Products; Ruling of the Constitutional Court of 5 March 2004 regarding the Regulations on Granting Social Benefits and their Payment. See for the texts of the Rulings: <http://www.lrkt.lt/angdoc.htm>.

European Commission. In the present author's opinion this ruling deserves special attention, as in fact the Court's main arguments were based on EU law.[61] Besides these two rulings, there have been some other decisions in which a reference is made to EU law.[62] Of course, after accession the Constitutional Court will have to reconsider the place of EU law in the national legal system and its impact on the Constitution.

2.2 Impact of EU accession on the structure, (rules of) procedure and practice of the national courts

Although it is clear that EU accession adds a totally new dimension to the work of the national ordinary courts, the court structure has remained intact after accession. However, at the normative level several amendments of national procedural rules took place. The Law on the Courts and the Law on Administrative Procedures[63] were supplemented with provisions concerning the rights and duties of national courts as regards the preliminary rulings procedure.[64] In addition, the Code of Criminal Procedure was amended and provisions

---

[61] Ruling of the Constitutional Court of 6 October 1999 on the compatibility of Parts 1, 2 and 3 of Art. 8 and Parts 7, 8 and 9 of Art. 16 of the Law of the Republic of Lithuania on Telecommunications with the Constitution of the Republic of Lithuania, available at: <http://www.lrkt.lt/angdoc.htm>.

[62] E.g., Ruling of the Constitutional Court of 13 February 1997 on the compatibility of Arts. 1 and 30 of the Law of the Republic of Lithuania on Alcohol Control, Arts. 1, 3 and 11 of the Law of the Republic of Lithuania on Tobacco Control and Resolution No. 179 of the Government of the Republic of Lithuania of 2 February 1996 on the Control of Alcohol Advertisements with the Constitution of the Republic of Lithuania; Ruling of the Constitutional Court of 11 November 1998 on the compatibility of Part 4 of Art. 38 of the Law of the Republic of Lithuania on Elections to the *Seimas* and Part 4 of Art. 36 of the Law of the Republic of Lithuania on Elections to Local Government Councils with the Constitution of the Republic of Lithuania; Ruling of the Constitutional Court of 14 March 2002 on the compatibility of para. 2 of Art. 11 of the Law of the Republic of Lithuania on Pharmaceutical Activities with the Constitution of the Republic of Lithuania; Ruling of the Constitutional Court of 23 October 2002 on the compatibility of Art. 8 and para. 3 of Art. 14 of the Law of the Republic of Lithuania on the Provision of Information to the Public with the Constitution of the Republic of Lithuania; Ruling of the Constitutional Court of 26 January 2004 on the Law of the Republic of Lithuania on Alcohol Control and the Rules for Licensing the Production of Alcohol Products; Ruling of the Constitutional Court of 5 March 2004 regarding the Regulations on Granting Social Benefits and their Payment. See for the texts of the Rulings, available at: <http://www.lrkt.lt/angdoc.htm>. For more details see also E. Kūris, *Ekstranacionaliniai veiksniai Lietuvos Respublikos Konstituciniam Teismui aiškinant Konstituciją* (Teisė, Mokslo darbai 2004) No. 50, pp. 87-91.

[63] See *supra* nn. 38 and 39.

[64] The Law on Courts: *Valstybės žinios*, 2002 No. 17-649; see for the electronic version (not incorporating later amendments), available at: <http://www3.lrs.lt/cgi-bin/preps2?Condition1=187988&Condition2=>. The Law on Administrative Proceedings: *Valstybės žinios*, 2000, No. 85-2566; see for the electronic version (not incorporating later amendments), available at: <http://www3.lrs.lt/cgi-bin/preps2?Condition1=162936&Condition2=>.

implementing Framework Decision 2002/584/JHA concerning the European arrest warrant and the surrender procedures between Member States were inserted. On the subject of the workload of the courts it is still too early to evaluate any possible changes. So far, the national courts have not yet referred questions for a preliminary ruling to the ECJ. Of course, it will take some time for national courts to accustom themselves to the procedure of preliminary rulings. Furthermore, many disputes which are currently pending before the courts relate to pre-accession situations and are thus not covered by the procedure.[65] It seems likely that the use of the preliminary rulings procedure by national courts will, at least at the beginning, depend heavily on the initiative of the parties to a dispute. The question of training judges, especially at lower levels within the judiciary is of enormous importance, now that the majority of judge are not yet that familiar with EU law, not to mention with the procedural aspects of the preliminary rulings procedure.

3. ROLE OF THE NATIONAL PARLIAMENT AND THE GOVERNMENT

3.1 **Preparedness for legal approximation**

From the beginning of the process of approximation of Lithuanian legislation with the *acquis* draft laws related to integration issues were given priority by the *Seimas*. Each year a separate EU agenda is drafted for the adoption of "integration" laws. Taking into account the fast pace of the integration's process it is quite usual for Parliament to use the expedited procedure for the adoption of EU-related laws. Further, in order to cope better with EU issues and ensure better coordination of decision-making a parliamentary European Affairs Committee was established in 1999. During the accession stage the primary aim of the European Affairs Committee was to coordinate the work of Parliament in the field of EU issues, to analyse various questions arising out of the accession process, to exercise parliamentary control of the accession negotiations, which were mainly conducted by the Government, and thus to ensure democracy in the making of the various decisions related to EU issues.

---

[65] See, for example, the ECJ ruling in Case C-321/97 *Andersson* [1999] *ECR* I-3551.

3.2 Control over decisions taken by ministers in the Council of the European Union

As was already mentioned one of the implications of Lithuania's accession to the EU is the change in the balance of powers between the Parliament and the Government. In Lithuania, once the decision was taken to amend the Constitution to prepare for accession, one of the main subjects of vivid debate was the relationship between the *Seimas* and the Government in the EU decision-making process. Parliament regarded itself as the guarantor of democratic legitimacy and wished to be fully involved in this process. As is demonstrated by paragraph 3 of the adopted Constitutional Act[66] this idea was to some extent reflected in the Act. On the one hand, the Act secures an important role for Parliament in the EU decision-making process by requiring that Parliament shall be given all relevant information and that it shall adopt a position on issues falling within its legislative competence. On the other hand, the Act leaves some discretion to the Government when it comes to defining a final position in the EU Council of Ministers. Needless to say, after receiving Parliament's position on a given subject the Minister concerned must show convincing reasons to depart from this position. Besides, this provision laid down the basis for simplification of the process of adoption of decisions within the Parliament itself, as it stipulates that when it comes to EU issues, decisions may be adopted by the European Affairs Committee or the Foreign Affairs Committee.[67] It is still too early to evaluate the actual practical interplay between the Parliament and the Government in this field, since the amendments of the Statute of the Parliament which introduced detailed provisions implementing the above-mentioned norms of the Constitutional Act were only adopted on 9 November 2004.[68] These amendments lay down detailed provisions defining how the European Affairs Committee and the Foreign Affairs Committee will deal with European issues. It provides that decisions in the field of the EU are as a rule adopted by the European Affairs Committee, or, when it comes to foreign and security issues or matters concerning foreign trade or the WTO, by the Foreign Affairs Committee. It establishes detailed provisions concerning cooperation between the two Committees and the specialized committees (all other committees of Parliament), as well as between the Committees and the Government. Separate provisions are devoted to the control of the subsidiarity principle. In this case specialized committees are required to supervise compliance with this principle in their own respective fields of competence. If there are doubts, the specialized committee

---

[66] See *supra* n. 32.

[67] Normally, these types of decisions are adopted by the entire Parliament.

[68] *Valstybės žinios*, 2004, No. 165-6025.

should refer the issue to the European Affairs Committee. In case the European Affairs Committee comes to the conclusion that the principle has been breached it is obliged to refer the issue to the plenary session of Parliament. Once the view is taken by Parliament that an EU proposal is not in conformity with the subsidiarity principle, this position must be transmitted to the Government, the national parliaments of other EU Member States and the relevant EU institutions.

Finally, the regulations of the Government concerning the coordination of EU affairs should be noted.[69] These lay down provisions concerning the definition of national positions concerning draft EU legislation and the implementation of the adopted *acquis* at the level of the executive branch. Among other things, it provides that draft laws, which implement relevant provisions of EU law, should be submitted by the Government to the Parliament not later than six months before the deadline of implementation of these EU acts. Such a period should leave enough time for the consideration of draft laws by Parliament.

4. EUROPEAN CONSTITUTION

4.1 Impact of the EU Constitution on the Community legal order

In Lithuania, at least in academic circles, there has not been that much debates concerning the legal nature of the European Constitution and its impact on the national legal system.

It is apparent that in some fields the supranational features of the EU are strengthened, but if the Constitution is ratified by all EU Member States and comes into force the EU would remain an organization displaying a mixture of intergovernmental and supranational features. Besides, a more precise delimitation of competences between the EU and the Member States, the restriction of the use of the "flexibility clause" and the provisions of Article 5(1) of Part I of the European Constitution with regard to the national identity of the Member States show that the "dialogue" between the ECJ and the constitutional courts of some Member States has produced certain results. The ECJ has already indicated that in some cases it is willing to take into account national constitutional traditions when interpreting EU law.[70] This could lead to increased horizontal understanding of the relationship between EU law and national law, despite the fact that the principle of the supremacy of EU law is clearly spelled

[69] See the Decree of the Government of 9 January 2004, No. 21. *Valstybės žinios*, 2004, No. 8-184.

[70] E.g., the ECJ decision of 11 March 2003 in Case C-186/01 *Alexander Dory* v. *Federal Republic of Germany* [2003] *ECR* 2479.

out in the Constitution.[71] Of course, any evaluation of the final outcome of the Convention depends very much on the perspective from which the Constitutional Treaty is viewed. On the one hand, some authors even make comparisons with the Philadelphia Convention in 1787.[72] However, in the present author's opinion, if we look at the Laeken declaration and the final document produced by the Convention, it is more appropriate to speak of consolidation, simplification and rationalization. In terms of the essence of the exercise, constitutionalization does not seem the correct term, but rather constitutional formalization, now that it is clear that the constitutional claims of the EU are already not to be ignored. One could agree with the proposition that adoption of the European Constitution does not indicate the aim to create a superstate but rather to maintain the delicate balance between the EU level and the national constitutional levels and their plurality (and perhaps even to re-emphasize it).[73]

Moreover, the inclusion of the Charter of Fundamental Rights in the Constitution and the strengthening of the position of the European Parliament and the reinforced powers of the national parliaments should also be welcomed. These changes should provide for a higher degree of legitimacy and mutual understanding between the different levels of decision-making.

On the other hand, the author is of opinion that the aim to produce a Constitution which would be comprehensible to ordinary people has failed, since the EU Constitutional Treaty remains a complex document.[74] In some cases, the same provisions seem to have been repeated, for example, the almost identical provisions with regard to EU citizenship that are included in both Article I-8 of Part I and Chapter V of Part II of the Constitutional Treaty.

4.2 Ratification

Lithuania was the first EU Member State to ratify the European Constitution. This was done on 11 November 2004, although there was much discussion concerning

---

[71] This insertion of provisions concerning the supremacy of EU law only reflects where EU law stands now (i.e., the current case law of the ECJ) and thus would have be more important form a political rather than a legal point of view. See also I. Jarukaitis, 'Europos Sąjungos Konstitucinė sutartis ir valstybių narių konstitucijos' [The EU Constitutional Treaty and Constitutions of the Member States], in *Konventas, Konstitucija ir Europos Sąjungos ateitis 2002-2003* (Vilnius, Firidas 2004).

[72] E.g., M. Rosenfeld, 'The European Convention and Constitution Making in Philadelphia', 1 *International Journal of Constitutional Law* (2003) pp. 375-376.

[73] M.P. Maduro, 'Is There Europe for a Constitution?', in J.H.H. Weiler, I. Begg, J. Peterson, eds., *Integration in an Expanding European Union: Reassessing the Fundamentals* (Oxford, Blackwell Publishing 2003).

[74] The question, of course, is whether this ambitious goal could have been achieved at all, but the idea of a short version of the Constitution (for example, containing only Parts I and II) seems attractive to some extent.

the mode of ratification (through Parliament or by referendum). Parliament decided that no referendum was needed and ratified the European Constitution using the ordinary procedure for the ratification of international agreements.[75] This decision was based on several facts and assumptions. First of all, the decision to become an EU Member State had already been the subject of a referendum in Lithuania only one year before[76] and as the Constitutional Treaty does not change the nature of the EU into an organization that is essentially different from the one to which Lithuania acceded on 1 May 2004 repeating the referendum was not considered necessary. Already before ratification of the Treaty the main political parties which were in power at the time expressed this view and that the EU Constitution could be ratified by Parliament. It was also argued that the honour of ratifying should go to Parliament which had played a major role in the accession process during the past four years.[77] By contrast, however, some opposition parties opposed this rapid ratification procedure arguing that both the Members of Parliament and the population as a whole should be given more time to familiarize themselves with the contents of the Constitutional Treaty. Several non-governmental organizations called for ratification of the Treaty by way of referendum arguing that the Treaty establishes radical changes in the EU which should be sanctioned by the people. Others suggested that the opinion of the Constitutional Court on the constitutionality of parliamentary ratification should be asked. However, neither Parliament, nor the President who signed the law on ratification referred the question to the Constitutional Court.[78]

Of course, the ratification of the Constitutional Treaty as such should be evaluated positively. It reflects Lithuania's positive attitude to the EU and the integration process in a wider sense. On the other hand, being in such a hurry may have some negative consequences. By pressing ahead so urgently, the feeling may be created that European issues have nothing to do with ordinary people, as speedy ratification precluded any wider public debate on the future direction of the Union. The adoption of the Constitutional Treaty would have been an excellent opportunity to discuss and promote European values and Europe's identity in all EU Member States. It remains to be seen how ordinary citizens will in future be informed about the changes brought by the Constitutional Treaty and its impact on their lives and what their perception of the EU Constitution will be.

---

[75] The Law on Ratification of the Treaty: *Valstybės žinios*, 2004, No. 170-6239; available at: <http://www3.lrs.lt/cgi-bin/preps2?Condition1=245599&Condition2=>.

[76] See *supra* n. 41.

[77] The new Parliament was elected in October 2004 and started work on 15 November 2004.

[78] Under Art. 106 of the Constitution of Lithuania Parliament and the President of Republic have the right, but not the duty to ask an opinion of the Constitutional Court concerning the constitutionality of international agreements.

Of course, theoretically the question of the constitutionality of the ratification of the EU constitutional treaty may still be raised by ordinary courts in concrete disputes related to the application of provisions of the Treaty.

MALTA

Peter G. Xuereb*

1. THE CONSTITUTION OF THE REPUBLIC OF MALTA

The Maltese Constitution[1] is the supreme law of the land. Until the recent amendment introduced by the European Union Act of 2003,[2] whereby the Treaty of Accession[3] was ratified according to Maltese law, the Constitution made no reference either to the international legal order in general or to the effects in law of the eventuality of Malta joining the European Union. The Maltese legal position was fully dualist, therefore. The matter of incorporation of treaties was governed by the Ratification of Treaties Act,[4] which provides that "no provision of a treaty shall become, or be enforceable as, part of the law of Malta except by or under an Act of Parliament." In effect, Parliamentary approval is necessary via ratification or authorization of ratification of any international treaty. The Maltese courts would only be able to give effect to international agreements insofar as these might have been incorporated into Maltese law by, or by virtue of, legislation passed by the House of Representatives for the purpose. The main relevant parts of Section 3 of the Ratification of Treaties Act state that:

> 1. Where a treaty to which Malta becomes a party after the coming into force of this Act is one which affects or concerns:
> (a) the status of Malta under international law or the maintenance or support of such status, or
> (b) the security of Malta, its sovereignty, independence, unity or territorial integrity, or
> (c) the relationship of Malta with any multinational organization, agency, association or similar body,

* Peter G. Xuereb, Professor of European and Comparative Law, Jean Monnet Chair, Chairman of the European Documentation and Research Centre, University of Malta. Author's note: Since this article was written, the Maltese House of Representatives approved a resolution by unanimity authorizing the ratification of the Constitutional Treaty.

1 Chapter 1 of the Laws of Malta.

2 Act V of 2003 (Chapter 460 of the Laws of Malta).

3 *OJ* L 236 of 23 September 2003.

4 Act V of 1983.

such Treaty shall not enter into force with respect to Malta unless it has been ratified or its ratification has been authorized or approved in accordance with the provision of this Act.

2. A Treaty to which subsection (1) of this Section applies shall be ratified or shall have its ratification authorized or approved as follows:
(a) where such treaty concerns a matter referred to in paragraph (a) or (b) of subsection 1 of this Section or contains any provision which is to become, or be enforceable as, part of the law of Malta, by Act of Parliament;
(b) in any other case, by Resolution of the House of Representatives.

3. No provision of a treaty shall become, or be enforceable as part of the law of Malta except by or under an Act of Parliament.

The procedure for ratification of international treaties, including the Treaty of Accession, was therefore ratification, or authorization of ratification, by legislation in the House of Representatives in accordance with the Ratification of Treaties Act. This was done, in the case of ratification of the Treaty of Accession, by the passage of the European Union Act of 2003,[5] which authorized the Government of Malta to proceed to the ratification of the Treaty of Accession and related agreements.[6] It is clear that joining the European Union involved the conclusion and ratification of treaties bearing on the sovereignty of Malta on a strict interpretation of such concept, possibly as perceived by some on the status of Malta in terms of its constitutionally enshrined position of neutrality[7] bearing in mind the possible evolution of the common and foreign security policy, and in general terms involving "the relationship of Malta with any multinational organization" in terms of section 3. The European Union Act was passed by majority in the House of Representatives, and enacted on 14 July 2003. Malta deposited the relative instruments of ratification with the Italian Government on 29 July 2003. It came into force on 1 May 2004. As the ratification of the Constitutional Treaty certainly affects or concerns the relationship of Malta with a "multinational organization" (the EU directly and other multinational organizations indirectly), and also involves that Treaty becoming enforceable as part of the law of Malta, and also has implications for Malta's security, etc., it is envisaged that the Treaty will be ratified in Malta via the passage of an Act of Parliament.

---

[5] European Union Act, Act V of 2003, Chapter 460 of the Laws of Malta.
[6] Ibid., Art. 6.
[7] Section 1 of the Constitution.

Before the coming into force of the European Union Act, section 65(1) of the Constitution provided that "Subject to the provisions of this Constitution, Parliament shall make laws for the peace, order and good government of Malta." There were those who argued that this precluded the transfer of legislative power to the law-making institutions of the Union, and that there was no authority under the Constitution to transfer legislative authority. In the result, and without this issue having been settled, since section 65 is not one of the provisions of the Constitution which, in virtue of that same Constitution, was subject to the two-thirds majority amendment rule, it was decided to amend section 65 to make provision for a "transfer of sovereignty". Section 65 was amended by Article 7 of the European Union Act of 2003. Section 65 now provides that:

> Subject to the provisions of this Constitution, Parliament may make laws for the peace, order and good government of Malta in conformity with full respect of human rights, generally accepted principles of international law and Malta's international and regional obligations in particular those assumed by the Treaty of Accession to the European Union signed in Athens on the 16th of April 2003.

The Constitutional amendment authorizes the Maltese Parliament to legislate where necessary to implement the obligations arising from the Treaty.

Supremacy

On the supremacy question, the Constitution provides in section 6 that "if any other law[8] is inconsistent with this Constitution, this Constitution shall prevail and the other law shall, to the extent of this inconsistency, be void." This is made subject in particular to the operation of section 66, which lays down the procedure for amendment of the Constitution (normally, but not in all cases, by a two-thirds majority of the House).

The effect of the amendment to section 65 of the Constitution would appear to be that should Parliament enact any laws which are inconsistent with Malta's obligations as a Member State of the Union, such laws will, to the extent of any incompatibility, be deemed null and void as being in breach of section 65. In effect, Union law is made supreme over any law passed by the Maltese Parliament including after the coming into force of the European Union Act and including over any subsequent Maltese law (i.e., no *lex posterior* rule would apply). The only remaining question is as to any conflict that may occur between

[8] I leave aside the question whether the reference to "any other law" is capable of an extended interpretation beyond the obvious reference to any law of the Maltese Parliament itself. The section was not drafted at a time when Union membership was an immediate prospect.

Union law (assuming it to be included in "any other law", where it be directly applicable according to Union law) and one or more provisions of the Constitution itself.

The general consensus in Malta is that there is no existing conflict between the *acquis* and any particular provision of the Maltese Constitution. The hypothetical question arises as to what the position would be should such a conflict occur in the future. It is not envisaged that the Maltese Constitution will ever be changed in order to create a conflict that did not previously exist. Were this to be done it would be unlikely to be deliberate, and the Maltese law would presumably be amended or repealed to bring it into line with Union law. Were it to be deliberate, the grounds would presumably be that the matter was of the essence of national identity (used in the sense of Article I-5 of the Draft Constitution) and there would no doubt be questions as to whether it was not the case that the Union had in some way encroached on essential matters intended to be safeguarded by the Union Constitution itself (assuming this was in force). In other words, there might be a question as to just who was failing in a duty of loyalty. But this is of course, to argue very hypothetically.

Therefore, leaving aside questions of encroachment on national identity, the question resolves itself into the question as to what the position would be as a matter of Maltese constitutional law should *new Union law* cause an *irreconcilable* (via interpretation and full dialogue) conflict to arise. The new section 65 might then be turned to for an answer as it may be read as expressing a duty on Parliament to try to bring the Constitution into line with Union law in such an event, if necessary via an amendment of the Constitution, despite the enabling terminology ("may") used in section 65; this in virtue of general principles, also referred to in section 65, including those of international law, which oblige Malta to abide by its international obligations, but presumably saving always the protection of the essence of national identity as recognized by the Draft Constitution itself.[9] It might therefore be argued that the recent Maltese enactments and amendments referred to above have secured to most intents and purposes, and for most foreseeable realistic eventualities, the effective resolution of any conflict of legal provision in favour of the application of Union law, in line with Malta's obligations under the Treaties and including under the new Union Constitutional Treaty, should this come into force, after its ratification including by Malta. It follows that the same provisions of Maltese law, including those of the European Union Act of 2003, should guarantee the effectiveness, including the direct effect, of relevant Union law in Malta according to the terms of applicability and effect of Union law under Union law.

---

[9] Draft Constitutional Treaty, Art. I-5.

The European Union Act of 2003 makes express provision on these points. Article 3 provides that:

> From the first day of May 2004, the Treaty and existing and future acts adopted by the European Union shall be binding on Malta and shall be part of the domestic law thereof under the conditions laid down in the Treaty. Any provision of any law which from the said date is incompatible with Malta's obligations under the treaty or which derogates from any right given to any person by or under the treaty shall to the extent that such law is incompatible with such obligations or to the extent that it derogates from such rights be without effect and unenforceable.

The reference in this provision to "any provision of any law" arguably has to be read subject to section 65 of the Constitution which in its latest version provides that "Subject to the provisions of the Constitution", Parliament may make laws in conformity with Malta's international obligations. However, I would recall here that the sense of Article I-5(1) of the Draft Constitutional Treaty is that the primacy rule as enshrined (for the first time in an agreed text) in Article I-6 of the Draft Constitution will itself have to be read subject to the same Article I-5, unless that latter provision is to be denied all legal effect, and that it is presumably intended that Union Law be valid, and only then supreme, provided that the Union has acted within the parameters of, *inter alia*, that provision.

There is a full definition of "the Treaty" in Article 2(1) of the European Union Act. This is expanded on by Article 2(2) which provides that "if the Prime Minister by order declares that a treaty specified in the order being a treaty entered into by Malta after the 16th April, 2003, is to be regarded as one with the treaty as herein defined, the order shall be conclusive that it is to be so regarded." It is further provided that no such order shall be made until a draft thereof has been approved by resolution of the House, and any such resolution be submitted for examination by the Standing Committee on European and Foreign Affairs.

2. THE JUDICIARY

By Article 4(1) of the European Union Act, "all such rights, powers, liabilities, obligations and restrictions from time to time created or arising by or under the Treaty, and all such remedies and procedures from time to time provided by or under the Treaty, that in accordance with the treaty are without further enactment to be given legal effect or used in Malta, shall be recognized and available in Law, and be enforced, allowed and followed accordingly."

Those familiar with the European Communities Act of the United Kingdom will see the parallel in terms of wording. Therefore, the Maltese courts will apply and give effect to Union law according to the terms of the Union *acquis*, in accordance with Article 4(1). The general view is that in sum, the provisions referred to above are fully able to cover the questions of "indirect effect" of Union law as they have arisen in the Union in the past. In other words, the Maltese courts will interpret any Maltese law relevant to a case in the light of Union law and in such a manner as to seek to give full effect to Union law whether prior or subsequent to the Maltese law.

Article 5(1) of the European Union Act provides, in terms that also parallel the provisions of the European Communities Act of the United Kingdom, that: "For the purposes of any proceedings before any court or other adjudicating authority, any question as to the meaning or effect of the Treaty, or as to the validity, meaning or effect of any instruments arising therefrom or thereunder, shall be treated as a question of law and if not referred to the Court of Justice of the European Communities, be for determination as such in accordance with the principles laid down by, and any relevant decision of, the Court of Justice of the European Communities or any court attached thereto." Article 5(2) and (3) deal with issues of judicial notice and evidentiary matters.

It is clear that the impact on the judiciary of accession to the Union will be as strong as in other new Member States. Of course, there is the experience of adaptation over many years in the "old" Member States to draw on. Nevertheless, procedures will need to be put in place to ensure the smooth and consistent operation of all related procedures. In particular, proper guidelines should be put in place with regard to the making of preliminary references such as under the current Article 234 of the European Community Treaty. At the time of writing, it is not clear what the preferred option on this score might be. In particular, there is the choice of legislating directly or, alternatively, of leaving it to the courts to establish their own rules of practice within a legislative framework. Within these options, there is the question as to whether one might do so by amendment of the Code of Organization and Civil Procedure (and perhaps other codes), or of legislating *ad hoc*. No clear proposals have as yet emerged, so the current position is that matters will be decided on a case-by-case basis. Of course, any judge faced with the issue of having to decide questions related to the making of a preliminary reference will be following the case law of the Court of Justice and be guided by the best practice of other Member States.

3. THE HOUSE OF REPRESENTATIVES (PARLIAMENT)

We know that the latest enlargement of the Union was different from all previous enlargements, not only in terms of the number of new members, but also in terms of the massive exercise of adoption of the bulk of the *acquis* prior to entry. Much of this required parliamentary action. Therefore, the Maltese Parliament, in the same way as the Parliaments of the other new members had already "worked" on transposing much of the *acquis* and adopting legislation ancillary to such transposition and adoption. Nevertheless, a task of a different order now presents itself in terms of the ongoing real-time scrutiny of Union legislative proposals and the analysis of policy proposals. In Malta, this task will fall for the most part on the Parliamentary Committee on European and Foreign Affairs. This Committee has the wider brief of following all international affairs, as suggestions to have two committees, with one exclusively devoted to European affairs, were not followed up. The Committee is getting to grips with its new role. Now that the five Maltese European Parliamentarians have taken their seats in the European Parliament, working relationships between them and the Committee are no doubt being forged. It is expected that the Committee and the European Parliamentarians will work closely with the Malta-EU Steering and Action Committee (MEUSAC), a body composed of civil society representatives that advised on the negotiations and adoption of the *acquis* in the run-up to accession.

Clearly, Government Ministers will be accountable to Parliament for their actions in the Council of the European Union. In part this will be through the European and Foreign Affairs Committee of Parliament. Parliament is composed of 65 members, with the government having a majority of 35 seats. The government is therefore very much in the "driving seat". The remaining seats are held by the Labour Party, which was opposed to membership but has changed its stance since losing the membership referendum and subsequent general election. The Labour Party has returned three of the five new Members of the European Parliament in the June 2004 European Parliament elections.

The European and Foreign Affairs Committee (EFAC hereafter) was set up in October of 2003. It is composed of nine members, drawn from both sides of the House and having a chairman. It has some research backup, but is still building up its EU law scrutiny capability. It will be organized into three working groups for the purpose. One will sift through the documentation and channel it through to one of the other two, depending on subject-matter. The relevant Government Minister will attend working group sessions. Under ongoing discussion, even while operations are under way, is the optimum working method of the working groups. The main challenge is to furnish the EFAC with the full resources needed to fulfil its dual tasks, in relation both to European Affairs and to Foreign Affairs. It is to be expected that the Committee will play a vital role in monitoring Government activity in the Council of the European Union.

4. THE EUROPEAN CONSTITUTIONAL TREATY

The agreement reached in Brussels by heads of state and government on 18 June 2004 on the Treaty establishing a Constitution for the Union, signed in October 2004, marks a historic development in terms of the Union's history. It will also have implications at the national constitutional level in all Member States, if ratified in accordance with the Member States' constitutional traditions.

In Malta, ratification involves the processes referred to above. There is no constitutional obligation for the holding of a referendum, and Parliament can therefore decide the question in accordance with the Constitution and the Ratification of Treaties Act.

As to the aftermath, the Constitution will of course deepen the involvement of national Parliaments on questions of subsidiarity and proportionality, and this will be a major area of scrutiny for the EFAC of the Maltese Parliament.

Thus far, the Constitution has received a general welcome in Malta. It cannot be said that there is familiarity with its detailed provisions at the level of the general public (an understatement this), but it is true to say that since the membership issue was settled, the focus of debate as far as Europe is concerned has begun to shift to the adoption of the Constitution, albeit this was against the backdrop of the European Parliament elections as until the end of June. The general consensus, barring the views of a small but vociferous "hard-line" "pro-sovereignty" group that operates outside the political parties, is that there are no legal obstacles, as indicated above, to the ratification of the European Constitution by the Maltese Parliament. The essential guarantees sought and obtained by Malta in the membership negotiations will still stand, in particular that as to the respect for Malta's constitutionally-enshrined neutrality status. However, the Labour Party in opposition is still studying the Draft Constitutional Treaty and has not yet taken a position as to whether or not in its opinion any amendment of the Constitution is required before the Treaty could be ratified. The Government's position is that an Act of Parliament passed by majority suffices.

There is a sense that the Constitution will strengthen the Union legal order, but that this consequence follows not so much from substantial federalization but rather from much-needed clarification of hitherto somewhat unclear parts of the *acquis*, as for example on the legal status of the Union, the "primacy rule", the legal effect of the Charter of Fundamental Rights, and the division of competences between the Union on the one hand and the Member States on the other. Certainly, the author would argue that the Constitution establishes the relationship between the Union and the Member States, between the Member States, and between the Union and the Union's "neighbours" on a clearer and sounder footing than do the present Treaties. Examples include Article I-2 on the values of the Union, including solidarity; Article I-5, which for the first time clearly establishes the duty of loyal cooperation as a two-way duty of loyalty between the Union and the Member States; and the many specific provisions requiring solidarity as a matter of process and substance, such as Articles III-130, 257(2), 259, 266(3), and 268.

Of particular interest to Malta are the provisions on the Union's relations with the wider world. I can refer here in particular to Article I-3(4) and to Article III-292(1). Malta has a particular concern, and in a sense feels a sense of responsibility now as a Member State sited right in the centre of the Mediterranean, for that same Mediterranean area; that is to say for the part it can play in securing peace and prosperity in the Euro-Mediterranean area. Article I-3(4) provides that: "In its relations with the wider world, the Union shall uphold and promote its values and interests. It shall contribute to peace, security, the sustainable development of the Earth, solidarity and mutual respect among peoples, free and fair trade, eradication of poverty and protection of human rights and in particular the rights of the child, as well as to the strict observance and development of international law, including respect for the principles of the United Nations Charter." Article III-292(1) provides that "the Union's action on the international scene shall be guided by the principles which have inspired its own creation, development and enlargement, and which it seeks to advance in the wider world: democracy, the rule of law, the universality and indivisibility of human rights and fundamental freedoms, respect for human dignity, equality and solidarity, and for international law in accordance with the principles of the United Nations Charter and international law." I dare say that this fits in perfectly with any agenda that Malta would have wished for the Union to have *vis-à-vis* its neighbours in the Mediterranean.

As far as institutional representation is concerned, the decision to raise to six (from five) the minimum number of members of the European Parliament allocated to Member States, which adds one to Malta's number, will make a difference in terms of the division of workload and general ability to cope with the demands of giving adequate input into that institution, with positive implications also for the work of the EFAC and of the national Parliament itself. Clearly, the Maltese Government felt that it could work within the institutional framework otherwise proposed in the Constitution.

The European Constitution therefore presents opportunities for Malta to give voice to its primary concerns, placing high up on this list Malta's wish for the development of cooperation and integration across the Euro-Mediterranean area, while at the same time embodying the concept of equality for all Member States, with due recognition of population size and on the other hand of the specificities and particular needs of each Member State, translated into a clear commitment to two-way loyalty and solidarity.

POLAND

Stanisław Biernat*

1. NATIONAL CONSTITUTION

1.1 Implementation of international law and transfer of legislative powers

The Constitution of the Republic of Poland of 1997[1] contains a basic provision granting constitutional authorization to conclude the Accession Treaty and accede to the European Union. According to Article 90 paragraph 1: 'The Republic of Poland may on the basis of an international agreement transfer to an international organization or international institution the powers of organs of the state authority in certain matters.'[2] It should be noted that neither the words "European Union" nor "European Community" are used in the provision in question. Article 90 paragraph 1 was deliberately formulated in a more general manner, so that it could be applied more broadly. However, in the light of the intentions of the framers of the Constitution there can be no doubt that the provision in question was meant to refer primarily to integration in the European Union. On the basis of such an agreement there thus takes place a shift to the international level – or perhaps it would be better to say in this context the "supranational" level – of powers which, on the basis of the Constitution and statutes, are typically assigned to state organs. It is to be assumed that the provision in question may concern the powers of all the categories of organs of state authorities mentioned in Article 10 of the Constitution,[3] and also to organs of local government or other forms of self-

* Stanisław Biernat, Professor at Jagiellonian University, Krakow. Jean Monnet Chair of European Law.

[1] The Constitution of the Republic of Poland, *Dziennik Ustaw* [Journal of Laws], 1997, No. 78, item 483.

[2] See, e.g., J. Barcz, 'Membership of Poland in the European Union in the Light of the Constitution of 2 April 1997. Constitutional Act of Integration', 23 *Polish Yearbook of International Law* (1997-1998) pp. 21-34; S. Biernat, 'Constitutional Aspects of Poland's Future Membership in the European Union', 36 *Archiv des Völkerrechts* (1998) pp. 398-424.

[3] Art. 10(1): 'The system of government of the Republic of Poland shall be based on the separation of and balance between the legislative, executive and judicial powers.' Art. 10(2): 'Legislative power shall be vested in the *Sejm* and the Senate, executive power shall be vested in the President of the Republic of Poland and the Council of Ministers, and the judicial power shall be vested in courts and tribunals.'

government. Article 90 paragraph 1 of the Constitution does not contain a formulation regarding a limitation of the sovereignty of the Republic of Poland as a result of concluding the international agreement there specified. The issue of the consequences of accession to the Union has nevertheless been discussed in Poland in such categories, and the question of the limiting of sovereignty has been raised particularly by sceptics or opponents of membership.

1.2 Supremacy and direct effect

The general provision specifying the position of international law in the constitutional order of the Republic of Poland is Article 9 of the Constitution.[4] On the other hand, Article 91 of the Constitution specifies the position of international treaties in the legal order of the Republic of Poland, as well as the relationship between the provisions found in international agreements and the norms of Polish law.[5] It should be noted at this point that the Polish Constitution does not differentiate between international law and Community (Union) law.

Article 91 paragraph 1 introduces the principle of the direct applicability in Poland of ratified international treaties. It should be stated in the context of Poland's membership of the European Union that direct applicability pertains not only to the provisions of the Accession Treaty itself, but to the entire *acquis communautaire* accepted in Poland by virtue of Article 2 of the Act concerning the conditions of accession.[6]

The obligation to observe the principle of direct applicability of Community law pursuant to Article 91 paragraph 1 of the Constitution rests on all organs of the Polish state: the legislative branch (*Sejm* and Senate), the executive branch (the Government and public administration), and the courts. It should be acknowledged that after Poland's accession to the European Union, Article 91 paragraph 1 has to be interpreted in the light of Community law and in particular with reference to the case law of the ECJ. Thus whether or not in a given situation the application of Community law "depends on the enactment of a statute" is not fully at the discretion of the Polish state organs as they have to use the criteria they themselves have established for recognizing certain norms as self-executing.

---

[4] Art. 9: 'The Republic of Poland shall respect international law binding upon it.'

[5] Art. 91(1): 'A ratified international agreement, upon its publication in *Dziennik Ustaw Rzeczypospolitej Polskiej* [Journal of Laws of the Republic of Poland], shall constitute part of the national legal order, and shall be applied directly, unless its application depends on the enactment of a statute.' Art. 91(2): 'An international agreement that has been ratified upon prior consent granted in a statute shall have primacy over a statute, if the statute in question cannot be reconciled with the agreement.' Art. 91(3): 'If an agreement, ratified by the Republic of Poland, establishing an international organization so provides, the law established by such organization shall be applied directly, and have primacy in the event of a collision with statutes.'

[6] *OJ* 2003 L 236/33.

The question arises as to whether or not the "direct applicability" of Community law, as referred to in Article 91 paragraph 1 of the Constitution, should be understood more broadly, so as to include also "direct effect". An affirmative answer is favoured here. Direct effect is in essence one of the consequences of the direct applicability of the norms of Community law.

Article 91 paragraph 2 of the Constitution covers a broad spectrum of international agreements; more specifically, it deals with treaties ratified by prior consent expressed in a statute. However, given the topic of this analysis, it is essential that this provision refers also to the Accession Treaty and indirectly to the Founding Treaties of the Union and the Community. Article 91 paragraph 2 of the Constitution proclaims the primacy of primary Community law over Polish statutes. Moreover, though this is not expressly stated, the primacy of Community law extends to legal acts of a lower rank than that of a statute in the hierarchy of the sources of law (for example, executive regulations and other normative acts of the Government, Ministers, or various organs of public administration). It is safe to assume that the term "primacy" used in the provision under discussion should be understood in the same way as in the previously established case law of the Court of Justice. In the event of contradictions between the norms of Community law and the norms of Polish statutes, as well as the norms of acts of lower rank, the Polish state organs are obliged to ensure that the norms of Community law are applied. The formulation used in Article 91 paragraph 2, to the effect that the primacy (supremacy) of an international agreement (here: Community law) comes into play "if the statutes cannot be reconciled with the agreement" should be understood as establishing the obligation to interpret the provisions of Polish law in such manner as to bring about the removal of contradictions with Community law, as far as possible.

Article 91 paragraph 3 regulates, among other things, the role of secondary EU law in the legal order of Poland which enjoys primacy over Polish statutes and is directly applicable.[7] It should be assumed that the term "direct applicability" found in Article 91 paragraph 3 is used in the same sense as in Article 91 paragraph 1, while the term "primacy" is used in the same meaning as in Article 91 paragraph 2. There is no need, then, to reinterpret these concepts at this point.

The provisions of Article 91 paragraphs 2 and 3 of the Constitution, discussed above, do not proclaim, however, the primacy of EU primary and secondary law over the Constitution itself. What is more, according to Article 8 of the Constitution: 'The Constitution is the supreme law of the Republic of Poland.'

---

[7] See C. Mik, 'Implementation of Primacy and Direct Effect Principles of Community Law in the Polish Constitutional System', *Droit Polonais Contemporain – Polish Contemporary Law* (1998) No. 1-4, pp. 5-17.

Various positions have been presented in the literature on the relationship between Community law and the Polish Constitution. According to some authors, in view of the clear wording of Article 8 referred to above, the primacy of Community law does not extend to cover the Constitution.[8] An opinion to the contrary is also expressed, that is to say that through the conclusion of the Accession Treaty upon the authorization contained in Article 90 of the Constitution, Poland took over the entire *acquis communautaire*, including the principle of primacy of Community law over the whole national legal order as developed in the case law of the ECJ.[9] Finally, a pragmatic approach is also represented, postulating the abandonment of a general definition of the relationship between the legal orders discussed and seeking ways of avoiding conflicts, especially using the suitable interpretation of the law.[10]

The Constitutional Tribunal in its judgment of 11 May 2005[11] held that also after accession to the Union the Constitution of the Republic of Poland shall remain the supreme law in Poland, and Article 8 thereof shall retain its full force and effect. If a conflict occurred between the Constitution and Community law which could not be solved through interpretation of the law, Poland would have three ways out of this situation: amending the Constitution, initiating modification of EC (EU) law or ultimately withdrawing from the European Union. In the opinion of the Constitutional Tribunal, the principle of primacy of Community law may not eliminate its competence of examining the compliance of EU law with the Constitution of the Republic of Poland. Particularly emphasized in that context was the unacceptability of reducing the level of protection of the rights and freedoms of individuals.

1.3 Amendments

For a number of years, there have been discussions in Poland pertaining to the need for an amendment to the Constitution before the ratification of the Accession Treaty and before actual accession to the European Union. Various views on this issue have been presented.[12] The ratification process lasted from April to July 2003 and no amendments to the Constitution were made before or during ratification.

---

[8] See L. Garlicki, 'Kilka uwag o konstytucyjnych aspektach przystąpienia Polski do Unii Europejskiej', in L. Garlicki, ed., *Konstytucja Wybory Parlament* (Warsaw 2000) p. 64.

[9] See J. Barcz, 'Akt integracyjny Polski z Unią Europejską w świetle Konstytucji RP', 4 *Państwo i Prawo* (1998) p. 12.

[10] See S. Biernat, 'Prawo Unii Europejskiej a Konstytucja RP i prawo polskie – kilka refleksji', 11 *Państwo i Prawo* (2004) pp. 23-25.

[11] Judgment of 11 May 2005, K 18/05, available at: <http://www.trybunal.gov.pl/eng/summaries/documents/K_18_04_GB.pdf>.

[12] K. Wojtowicz, 'Proposed Changes in the Polish Constitution of 1997 ahead of Poland's Accession to the European Union', 25 *Polish Yearbook of International Law* (2001) pp. 27-44; S. Biernat,

1.4 Provisions contrary to the *acquis communautaire*

In the aforementioned discussions, the opinion has prevailed that there was no need to amend the Constitution in connection with the accession of Poland to the EU. Personally I have also subscribed to this opinion.[13] It is nevertheless worth giving an account of several debatable issues where some authors have suggested that there was a contradiction between the constitutional order in Poland and the *acquis communautaire.*

As was mentioned earlier, the provisions of Article 91 paragraphs 2 and 3 of the Constitution proclaim the primacy of EC law only over statutes, and, as indirectly follows from this, over normative acts of lower rank as well. The legal literature has included some postulates for extending the primacy of EU law over the entire legal order in Poland, including the Constitution.[14] This postulate would be difficult to implement, for political reasons, but also because of the wording of Article 8 paragraph 1 of the Constitution, in particular in the light of the judgment of the Constitutional Tribunal referred to above.[15]

Another debated issue was that of the right to vote for citizens of other Member States in the local elections in Poland. Article 62 of the Constitution grants these rights to Polish citizens.[16] Some commentators pointed at the incompatibility of this provision with Article 19 EC and postulated an amendment to the Constitution. Again the view prevailed that it is sufficient when the right to vote in local elections is granted to the citizens of other Member States in a statute.[17] Such a statute was adopted in March 2004.[18] The Constitutional Tribunal in its judgment of 11 May 2005 held that the provisions of the statute were in conformity with the Constitution. The constitutional guarantees in that regard for Polish citizens constitute a minimum; they do not exclude the extension of election

---

'The Openness of the Constitution of the Republic of Poland towards European Integration', in G. Amato, G. Braibant and E. Venizelos, eds., *The Constitutional Revision in Today's Europe* (London, Esperia 2002); J. Barcz, ed., *Czy zmieniać konstytucję? Ustrojowo-konstytucyjne aspekty przystąpienia Polski do Unii Europejskiej* (Warsaw 2002).

13 S. Biernat, 'Polen vor der Mitgliedschaft in der Europäischen Union: Steht die polnische Verfassung dem Beitritt entgegen?', in J. Stelmach and R. Schmidt, eds., *Krakauer-Augsburger Rechtsstudien – Probleme der Angleichung des Europäischen Rechts* (Krakow-Munich 2004) pp. 73-92.

14 See J. Barcz, '*Członkostwo Polski w Unii Europejskiej a Konstytucja z 1997 r.*', in J. Barcz, *supra* n. 12, p. 28.

15 See *supra* n. 11.

16 Art. 62(1): 'If, no later than on the day of voting, he has attained 18 years of age, a Polish citizen shall have the right to participate in a referendum and the right to vote for the President of the Republic of Poland as well as representatives to the *Sejm* and Senate and organs of local government.'

17 See Biernat, *supra* n. 13, pp. 87-92; K. Działocha, 'Zgodność zmian w prawie wyborczym z Konstytucją RP (w związku z przystąpieniem Polski do Unii Europejskiej)', 11 *Państwo i Prawo* (2003) pp. 13-21.

18 *Dziennik Ustaw*, No. 102, item 1055.

rights to citizens of other Member States so as to secure compliance with Community law. The Tribunal stated that the principle of sovereignty of the nation proclaimed in Article 4 of the Constitution[19] shall not extend to cover local elections. Furthermore, Article 16 of the Constitution[20] does not make belonging to a local government community dependent on holding Polish citizenship.

Another controversy was caused by the implementation in Polish law of the provisions of the Council framework decision 2002/584 of 13 June 2002 on the European arrest warrant and the surrender procedures between Member States.[21] The Constitution of the Republic of Poland contains a provision in Article 55 paragraph 1 that states: 'The extradition of a Polish citizen shall be forbidden.' Some authors were of the opinion that the implementation of the framework decision in question was impossible without prior amendment to the Constitution. However, the view prevailed in the literature which deemed "surrender" in the execution of the European arrest warrant, as applied to Polish citizens, to be a legal construction different from that of "extradition", making the constitutional change unnecessary.[22] In March 2004, the Polish Code of Criminal Procedure was amended, implementing framework decision 2002/584.[23]

In its judgment of 27 April 2005,[24] the Constitutional Tribunal held, however, that the provision of the Code allowing the surrender of a Polish citizen is contrary to Article 55 of the Constitution. The Tribunal admitted that the European arrest warrant is a useful instrument of judicial cooperation between Member States, and the surrender of citizens under the framework decision in question does indeed display a number of specific features compared to traditional extradition. However, this is still the same legal construction comprised in the prohibition formulated in Article 55 of the Constitution. The principle of interpretation of the Polish Constitution in conformity with Community law has its impassable limits. The Constitutional Tribunal used, however, the possibility provided for in Article 190 paragraph 3 of the Constitution[25] and postponed the

---

19 Art. 4(1): 'Supreme power in the Republic of Poland shall be vested in the Nation.' Art. 4(2): 'The Nation shall exercise such power directly or through its representatives.'

20 Art. 16(1): 'The inhabitants of the units of basic territorial division shall form a self-governing community in accordance with the law.'

21 *OJ* 2002 L 190/1.

22 See, e.g., E. Piontek, 'Europejski nakaz aresztowania', 4 *Państwo i Prawo* (2004) pp. 33-42.

23 *Dziennik Ustaw*, No. 69, item 626.

24 Judgment of 24 April 2005, P 1/05, available at: <http://www.trybunal.gov.pl/eng/summaries/documents/P_1_05_GB.pdf>.

25 Art. 190(3): 'A judgment of the Constitutional Tribunal shall take effect from the day of its publication, however, the Constitutional Tribunal may specify another date for the end of the binding force of a normative act. Such time period may not exceed 18 months in relation to a statute or 12 months in relation to any other normative act. Where a judgment has financial consequences not provided for in the Budget, the Constitutional Tribunal shall specify the date for the end of the binding force of the normative act concerned, after seeking the opinion of the Council of Ministers.'

date on which the provision of the Code of Criminal Procedure is to lose its binding force by 18 months. This time period is intended to be used for the fulfilment of the conditions for the implementation of framework decision 2002/584. This basically means the need to amend the Constitution. One may nevertheless doubt whether such an amendment can be effected in the political situation which can be expected in the coming years. It is worth adding that in the opinion of the Tribunal, Polish courts during the above-mentioned period of 18 months should simply apply the provision of the Code of Criminal Procedure concerning the surrender of Polish citizens in the procedures for the execution of the European arrest warrant. The practice of the courts varies, though, and some of them refuse to adjudicate on the surrender of Polish citizens.

Article 227 of the Constitution stipulates: 'The central bank of the State shall be the National Bank of Poland. It shall have the exclusive right to issue money as well as to formulate and implement monetary policy. The National Bank of Poland shall be responsible for the value of the Polish currency.' Views have been voiced that this provision would have to be changed before Poland's accession to the Economic and Monetary Union.[26] As this is to take place only after several years the aforementioned provisions was not regarded as an obstacle for the accession of Poland to the European Union.

1.5 Procedures to be followed to adapt the national constitution to the *acquis communautaire*

As indicated above, doubts pertaining to the conformity of the constitutional order with the *acquis communautaire* have so far been dispelled mainly through the interpretation of constitutional provisions in accordance with EU law. This kind of interpretation has been definitely facilitated by the openness of the Constitution of the Republic of Poland towards international law and European integration, expressed particularly in Articles 9 and 90 paragraph 1 referred to above. The case law of the Tribunal to date has demonstrated its pro-European attitude.[27] In the fields where the Constitution shows lacunae, or where the constitutional provisions leave space for diverse interpretations, suitable statutes have been adopted by Parliament and their compatibility with the Constitution has been reviewed by the Constitutional Tribunal. These methods of ensuring the conformity of Poland's constitutional order with the *acquis communautaire* have proven effective. Lack of conformity with the Constitution has so far been found

[26] The Constitutional Tribunal indicated this issue *obiter dicta* in its judgment of 11 May 2005 referred to above, *supra* n. 11.

[27] See judgment of 27 May 2003, K 11/03, available at: <http://www.trybunal.gov.pl/eng/summaries/K_11_03_GB.pdf> or of 31 May 2004, K 15/04, available at: <http://www.trybunal.gov.pl/eng/summaries/K_15_04_GB.pdf>.

only once in the case of the above-mentioned issue concerning the Code of Criminal Procedure and the implementation of framework decision 2002/584.

2. ROLE OF THE JUDICIARY (NATIONAL COURTS, INCLUDING SPECIAL BODIES WITH JUDICIAL FUNCTIONS)

2.1 Europe Agreement

In the period preceding accession, Polish courts have repeatedly referred to and applied the Europe Agreement.[28] This has been done, *inter alia*, by the Constitutional Tribunal, the Supreme Court, the Supreme Administrative Court, and the Anti-Monopoly Court (now renamed the Competition and Consumer Protection Court). Polish courts have referred most frequently to the obligation to approximate Poland's existing and future legislation to that of the Community pursuant to Article 68 of the Europe Agreement.[29] Sometimes the courts referred to other provisions of the Europe Agreement, e.g., in customs-related cases.

2.2 Supremacy and direct effect

In the period preceding the accession, Polish courts clearly stressed that European law did not have binding force in Poland.[30] For this reason the primacy (supremacy) *vis-à-vis* Polish law and the direct effect of provisions of EC (EU) law were not admitted. The courts did recognize, however, the binding force of the Europe Agreement as a ratified international agreement.[31] After accession to the EU Community law enjoys primacy over Polish statutes pursuant to Article 91 paragraph 2 of the Constitution, as already discussed.

---

[28] See the surveys of the case law of Polish courts: S. Biernat, '"European" Rulings of Polish Courts Prior to Accession to the European Union', 1 *The Polish Foreign Affairs Digest* (2005) pp. 127-149; S. Biernat, 'Die "europäische" Rechtsprechung polnischer Gerichte vor dem Beitritt zur Europäischen Union', in J. Masing and W. Erbguth, eds., *Die Bedeutung der Rechtsprechung im System der Rechtsquellen: Europarecht und nationales Recht* (Stuttgart 2005) pp. 191-207; I.G. Gęsior, 'Zasada przychylności prawu wspólnotowemu w orzecznictwie Trybunału Konstytucyjnego', in J. Barcz, ed., *Efektywność prawa wspólnotowego w Polsce* (Warsaw 2005) pp. 67-85; A.E. Kellermann, 'Direct effect of Europe Agreements in the pre-accession period', 2 *Revista romana de Drept Comunita* (2004).

[29] See, e.g., judgments of the Constitutional Tribunal: K 12/00, OTK 2000, No. 7, item 255; K 35/99, OTK 2000, No. 8, item 295 or K 15/99, OTK 2000, No. 5, item 137; and of the Supreme Court: I CKN 121/98, III RN 240/01, OSNP 2004, No. 3, item 42; I CKN 308/01, Lex No. 80243.

[30] See judgment of the Supreme Court: III RN 240/01, *supra* n. 29.

[31] See judgments of the Constitutional Tribunal: K 12/00, *supra* n. 29; K 35/99, *supra* n. 29; K 15/99, *supra* n. 29 or of the Supreme Court: I CKN 1217/98, OSNC 2002, No. 1, item 13; III RN 240/01, *supra* n. 29; I CKN 308/01, *supra* n. 29.

2.3 Indirect effect

In the period preceding the accession, the Polish courts (particularly those mentioned earlier in this text) have often referred to the provisions of both primary and secondary EC law. They have done so primarily in connection with the obligation of the approximation of Polish law with the requirements of the *acquis communautaire* as proclaimed in Article 68 of the Europe Agreement. The norms of EC (EU) law were used by Polish courts as an aid in the interpretation of Polish law. The courts emphasized that in the cases where various interpretations were possible, the option chosen should be the one enabling the conformity of Polish law with European law.[32]

The Constitutional Tribunal has held in its judgments that the interpretation of statutes should take into account "the constitutional principle of supporting the process of European integration" expressed in the Preamble and Article 9 of the Constitution.[33] Article 90 should also be mentioned in this context. Thus an interpretation of the law which serves the purpose of applying this principle is "constitutionally preferable." In another judgment, the Constitutional Tribunal declared that in certain situations it was appropriate to refer to European law in order to establish the contents of constitutional provisions.[34] Similar – although less strongly worded – statements on the role of EC law in the interpretation of Polish statutes before the accession can be found in the decisions of the Supreme Court[35] and the Supreme Administrative Court.[36]

2.4 Cases

References to Community law were made in judgments of the Constitutional Tribunal and various Polish courts even before Poland acceded to the EU, at a time when it was a state associated with the Community under the Europe Agreement. In more than ten judgments, in which the Constitutional Tribunal examined the conformity of statutes with the Constitution, references were made to the Europe Agreement, and sometimes, through it, to primary or secondary Community law and to the case law of the ECJ. In this way the substantive rules of Community law served to interpret Polish law in various areas. The Constitutional Tribunal referred to EC law while examining the conformity with the Constitution of the provisions of statutes pertaining to the different retirement age

---

[32] See judgment of the Constitutional Tribunal K 2/02, OTK-A 2003 No. 1, item 4 or of the Supreme Court: I CKN 308/01, *supra* n. 29; III RN 54/01, OSNAP 2002, No. 14, item 321.

[33] See judgment K 11/03, *supra* n. 27.

[34] See judgment K 2/02, *supra* n. 32.

[35] See judgment I CKN 308/01, *supra* n. 29 or III RN 54/01, *supra* n. 32.

[36] See judgment V SA 305/00, Lex No. 51327.

of women and men.[37] Various courts referred to EC law in the course of interpreting Polish statutes in the field of labour law,[38] the free movement of goods, competition law, admissibility of control in advertising, in customs law, banking law, tax law, consumer protection and others.[39] References to Community law before accession were auxiliary in their nature, and the Constitutional Tribunal emphasized that Community law had no binding force in Poland yet. During that period the Constitutional Tribunal relied for the first time on the principle of interpretation of national law in conformity with EC (EU) law.[40]

Also before accession to the EU or soon afterwards, the Constitutional Tribunal issued three judgments of major systemic importance for the clarification of doubts as to the procedure of accession, and for the adaptation of Poland's system to enable it to conform to the conditions of membership. These were judgments in cases concerning the compliance with the Constitution of the statutes on the national referendum,[41] elections to the European Parliament[42] and the cooperation between executive and legislative powers.[43]

Regular mention has already been made of the landmark judgment of the Constitutional Tribunal on the compliance with the Polish Constitution of the Accession Treaty and the EC and EU Treaties. The judgment was the result of an application to the Court by three groups of right-wing deputies in the *Sejm*. It should be recalled that in the judgment concerned the Tribunal emphasized clearly that the Constitution of the Republic of Poland remains the supreme law in Poland and that the primacy of EC law does not extend to the Constitution. At the same time, however, the Constitutional Tribunal held that the Accession Treaty and primary EU law comply with the Polish Constitution. It should be noted at this point that the extent of the claims made by the applicants against EU law was very broad and varied. They concerned, amongst other things, breach of sovereignty and independence of Poland, infringement of the principle of separation of powers, loss of independence of Polish courts, etc. In addition to allegations of a

---

37 See judgment K 15/99, *supra* n. 29; K 35/99, *supra* n. 29; K 15/97, OTK 1997, No. 3-4, item 37; or K 27/99, OTK 2000, No. 2, item 62.

38 See judgment of the Constitutional Tribunal: K 12/00, *supra* n. 29 or of the Supreme Court III ZP 21/97, OSNAP 1998, No. 5, item 143.

39 See for a discussion of these judgments the works quoted *supra* n. 28.

40 See judgment K 2/02, *supra* n. 32 or judgment of 21 April 2004, K 33/03, available at: <http://www.trybunal.gov.pl/eng/summaries/documents/K_33_03_GB.pdf>.

41 See Act of 14 March 2003 on the nationwide referendum, *Dziennik Ustaw*, No. 57, item 507 as later amended and judgment of 27 March 2003, K 11/03, *supra* n. 27.

42 See Electoral Law to the European Parliament Act of 23 January 2004, *Dziennik Ustaw*, No. 25, item 219; and judgment of 31 May 2004, K 15/04, *supra* n. 27.

43 See statute on the cooperation between Poland's Council of Ministers and the *Sejm* and Senate, in matters connected with the membership of the Republic of Poland in the European Union of 11 March 2004, *Dziennik Ustaw*, No. 52, item 515, and judgment of 12 January 2005, K 24/04, available at: <http://www.trybunal.gov.pl/eng/summaries/documents/K_24_04_GB.pdf>.

general nature, there were also a number of detailed ones. The Tribunal dismissed all of these, analysing, one after another, the content of the rules of EU law objected to and comparing them with the rules of the Constitution of the Republic of Poland. Furthermore, the Tribunal emphasized strongly the authorization for Poland to join the Union under Articles 9 and 90 paragraph 1 of the Constitution, as well as the democratic legitimization of the accession decision itself; that decision was made, after all, directly by the nation as a holder of the sovereign right in a referendum.

2.5 Structure, procedures and practice

The accession of Poland to the EU has not affected the structure of the Polish judiciary.

There has been some discussion in the legal literature whether it should be necessary or purposeful to include in the rules of procedures of civil, criminal and administrative courts, specific provisions on the preliminary references of the Polish courts to the Court of Justice based on Article 234 EC.[44] However, no amendments have been introduced in the relevant statutes, possibly presuming that Article 234 EC will be regarded in the practice of Polish courts as a directly applicable provision of law with primacy over Polish law. The first experiences of the courts after accession to the Union will demonstrate whether it is necessary to supplement the procedural statutes. Doubts have already arisen as to whether a preliminary reference to the ECJ should result in a staying of the proceedings or adjournment of the trial. Moreover, discussions are going on as to whether in the case of a reference to the ECJ or a refusal to make one a remedy is available to the dissatisfied party to a court of higher instance.

In June 2005, the administrative court in Warsaw was the first Polish court to submit a preliminary reference to the ECJ.[45]

It is difficult to predict at this time whether the application of European law is to increase the caseload of the courts. This is likely to happen in cases involving refugees, now that Poland as an EU Member State will become more attractive to applicants seeking refugee status. So far, there have not been many cases submitted to the administrative courts challenging the decision of the National Board for Refugees, although this situation may change.[46] It should be noted that, irrespective

---

[44] See M. Szpunar, 'Wpływ członkostwa Polski w Unii Europejskiej na sądownictwo – zagadnienia wybrane', in S. Biernat, S. Dudzik and M. Niedźwiedź, eds., *Przystąpienie Polski do Unii Europejskiej. Traktat akcesyjny i jego skutki* (Zakamycze 2003) pp. 277-301.

[45] This pertains to the interpretation of Arts. 25, 28 and 90 EC in connection with doubts as to whether Polish fiscal law contains discriminatory provisions.

[46] See, e.g., J. Chlebny, 'Ochrona sądowa w sprawach dotyczących osób ubiegających się o nadanie statusu uchodźcy – doświadczenia i perspektywy', VII *Miscellanea Iuris Gentium* (2004) pp. 19-33.

of the membership of the EU, many courts in Poland are already struggling with an excessive caseload and Poland as a result has lost a number of cases before the ECtHR for infringement of Article 6 of the ECHR.[47]

3. ROLE OF THE NATIONAL PARLIAMENT

3.1 Preparedness for legal approximation

In February 2004, the Rules of Procedure of the *Sejm* (the first Chamber of Parliament) were amended.[48] The Rules provide for a special procedure to handling Bills for the implementation of EU law. These Bills are conducted through "fast-track" procedures for the enactment of legislation by the *Sejm*. The Rules contain provisions ensuring the speedy and efficient consideration of the Bills in question by the Committee for the European Union and other competent parliamentary committees. Similar provisions were also in force before accession when Poland was adapting national law to harmonize it with the *acquis communautaire* in order to meet the requirements for membership.[49] Special provisions pertaining to "European" Bills are also included in the Rules of Procedure of the Senate (the second Chamber of Parliament).[50]

Under a statute enacted in March 2004 (which will also be referred to further below) the Council of Ministers is obliged to submit to the *Sejm* any Bills implementing EU law on precisely scheduled dates, thereby enabling these Bills to be passed in time so as to avoid infringing the requirements of EU law.

3.2 Control over decisions taken by ministers in the Council of the European Union

The Constitution of the Republic of Poland does not include any special provisions on the competences to present the position of Poland to the institutions and organs of the European Union. According to Article 146 paragraph 1 of the Constitution: 'The Council of Ministers shall conduct the internal affairs and foreign policy of the Republic of Poland.' This provision is deemed to pertain

---

47 In 1997-2004, the European Court of Human Rights at Strasbourg delivered 178 judgments in cases against Poland. In 112 of these, i.e., over 60 per cent, the Court found a violation of the right to trial within a reasonable time, contrary to Art. 6 § 1 of the European Convention on Human Rights.

48 *Monitor Polski* [Official Gazette] 2004, No. 12, item 182.

49 See S. Biernat, 'The Impact of European Integration on the Organization and Functioning of Poland's Legislative and Executive Authorities', 9 *Revue Européenne de Droit Public* (1997) No. 4, pp. 1187-1208.

50 *Monitor Polski*, 2004, No. 18, item 302.

also to Poland's relations with the European Union and its institutions. Prior to enlargement, legal literature presented various proposals concerning the position of Parliament in European matters.[51]

In March 2004, a statute on the cooperation between Poland's Council of Ministers and the *Sejm* and Senate, in matters connected with the membership of the Republic of Poland in the European Union, was adopted and came into force.[52] The statute obliges the Council of Ministers[53] to present to the *Sejm* and Senate information on the participation of Poland in the activities of the European Union at least once every six months. Upon request, the Council of Ministers is also obliged to provide information on all matters connected with EU membership. The internal organ of the *Sejm* which considers the documents submitted to it and provides opinions on them is the Committee for the European Union. It was set up pursuant to the Rules of Procedure of the *Sejm* as amended in 2004. The Committee has 46 members which comprises one-tenth of the total number of deputies in the *Sejm*. The Committee is composed on the basis of strict proportion so as to reflect precisely the distribution of political forces in the Chamber. Subcommittees, both permanent and *ad hoc*, shall be set up within the Committee. A corresponding committee was set up in the Senate.

The statute stipulates that the Council of Ministers promptly submits to the *Sejm* and Senate (or, more precisely: the above-mentioned parliamentary committees) various documents received from the European Union. This obligation covers, e.g., White and Green Papers, the Action Plans of the Council of the European Union, the annual legislative plans of the European Commission, the drafts of international agreements to which the EU, EC or Member States are to be parties, the drafts of acts of the representatives of the Member States meeting in the Council, as well as the drafts of other acts including those which do not have legal force, such as guidelines on employment.

The drafts of legal acts of the European Union constitute a special category, which the Council of Ministers is obliged to send promptly to the *Sejm* and Senate. In addition, the Council of Ministers is also obliged to present the draft versions of its positions on drafts of the EU legal acts. The *Sejm* and Senate Committees for the EU may issue opinions on the submitted documents or drafts of the European Union institutions. Failure to issue an opinion within the time

---

[51] See J. Barcz, 'Parlament polski w procesie decyzyjnym w sprawach integracyjnych. Wnioski de lege ferenda', 3 *Kwartalnik Prawa Publicznego* (2002) S. 7-52; R. Grzeszczak, 'Wpływ członkostwa Polski w Unii Europejskiej na Sejm i Senat RP', in Biernat, Dudzik and Niedźwiedź, *supra* n. 44, pp. 215-230.

[52] See *supra* n. 43.

[53] In order to avoid misunderstanding it should be explained that here "the Council of Ministers" means the Government of Poland and not the EC institution.

limit provided in the statute is equal to a "no objection" statement from the Committee.

The statute provides for special treatment of the drafts of legal acts which are to be considered by the Council of the European Union. These drafts, together with the drafts of the Polish Government's positions are obligatorily submitted to the Committee for the EU of the *Sejm* for opinion. An issue that was widely discussed prior to the adoption of the statute was the legal force of the opinion on the draft of an EU legal act and the position of the Council of Ministers. The statute stipulates that the Committee's opinion should "provide a basis for the position of the Council of Ministers." If the latter is not going to take into account the opinion, it is under obligation to promptly explain the grounds for taking such a divergent position. Thus, the opinion of the Committee is not absolutely legally binding. Granting binding legal force to the position of the *Sejm* or its Committee would be irreconcilable with the constitutional principle of the separation of powers.

The statute discussed herein does not provide for corresponding consulting powers for the Senate committee. The Constitutional Tribunal held that the applicable provision of the statute did not conform with the Constitution as it did not guarantee equal treatment to both Chambers of Parliament.[54] The Tribunal concluded that the consulting by parliamentary committees of draft positions of the Polish Government to be presented in the forum of EU institutions meant the performance of legislative functions of Parliament and not the control functions over the executive branch. This is why the granting of the same powers to the *Sejm* and the Senate is required. As a result of the judgment of the Constitutional Tribunal under discussion the statute was amended in 2005.

It should be pointed out that the proper functioning of the Parliamentary Committees for the EU is of paramount importance. According to Articles 87 and 92 of Constitution, the statutes passed by Parliament are the principal source of law whereas regulations and other legal acts issued by executive authorities are only implementing pieces of legislation issued on the basis of specific authorization contained in relevant statutes. In this situation the broad and early involvement of the Committee for the EU and other parliamentary committees in shaping the position to be presented by Poland in the EU forum should enhance the chances for the proper and timely adoption of the necessary statutes implementing EU law in the Polish legal order.

---

[54] See *supra* n. 43. It is worth adding that three judges submitted a dissenting opinion.

4. EUROPEAN CONSTITUTION

4.1 Impact of the EU Constitution on the Community legal order and accession

After it was signed in October 2004, the European Constitution met with a varied response in Poland. Discussions on the subject had begun earlier, following the submission of the draft Constitution by the European Convention.

In the opinions of its supporters, the European Constitution definitely represents progress by improving the legal bases on which the Union is founded. It is also beneficial from the viewpoint of newly acceding Member States and their nationals.[55] The following advantages of the draft Constitution may be listed: simplification of the Union's primary law; increased democratization of the Union owing to the enhanced roles of the European Parliament and national Parliaments; more profound integration within the Union through the formal abandoning of the division into Pillars and endowing the Union with legal personality; division of competences between the Union and the Member States; reform of decision-making procedures; rendering the Charter of Fundamental Rights binding; and declaring the possibility for a Member State to withdraw from the European Union; the latter issue may be of importance to Eurosceptics.

The discussion was dominated, however, by rather critical opinions in Poland with respect to the document in question. They were expressed particularly by right-wing or centrist parties. The most significant reservations pertained to the lack of reference in the preamble of the Constitution to the Christian tradition of Europe,[56] and to the change of the voting system in the future Council of Ministers to the disadvantage of Poland, when compared with the arrangement agreed in political terms in Nice in 2000 and legally guaranteed in the Accession Treaty in 2003.[57] The European Constitution was criticised also for being a long and

---

[55] See S. Biernat, 'Europe, its Member States and Citizens – do they need a Constitution?', 2 *Irish Journal of European Law* (2004) pp. 340-345; S. Biernat, 'The European Constitution from the Perspective of the New Member States', Walter-Hallstein Institut für Europäisches Verfassungsrecht, available at: <http://www.rewi.hu-berlin.de/WHI/deutsch/fce/index05.htm#fce105>.

[56] It is worth noting that during the IGC, Poland advocated the inclusion in the preamble to the European Constitution of a reference to the Christian heritage of Europe and not of *invocatio dei.* Prior to that some of the members of the Convention proposed inclusion of the *invocatio dei* modelled on the preamble to the 1997 Polish Constitution, which has been considered a particularly successful formula: "We, the Polish Nation – all citizens of the Republic, Both those who believe in God as the source of truth, justice, good and beauty, As well as those not sharing such faith but respecting those universal values as arising from other sources...". For a positive assessment of this formula see J.H.H. Weiler, *Chrześcijańska Europa* (Poznań 2003); English edition *A Christian Europe* (forthcoming).

[57] See Art. 205 EC paras. 2 and 4 as amended (with effect from 1 November 2004) by Art. 12 of the Act concerning the conditions of accession.

fuzzy document, hard to understand by citizens. Varied opinions were voiced as to the political, economic and social visions of the Union to emerge after the coming into force of the Constitution.

4.2 Obstacles to ratification of the European Constitution

The opinion prevails that the legal character of the European Constitution does not differ from that of the current Founding Treaties of the Community and the Union. The most serious doubt relating to the constitutional reform of the Union judged in the light of the Constitution of the Republic of Poland concerns Article I-6 of the Constitutional Treaty, proclaiming the principle of primacy of the European Constitution and EU law over the law of the Member States. Some have observed that this provision cannot be reconciled with the aforementioned Article 8 paragraph 1 of the Polish Constitution. One should point out, however, that the principle of the primacy of EC law is already binding, even though this fact might have escaped the attention of some of the opponents of the Constitutional Treaty. At present the primacy of EC law does not stem from any direct Treaty provision but from the established case law of the Court of Justice.[58] It could therefore be assumed, that in legal terms the Constitutional Treaty does not introduce any fundamental change in this matter. In political and social terms the changes are nevertheless obvious.

Undoubtedly, however, the primacy of EU law, expressed directly in the European Constitution, could in Poland end up on a tense footing with the supreme position of the Constitution of the Republic of Poland in the system of the sources of law, as understood by the Constitutional Tribunal in its judgment of 11 May 2005 which has been referred to a number of times above.

The Constitutional Treaty is commonly treated as an international agreement concluded in accordance with Article 90 paragraph 1 of the Constitution of Poland, which 'transfers to an international organization or international institution the powers of organs of the state authority in certain matters'. Thus the procedure pursuant to Article 90 paragraphs 2 through 4 of the Constitution shall apply.[59] This means that the same ratification procedure as applied to the Accession

---

[58] See, e.g., the well-known judgments of the ECJ 6/64 *Costa* v. *ENEL* [1964] *ECR* 585; 106/77 *Amministrazione delle Finanze dello Stato* v. *Simmenthal* [1978] *ECR* 629 or C-213/89 *R.* v. *Secretary of State for Transport ex parte Factortame* [1990] *ECR* I-2433.

[59] Art. 90 paras. 2-4 of the Constitution: '(2) A statute granting consent for ratification of an international agreement referred to in para. 1, shall be passed by the Sejm by a two-thirds majority vote in the presence of at least half of the statutory number of Deputies, and by the Senate by a two-thirds majority vote in the presence of at least half of the statutory number of Senators. (3) Granting of consent for ratification of such agreement may also be passed by a nationwide referendum in accordance with the provisions of Article 125. (4) A resolution in respect of the choice of procedure for granting consent to ratification shall be taken by the Sejm by an absolute majority vote taken in the presence of at least half of the statutory number of Deputies.'

Treaty must be applied to the Constitutional Treaty.[60] Under the provisions of Article 90 paragraph 4, the *Sejm* has to select one of two methods for expressing its consent to the ratification: either by a ratification statute (Art. 90 para. 2) or by national referendum (Art. 90 para. 3). It was a political certainty that as in the case of the Accession Treaty the referendum procedure would be chosen to ratify the Constitutional Treaty. The President of the Republic of Poland together with left-wing parties supporting the Constitutional Treaty have suggested that the referendum on the Treaty should be held in autumn 2005 and should be combined with the presidential election and possibly also the parliamentary elections. Opposition right-wing parties preferred a later date.

The situation changed as a result of the rejection of the European Constitution in the referenda in France and the Netherlands in May and June 2005, respectively, and the conclusions of the European Council of June 2005. At the beginning of July 2005, the *Sejm* voted to put off a decision on how to ratify the Constitutional Treaty.[61] The process of ratification has been suspended until after the September parliamentary elections at the earliest.

The resumption of the process of ratification of the Constitutional Treaty in Poland and its further progression can be expected to depend, on the one hand, on the developments in other Member States and possible further decisions made in the forum of the European Council and, on the other hand, the political situation in Poland itself.

In this context, it is only possible to formulate a few diverse comments on future developments. There seems to be no doubt that the referendum path will be selected for the ratification of the Constitutional Treaty or another treaty which will possibly be negotiated by the Member States. Such a procedure involves certain risks related to the strict requirements set out by the Polish Constitution, one of them being that the referendum must be of a decisive and not just a consultative nature and that the outcome is binding under strict conditions.[62] Given the slight public interest in public affairs of the Polish population,[63] one concern is that the turnout in the referendum on the ratification of the Constitutional Treaty will not exceed the 50 per cent threshold which would result in the

60 See S. Biernat, 'Are the acceding states constitutionally prepared to become members of the European Union?', in N. Neuwahl, ed., *European Union Enlargement: Law and Socio-Economic Changes* (Montreal, Thémis 2004) pp. 63-85.

61 A. Rettman 'Poland kicks EU Constitution into uncertain future', *Euobserver*, 6 July 2005, available at: <http://euobserver.com/?sid=18&aid=19508>.

62 Art. 125 para. 3 of the Constitution: 'The result of a nationwide referendum shall be binding, if more than half of the number of those having the right to vote have participated in it.'

63 For example, the turnout in the June 2004 election for the European Parliament was about 21 per cent. The participation in the Polish referendum of June 2003 which approved the ratification of the Accession Treaty was however about 59 per cent. By Polish standards, this was an exceptionally high turnout, which is believed to be very difficult to reach again.

outcome not being binding. In that case, a further ratification procedure will have to be decided by the *Sejm* in accordance with Article 75 of the statute *on* the nationwide referendum of March 2003.[64] The *Sejm* could then either declare another referendum or decide that the consent to ratification should be given through a ratification statute.[65]

Considering the unstable political climate in Poland, it cannot be excluded that the referendum will result in the rejection of a new treaty. It is more likely, however, that the referendum may not be of a binding character because of an insufficient turnout. In that case it is expected that in accordance with the relevant provisions of the statute on the referendum as set out above, the decision to ratify the Constitutional Treaty will be made by Parliament through the enactment of a ratification statute. However, Article 90 paragraph 2 of the Constitution sets high standards for the statute approving the ratification of agreements referred to in Article 90 paragraph 1 of the Constitution. It is worth recalling that the adoption of the ratification statute requires the rigorous qualified majority of the votes of all deputies to the *Sejm* and the Senate.[66] It is difficult to predict whether such a majority willing to support the European Constitution or its equivalent will be present in a future Parliament.

---

64 *Dziennik Ustaw*, No. 57, item 507. Art. 75: 'If the result of the referendum on the consent to the ratification of an international agreement is not binding, the Sejm may again adopt a resolution on the choice of procedure for granting consent to the ratification of the agreement.'

65 Art. 75 of the statute on referendum was challenged in the Constitutional Tribunal. However, in May 2003, the Tribunal decided that the provision in question is compatible with the Constitution. See judgement K 11/03, *supra* n. 27.

66 See *supra* n. 59.

SLOVAK REPUBLIC

Miroslav Slastan*

1. NATIONAL CONSTITUTION

1.1 Implementation of international law and transfer of legislative powers

The first article of the Slovak Constitution No. 460/1992 of the Collection of Laws (Coll.)[1] defines "the Slovak Republic as a sovereign, democratic state governed by the rule of law, which it is not bound to any ideology or religion". The second paragraph of this Article emphasizes that "the Slovak Republic acknowledges and adheres to general rules of international law, international treaties by which it is bound, and its other international obligations". From this reference to international law in the opening provision of the Constitution we may assume a strong emphasis on and the precise constitutional regulation of international obligations, whether they arise from treaties, conventions or pacts to which the Slovak Republic is a contracting party, or from acts of institutions or bodies of international organizations of which Slovakia is a member.

This approach was not an original feature of the Slovak Constitution. It was introduced after much controversy and discussion among constitutional legal experts and the Members of the National Council of the Slovak Republic ("the Slovak Parliament" or "Parliament") after Slovakia was given the opportunity to become a member of NATO and after the December 1999 Helsinki Summit of the European Council when it was finally decided to enter into negotiations on the accession of the Slovak Republic to the European Union.[2]

* Department of Constitutional Law, Faculty of Law, Matej Bel University, Banská Bystrica, SK.

[1] The Constitution of the Slovak republic No. 460/1992 of the Collection of Laws, adopted on 1 September 1992, entered into force on 1 October 1992, except several provisions which have entered into force since 1 January 1993 (amended and completed by Constitutional acts No. 244/1998 Coll., 9/1999 Coll., 90/2001 Coll., 140/2004 Coll. and 323/2004 Coll.). Other terms used in this text: "the Slovak Constitution" or "Constitution". When referring to the article without *expressis verbis* named act, consider as the Constitution of the Slovak republic No. 460/1992 Coll.

[2] See Helsinki European Council 10 and 11 December 1999, Presidency Conclusions point I.; see <http://europa.eu.int/council/off/conclu/dec99/dec99_en.htm>.

Before this, there was only Article 7 of the Slovak Constitution dealing with such matters, which read that "the Slovak Republic may, by its own discretion, enter into a state union with other states. The right of secession cannot be restricted. A constitutional law, which shall be confirmed by a referendum, shall decide upon entry into a state union or on secession from such a union". Nothing was said about the possibility of transferring competences (of the legislative, executive or judicial bodies of the Slovak Republic) to international organizations or related legal concepts. A subsequent Article 11 (within the second heading on "fundamental rights and freedoms") only stated that "international treaties on human rights and fundamental freedoms which the Slovak Republic has ratified and which were promulgated in the manner laid down by law before the entry into force of this constitutional act, shall be a part of its legal order and shall have precedence over laws if they provide a greater scope of constitutional rights and freedoms".[3]

The incorporation and implementation in the national legal order of international law other than such treaties was thus effected through a dualistic doctrine of the relationship between international law and the national legal order, without there being a general reception clause for international obligations in the Slovak legal order. In addition, any international treaties mentioned in Article 11 which were not promulgated in the manner laid down by act No. 1/1993 Coll. did not have the character of a national source of law (e.g., the General Declaration of Human Rights of 1948).[4] Except for the above-mentioned international treaties on human rights and fundamental freedoms, until 2001 no general constitutional provision existed which regulated the relationship between international obligations and the Constitution of the Slovak Republic.

The implementation of international treaties in the Slovak legal order by means of laws was explicitly prescribed by Article 86 sub (e).[5] Before this there was (and still is) a practice of including individual reception clauses in legislation, such as § 99 of Act No. 511/1992 Coll. on the administration of taxes and charges which provides that: "the provisions of this act shall be applicable, unless an international treaty, which is binding on the Slovak Republic [i.e., which has been ratified by the President of the Slovak Republic and promulgated in the Collection of Law], provides otherwise", which is true for several international treaties.[6]

---

3 Now Art. 154c para. 1 of the Slovak Constitution.

4 See cases II. ÚS 28/96 and II ÚS 41/99, Collection of Sentences and Decisions of the Constitutional Court of the Slovak Republic, Košice 1996, 1999.

5 Art. 86 alinea (e) of the Constitution states: [The powers of the National Council of the Slovak Republic shall be particularly] "before ratification to approve international political treaties, economic treaties of general nature, as well as international treaties for whose implementation a law is necessary".

6 See also § 756 Act No. 513/1991 Coll. of the Commercial Code of the Slovak Republic.

The new constitutional situation in this respect was established by the adoption of the final amendment of the Slovak Constitution so far on 23 February 2001.[7] Constitutional Act No. 90/2001 which amended the Constitution of the Slovak Republic came into force on 1 July 2001[8] and prepared the Slovak Republic for its membership in the European Union and NATO. It also extended the direct applicability of international treaties in the Slovak legal order and regulated their precedence over Slovak laws.

First of all, the following provision was added to Article 1: "the Slovak Republic acknowledges and adheres to general rules of international law, international treaties by which it is bound, and its other international obligations" corresponding to the standard of other Constitutions of the EU Member States.[9]

After the adoption of Constitutional Act No. 90/2001 Coll. the former concise *Article 7* became the central provision regulating the relationship between international treaties and the Slovak legal order with special regulations (after considerable controversy) for the *acquis communautaire*.

Paragraph 1 of Article 7 now states that "the Slovak Republic may, by its own discretion, enter into a state union with other states. A constitutional law, which shall be confirmed by a referendum, shall decide on entry into a state union or on secession from such a union". The words "the right of secession cannot be restricted" were eliminated. However, this does not describe the case of European integration.

Paragraph 3 of Article 7 provides for, for example, Slovak NATO membership by stating that: "for the purpose of maintaining peace, security and the democratic order, under conditions established by an international treaty, the Slovak republic may join an organization of mutual collective security".

The general reception clause for incorporating international obligations into the Slovak legal order was introduced by paragraph 5 of Article 7: "international treaties on human rights and fundamental freedoms and international treaties for whose exercise a law is not necessary, and international treaties which directly confer rights or impose duties on natural persons or legal persons and which were ratified and promulgated in the way laid down by law shall have *precedence over laws*" and form an integral part of the Slovak legal order. However, this does not create an automatic mechanism for incorporation, now that paragraph 4 of Article 7 emphasizes that "the *validity* of international treaties on human rights and fundamental freedoms, international political treaties, international treaties of a military character, international treaties from which the membership of the Slovak Republic in international organizations arises, international economic treaties of a general character, international treaties for whose implementation a law is

---

[7] Slovakia became member of NATO on 29 March 2004 and a member of the EU on 1 May 2004.

[8] Except several provisions which came into force on 1 January 2002.

[9] See, e.g., Art. 25 of the Constitution (Basic Law) of the Federal Republic of Germany from 23 May 1949.

necessary and international treaties which directly confer rights or impose duties on natural persons or legal persons, *require* the *approval* of the National Council of the Slovak Republic before ratification".

This leads us to the conclusion that (a) *any* international treaty on human rights and fundamental freedoms, (b) all international treaties for whose implementation a law is not necessary, and (c) international treaties which directly confer rights or impose duties on natural persons or legal persons, are *incorporated* in the Slovak legal order (as an original source of law) provided that they are:

(1) ratified by the President (Art. 102 para. 1, alinea (a) of the Constitution);
(2) approved by the National Council of the Slovak Republic before ratification;[10] and
(3) promulgated in the way laid down by law (Act No. 1/1993 Coll.).

The Slovak Constitution also states that these three categories of international treaties, after fulfillment of the abovementioned conditions, shall have precedence over laws of the Slovak Republic. Article 86 sub (d) recognizes that only the Slovak Parliament has the power to determine whether the international treaty falls within the scope of paragraph 5 of Article 7. Article 144, paragraph 1, of the Slovak Constitution further provides that "judges, in the performance of their function, shall be independent and, in decision making shall be bound by the Constitution, by constitutional law, by international treaties pursuant to Article 7, paragraphs 2 and 5, and by law". Under Article 13 the situation is dealt with where an international treaty imposes duties on natural persons or legal persons. According to Article 13, paragraph 1, (in Title 2 headed "fundamental rights and freedoms") duties can be imposed (a) by a law or on the basis of a law, within the limits it imposes and having due regard to fundamental rights and freedoms, (b) by an international treaty according to Article 7, paragraph 4, which directly confers rights and imposes duties on natural persons or legal persons, or (c) by regulations of the Government according to Article 120, paragraph 2.

Any other international treaties, especially those mentioned in Article 7, paragraph 4, i.e., international political treaties, international treaties of a military character, international treaties from which the membership of the Slovak Republic in international organizations arises (but expressly not the Treaty on Accession and the EU Treaty), international economic treaties of a general character, international treaties for whose implementation a law is necessary and international treaties which directly confer rights or impose duties on natural persons or legal persons, even if they are approved by the Slovak Parliament and promulgated in the Slovak Collection of Laws (i.e., incorporated in the Slovak

---

10 Except for international treaties for whose implementation a law is not necessary, as they are not mentioned in Art. 7 para. 4 or Art. 86 sub (d) of the Slovak Constitution.

legal order) shall *not* have precedence over laws of the Slovak Republic, which means among other things that judges are not bound by them in deciding cases.

Secondly, Constitutional Act No. 90/2001 amending the Constitution of the Slovak Republic on 23 February 2001 extended the legislative powers of the Government of the Slovak Republic in *Article 7, paragraph 2*. This provision deals with two special international treaties concerning the European Union, namely the Treaty on Accession and the Founding Treaties (TEC/TEU),[11] which are incorporated into the Slovak legal order by Article 7, paragraph 5, as will be discussed below. Paragraph 2 provides that "legally binding acts of the European Communities and of the European Union shall have precedence over laws of the Slovak Republic". This means that secondary EC/EU legislation shall be part of the Slovak legal order. The final sentence of paragraph 2 regulates that "the transposition of legally binding acts which require implementation (still secondary EC/EU law) shall be realized through a law or regulations of the Government according to Article 120, paragraph 2".

Thus, according to Article 120 of the Slovak Constitution, the Government shall have the power not only to issue regulations to implement laws within the limits laid down by the law (para. 1), but also if laid down by a law, to issue regulations on the implementation of the Europe Agreement Establishing an Association between the European Communities and their Member States on the one part, and the Slovak Republic on the other part (this is already an obsolete provision), and "on the implementation of international treaties according to Article 7, paragraph 2".[12] Now it is not clear (from Art. 7, para. 2, last sentence and Art. 120, para. 2) if the Government is only entitled to issue regulations on the implementation of secondary EC/EU law (Art. 7, para. 2) or also on the implementation of international treaties and thereby primary EC/EU law (Art. 120, para. 2).

Regardless of this dilemma, Parliament adopted an implementing law which includes detailed provisions on these approximation regulations, namely Act No. 19/2002 Coll. of 18 December 2001 on the conditions for the adoption of approximation regulations of the Government of the Slovak Republic,[13] which entitles the Slovak Government in addition to Parliament to independently implement several international obligations (now obligations which result from the Treaty on Accession, ergo the Founding Treaties).[14]

---

[11] "The Slovak Republic may, by an international treaty, which was ratified and promulgated in the way laid down by law, or on the basis of such a treaty, transfer the exercise of a part of its powers to the European Communities and the European Union."

[12] Art. 120, para. 2, of the Slovak Constitution.

[13] Amended by Acts Nos. 207/2002 Coll. and 607/2004 Coll.

[14] These approximation regulations can be adopted by the Slovak Government in the field of customs law, banking law, accounting law, company tax law, law of intellectual property, etc.; it may not regulate the limits of fundamental rights and freedoms, the state budget, and matters which have to be regulated by law according to the Constitution, and it may not create new state institutions.

As far as the transfer of powers to international organizations is concerned, it has to be observed that the Constitution of the Slovak Republic only provides for this in one specific case, namely that of the European Union. As we have pointed out, according to the first sentence of Article 7, paragraph 2, "the Slovak Republic may, by an international treaty, which was ratified and promulgated in the way laid down by law, or on the basis of such a treaty, transfer the exercise of a part of its powers to the European Communities and the European Union". There was much debate between Slovak political parties which, particularly for the benefit of the public, argued over the question of whether membership meant loss of our sovereignty or not, where one side contended that it did not as the transfer only concerned "part of the powers" and only their "exercise".

1.2 Supremacy and direct effect

As we have pointed out, international treaties on human rights and fundamental freedoms, international treaties which directly confer rights or impose duties on natural persons or legal persons (after approval by the National Council of the Slovak Republic before ratification) and international treaties for whose implementation a law is not necessary and which were ratified and promulgated in the way laid down by law shall have precedence over laws according Article 7, paragraph 5. Its first and foremost meaning is that "Slovak judges, in the performance of their function, shall be independent and, in decision making, shall be bound by the Constitution, by constitutional law, by international treaties pursuant to Article 7, paragraphs 2 and 5, and by law".[15] From this provision it is clear that international treaties pursuant to Article 7, paragraph 5, of the Constitution do not have precedence over the Constitution or constitutional law.

Thus the Constitutional Court shall decide on the conformity of laws, government regulations, generally binding legal regulations of Ministries and other central state administration bodies, generally binding regulations pursuant to Article 68 (regulations of the local bodies), generally binding legal regulations of the local bodies of state administration and generally binding regulations of the bodies of territorial self-administration pursuant to Article 71, paragraph 2, with the Constitution, with constitutional laws and with the international treaties to which the National Council of the Slovak Republic has expressed its assent and which were ratified and promulgated in the manner laid down by law, except where another court shall decide on their conformity.[16] This means that the Constitutional Court is obliged to review all international treaties mentioned in Article 7, paragraph 4, not only those with precedence over Slovak national law under paragraph 5.

---

[15] Art. 144, para. 1, of the Slovak Constitution.
[16] Art. 125, para. 1, of the Slovak Constitution.

A contrario sensu the Slovak Constitutional Court shall decide on the conformity with the Constitution and constitutional law of draft international treaties to which the assent of the National Council of the Slovak Republic is necessary (Art. 7, para. 4) prior to the submission of the draft treat to Parliament.[17] If the Constitutional Court holds that the international treaty in question is not in conformity with the Constitution or constitutional law, it cannot be ratified.

The Slovak Constitution does not deal with the situation where, for example, a judge on a district or county court is confronted with an international treaty which is incompatible with the Constitution or constitutional laws. The Slovak Republic is a party to the Vienna Convention on the Law of Treaties,[18] which in Article 26 provides the basic principle of international law that *pacta sunt servanda* ("every treaty in force is binding upon the parties to it and must be performed by them in good faith"). In addition, according to Article 27 of the Vienna Convention: "a party may not invoke the provisions of its internal law as justification for its failure to perform a treaty". With reference to Article 1, paragraph 2, mentioned above, we must conclude that the Slovak judge in our example will be bound by the international treaty concerned, despite its non-conformity with the Constitution.

The supremacy of international law over national law is also complicated by Article 86 sub (d) of the Constitution, which states that only the National Council of the Slovak Republic shall be competent (to the exclusion of the Constitutional Court or any other courts) to decide on whether the international treaty falls within the category of treaties intended under Article 7, paragraph 5. A decision of Parliament that an international treaty shall have precedence over laws is an integral part of the treaty's promulgation in the Collection of laws.[19]

Article 7 of the Slovak Constitution contains special regulations in respect of the European Union. As was mentioned above, according to paragraph 2 of Article 7: "the Slovak Republic may, by an international treaty, which was ratified and promulgated in the way laid down by law, or on the basis of such a treaty, transfer the exercise of a part of its powers to the European Communities and the European Union". The same paragraph states, that "legally binding acts of the European Communities and of the European Union shall have precedence over laws of the Slovak Republic. The transposition of legally binding acts which require implementation shall be realized through a law or a regulation of the Government according to Article 120, paragraph 2". Several risks potentially present themselves through this provision.

---

17 Art. 125a, paras. 1 and 2 of the Slovak Constitution.

18 Vienna Convention on the Law of Treaties of 22 May 1969, entered into force for the Slovak Republic valid on 28 August 1987, promulgated in the Collection of Laws under notification of the Ministry of Foreign Affairs No. 15/1988 Coll. See also <http://www.un.org/law/ilc/texts/treaties.htm>.

19 Para. 6, sub 2 of Act No. 1/1993 Coll.

It was clearly the intention of the legislator to make primary and secondary EC/EU legislation directly applicable in the Slovak legal order and give it precedence over national law. However, the wording of this provision does not seem to include the case law of the Court of Justice of the European Communities, for example. For this reason, we have the following reservations concerning this provisions:

(a) The term "legally binding acts of the European Communities and of the European Union" in accordance with the linguistic interpretation means *only secondary* legislation of the EC/EU law, therefore omitting further sources of EC/EU law, such as the primary law, the general principles of Community law, the international agreements concluded by the Community and agreements involving the Community and the case law of the Court of Justice.[20]

(b) The term "*legally binding acts* of the European Communities and of the European Union" indicating secondary EC/EU legislation might create uncertainty in some situations as to the extent to which according to Article 249 TEC a given Directive is a legally binding in respect of its scope and subject matter, as to which acts of the Second and Third Pillar fall within the scope of this term (e.g., decisions according to Art. 34, para. 2, sub (b), (c) or (d) TEU); or as to the position of external agreements (commercial agreements under Art. 133 TEC, Association Agreements under Art. 310 TEC, agreements on cooperation under Art. 300 TEC, etc.),

(c) Finally, the term "shall have precedence over *laws* of the Slovak Republic" in accordance with the grammatical interpretation and with Article 125, paragraph 1, sub (a) means that secondary legislation (particular binding acts under Art. 249 TEC) shall have precedence over *laws* and implicitly over other generally binding legal regulations with the exception of the Constitution and the constitutional laws.

All Acts and generally binding legal regulations shall enter into effect (in accordance with Act. No. 1/1993 Coll., not by international law) on the date of their promulgation. Details on the promulgation of Acts, of international treaties and of legally binding acts of an international organization pursuant to Article 7, paragraph 2, have to be laid down by law.[21] The promulgation of Acts, other generally binding legal regulations and of international treaties is consequently

20 For the sources of EC/EU law see, e.g., D. Simon, *Le système juridique communautaire*, 3rd edn. (Paris, P.U.F. 2001) p. 302; J.-M. Favret, *Droit et pratique de l'Union européenne*, 4th edn. (Paris, Gualino 2003) pp. 315 et seq.; S. Raepenbusch, *Droit institutionnel de l'Union et des Communautés européennes*, 3rd edn. (Brussels, De Boeck Université 2001) pp. 283 et seq.

21 See Art. 87, para. 4, of the Slovak Constitution.

regulated by Act No. 1/1993 Coll. on the Collection of Laws. In connection with secondary EC/EU law, the Slovak Parliament on 24 June 2004 adopted Act No. 416/2004 Coll. on the Official Journal of the European Union. The purpose of this Act is to establish a conclusive presumption of knowledge of legally binding acts of the European Union and the European Communities and to complement the competences of the Ministry of Justice of the Slovak Republic for the purpose of ensuring public access to the Official Journal of the European Union. Paragraph 1 of the Act states that legally binding acts of the European Communities and of the European Union which are promulgated in the Official Journal of the EC/EU comply with international treaties[22] in force on the territory of the Slovak Republic.

Finally, how does the Constitution of the Slovak Republic deal with the primary law of the European Union? As Article 7, paragraph 2, does not refer to the primary law of the EU, it must be concluded that primary law falls under the scope of paragraph 5, as the Founding Treaties are international treaties which directly confer rights or impose duties on natural persons or legal persons.[23]

1.3 Amendments

Practically all necessary constitutional amendments for the ratification of the Treaty on Accession (and where necessary also for that of the EU Treaty (TEU), the EC Treaty (TEC) and the Euratom Treaty) were introduced by the abovementioned constitutional Act No. 90/2001 to amend the Constitution (known as the "integration amendment").

Not only Article 1, paragraph 2, and Article 7, paragraphs 2, 4 and 5 and Article 144, paragraph 1, enabled the implementation of primary and secondary EC/EU law from 1 May 2004, but several other provisions were also involved. *Exempli gratia*, the former Article 23 of the Slovak Constitution (freedom of movement) in paragraph 4 stated that Slovak citizens may not be forced to leave their homeland and cannot be deported or extradited. Constitutional Act No. 90/2001 repealed the word "extradite" so as to enable the implementation of Council Framework Decision 2002/584/JHA of 13 June 2002 on the European arrest warrant and the surrender procedures among the Member States.[24]

Another provision was added by Constitutional Act No. 90/2001 to comply with Article 19 TEC, providing the right of citizens of the Union residing in a Member State of which they are not a national to vote and to stand as a candidate at municipal elections in the Member State in which they reside. Now the second

---

[22] See Art. 254, paras. 1 and 2 TEC and Art. 2 of the Treaty on Accession of the Slovak Republic to the European Union.

[23] See also decision No. 365 of the National Council of the Slovak Republic of 1 July 2003 to approve the Treaty on Accession.

[24] See § 14 sect. 4 of Act No. 403/2004 Coll. of 24 June 2004 on the European Arrest Warrant.

sentence of Article 30, paragraph 1, states that aliens with permanent residence in the territory of the Slovak Republic shall have the right to vote and to be elected to bodies of local self-administration (municipalities and higher territorial units).[25]

Further amendments to the Slovak Constitution to align it with the *acquis communautaire* are not excluded. In fact, some constitutional provisions may be considered to be contrary to EC/EU law.

For the eventuality that a new treaty is adopted amending the Treaty on European Union (TEU) and the Treaties establishing European Communities (or related acts) a ratification procedure has been laid down in the Constitution (Arts. 102 a and 7, para. 4 taken together with Art. 86 sub (d). A special constitutional provision is Article 84, para. 4, of the Slovak Constitution. Regarding parliamentary consent prior to ratification by the President in the approval of international treaties according to Article 7, paragraph 2 (Treaty on Accession as well as the Treaties making up primary EC/EU law), this consent must be given by a three-fifths majority of all Members of Parliament.[26] The same majority of all Members of Parliament shall be required for the purpose of adopting or amending the Constitution.

1.4 Provisions contrary to the *acquis communautaire*

As we observed above, according to Article 7, paragraphs 2 and 5 and Article 125a, paragraph 1, the precedence of primary and secondary EC/EU law is excluded with respect to the Constitution and constitutional laws.[27]

Secondly, under Article 30, paragraph 1, citizens shall have the right to participate in the administration of public affairs directly or through freely elected representatives. Aliens with permanent residence in the territory of the Slovak Republic shall have the right to vote and to be elected to local self-governing bodies. Nevertheless, paragraph 4 of Article 30 only guarantees access to elected and public offices under equal conditions for Slovak citizens.

Questions may arise from the subdivision of international treaties according to Article 144, paragraph 1: "judges, in the performance of their function, shall be independent and, in decision making shall be bound by the Constitution, by the constitutional law, by the international treaty pursuant to Article 7, paragraphs 2 and 5, and by law". If a Slovak court in a case pending before it suspects that

---

25 The right to vote and to stand as a candidate in elections to the European Parliament (Art. 19, para. 2, TEC) is implemented by §§ 2 and 3 of Act No. 331/2003 Coll. on elections to the European Parliament.

26 This was, e.g., the case in the decision of the National Council of the Slovak Republic No. 1596 of 11 May 2005 which expresses its approval of the Treaty establishing a Constitution for Europe.

27 See the established case law of the Court of Justice in cases 6/64 *Costa*, e.g., 11/70 *Internationale Handelsgesellschaft*, 106/77 *Simmenthal SpA*, C-285/98 *Tanja Kreil*, etc.

other generally binding legal regulations are (partly) contrary to the Constitution, constitutional laws, or international treaties pursuant to Article 7, paragraph 5 or to a law, it must stay the proceedings and submit an application for the commence of proceedings according to Article 125, paragraph 1. The opinion of the Constitutional Court of the Slovak Republic contained in the decision shall be binding upon the Court. However, Article 7, paragraphs 2 and 5 of the Constitution does not distinguish between two different categories of international treaties. Also approval decision of the National Council of the Slovak Republic No. 365 from 1 July 2003 with the Treaty on Accession of the Slovak Republic to the European Union states, that Treaty on Accession falls under paragraph 5 of Article 7 and implicitly also TEC and TEU. Consequently, if any Slovak judge assumes that any provision of a generally binding legal regulation contradicts the Treaty on Accession, TEC or TEU, it shall suspend the proceedings and shall submit a proposal for the commence of proceedings to the Constitutional Court. Is it thus the legal opinion of the Constitutional Court (not of the European Court of Justice) that is binding for the Slovak judges according to the Slovak Constitution? This would be absolutely contrary to the Articles 234, 244, 256 and 10 TEC.

It is our opinion that international treaties under Article 7, paragraph 2, are of a different category than treaties in paragraph 5 (international treaties which directly confer rights or impose duties on natural persons or legal persons). The decision to approve the Treaty of the National Council of the Slovak Republic No. 365 from 1 July 2003, which states that the Treaty on Accession falls under paragraph 5 of Article 7 does not extend the rights of the Slovak Constitutional Court in Article 144, paragraph 2, to interpret primary EU law instead of the European Court of Justice.

1.5 Procedures to be followed to adapt the national Constitution to the *acquis communautaire*

The basic changes were made prior to the Slovak membership of the European Union (constitutional Act No. 90/2001 Coll.). The powers of the National Council of the Slovak Republic (acting as constituent power) shall be particularly to adopt the Constitution and constitutional laws, and amendments of these.[28] For the purpose of adopting or amending the Constitution or a constitutional law, the consent of a three-fifths majority of all Members of Parliament is required.[29] The same procedure was prescribed by Article 84, paragraph 4, for the Treaty on Accession before it could be ratified by the President and promulgated in the Collection of Laws.

---

28 Art. 86 sub (a) of the Slovak Constitution.

29 Art. 84, para. 4, of the Slovak Constitution.

Despite the fact that an obligatory referendum is not provided for by the Constitution in this respect, a referendum on the membership of the Slovak Republic in the EU (to approve the Treaty on Accession) was held after a resolution of Parliament (in consensus with the Government) on 16 and 17 May 2003.[30] Under Article 93, paragraph 2, of the Constitution "a referendum may also be used to decide on other crucial issues of public interest". A referendum shall be declared by the President of the Slovak Republic upon a petition submitted by at least 350,000 citizens, or upon a resolution of the National Council of the Slovak Republic.[31] The results of a referendum shall be valid provided an absolute majority of eligible voters have participated and the issue has been decided by an absolute majority of votes.[32] The referendum on EU membership has been the only valid referendum in the Slovak Republic since this instrument has been applied due to the 52.15 per cent turnout and the total of 92.46 per cent of votes cast favouring accession. It had been argued, however, that even if a majority of eligible voters failed to participate in the referendum this would not change anything, now that the referendum was not mandatory and could therefore only have an advisory function.

Some hesitation has therefore arisen in connection with Article 7, paragraph 1. According to this provision "the Slovak Republic may, by its own discretion, enter into a state union with other states. A constitutional law, which shall be confirmed by a referendum, shall decide on the entry into a state union, or on the secession from such union". Two political parties in Parliament (the Christian Democrats and the Communist Party), whose political programmes are fairly cautious with respect to the European Union and integration,[33] argued that the EU constituted a state union already and that a referendum was therefore mandatory and its result legally binding.

2. ROLE OF THE JUDICIARY

2.1 Europe Agreement

The Europe Agreement establishing an Association between the European Communities and their Member States on the one part, and the Slovak Republic on the other part was signed in 1993 and entered into force on 1 February 1995, but was not promulgated until 1997[34] and therefore only its provisions on human

---

[30] See decision of the President of the Slovak Republic of 17 February 2003 on the promulgation of the referendum, published under No. 49/2003 Coll.

[31] Art. 95, para. 1, of the Slovak Constitution.

[32] Art. 98, para. 1, of the Slovak Constitution.

[33] See <http://www.kdh.sk> and <http://www.kss.sk>.

[34] See notification of the Ministry of Foreign Affairs No. 158/1997 Coll.

rights and fundamental freedoms were directly applicable within the Slovak legal order. After the adoption of constitutional Act No. 90/2001 Coll. the Europe Agreement finally formed an integral part of the Slovak legal order. Given the brief period that it has been applicable, therefore, little is known about its application by the Slovak national courts in civil, commercial, administrative or criminal proceedings. To illustrate this: the Slovak Government was directly authorized by the Constitution to issue regulations on the implementation of the Europe Agreement and was therefore practically the only institution to apply the agreement.

2.2 Supremacy and direct effect; indirect effect; cases

As we have mentioned above, Slovak courts under Article 144, paragraph 1, of the Constitution have to recognize all the provisions of the Treaty on Accession and the Founding Treaties. Supremacy of these Treaties only means, however, that they have precedence in the application of legal rules (Art. 7, para. 5), not that they rank higher than the Constitution. Supremacy of secondary EC/EU law means the same (pursuant to Art. 7, para. 2). There have been several cases, also before the lower courts, which indicate that secondary EC law (mostly Regulations) is being duly applied. With respect to the principle of indirect effect we have to underline that there is no clear legal basis (except for ECJ case law) which allows the Slovak courts to apply this principle. As Slovak courts are accustomed to applying only the traditional methods of legal interpretation, the first case acknowledging indirect effect will most likely be decisive.

The Constitutional Court of the Slovak Republic is vested with the mandate to protect the constitutionality of laws according to Article 124 of the Slovak Constitution and therefore the first direct confrontation of generally binding legal regulations of the Slovak Republic (especially the Constitution) with EC/EU law is expected to take place here. There has already been one case of the Slovak Constitutional Court in which the Court in its reasoning also mentioned EU law (concerning the EU Directives on advertising).[35]

2.3 Structure, procedure and practice

Slovak courts are not only entitled from 1 May 2004 to request the European Court of Justice to give a preliminary ruling according to Article 234 TEC, but from 1 October 2004 also with reference to § 109, paragraph 2, sub (c) of the Slovak Code of Civil Procedure (Act No. 99/1963 Coll.).[36] District and regional

[35] See PL. ÚS 37/99 Collection of Sentences and Decisions of the Constitutional Court of the Slovak Republic, Košice 2000.

[36] Appropriate amendments to the Slovak Code of Civil Procedure were introduced by Act No. 428/2004 Coll. of 24 June 2004 which entered into force on 1 October 2004.

courts as wells as the Supreme Court of the Slovak Republic must stay the proceedings if they decide to refer matters for a preliminary ruling from the European Court of Justice subject to Article 234 TEC.

The provisions of § 121 of Act No. 99/1963 Coll. also state that during civil proceedings there is no need to demonstrate facts of common knowledge or facts known to the court due to the performance of its functions, nor do legal regulations promulgated or announced in the Collection of Laws of the Slovak Republic or legally binding acts which were promulgated in the Official Journal of the EC/EU have to be proven.

The manner of enforcing decisions of the Council or of the Commission as envisaged in Article 256 TEC is *expressis verbis* provided in § 275a. The same provisions that regulate the enforcement of judgments of the Slovak courts in § 251 to § 271 of the Slovak Code of Civil Procedure also apply to the enforcement of Council and Commission decisions. The Code does not, however, refer to Article 244 TEC and the enforcement of the judgments of the European Court of Justice.

To date, there have only been proposals to request a preliminary ruling according to Article 234 TEC, mostly raised before the Supreme Court of the Slovak Republic. The application of primary EC/EU law by the Slovak courts is also to be awaited.

3. ROLE OF THE NATIONAL PARLIAMENT

3.1 **Preparedness for legal approximation**

The legal approximation of the national legislation with EC/EU law started partly after the Europe Agreement entered into force on 1 February 1995.[37] This process was rapidly speeded up after negotiations on accession of the Slovak Republic to the European Union in February 2000. Both legislative actors (Parliament and the Government) have adapted their procedures on the legislative procedure (Rules on Law-making). All Acts drafted by the Government or by a parliamentary committee or a Member of Parliament shall include a compatibility clause[38] in the

[37] Europe Agreement establishing an association between the European Communities and their Member States, of the one part, and the Slovak Republic, of the other part was signed on 4 October 1993. See notification No. 158/1997 Coll.

[38] The compatibility clause first of all states the commitment of the Slovak Republic towards the European Communities and the European Union:
(a) identification of the subject matter of the draft legal regulation from the point of view of the European Agreement on Association, the National Programme for the Adoption of the *acquis communautaire*, the Accession Partnership, the White Paper, the screening and the plan of legislative tasks of the Government of the Slovak Republic,

explanatory memorandum to indicate the compliance of the draft rules with EC/EU law.[39] The detailed requirements imposed under this clause are still specified in the Rules on Law-making of the National Council of the Slovak Republic (No. 19/1997 Coll.) in case a Bill is introduced by a Member of Parliament or a parliamentary committee[40] and in the Rules on Law-making of the Government of the Slovak Republic (resolution No. 241 of 8 April 1997,[41] last amended by resolution No. 1097 of 19 November 2003) in case a Bill is introduced by the Government.

Contrary to what is provided under the Rules on Law-making of Parliament, the Government is by its rules obliged in addition to the compatibility clause to work out what is termed a concordance table showing how the Government Bill concords with the law of the European Communities and the law of the European Union as an update of approximation. All draft rules have to be divided into individual parts (e.g., article, section, paragraph, sentence and number) and compared to the corresponding provision in the *acquis communautaire*. It also has to include further information, such as methods of transposition (ordinary transposition, transposition with option as to method, transposition at discretion, concordance, administrative infrastructure, stage of the legislative process, timetable, notes, etc.). The Government of the Slovak Republic bears the main responsibility when it comes to the approximation of the Slovak legislation to EC/EU law. For this purpose, the necessary administrative capacity was created (e.g., by the establishment of the Institute for the Approximation of Law at the Office of the Government of the Slovak Republic). On the other hand, the Government alone without the effective cooperation of Parliament cannot always be held responsible for possible failures during the implementation process. During the legislative procedure in Parliament, all Members of Parliament as well as any parliamentary committee have the right to propose modifications to the Government Bill.[42]

The administrative capacity of the National Council of the Slovak Republic to deal with the implementation of the *acquis communautaire* is limited. The

---

(b) identification of the commitments resulting from the adopted negotiating positions in the respective chapter, which is the subject of the draft legal regulation (point 3).

The degree of compatibility of the draft legal regulation with the law of the European Communities and the law of the European Union: (a) full, (b) partial, (c) none, (d) the draft legal regulation is incompatible (point 5).

It is obvious at a glance that the compatibility clause is completely redundant, too general and out of date.

39 See § 68, para. 3, of Act No. 350/1996 Coll. on Parliament.

40 See Art. 2, para. 1, Art. 3 and annex I to resolution No. 519 of 18 December 1996 promulgated in the Collection of Laws under No. 19/1997.

41 See Arts. 3, 3a, 3b, 12, para. 3, and annex I.

42 See Act No. 350/1996 Coll.

Committee on European Affairs[43] of the Slovak Parliament and its secretariat – the Section for European Affairs – is responsible for monitoring EC/EU legislation and has to elaborate analyses and proposals for the Slovak position in this process. In 1993, a Commission for the Harmonization of Slovak Law with EC law was created as an advisory body to the Constitutional Law Committee which was later replaced by the Legal Compatibility Commission of the Legislation Section of the Office of Parliament. This is now the Department of Approximation of Law within the Section for Legislation and Approximation of Law whose function is to monitor all Government and Parliamentary Bills, to advise on their compatibility with the *acquis communautaire* and to suggest any appropriate amendments to the Members of Parliament and committees.

There is no special legislative procedure to be used by the National Council of the Slovak Republic with respect to the approximation of Slovak legislation to EC/EU law. All the general provisions, including those on the discussion of Bills in parliamentary committees or in plenary, the voting, the submission of comments by the President to the National Council of the Slovak Republic, the expedited procedure and promulgation in the Collection of Laws may be applied in these situations as well.

3.2 Control over decisions taken by ministers in the Council of the European Union

According to Article 72 of the Slovak Constitution, "the National Council of the Slovak Republic shall be the sole constitutional and legislative body of the Slovak Republic". On the other hand, Article 13, paragraph 1, states that duties can also be imposed on natural persons or legal persons by regulations of the Government according to Article 120, paragraph 2.

The powers of the Slovak Parliament are non-exhaustively listed in for the most part Article 86 of the Constitution which mentions the following: "(a) to adopt the Constitution, constitutional laws and other laws, and to supervise their implementation, (b) to approve treaties on the union of the Slovak Republic with other states and the repudiation of such treaties by a constitutional law (...), (d) before ratification to approve international treaties on human rights and fundamental freedoms, international political treaties, international treaties of a military nature, international treaties from which the membership of the Slovak Republic in international organizations arises, international economic treaties of a general nature, international treaties for whose exercise a law is necessary, and international treaties which directly confer rights or impose duties on natural persons or legal persons, and at the same time to decide on whether they are international

43 Formerly the Committee on European Integration which was created in 1996 according to the Polish and Hungarian model.

treaties according to Article 7, paragraph 5, (e) to establish Ministries and other governmental bodies, (f) to deliberate on the Government's Programme, monitor the activities of the Government, and deliberate on votes of no confidence with respect to the entire Government or one of its members (...), and (h) to deliberate on fundamental issues relating to domestic, international, economic, social and other policies (...)".

In the constitutional and political system of the Slovak Republic, the Slovak Government both as a whole, as well as its individual members (the Prime Minister, the Vice-Prime Minister and all other Ministers) are politically accountable to the Slovak Parliament. The Government of the Slovak Republic shall be accountable to the National Council of the Slovak Republic for the exercise of governmental powers. The National Council of the Slovak Republic may take a vote of no confidence at any time.[44] Members of the Government shall be individually accountable to the National Council of the Slovak Republic for the discharge of their function.[45]

It would be contrary to this system of division of powers within the Slovak political and constitutional system, if the Slovak Parliament did not retain control over decisions taken by Ministers in the Council of the European Union to a certain extent. This was one of the reasons for the adoption by the Slovak Parliament on 24 June 2004 of Constitutional Act No. 397/2004 Coll. on the cooperation between the National Council of the Slovak Republic and the Government of the Slovak Republic in affairs concerning the European Union.[46] This Constitutional Act lays down new obligations for the Government of the Slovak Republic as well as for its individual Members who:

(1) have to submit any "proposals of legal binding acts and other acts of the European Communities and European Union, which shall be discussed by the representatives of Governments of the EU Member States" to Parliament;

(2) also have to inform the Slovak Parliament of any "others matters related to the Membership of the Slovak Republic in the European Communities and the European Union"; and finally

(3) have to submit to Parliament "timely information concerning the position Slovakia intends to adopt" with respect to proposals or acts mentioned under point (1), the essence of which shall be "to estimate the effects of such acts for the Slovak Republic".

---

44 Art. 114, para. 1, of the Slovak Constitution.
45 Art. 116, para. 1, of the Slovak Constitution.
46 Constitutional Act No. 397/2004 Coll., entered into force on 1 August 2004.

The National Council further has the power to approve the mandate (positions) of the Government concerning proposals of legally binding acts and other acts of the European Communities and the European Union which shall be discussed by the representatives of Governments of the EU Member States. This mandate binds all members of the Government during the voting in the EU Council.[47] If the Slovak Parliament is unable to adopt a decision at all or within two weeks, the member of the Government concerned is bound by the proposal in this matter as adopted by the Government.[48] He or she may deviate from it only in case of emergency and having due regard to the interests of the Slovak Republic, after which he/she immediately has to inform Parliament and state the reasons for the deviation.

The National Council may also authorize a committee by law to exercise the abovementioned powers. The Committee on European Affairs of the Slovak Parliament was established after almost one year by a revision of the Act on Parliament No. 350/1996 Coll. (Standing Orders of Parliament).[49] Its main task is to monitor closely the decision-making process in the European Union and the activities of the Slovak Government in the different Council meetings.[50] Detailed rules of cooperation between the National Council of the Slovak Republic and the Government are to be laid down in an ordinary law,[51] which has yet to be adopted.

One concern arising from the organization of this process is that it may entail a political risk. The eleven Members of Parliament are currently able to determine the voting of the Slovak Republic in the Council of the EU. However, the position approved by the parliamentary committee may be too restrictive for the Ministers in question and may in the end prove to be counterproductive by excluding the Slovak Ministers from the discussion in the Council. On the other hand, how can this philosophy of the "imperative mandate" ever ensure the efficiency of the EU legislative process if all 25 Members of the Council from the present EU Member States have different instructions? Moreover, the discussion in the Council of Ministers as intended by the Slovak law is only the final stage of the EU legislative process. Many key decisions have already been adopted within Coreper by the Member States' ambassadors in Brussels. The words "member of the Government" in Article 2, paragraphs 4 and 5 of Constitutional Act No. 397/2004 Coll. in our opinion do not cover the representatives voting in Coreper. Finally, the few Members of the Slovak Parliament, let alone the National Council of the Slovak Republic on its own, are in practical terms unable to respond to the

---

[47] See, e.g., Decision of the National Council of the Slovak Republic No. 1340 of 30 November 2004 on the proposed position of the Slovak Republic on the initiating of negotiations on accession with Turkey.

[48] See Art. 2, para. 4, of Act No. 397/2004 Coll.

[49] See Act No. 253/2005 Coll. of 24 May 2005.

[50] For details see para. 58a of Act No. 350/1996 Coll.

[51] Art. 3 of Act No. 397/2004 Coll.

enormous amounts of EU legislation adopted every year in addition to exercising their everyday functions.

4. EUROPEAN CONSTITUTION

4.1 Impact of the EU Constitution on the Community legal order and accession

The architecture of the European Treaty is the DOS or Windows software of European integration. If it is unclear or shows gaps it will lead to instability. One of the reasons that primary EC/EU law is so complex is that the original Community Treaties and the Maastricht Treaty on European Union have been amended on numerous occasions by successive revisions. It has become almost impossible for practitioners to work with all these Treaties, even though they are the only instruments with authentic status. This situation has arisen as a result of the fact that the Treaties have never been "codified". A Treaty establishing a Constitution for Europe both with respect to the antecedent and contemporary EU/EC primary law therefore has the particular objective of:

- improving the linguistic quality and (by rearranging the provisions) also the logical structure of the Treaties;
- cleaning up the Treaties editorially, in particular deleting obsolete provisions;
- distinguishing between institutional provisions and the various policies, and finally
- bringing together the three Communities and the Union's areas of activity into a single Treaty, setting general principles, constitutional provisions and European fundamental rights at the beginning.[52]

However, although the Constitution for Europe would replace the Three Pillars structure, its linguistic quality, its size (almost 800 pages) and its structure are still far from perfect, and have not yet resulted in a clear and concise international treaty.

4.2 Obstacles to ratification of the European Constitution?

According to Article 102, paragraph 1 of the Slovak Constitution, the President shall represent the Slovak Republic externally, negotiate and ratify international treaties, but before ratification of international treaties listed in Article 7, paragraph 4 (e.g., international treaties from which a membership of the Slovak

---

[52] *OJ* C 151/51, No. 2, p. 14.

Republic in international organizations arises and international treaties which directly confer rights or impose duties on natural persons or legal persons), i.e., also the Treaty establishing a Constitution for Europe, approval by the National Council of the Slovak Republic is required.

The National Council of the Slovak Republic approved the Treaty establishing a Constitution for Europe on 11 May 2005 by qualified majority of its members. This means, that the Slovak parliament, as the supreme legislative body, has approved the ratification of this treaty. As the President was already prepared to ratify the Constitution for Europe, suddenly the Slovak Constitutional Court has accepted according to Article 127, paragraph 1 of the Constitution, a petition of several persons (Slovak citizens) and suspended the enforceability of National Council decision (approval) No. 1596, thus forbidding the president to ratify the Constitution for Europe. This petition was based on violation of the Article 30, paragraph 1 ("citizens shall have the right to participate in the administration of public affairs directly or through freely elected representatives…") in connection with Article 7, paragraph 1 ("The Slovak Republic may, by its own discretion, enter into a state union with other states. A constitutional law, which shall be confirmed by a referendum, shall decide on the entry into a state union, or on the secession from such union…") and Article 93, paragraph 1 (process of referendum). This means that the Constitutional Court will now need to decide if the European Union is a "state union" and thus whether an obligatory referendum for the ratification of the Treaty establishing a Constitution for Europe is necessary. It is not clear yet how the Constitutional Court will decide.

ANNEX: PROGRAMME OF THE FINAL CONFERENCE OF THE MATRA MULTI-COUNTRY PROJECT

The Impact of Accession on the National Legal Orders of New EU Member States and (Pre-)Candidate Countries

The Hopes and Fears of New Member States and (Pre-)Candidate Countries

Views on the EU Constitution

INTRODUCTION

In December 2002, the Dutch Ministry of Foreign Affairs approved the Matra Multi-Country Project entitled "The Impact of Accession for the Acceding Member States and (Pre-)Candidate Countries." The Project is a follow-up to the Asser Colloquium on European Law of September 2000 entitled "The Constitutional Impact of EU enlargement at the EU and National Levels."

The Ministry of Foreign Affairs selected the following countries as participants: Slovenia (new Member State), Croatia (applicant country), Serbia and Montenegro ((pre-)candidate country), Bulgaria, Romania and Turkey (candidate countries).

The Project, which runs from January 2003 until December 2004, will conclude with a Final Conference entitled "The Hopes and Fears of New Member States and (pre-)candidate countries" on 13 October 2004.

Recent developments culminating in the Draft Constitution of the European Union bring about the need for acceding and (pre-)candidate Member States to comment on and review the Draft. National rapporteurs from each participating country have been invited to present their views through country reports on the basis of an extensive questionnaire. The Matra Multi-Country Project representatives will give their presentations during Parallel session 1A.

As only one of the New Member States participated in the Matra Multi-Country Project, the organization has decided to also include the other new Member States in the Final Conference. They have been invited to express their perspective on the EU Constitution and will present their accomplishments with regard to the Copenhagen accession standards. National rapporteurs from these countries will present their views through conference papers on the basis of a more limited questionnaire during Parallel Session 1B.

The participants of the Final Conference of the Matra Multi-Country Project are also invited to participate in the XXXIV Session of the Asser Colloquium on European Law, organized on 14, 15 and 16 October. This Colloquium, which bears the title "The EU Constitution: The Best Way Forward" is organized during the Dutch Presidency of the EU and will focus on the EU Constitution and its contribution to the legal order of the Union and the national legal orders. Several reporters who will present their country reports at the Final Conference of the Matra Multi-Country Project have also been invited to speak at the Colloquium.

WEDNESDAY 13 October 2004

PLENARY OPENING SESSION

13.30-13.35	Opening of the Matra Conference by **L.P.M. van Geel**, Director Matra, Netherlands Ministry of Foreign Affairs, The Hague
13.35-13.45	Welcome and opening remarks by **Frans Nelissen**, General Director T.M.C. Asser Instituut, Professor University of Groningen
13.45-13.55	The results and impact of the Matra Multi-Country Project by **Alfred E. Kellermann**, General Secretary T.M.C. Asser Instituut, Director Matra Multi-Country Project; visiting Professor in the law of the EU
13.55-14.10	Introduction on the Impact of the EU Constitution on the Courts (Matra Multi-Country General Report) by **Jenö Czuczai**, Vice-President European Law Academy Budapest, Jean Monnet Professor, College de Bruges
14.10-14.20	Introduction on the role of national Parliaments by **Anneli Albi**, lecturer University of Kent
14.20-14.30	Introduction on the role of the governments and administrations by **Steven Blockmans**, T.M.C. Asser Instituut

All representatives of the new Member States and (pre-)candidate countries accredited in The Hague will be invited to attend the plenary opening session.

THE IMPACT OF EU ACCESSION ON THE NATIONAL LEGAL ORDER IN THE LIGHT OF EU CONSTITUTIONALIZATION

PARALLEL PANEL SESSION I.A

Chair: **Alfred E. Kellermann**, General Secretary T.M.C. Asser Instituut

New Member State

15.00-15.15	Specific legal and constitutional problems in Slovenia, by **Primoz Vehar**, National Assembly, Ljubljana and **Miha Pogacnik**, Ljubljana, Slovenia

(Pre-)Candidate Countries

15.15-15.30 Specific legal and constitutional problems in Bulgaria, by **Evgeni Tanchev**, Member Constitutional Court, Sofia, Bulgaria and **Jenia Peteva**, Assistant Professor Sofia University, Sofia, Bulgaria

15.30-15.45 Specific legal and constitutional problems in Romania, by **Victor Duculescu**, Professor of Constitutional Law, Bucharest University, Bucharest, Romania

15.45-16.00 Specific legal and constitutional problems in Turkey, by **Kemal Baslar** (Constitutional Court, Ankara) and **Erdogan Ishakoglu** (Ministry of Justice, General Directorate for EU Affairs, Ankara)

Applicant Country

16.00-16.15 Specific legal and constitutional problems in Croatia, by **Siniša Rodin**, Professor and **Tamara Capeta**, Assistant Professor, University of Zagreb

(Pre-)Candidate Country

16.15-16.30 Specific legal and constitutional problems in Serbia and Montenegro, by **Dusko Lopandic**, Assistant Minister, Ministry of International Economic Relations, Belgrade, Republic of Serbia

16.30-17.00 Questions / Discussion

PARALLEL PANEL SESSION I.B

Chair: **Jaap W. de Zwaan**, Vice-President of the T.M.C. Asser Institute, Professor at the Erasmus University Rotterdam

New Member States

15.00-15.10 Specific problems in the Estonian constitutional and legal order, by **Anneli Albi**, Estonia

15.10-15.20 Specific problems in the Latvian constitutional and legal order, by **Anita Usacka**, Professor, Ph.D; Judge of the International Criminal Court, The Hague and Former Judge of the Constitutional Court, Riga, Latvia

15.20-15.30 Specific problems in the Lithuanian constitutional and legal order, by **Irmantas Jarukaitis**, Deputy Director-General, European Law Department, Ministry of Foreign Affairs, Vilnius, Lithuania

15.30-15.40 Specific problems in the Cyprus constitutional and legal order, by **Nicholas Emiliou**, Ambassador, Permanent Representative for Cyprus, EU, Brussels (not present)

15.40-15.50	Specific problems in the Maltese constitutional and legal order, by **Peter X. Xuereb**, University of Malta, Malta
15.50-16.00	Specific problems in the Czech constitutional and legal order, by **Jiri Zemanek**, Charles University, Prague, Czech Republic
16.10-16.20	Specific problems in the Hungarian constitutional and legal order, by **Jenö Czuczai**, Vice-President, European Law Academy, Budapest, Jean Monnet Professor, Hungary,
16.20-16.30	Specific problems in the Slovak constitutional and legal order, by **Vlasta Kunova**, Comenius University, Slovak Republic (not present)
16.30-16.40	Specific problems in the Polish constitutional and legal order, by **Stanislaw Biernat**, Jagiellonian University of Cracow, Jean Monnet Professor, Poland
16.40-17.00	Questions / Discussion

PLENARY FINAL SESSION

17.00-18.00	Round Table Discussion chaired by **Alfred E. Kellermann** and **Jaap de Zwaan** Members of the Panel: **Stanislaw Biernat; Victor Duculescu; Jenö Czuczai; Slobodan Samardzic**

THURSDAY 14 October 2004

PLENARY SESSION I

THE PROCESS AND IMPACT OF EU CONSTITUTION MAKING: VOICE AND EXIT

Chair: **Deirdre Curtin**, Chairperson of the Commission for European Law of the T.M.C. Asser Institute

09.00-09.05	How to convince the European citizens to ratify the EU constitution?, by **Alfred E. Kellermann**, General Secretary T.M.C. Asser Instituut
09.05-09.10	Introduction to the subject by **Deirdre Curtin**, Professor University of Utrecht
09.10-09.30	The EU Constitution and the European Parliament, by **the President of the European Parliament** (Strasbourg, Brussels)

09.30-10.00	Keynote Speech "The process of EU Constitution-making and the voice of the citizens", by **Joseph H.H. Weiler**, Professor New York Law School, New York
10.00-10.30	The process of ratification and the exit options: a legal perspective, by **Bruno de Witte**, Professor, European University Institute (EUI), Florence
10.30-10.55	Questions / Discussion
11.25-12.15	Panel and General Discussion: - **Anne Peters**, Professor University of Basel - **Jo Shaw**, Professor and Jean Monnet Chair, University of Manchester - **Peter-Christian Müller-Graf**, Professor University of Heidelberg - **Evgeni Tanchev** (Member of the Constitutional Court, Sofia)
14.00-14.30	The EU Constitution and the experiences of the Irish Presidency, by **Dick Roche T.D.**, Minister of State with responsibility for European Affairs at the Department of the Taoiseach, Dublin (invited)
14.30-15.00	The EU Constitution and the Priorities of the Dutch Presidency, by **Atzo Nicolai**, State Secretary of the Netherlands for European Affairs, Ministry of Foreign Affairs, The Hague

PLENARY SESSION II

TRANSPARENCY AND LEGAL INSTRUMENTS IN THE EU CONSTITUTION

Chair: **Jenö Czuczai**, Vice-President European Law Academy Budapest, Jean Monnet Professor College of Europe, Bruges

15.00-15.20	New legal instruments, by **Armin von Bogdandy**, Professor University of Heidelberg and **Juergen Bast**, Director and Staff Member Max Planck Institute for Comparative Law and International Law, Heidelberg
15.20-15.40	Executive acts and control mechanisms, by **Michelle Everson**, Birbeck College, London
16.00-16.20	Operational collaboration on justice, security and policing in the constitutional framework, by **Steve Peers**, Professor University of Essex
16.20-16.40	Drawing the threads together from parts 1 and 111 of the EU Constitution, by **Jan Wouters**, Professor at Leuven University

16.40-17.30 Panel and General Discussion:
- **Piet Eeckhout**, Professor Kings College London
- **Jörg Monar**, Professor University of Sussex
- **Nicholas Emiliou**, Permanent Representative for Cyprus, Council of Europe,
- **Siniša Rodin**, Professor University of Zagreb

20.00-22.00 Conference Dinner Thursday Evening

Speakers
Piet Hein Donner, Minister of Justice of the Kingdom of the Netherlands, The Hague
Jacek Saryusz-Wolski, Warsaw, Member of the European Parliament, Strasbourg (invited)

FRIDAY 15 October 2004

PARALLEL SESSION III.A

THE DEMOCRATIC LIFE OF THE EUROPEAN UNION

Chair: **Deirde Curtin**, Professor Universoty of Utrecht
Walter van Gerven, Former Advocate General European Court of Justice, Luxembourg (invited)

09.00-09.30 The role of parliaments in the EU constitutional framework: partnership or rivalry? by **Heidi Hautala**, ex-MEP and member of Finnish Parliament
09.30-10.00 Theory and reality of public access to EU information, by **Lorenzo Cotino**, University of Valencia
10.00-10.30 Giving substance to participation; the social model, by **Adelina Adinolfi**, University of Florence (invited)
11.00-11.30 The European Ombudsman and the European Constitution, by **Nikiforos Diamandouros** (European Ombudsman), Strasbourg
11.30-12.30 Panel and General Discussion:
- **Tom Eijsbouts**, In defence of the European Parliament, Professor of European Constitutional Law, University of Amsterdam
- **Roel Fernhout**, Ombudsman of the Netherlands, The Hague
- **Gerard van der Wal**, Houthoff Buruma, Brussels

PARALLEL SESSION III.B

IMPROVING THE EFFICIENCY AND QUALITY OF LEGISLATION EXPANSION OF EXECUTIVE, JUDICIAL AND LEGISLATIVE POWERS

Chair: **Francis Jacobs**, Advocate General European Court of Justice, Luxembourg

09.00-9.30 The evolution in the role and powers of the European Council and the Council of Ministers, by **Jan Werts**, European Correspondent in Brussels

09.30-10.00 The evolution in the role and powers of the European Commission, by **Michel Petite**, Director General Legal Service of the European Commission, Brussels

10.00-10.30 The expanding role of the European Parliament, by **Ricardo Passos**, Member of the Legal Service, European Parliament, Luxembourg

11.00-12.30 Panel Discussion
- **Stanislav Biernat**, Professor Jagiellonian University, Cracow, Poland
- **Christiaan W.A. Timmermans**, Judge at the European Court of Justice
- **Miguel Maduro**, Advocate General Court of Justice, Luxembourg
- **Paul Craig**, Professor University of Oxford (invited)

PLENARY SESSION IV

ACCESS TO JUSTICE AND THE EU CONSTITUTION

Chair: Prof. **Sacha Prechal**, Professor University of Utrecht

14.00-14.30 The workload of the Luxembourg Courts and the citizens right to a judge, by **Denis Waelbroeck**, Brussels

14.30-15.00 The expanding role of the national courts and the EU constitutional system, by **Jutta Limbach**, President of the Goethe Institute, Munich, former President of the Bundesverfassungsgericht, Karlsruhe

15.00-15.30 The complementary roles of Strasbourg and Luxembourg, by **Rick Lawson**, Professor University of Leiden

16.00-16.30 The expanding jurisdiction of the Court of Justice, by **Ad Geelhoed**, Advocate General European Court of Justice, Luxembourg

16.30-17.30 Panel and General Discussion:
- **Arjen Meij**, Judge in the Court of First Instance, Luxembourg
- **Anita Usacka**, Staff Member ICC, The Hague; Former Judge Constitutional Court, Riga, Latvia
- **Piet van Nuffel**, Brussels
- **Onno Brouwer**, CCBE (Council of the Bars and Law Societies of the EU), Chairman of the Permanent Delegation to the European Court of Justice

20.00-22.00 Conference Dinner Friday Evening

Speakers:
János Martonyi, former Minister of Foreign Affairs of Hungary and Hungarian representative in the European Convention, Budapest
Thom de Graaff, Vice-Prime Minister of the Kingdom of the Netherlands, The Hague (invited)

SATURDAY 16 October 2004

FINAL SESSION

Chair: **Jan Jans**, Professor University of Amsterdam

09.30-10.30 Summaries and reports of the Plenary Sessions I, II and IV and the Parallel Sessions IIIA and IIIB, by **Deirdre Curtin, Jenö Czuczai, Walter van Gerven, Francis Jacobs** and **Sacha Prechal**

11.15-12.45 Round Table Chaired by **Deirdre Curtin**
Suggestions and Recommendations by:
- **Ayse Saadet Arikan**, Ankara (view of (pre)candidate countries)
- **Jaap de Zwaan**, Professor Erasmus University Rotterdam (view of New Member States)
- **Paul Magnette**, Professor Universite Libre Brussels, Belgium
- **Marko Starman**, State Secretary, Ministry of Justice, Ljubljana, Slovenia
- **Mark Entin**, Professor Moscow State Institute for International relations, Director European Law Institute MGIMO, Moscow (view from a neighbouring non-Member State), and

	- representatives of the European Parliament, Court of Justice, Council and Commission
12.45-13.00	Closing Remarks and Follow-up, by **Alfred E. Kellermann**, General Secretary, T.M.C. Asser Instituut.

The conclusions, recommendations and suggestions of this event were forwarded to the Dutch EU Presidency.

MIX
Papier aus verantwortungsvollen Quellen
Paper from responsible sources
FSC® C105338

If you have any concerns about our products,
you can contact us on
ProductSafety@springernature.com

In case Publisher is established outside the EU,
the EU authorized representative is:
Springer Nature Customer Service Center GmbH
Europaplatz 3, 69115 Heidelberg, Germany

Printed by Libri Plureos GmbH
in Hamburg, Germany